2006-2012   KENGO KUMA

Copyright © 2012 A.D.A. EDITA Tokyo Co., Ltd.
3-12-14 Sendagaya, Shibuya-ku, Tokyo 151-0051, Japan
All rights reserved. No part of this publication may be reproduced,
stored in a retrieval system, or transmitted, in any form or by any means,
electronic, mechanical, photocopying, recording, or otherwise,
without permission in writing from the publisher.

Copyright of photographs except as noted
©2012 GA photographers
Copyright of drawings and renderings except as noted
©2012 Kengo Kuma and Associates

Logotype : Gan Hosoya

First published 2012
Reprinted 2020

Printed and bound in Japan

ISBN978-4-87140-433-4 C1352

KENGO KUMA
2006-2012

Edited by Yukio Futagawa
Text by Kengo Kuma

企画・編集:二川幸夫　序文・作品解説:隈研吾

A.D.A. EDITA Tokyo

KENGO KUMA

1954	Born and grew up in Yokohama, Kanagawa Prefecture, Japan
1979	University of Tokyo, M. Arch.
1985-86	Visiting Scholar Graduate School, Columbia University and Asian Cultural Council
1987	Established Spatial Design Studio in Tokyo
1990-	Established Kengo Kuma & Associates
1995	Grand Prize, JCD Design Award'95 Cultural/Public Institutions (for "Kiro-san Observatory")
1997	Annual Prize, Architectural Institute of Japan Award (for "Noh Stage in the Forest")
	First Prize, AIA DuPONT Benedictus Award (for "Water / Glass")
1998-99	Professor of the Faculty of Environmental Information, Keio University
1999	Honorable Mention, Boston Society of Architects Unbuilt Architecture Design Award
2000	Grand Prize, INTER INTRA SPACE design selection (for "Kitakami Canal Museum")
	Director General of Forestry Agency Award (for "Museum of Ando Hiroshige")
2001	Professor of the Faculty of Science and Technology, Keio University
	International Stone Architecture Award, Italy (for "Stone Museum")
	Togo Murano Award (for "Museum of Ando Hiroshige")
2002	Spirit of Nature Wood Architecture Award, Finland
2005	The Marble Architectural Awards, Italy
2008	Energy Performance + Architecture Award (France)
	Bois Magazine International Wood Architecture Award (France)
2009	Decoration Officier de L'Ordre des Arts et des Lettres (France)
2010	Mainichi Art Award for "Nezu Museum"
2011	The Minister of Education, Culture, Sports, Science and Technology's Art Encouragement Prize for "Yusuhara Wooden Bridge Museum"

1954	神奈川県横浜市生まれ,横浜育ち
1979	東京大学工学部建築学科大学院修了
1985-86	コロンビア大学建築・都市計画学科客員研究員
	Asian Cultural Council給費研究員
1987	空間研究所設立
1990-	隈研吾建築都市設計事務所主宰
1995	JCDデザイン賞文化・公共施設部門最優秀賞「亀老山展望台」
1997	日本建築学会賞「森舞台 登米町伝統芸能伝承館」
	AIAベネディクタス賞「水／ガラス」
1998-99	慶應義塾大学環境情報学部特別招聘教授
1999	ボストン・ソサエティ・オブ・アーキテクツ・アンビルト・アーキテクチャー・デザイン・アワード
2000	インター・イントラ・スペース・デザイン・セレクション大賞「北上運河交流館」
	林野庁長官賞「那珂川町馬頭広重美術館」
2001	慶應義塾大学理工学部教授
	インターナショナル・ストーン・アーキテクチャー・アワード「石の美術館」
	村野藤吾賞「那珂川町馬頭広重美術館」
2002	スピリット・オブ・ネイチャー 木の建築賞
2005	マーブル・アーキテクチャー・アワード
2008	エネルギー・パフォーマンス — アーキテクチャー・アワード［フランス］
	Bois Magazine 国際木の建築賞［フランス］
2009	芸術文化勲章オフィシエ［フランス］
2010	毎日芸術賞「根津美術館」
2011	芸術選奨文部科学大臣賞［美術部門］「梼原・木橋ミュージアム」

2006-12 Contents
KENGO KUMA 2006-2012

8	Small Architcture / Kengo Kuma	162	Bamboo/Fiber / Japan, 2008-10
12	Ginzan-Onsen Fujiya / Yamagata, Japan, 2002-06	168	The Momofuku Ando Center of Outdoor Training
16	Z58 / Shanghai, China, 2003-06		Nagano, Japan, 2008-10
22	Asahi Broadcasting Corporation / Osaka, Japan, 2003-08	174	Prostho Museum Research Center / Aichi, Japan, 2008-10
28	Hoshinosato Annex / Kudamatsu, Yamaguchi, 2004-06	178	Lake House / Japan, 2008-11
32	Y Hütte / Japan, 2004-06	184	Xinjin Zhi Museum / Sichuan, China, 2008-11
36	Yusuhara Town Hall / Kochi, Japan, 2004-06	194	Aore Nagaoka / Niigata, Japan, 2008-12
40	Chokkura Plaza / Tochigi, Japan, 2004-06	202	Kabuki-za Building / Tokyo, Japan, 2006-13
46	Suntory Museum of Art / Tokyo, Japan, 2004-07	204	Lucien Pellat-Finet Shinsaibashi / Osaka, Japan, 2009
52	Kure City Ondo Civic Center / Hiroshima, Japan, 2004-07	206	Community Market Yusuhara / Kochi, Japan, 2009-10
58	Steel House / Tokyo, Japan, 2004-07	210	Yusuhara Wooden Bridge Museum / Kochi, Japan, 2009-10
62	Nezu Museum / Tokyo, Japan, 2004-09	214	Stone Roof / Nagano, Japan, 2009-10
68	Tokyu Capitol Tower / Tokyo, Japan, 2004-10	220	Museum at The China Academy of Art / Hangzhou, China, 2009-
74	Yien East / Japan, 2005-07	222	Granatum-Granada Performing Arts Centre / Granada, Spain, 2009-
80	Hoshakuji Station / Tochigi, Japan, 2005-08	226	Mesh/Earth / Japan, 2009-11
82	The Opposite House / Beijing, China, 2005-08	232	Asakusa Culture Tourist Information Center / Tokyo, Japan, 2009-12
92	T-Room / Ishikawa, Japan, 2005	236	Jeju Ball / Jeju, South Korea, 2009-12
93	Kenny Heights Museum / Kuala Lumpur, Malaysia, 2006-	244	Shang Xia / Shanghai, China, 2009-10
94	Sake no Hana / London, U.K., 2006-07	246	Ceramic Cloud / Reggio Emilia, Italia, 2009-10
98	Ryotei Kaikatei Annex "sou-an" / Fukui, Japan, 2006-08	248	Chikugo Art and Culture Center / Fukuoka, Japan, 2010-
102	Wood/Berg / Japan, 2006-08	252	Teikyo University Elementary School / Tokyo, Japan, 2010-12
110	Museum of Kanayama Castle Ruin, Kanayama Community Center	258	V&A at Dundee / Scotland, U.K., 2010-
	Gunma, Japan, 2006-09	260	Garden Terrace Miyazaki / Miyazaki, Japan, 2010-12
116	Shimonoseki City Kawatana-Onsen Visitor Center and Folk Museum	266	Starbucks Coffee Dazaifu-Tenmangu Omotesando
	Yamaguchi, Japan, 2006-09		Fukuoka, Japan, 2011
122	Glass/Wood / U.S.A., 2006-10	269	Bubble Wrap / Osaka, Japan, 2011
127	Tee Haus / Frankfurt, Germany, 2005-07	270	Polygonium House / Tokyo, Japan, 2011
128	Tiffany Ginza / Tokyo, Japan, 2007-08	272	Green Cast / Kanagawa, Japan, 2009-11
131	Fu-an / Shizuoka, Japan, 2007	274	Iiyama Plaza / Nagano, Japan, 2012-
132	Garden Terrace Nagasaki, Nagasaki, Japan, 2007-09	276	Towada City Plaza for Social Communication / Aomori, Japan, 2011-
138	Akagi Jinja & Park Court Kagurazaka / Tokyo, Japan, 2007-10	278	Under One Roof / Lausanne, Switzerland, 2012-
142	Sanlitun SOHO / Beijing, China, 2007-10	282	Susa International Train Station / Turin, Italy, 2012-
150	Water/Cherry / Japan, 2007-12	284	Tomioka City Hall / Gunma, Japan, 2012-
158	Cavamarket Headquarters Project / Campania, Italy, 2007-09	286	Besançon City Arts and Culture Center / Doubs, France, 2007-13
160	Casa Umbrella / Milan, Italy, 2007-08	290	List of Works 2006-2012
161	Water Branch House / New York, U.S.A., 2008-		

8	小さな建築／隈研吾		162	Bamboo/Fiber　東日本, 2008-10年
12	銀山温泉 藤屋　山形県尾花沢市, 2002-06年		168	安藤百福記念自然体験活動指導者養成センター
16	Z58　中国, 上海, 2003-06年			長野県小諸市, 2008-10年
22	朝日放送　大阪府大阪市, 2003-08年		174	プロソミュージアム・リサーチセンター　愛知県春日井市, 2008-10年
28	ほしのさとアネックス　山口県下松市, 2004-06年		178	Lake House　日本, 2008-11年
32	Y Hütte　東日本, 2004-06年		184	新津 知・芸術館　中国, 成都, 2008-11年
36	梼原町総合庁舎　高知県高岡郡, 2004-06年		194	アオーレ長岡　新潟県長岡市, 2008-12年
40	ちょっ蔵広場　栃木県塩谷郡, 2004-06年		202	(仮称)歌舞伎座ビル　東京都中央区, 2006-13年
46	サントリー美術館　東京都港区, 2004-07年		204	ルシアン・ペラフィネ 心斎橋店　大阪府大阪市, 2009年
52	呉市音戸市民センター　広島県呉市, 2004-07年		206	まちの駅「ゆすはら」　高知県高岡郡, 2009-10年
58	鉄の家　東京都文京区, 2004-07年		210	梼原・木橋ミュージアム　高知県高岡郡, 2009-10年
62	根津美術館　東京都港区, 2004-09年		214	Stone Roof　長野県, 2009-10年
68	東急キャピトルタワー　東京都千代田区, 2004-10年		220	中国美術学院博物館　中国, 杭州, 2009年-
74	Yien East　日本, 2005-07年		222	グラナトゥン　スペイン, グラナダ, 2009年-
80	宝積寺駅　栃木県塩谷郡, 2005-08年		226	Mesh/Earth　日本, 2009-11年
82	The Opposite House　中国, 北京, 2005-08年		232	浅草文化観光センター　東京都台東区, 2009-12年
92	t-room　石川県金沢市, 2005年		236	Jeju Ball　大韓民国, ジェジュ島, 2009-12年
93	ケニー ハイツ ミュージアム　マレーシア, クアラルンプール, 2006年-		244	「上下」上海店　中国, 上海, 2009-10年
94	Sake no Hana　イギリス, ロンドン, 2006-07年		246	Ceramic Cloud　イタリア, レッジオエミリア, 2009-10年
98	料亭開花亭別館「sou-an」　福井県福井市, 2006-08年		248	筑後広域公園芸術文化交流施設(仮称)　福岡県筑後市, 2010年-
102	Wood/Berg　日本, 2006-08年		252	帝京大学小学校　東京都多摩市, 2010-12年
110	史跡金山城跡ガイダンス施設, 太田市金山地域交流センター		258	ヴィクトリア&アルバート・ミュージアム・ダンディ
	群馬県太田市, 2006-09年			イギリス, スコットランド, 2010年-
116	下関市川棚温泉交流センター「川棚の社」　山口県下関市, 2006-09年		260	ガーデンテラス宮崎　宮崎県宮崎市, 2010-12年
122	Glass/Wood　アメリカ, 2006-10年		266	スターバックスコーヒー太宰府天満宮表参道店
127	Tee Haus　ドイツ, フランクフルト, 2005-07年			福岡県福岡市, 2011年
128	ティファニー銀座　東京都中央区, 2007-08年		269	Bubble Wrap　大阪府大阪市, 2011年
131	浮庵　静岡県静岡市, 2007年		270	ポリゴニウム・ハウス　東京都千代田区, 2011年
132	ガーデンテラス長崎　長崎県長崎市, 2007-09年		272	グリーン・キャスト　神奈川県小田原市, 2009-11年
138	赤城神社・パークコート神楽坂　東京都新宿区, 2007-10年		274	(仮称)飯山ぷらざ　長野県飯山市, 2012年-
142	三里屯SOHO　中国, 北京, 2007-10年		276	(仮称)十和田市民交流プラザ　青森県十和田市, 2011年-
150	Water/Cherry　日本, 2007-12年		278	Under One Roof　スイス, ローザンヌ, 2012年-
158	カヴァマーケット・ヘッドクォータース		282	スーザ国際駅　イタリア, トリノ, 2012年-
	イタリア, カンパニア, 2007-09年		284	富岡市新庁舎　群馬県富岡市, 2012年-
160	Casa Umbrella　イタリア, ミラノ, 2007-08年		286	ブザンソン芸術文化センター　フランス, ブザンソン, 2007-13年
161	Water Branch House　アメリカ, ニューヨーク, 2008年-		290	作品リスト　2006-2012年

Small Architecture
小さな建築

Kengo Kuma
隈研吾

What triggers architecture to evolve? What triggers the history of architecture to change its course?

Traditional architecture textbooks use the logic of Darwinian theory of evolution to explain what defines the current of architectural design. I call this 'evolutionary history of architecture.' A familiar theory stating that the emergence of new techniques and materials such as concrete and steel have triggered evolution in architecture. History of modern architecture has been explained based on this logic, that technology was key to the evolution of architecture, making it stronger, bigger and brighter.

Now in the wake of the Great East Japan Earthquake on March 11, 2011, we can clearly deny this 'evolution theory.' Architecture's driving force is not progress in technology. Great disasters have been transforming and altering the course of architecture.

The reason is simple. Fear motivates people. People rarely bother to change in times of happiness. When people are happy, they only repeat their own past and are reluctant to make a big change. Humans are essentially negligent and lazy.

But once life is at stake, the living creature in us awakens. Sensing an imminent death, it truly strives to change. It is in this way that architecture has been changing its direction: out of big disasters. The history of architecture has been driven by great tragedies. Catastrophes have played major roles in politics and economy, as well as in philosophy and science, but especially in the history of architecture. Because architecture has always been considered as a protective shelter and people held on to it. When people fear for their lives they try to hold on to architecture, and such desperate yearning has triggered change in the history of architecture.

One representative case is the Great Lisbon Earthquake that occurred on November 1st, 1755. At a time when world population was 700 million, 50 to 60 thousand people perished. Those who survived plunged in the depths of horror. People were struck with terror that God might have finally abandoned them. An unprecedented type of horror, of unprecedented intensity.

People who felt abandoned by God turned to architecture to rely on. The huge earthquake destroyed small, vulnerable buildings that used to fill the city of Lisbon, burned them, and took people's lives. If only those buildings can be bigger and stronger, architecture might be able to protect us, in place of God, people thought: hence the beginning of a new era of architecture.

Those who were most sensitive and responsive to the disaster were a group of French avant-garde architects called the 'Visionnaires' (visionaries), who soon began to draw pictures of architectures that have nothing to do with God. Pictures of big, strong architectures based on rational science and mathematics.

They believed that small, vulnerable architecture in Lisbon killed all these people. And tried to protect vulnerable humans with big, strong architecture.

The history of modern architecture started from this Visionnaire concept and saw architecture undergo a complete change. Even though Visionnaires didn't know concrete nor steel, they started to draw energetically, lead by their intuition that big, strong architecture will save lives. Which was then followed by technology. Modern architecture movement at the beginning of the 20th century is a product of Visionnaire concept and its follow-up scientific technology. Technology did not take the lead — horror and disaster did, and technology tagged along.

Even after Lisbon, horror and disaster con-

建築は何をきっかけとして，変化していくのだろうか。建築史は，何をきっかけとして，方向を変えるのだろうか。

従来の建築の教科書の多くは，ダーウィンの進化論のロジックを用いて，建築のデザインの流れが決定されてきたと説明する。ぼくはこれを「進化論的建築史」と呼ぶ。例えばコンクリート，鉄といった新しい材料，新しい技術の登場をきっかけとして，建築が進化してきたとする聞きなれた説である。近代建築史は，このロジックに基づいて説明されてきた。技術が建築を進歩させ，建築をより強く，より大きく，より明るいものにしてきたという説明である。

2011年，3月11日の東日本大震災の後，われわれははっきりと，この「進化論」を否定することができる。建築を動かしてきたのは技術の進歩ではない。大きな災害をきっかけとして建築は流れが変わり，転換してきたのである。

理由は簡単である。恐怖が人を動かすからである。幸福な時に，人は変わろうとはしない。幸福な時，人は過去の自分をリピートするだけで，大きく変わろうとはしない。人間は本質的に怠慢であり，怠惰である。

しかし，生命が危機にさらされた時，生物は目をさます。このままでは死んでしまうと感じた時，生物は本気で変わろうとする。建築はそのような形で，大災害によって方向を変えてきた。大きな悲劇が建築の歴史を動かしてきた。政治経済においても，哲学や科学においても，大災害が果たした役割は大きいが，建築史では，特に大災害が重要な役割を果たした。なぜなら建築というものが，人を守るシェルターだと考えられていて，人はそれにすがろうとしたからである。生命が危ないと感じた時，人は建築にすがろうとして，その切実な気持が建築史を転換してきた。

代表的な事例は1755年11月1日の，リスボン大地震であった。世界人口7億人の時代に，5万人から6万人の人々が亡くなった。生き残った人々も，恐怖の底につき落とされた。神がついに人間を見捨てたのではないかという恐怖が，人々を襲ったのである。かつてない種類，かつてない強さの恐怖であった。

神に見捨てられたと感じた人々は，建築に頼ろうとした。大地震はリスボンの街を埋め尽くしていた弱く小さな建築群を壊し，燃やし，人々の命を奪った。建築がより強くて大きかったならば，建築は神に換わって自分たちを守ってくれるかもしれないと，人々は感じた。そこから，建築の新しい時代が始まった。

最も感度が高く，災害に敏感に反応したのが，ヴィジョネール（幻視者）と呼ばれる，フランスの一群のアヴァンギャルド建築家たちである。彼らは神とはまったく無関係な建築の絵を描き始めた。合理的な科学と数学とに基づく，強く，大きな建築の絵を描き始めた。

弱く，小さなリスボンの建築が人々を殺したと，彼らは考えた。強く，大きな建築によって弱い人間を守ろうとしたのである。

このヴィジョネールの構想から，近代建築史はスタートし，建築がらっと変わり始めたのである。ヴィジョネールたちは，コンクリートも鉄も知らなかったが，強く，大きな建築が生命を救うという直観に導かれて，猛然と絵を描き始めた。その後に技術がついてきたのである。20世紀初頭の近代建築運動は，ヴィジョネールの構想と，それを後追いした科学技術の産物である。技術が先導したのではなく，恐怖が先導し，大災害が先導し，技術が後を追いかけたのである。

リスボンの後も，災害と恐怖が建築史を導いた。ナポレオンⅢ世は，狭い路地をアジトとするテロを恐れ，路地によって燃え広がる大火を恐れ，「小さなパリ」を捨てて，大通りのモニュメントと大きな建築で構成する「大きなパリ」をめざし，1853年から1870年にかけて，

tinued to lead the history of architecture. Napoleon III, in fear of terrorism that nestled among narrow streets, in fear of conflagration that would spread through the network of alleyways, put away the idea of a 'small Paris' to go for a 'big Paris' made up of monuments on boulevards and large architectures. From 1853 through 1870 he commissioned Haussmann to achieve a major renovation of Paris to create a 'big Paris.'

The Great Chicago Fire in 1871 uncovered the vulnerability of overcrowded small wooden architectures. Death toll was in the range of several hundreds, but 30% of the city was consumed by fire. In an attempt to rebuild cities with large structures made of concrete and steel, American cities changed their course of progress. From the ruins emerged a set of high-rise buildings named the Chicago School, that lead to the creation of a number of skyscrapers in New York in the early 20th century. Skyscrapers in New York became a model for metropolis around the world, an urban prototype of the 20th century. A catastrophic event triggered a change in the course of history, heading for bigger, stronger architecture.

Similar things had happened in Japan. Following the Great Kanto Earthquake in 1923, everything began to shift toward bigger, stronger architecture. A crammed Tokyo with small low-rise wooden structures was denied; a city with a human scale that Tokyo has inherited from Edo was totally denied; and a project to rebuild Tokyo with large concrete structures began to take place. Big, strong architectures were constructed at a furious pace. World War II accelerated its speed.

Then what will 3.11 bring to us today? My opinion is that 3.11 was a type of disaster that is definitely different from the past ones.

3.11 taught us that, be it big or strong, architecture is utterly powerless and undependable in front of the mighty forces of nature. A concrete structure did not stand a chance against the forces of nature. In that sense, 3.11 was different from previous disasters. It brought people senses of exhaustion and resignation. Instead of working hard toward the bigger and stronger, all we could do was to tremble in despair and pray in humility.

Tragedy of the nuclear plant in Fukushima worsened the devastation. Even the biggest and strongest architecture was absolutely ineffective against radiation contamination. Strength and size did not matter: nuclear radiation showed no mercy. Desperation deepened. We looked for strength and size, ran short of electricity, and ended up with nuclear energy. It even felt like a divine punishment for having been so ungodly. Punished for the 250 years since Lisbon. If big, strong architecture were not dependable in the least, then what is left for us to rely upon?

My answer is to make architecture small. Our arrogance in believing that big, strong architecture is safe and makes people happy has chased away our sense of awe toward nature, giving way to an arrogant, fragile society dependent on a 'big technology' cut off from Mother Nature that was the nuclear power.

In the information society, the era of 'big systems' and 'big computers' has ended as early as in the 1970s to give way to the era of 'small computers'. 'Grass-roots' movement emerged among those wishing to face the world directly and deal with it with their own small hands and their own small head, using 'small computers.' Alan Kay came up with the idea of personal computers and Steve Jobs designed 'small devices' to materialize it. A 'democratic system' to face the world in a direct manner has dramatically changed the world of information.

Then, what is possible for architecture to do? I am thinking that there has to be two types of smallness in architecture.

One is physical smallness. Big and strong architecture was, before something as overwhelming as nature, utterly powerless and nothing but trouble. It is not easy to safely evacuate people from 'big architectures,' the high-rise buildings. People have forgotten, for 250 years after Lisbon, the cost, energy and mental strain

彼はオスマンを使ってパリの大改造をなしとげ、「大きなパリ」をつくった。

1871年のシカゴ大火は、木造の小さな建築が密集する弱さを露呈した。死者こそ数百人だったが、都市の30％が焼失した。コンクリートと鉄でできた大きな建築を単位として都市をつくり直そうと、アメリカの都市は流れを変えた。焼け跡には、シカゴ派と呼ばれる高層建築群が登場し、その流れは20世紀初頭のニューヨークの超高層建築群を生み出した。ニューヨークの超高層は世界の大都市のモデルとなり、20世紀の都市の原型をつくった。大災害によって、強く大きな建築へと、歴史の流れが変わったのである。

日本でも似たようなことが起こった。1923年の関東大震災によって、強く大きな建築へ、すべてが流れ始めた。低層の木造建築が密集する、小さくごちゃごちゃとした東京は否定され、江戸から東京へと続いてきたヒューマンスケールの都市は全否定され、コンクリートの大建築で東京をつくり直す作業が始まった。大きく強い建築が、恐ろしい勢いで建設され始めた。第2次世界大戦が、そのスピードを加速した。

では3.11は、何をわれわれにもたらすだろうか。過去の大災害と3.11は、決定的に違う種類の災害であると、ぼくは考える。

強かろうと、大きかろうと、自然の大きな力の前では、建築はまったく無力であり、頼りにならないことを、3.11はわれわれに教えてくれた。コンクリートだろうと、自然の大きな力の前では、ひとたまりもなかった。その意味で、3.11は、かつての大災害とは質の違う大災害であった。人を脱力させ、大きな諦めがもたらされた。我々は、強さと大きさに向かってがんばるのではなく、絶望して震え、謙虚に祈るしかなかった。

さらに福島の原子力発電所の悲劇が、あと押しをした。いかに強く大きな建築も、放射能の前ではまったく無力であった。強さも大きさも無関係であり、放射能は容赦がなかった。絶望はさらに深くなった。強さと大きさを求めたから電気が足りなくなり、原子力にいきついたのである。神を恐れぬことへの、天罰とすら思えた。リスボン以来の250年に、天罰が下ったのである。では、強く大きな建築が、少しも頼りにならないとしたら、われわれは何に頼ったらいいのだろうか。

ぼくの解答は、建築を小さくすることである。強く大きくすれば安全であり、人間は幸福になれるという傲慢によって、自然への畏敬の念は失われ、大地とは縁の切れた原子力という「大きな技術」に頼る、傲慢で脆弱な社会が生まれたのである。

情報の社会では、はやくも1970年代に「大きなシステム」や「大きなコンピュータ」の時代が終わり、「小さなコンピュータ」の時代が始まった。「小さなコンピュータ」によって、自分の小さな手で、自分の小さな頭でじかに世界と向き合おうとする「草の根」の動きが始まった。アラン・ケイがパソコンという考え方を打ち出し、スティーブ・ジョブスはそのための「小さなキカイ」をデザインし、世界と直接に向かい合う「民主的システム」で、情報の世界は大きく転換した。

では、建築に、何が可能だろうか。ぼくは、建築には2種類の小ささが必要だろうと考えている。

ひとつは、物理的な小ささである。強くて大きな建築は、自然というとてつもないものの前では、まったく無力でやっかいなだけの存在であった。高層ビルという「大きな建築」から、人々を安全に避難させることは簡単ではない。大きさのためにかかるコスト、エネルギー、精神的負担のことを、リスボン後の250年間、人々は忘れていた。見て見ないふりをしていた。大きさは、人間と自然とを遠ざけるだけで、生命をあやうくするのである。

さらに、大きいものが目の前にあるだけで、人は威圧

that bigness has to pay. Pretended not to see. Bigness only alienates humans and nature: it in fact endangers lives.

Furthermore, just standing in front of something big makes people intimidated and daunted. To take big architectural volumes apart into small parts has been my subject theme for the last 15 years that is covered in this anthology. 'Asakusa Culture Tourist Information Center' is an attempt to break down a 38.9-meter tower into eight wooden one-story buildings. The opera house 'Granutun' in Granada is an attempt to break down a 1,500 capacity hall into 30 hexagons using 30 and 60-degree geometries.

As I went along with breaking down big things into small parts, it gradually came to me that a thorough continuation of this labor will eventually take me to a problem of 'how to produce architecture,' which consists of identifying the smallest unit size in the production. For example, in the 'Prostho Museum Research Center,' I came up with a method of taking a thin, 2m-long wooden bar with a 6cm x 6cm section as a unit and assembling them. The moment when I finally stumbled upon this unit size, I knew for sure that the rest could be left to this small bar as it will connect the world with people on its own. This very wooden bar is in fact the personal computer, the 'small architecture' itself.

In 'V&A Dundee', I spent most of my time studying the details of piling up pre-cast concrete bars with a 250mm x 250mm section. Once I can manage to design this bar properly, the 'small' architecture will be given a spark of life.

Breaking down architecture into small parts does not mean simply smashing a big architecture to small pieces: it implies discovery of the path that connects that minimal unit size with the incredibly enormous world. And the moment that path is discovered, all of a sudden, what used to be a mere grain transforms into a 'small architecture.' And that is what I believe to be the democracy of architecture. When each one of us comes to discover a circuit that connects one's alias with the world, democracy is born. Democracy is not about majority: it is all about smallness.

Continuous assemblage of units is not the only labor that connects the unit with the world. Tearing down a once finished assemblage then re-assembling is also an extremely important labor. Concrete was not at all good at this 'tearing down' and 're-assembling,' as a small fix meant destroying everything and starting all over. What I am proposing instead is fixable, flexible architecture that is reparable. For example, in the 'Prostho Museum' the simple gesture of twisting a wooden bar clenches the joint, and twisting in the other direction disjoints it. By alternating between 'small construction' and 'small destruction' one gets closer to the right answer in one way or another, which is also one of the important techniques of the 'small architecture.'

One other thing that cannot be left out is the fact that physically small units are substantially small in terms of economics as well. Economic smallness is a situation where that unit, rather than being dependent on the 'big economy' such as national economy or global economy, becomes incorporated into the local network of 'small economy' as an indispensable member and contributes to the survival of that economy.

For instance, it is preferable that materials used in such 'small architecture' are of local origin as much as possible. Lumber used in 'Aore Nagaoka' which is also the Nagaoka City Hall is Japanese cedar that came from within the radius of 15km. Not just any trees but only the local ones are used in an attempt to revitalize the local 'small economy.' Added to this was local-made silk fabrics called Tochio Tsumugi (Pongee) used for the Nagaoka City Hall's counter, which resulted in a drastic change in the atmosphere of the place.

Material is not the sole element that has to do with economy. Energy flow as well is the epitome of economic flow. Being dependent on electricity and gas supplied by the Japanese state is the same as being dependent on a 'big economy' called Japan and being constrained by it. As

---

され，萎縮するのである。大きな建築的ヴォリュームを，小さなものに分解することが，この作品集がカバーするこの15年間のぼくのテーマであった。「浅草文化観光センター」では，38.9mの高さの塔を，八つの木造平屋建築へと分解しようと試みた。グラナダのオペラ座「Granatum」では，1,500人のキャパのホールを，30度と60度の幾何学を用いて，30個の六角形（ヘキサゴン）へと分解しようと試みた。

大きなものを小さなものへと分解する作業を続けているうちに，この作業を徹底していけば「建築をどう生産するか」という，その生産の最小単位の問題にまできつくことが次第に見えてきた。例えば「プロソミュージアム・リサーチセンター」では，6cm×6cmの断面を持つ，長さ2mの細い木の棒を単位にして，その棒を組み上げていくという方法を発見した。その単位にたどり着けた時，後はこの小さな棒が勝手に世界と人間をつないでくれるだろうと，確信した。この木の棒こそが，パソコンなのであり，「小さな建築」そのものなのである。

「V&A Dundee」では，250mm×250mmの断面を持つプレキャスト・コンクリートの棒を積み上げていくディテールばかりをずっとスタディしていた。この棒が上手にデザインできれば，「小さな」建築に生命が宿るのである。

建築を小さく分解することは，単に大きな建築を小さく砕くことではなく，その小さな単位と，世界というとてつもなく大きなものをつなぐ道筋を，発見することなのである。この道筋が発見された時，突如として，ただの粒子であったものが，「小さな建築」へと変身をとげる。それが建築の民主主義であるとぼくは考える。一人ひとりが自分の別名と世界とをつなぐ回路を発見できた時，そこに民主主義が生まれる。民主主義とは多数決のことではなく，小ささである。

単位を組み上げ続けるだけが，単位と世界をつないでいるわけではない。一旦組み上がったものを壊し，組み直すことも極めて重要な作業である。コンクリートは，この「壊し」，「直す」作業がまったく苦手であった。ちょっと直そうと思ったら，全部を破壊して，一からやり直さなければならなかった。それに対し，ぼくが提案しているのは，直せる建築，取り返しがつく柔軟な建築である。例えば「プロソミュージアム」は，木の棒をひねるという単純な動作によってジョイントが固定され，逆向きにひねることによって分解される。「小さな建設」と「小さな破壊」を繰り返すことで，だましだまし正解に到達していくというのも，「小さな建築」の大事な技のひとつなのである。

さらにもうひとつ忘れてならないことは，物理的に小さな単位が，経済的にも充分に小さいということである。経済的な小ささとは，その単位が，国の経済やグローバル経済などの「大きな経済」に依存せずに，その場所に網を張っている「小さな経済」に組み込まれ，「小さな経済」のなくてはならない要員として，その経済の存続に貢献している状態のことである。

例えば「小さな建築」で使う材料は，なるべく地元の材料であることが望ましい。長岡市役所でもある「アオーレ長岡」で使われている木材は，15km圏内の杉材とした。木ならばどこのものでもいいというわけではなく，地元の木材を用いて，地元の「小さな経済」を活性化しようとしたのである。さらに，「長岡」の市役所カウンターに栃尾紬という地元産のシルクの織物を使ったら，その場所の空気が一変した。

材料だけが，経済と関係あるわけではない。エネルギーの流れもまた，経済の流れそのものである。日本国から供給される電力やガスに頼るということは，日本国という「大きな経済」に依存し，それに拘束されるということである。国際的な平均価格と大きくかけ離れた，日本特有の「高い電気」，「高いガス」に頼っていては，

long as one relies on Japan's typically 'expensive electricity' and 'expensive gas' that by far exceed the international average price, no matter how thoroughly an architecture is disassembled, it will still be unable to break away from the 'big architecture.'

Will it be right to take part in this country's unworthy 'big' system and lend one's hand to its survival by building a piece of architecture?

'Water Block' started out as a project of physically breaking down an architecture into small blocks. But as the prototype developed, it became clear that I would never be content with just the physical smallness which compelled me to expand into the area of 'economic smallness', and ended up renaming the project 'Water Branch.'

Whereas 'Water Block' was just a small plastic tank, with 'Water Branch' it became possible to connect units and run water through them. With hot water running through the architecture the building itself can be heated, or effectively air-conditioned by running cold water. And we no longer need to rely on electricity or gas to heat or cool the water. An effective use of sunlight can either heat it or cool it.

The transition from 'Water Block', a simple conversion of plastic tank, to 'Water Branch' with running water, was of great significance. It reminded me that the presence of a flow transforms so much the very meaning that an object has in its essence. With water flowing in the architecture itself, that is, circulating inside the architectural body, what was supposed to be an architecture is reborn as a living creature. Plastic tanks are transformed into molecular cells. Frankly, it has never occurred to me that a transition of this magnitude would happen as a result of such simple thing.

All you need is to create a flow, and architecture is reborn as a living creature. 'Small architecture' might be, after all, another name for living creature. The Metabolism movement had been going on the right track, but been missing the whole point. They believed that by conceiving architecture as an ensemble of small capsules where these capsules can be replaced in the manner of metabolism, one can breathe life into architecture.

With my desire to disassemble 'big architectures' to 'small architectures,' we are all in the same team. But Metabolists never came to realize the importance of a flow. Instead, they went for the idea of metabolism. They went out of their way to replace capsules when they became old. Replacing capsules is the equivalent of organ transplantation. It inflicts too much damage on the body. All it takes is to let them grow old and get dirty. They grow old exactly because they are living creatures. There is no need to force them to metabolize. As long as there is a flow, they will not die.

What is more important is to create that flow. Create a flow and connect architecture to the outside world. As liquid flows, energy flows and matter flows, architecture turns into a living creature and becomes one with the environment.

And that is when a 'small architecture' becomes a 'small living creature.' The smaller the creature is, the stronger it is. Of the several million types of living creatures that exist on this planet, why is it that 80% of them are insects? It is because insects are small. From a point of view of a small presence, the world is a rich environment filled with diversity. Small insects can live in spaces between stones, or in some cases, even live inside a stone. Contrastingly, the smaller one can be in size, the richer, bigger and more tolerant the world is. On the contrary, the bigger one can be in size, the narrower, more cramped and less comfortable the world is to live. No more room for big, arrogant living creatures. 21st century architecture has to be small. It has to be connected to the world by being small and ever-flowing. It has got to be small to survive.

建築がいかに分解できたとしても，依然として「大きな建築」から脱却できない。

建築をひとつ建てることによって，この国の低劣な「大きな」システムに加担して，その存続に手を貸していいだろうか。

「Water Block」では，建築を小さなブロックに物理的に分解するプロジェクトとしてスタートしたが，試作を進めているうち，物理的小ささだけでは満足しきれなくなって，「経済的小ささ」の領域にまで手を出すことになって「Water Branch」と，名前まで変えてしまった。

「Water Block」はただの水を入れる小さなポリタンクであったが，「Water Branch」では，ユニットとユニットをつなぐことが可能となり，そこに水を流すことができるようになったのである。温水を建築の中に流せば，建物自体が温まるし，冷水を流せば，効率的な冷房が可能となる。水を暖めたり冷やすにも，電気やガスに頼る必要はもはやない。太陽の光を効率的に利用するだけで，水は暖かくも冷たくもなるのである。

ただのポリタンクの転用であった「Water Block」から，水の流れる「Water Branch」への転換には大きな意味があった。流れが発生することによって，かくも本質的に物体の持っている意味自体が転換するということを思い知らされた。建築自体に水が流れることによって，すなわち建築の体内を水が流れることによって，簡単にいえば，建築であったはずのものが，生き物へと生まれ変わるのである。ポリタンクが細胞へと変身をとげるのである。そんな単純なことで，これほど大きな転換が起こるとは，実のところ想像してはいなかった。

流れをつくり出すだけで，建築は生物に生まれ変わるのである。「小さい建築」とは，結局のところ生物の別名なのかもしれない。メタボリズムはいいところまでいっていたが，肝心なところを見落としていた。建築を小さいカプセルの集合体にして，カプセルが「取り替え」という形で新陳代謝すれば建築は生命になると，彼らは考えていた。

「大きな建築」を「小さな建築」に分解しようという気持ちにおいて，彼らはぼくの仲間である。しかし，メタボリストは流れの重要性に気付かなかった。代わりに新陳代謝を考えた。古くなったら，カプセルを取り替えようと無理をした。カプセルの取り替えは臓器移植である。身体にとって，無理が大きすぎる。古びて汚れていくにまかせればいいのである。古びいくからこそ，生物なのであって，無理に新陳代謝などさせる必要はない。流れがあるかぎり，死ぬことはない。

それよりも大事なことは，流れをつくり出すこと。流れをつくり出して，建築を外の世界につないでやることなのである。液体が流れ，エネルギーが流れ，物質が流れれば，建築は生き物となり，環境と一体になるのである。

その時「小さな建築」は「小さな生き物」となる。生き物は小さいほど強い。地球上に数100万種の生物がいて，その80％が昆虫であるのはなぜか。昆虫が小さいからである。小さな存在から見れば，世界は多様性に満ちた，豊かな環境である。小さな虫は石と石との隙間にも住めるし，場合によっては，石の中にだって住める。自分が小さければ小さいほど，逆に世界は豊かであり，大きいし，寛容である。逆に自分が大きければ大きいほど，世界は狭苦しく，住みにくい。大きくて，傲慢な生物には居場所がない。21世紀の建築は小さくなければならない。小さくて，しかも流れ続けることで，世界とつながっていなくてはいけない。小さくなければ生きていけない。

2002-06　**Ginzan-Onsen Fujiya**
Yamagata, Japan

Site plan

Overall view over Ginzan river　銀山川越しに見る全景

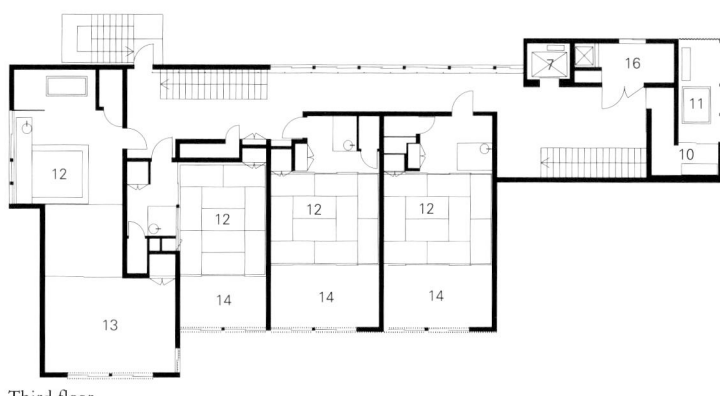
Third floor

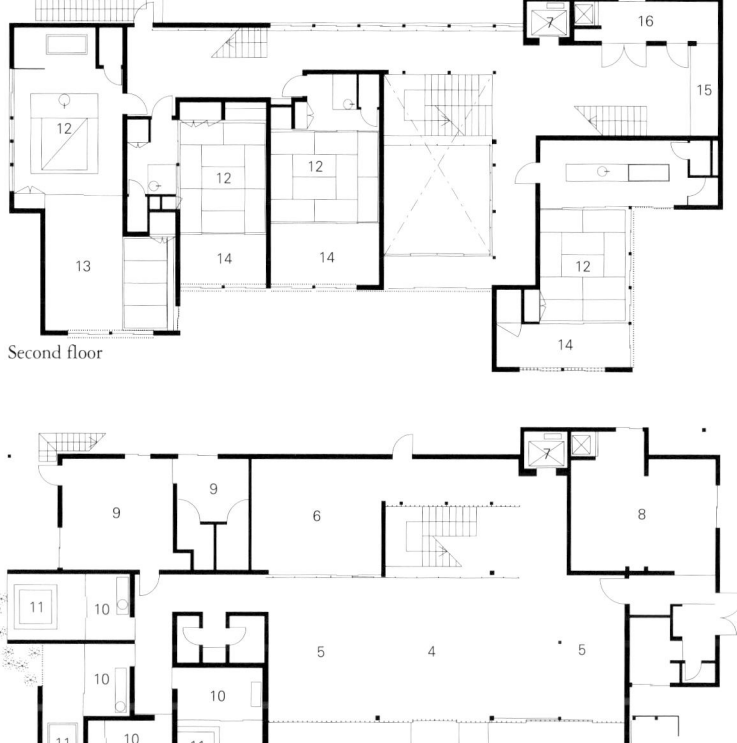
Second floor

First floor S=1:300

1	BASIN
2	APPROACH
3	CAFE
4	ENTRANCE HALL
5	LOUNGE
6	OFFICE
7	ELEVATOR
8	KITCHEN
9	STAFF ROOM
10	DRESSING ROOM
11	BATH ROOM
12	GUEST ROOM
13	DINING ROOM
14	VERANDA
15	GALLERY
16	PANTRY
17	GINZAN RIVER

The project is a four-storey wooden hot spring hotel built at the bottom of a deep valley in a snow country. As the one hundred years old building became obsolete, it was restored and the figure of one hundred years ago was revealed after as many usable wooden columns and beams as possible were reused and aluminum sashes and concrete walls were eliminated. For the interior, an atrium was inserted and internal space was recomposed, centering this vertical space. A delicate screen (sumushiko) that is made of 4 mm-wide bamboo wrapped the atrium and made it possible to induce gentleness that ordinal wooden lattice do not offer. Stained-glass that is exceedingly transparent used in Cistercian monastery in the middle age was applied for an opening of the first floor facing the outside. Accordingly, the interior and the exterior space were gently connected. Modern stained-glass is usually made with 3 mm-thick glass, but this time we specially asked craftsman of Saint-Gobain in France to use 4 mm-thick glass. Thus, the stained glass alone separates the outdoor and the indoor without protection of other glass. By the series of delicate screens that are positioned between transparency and opaqueness, tender light is filled with darkness inside. The space heals us, as if hot spring heals our bodies.

銀山温泉 藤屋

雪国の深い谷の底に建つ、木造4階建ての温泉旅館。100年の歴史を持つ建物が老朽化したため、使える木の柱や梁を可能な限り再利用し、アルミサッシやコンクリートの壁を取り除いて、100年前の姿を再生した。インテリアにおいては、アトリウムを挿入し、その垂直的空間を中心として内部空間を再構成した。アトリウムを4mm幅の竹を用いた繊細なスクリーン(簾虫籠)で包み込むことによって、従来の木製の格子には無いやわらかさを、室内に導入することが可能となった。外部に面した1階の開口部には、中世にシトー派修道院で多用された限りなく透明に近いステンドグラスを填め、室内と室外をやわらかく接続した。通常、現代のステンドグラスは厚さ3mmで吹かれるが、ここでは特別にフランスのサンゴバンの職人たちに依頼して、4mm厚のステンドグラスをつくり、他のガラスに保護されることなく、そのステンドグラス1枚で、外部と内部とが仕切られている。これらの透明と不透明との中間に位置する繊細なスクリーン群によって、室内はやさしい光と影に満たされ、身体は温泉に癒されるように空間に癒される。

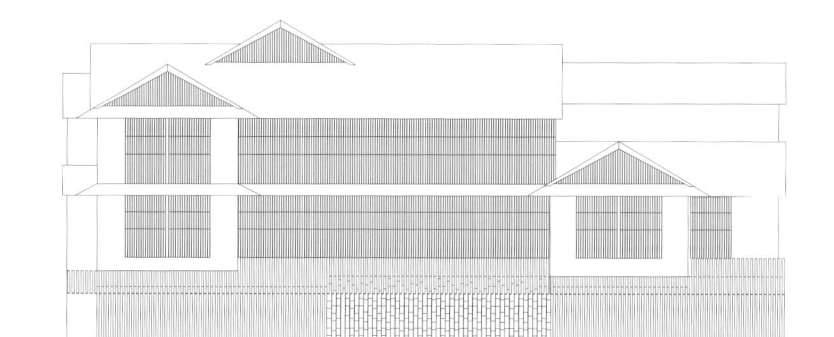
North elevation S=1:300

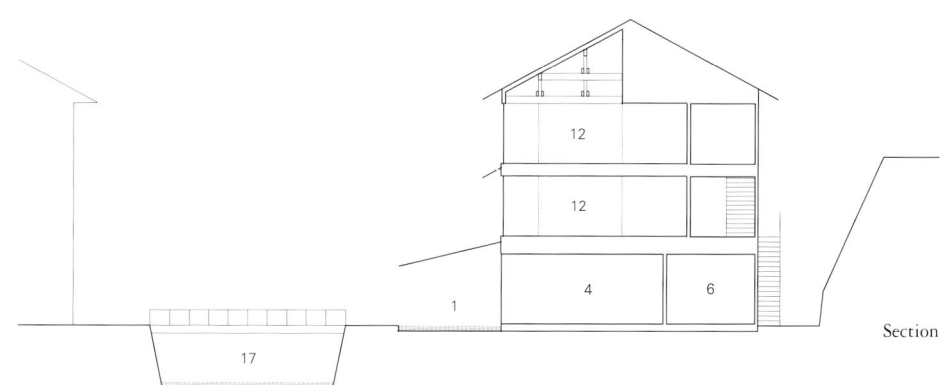
Section

Staircase　階段室

Corridor on second floor　2階廊下

Entrance hall and lounge on first floor　1階エントランスホールとラウンジ

Guest room on third floor　3階客室

View toward entrance hall from lounge　ラウンジよりエントランスホールを見る

Guest room on second floor　2階客室

2003-06 Z58
Shanghai, China

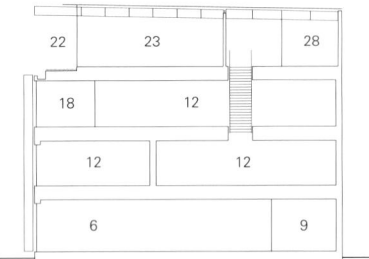

East elevation

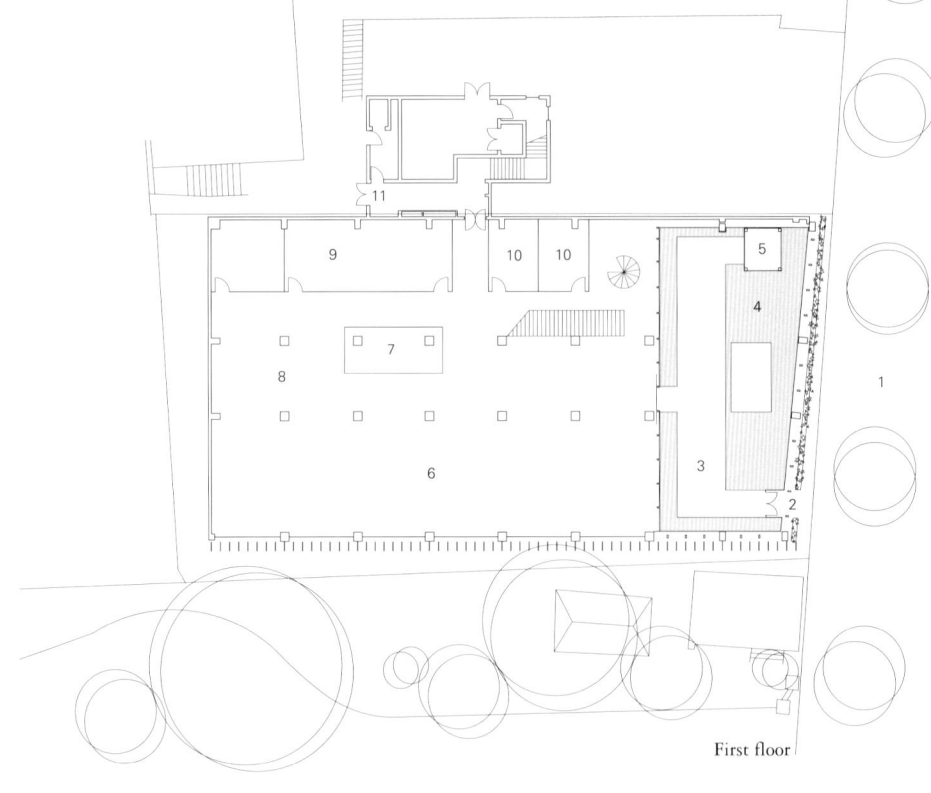

First floor

Section S=1:500

1 PANYU ROAD	16 BRIDGE FOR ELEVATOR
2 MAIN ENTRANCE	17 DESIGN STUDIO
3 RECEPTION	18 OFFICE (PRIVATE)
4 BASIN / ATRIUM	19 MEETING ROOM
5 ELEVATOR	20 CLOSET
6 SHOP / SHOWROOM	21 PANTRY
7 BAR	22 BASIN
8 CAFE	23 GUEST ROOM
9 BUSINESS LOUNGE	24 BASIN LOUNGE
10 OFFICE (SALES PART)	25 LOUNGE / BOOK SHELVES
11 ENTRY FOR STAFF	26 BATHROOM
12 OFFICE	27 SAUNA
13 STORAGE	28 FITNESS ROOM
14 WC FOR STAFF	29 KITCHEN
15 VOID	

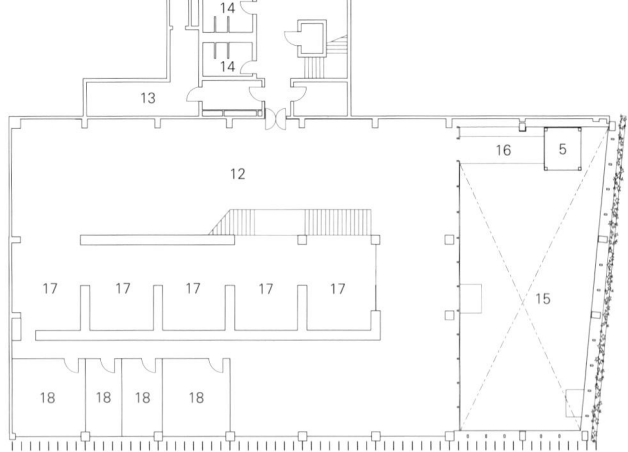

Second floor

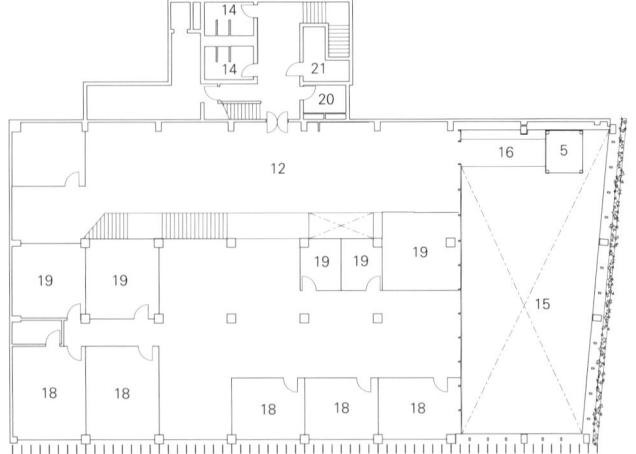

Third floor

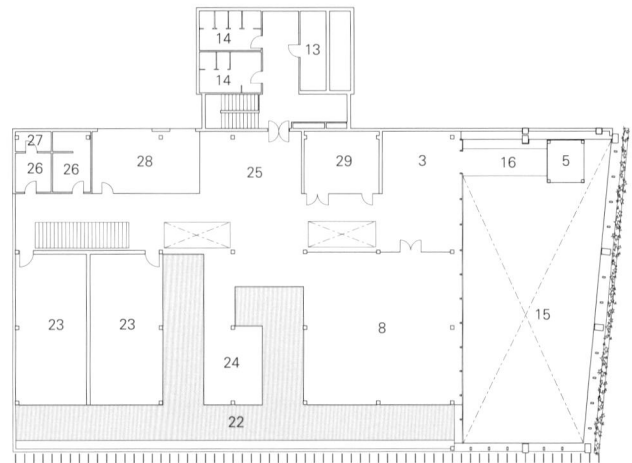

Fourth floor S=1:500

We made an office that gives oasis-like peace to people in the historical district of Shanghai. We wanted to restore nature in the office abundant of water and greenery. In detail, we made a stainless steel plant box between the road and the building. Ivy was planted there that cuts off noise from the street. The polished stainless steel plant box reflects the street and erases the architecture. Only the ivy creates a boundary between the street and the building. Furthermore, on the backsides, we inserted a second filter made with glass and a waterfall. By inserting two filters between the urban and the building, we reconstructed nature in the office interior. On the highest floor, we inserted a large water surface. The broken light particles created by the upper aluminum louver blades resonate with the water surface. We were able to recreate another nature that is filled with light particles on the interface of the sky and the architecture.

Z58

上海の旧市街地に，オアシスのような，人に安らぎを与えるオフィスをつくった。水と緑に溢れたオフィスの中に自然を取り戻したいと考えた。具体的には，道路と建物との間にステンレスでプラントボックスをつくり，そこにツタを植えて，ストリートのノイズをカットした。鏡面仕上げのステンレスでできたプラントボックスは，道路を映し込み，建築は消去されて，ツタだけが道路と建築との境界を形成している。さらにその裏側に，ガラスと滝でつくった2番目のフィルターを挿入した。二つのフィルターを都市と建築との間に挿入することによって，オフィスの内部に自然を再創造した。最上階では大きな水面を建築に挿入し，上部のアルミルーバーによって砕かれた光の粒子と水面とが響きあって，粒子状の光に溢れたもうひとつの自然を，空と建築との境界面に再生することができた。

Overall view from Panyu Road　番禺路より見る全景

Atrium on first floor. View of planter boxes over basin
1階アトリウム。水盤越しにプランター・ボックスを見る

Ribbed glass wall of atrium　アトリウムのガラス・リブ壁面

Atrium on first floor　1階アトリウム

View of basin from lounge on fourth floor　4階ラウンジより水盤を見る

Bridge for elevator on third floor　3階エレベータ・ブリッジ

Atrium. View toward elevator shaft　アトリウム。エレベータ・シャフト方向を見る

2003-08 Asahi Broadcasting Corporation
Fukushima, Osaka, Japan

Overall view from Dojima river　堂島川越しに見る全景

Overall view from southeast　南東より見る全景

View of west elavation over Naniwa street　なにわ筋越しに見る西立面

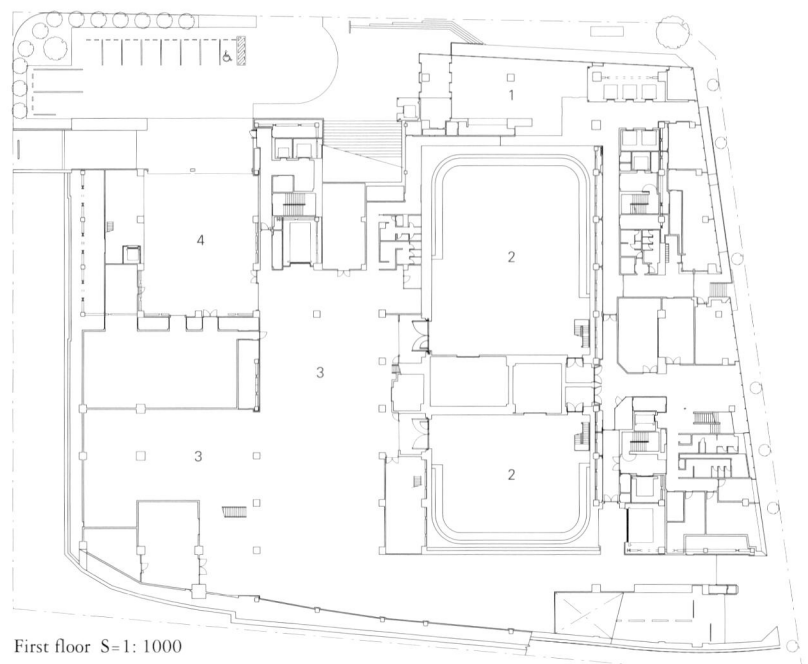
First floor S=1: 1000

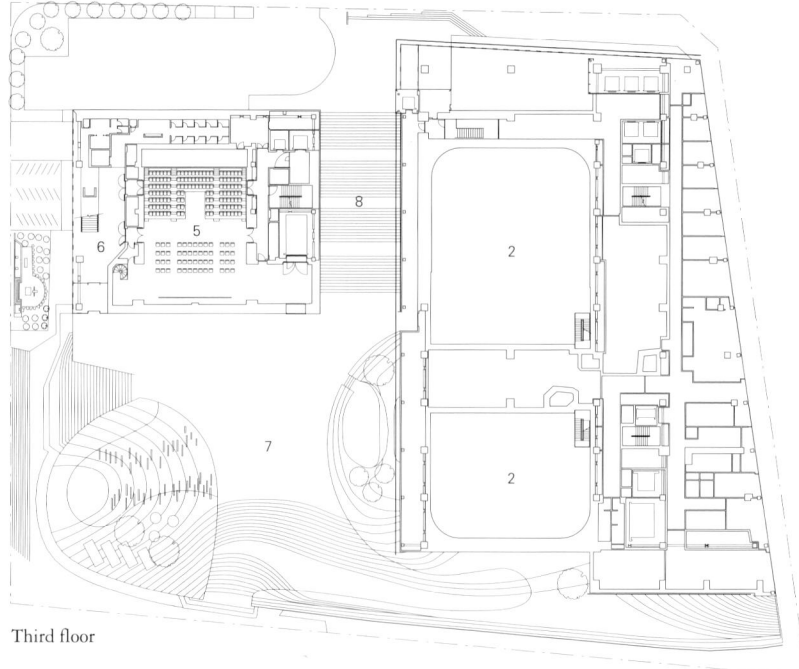
Third floor

We proposed a gateway style broadcasting station building which connects nature and the city at a site facing the Doutombori River which flows through the center of Osaka city. For security reasons broadcasting stations usually tend to be black boxes showing their backs to the city, however on this project we aimed to design a station that was open to the city and create a new flow of people in the city. The river and the broadcasting station are connected with a mounded geometric square. Naniwa Street on west which is the main street of Osaka city and the broadcasting station is connected with a 'Hollow' space at the lower part of the building. Thus we could achieve an open and familiar facility for the citizens of Osaka. In the square, there is a hall where a live audience show can be recorded and this has become another interface to connect the broadcasting station and the city.

The exterior is covered with a hound's tooth pattern made of recycled timber panels, which helps to bring a soft and warm atmosphere that usual office buildings do not have, and it adds a new face to the Japanese waterfront which lacks richness.

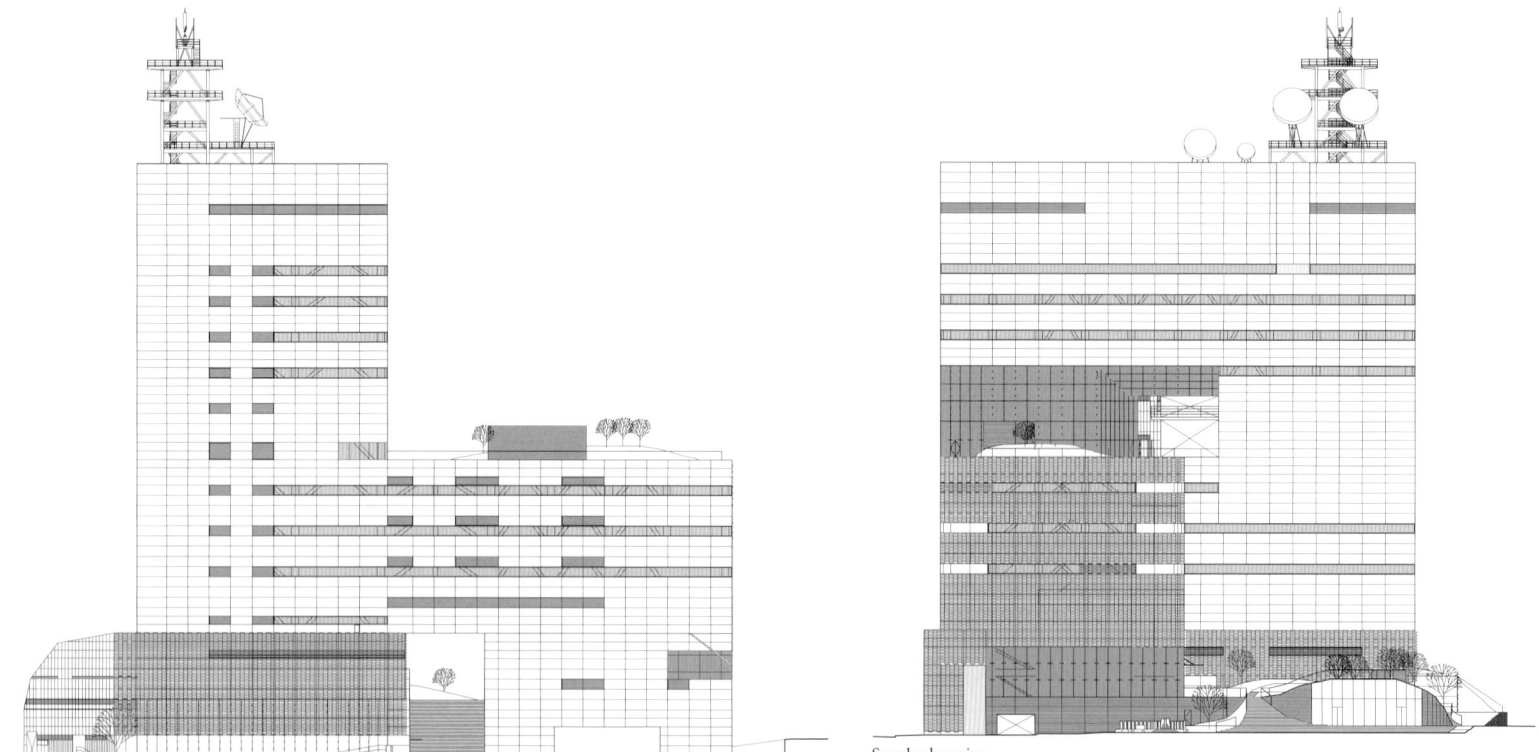

West elevation S=1:1000

South elevation

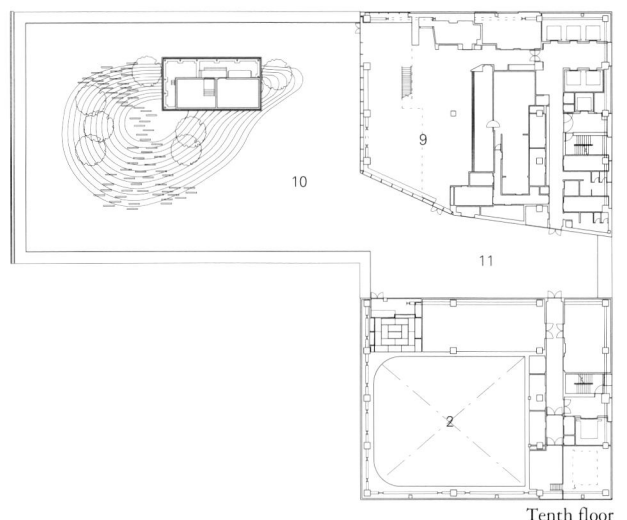
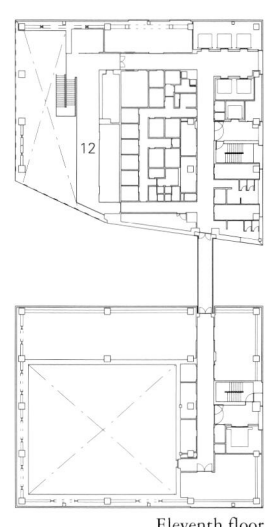

Tenth floor　　　Eleventh floor　　　Twelfth floor

1　ENTRANCE HALL
2　STUDIO
3　STORAGE (SET)
4　GARAGE (BROADCAST)
5　ABC HALL
6　FOYER (ABC HALL)
7　WOODEN DECK
8　STEPPED OPEN SPACE
9　DINING ROOM
10　TERRACE
11　AIR HOLE
12　PARLOR
13　OFFICE
14　MEETING ROOM (LARGE)

朝日放送

大阪の中心を流れる道頓堀川に面した敷地に,自然と都市とをつなぐゲート型の放送局を構想した。通常,放送局は,セキュリティ重視のあまり,都市に背を向けたブラックボックスとなりやすい。今回のプロジェクトでは,逆に都市に開かれ,都市に新しい人の流れをつくり出す放送局を目的とした。川と放送局は,マウンド状の広場によってつながれ,西側の大阪の主要幹線なにわ筋と放送局は,低層部にあけられた「孔」状の空間によってつながれる。この「孔」を媒介として広場は都市につながれ,市民に親しまれる開かれた放送局が実現した。広場に面しては,視聴者参加型の番組収録が行われるホールが配置され,放送局と都市をつなぐもうひとつの接点となっている。

外壁には再生木材を用いたパネルを千鳥状にレイアウトすることで,通常のオフィスビルにはないようなやわらかさや暖かさを達成し,潤いの欠けた日本のウォーターフロントに新しい顔をつけ加えた。

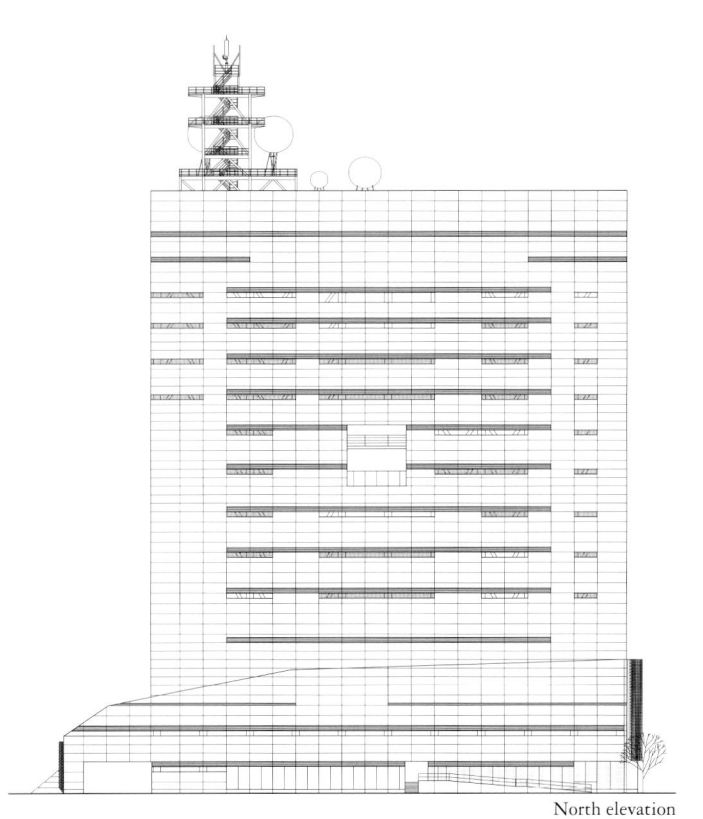

North elevation

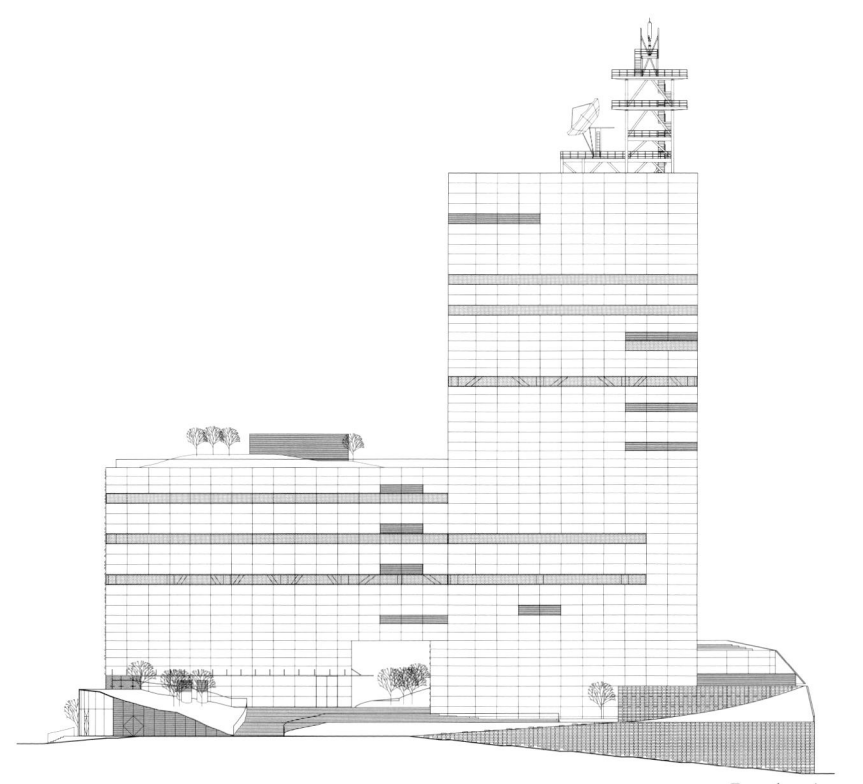

East elevation

Entrance hall エントランス・ホール

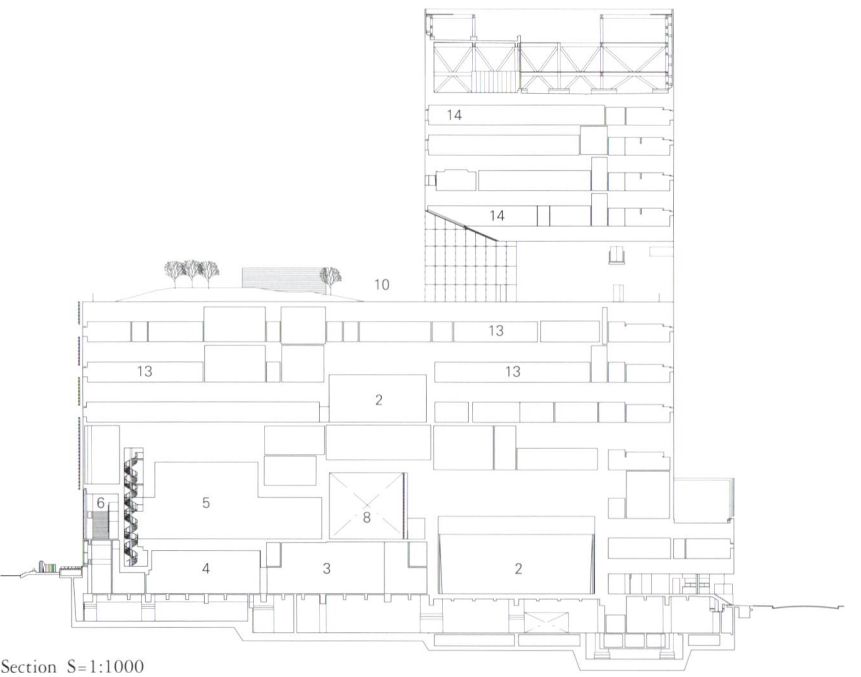

Section S=1:1000

Entrance hall. View toward Naniwa street　エントランス・ホール。なにわ筋方向を見る

Dining room for staff on tenth floor　10階社員食堂

Evening view of dining room for staff from terrace　スカイテラスより食堂を見る。夕景

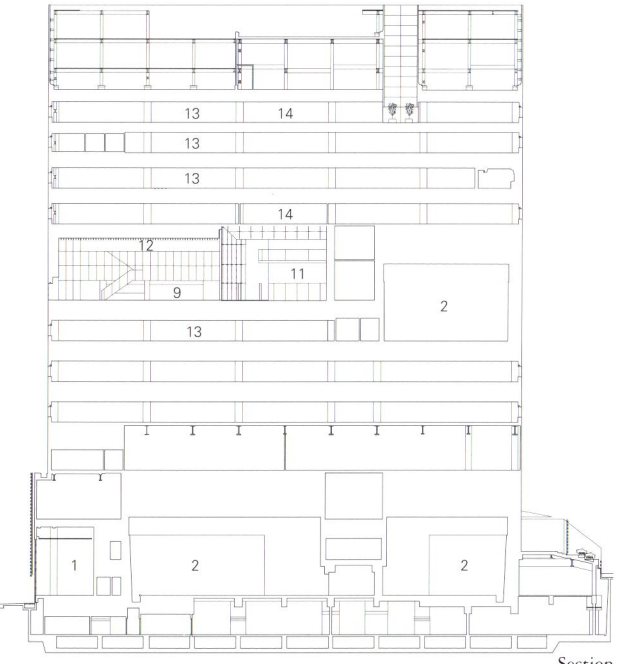
Section

2004-06   Hoshinosato Annex
Kudamatsu, Yamaguchi, Japan

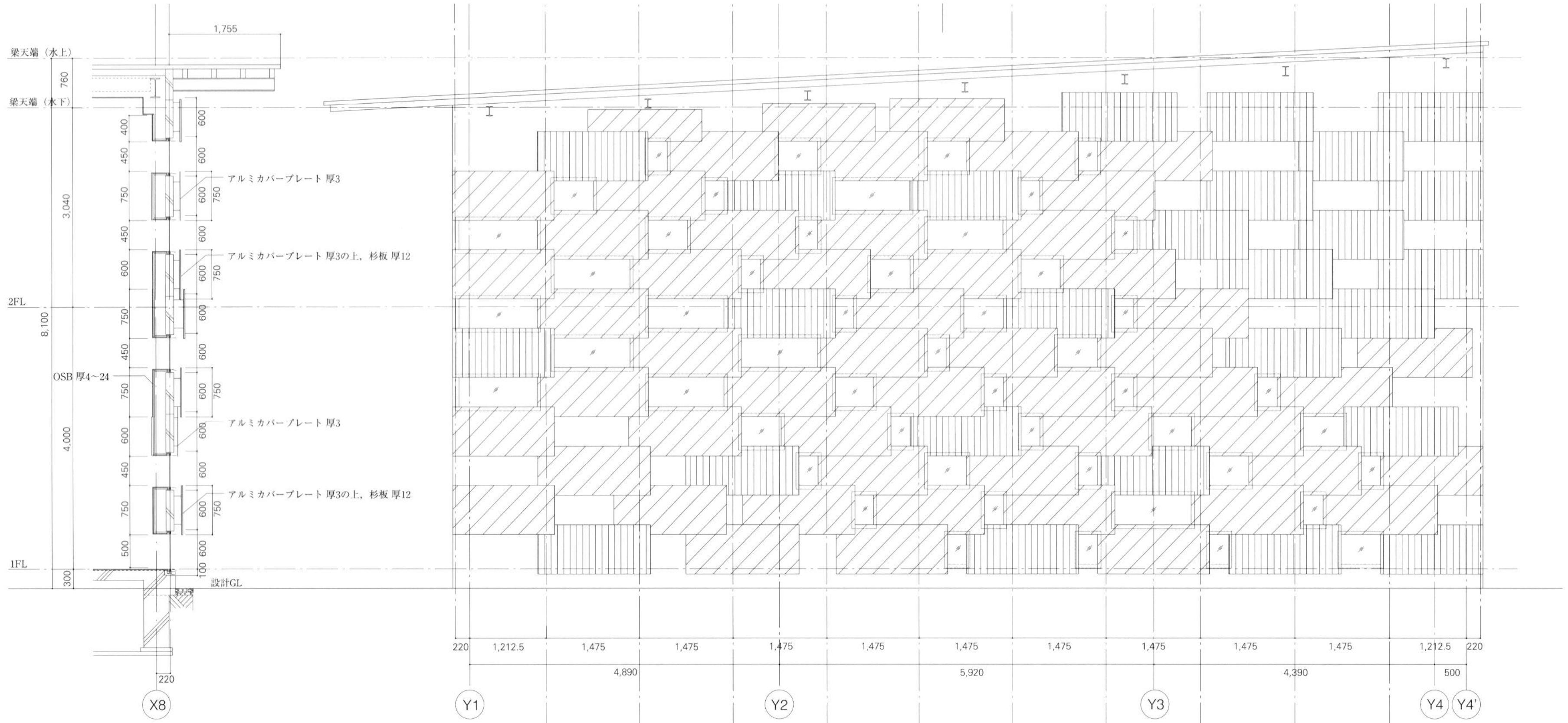

East elevation S=1:100

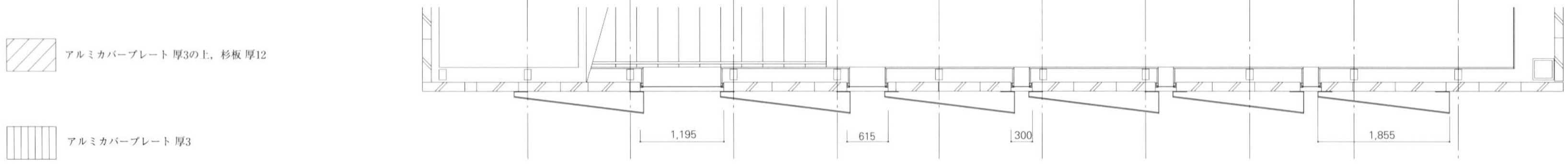

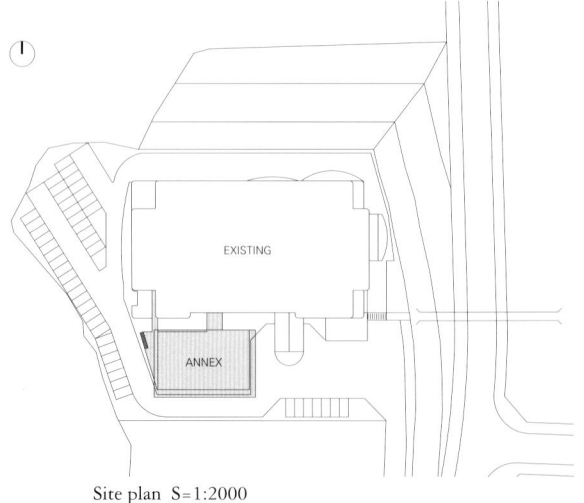

Site plan S=1:2000

The building is an extension project of a special nursing home for elderly people located in Kudamatsu city, Yamaguchi prefecture. We intended a 'house', which cordially welcomes the elderly and in which they can relax. In order to fulfill the purpose, we comprehensively used natural materials also to the exterior. Furthermore, natural materials were divided into smaller human-scale unit and we tried to design the facility closer to 'home'. The exterior wall was consisted of particles in a small unit made of cedar and aluminum boards. The gap created by shifting the components was detailed to function as an opening. The elements overlap in different levels like fish scale, so that the existence of the unit will look apparent. Although there were parts that cannot use wood for the exterior wall because of the legal restriction, those areas were gradationally covered by aluminum and wood and prevented only the part to be enclosed with aluminum panels. In that way, it was possible to gain loose and gentle change of texture that is found in the natural world.

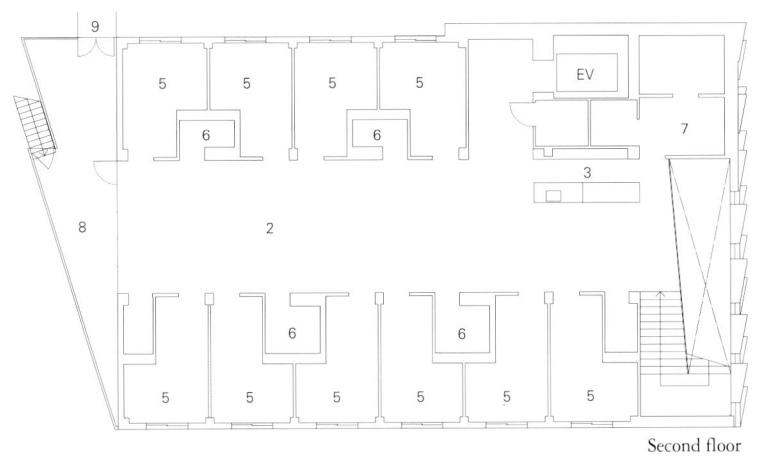

Second floor

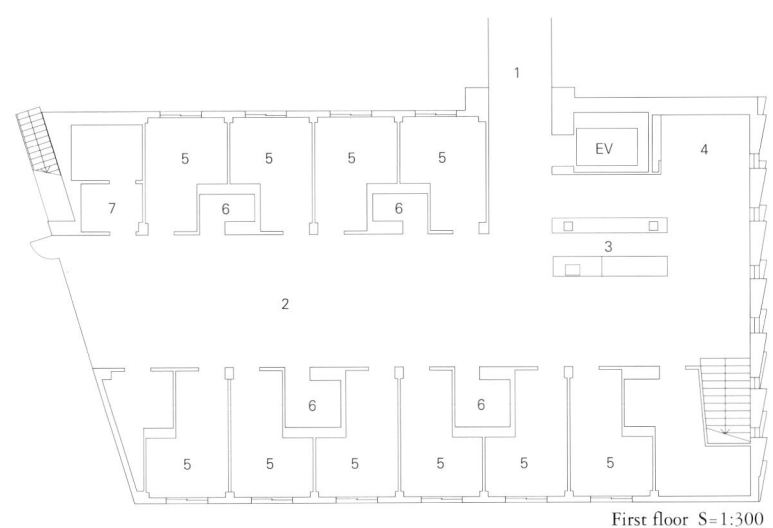

First floor S=1:300

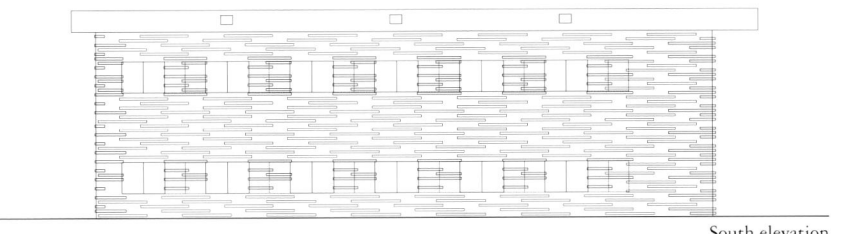

South elevation

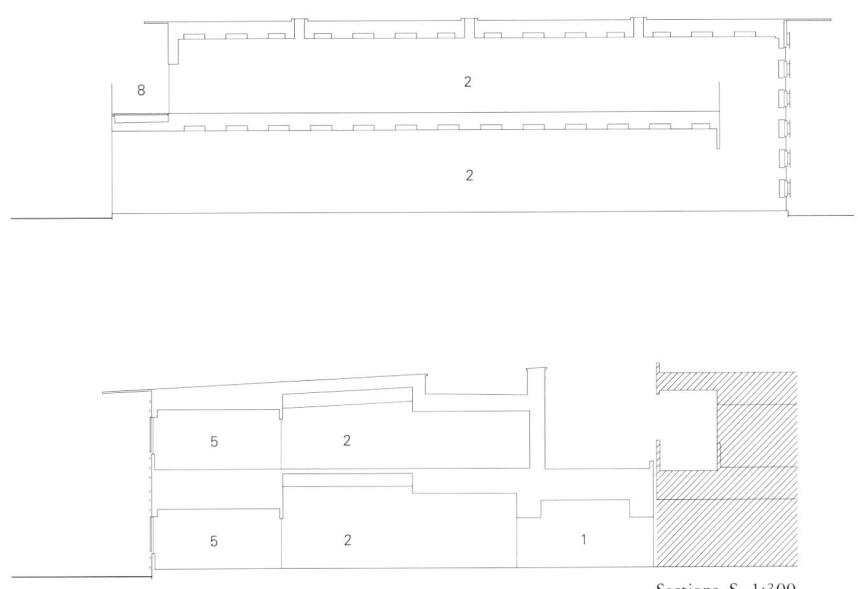

Sections S=1:300

ほしのさとアネックス

山口県下松市にある特別養護老人ホームの増築計画。老人を暖かく迎え、老人が心安らぐ「家」を目指し、外装にも自然素材を多用した。しかも自然素材をヒューマンスケールを持つ小さな単位へと分解することで、「家」へと近づけようとした。外装は杉板とアルミ板でできた小さな粒子で単位を構成し、その単位ユニットをずらすことによってできる隙間を、開口部とするディテールとした。ユニット同士は、魚のウロコのように段差をつけながら重ね合わされ、単位の存在を浮き上がらせるディテールとした。外壁には、法律上の規制で木を使えない部分が存在するが、その部分だけ突然アルミ板貼りとするのではなく、アルミと木とをグラデーショナルに切り換えていくことによって、自然界にあるような、ゆるやかでやわらかいテクスチャーの変化を獲得することが可能となった。

1 CORRIDOR
2 GROUP LIVING ROOM
3 PANTRY
4 COMMUNICATION ROOM
5 ROOM
6 WC
7 DRESSING ROOM
8 TERRACE
9 BRIDGE

Overall view from southeast　南東より見る全景

View of staircase from communication room　談話室より階段室を見る

Pantry and communication room on first floor　1階パントリーと談話室

Group living room on second floor　2階共同生活室

2004-06 Y Hütte
Japan

Overall view from south 南より見る全景

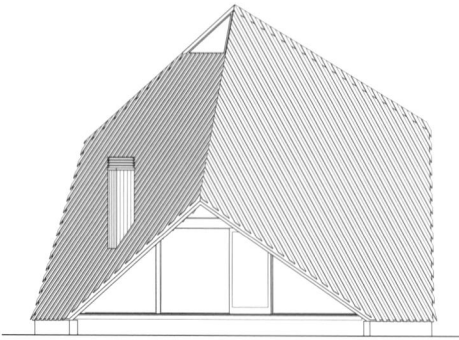
South elevation

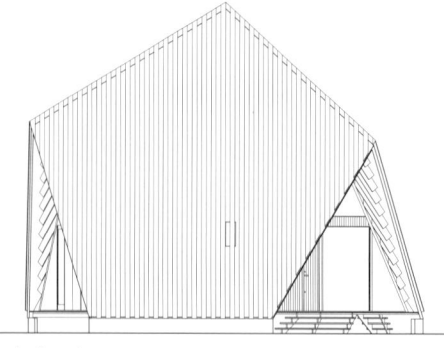
North elevation

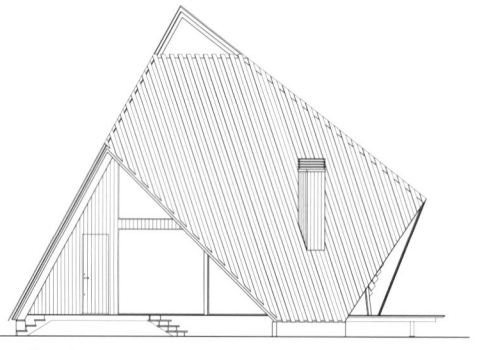
West elevation

View from west　西より見る

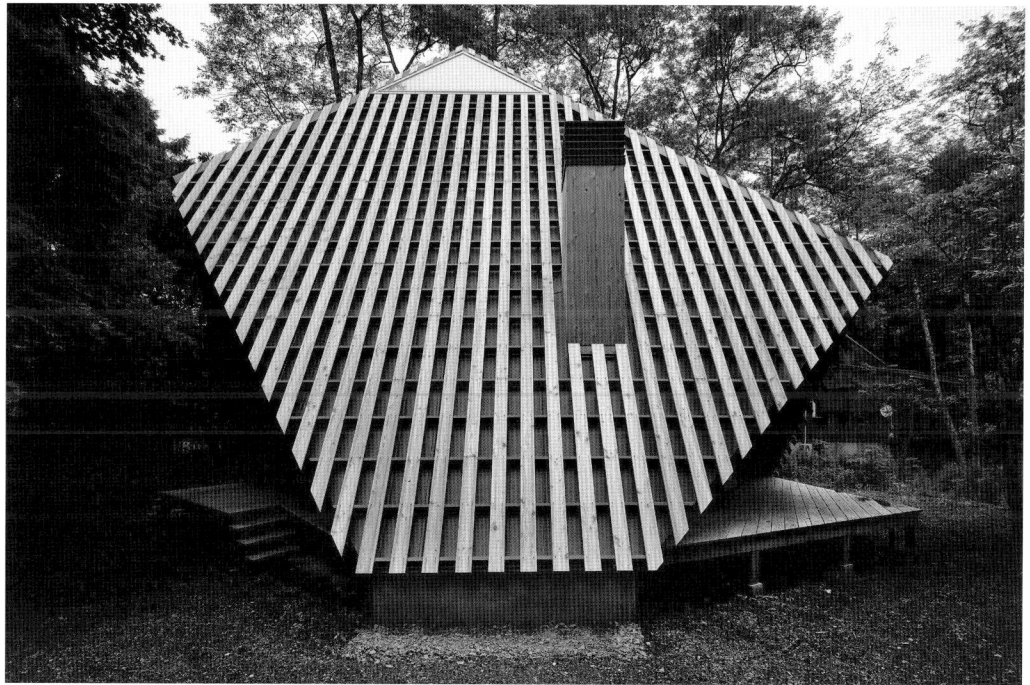

Southwest elevation. Vertical siding roof　南西立面。縦羽目板張の屋根

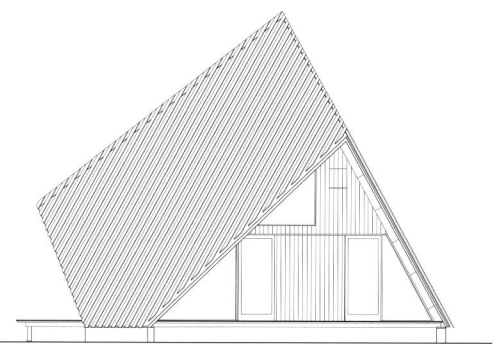

East elevation S=1:200

I reflected upon how a hut in a forest should be.

A quadrilateral plan drawn on a perpendicular Cartesian coordinate system would restrict the direction and would be too artificial and constructive in the natural forest. I am more interested in an architecture that is "close to nature". So I came up with a form structured by resting three panels on each other to produce a triangular pyramid and cutting its corners. A large single-space is created by the three panels.

The panels, functioning as both roof and wall, are held by wooden ribs at 300 mm pitch, and these ribs give an effect of diffusing light just like the branches and leaves of a tree. The slanted panels meet together in a tree-like manner, giving it an impression of top branches of trees tied together. This effect is the reason why Frank Lloyd Wright and Buckminster Fuller preferred triangular to rectangular form for its quality of resembling nature. The plan becomes a hexagon, and when each edge is given different elements; dining set, fire place, piano, kitchen counter, bed, writing table, the elements are adjoined in obtuse angles and dispersed in the space creating a loosely partitioned room.

As a heating device, an "Ondor-type (Korean floor heater)" floor heating system is introduced. Hot air is sent under the space between the doubled-floor, and vented through the slit opened near the window to prevent condensation.

In summer, air conditioning is limited to ventilation considering the cool climate. The tilted panels and high ceiling enables ventilation through natural gravity. In addition, the skylights are positioned corresponding to the dominant wind which cools down and thus creating effective ventilation.

This hut, designed through the investigation of the form, "close to nature", somehow resembles Laugier's "Primitive Hut" and ancient pit dwellings.

Y Hütte

森の中の小屋は、どうあるべきかを考えた。

　直交デカルト座標による四角形の平面は向きを規定してしまい、森の中では人工的で、また構築的である。より「自然に近い」建築のあり方に興味がある。そこで3枚のパネルを互いにもたせかけ三角錐をつくり、その角を切り落とした形態を採用することにした。結果として、3枚のパネルによる大きな一室空間が現れる。

　屋根でも壁でもあるパネルは、300mmピッチの木製のリブにより支えられていて、このリブは樹木の枝葉のように光を拡散する効果を与える。パネルの勾配が樹形に重なり、あたかも樹木の先端をつないだような印象となる。フランク・ロイド・ライトやバックミンスター・フラーが三角形にこだわり、三角形が四角形よりも自然に近い形態だと考えた理由もここにある。その平面は六角形となり、各辺に六つの要素(ダイニングセット、暖炉、ピアノ、キッチンカウンター、ベッド、書斎机)を配することにすると、要素が鈍角で隣り合うため向きが分散し、一室空間を緩やかに分節する。

　また、暖房はオンドル型の床暖房を採用した。二重床の床下空間に温風を送り込み、空気式の床暖房として利用した後、窓際に設けたスリットから吹き出させる。窓際から吹き出すことにより、結露防止も期待できる。夏季は冷涼な気候を考慮し、換気のみとしている。パネルの勾配と高い天井高は重力換気を促す。さらに、屋根の頂点近くのトップライトは、卓越風向にあわせて設けることで、吸引効果による効率的な換気をもたらす。

　「自然に近い」あり方を探求したこの小屋は、なぜかしらロージェの「原初の小屋」や「竪穴式住居」を想起させることとなった。

View toward bedroom from living room　居間より寝室方向を見る

View toward entrance. Natural light through skylight　玄関方向を見る。天窓から差す自然光

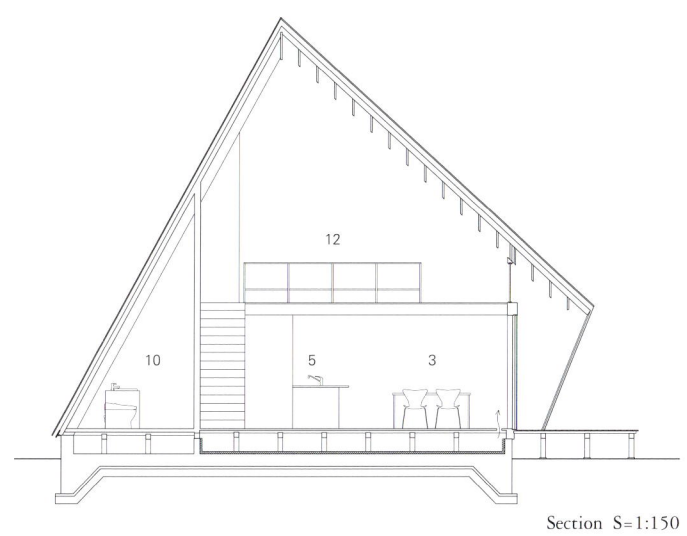

1 TERRACE
2 ENTRANCE
3 KITCHEN
4 MUSIC ROOM
5 LIVING ROOM
6 DINING ROOM
7 STUDY
8 BEDROOM
9 STORAGE
10 WC
11 BATHROOM
12 GUEST ROOM
13 VOID

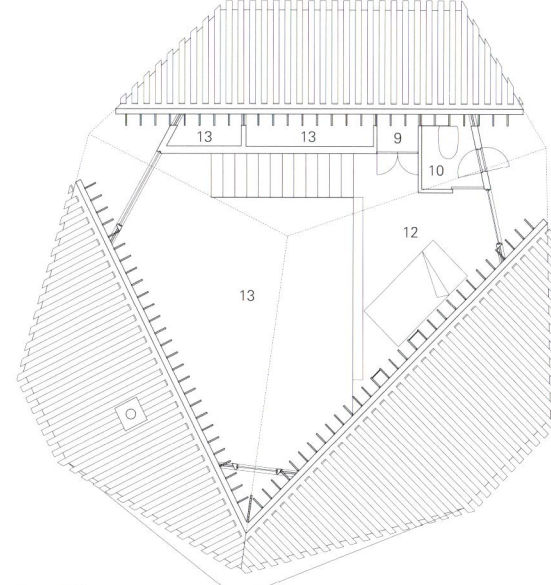

Second floor

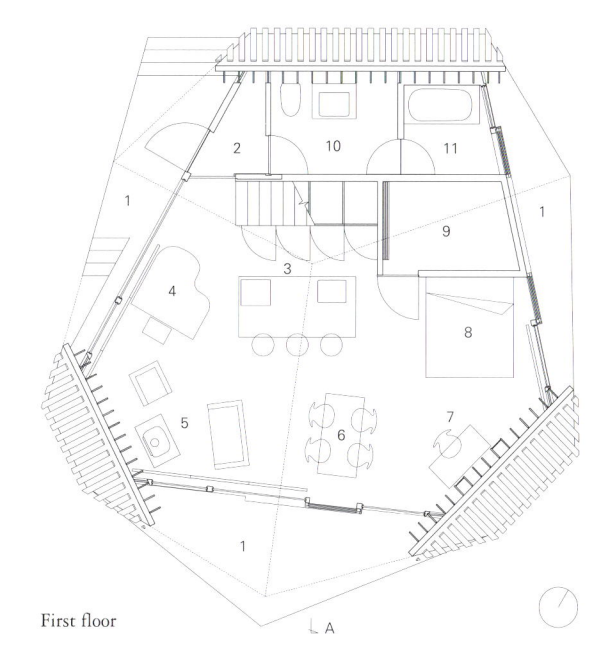

First floor

Section S=1:150

35

2004-06 Yusuhara Town Hall
Takaoka, Kochi, Japan

Overall view from southwest 南西より見る全景

Atrium　アトリウム

Pillars and beams　柱と梁

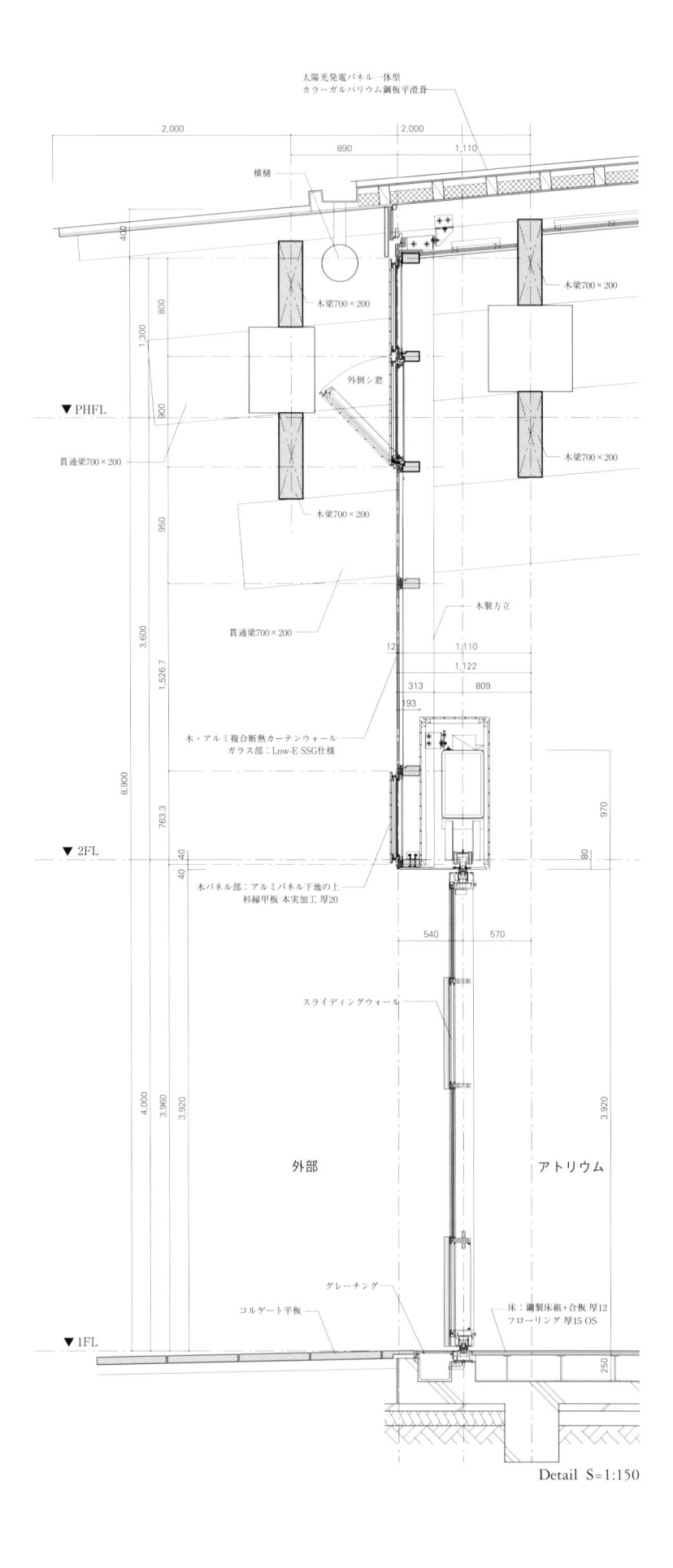

Detail S=1:150

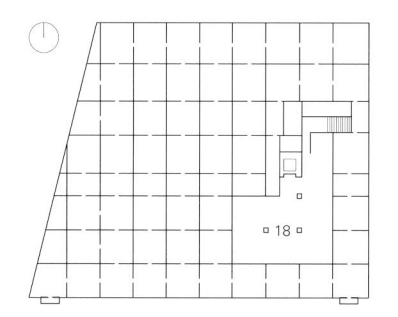

Basement S=1:1000 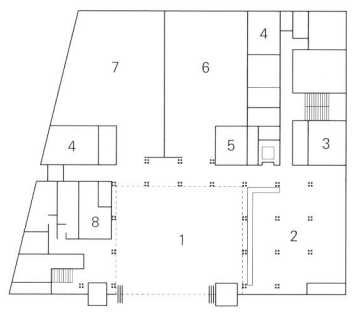   First floor 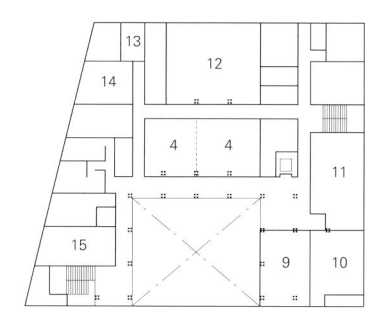   Second floor 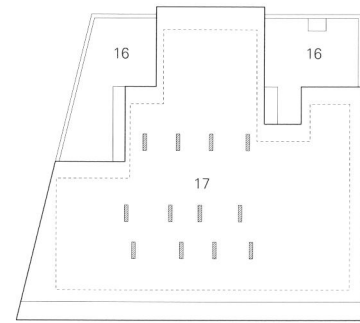   Third floor

This is a town hall project which becomes a new community starting point for the city of Yusahara in Kochi Prefecture. This town is known for its urban development using 'Japanese Cedar'. In consideration of the heavy snow falls, a generous atrium is prepared for the spaces of daily facilities such as the bank, the local agricultural association, the local chamber of commerce and industry etc. This square is also used for a traditional performance called 'Kagura' and other festivals as well.

Local cedar is used for the structure and an 18 m span was achieved by doubling the lattice beams. We aimed to show the simplicity and beauty of Japanese timber structures by exposing this structure of double beams sandwiching the columns.

The interior and exterior squares are divided by large sliding doors which are usually used for airplane hangars, and it is kept open from April to October to unite the inside and outside without any air-conditioning. The roof is covered with solar panels and a 'cool-tube' system is laid underground to bring in stable warm air from underground in winter.

梼原町総合庁舎

「杉」による街づくりで知られる、高知県梼原町の新しい交流の起点となる「木の町役場」（総合庁舎）。雪の多い気象条件への対応として、内部に大きなアトリウムを設け、銀行、農協、商工会など町民が日常生活で必要とする施設を内包する、巨大な室内広場をつくった。この広場は、神楽と呼ばれる伝統的なパフォーマンスや、祭りのための空間としても機能する。

構造には地元産の杉材を用い、18mという大スパンをダブルラチス梁構造で可能とした。柱を2本の梁が挟んで建築を支えている様子を可視化し、日本の木構造の簡潔な美しさを人々が再確認できるような建築をめざした。

室内広場と外部の広場は、飛行機の格納庫に用いる巨大なスライディングドアで区切られ、4月から10月の間のスライディングドアは開け放たれ、室内と室外は完全に一体化され、その間は空調を行わない。屋根は太陽光発電パネルで覆われ、地下にはクールチューブシステムが配備され、冬季は地中の安定した空気を用いた省エネルギーの空調が行われる。

1 ATRIUM
2 GENERAL AFFAIRS AND INDUSTRIAL PROMOTION SECTION
3 DEPUTY MAYOR'S OFFICE
4 MEETING ROOM
5 CASHIER'S SECTION
6 KOCHI BANK
7 ZEN-NOH'S OFFICE
8 NIGHT WACHMAN'S ROOM
9 MAYOR'S OFFICE
10 MEETING ROOM (EMERGENCY SUPORT)
11 ENVIRONMENTAL MAINTENANCE SECTION
12 ASSEMBLY HALL
13 CHAIRPERSON'S OFFICE
14 ASSEMBLY SECRETARAIT
15 CHAMBER OF COMMERCE AND INDUSTRY
16 MECHANICAL
17 SOLAR PANEL
18 BOOK STACK

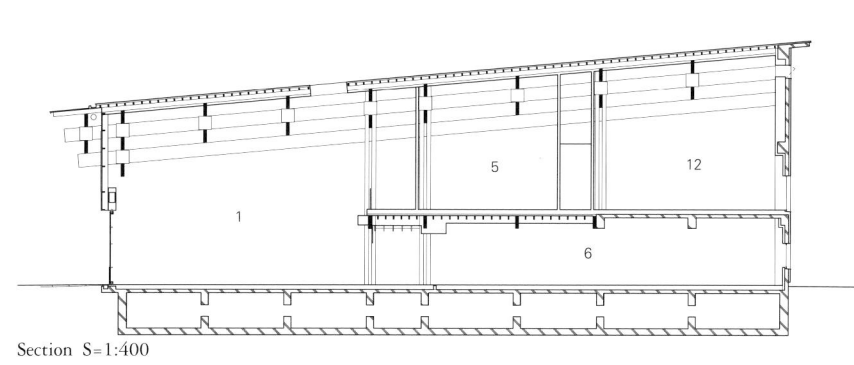

Section S=1:400

Meeting room　会議室

2004-06
Chokkura Plaza
Takanezawa, Tochigi, Japan

We restored a stone warehouse that was built about a hundred years ago made out of Oya stone. We designed the building that the old and the new, and the opaque and the transparent gradationally coexist. Blocks made of Oya stone were joined with 6 mm-thick steel plates. A new integral structure system enabled the gradational condition. Letting stone to bear compression load and steel to tolerate tension load, masonry and a steel frame structure were gradually merged. It was possible to create a porous natural body that a rich texture of the stone and lightness of the steel coexist.

At one time Frank Lloyd Wright was attracted by spongy and tender appearance of Oya Stone and used in Imperial Hotel (1923) in spite of surroundings oppositions. Wright considered a porous substance becomes much tender by the shades produced in the holes and it then unifies with the earth. Wright further gave rough texture to the originally porous Oya stone, so the Oya stone's shades became much intense. In this project, the integral structure allowed a hole to penetrate the wall and the permeable character of Oya stone further evolved. Sunlight and wind flow into the architecture through the holes. Mediating the holes, the architecture, the earth and the sky were connected much deeply and strongly.

Chokkura hall: west elevation　ちょっ蔵ホール：西立面

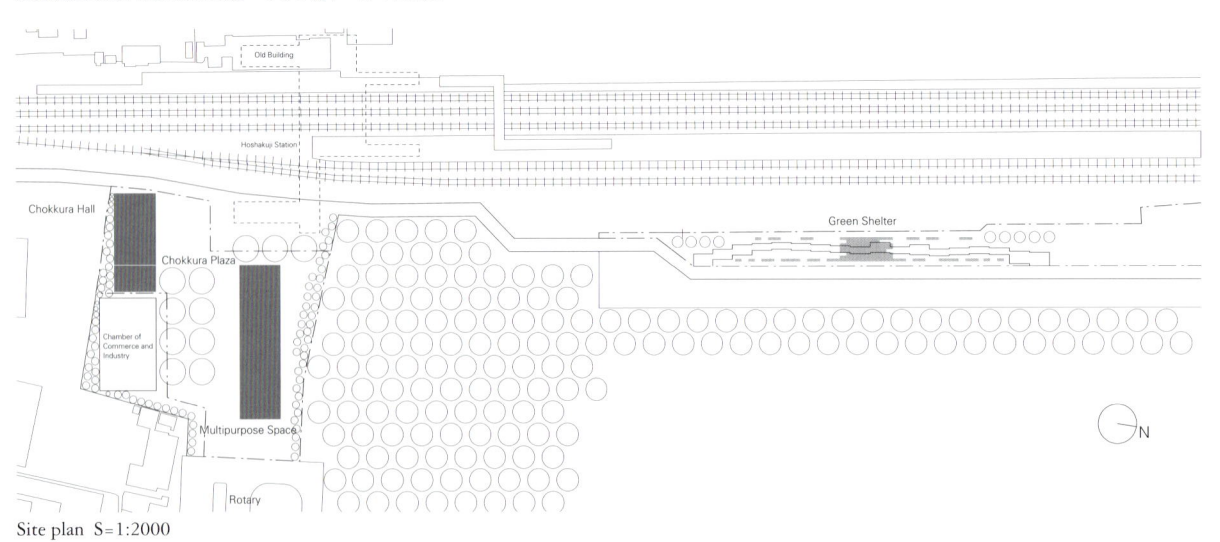

Site plan　S=1:2000

Multipurpose space: view from southeast　多目的展示場：南東より見る

Multipurpose space: south elevation

East elevation

Multipurpose space: north elevation

West elevation

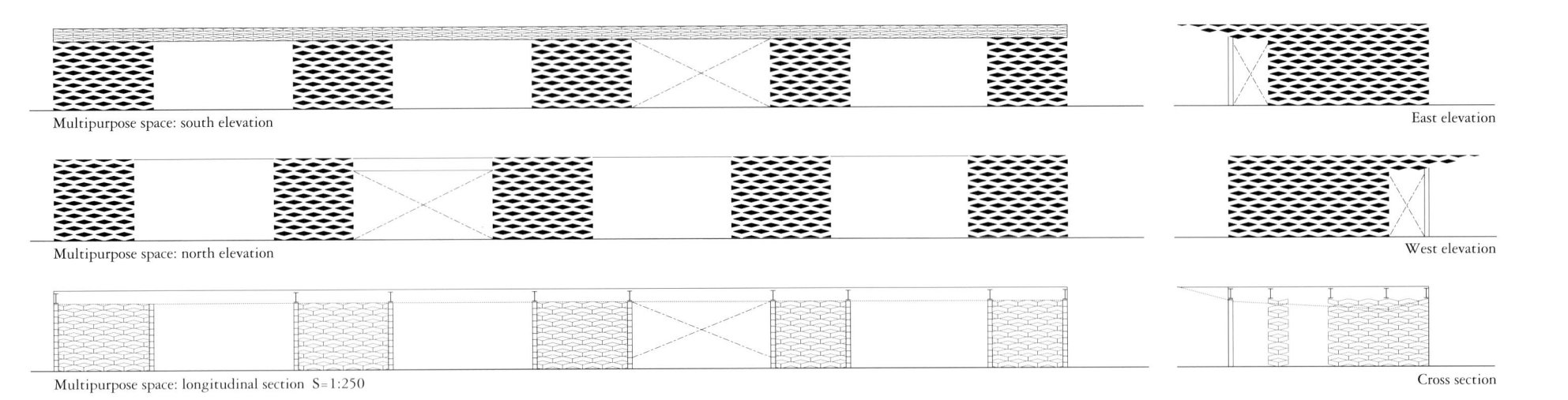

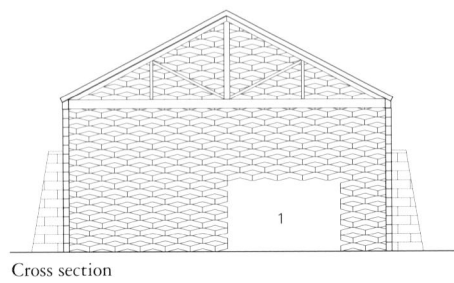

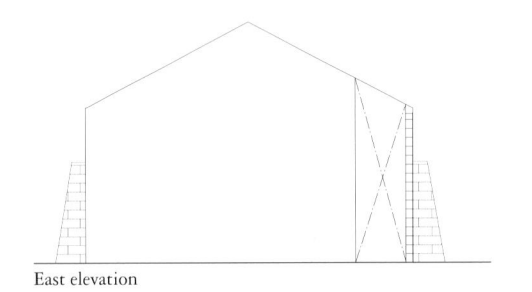

Multipurpose space: longitudinal section S=1:250

Cross section

Chokkura hall: west elevation S=1:250

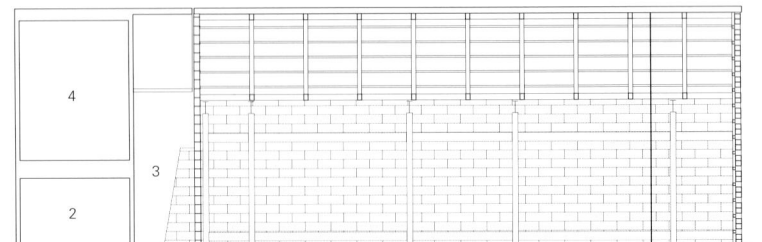

Cross section

East elevation

Chokkura hall: north elevation

Longitudinal section

1 CHOKKURA HALL
2 WC
3 STORAGE
4 MECHANICAL

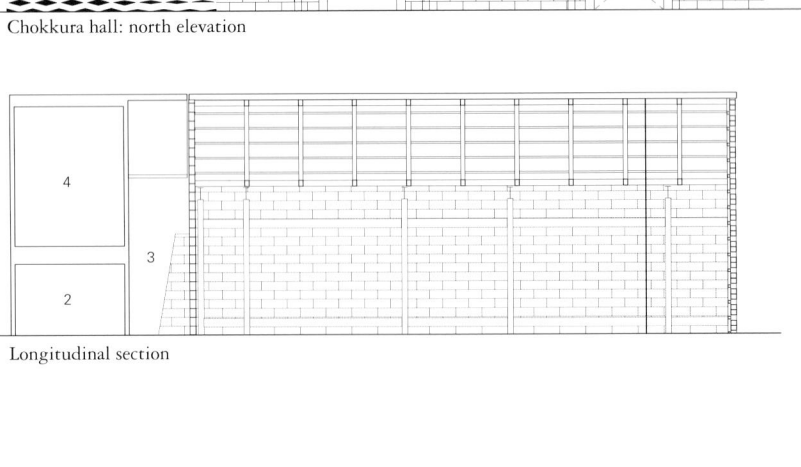

Multipurpose space: view of center corridor from south   多目的展示場：南より中央通路を見る

Multipurpose space: view toward center corridor　多目的展示場：中央通路方向を見る

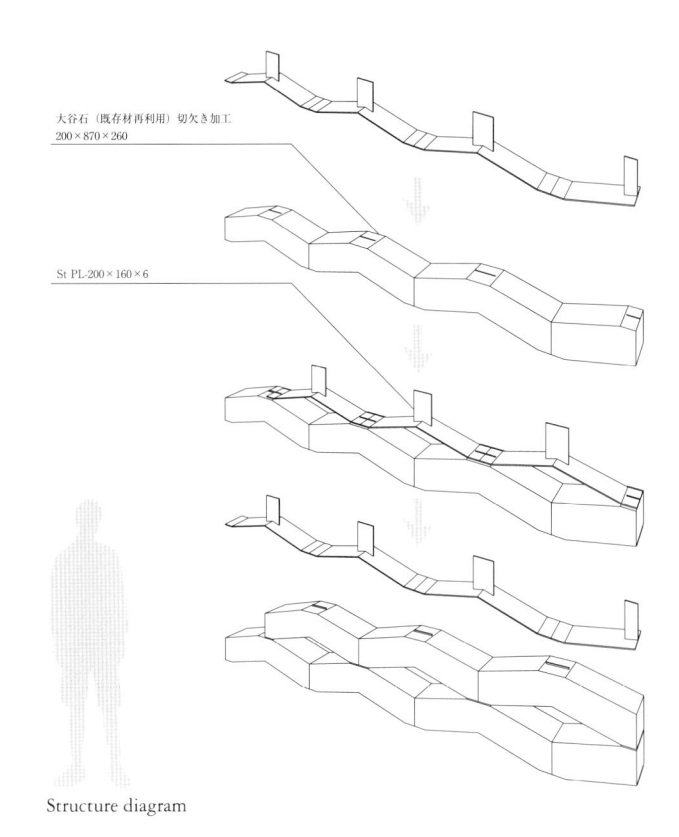

Structure diagram

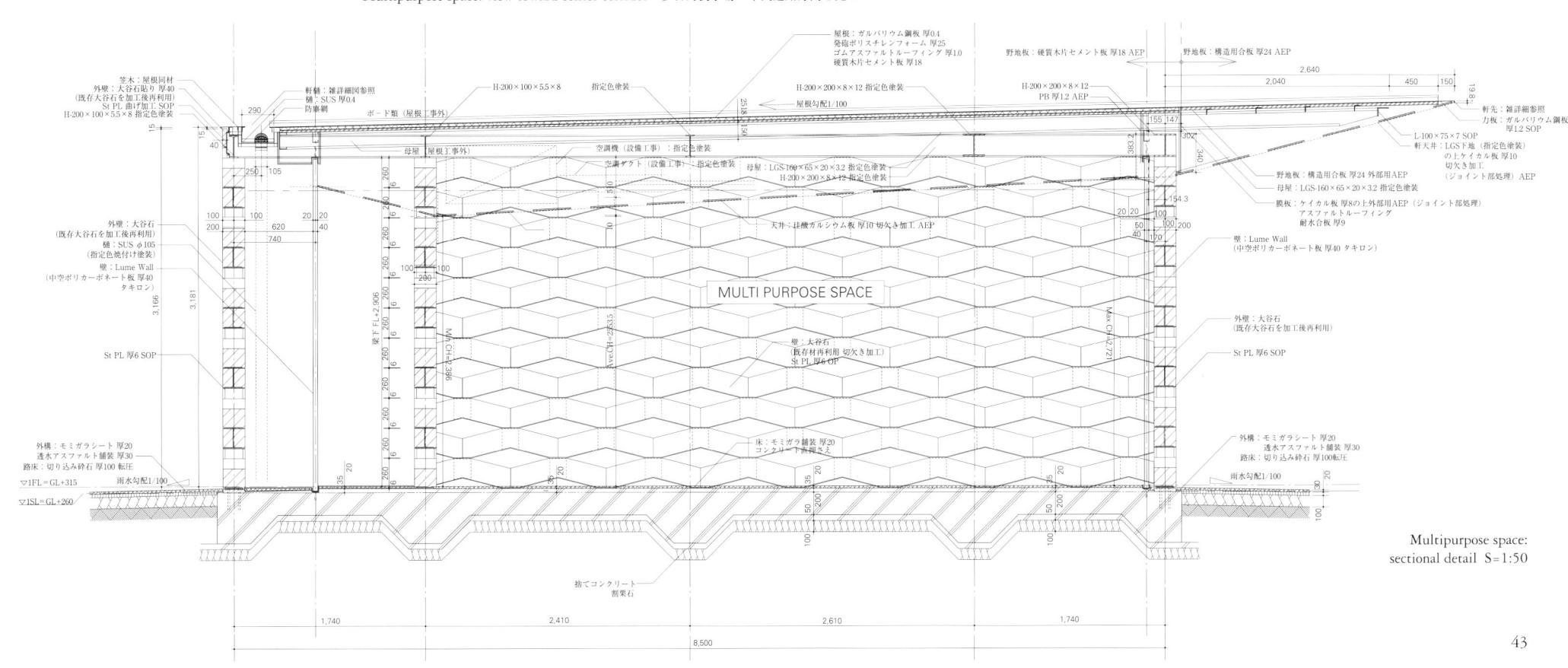

Multipurpose space: sectional detail　S=1:50

43

ちょっ蔵広場

約100年前に建設された大谷石の石蔵を改修し、古いものと新しいもの、不透明なものと透明なものがグラデーショナルに併存する建築をつくった。大谷石のブロックと鉄板(厚さ6mm)とを組み合わせた。新しい複合的構造システムによって、このグラデーショナルな状態が可能となった。石に圧縮力を負担させ、鉄に引張力を負担させることで、組積造と鉄骨造とを有機的に合成させた。石の豊かな質感と、鉄の軽やかさとが共存する、多孔質な有機体をつくることが可能となった。

かつてフランク・ロイド・ライトは、大谷石の多孔質でやわらかな表情に惹かれ、周囲の反対を押し切って、「帝国ホテル」(1923年)を大谷石でつくり上げた。多孔質の物質は、その孔に生じる影によって、よりやさしく、やわらかな存在となり、大地と同化するというのがライトの考え方であった。そもそも多孔質である大谷石に、ライトはさらに凹凸をつけ、大谷石の陰影はさらに濃くなった。今回の複合構造によって孔は壁を貫通し、大谷石の多孔質な性格をさらに進化させた。孔を通じて光と風が建築に流れ込み、孔を媒介として、建築と大地と空は、より深く、強く接続された。

Chokkura hall: main entrance　ちょっ蔵ホール：主玄関

Green shelter　グリーン・シェルター

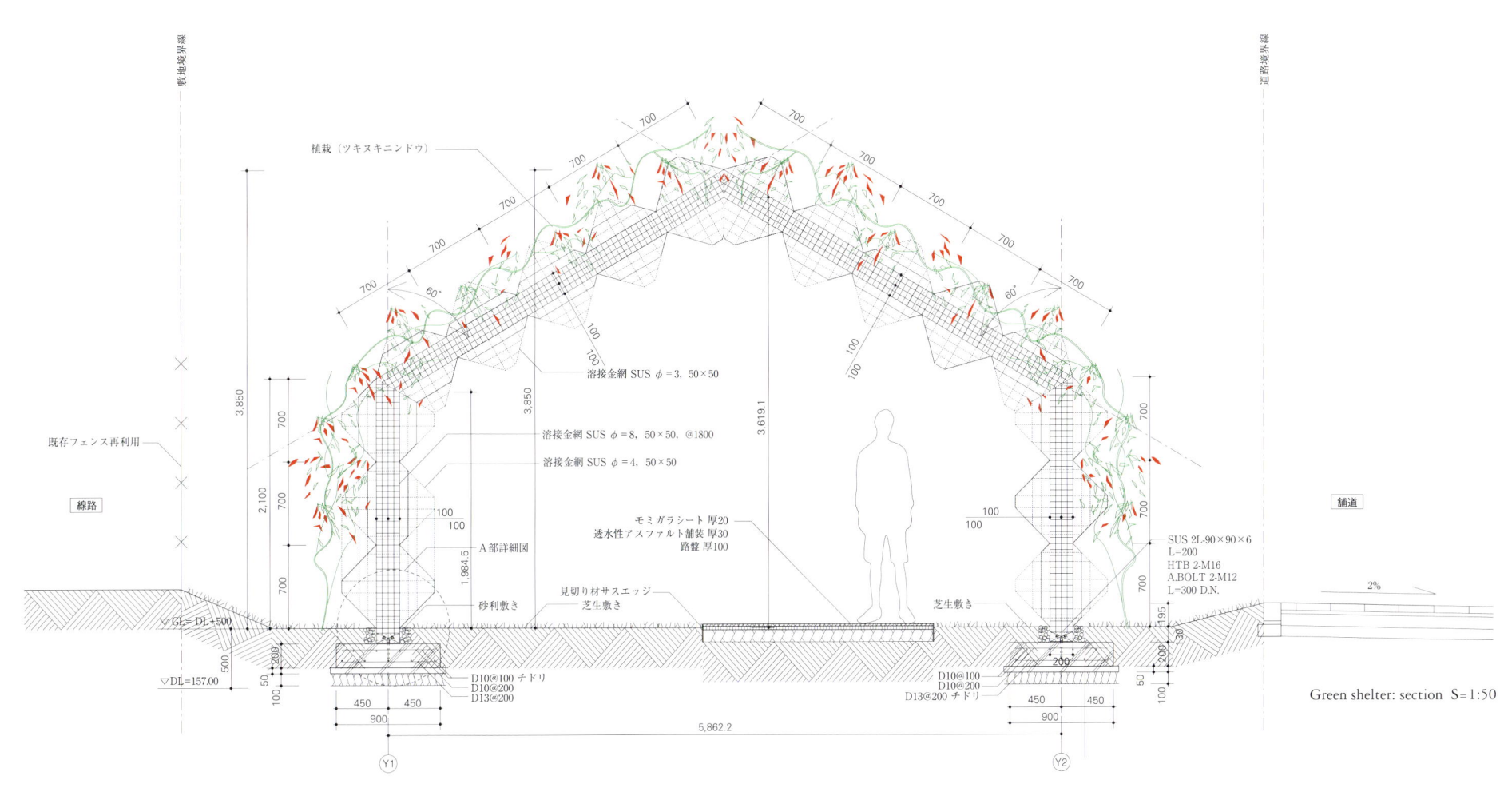

Green shelter: section　S=1:50

2004-07 Suntory Museum of Art
Minato, Tokyo, Japan

We created a gentle and warm museum by using timber in the center of a city. The recycled white oak flooring was once used for whisky barrels, and the timber ceiling is made from Paulownia, which controls moisture levels very well.

The traditional detail called Muso-Koshi, which can be seen in the old Japanese 'Minka' (Old house) was used for the openings before glass had been introduced. This Muso-Koshi controls the passage of light and wind with two vertical timber screens that can slide past each other, allowing different degrees of environmental transparency. We tried to create a variety of lighting conditions inside by mechanically sliding two screens.

The 35 cm deep ceramic tile louvers are installed on the exterior wall. Combining the tile and aluminum fixing allowed the edge of the louvers to be very thin. This approach which uses thin tiles to be expressed as a material was further developed in the project Ceramic Cloud (2010) in Italy.

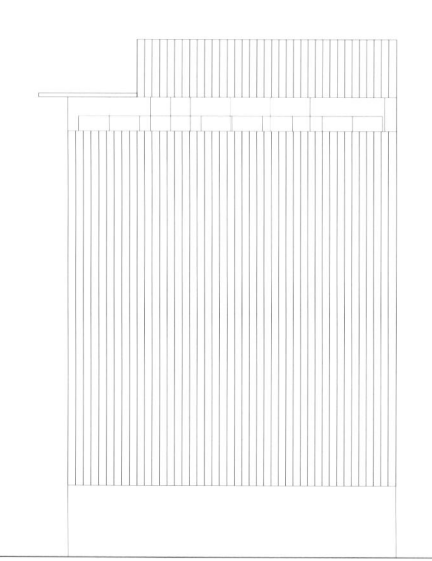

West elevation S=1:600

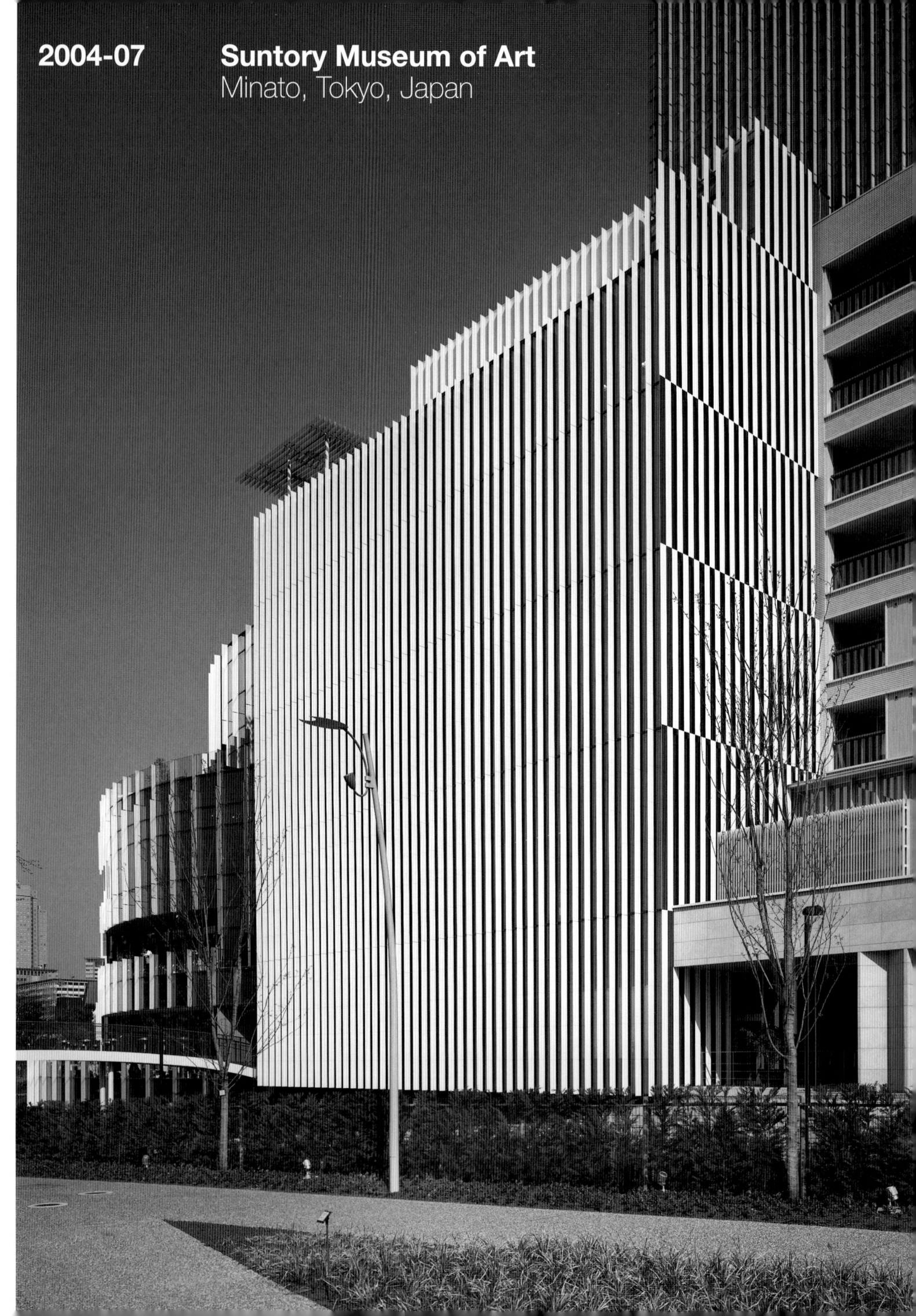

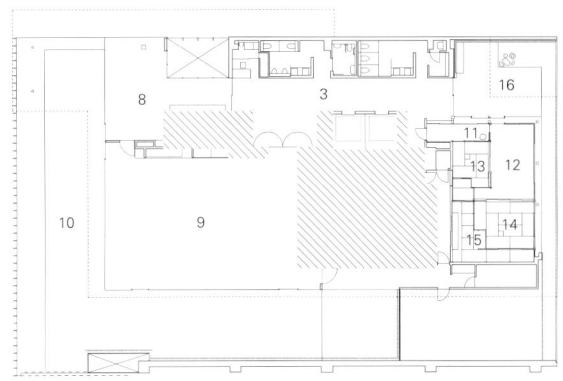

Sixth floor

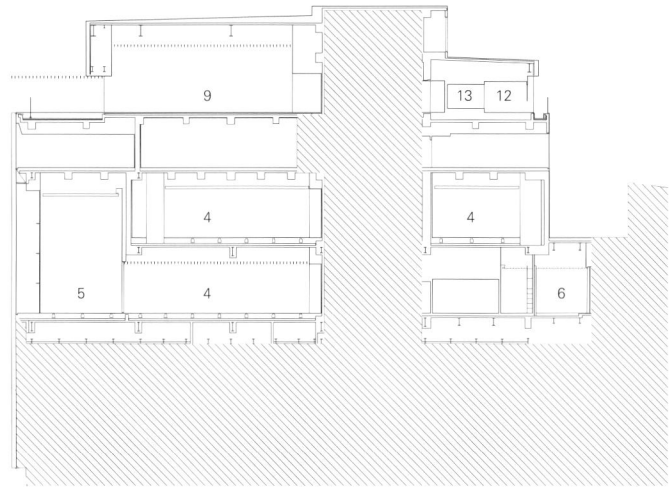

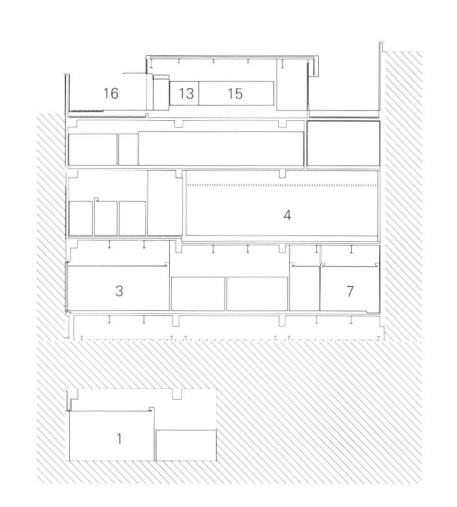

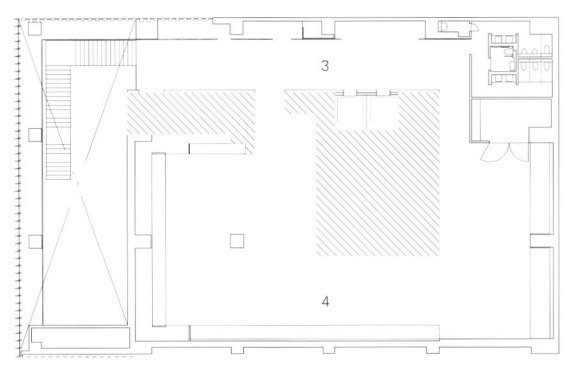

Fourth floor

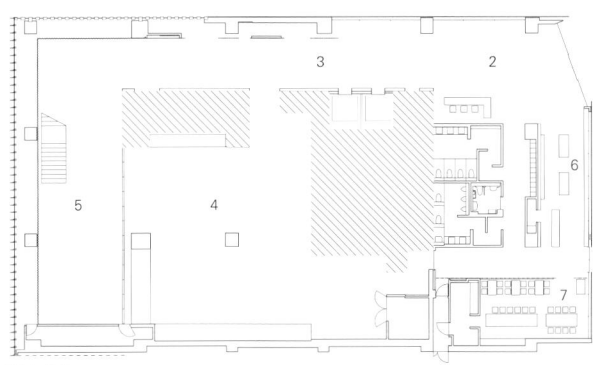

Third floor

Sections S=1:600

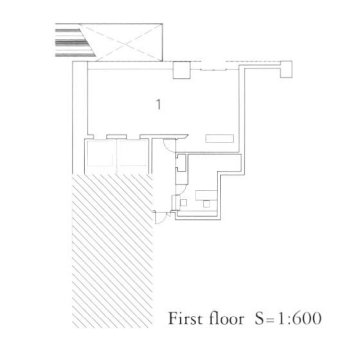

First floor S=1:600

1 ENTRANCE
2 MAIN ENTRANCE
3 LOBBY
4 EXHIBITION SPACE
5 VOID GALLERY
6 SHOP
7 CAFE
8 MEMBER'S SALON
9 HALL
10 DECK
11 ROJI (CORRIDOR)
12 TEAROOM
13 KOMA (SMALL TATAMI ROOM)
14 HIROMA (LARGE TATAMI ROOM)
15 MIZUYA (WASHING PLACE)
16 TERRACE

サントリー美術館

都市の中心に, 木を用いたやさしく暖かな美術館を創造した。床にはウイスキーの樽に用いられたホワイトオーク材が再利用され, 天井には湿度調整機能を有する桐材が用いられた。

開口部には, 無双格子と呼ばれる, 日本の民家に伝わる伝統的なディテールが採用された。無双格子とは, 2枚の格子をスライドさせることによって, 光や風の導入をコントロールする仕掛けであり, ガラスが導入される前の日本の民家は, この仕掛けで室内外の環境を調整していた。今回は2枚の格子を電動でスライドさせることによって, 室内に様々な光の状態を創造しようと試みた。

外壁には, 大版のタイルを用いたデプス35cmのルーバーが取り付けられている。タイルとアルミの押し出し材を組み合わせることで, ルーバーの先端を薄くするディテールが可能となった。素材としてのタイルの薄さ自体を表現とする方法は, その後「セラミック・クラウド」(2010年)でさらに展開された。

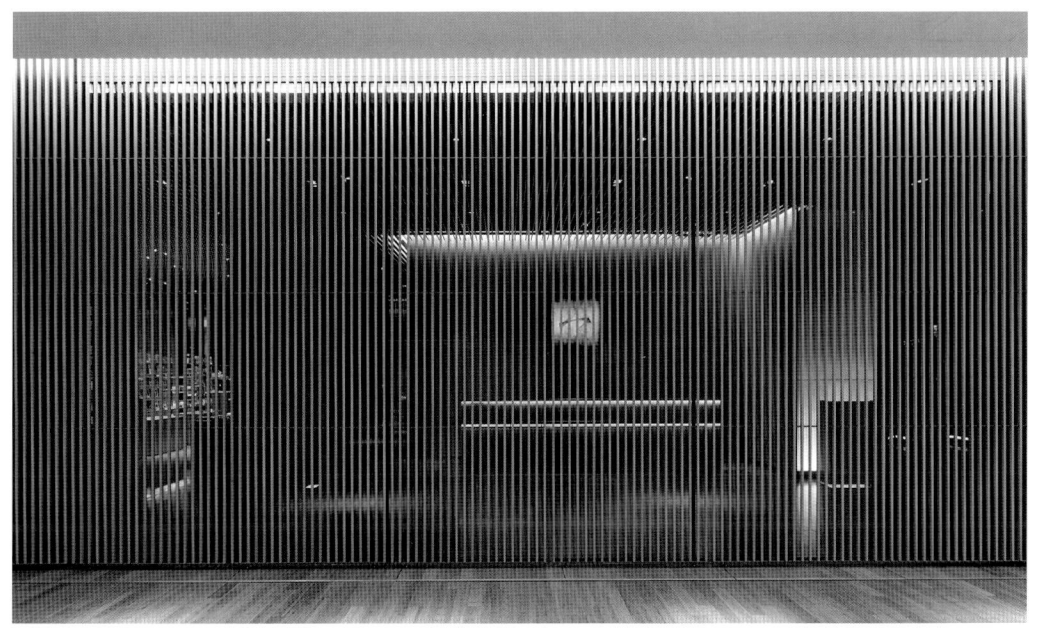

Wooden louver of entrance on third floor　3階エントランスの木ルーバー

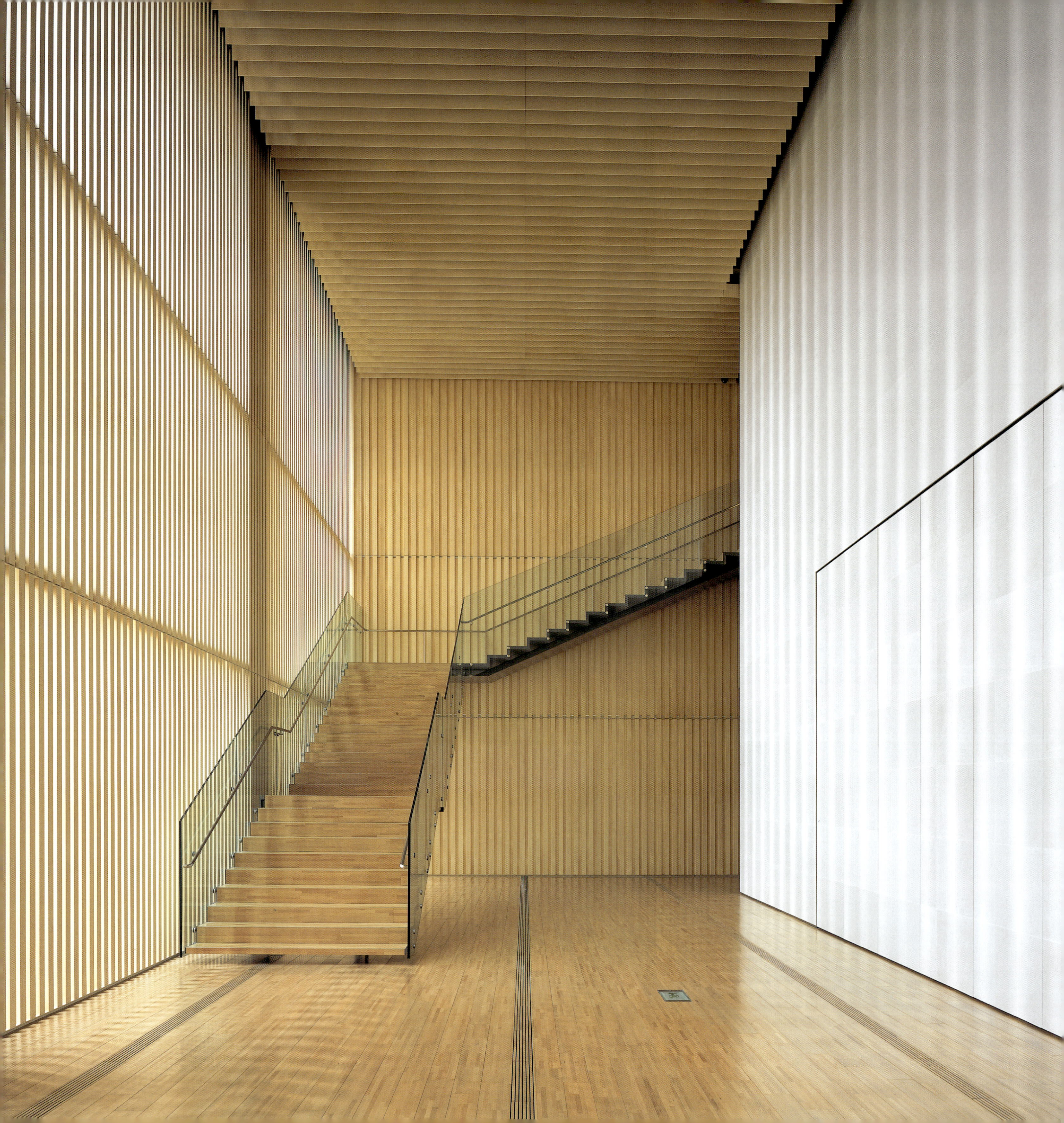

Lobby on fourth floor　4階ロビー

△▽ Exhibition space on fourth floor　4階展示室

◁ Void gallery on third floor　3階吹抜けギャラリー

49

Terrace of tearoom 'Gencho-an'　茶室「玄鳥庵」のテラス

Tearoom　茶室

Roji (corridor) of 'Gencho-an'　「玄鳥庵」の露地

Shopping mall 'Garden terrace': void of entrance
「ガーデンテラス」：エントランスの吹抜け

Void of 'Garden terrace'　「ガーデンテラス」の吹抜け

51

2004-07　Kure City Ondo Civic Center
Kure, Hiroshima, Japan

View of west wing　西棟を見る

Site plan　S=1:2000

This is a public building located on the coast of one of the islands in the Seto Inland Sea. This complex houses the local government office, library and gymnasium and becomes a new 'center' for people on the island. We thought that we should put traditional Japanese tiles on the roof for this 'New House' for the people. The main element of the villages on the islands in the Seto Inland Sea used to be the roofs covered with Japanese tiles, therefore we thought it was important for the local government to lead in the revival of this scenery.

The biggest issue is how the edge of the roof can be lowered to bring it close to the ground when the roof is put on a large public building. We believe that the roof is a tool to connect the architecture to the ground, and to achieve that the height of the eave should be as low as possible. However there is a risk that the space underneath will be dark if the eaves are lowered too much. To solve this problem, we developed a new detail. It is a steel frame louver with the Japanese tile installed by cement. This louver detail reduces the strong sunlight and makes it possible to create a deep and bright human scale beneath the eaves.

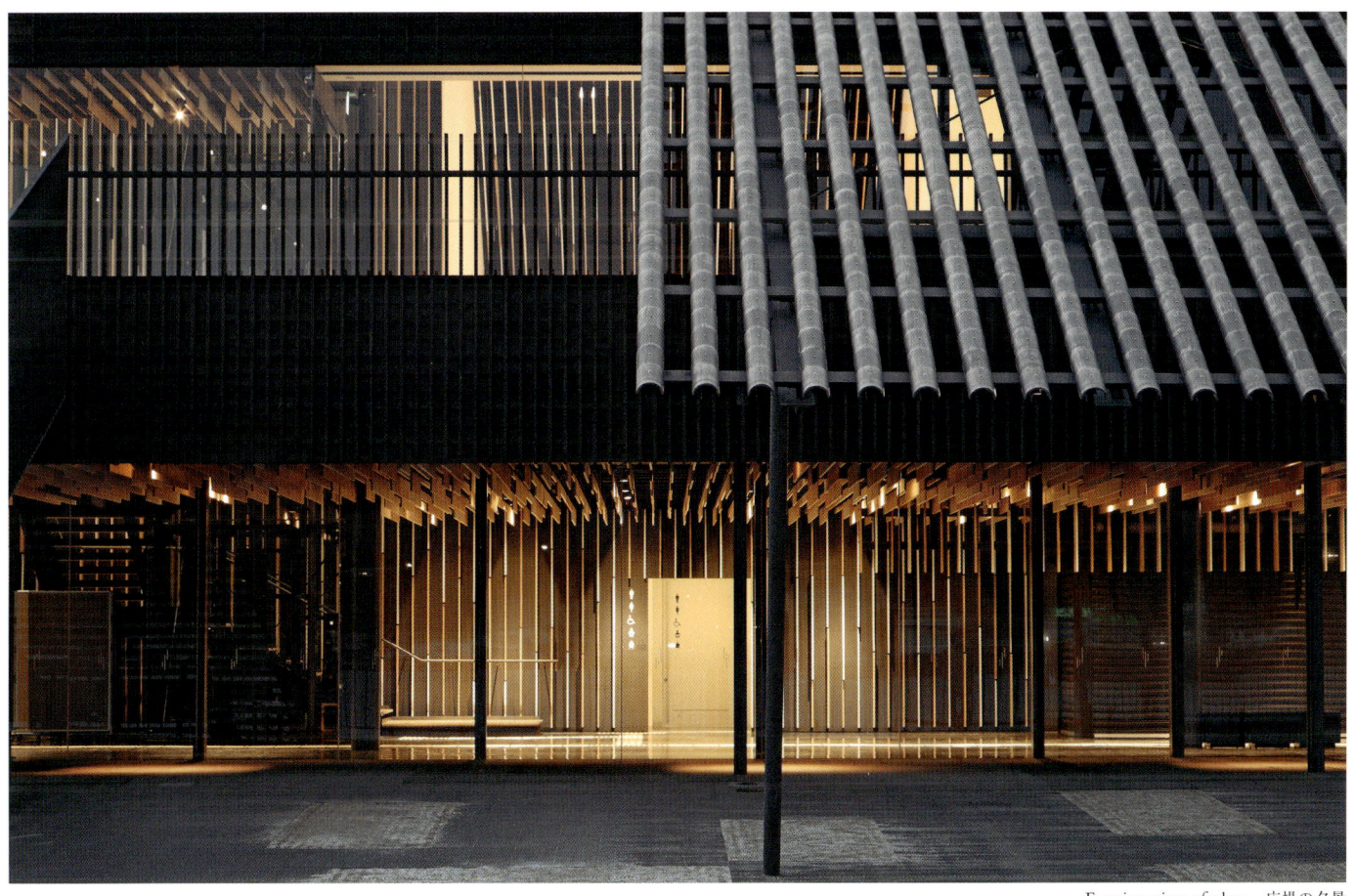

Overall view from Ondo fishing port　音戸漁港より見る全景

Evening view of plaza　広場の夕景

Terrace on second floor　2階テラス

Bridge　ブリッジ

呉市音戸市民センター

瀬戸内の島の浜辺に建つ公共建築。役場、図書館、体育館が複合し、島の生活の新しい核となる。島民のための「新しい家」には、本瓦の屋根をのせるべきだと考えた。瀬戸内の島の集落の基本要素は、本瓦の屋根の連なりであり、その集落の風景を役場こそが率先して復活させなければならないと考えた。

最大の課題は、公共建築の大きなヴォリュームに屋根をのせた時、いかに軒の先端を低くして、大地に屋根を近づけられるかである。屋根は建築というヴォリュームを地面に接続するためのツールであり、そのために軒の高さは可能な限り低くしなければならない。しかし、無理に軒を深くすると、暗い軒下空間をつくる危険がある。その解決のため、スティールのフレームに本瓦をセメントを用いて取り付けた、本瓦のルーバーという新しいディテールを開発した。このルーバーによって、瀬戸内の強い日差しをさえぎり、明るくヒューマンな深い軒下空間をつくることが可能となった。

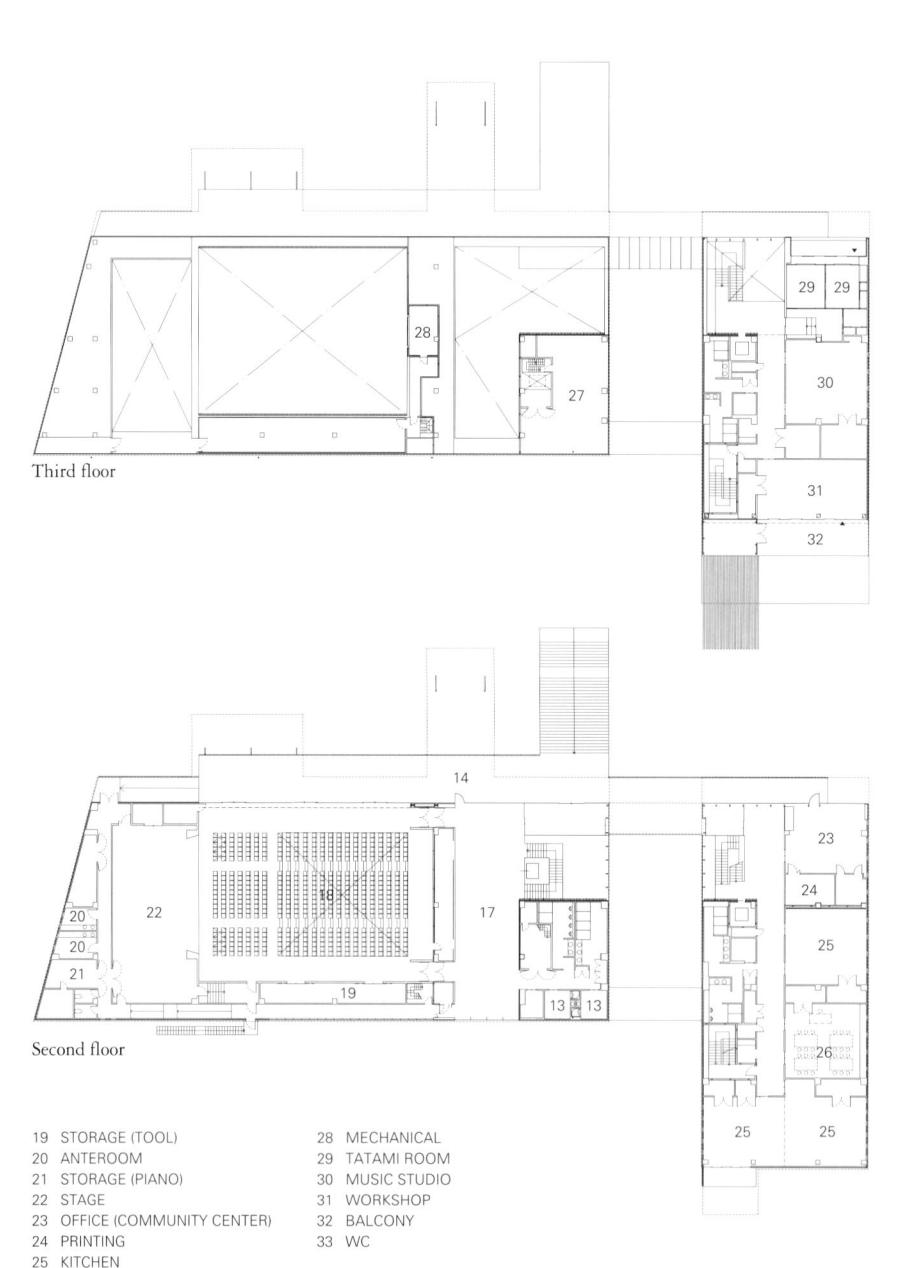

Third floor

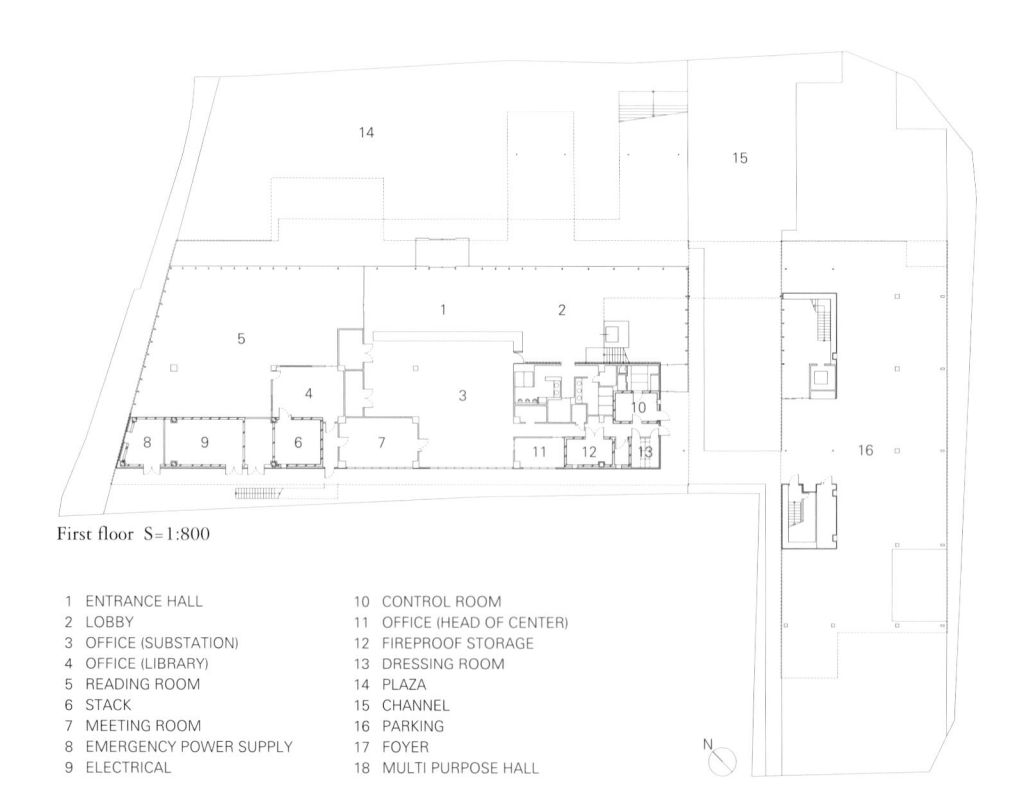

First floor　S=1:800

Second floor

1	ENTRANCE HALL	10	CONTROL ROOM	19	STORAGE (TOOL)	28	MECHANICAL
2	LOBBY	11	OFFICE (HEAD OF CENTER)	20	ANTEROOM	29	TATAMI ROOM
3	OFFICE (SUBSTATION)	12	FIREPROOF STORAGE	21	STORAGE (PIANO)	30	MUSIC STUDIO
4	OFFICE (LIBRARY)	13	DRESSING ROOM	22	STAGE	31	WORKSHOP
5	READING ROOM	14	PLAZA	23	OFFICE (COMMUNITY CENTER)	32	BALCONY
6	STACK	15	CHANNEL	24	PRINTING	33	WC
7	MEETING ROOM	16	PARKING	25	KITCHEN		
8	EMERGENCY POWER SUPPLY	17	FOYER	26	OFFICE		
9	ELECTRICAL	18	MULTI PURPOSE HALL	27	LECTURE ROOM		

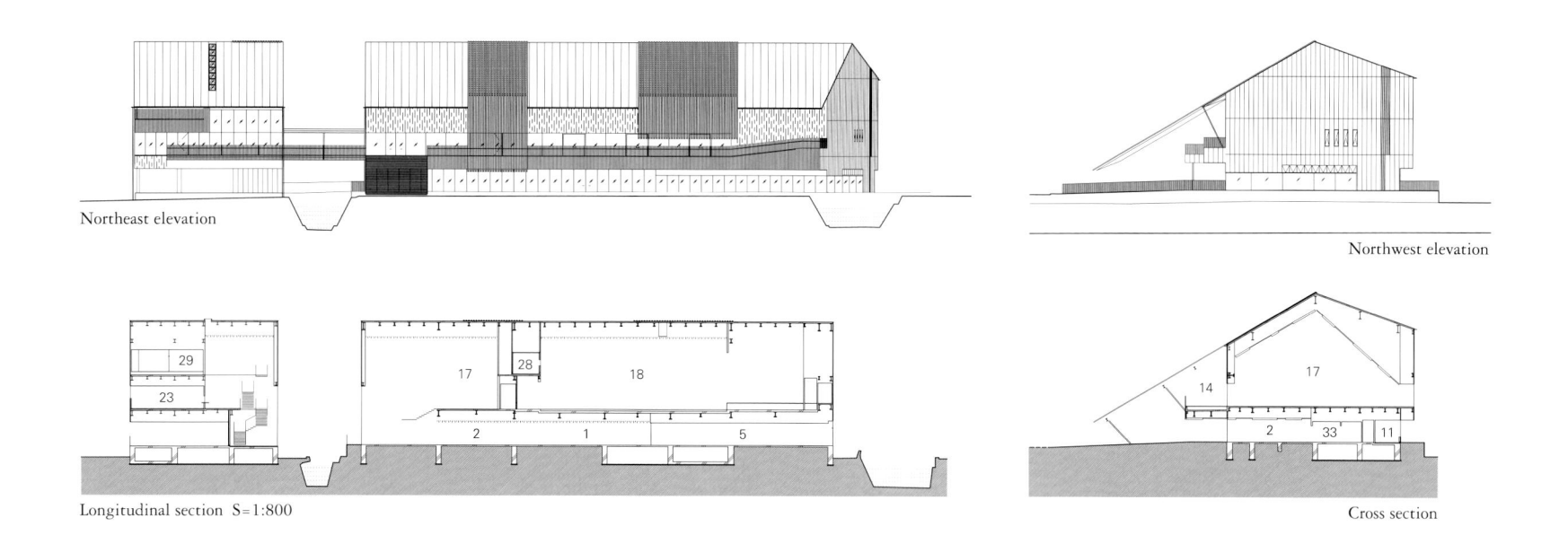

Northeast elevation

Northwest elevation

Longitudinal section S=1:800

Cross section

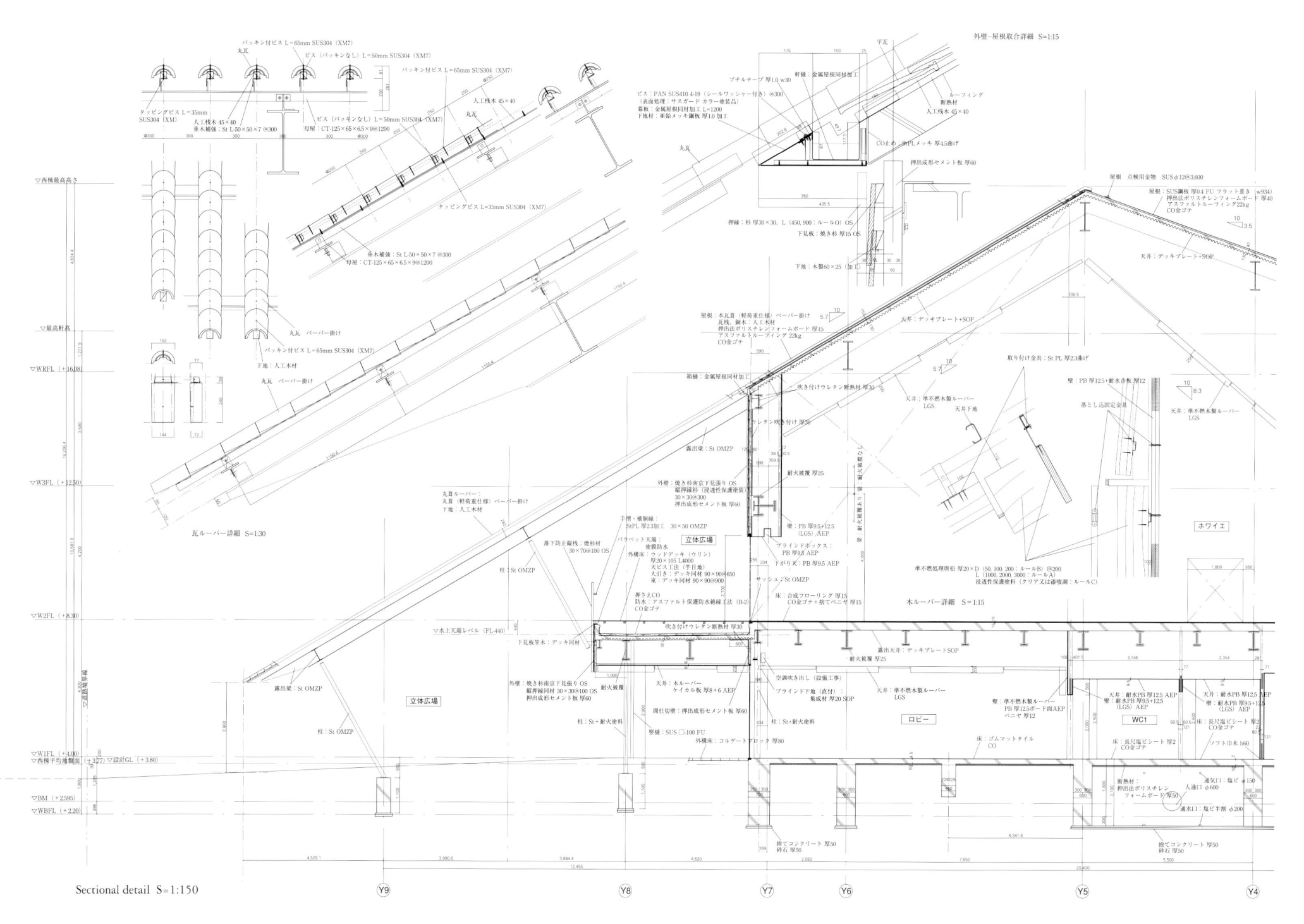

Sectional detail S=1:150

Evening view of entrance hall from plaza　夕景。広場よりエントランスホールを見る

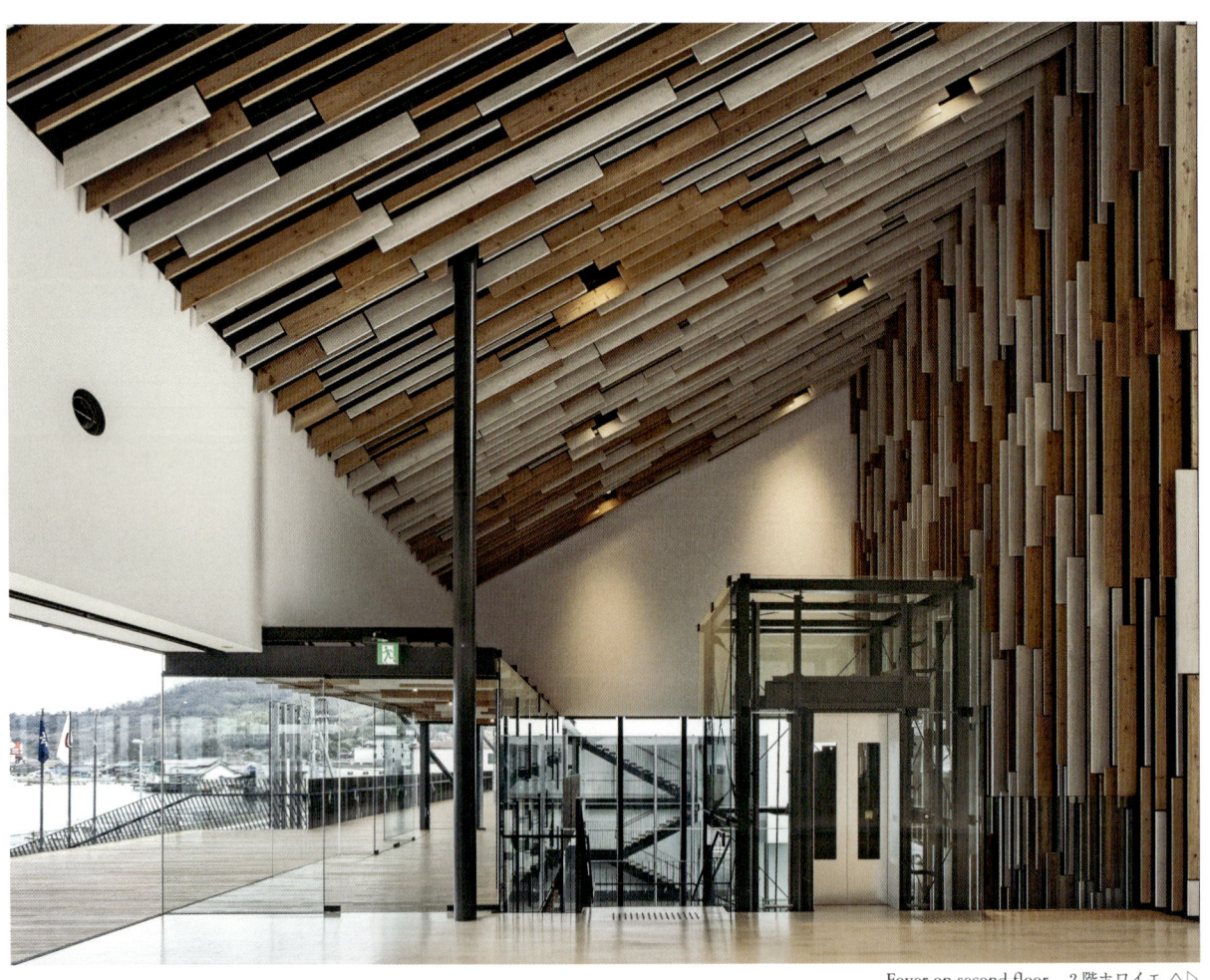

Foyer on second floor　２階ホワイエ △▷

△▽ Multipurpose hall on second floor　2階多目的ホール

2004-07 Steel House
Bunkyo, Tokyo, Japan

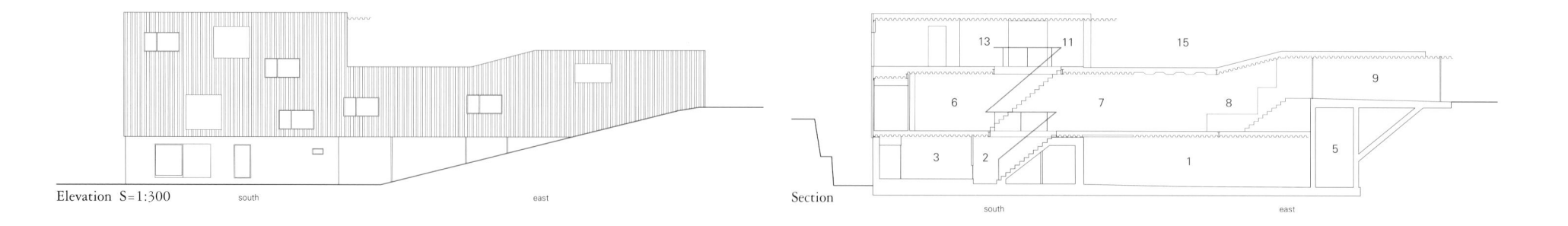

Overall view from southeast　南東より見る全景

Elevation S=1:300

Section

Pilotis　ピロティ

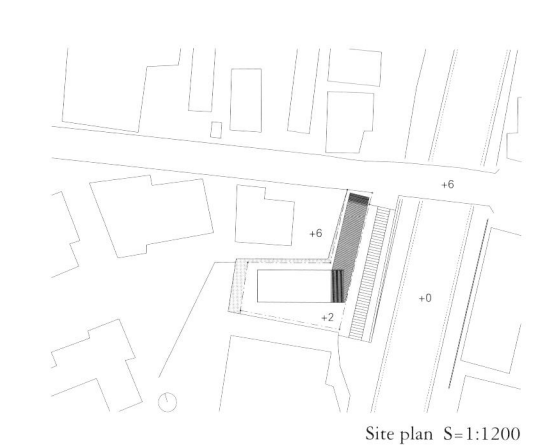

1	PILOTIS
2	ENTRANCE HALL
3	TATAMI ROOM
4	MIZUYA (WASHING PLACE)
5	STORAGE
6	LIVING ROOM
7	DINING ROOM
8	KITCHEN
9	GARAGE
10	CORRIDOR
11	BEDROOM
12	CLOSET
13	MASTER BEDROOM
14	BATHROOM
15	TERRACE

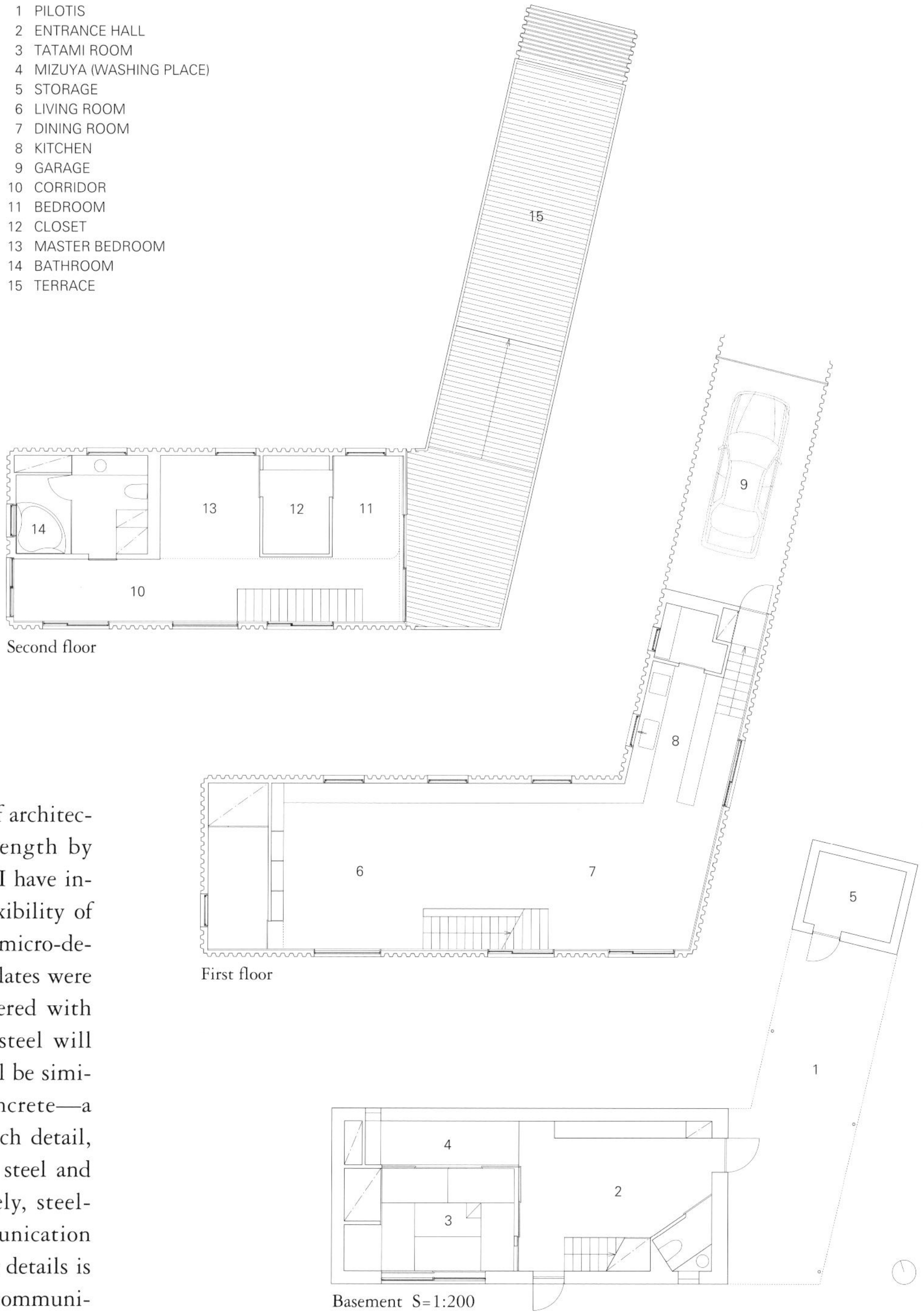

Site plan S=1:1200

Second floor

First floor

Basement S=1:200

A house in monocoque structure, pillarless like a freight wagon, made of 3.2 mm-thick corrugated steel plates. The client, Professor Hirose, has been an avid railroad fan from his childhood, and keeps a collection of several thousand model trains in his house. His wish has been to live inside a train wagon. Following the peculiar, L-shaped form of the site, the house resembles a long train halting on a slope, bent in an L shape.

Originally, train wagons had been designed based on the concept of frame + membrane. Today, the frame and membrane are no longer separate categories and wagons are designed based on the concept of monocoque. In that sense, this house is a statement criticizing the presence of modern-day architecture, which is yet to rid itself of the frame structure of columns and beams.

Here, the basic idea in terms of architectural structure is to increase its strength by bending the steel plates. In doing so, I have intended to convey the softness and flexibility of this material that is steel, through the micro-details of the bent sections. If the steel plates were to be used without bending and covered with paint, the fact that this material is steel will never be known to us. Its presence will be similar to that of plaster boards and concrete—a mere white, abstract surface. With such detail, communication between the material steel and us will never be established. Inversely, steel-bending details will establish communication between steel and us. Every one of our details is designed for the sake of establishing communication between materials and people.

鉄の家

3.2mm厚のコルゲートの鉄板を用いて,柱梁のない,鉄道の貨車のようなモノコック構造の家をつくった。クライアントである廣瀬通孝教授は子供の頃からの鉄道の熱烈なファンであり,家の中には数千台の鉄道模型が保管されている。彼も貨車の中に暮らすような生活を望んでいた。L字形の特殊な敷地形状に合わせて,細長い貨車がL字形に折れ曲がって坂道に停車したような姿の家となった。

鉄道の車体もそもそもは構造体＋皮膜という設計思想に基づいてデザインされていたが,今日では構造体と皮膜という区分は消え,モノコックの考えに基づいて設計されている。その意味でこの家は,柱梁のフレーム構造から未だに抜け出すことのできない現代建築という存在そのものに対する,ひとつの批判である。

鉄板を折り曲げることで強度を上げるのが,この建築の構造の基本的な考え方である。折り曲げることで,その曲げた部分のミクロのディテールから,鉄という素材のやわらかさ,しなやかさを伝えたいと考えた。もし,鉄板を曲げずに用い,その表面を塗装してしまったならば,その素材が鉄であることはわれわれには伝わらない。プラスターボードやコンクリートと同じ,白い抽象的な面が,そこに存在するだけである。そのディテールでは,鉄という物質とわれわれとの間のコミュニケーションは成立しないのである。逆に,鉄を曲げるディテールによって,鉄とわれわれとの間に,コミュニケーションが成立する。素材と人間との間に,いかにコミュニケーションを成立させるかを目指して,われわれのあらゆるディテールはデザインされている。

Living/dining room on first floor. Models of train displayed on left　1階居間／食堂。左は鉄道模型の展示棚

Living/dining room　居間／食堂

Tatami room and entrance hall on basement　地階，和室とエントランス・ホール

Steel stairs on first floor　1階スティールの階段

Corridor on second floor　2階廊下

Bedroom and corridor: partitioned with curtain
寝室と廊下：カーテンで仕切られる

2004-09 **Nezu Museum**
Minato, Tokyo, Japan

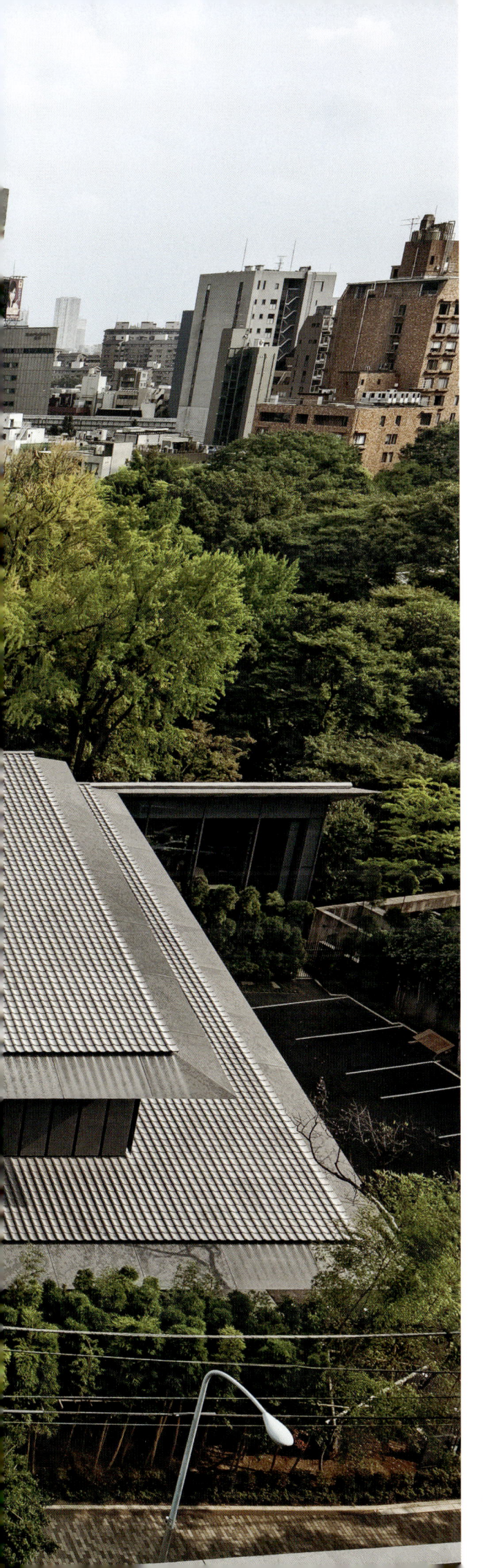

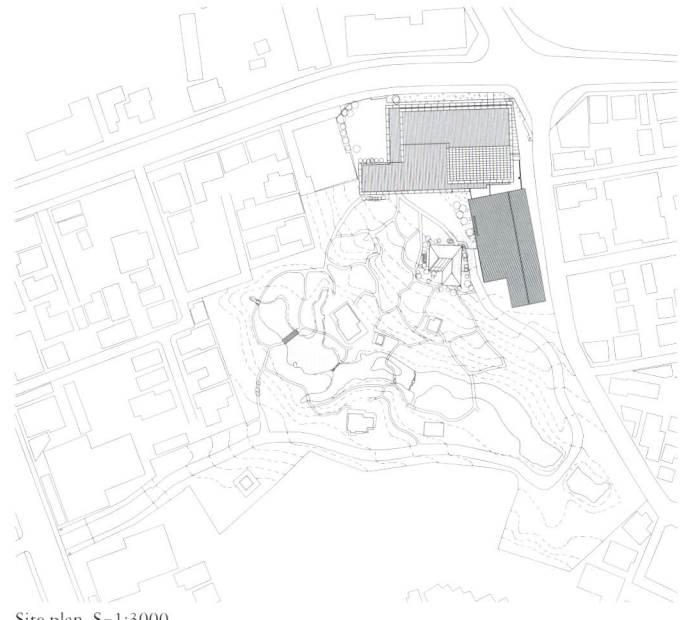

Site plan S=1:3000

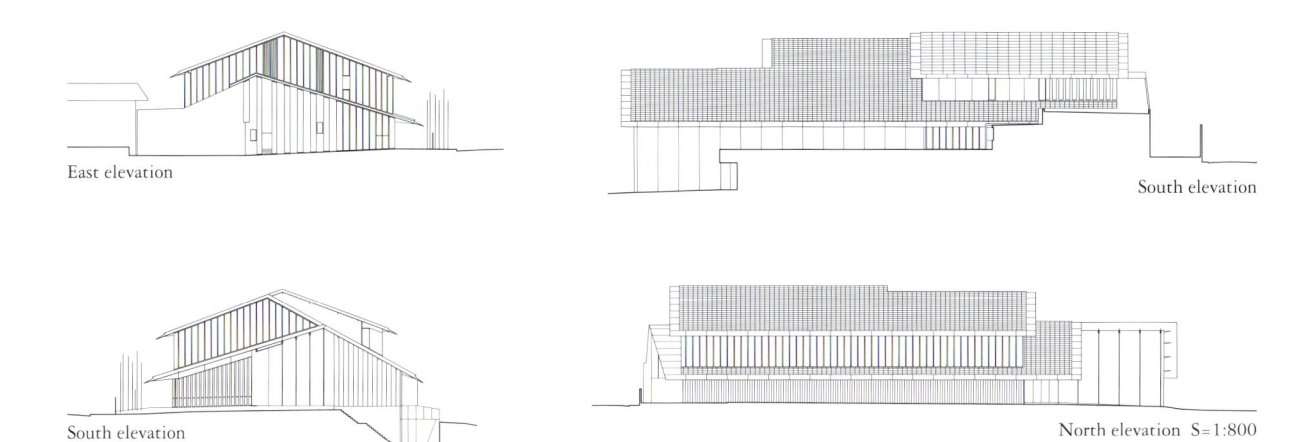

East elevation

South elevation

South elevation

North elevation S=1:800

Our goal in the project was to create a museum integrated with garden that lives together with nature in a highly dense urban setting. In the first place, we thought Japanese traditional art do not get along with 20th century's closed box-type museums. In Japan, a garden, architecture and art is a united being and to create a merged state of the three was the target of the museum. Likewise, we wanted to overcome the weak points of 20th century art such as the separation of art pieces from locale and commercialization of artistic works.

In order to unite a garden, architecture and art, we used a vocabulary of roof. We made a large glass opening under the roof and integrated the garden and the exhibition space.

On the approach, two-storey volume was first divided into two using the roof and eaves, and gained human scale. Then, dark half-outdoor space under 4 m-long cantilevered deep eaves was turned two times and approached to the building. The approach similar to tearoom manners gradually invited people from the noisy Omotesando to the calmness of the Japanese garden.

Bird's eye view toward southeast　鳥瞰。南東方向を見る

Southwest elevation 南西立面

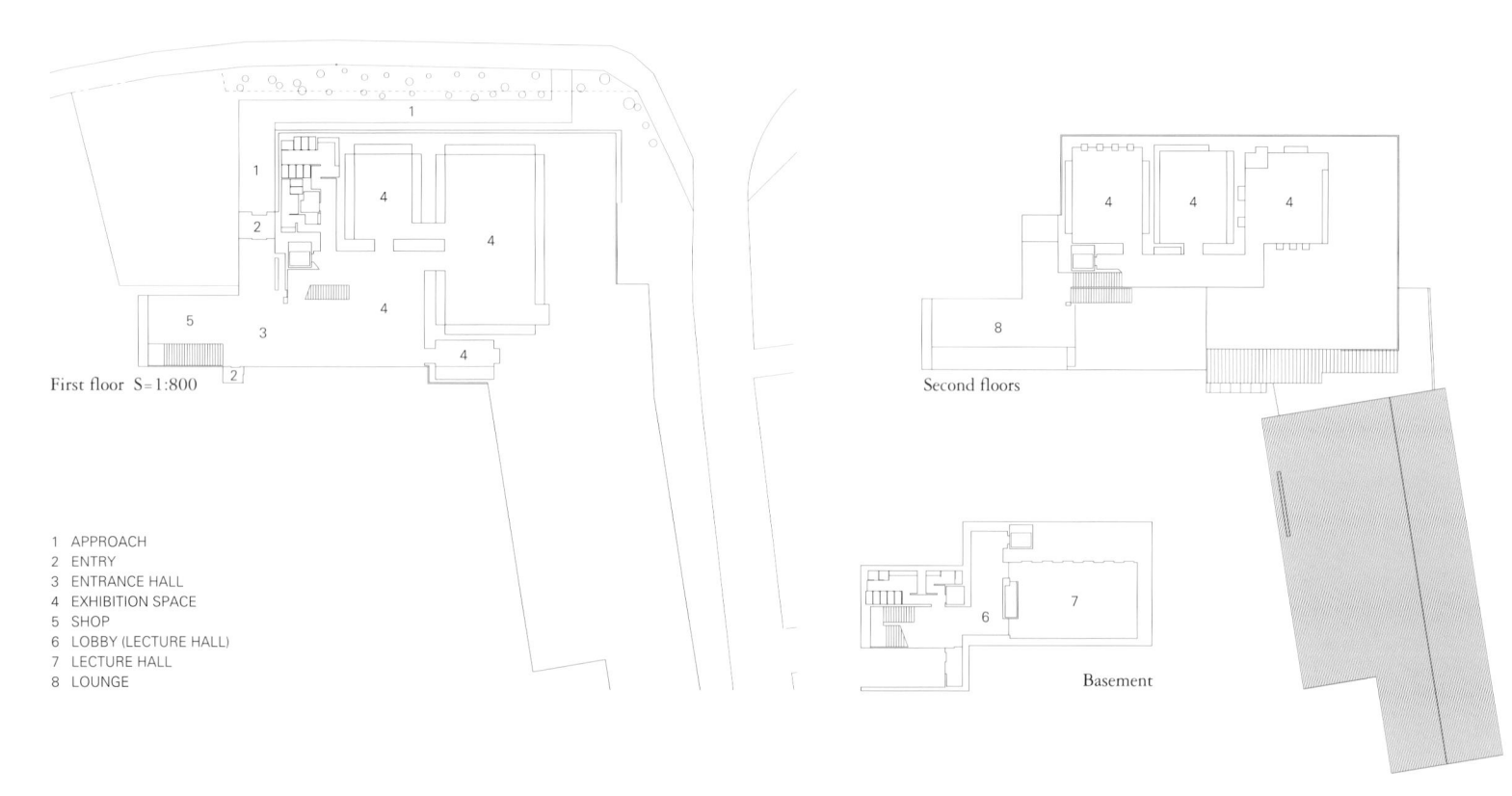

First floor S=1:800

Second floors

Basement

1 APPROACH
2 ENTRY
3 ENTRANCE HALL
4 EXHIBITION SPACE
5 SHOP
6 LOBBY (LECTURE HALL)
7 LECTURE HALL
8 LOUNGE

根津美術館

高密度の都市的環境の中に, 自然環境と共生した, 庭園と一体化した美術館をつくることを目標にした。日本の伝統的美術は, そもそも20世紀の閉鎖したハコ型の美術館と相性が悪いとわれわれは考えた。日本において庭園と建築と美術は不可分の一体の存在であり, その三者が融合した状態をつくることがこの美術館の目標であった。そのようにして三者を融合することで, 20世紀の美術の弱点であった作品と環境の分離, 作品の商品化といった問題を乗り越えようと考えた。

庭園, 建築, 美術を一体化するために, われわれが用いたのは屋根というヴォキャブラリーである。屋根の下に大きなガラスの開口部を設けて, 庭園と展示空間を一体化した。

アプローチにおいても, 屋根と庇を用いて2階建てのヴォリュームをまず二つに分解してヒューマンスケールを獲得し, さらに4mのキャンティレバーとなる深い庇下に生まれた半屋外の薄暗い空間を, 2度転回させながら建物にアプローチさせた。この茶室的なアプローチによって, 表参道の喧騒からグラジュアリーに日本庭園の静けさの中へと, 人々を誘った。

Approach under eaves 軒下のアプローチ

Evening view from garden 庭園より見る夕景

65

Exhibition hall on first floor　1階展示ホール

Sectional detail S=1:250

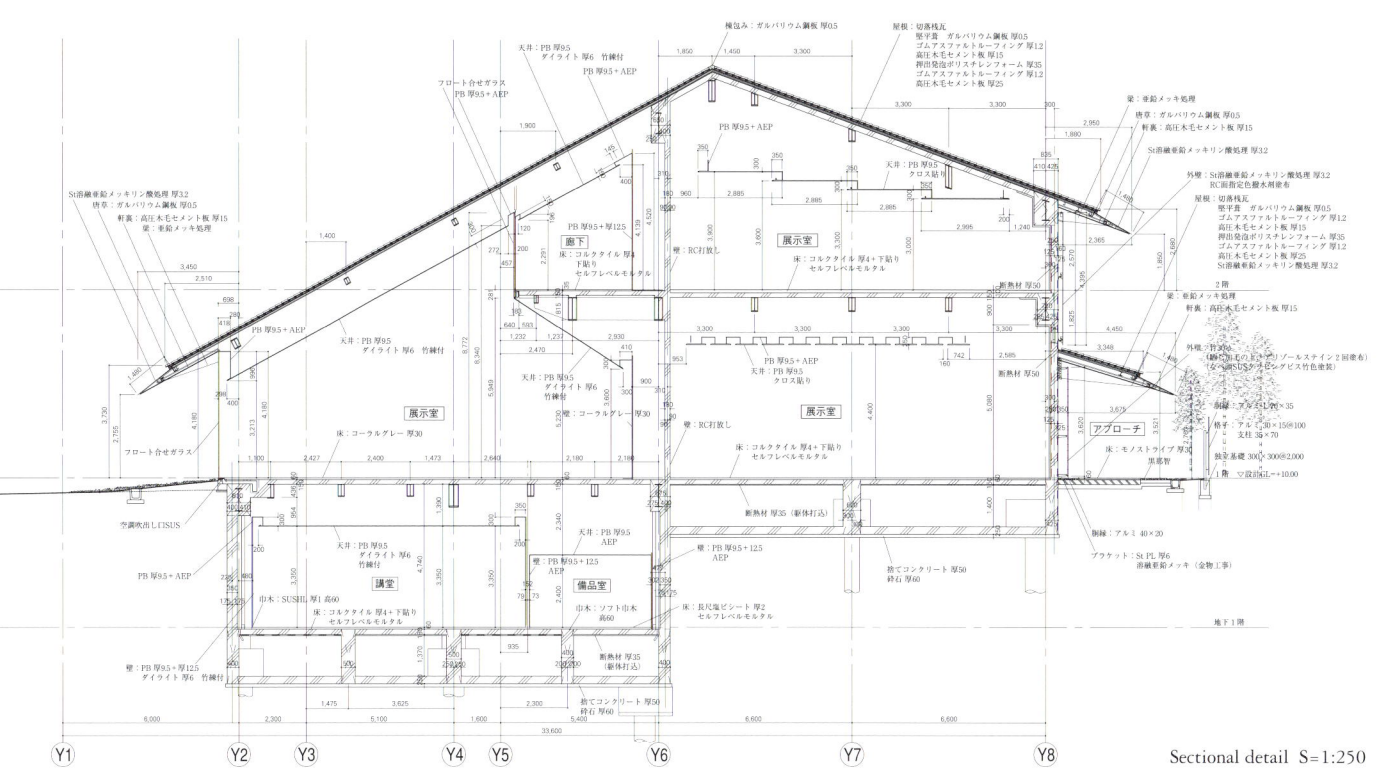

Exhibition room on second floor　2階展示室

2004-10 Tokyu Capitol Tower
Chiyoda, Tokyo, Japan

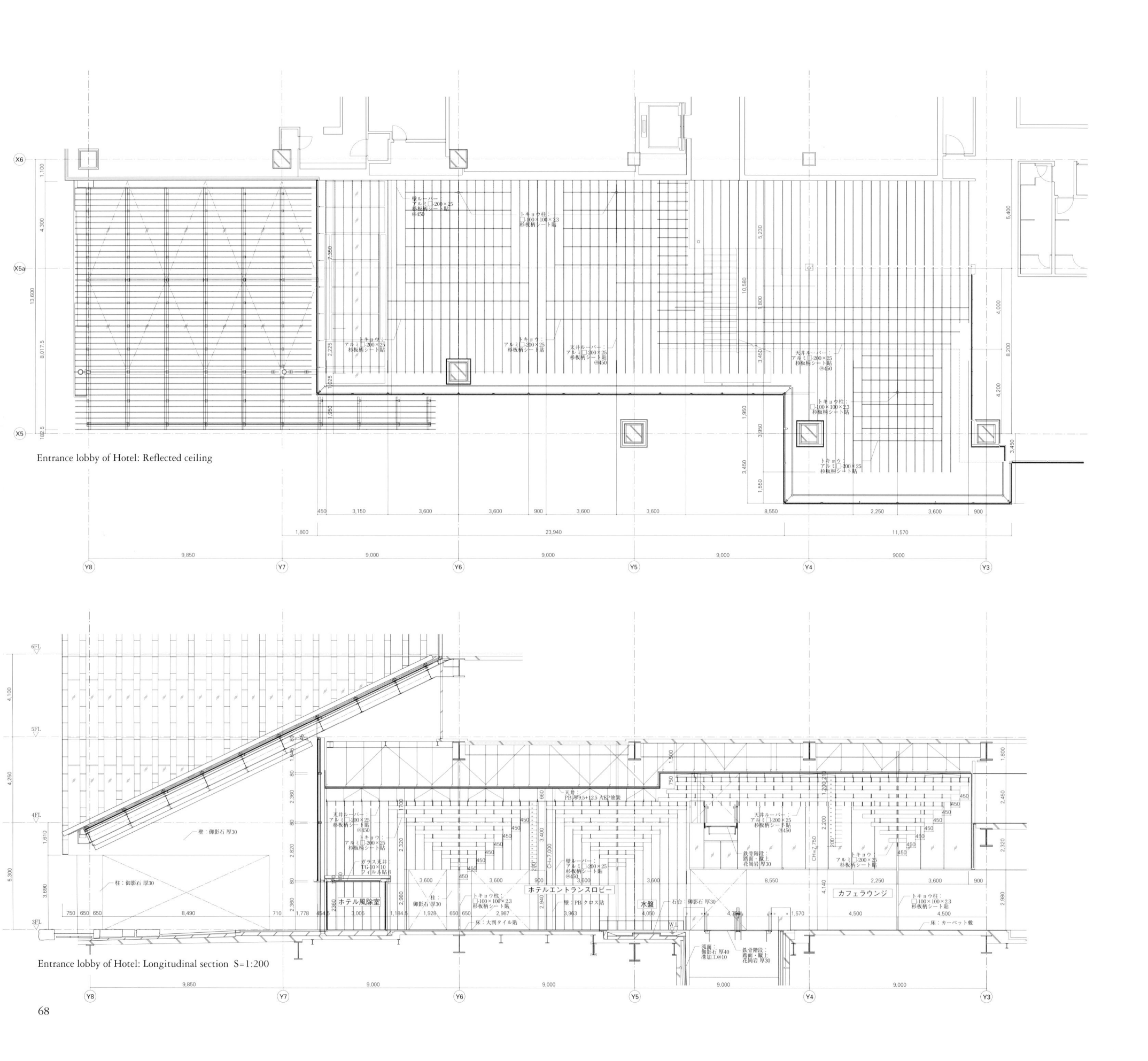

Entrance lobby of Hotel: Reflected ceiling

Entrance lobby of Hotel: Longitudinal section S=1:200

Canopy on hotel entrance　ホテルのエントランスに掛かるキャノピー

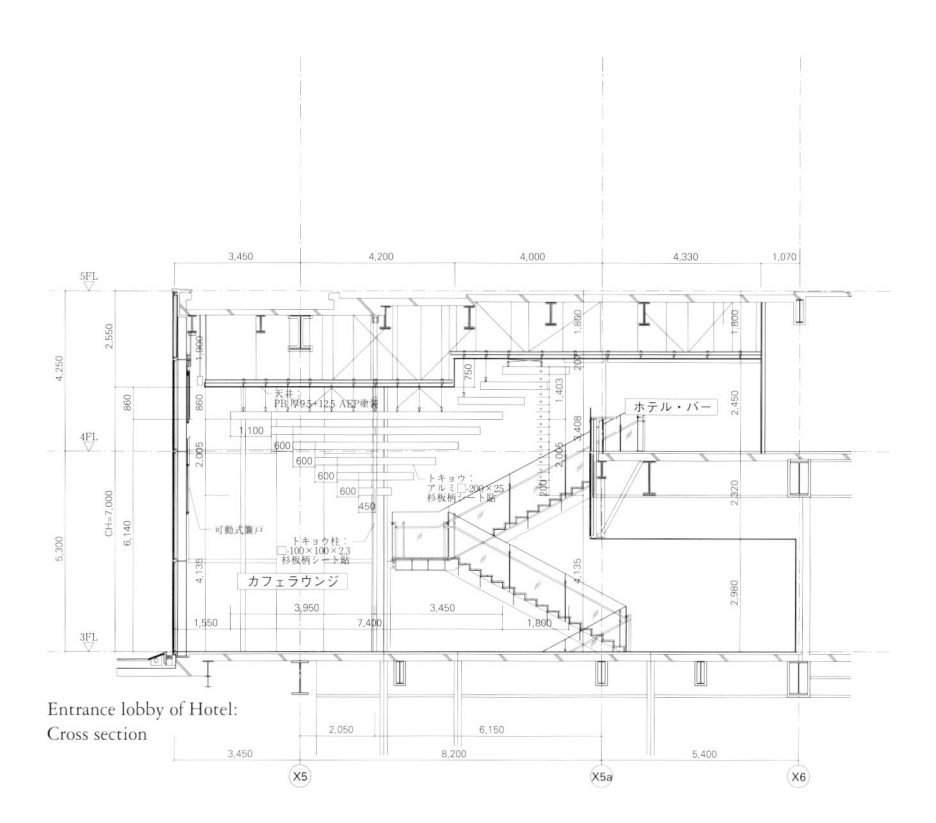

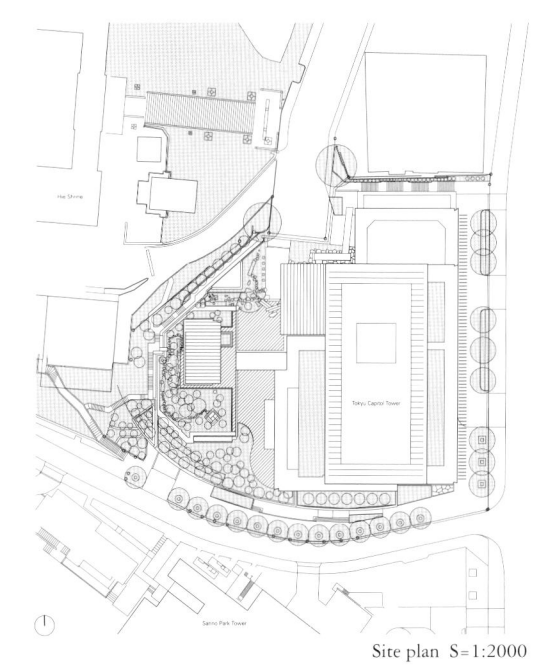

Entrance lobby of Hotel:
Cross section

Site plan　S=1:2000

Entrance of hotel　ホテルのエントランス

Evening view of basin　水盤の夕景

In the design of the high-rise hotel located in the city center, I sought to regain weightlessness that wooden architecture originally had. On the higher part of the facade we attempted a light exterior wall design that can feel as 'stone lattice' rather than 'stone wall'. We chose a detail that dry fixes stone to aluminum curtain wall, in order to avoid heaviness in spite of the use of stone. Eventually, we achieved a sensitive scale of 300 mm-wide stone lattice.

On the lower part of the hotel, we used a traditional Japanese architecture's vocabulary of 'Geya' (attached eave) and 'hanare' (annex) and integrated the architecture and the garden. The garden is not completed within the site, but is unified with the neighboring Hie Shrine's thick forest. The sectional plan was designed to bury the hotel's annex in the Hie Shrine's forest. In the interior space a bracket unique to traditional wooden architecture called 'to-kyo' was inserted. Hence, introducing light secondary scale in the heavy concrete skeleton attained lightness and warmth. The screen of the 'annex' was detailed by hanging stone directly with metal. Water was inserted in the stone lattice and creates an artificial waterfall. By accumulating the extraordinary details, we applied a method of creating a screen out of material itself, which we tried in other small buildings, to a large-scale high-rise building.

Stone louver wall of annex　離れの石ルーバー壁

東急キャピトルタワー

都心部の高層ホテルに，木造建築が持っていたような軽やかさを取り戻そうと考えた。高層部ファサードにおいては，「石の壁」ではなく「石の格子」と感じられるような軽やかな外壁デザインを試みた。石を使いながら重さを回避するために，アルミカーテンウォールに石を乾式で取り付けるというディテールを採用し，300mm幅の石の格子という繊細なスケールを達成した。

ホテル低層部では，「下屋」と「離れ」という日本建築の伝統的ヴォキャブラリーを用いて，建築と庭園を一体化させた。庭園は敷地内で完結させず，隣接する日枝神社の深い森と一体のものとしてデザインし，日枝神社の森の中に，ホテルの「離れ」を埋め込むような断面計画とした。内部空間において，斗栱と呼ばれる伝統的木造建築固有の骨組みを挿入し，コンクリートの重いスケルトンの中に軽やかな2次的スケールを導入し，空間に軽やかさ，暖かさを導入した。「離れ」のスクリーンは石を直接金属でつり下げるディテールとし，その石の格子に水を流し，人工の滝とした。これらの特殊なディテールを重ね合わせることによって，これまで小さな建物でわれわれが挑戦してきた素材自体をスクリーン化する方法を，大規模な高層建築に適用した。

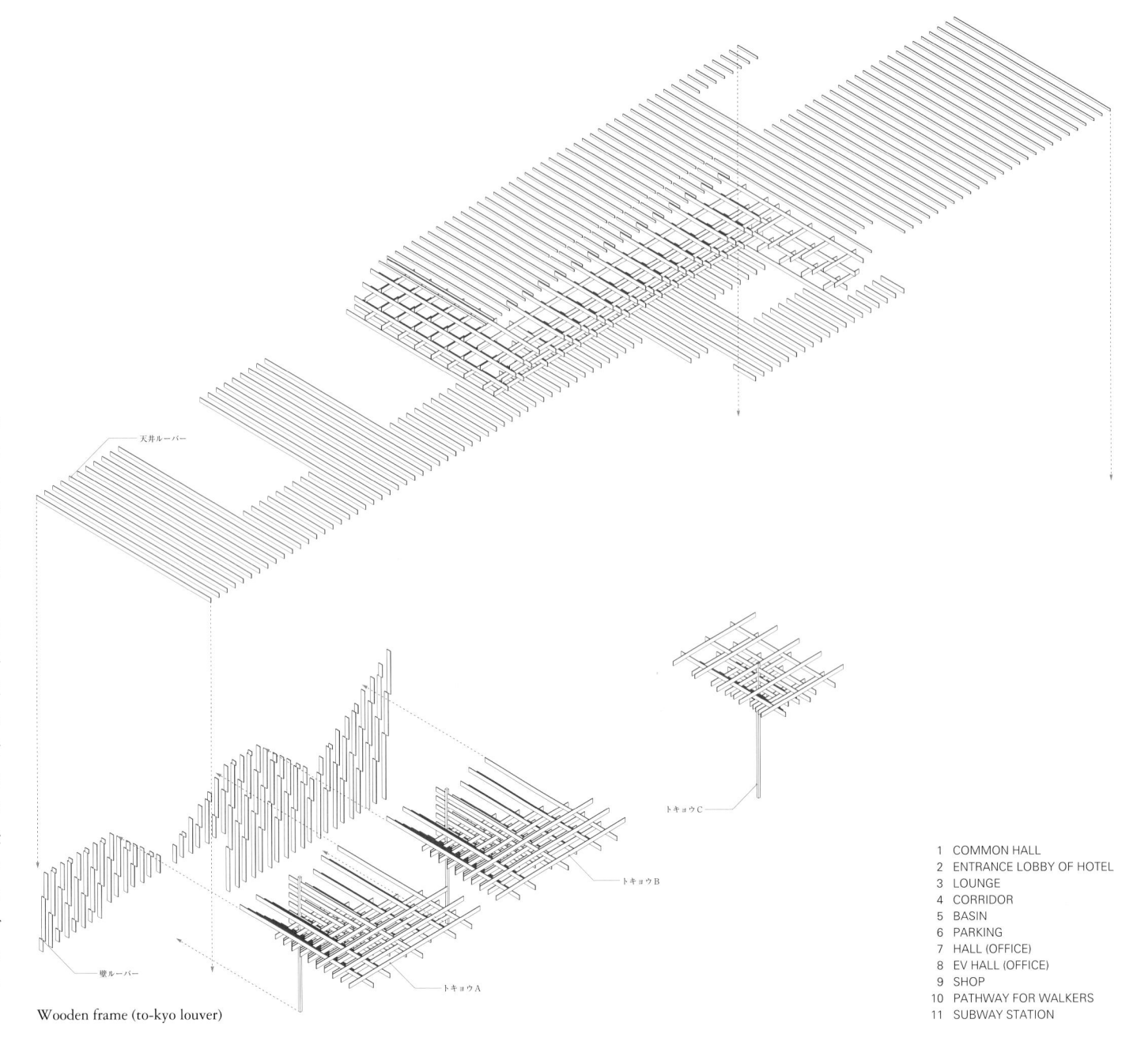

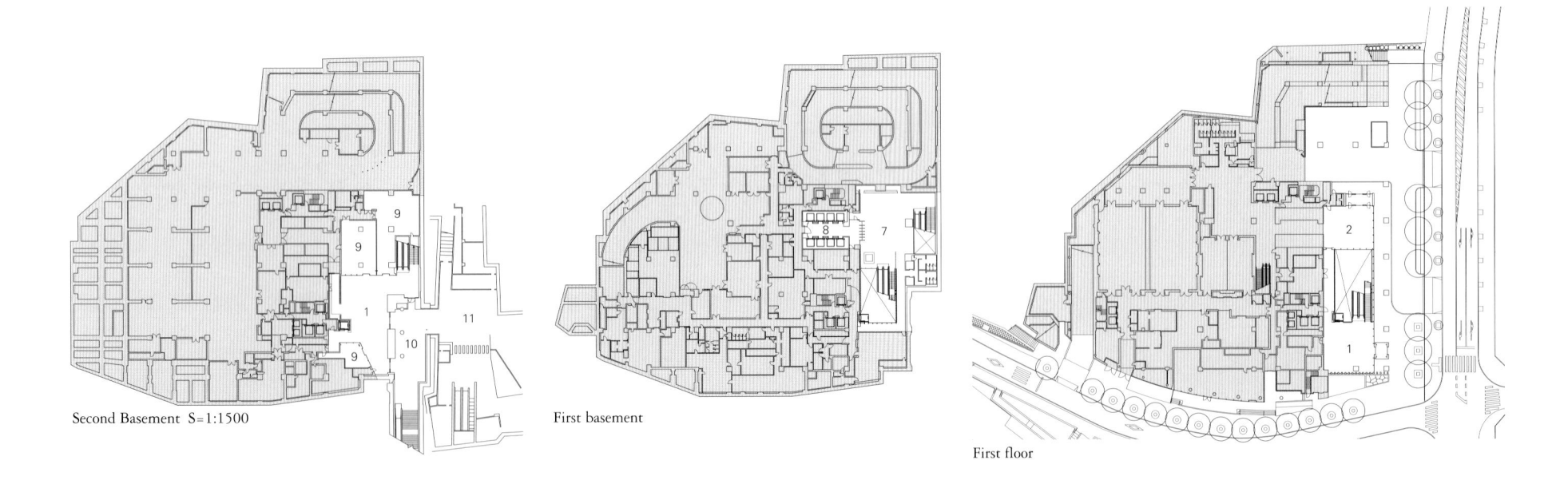

天井ルーバー
トキョウC
トキョウB
トキョウA
壁ルーバー

Wooden frame (to-kyo louver)

1 COMMON HALL
2 ENTRANCE LOBBY OF HOTEL
3 LOUNGE
4 CORRIDOR
5 BASIN
6 PARKING
7 HALL (OFFICE)
8 EV HALL (OFFICE)
9 SHOP
10 PATHWAY FOR WALKERS
11 SUBWAY STATION

Second Basement S=1:1500

First basement

First floor

△▽ Entrance lobby of hotel　ホテルのエントランス・ロビー

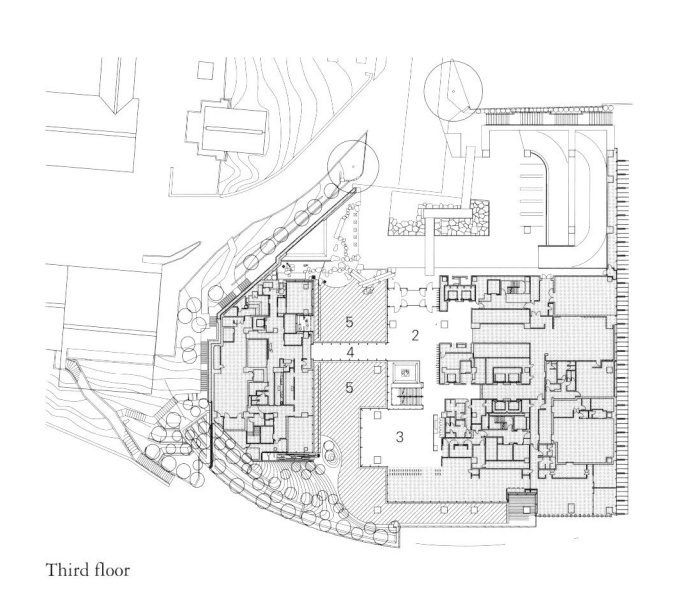

Third floor

73

2005-07　Yien East
Japan

Overall view　全景

View from annex wing toward main wing　離れより母屋を見る

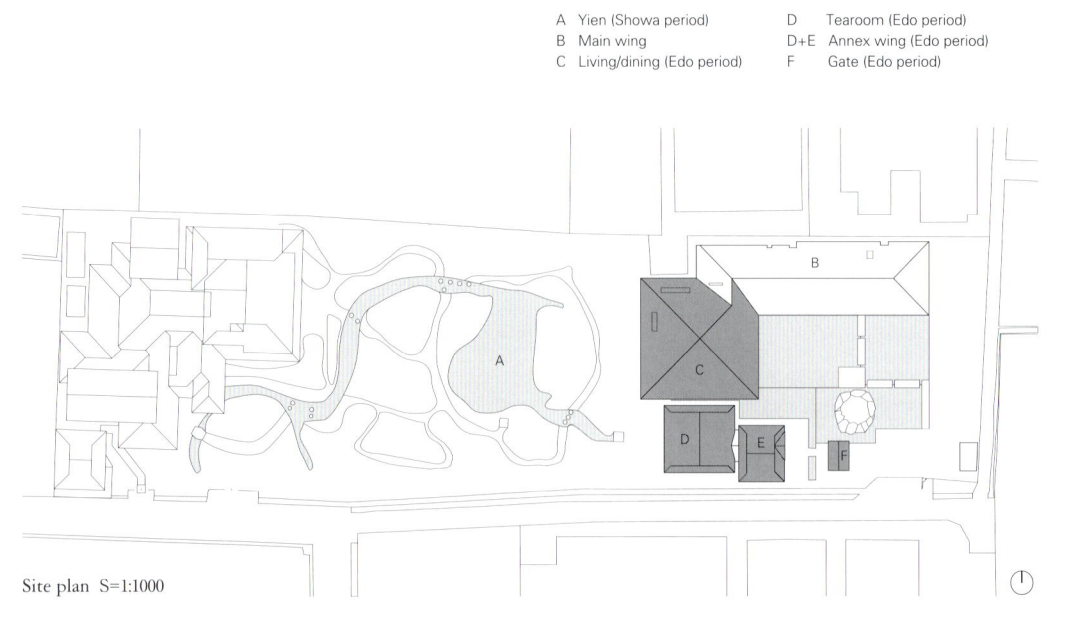

A　Yien (Showa period)
B　Main wing
C　Living/dining (Edo period)
D　Tearoom (Edo period)
D+E　Annex wing (Edo period)
F　Gate (Edo period)

Site plan　S=1:1000

Architectures that straddle five time periods and locations were brought together in one place to form a string of smooth continuity—namely, the gate from Taima-dera Temple in Nara (Edo period), the entrance and 'shoin' (drawing room) from Hannya-ji Temple in Nara (mid-Edo), and the Noh stage from Yokoyama residence in Kanazawa (late Edo) were first gathered in Shiroganedai in Tokyo then cut-and-pasted onto this site.

Horizontal elements, that is, smooth continuum between the floor and the roof, were of major concern when putting together different time periods. Once the horizontal elements were connected in a smooth manner, human activities experienced on them will flow in like manner. Vertical elements were expressed as details that do not interfere with the continuity of horizontal elements using materials such as stainless mesh. Life will flow in beauty no matter how disparate things are placed on these horizontal surfaces. Modernists have learned from Japanese architecture that spatial transparency is in fact such continuity of horizontal surfaces. This architecture is a reaffirmation of this fact.

Main wing　母屋

View toward annex wing from bedroom　離れより寝室を見る

Washbasin　つくばい

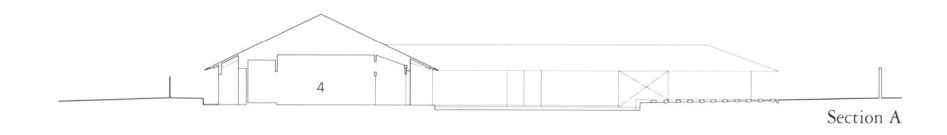

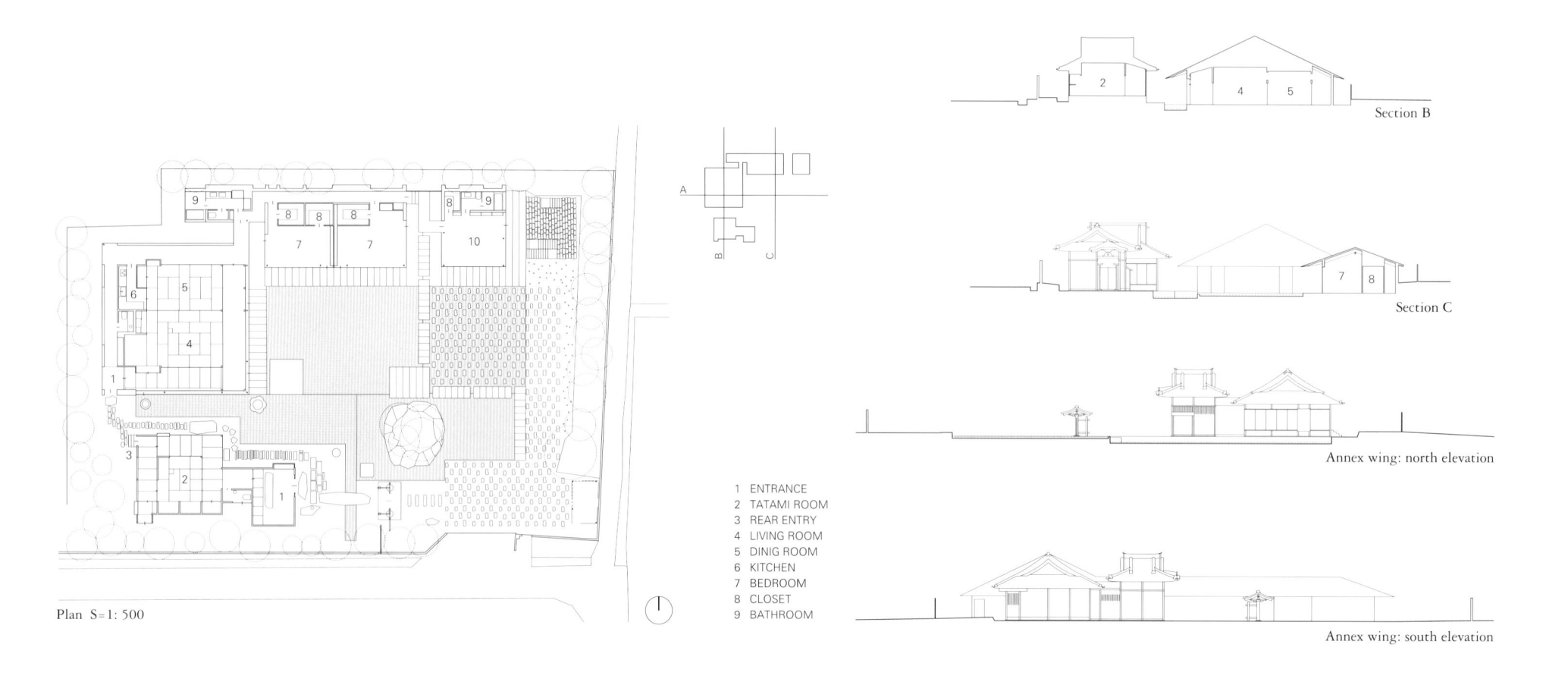

Plan S=1:500

1 ENTRANCE
2 TATAMI ROOM
3 REAR ENTRY
4 LIVING ROOM
5 DINIG ROOM
6 KITCHEN
7 BEDROOM
8 CLOSET
9 BATHROOM

Section A

Section B

Section C

Annex wing: north elevation

Annex wing: south elevation

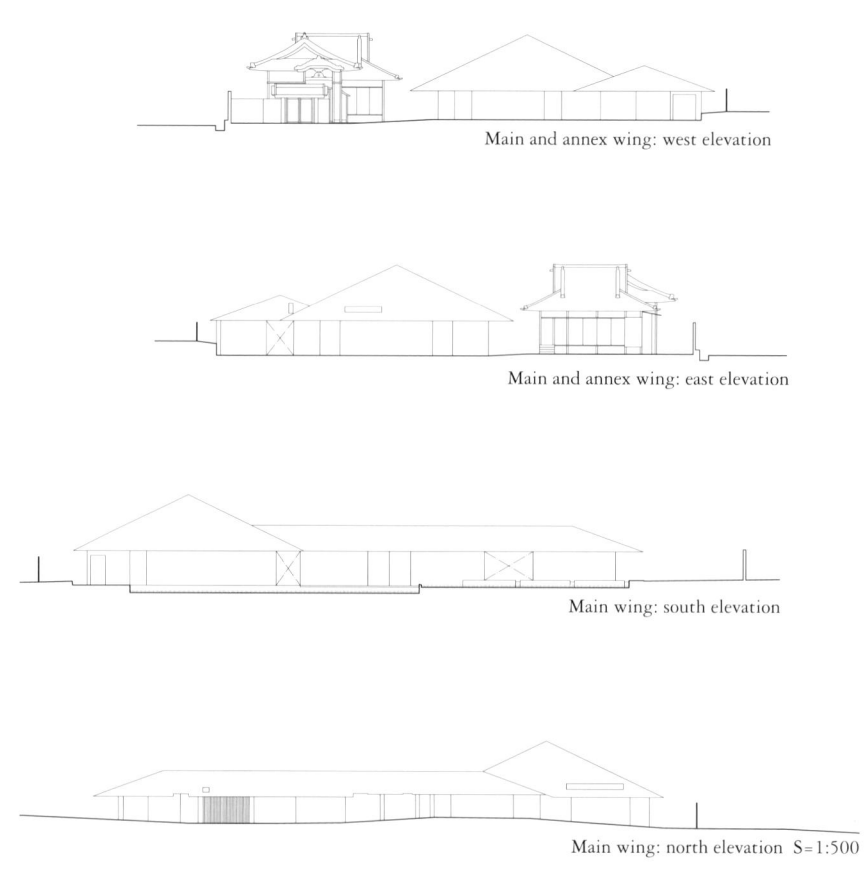

Main and annex wing: west elevation

Main and annex wing: east elevation

Main wing: south elevation

Main wing: north elevation S=1:500

Relations of main wing (left) and annex wing (right)　母屋（左）と離れ（右）の関係

Annex wing　離れ

View toward annex wing from living room of main wing　母屋の居間より離れを見る

In-between space of bedroom and study　寝室と書斎の隙間

View from bedroom toward study　寝室より書斎を見る

View from study toward bedroom　書斎より寝室を見る

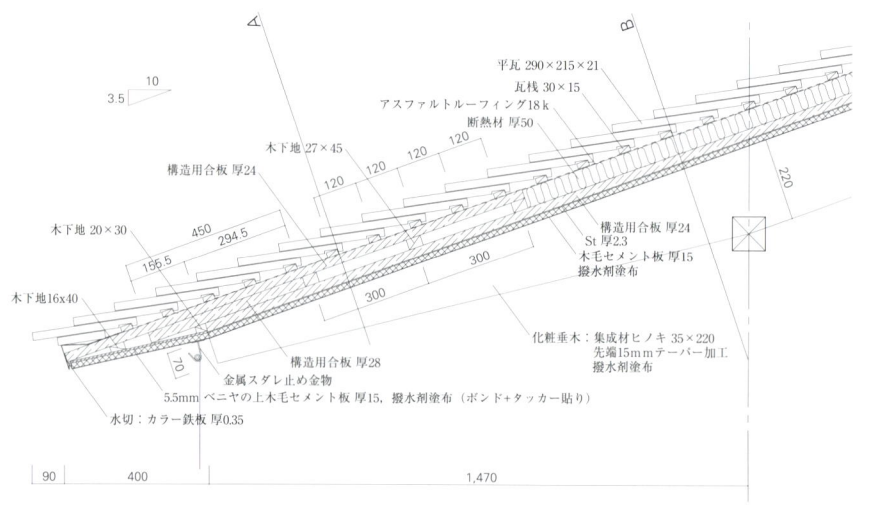

In-between space of bedroom and living room　寝室と居間の隙間

Sectional detail of eaves　S=1:20

Eaves of study: view toward bamboo grove　書斎前の軒下：竹林方向を見る

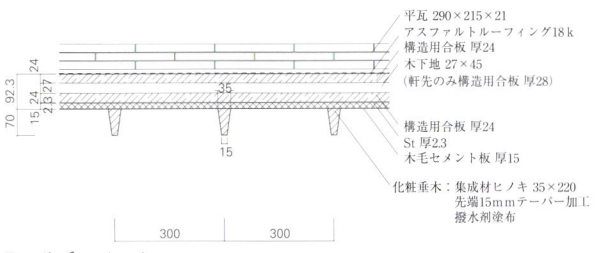

Detail of section A

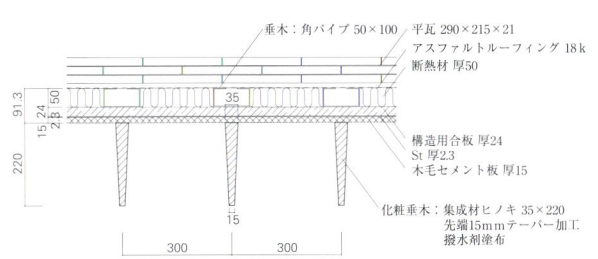

Detail of section B　S=1:20

Yien East

五つの時代，場所にまたがる建築をひとつの場所に集め，ひとつながりのスムースな連続性をつくった。具体的には，奈良当麻寺門（江戸時代），奈良般若寺玄関，書院（江戸時代中期），金沢横山家能舞台（江戸時代後期）を一旦，ある文人が東京の白金台に集め，さらに今回，それがこの地にカット＆ペーストされた。

複数の時間の集合において最も留意したのは，水平エレメント，具体的には床と屋根とをスムースに連続させていくことである。水平エレメントさえスムースにつながれば，その上で行われる人間の体験は，スムースに淀みなく流れていく。垂直エレメントはステンレス・メッシュなどを用い，水平エレメントの連続性を妨げないディテールとした。水平面の上にどんな異質なものを置かれようと生活は美しく流れていく。空間の透明性とはそのような水平面の連続性であることを，モダニストたちは日本建築から学んだ。この建築は，その事実を再確認させてくれた。

2005-08 Hoshakuji Station
Takanezawa, Tochigi, Japan

In front of Hoshakuji station of JR Tohoku Line, we designed a group of community facilities called Chokkura Plaza (2006) and then we designed a station building. In Chokkura Plaza we challenged a porous masonry using a mixed structural system combining local Oya stone and diagonal shaped steel plates. For the station building, we extended the diagonal pattern, but changed the material to lighter and warmer one (steel pipe and structural plywood). We tried to create a harmony of the entire facility, centering the station building. As a result, the open space and the station building were solved using the same geometry, but reproduced a lightness and gentleness that the old wooden station building once had and is analogous to wooden houses. The roof of the station building is a diagonal coffered ceiling using structural plywood. Lighting fixtures were installed in the slit between the plywood. The ceiling that has shades and a sense of volume give warmth and rhythm to the passage space, which tends to be cold, and at the same time function as a structure to support the roof.

Bridge　自由通路

East exit　東口

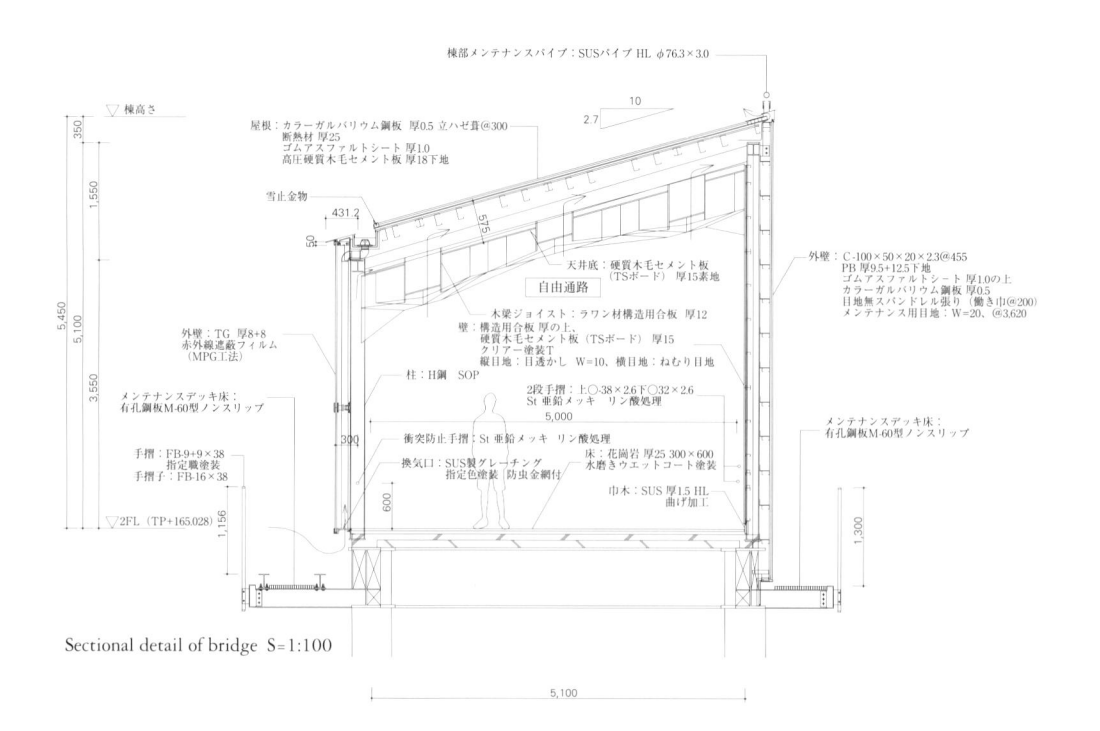

Sectional detail of bridge　S=1:100

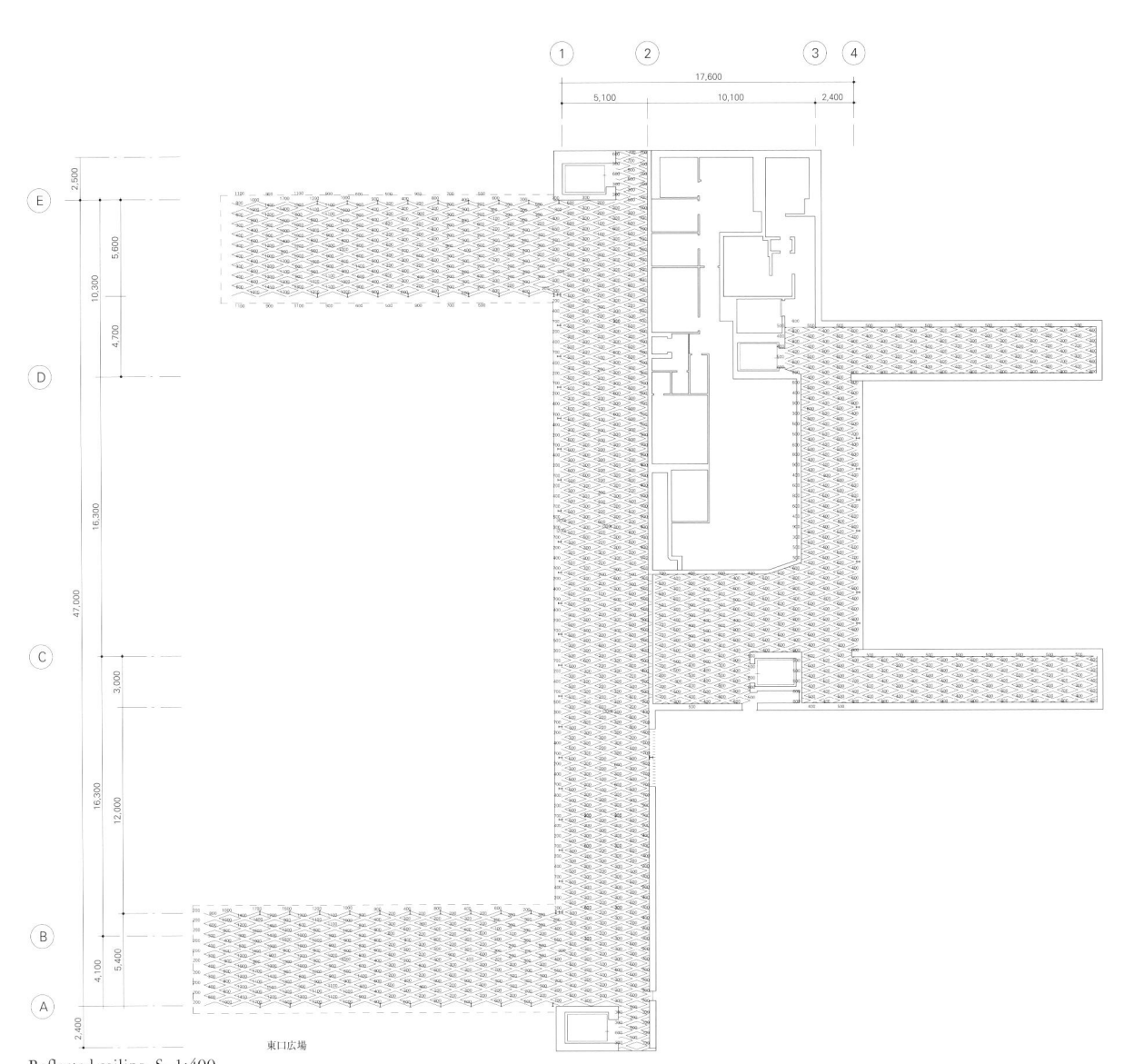

Reflected ceiling S=1:400

Wooden beam detail S=1:20

Detail of wooden beam　木梁のディテール

Staircase of east exit　東口昇降階段

宝積寺駅

東北本線宝積寺駅前に、「ちょっ蔵広場」(2006年)と呼ばれるコミュニティ施設群を設計し、続いて駅舎を設計した。「ちょっ蔵広場」では、地元産の大谷石とダイアゴナルな形状の鉄板とを組み合わせた混構造システムを用いた、多孔質な組積造に挑戦した。駅舎でもそのダイアゴナルなパターンを延長しながら、しかも材料をより軽く暖かいもの(鉄パイプと構造用合板)に切り換えた。そうすることで、駅舎を中心とする施設全体の調和をつくり出そうとした。結果、広場と駅舎とを同一のジオメトリーで解きながら、しかも昔の木造の駅舎が持っていた、木造住宅にも通じる軽やかなやわらかさを再生した。駅舎天井は構造用合板を用いたダイアゴナルな格天井とし、合板と合板のスリットに照明器具をセットした。陰翳と質感のある天井は、冷たくなりがちな通路空間に暖かさとリズムを与え、同時に屋根を支える構造としても機能している。

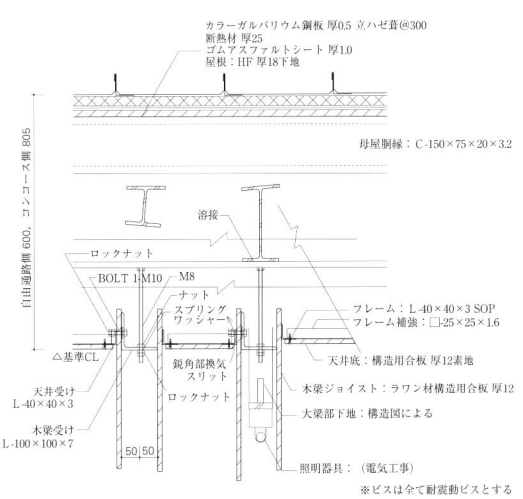

2005-08 The Opposite House
Beijing, China

Southeast view: entrance on right　南東より見る。右にエントランス

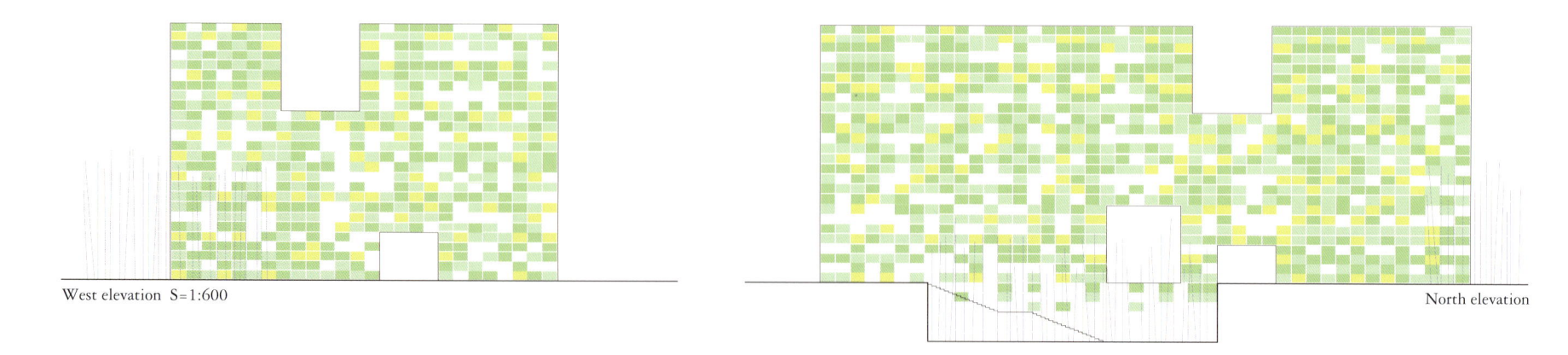

West elevation S=1:600

North elevation

Site plan　S=1:5000

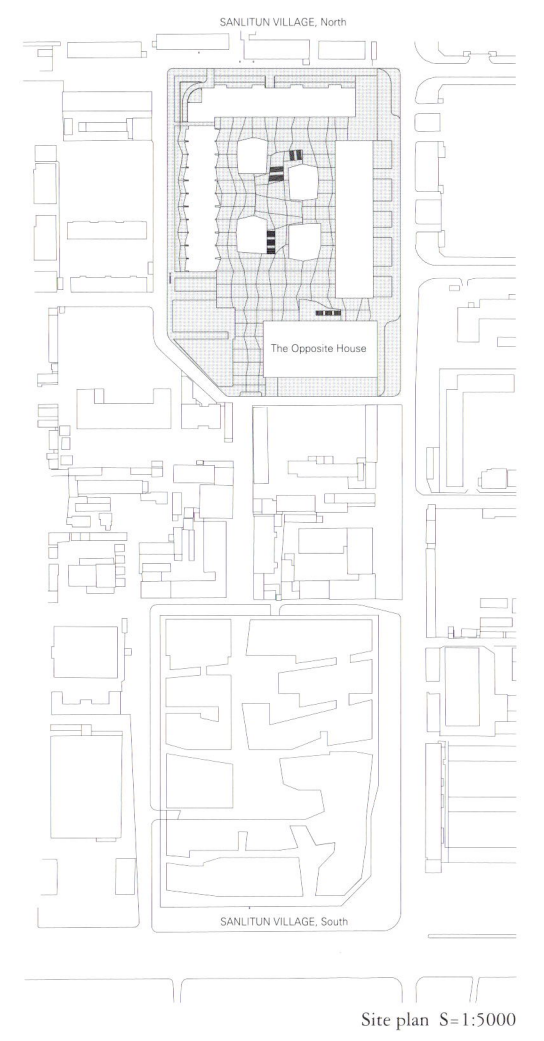

Atrium/gallery: view toward entrance　アトリウム／ギャラリー：エントランス方向を見る

83

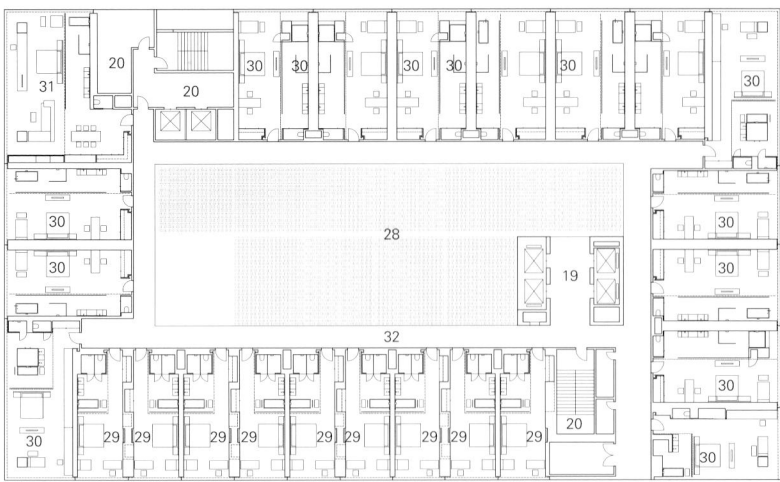

Typical floor

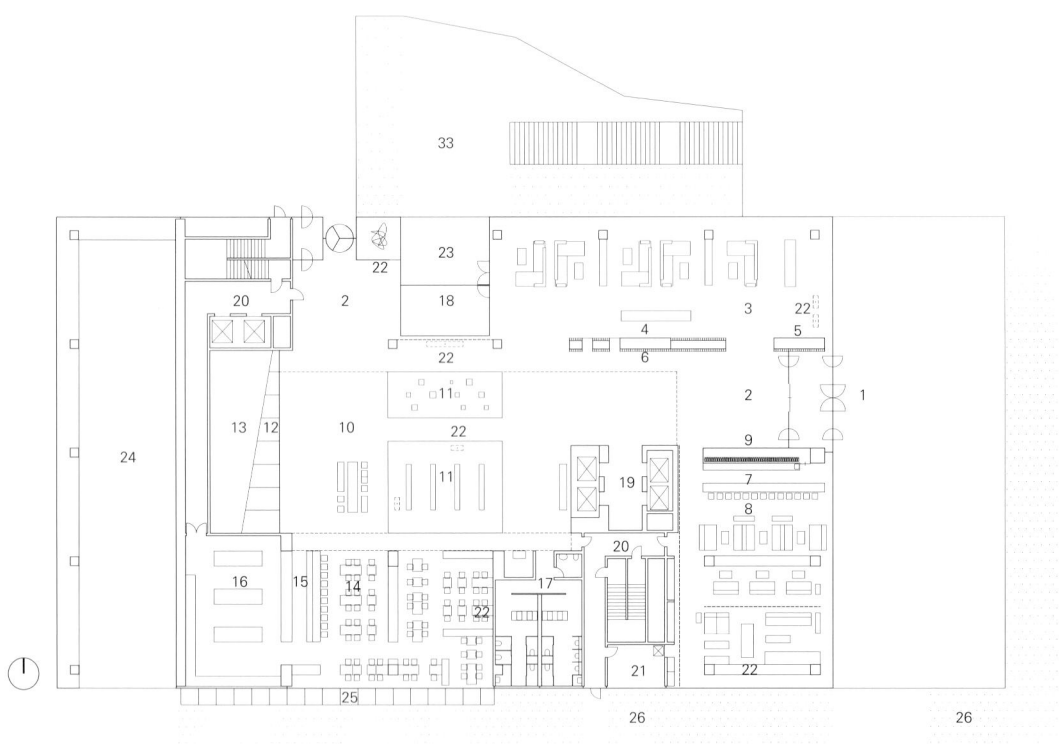

First floor S=1:600

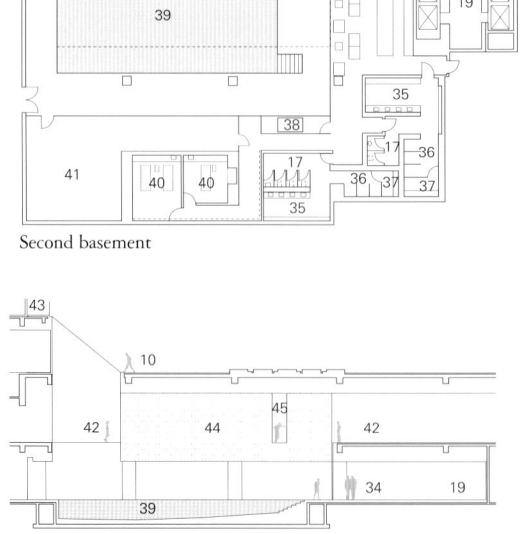

Second basement

Partial section: basement S=1:600

1	ENTRANCE
2	VESTIBULE
3	RECEPTION
4	STAFF WORK STATION
5	LUGGAGE STORAGE
6	ART DISPLAY WALL
7	BAR
8	BAR - SEATING AREA
9	BAR - WINE CELLAR
10	ATRIUM / GALLERY
11	REFLECTING POOL
12	SLANTED GLASS WALL
13	OPEN TO SWIMMING POOL
14	CAFE
15	ESPRESSO BAR
16	KITCHEN
17	TOILET
18	OFFICE
19	ELEVATOR LOBBY
20	SERVICE
21	MECHANICAL ROOM
22	ART DISPLAY
23	TERRACE
24	PARKING RAMP
25	SKYLIGHT
26	BAMBOO GARDEN
27	VEGETATION / TREE
28	ATRIUM / MESH SCREEN
29	GUEST ROOM - STUDIO 45
30	GUEST ROOM - STUDIO 70
31	GUEST ROOM - STUDIO 95
32	HALLWAY
33	SUNKEN GARDEN
34	JUICE BAR
35	POWDER ROOM
36	SHOWER ROOM
37	SAUNA
38	FOOT BATH
39	SWIMMING POOL
40	TREATMENT ROOM
41	GYM
42	B1 RESTAURANT
43	2F HALLWAY
44	FIBER OPTICS LIGHTING
45	GLASS BRIDGE

A	ATRIUM / GALLERY
B	TERRACE
C	GM OFFICE
D	CAFE
E	GUEST ROOM
F	HALLWAY
G	SKYLIGHT
H	RESTAURANT
I	SWIMMING POOL
J	GYM
K	MECHANICAL ROOM
L	SUNKEN GARDEN
M	BAMBOO GARDEN
N	PARKING

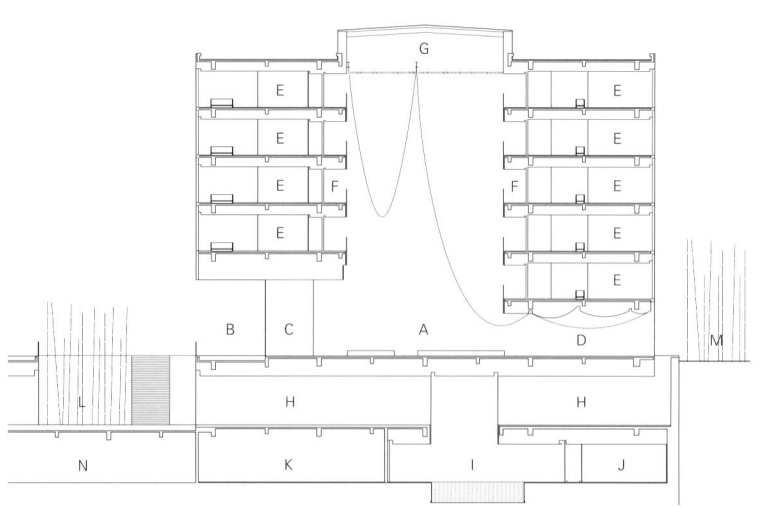

Cross section S=1:600

We challenged to create a new style for a city-type hotel, motivated by Siheyuan, a courtyard residence, which is a traditional residential style in northern China. Opposite House is an English translation of guest space in a part of Siheyuan.

Siheyuan uses diverse lattices and screens and they contribute to win surprising quietness even in a large city like Beijing. In the project, ceramic fritted glass and metal mesh were used and directed to gain the same thick sense of atmosphere and tranquility as Siheyuan. The facade glass was ceramic fritted twice with an abstracted traditional Chinese pattern that gradationally controls light penetration to the room and privacy.

In the upper part of the atrium that was equated as a courtyard, metal mesh was hanged and the entire atrium was filled with special light that filtrated through the mesh.

The light fell from the sky penetrates glass floor on the ground floor and reaches to the underground pool. The atrium that is filled with special light connects the sky and the ground, just like old Siheyuan's courtyard was once a communication place of the sky and the ground.

Reception　レセプション

Bar entrance on first floor, displayed wine cellar on left
1階バー・エントランス。左はディスプレイされたワイン・セラー

Bar: interior with mesh screen and translucent curtain
バー：メッシュ・スクリーンと半透明のカーテンで構成されたインテリア

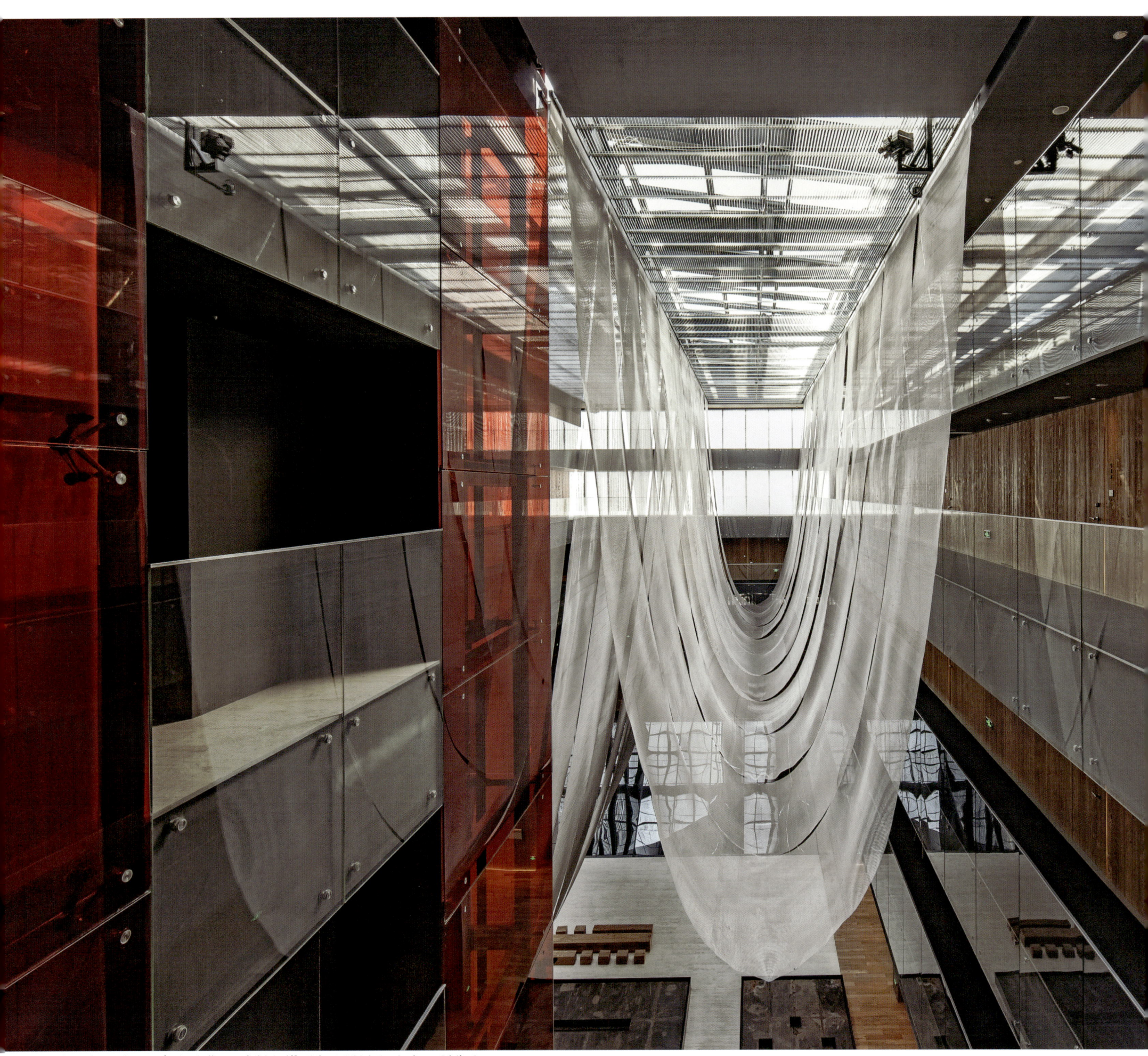

Mesh stainless-steel screen of atrium/gallery　アトリウム／ギャラリーのステンレス・メッシュ・スクリーン

Atrium/gallery with mesh screen: view toward cafe　メッシュ・スクリーンの垂れ下がるアトリウム／ギャラリー：カフェを見る

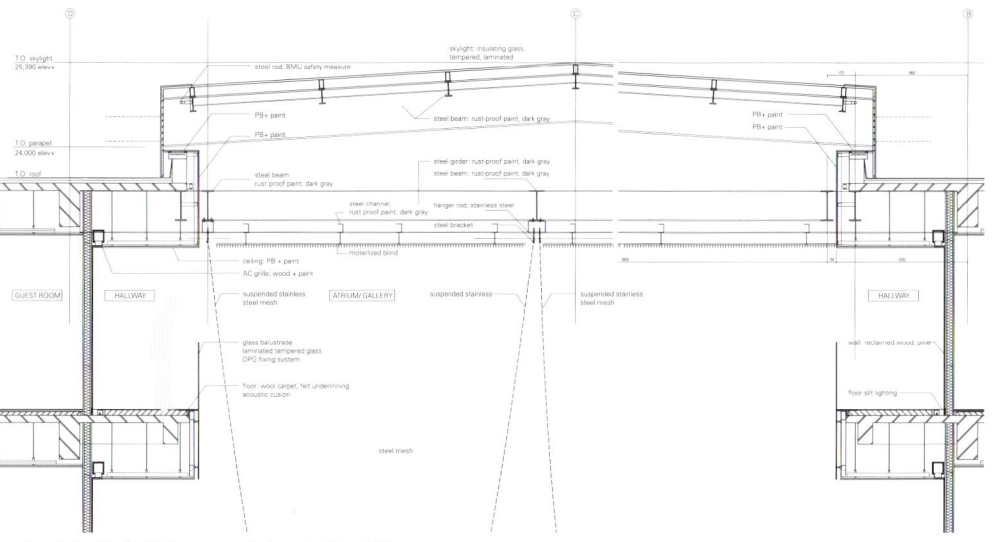

Sectional detail: skylight, suspended mesh S=1:120

The Opposite House

中国北方の伝統的な住居のスタイルである,四合院と呼ばれる中庭型住宅にヒントを得て,新しい都市型ホテルの形式を創造しようと試みた。「The Opposite House」は,四合院の一部である客用スペース「対院」の英訳である。

四合院は,様々な格子やスクリーンを用いて,北京のような大都市の中にありながら,驚くべき静謐さを獲得している。本プロジェクトでも,セラミックプリントを施したガラスと金属製のメッシュを用いて,四合院と同じような濃密な空気感,静謐さの獲得を目標とした。ファサードのガラスに中国の伝統的なパターンを抽象化したセラミックプリントを二重に施すことによって,室内へ射し込む光とプライバシーとをグラデーショナルにコントロールした。

中庭と見立てたアトリウム上部には,メタルメッシュを吊り下げ,アトリウム全体をメッシュで濾過させた特殊な光で満たした。

その天から降り注ぐ先は,1階のガラスの床を透過して地下のプールにまで到達し,かつての四合院の中庭が天と地との交信の場であったように,ここでは特別な光に満たされたアトリウムによって天と地とがつながれる。

Elevator　エレベータ

Swimming pool on second basement: fiber optics lighting above
地下2階スイミング・プール：天井の吹抜けから光ファイバーによる照明がほのかに照らす

Swimming pool, gym on left　スイミング・プール，左はジム

1	BEDROOM
2	STUDY
3	BATHROOM
4	TOILET
5	SHOWER
6	WARDROBE
7	LIVING
8	DINING
9	TERRACE
10	JACUZZI
11	PANTRY
12	BAR
13	COAT CLOSET
14	REFLECTING POOL

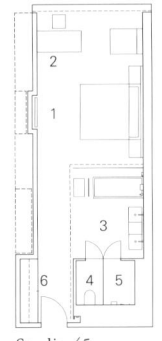

Studio 45

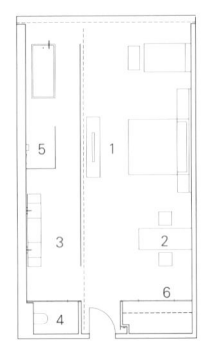

Studio 70

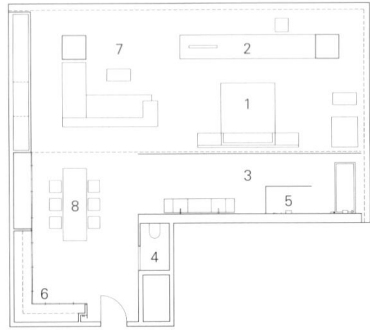

Studio 95

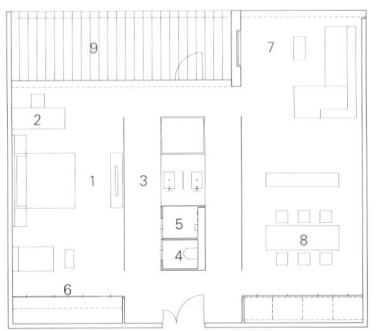

Studio 115

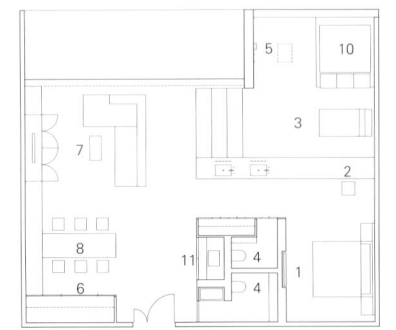

Studio 115　S=1:250

Guest room: studio 70-A　客室：スタジオ70m²-A

Guest room: studio 95　客室：スタジオ95m²

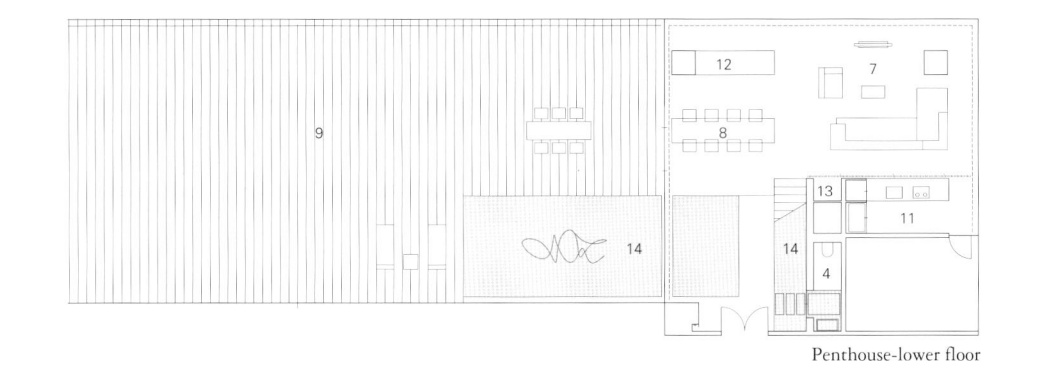

Penthouse-lower floor 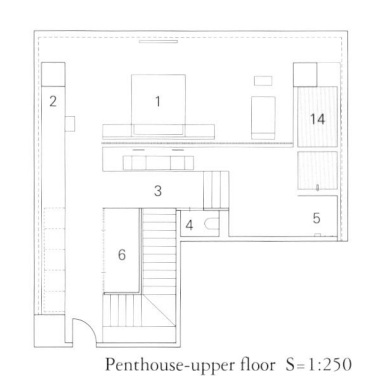   Penthouse-upper floor S=1:250

Penthouse: upper floor for bedroom and bathroom
ペントハウス：上階（寝室／浴室）

2005 T-Room
Ishikawa, Japan

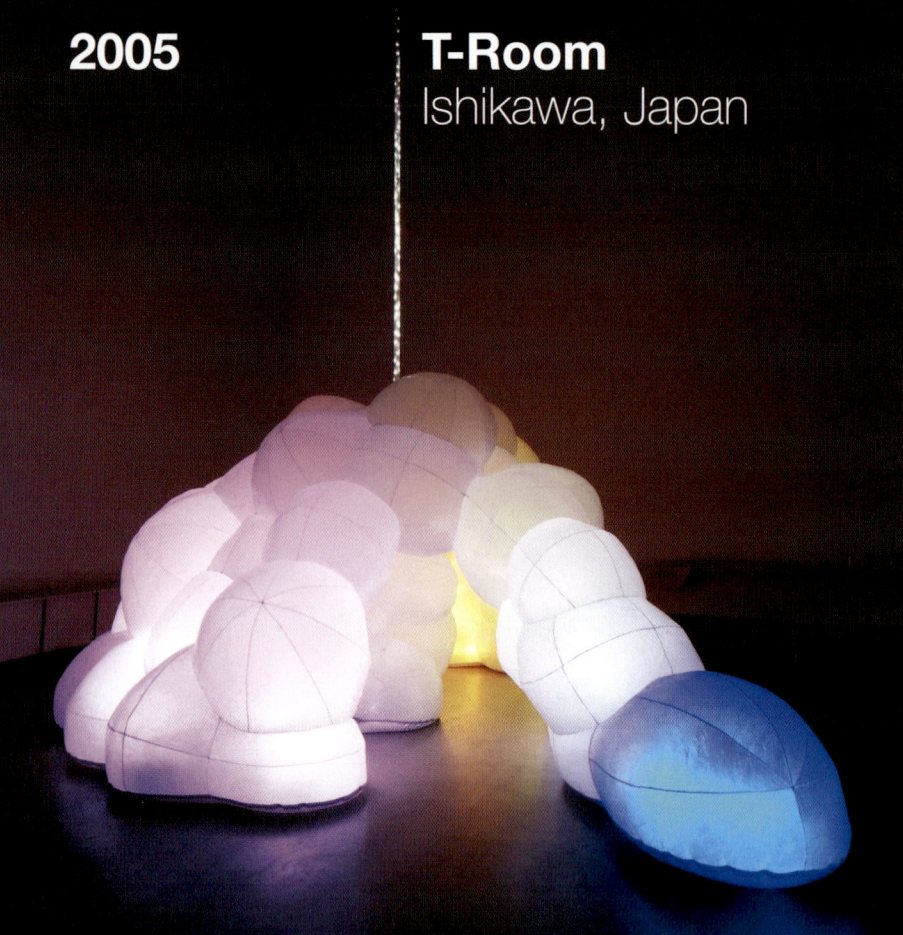

It came into my mind to create an extremely tender tearoom. In the first place, tearoom was initiated as an antithesis to an architectural style of Shoinzukuri that determines 'hard and square'. Therefore, Rikyu finished the internal corner of Taian's soil wall round and tried to make the space tender as much as possible.

We pursued the tenderness further than Taian. We considered that tenderness is not just about round shape, but is soft when touched and is keep on changing softly by itself. We re-defined tenderness in that way.

In order to accomplish the new tenderness, firstly, we made a covering that has mysterious texture like an organism's mucous membrane by applying sticky silicone to polyester mesh. Then, a balloon-shaped structure was formed with the membrane. By inflating and deflating air, we let the architecture itself move softly and flabby like a creature.

t-room
徹底的にやわらかい茶室をつくろうと考えた。そもそも茶室は,「固く四角い」書院造という建築様式に対するアンチテーゼとして始まったからである。だから,利休は待庵の壁の入り隅の土壁をまるく仕上げ,空間を可能な限りやわらかくしようと試みたのである。

われわれは待庵のさらに先のやわらかさを追及した。やわらかさとは,単に形がまるいだけではなく,さわってやわらかく,自分自身でやわらかく変化し続けることではないかと考えた。そのようにして,やわらかさを再定義した。

その新しいやわらかさを実現するため,まずポリエステルのメッシュに,ネバネバしたシリコンを塗って,生物の粘膜のような不思議な質感のある膜材をつくった。その膜材で,風船状の構造体をつくり,そこに空気を出し入れすることで,建築自体が生物のようにブヨブヨと動く仕組みとした。

LED light falls into t-room. 'LED light/sound' by Toshio Iwai
LEDの光がt-roomに落ちる。岩井俊雄による「LED light/sound」

Interior　t-roomの内部

Process of change color　変色過程

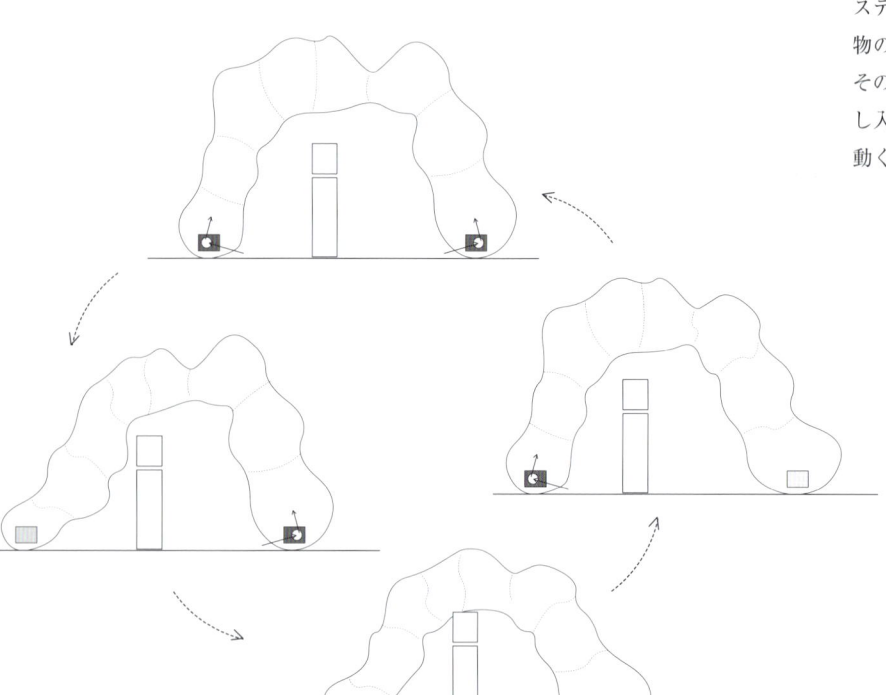

Time cycle diagram

Section　S=1:200

2006- Kenny Heights Museum
Kuala Lumpur, Malaysia

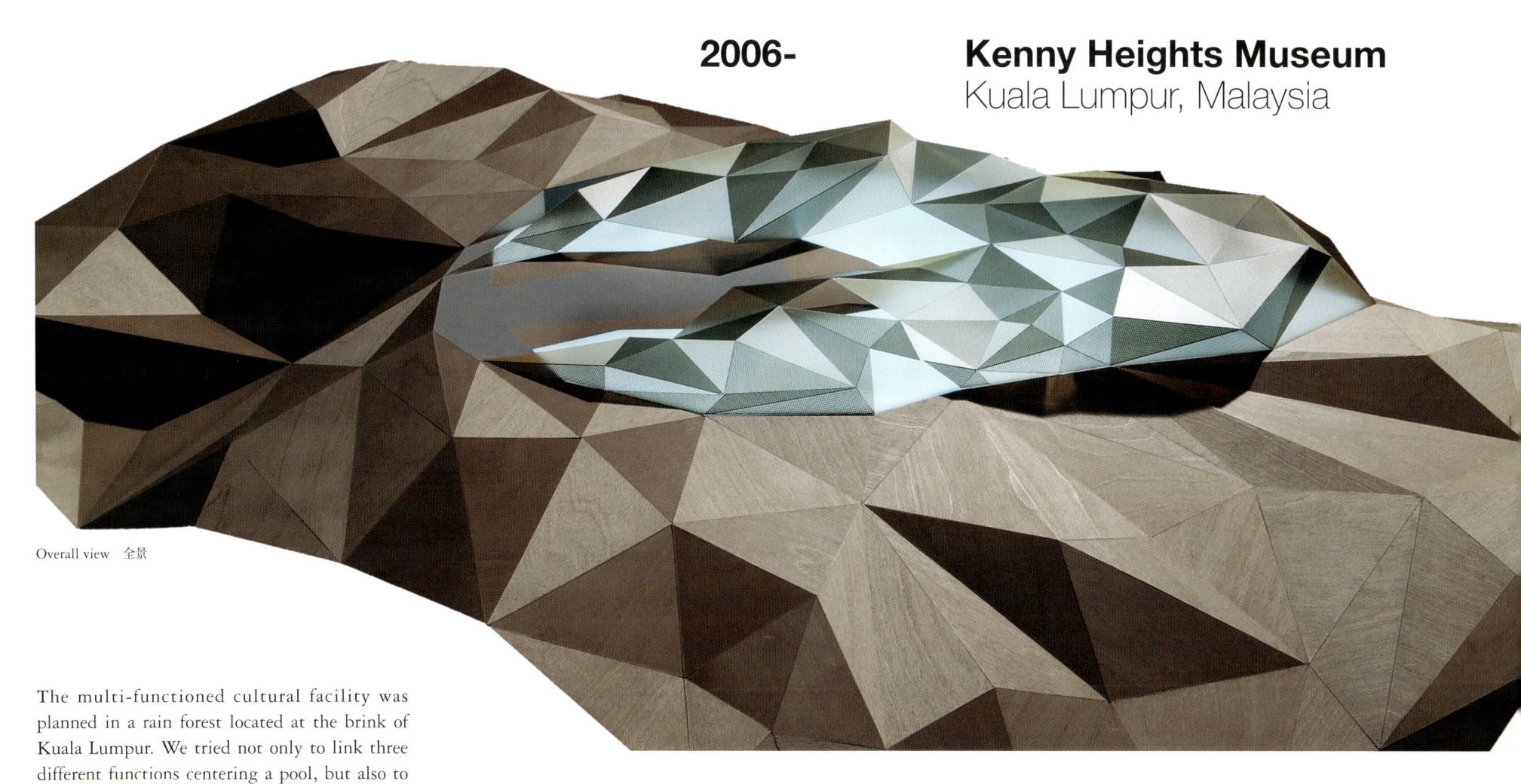

Overall view 全景

The multi-functioned cultural facility was planned in a rain forest located at the brink of Kuala Lumpur. We tried not only to link three different functions centering a pool, but also to connect to the scenery of the center of Kuala Lumpur by mediating the pool's water surface and using a roof as a frame.

For the exterior and the interior wall, sandwiched panels composed of a paper-made honeycomb core and plastics, which we used in Paper Snake (2005) in Anyang Korea, were applied, so as to mitigate tropics' strong sunlight. The roof is divided into polygons. We tried to create dense space that light and darkness coexist in a jungle where opaque and transparent triangles randomly appear.

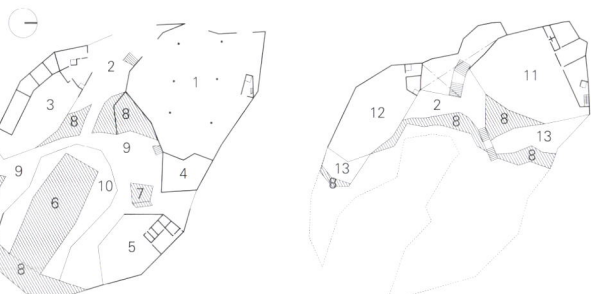

First floor S=1:3000 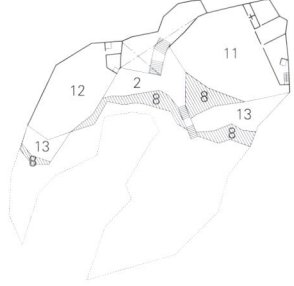   Second floor 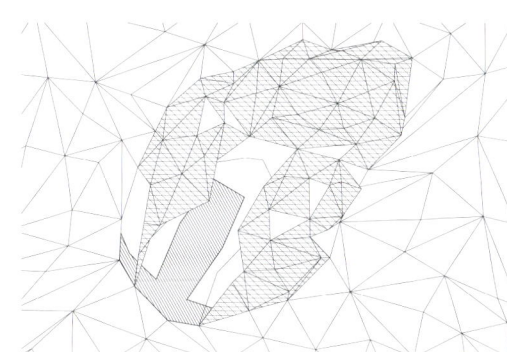   Roof

1 PARKING
2 ENTRANCE
3 SPA
4 MACHINE ROOM
5 CAFE
6 POOL
7 CHILDREN POOL
8 POND
9 WOODDECK
10 SAND
11 GALLERY
12 SHOWROOM
13 VIEW AREA

ケニー ハイツ ミュージアム

クアラルンプール外縁の熱帯雨林の中に計画された複合型文化施設。プールを中心として三つの異なる機能を接続するだけでなく,プールの水面を媒介にし,屋根をフレームとして利用することで,クアラルンプール中心部の景観との接続を試みた。

外部,内部は,韓国アニャンの「ペーパースネーク」(2005年)にも用いた紙製のハニカムコアをプラスチックでサンドイッチしたパネルによって,熱帯の強い光をやわらげる。屋根はポリゴン分割するだけでなく,不透明な三角形と透明な三角形とがランダムに出現し,光と闇とが混在した濃密な空間をジャングルの中につくり出そうと考えた。

View of pool from wooden deck ウッド・デッキよりプールを見る

2006-07 Sake no Hana
London, U.K.

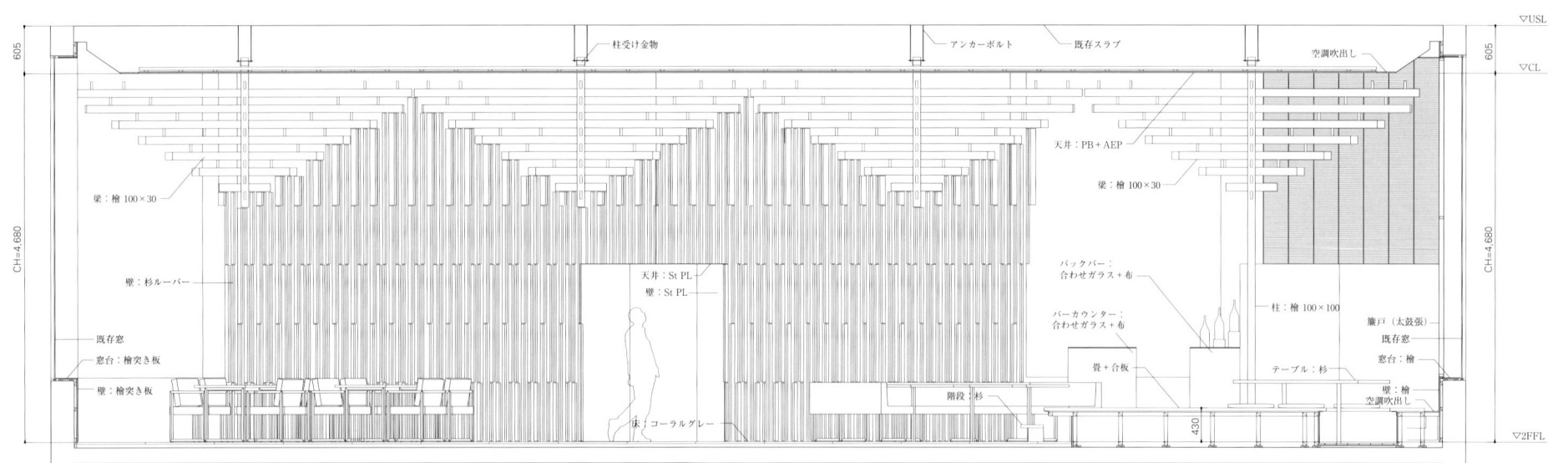

Longitudinal section: second floor

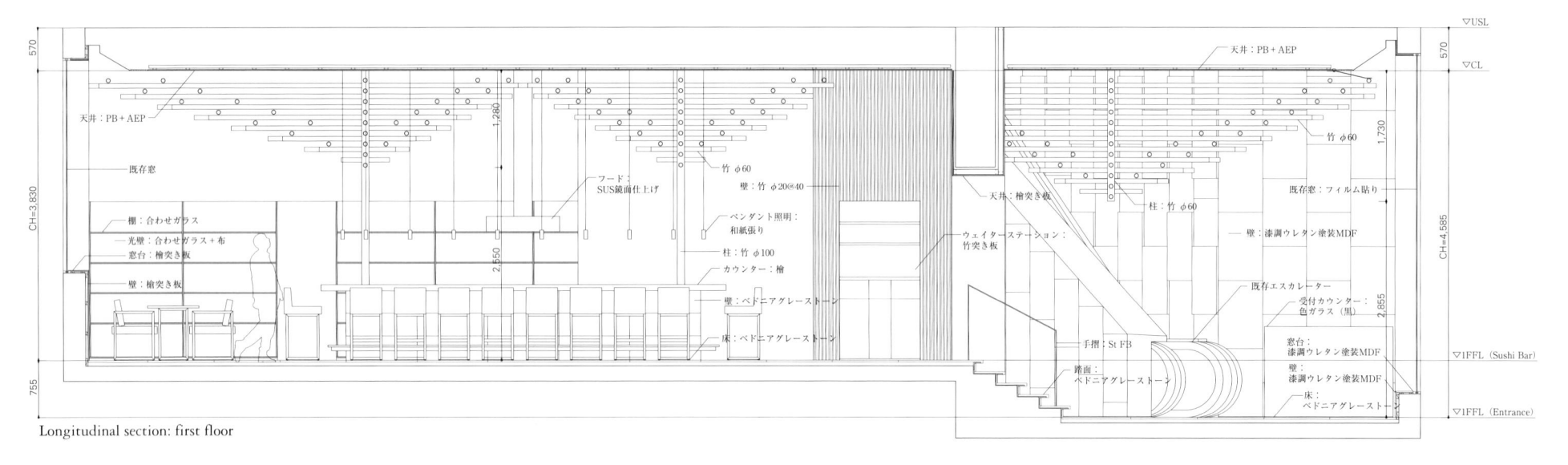

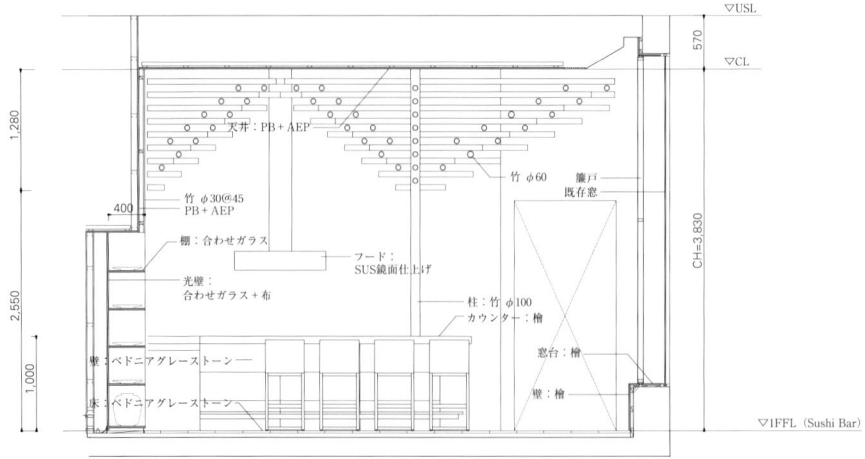

Longitudinal section: first floor

Cross section: first floor S=1:80

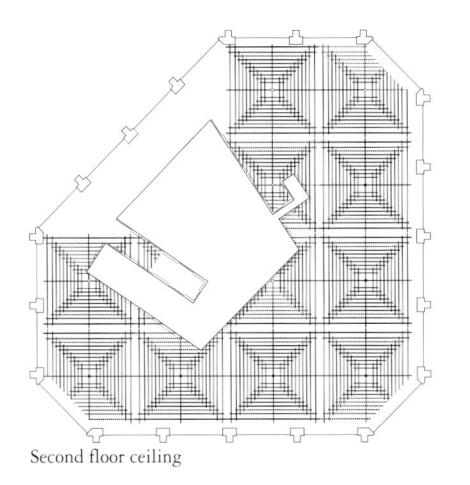

Second floor ceiling

Second floor

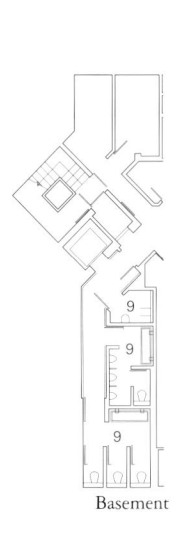

Basement

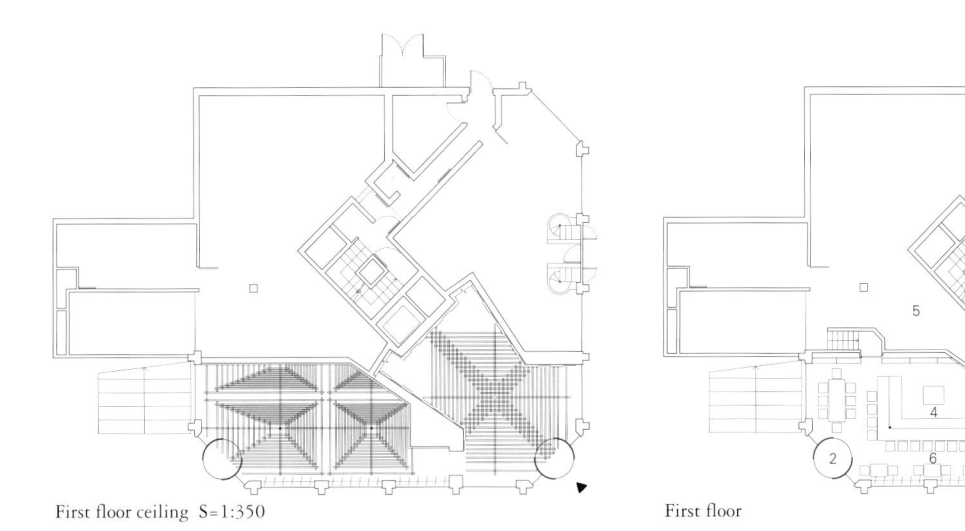

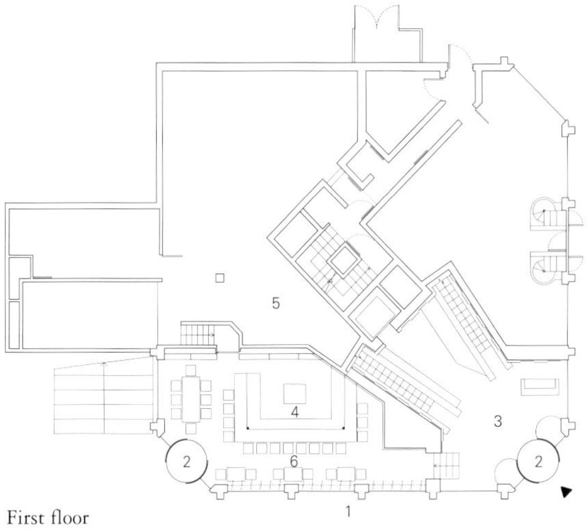

First floor ceiling S=1:350

First floor

Entrance hall on first floor　1階エントランス・ホール

1 ST JAME'S STREET
2 ENTRANCE
3 RECEPTION
4 COUNTER
5 KITCHEN
6 RESTAURANT
7 HOLDING BAR
8 VIP ROOM
9 WC

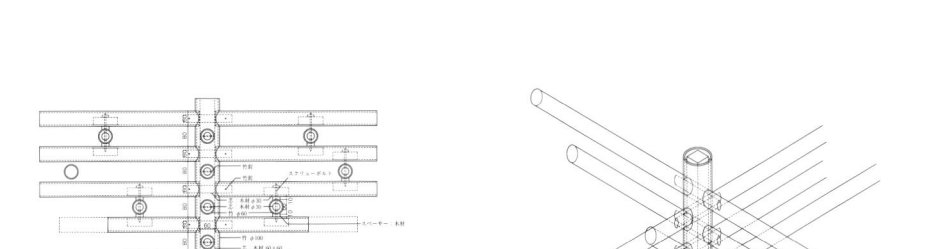

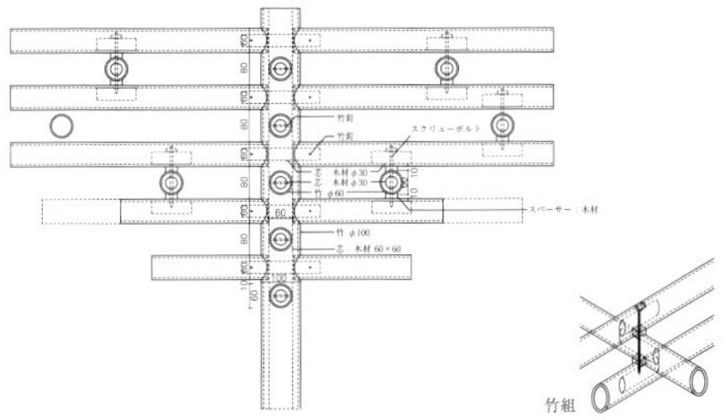

Bamboo frame ceiling: detail and diagram S=1:30

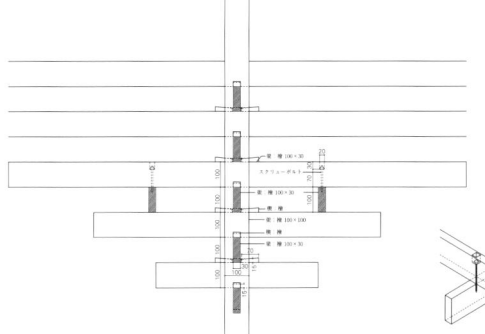

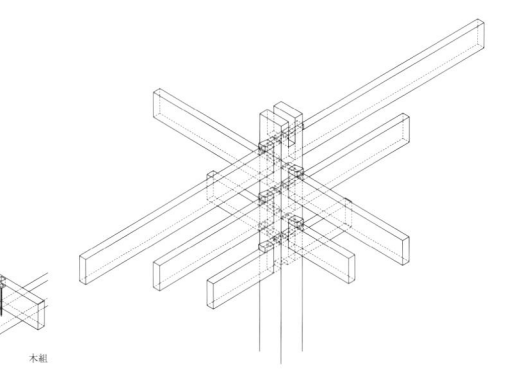

Wooden frame ceiling: detail and diagram S=1:30

Restaurant on second floor　2階レストラン

The project is a renovation of the first floor of Economist Building (1951) designed by Peter Smithson. Smithson tried a unique detail to tilt square columns for 45 degrees in the Economist Building. The detail is called renjikoushi in Japan. Smithson intended to rarefy the presence of structural supports by tilting and showing the edge and not the surface. Further, Smithson did not use Portland stone as a finishing material attached on concrete, but used as a solid stick material and fixed them by employing a special detail on the concrete body.

Smithson criticizes here modernism through how he treated the material. His opinion in Team X was to free architecture from solidified objects and let them float in an urban sea. In this way, he criticized Le Corbusier's modernism. Economist Building is a practice of criticism on modernism over a detail. The objective of the project was to revive the Smithson's spirit in the contemporary. Using stick-shaped materials such as wood and bamboo, we aimed at floating substances in lines and in particles in the city. It was idealized that not the architectural unit but smaller elements drift in the city and intercourse with human lives.

In the context, we looked into fundamental composition of wooden architecture in China and Japan. Brackets are combination of thin and delicate solid substances and they reach to a larger whole. We tried to revitalize the common method as Smithson in brackets in the present.

Sushi bar on first floor　1階寿司バー

Bamboo screen on first floor　1階の簾戸

Sake no Hana

ピーター・スミッソン設計の「エコノミストビル」(1951年)の1階の改修。スミッソンは「エコノミストビル」で,四角い柱を45度傾けるというユニークなディテールを試みた。日本でいえば連子格子と呼ばれるディテールである。傾けることで,面ではなくコーナーを正面に向け,構造体の存在感を希薄にするのがスミッソンの狙いであった。さらにスミッソンは,ポートランドストーンをコンクリートの表面に貼られた仕上げ材として扱わずに,無垢の棒状素材としてコンクリート躯体に特殊なディテールを用いて固定している。

スミッソンはここで,物質の取り扱い方を通じてモダニズムを批判している。チームX(チーム・テン)での彼の主張は,建築を孤立したオブジェクトから開放して,都市の海の中に浮かすことであった。そのようにして,コルビュジエ流モダニズムを批判したのである。「エコノミストビル」は,ディテールにおけるモダニズム批判の実践である。このスミッソンの精神を現代によみがえらせることが,本プロジェクトの目標であった。木,竹などの棒状の材料を用いて,物質を都市の中に線的に粒子的に浮かすことが本プロジェクトの目標であった。建築という単位が都市の中に漂うのではなく,より小さなエレメントとして都市の中に漂い,人間の生活と対話する状態が理想である。

その時,中国,日本の木造建築の基本的構成システムである組物に注目した。組物は,細く繊細な無垢の物質を組み合わせていくことで,大きな全体に到達する方法である。組物とスミッソンに共通の方法を現代によみがえらすことを試みた。

2006-08 Ryotei Kaikatei Annex "sou-an"
Fukui, Japan

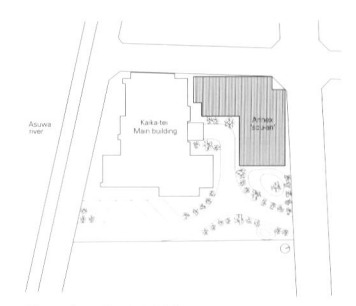

Site plan S=1:1500

Evening view of north elevation 北側ファサードの夕景

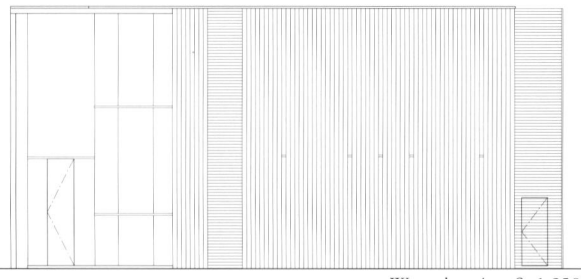

West elevation S=1:250

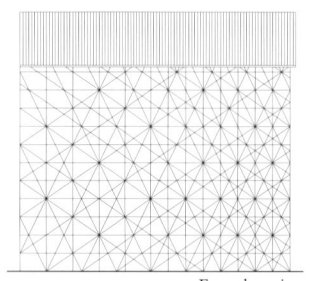

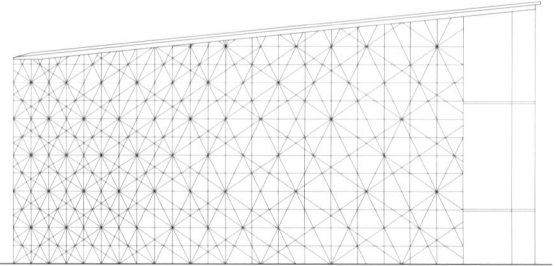

East elevation

North elevation

Overall view from northwest　北西より見る全景

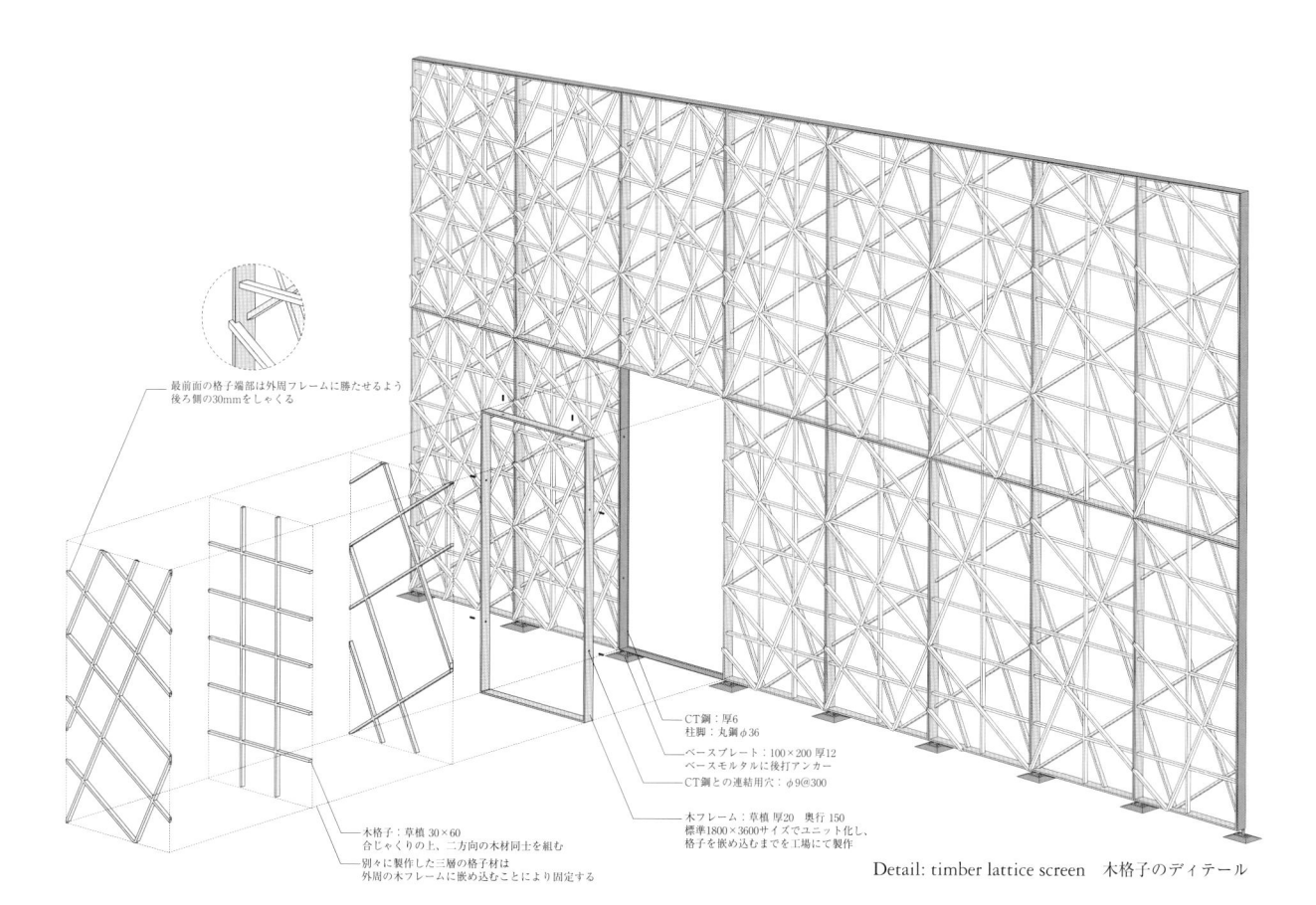

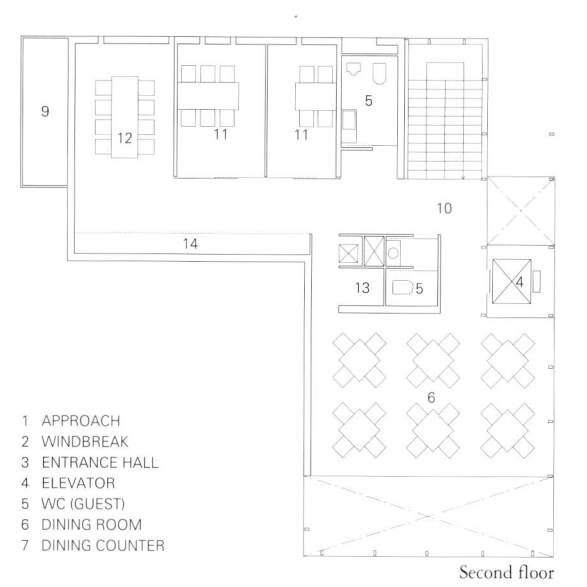

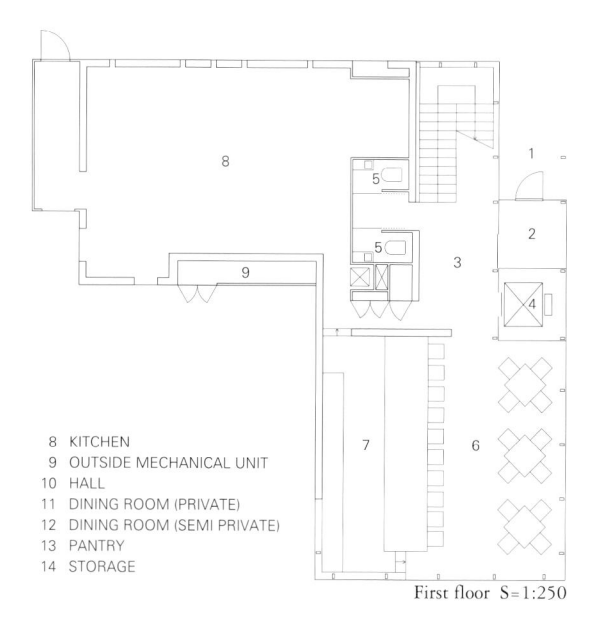

1　APPROACH
2　WINDBREAK
3　ENTRANCE HALL
4　ELEVATOR
5　WC (GUEST)
6　DINING ROOM
7　DINING COUNTER

Second floor

8　KITCHEN
9　OUTSIDE MECHANICAL UNIT
10　HALL
11　DINING ROOM (PRIVATE)
12　DINING ROOM (SEMI PRIVATE)
13　PANTRY
14　STORAGE

First floor　S=1:250

Detail: timber lattice screen　木格子のディテール

最前面の格子端部は外周フレームに勝たせるよう
後ろ側の30mmをしゃくる

木格子：草櫨 30×60
合じゃくりの上、二方向の木材同士を組む
別々に製作した三層の格子材は
外周の木フレームに嵌め込むことにより固定する

CT鋼：厚6
柱脚：丸鋼 φ36
ベースプレート：100×200 厚12
ベースモルタルに挽打アンカー
CT鋼との連結用穴：φ9@300

木フレーム：草櫨 厚20 奥行 150
標準1800×3600サイズでユニット化し、
格子を嵌め込むまでを工場にて製作

In-between space of glazed wall and timber lattice screen
ガラス壁と木格子の隙間

99

Dining room (semi private) on second floor　2階半個室

First floor: dining room on left, dining counter on right　1階：左が客室，右がカウンター席

Dining room on second floor　2階客室

This is a new light annex building located in the garden of an old Japanese restaurant. We aimed to design a light and transparent building that was also warm and friendly. We designed a glass box covered by a random lattice made from Buddhist pine. This random lattice pattern is repeated on the ceiling and walls inside to form a consistent theme. Based on a traditional pattern used in Japanese architecture and Kimono, we gave a randomness to it, breaking the symmetry and completeness of the original pattern. We tried to give a new openness to the glass box. Also, steel diagonal bracing within the timber lattice helped increase the building's rigidity.

The original building for the restaurant is set back from the alley, however we aim to activate the alley in the front and invite the flow of people into this alley by inserting this glass box and showing the active crowd inside. Indeed this glass box annex has become a trigger and the alley has been repaved with stone, and night lighting added. This old city is gaining a new life.

料亭開花亭別館「sou-an」
老舗の料亭の庭に計画された，軽やかなアネックス。軽やかで透明でありながら，しかも暖かくやさしい建築をつくろうと心掛け，クサマキの木でつくられたランダムな格子で覆われたガラスボックスを計画した。そのランダムな格子パターンは，室内の天井や壁のデザインにおいても反復され，この建築の通奏低音を形成している。このパターンは，日本の建築や着物に用いられた伝統的パターンをもとにして，それにランダムネスを与えて生成されたものであり，伝統的パターンのシンメトリーと完結性を崩すことで，ガラスボックスに新しい開放感を与えようと考えた。また，木の格子の一部にスティールの斜材を混ぜることで，この格子自体が構造的に建築の剛性を高める役割を果たしている。

料亭本体の建築は路地からセットバックしていたが，このガラスボックスを挿入することで，ボックス内部のにぎわいが前面の路地を再活性化し，人の流れを路地に呼び戻すことをねらった。実際にこのガラスボックスがひとつのきっかけとなって，路面の石畳化や夜間照明の整備が進み，旧市街地が新しい生命を獲得しつつある。

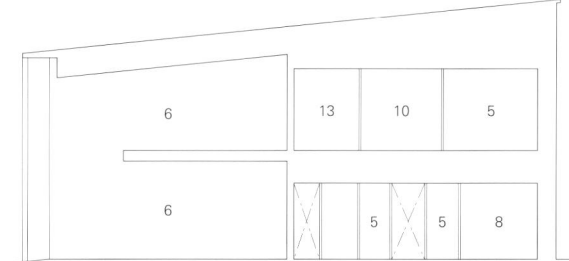

Section S=1:250

Void of dining room　客室の吹抜け

2006-08 Wood/Berg
Japan

Overall view from southwest 南西より見る全景

The goal of the project was to make middle floors (five layers) gentle. Paying attention to elements of balcony and eaves and carefully inserting the two elements between the building and the setting, we tried to make the architecture gentle. Although the main building structure is steel, tenderness and lightness that cannot be found in ordinary concrete balcony and eaves were introduced by attaching a balcony produced by wooden louvers and eaves to the steel structure. The balcony's floor and balustrade are created with a similar dimensional system as eaves as much as possible. As for details of particles such as louvers, the whole building feels more tender and light by truing up the size of particles.

In the old day Tokyo, tenderness was introduced to urbanity by inserting fragile secondary wooden elements such as rooftop clothes drying place and a second floor balcony between architecture and environment. We tried to prove that it is possible to make the city tender again, using such a method in the contemporary Tokyo.

Southwest elevation　南西立面

Basin 水盤

Entrance 玄関

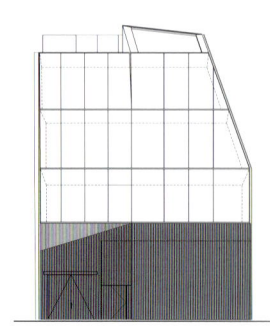

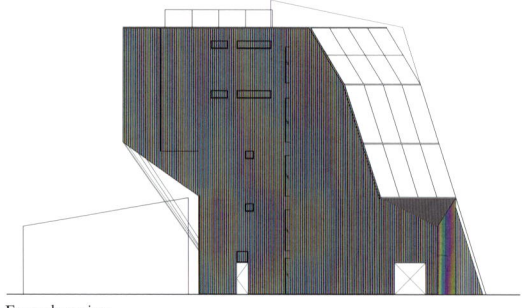

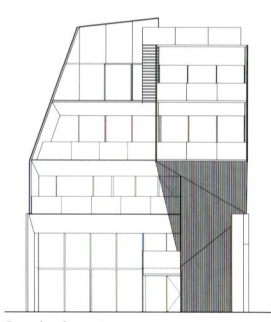

North elevation S=1:500

West elevation

East elevation

South elevation

Living room: view toward meeting room　居間：会議室方向を見る

Living room: view toward study　居間：書斎方向を見る

Wood/Berg

中層（5層）の住宅をやわらかくすることを目標にした。バルコニーと庇という要素に着目し，この二つのエレメントを建築と環境との間に注意深く挿入することで，建築をやわらかくしようと試みた。建築の主要構造は鉄骨であるが，鉄骨の構造体に木製のルーバーを用いて製作したバルコニーと庇をとりつけることで，従来のコンクリート製のバルコニーや庇にはない，やわらかさと軽さを導入した。バルコニーの床も手摺も，可能な限り庇と類似した寸法体系で製作した。ルーバーのような粒子状のディテールにおいては，粒子の粒を揃えることで，全体がよりやわらかく，軽く感じられるのである。

　かつての東京も，屋上の物干し台や2階のバルコニーなど，木でつくられた繊細な2次的エレメントを建築と環境の間に挿入することで，都市にやわらかさを導入していた。現代の東京においても，このような手法で，都市を再びやわらかくすることが可能であることを，ここで実証しようとした。

Terrace on playroom floor: view toward southeast　遊戯室階のテラス：南東方向を見る

Playroom　遊戯室

Terrace on playroom floor　遊戯室階のテラス

Swimming pool　プール

Sections　S=1:500

First floor

Basement　S=1:500

Roof

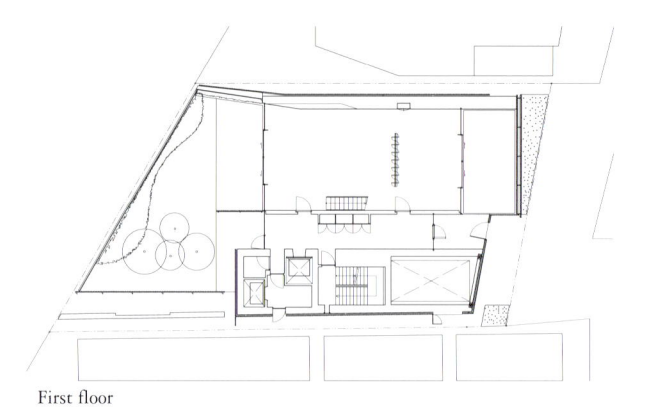

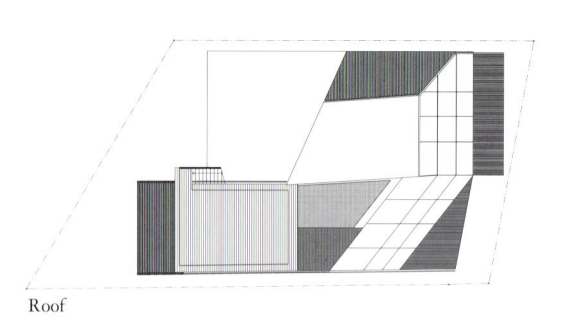

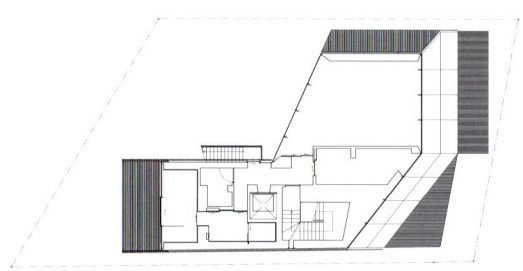

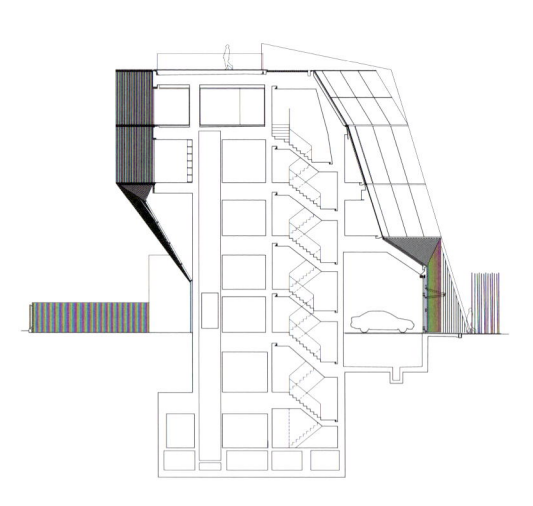

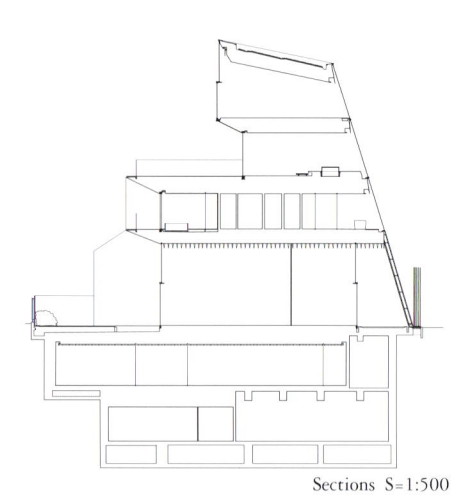

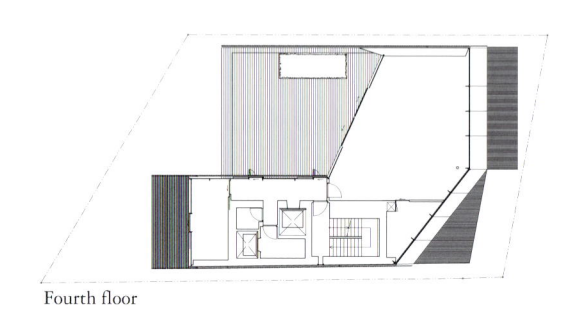

Fifth floor

Fourth floor

Third floor

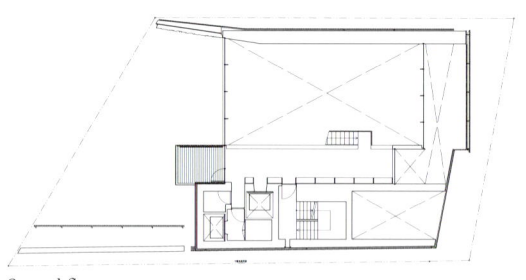

Second floor

Staircase 階段室

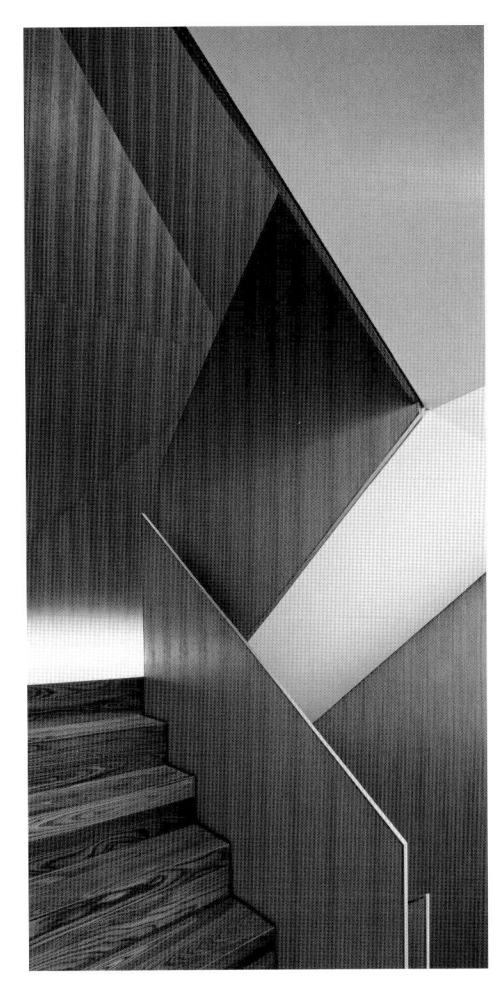

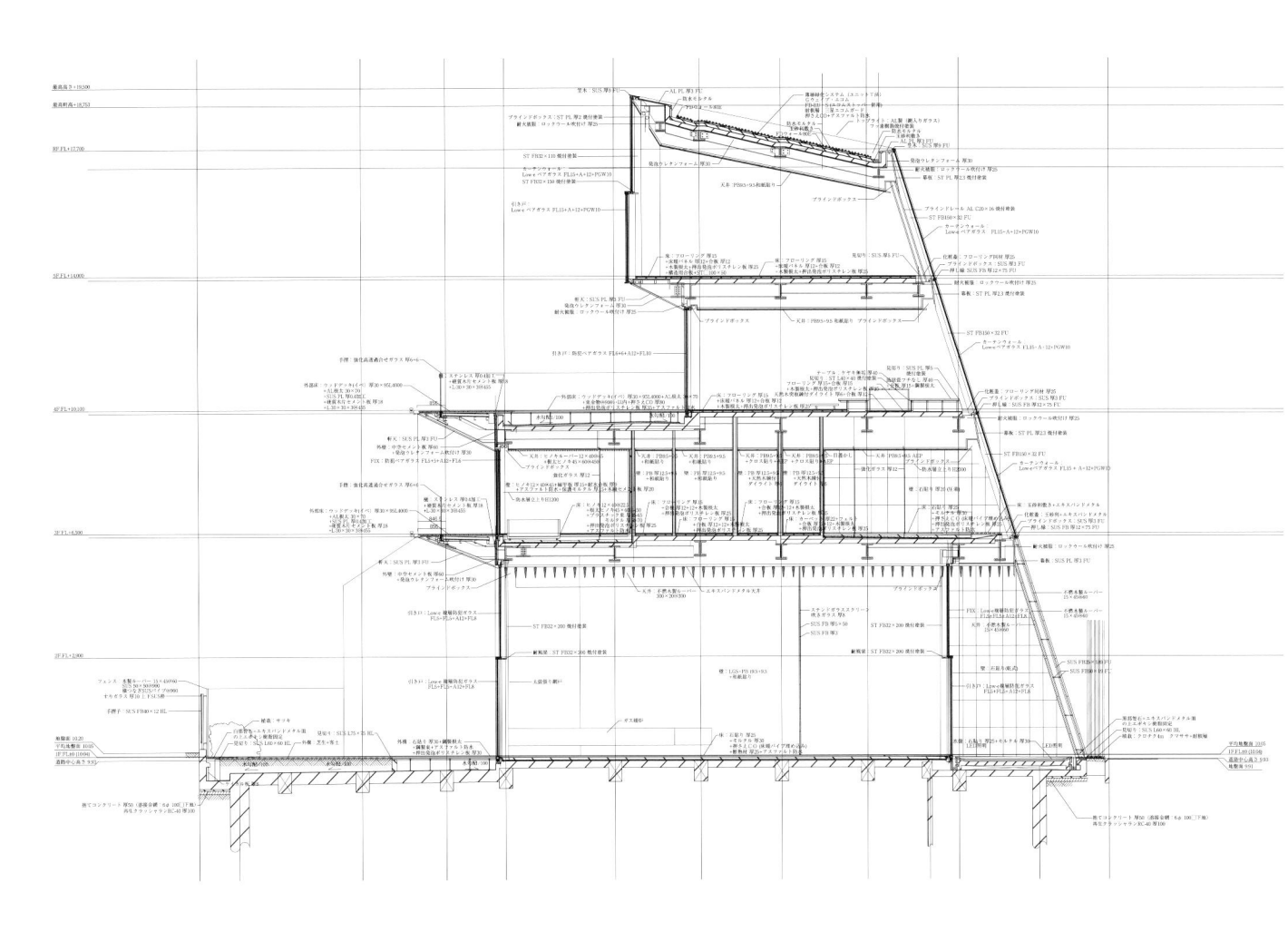

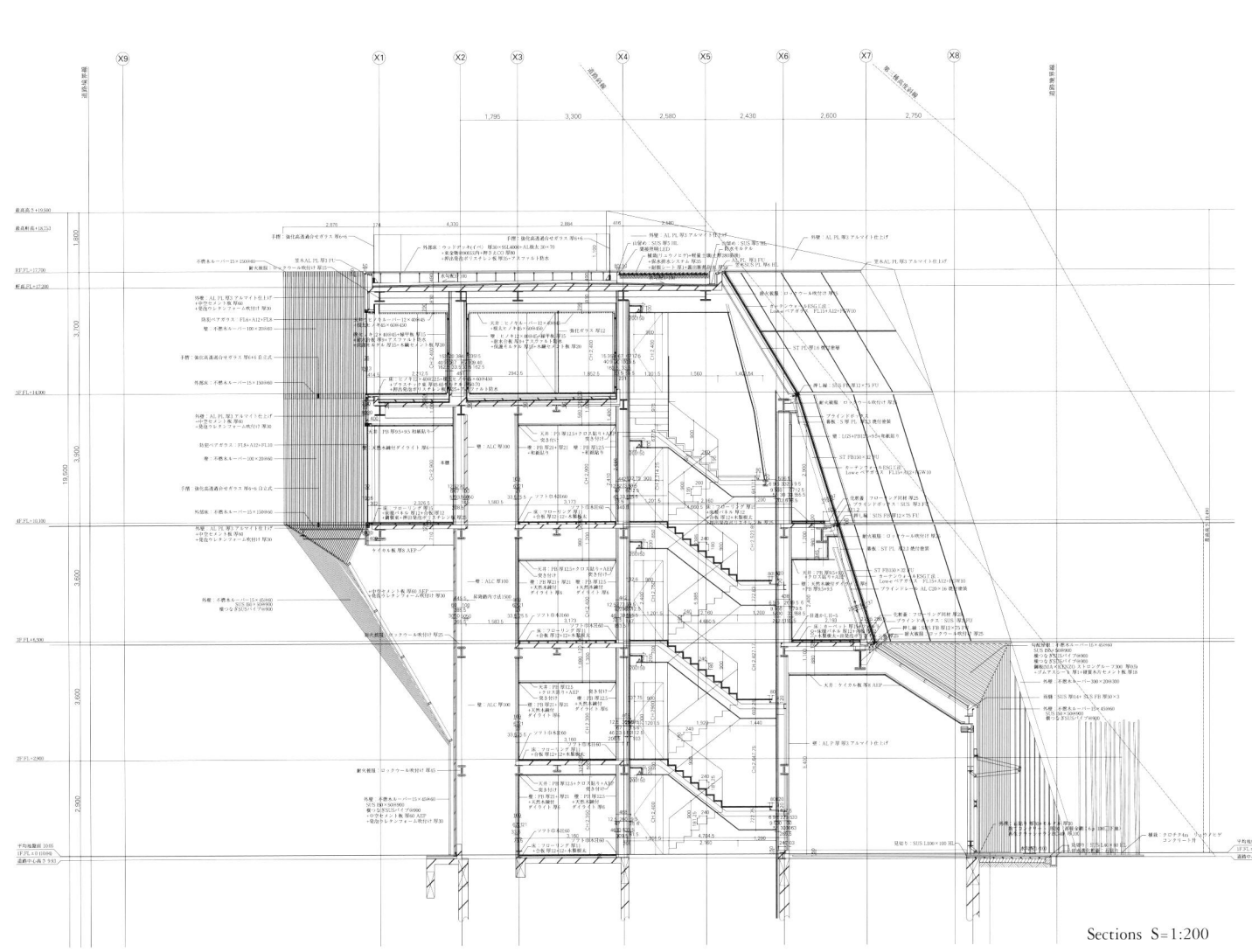

Sections S=1:200

109

2006-09 Museum of Kanayama Castle Ruin, Kanayama Community Center
Ota, Gunma, Japan

Overall view from southwest　南西より見る全景

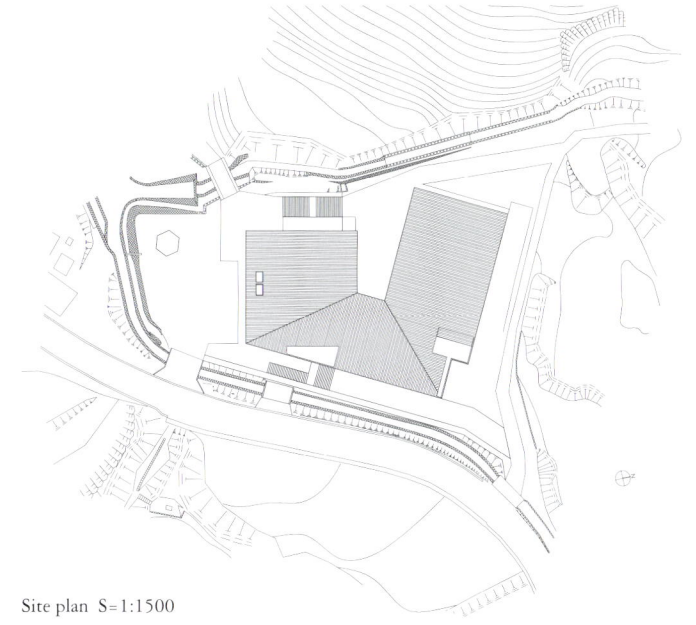

Site plan S=1:1500

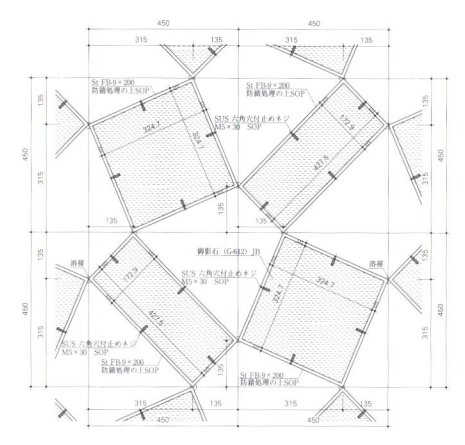

△▽ Stone screen detail

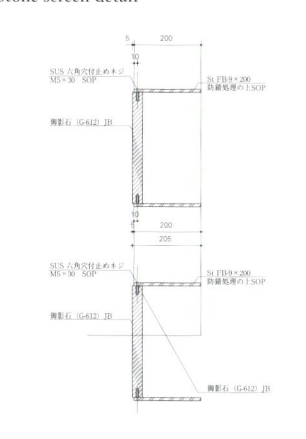

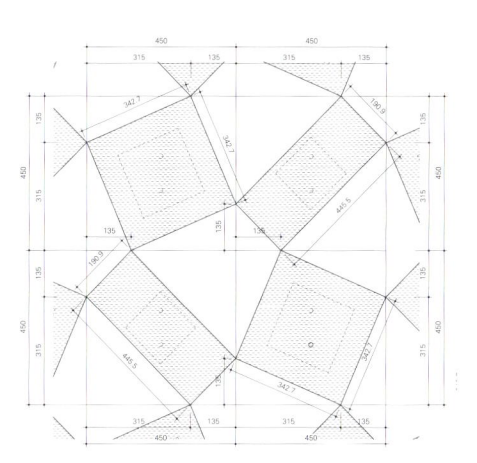

△▽ Stone tiled wall detail

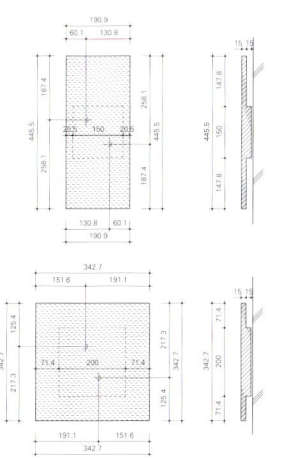

Stone screen ストーン・スクリーン

111

1 ENTRANCE HALL
2 COMMUNITY ROOM
3 MULTIPURPOSE HALL
4 STUDIO
5 GALLERY
6 INFORMATION SALON
7 GUIDANCE ROOM
8 REFERENCE ROOM
9 SMOKING ROOM
10 GATE
11 OFFICE
12 UNLOADING
13 STORAGE
14 MECHANICAL

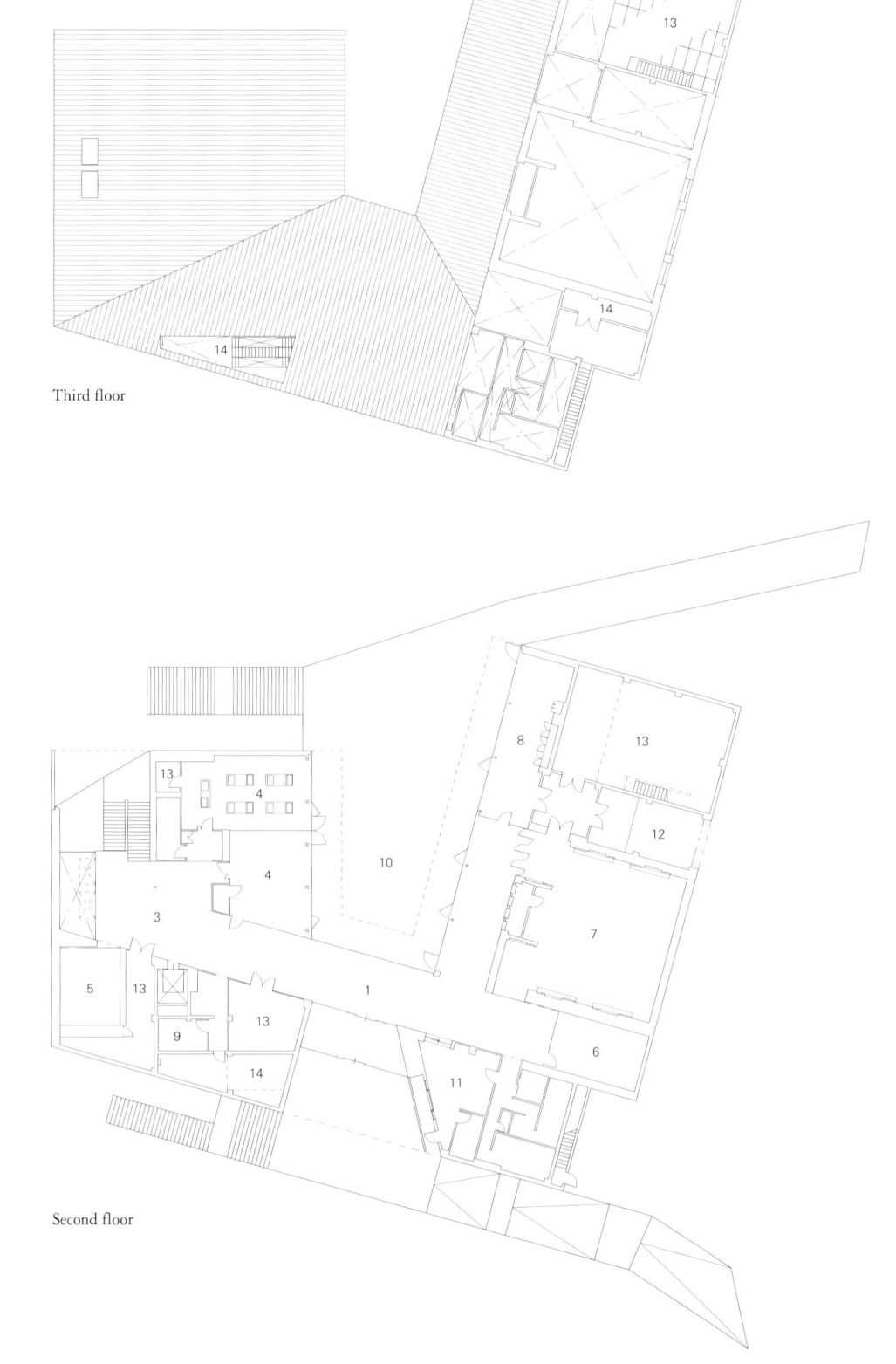

View toward entrance from outside stairs　外階段よりエントランス方向を見る

This is a complex facility housing a museum and craft workshops at the ancient site of Kanayama castle. On this site there is a significant height difference and so we proposed a continuous architecture to bridge this difference of levels. By perceiving the building as a retaining wall that is an architectural instrument, it became possible to connect the discontinuous environment smoothly. The facade screen is inspired by the historical stone walls of the castle. The 30 mm thick stone pieces are individually fastened to the building with stainless bolts. This stone wall pattern is repeated on the interior ceiling and the handrail around the atrium with another material (cemented excelsior board), and it gave another identity which is connected with the castle stone wall.

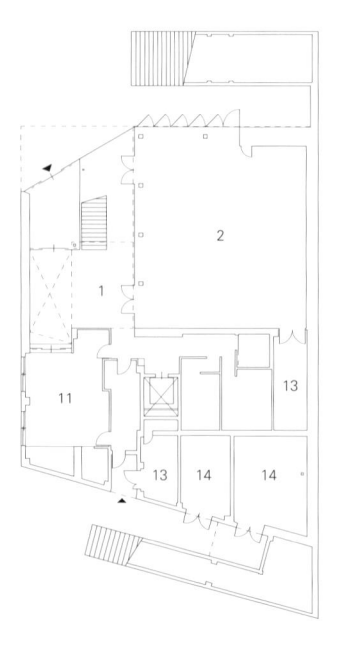

Third floor

First floor S=1:500

Second floor

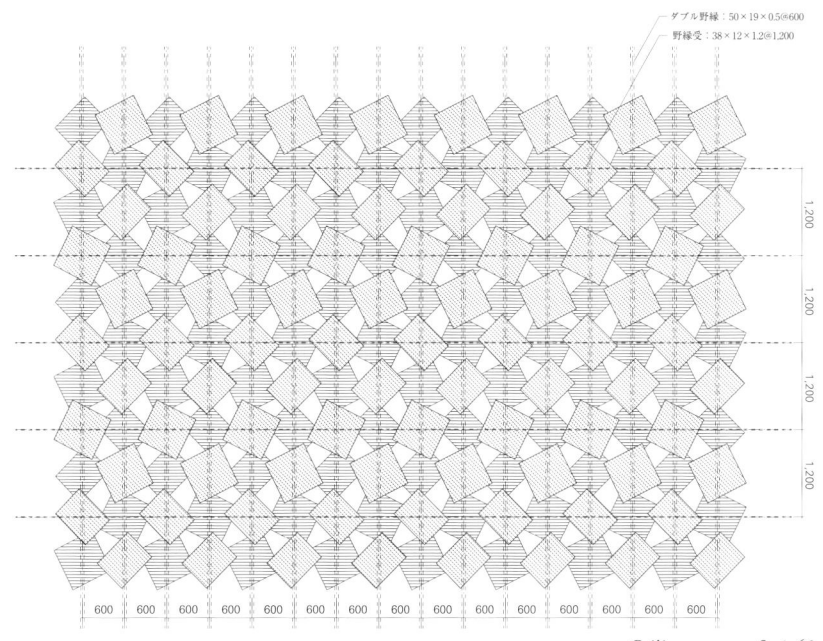

Ceiling pattern S=1:65

Entrance hall on first floor　1階エントランス・ホール

Staircase of entrance hall　エントランス・ホールの階段室

113

View of community square from entrance hall on second floor　2階エントランス・ホールよりコミュニティ・スクエアを見る

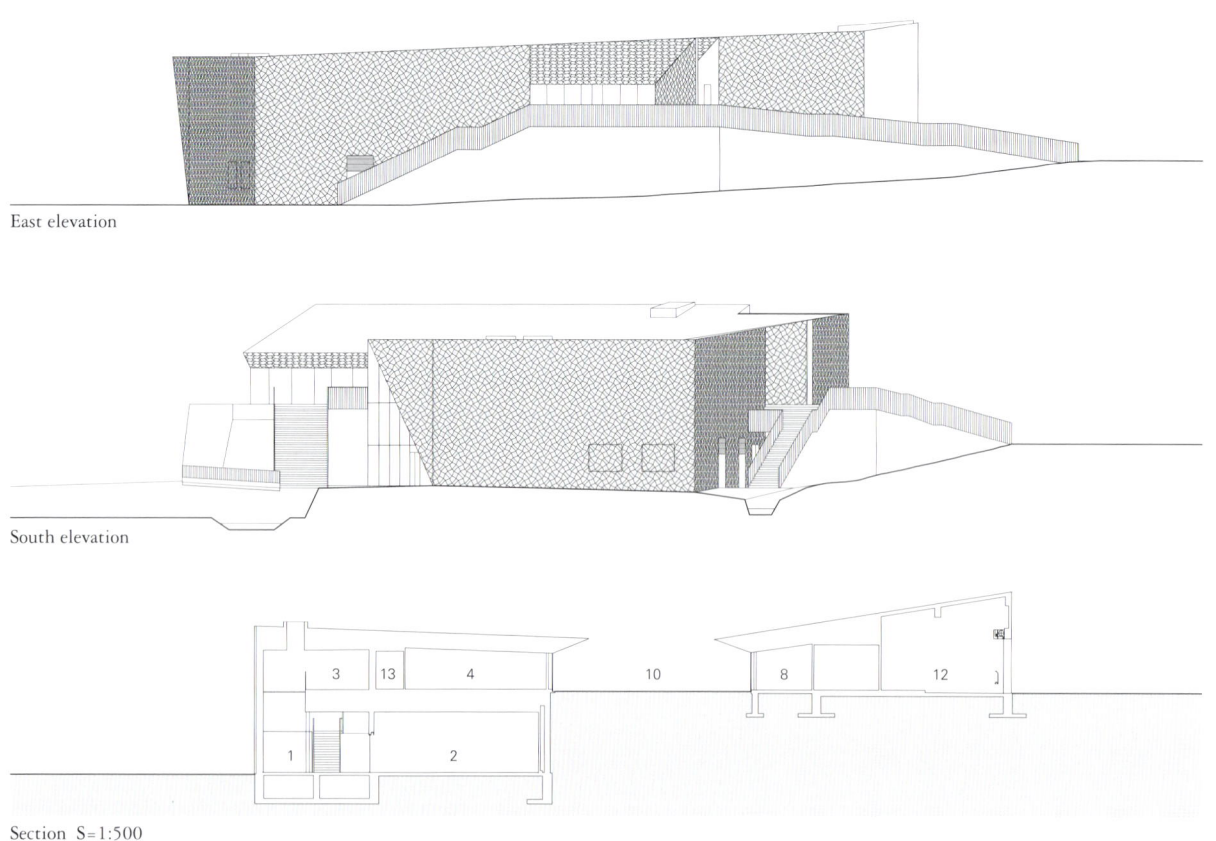

史跡金山城跡ガイダンス施設,
太田市金山地域交流センター

中世の山城である金山城の跡地に企画された, ミュージアムと工芸ワークショップとの複合施設。レベル差のある敷地の上に地面のギャップをまたがるように, ひとつの連続的建築をたてた。建築の擁壁化ともいうべきこの方法の採用で, 建築を道具として, 不連続な環境をスムーズにつなげることが可能となった。城の石垣の形状にインスパイアされた石のスクリーンで, ファサードは構成されている。30mmの厚みの石は, ステンレス製のボルトでひとつ一つ躯体に取り付けられている。この石垣のパターンは内部の天井や, 吹き抜けまわりの手摺りにおいても, 別の素材(木毛セメント板)を用いて反復され, 建築全体に古城の石垣と連続するひとつのアイデンティティを与えている。

East elevation

South elevation

Section　S=1:500

Community square: evening view　コミュニティ・スクエア：夕景

Community square: east view　コミュニティ・クスエア：東を見る

115

2006-09 Shimonoseki City Kawatana-Onsen Visitor Center and Folk Museum
Shimonoseki, Yamaguchi, Japan

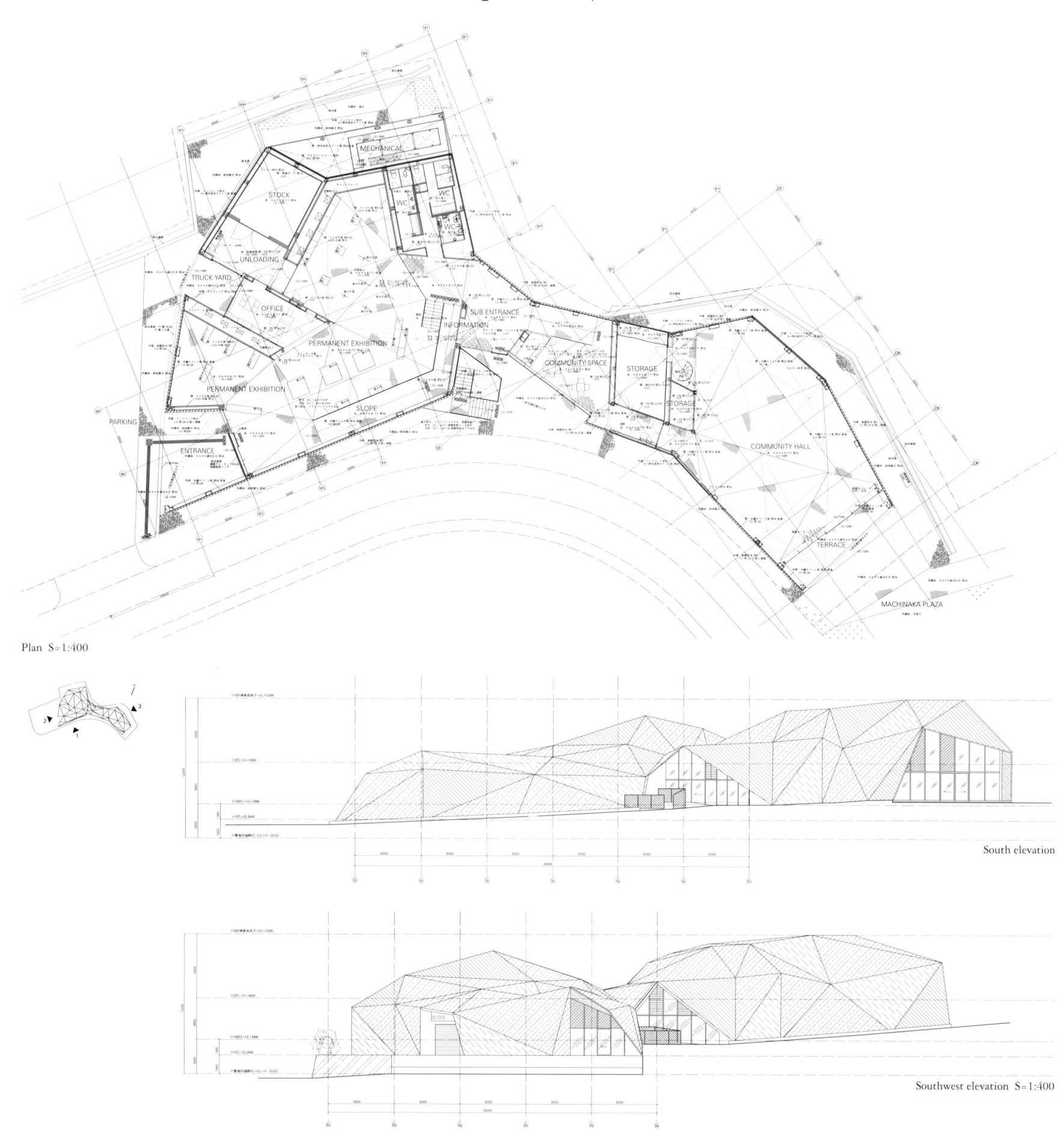

Plan S=1:400

South elevation

Southwest elevation S=1:400

A-A' section

B-B' section

C-C' section

D-D' section

E-E' section

F-F' section

North elevation S=1:400

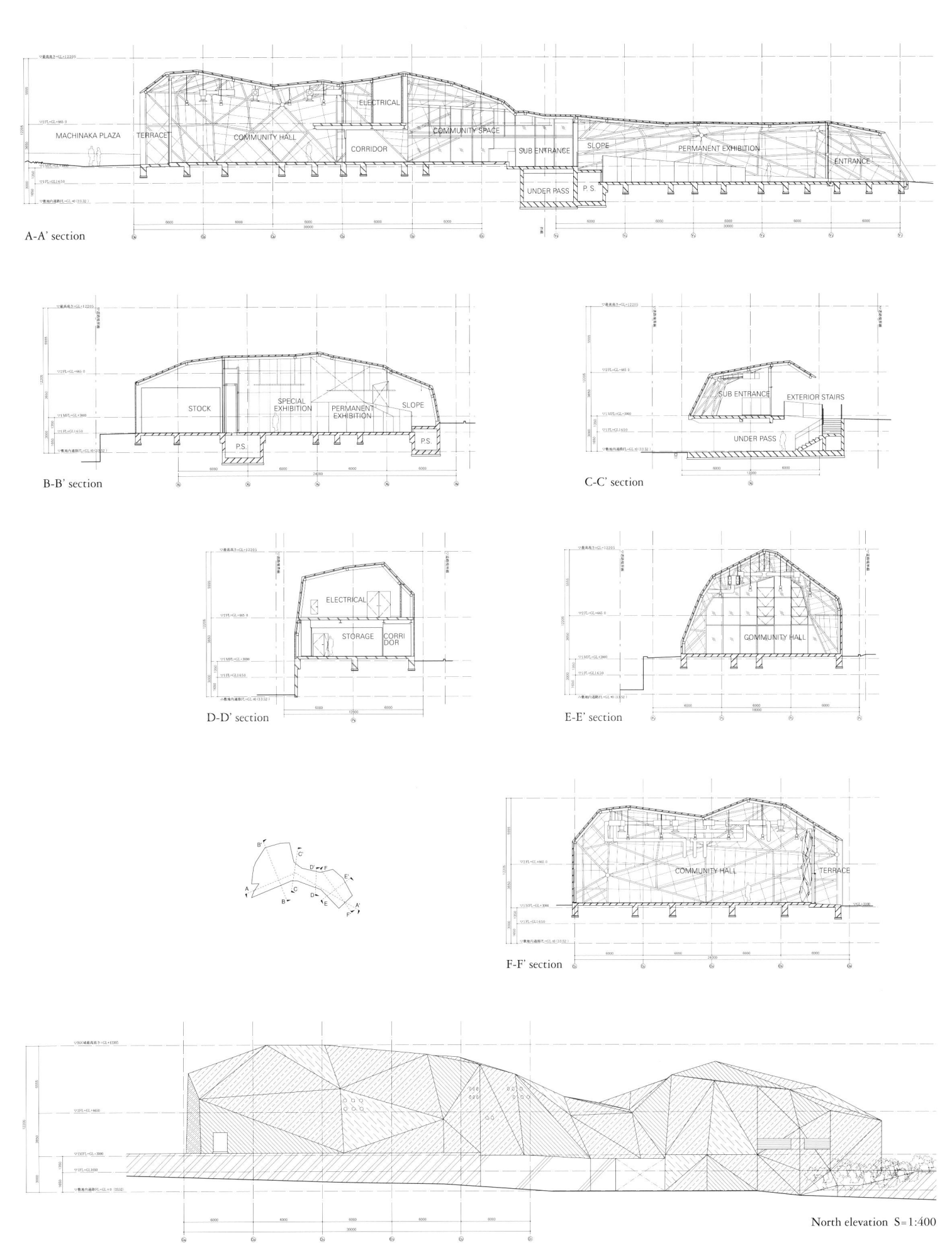

It was tried to abstract the mountain shape that extends to the surrounding site and to include and fuse plural functions such as musical room and museum in an artificial 'mountain'. We thought a public building akin to 'mountain' is more suitable rather than a box in an environment where local thatch-roofed houses are crowded. The 'mountain' is divided into polygons and the divided triangles were painted in three slightly different colors. The difference is so subtle that it is vague to judge the cause whether by the color difference or the way light shine. We thought that the state is suitable to the 'mountain', 'nature' and a modest solid body sense.

Casting 12 cm-thick concrete on a structural framework assembled by steel pipes completed the 'mountain' structurally. Steel frame is a main structure and thinness was accomplished by a structural style using concrete for securing surface solidity and soundproofing. Natural mountains gain lightness and tenderness by covering trees. In order to afford weightlessness and gentleness to the 'mountain', the structural style and the color were selected.

下関市川棚温泉交流センター（川棚の杜）

敷地周辺に広がる山の形状を抽象化して、その人工の「山」の中に音楽室とミュージアムという複数の機能を落とし込み融合させようと考えた。瓦葺きの民家が密集する環境の中には、ハコではなく、「山」のような公共建築がふさわしいと考えた。「山」はポリゴン分割され、分割されてできたそれぞれの三角形に対して、わずかな差異をもつ3色の色彩を施した。色の差は微妙で、それが色彩の差によるものか、光の当たり方の差によるかが判然としない曖昧な状況が生じる。その状態こそが、「山」にふさわしく、「自然」にふさわしい、慎ましやかな立体感であると考えた。

構造的には、鉄骨のパイプを組んだ骨組の上に厚み12cmのコンクリートを打つことで、この「山」はできあがった。鉄骨を主要構造とし、面剛性の確保と遮音性能確保のためにコンクリートを用いる構造形式によって、この薄さが実現した。自然の山は樹木に覆われることで、軽さとやわらかさを獲得している。この「山」にも、軽やかさとやわらかさを与えるために、この構造形式と色彩が選択された。

Overall view from south 南より見る全景

Evening view of community hall from southeast　大交流室の夕景。南東より見る

View toward permanent exhibition from entrance　エントランスより常設展示室方向を見る

Community hall　大交流室

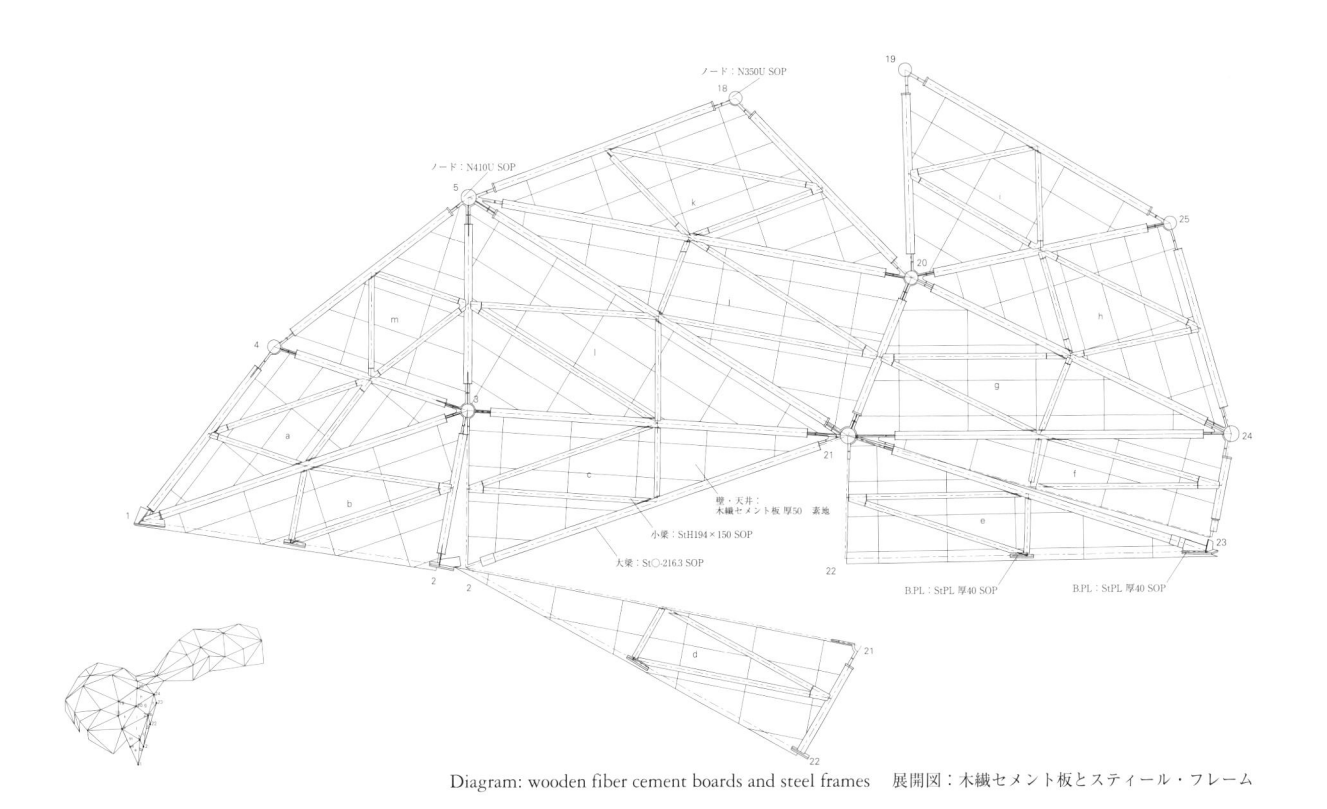

Diagram: wooden fiber cement boards and steel frames　展開図：木繊セメント板とスティール・フレーム

2006-10 Glass/Wood
U.S.A.

North elevation of addition: existing house on left　北側外観：左に既存母屋

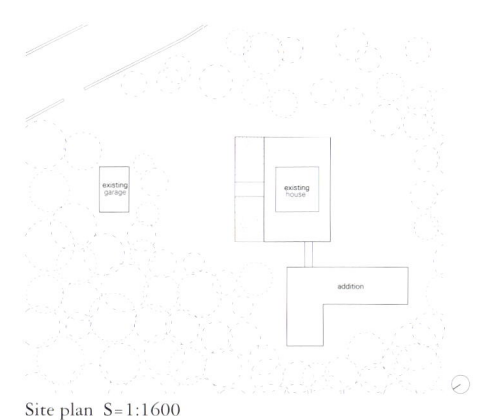

The site is located in Connecticut, U.S.A. The project is a renovation of the existing architecture and an addition of a new building accompanied with change in family composition. In New Canaan where the site is situated there are many residences that were designed by architects such as Philip Johnson and Marcel Breuer. Built in 1956, the existing house on the site is a house of the architect, John Black Lee, who was a friend of Johnson. It destined a succession of the beautiful glass covered architecture's spirit—New Canaan spirit. This was the second renovation following by Toshiko Mori in 1992.

Though the existing building was symmetric Palladian villa that stands alone in a forest, we tried to create 'intimacy' in the forest by adding perpendicularly placed new building and enclosing the territory in L-shape. (Johnson's Glass House is also built isolated.) L-shape is considered a model of the style in Japanese architecture which is similar to flight formation of geese. It enables two intersecting axes, framing of various spaces, lifting feeling of corners and a jump of consciousness by a rotating action.

In the new building, as a part of 'intimacy' we adopted a kind of mix structure that is made of wooden joist roof structure that sits on 3-inch by 6-inch steel flat-bar columns. Furthermore, by slightly placing columns away from corners, we tried to accelerate corners' transparency and a shift of notion by changing a direction.

In the existing building we substantially changed the inner plan, excluded symmetry and covered the exterior walls with louvers, so as to attain 'intimacy'. As substitute of isolated transparency achieved in 1950's we aimed at 'intimate transparency' and 'warm transparency'.

Site plan S=1:1600

Porch: view toward dining room　縁側：食堂方向を見る

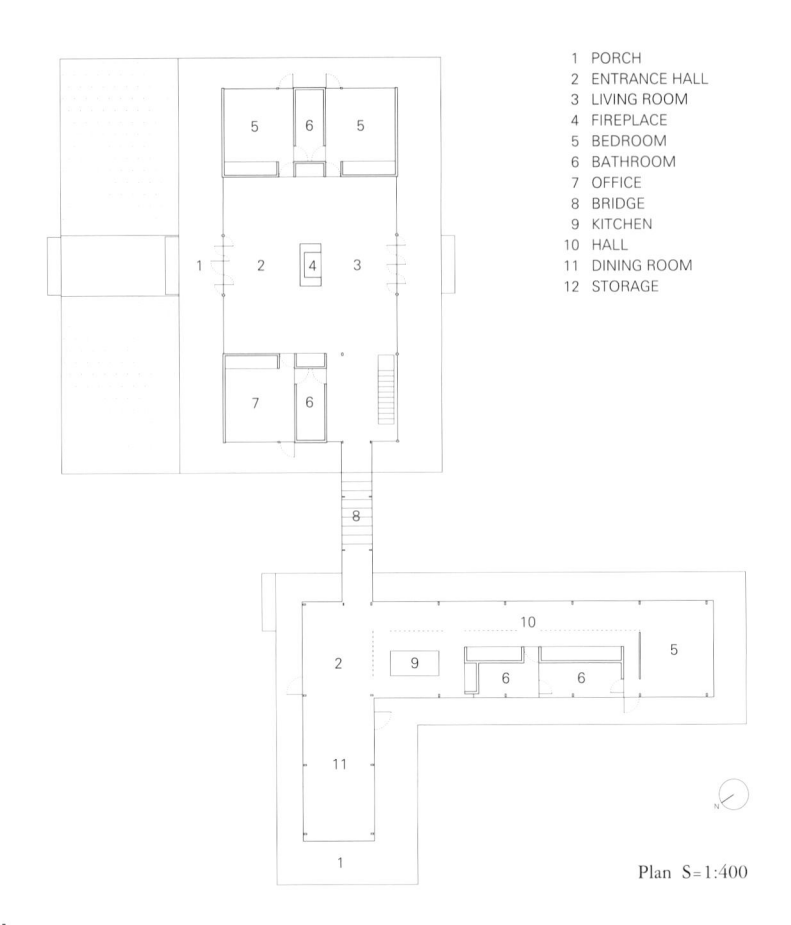

1	PORCH
2	ENTRANCE HALL
3	LIVING ROOM
4	FIREPLACE
5	BEDROOM
6	BATHROOM
7	OFFICE
8	BRIDGE
9	KITCHEN
10	HALL
11	DINING ROOM
12	STORAGE

Plan S=1:400

North-south section

East-west section

North elevation

West elevation S=1:400

Glass/Wood

敷地は，アメリカ，コネチカット州。家族構成の変化に伴う既存建築の改修と，新棟の増築である。敷地のあるニューキャナンという町は，1950年代にフィリップ・ジョンソンやマルセル・ブロイヤーをはじめとする建築家が設計した住宅が数多く残る町であり，敷地に建つ既存建築もジョンソンと交友のあった建築家ジョン・ブラック・リーの自邸（1956年）で，その美しいガラス張りの建築の精神──ニューキャナンの精神──の継承をめざした。今回の改修は2度目で，1992年にトシコ・モリの設計で一度改修されている。

既存建築は，森の中に孤立するシンメトリーなパラディオ形式のヴィラ建築であったが，直交する新棟の増築によってL字型に領域を囲い取り，森の中に一種の「親密さ」を創造しようと試みた（ジョンソンのガラスの家も同様に孤立型である）。L字型は日本建築の雁行型配置の原型とも考えられ，二つの交差する軸線，様々な空間のフレーミング，コーナーの浮遊感，回転による意識のジャンプなどが可能となる。

その「親密化」の一部として，新棟では3 inch×6 inchの鉄のフラットバーの柱の上に木のジョイスト構造の屋根が載るという，一種の混構造を採用した。さらに，コーナー部分では柱を隅部から微妙にずらすことでコーナーの透明性，方向転換による意識の転回をさらに加速しようと試みた。

既存棟も内部プランを大幅に変えてシンメトリーを排し，外壁を木のルーバーで覆うことによって「親密化」を行った。1950年代の孤立した透明性に代わって，「親密な透明性」，「暖かい透明性」の実現をめざした。

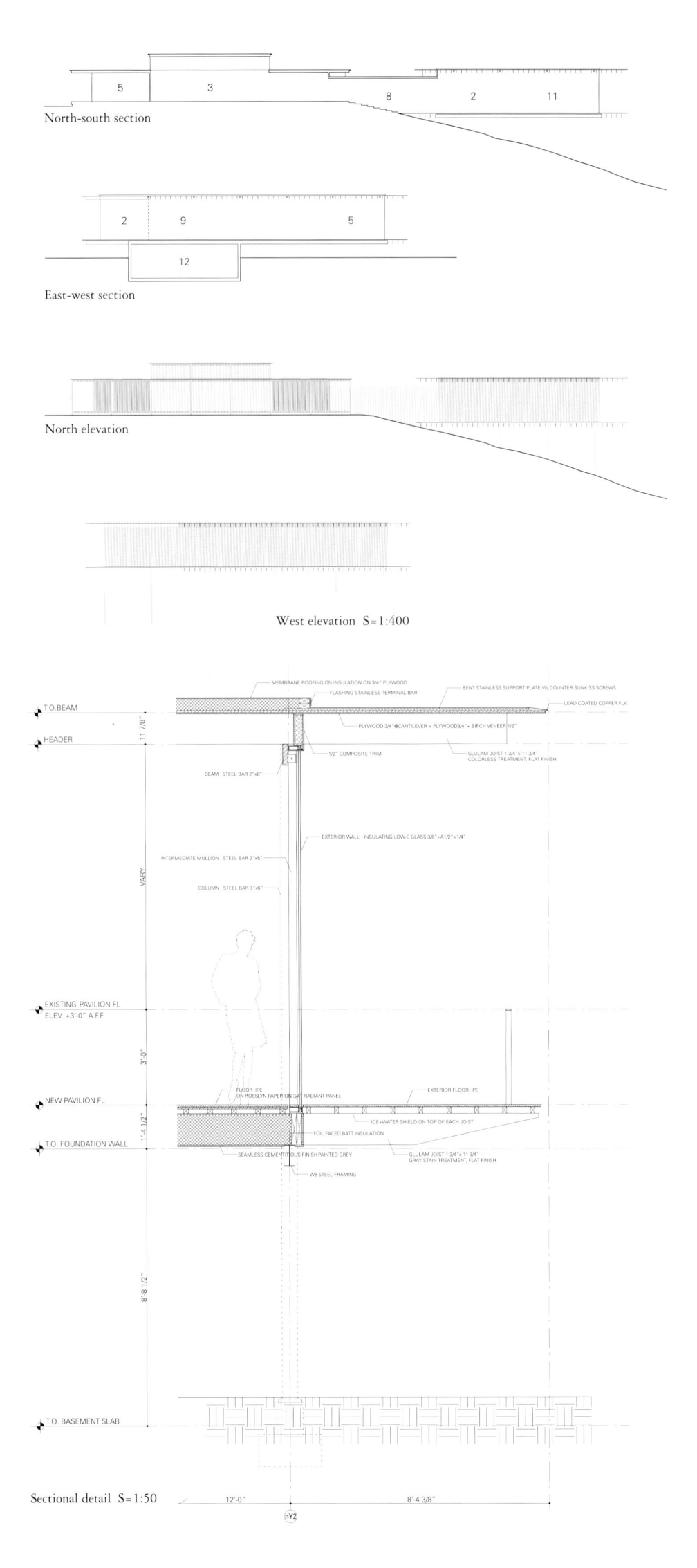

Sectional detail S=1:50

Two layers of eaves: glued laminated timber joists　二重の軒：構造用集成材による梁

Porch on east: existing house on right　東側のポーチ：右に既存母屋

Existing house: living room and fireplace　既存母屋：居間と暖炉

Connecting corridor: view toward existing house　連結廊下：既存母屋を見る

View toward entry of addition from kitchen　台所より増築棟の玄関を見る

Kitchen: looking through steel mesh　台所：スティール・メッシュ越しに見る

2005-07
Tee Haus
Frankfurt, Germany

Set up diagram
1. Exposed concrete base
2. Lay out tatami
3. After stretched membrane, ventilation

Plans S=1:200

Elevations

Sections

1 NIJIRIGUCHI (SMALL ENTRANCE)
2 ENTRANCE (WASHING PLACE)
3 TEAROOM
4 WASHING PLACE
5 LED LIGHTING

Overall view　全景

Interior　内観

The temporal tearoom was planned in the garden of Frankfurt Museum of Applied Art designed by Richard Meier. Usually, the tearoom is kept in storage. Several times a month when it is in use, the architecture emerges by inflating the air with a blower. One step forward to 'defeated architecture', I desired to create 'breathing architecture'. 'To be defeated' means one-way passivity towards environment. To 'breathe' means an interactive exchange with environment. At one time it shrinks as if holding one's breath and in another time it grows large as if fully inhaling air in one's chest. I considered a way for such a mutable architecture.

Using a new membrane material called Tenara, the structure was made of double membrane inflated with air in the middle. The two membranes are connected with polyester string. The string arranged in about 600 mm interval and the membrane joints appear on surface as dots. Tenara differs from ordinal membrane that bases glass fiber. Therefore, it is soft and light. In this project, the membrane swells and shrinks many times as if it breathes, so ordinal membrane that bases glass fiber had a problem with durability. That is why we chose Tenara. Tenera is highly transparent, so it was possible to gain a unique materiality that is in between reality and fantasy.

Tatami mats were laid in the room so that the space can hold tea ceremonies. A tearoom originated as a temporary space called 'enclosure'. The 'breathing architecture' is a trial to approach the model of tearoom. We expected to create the extreme opposite of the 20th century's concrete architecture that never breathes.

Tee Haus

リチャード・マイヤーの設計による，フランクフルト工芸デザインミュージアムの庭園に計画された仮設の茶室。通常は倉庫に収納され，月に数回の使用時のみ，ブロアーで空気を吹き込むことで建築が出現する。「負ける建築」を一歩進めて，「呼吸する建築」をつくりたいと考えた。「負ける」とは環境に対する一方的な受動性である。「呼吸する」とは，環境との間のインタラクティブなやりとりである。ある時は息を潜めて小さくなり，またある時は胸いっぱいに空気を吸込んで大きくなる。そのような可変的な建築のあり方を考えた。

テナラと呼ばれる新素材の膜を用いて，中間に空気を入れた二重膜構造とした。二重膜の間はポリエステル製の紐で結ばれ，約600mmピッチで配置されたその紐と膜材のジョイントが膜の上にドットとしてあらわれる。テナラは通常の膜材とは異なり，グラスファイバーを基材として使用していないため，やわらかく，しかも軽い。今回のプロジェクトは膜が呼吸するようにして何回も膨らんだり縮んだりするため，通常のグラスファイバーを基材とする膜材では，耐久性で問題が発生するため，テナラを選択した。また，テナラは透明性が高いため，現実と非現実との中間ともいえるような，独特の質感を獲得することができた。

内部には畳を敷き詰め，Tea ceremonyのためのスペースとして設定した。茶室はもともと「囲い」と呼ばれるテンポラリーなスペースから出発した。この「呼吸する建築」は茶室の原型に近づく試みでもあり，20世紀の呼吸することのないコンクリート建築の対極を目指した。

2007-08　Tiffany Ginza
Tokyo, Japan

It was a project to renovate an ordinary leasing building into a flagship shop of a world-renowned brand. The building was furnished with an altered identity by attaching 292 sheets of glass panels equipped with legs (we named it facet panel or a hermit crab panel) in 80 cm depth space between the existing building and the site boundary. The facet panel is composed of two glass panels sandwiching two aluminum honeycomb panels produced for airplanes. The overlapping of the two honeycomb panels in different density creates unique interference of light. The honeycomb panels also keep sights from the inside and have an effect of energy savings by cutting sunlight.

The facet panels have four legs produced for a special latch used in automobiles' hatchback doors. As a result, it is possible to offer a decent office space for tenants on the upper floors. Using the flexibility of the latch, they are fixed to the existing building's wall surfaces each in a different angle. As if small hermit crab freely live on big trees, only one kind of panel live on the existing building each in their own way. We aimed at a system that enables a free and loose renovation. The interior as well was designed to maximize the effect of small light particles that is gained from facet panels. The famous stainless big door of Tiffany in New York was redesigned with transparent acrylic and we also developed a gentle wooden wall's detail called wood drape.

Overall view from northwest　北西より見る全景

Facet panel's detail: axonometric

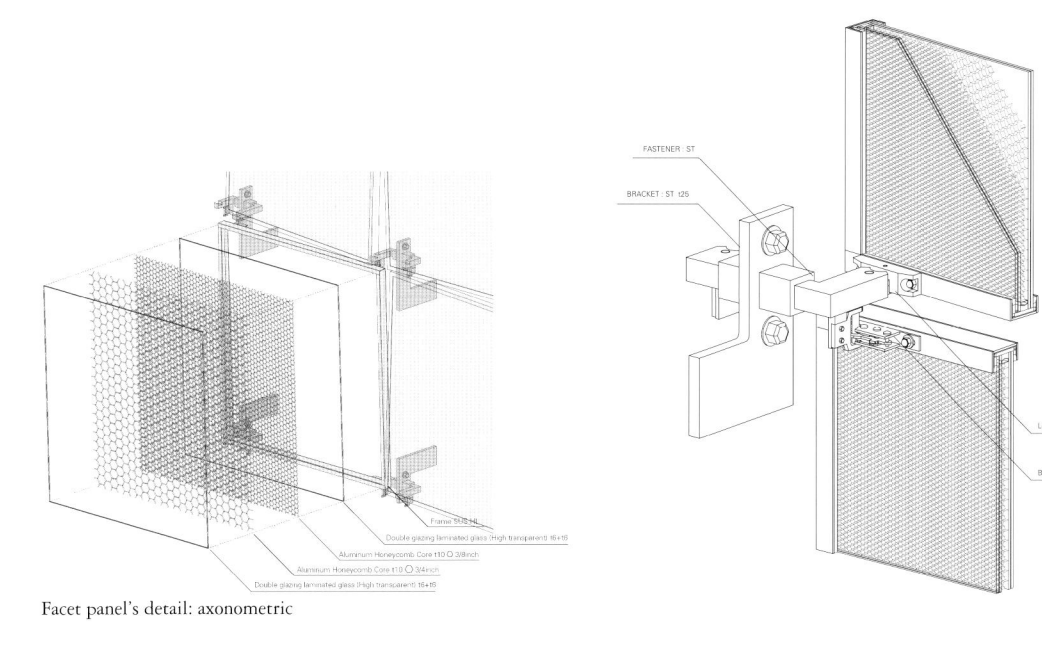

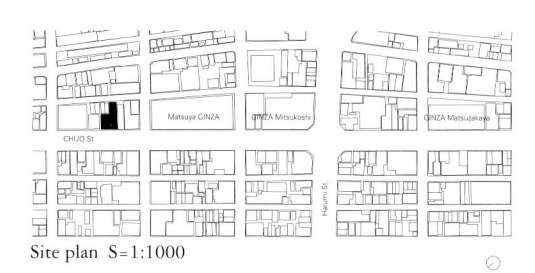

1 PRIVATE SALES
2 GUEST LOUNGE
3 CUSTOMER SERVICE
4 REST ROOM
5 BACK OFFICE AREA
6 CHANDELIER

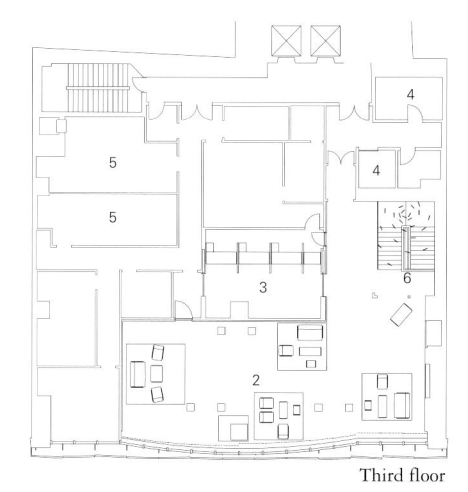

Site plan S=1:1000

Third floor

Facet panel's detail: horizontal detail S=1:150

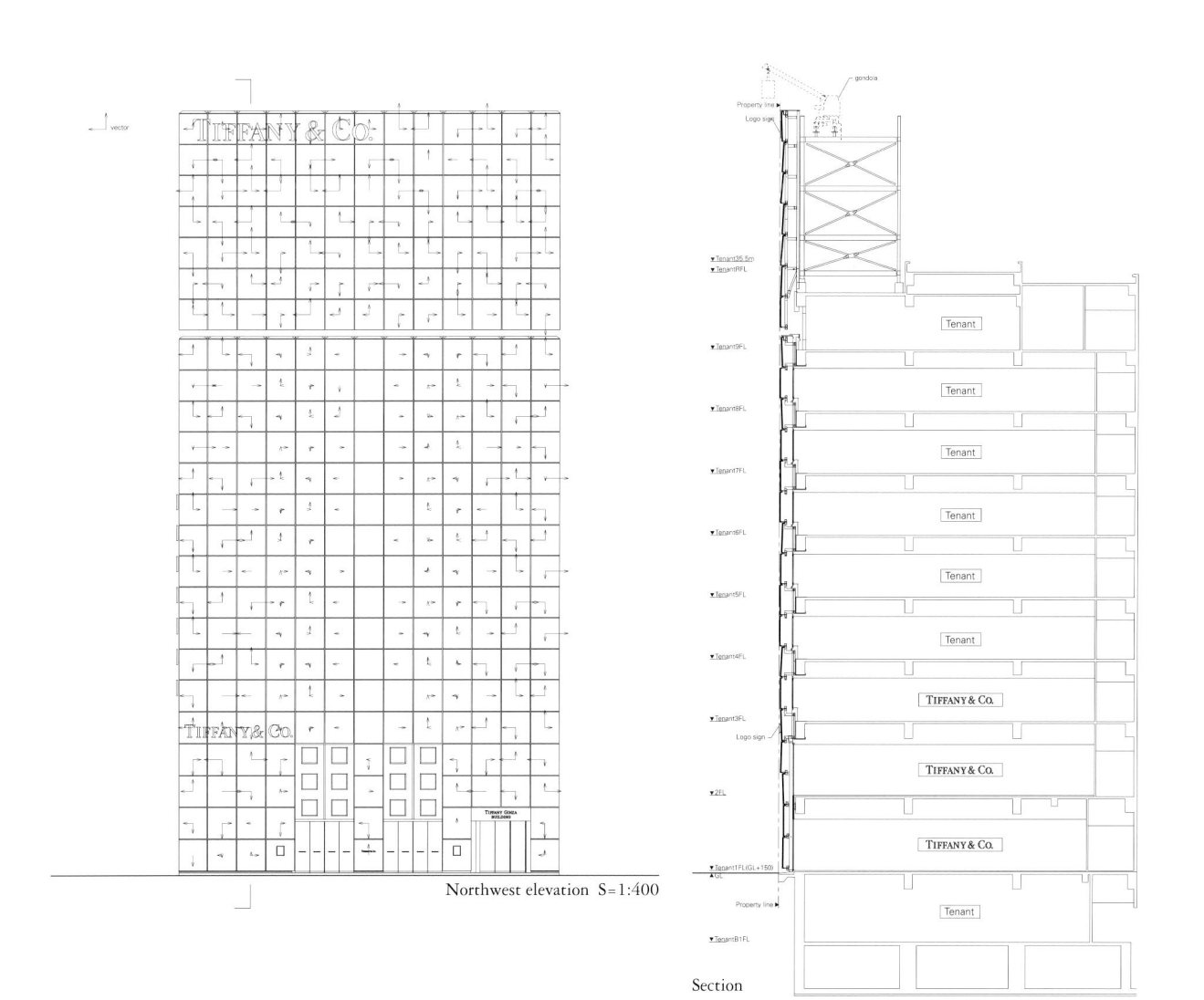

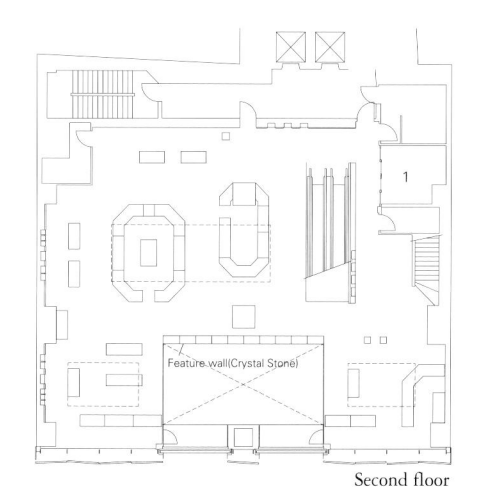

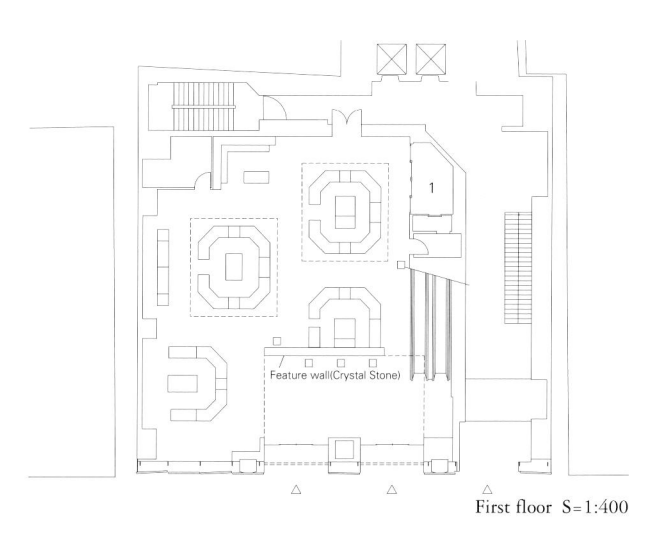

Second floor

Northwest elevation S=1:400

Section

First floor S=1:400

Evening view of facet panel　ファセット・パネルの夕景

Entrance　玄関

Crystal stone wall　クリスタル・ストーンの壁

ティファニー銀座

ありふれたテナントビルを,世界ブランドのフラッグシップショップへとリノベーションするプロジェクト。既存ビルと敷地境界線との間,80cmのスペースに,292枚の脚のついたガラスパネル(ファセットパネル,あるいはヤドリギパネルと名づけた)を取り付けることで,ビルに別のアイデンティティを与えた。ファセットパネルは,2枚のガラスパネルの間に航空機の機体用に製作されたアルミハニカムパネルを2枚挿入したもので,密度の異なる2枚のハニカムが重なり合うことで独特の光の干渉が生まれる。ハニカムパネルは,部屋内からの視線を確保しながら太陽光をカットして,省エネルギー化を達成する効果もある。

ファセットパネルは自動車のハッチバックドアなどに用いる特殊ラッチを用いて製作した4本の脚を持ち,その結果,上層階のテナントに対しても良好なオフィス空間を提供することが可能となる。そのラッチのフレキシビリティを利用して,それぞれに異なる角度で既存ビルの壁面に固定されている。小さなヤドリギが自由に大木に寄生するように,たった1種類のパネルが既存ビルに思い思いに寄生することで,自由でゆるいリノベーションが可能となるシステムを目指した。インテリアも,ファセットパネルで得られる細かな光の粒の効果の最大化を目的としてデザインされた。ニューヨークのティファニーの有名なステンレスの大扉は,透明アクリルでリデザインされ,ウッドレープと呼ばれるやわらかな木製の壁のディテールも開発した。

2007

Fu-an
Shizuoka, Japan

Study of setting 設置の試行

The idea was to create an extremely light architecture. The material used was so-called the lightest fabric in the world, super organza, which weighs only 11 g/m². By covering a transparent balloon filled with helium with the light cloth, the textile's weight of 1kg and the buoyancy of the balloon were balanced. Super organza is more rarefied existence similar to fog or haze rather than just a fabric. The tearoom space created in the haze feels more vague and boundary-less place rather than architecture.

Incidentally, the tearoom can be stored in a suitcase by folding the super-organza and the balloon. It is a portable, extremely light and tender tearoom.

浮庵

究極の軽い建築をつくろうと考えた。用いた材料は、世界で最も軽い布と呼ばれるスーパーオーガンザで、重量はわずか11g/m²である。ヘリウムガスを封入した透明な風船にこの軽い布を被せることで、布の1kgという重量と、風船の浮力とをバランスさせた。スーパーオーガンザは、布というより霧やカスミのように稀白な存在であり、その中に生成される茶室空間は、建築というよりも曖昧で輪郭のない場そのもののように感じられる。

ちなみにこの茶室は、スーパーオーガンザと風船をたたむことによって、スーツケースの中にも収納可能である。携帯可能な、究極の軽くやわらかな茶室である。

Completed 完成

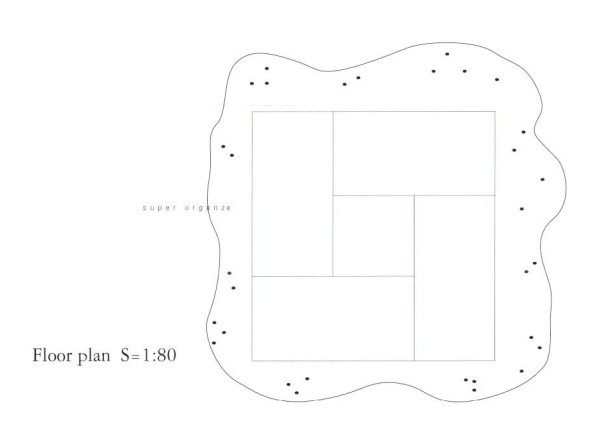

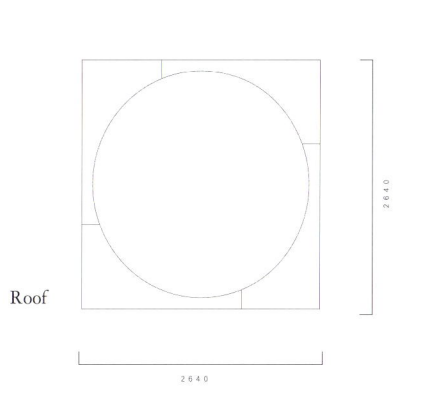

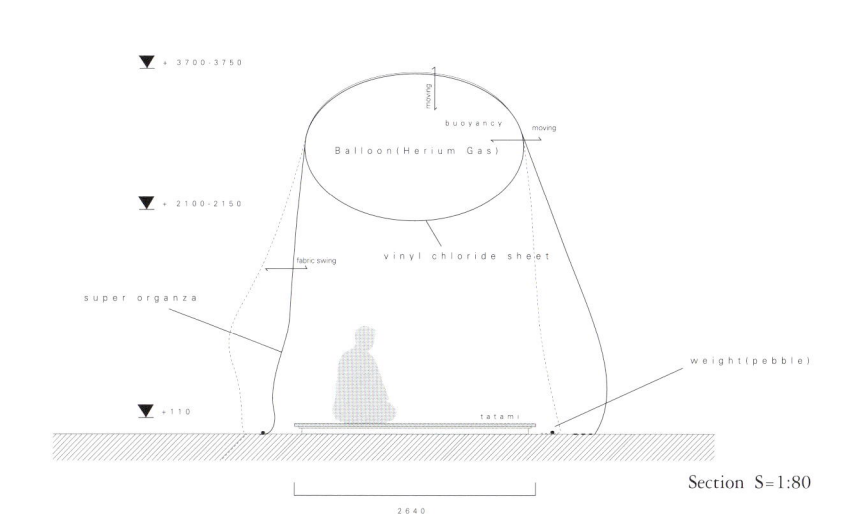

Floor plan S=1:80

Roof

Section S=1:80

2007-09 Garden Terrace Nagasaki
Nagasaki, Japan

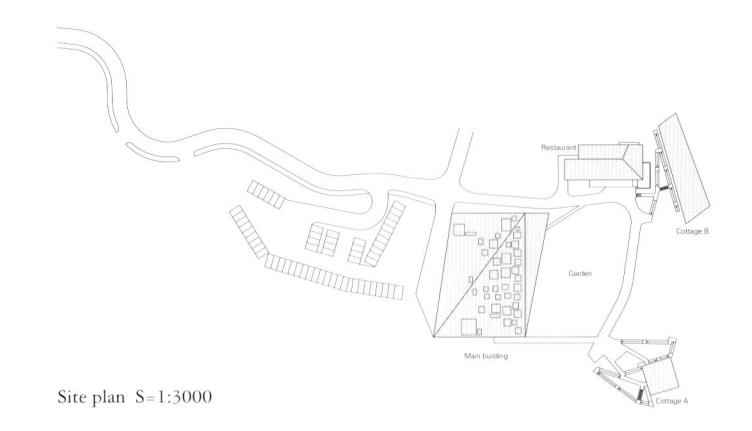

Site plan S=1:3000

Distant view from east　東側遠景

MAIN BUILDING

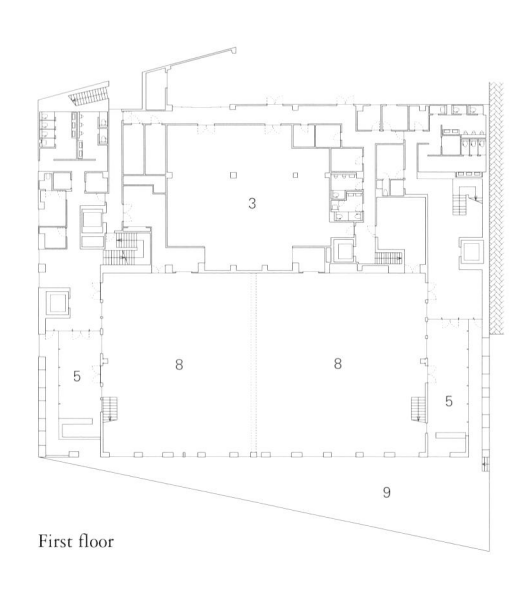

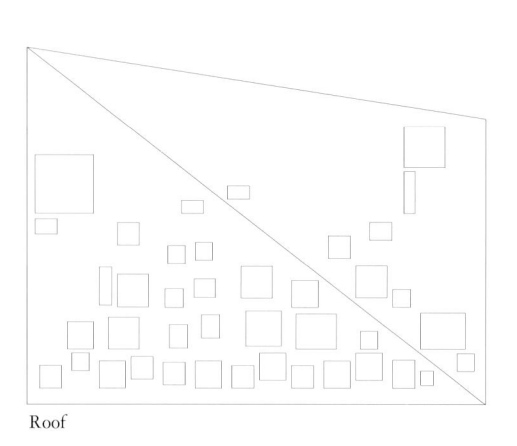

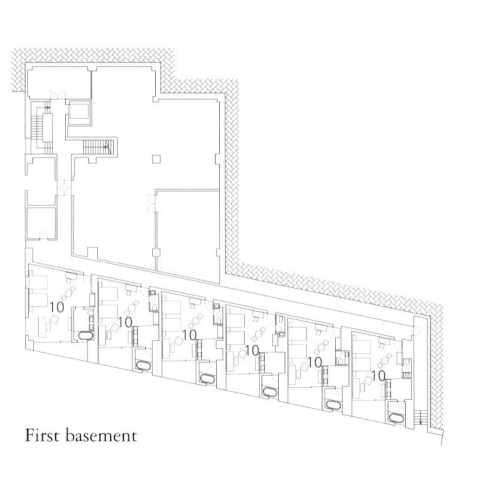

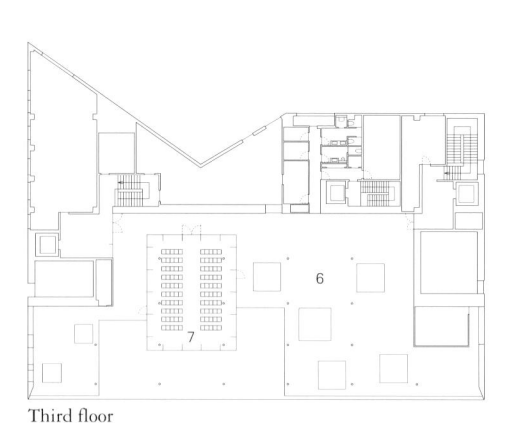

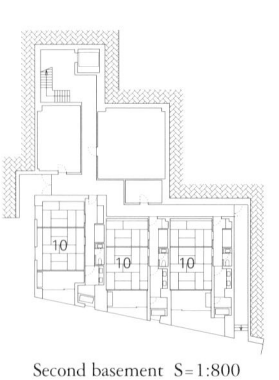

First floor

Roof

First basement

Third floor

Second basement S=1:800

Second floor

1 LOBBY
2 RESTAURANT
3 KITCHEN
4 OFFICE
5 FOYER
6 ROOF TERRACE
7 CHAPEL
8 BANQUET ROOM
9 TERRACE
10 GUEST ROOM

West elevation S=1:800

North elevation

East elevation

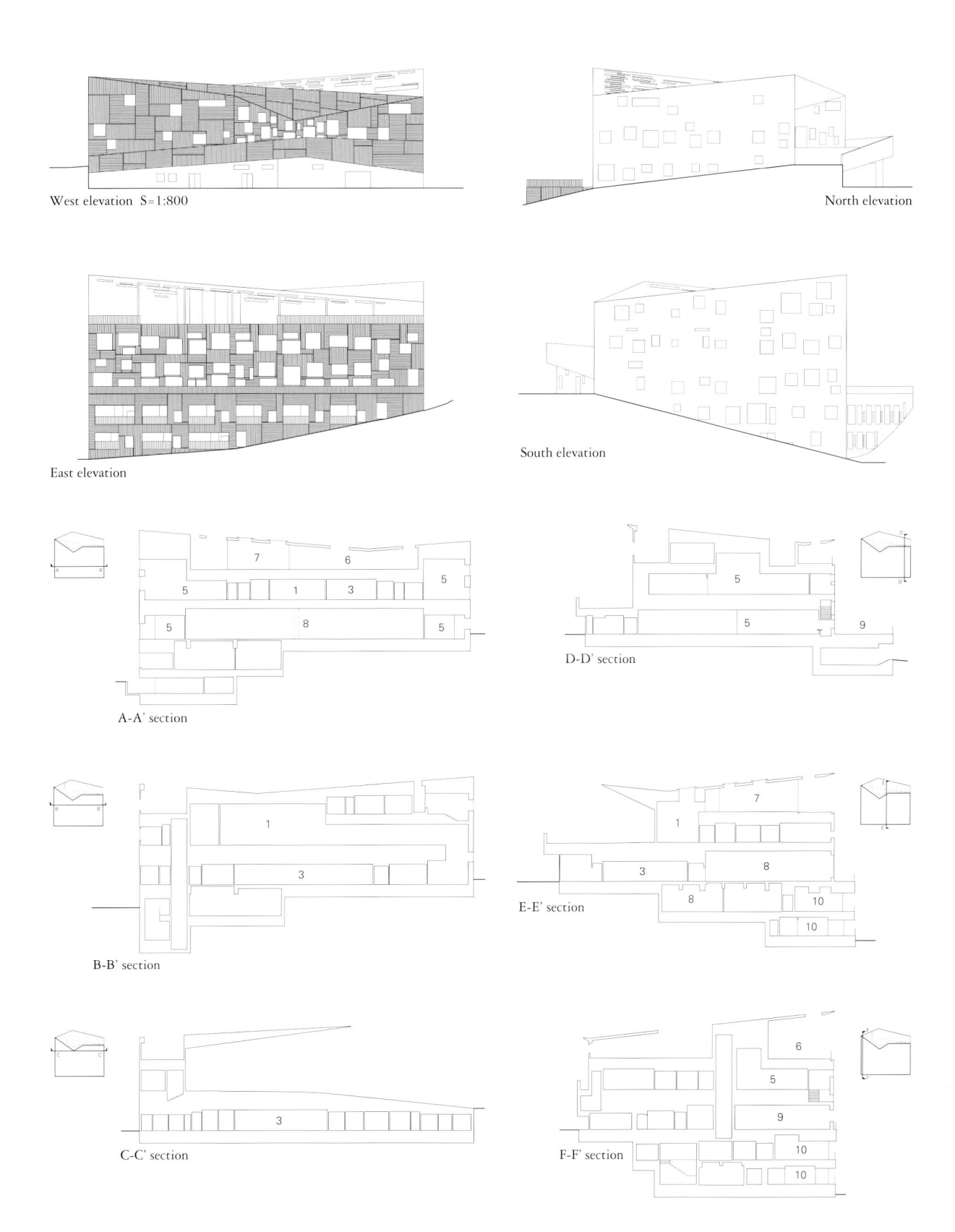

South elevation

A-A' section

D-D' section

B-B' section

E-E' section

C-C' section

F-F' section

A wooden hotel planned on top a hill overlooking the port of Nagasaki. In order that an architecture with a certain volume can be perceived as a 'wooden architecture,' simply pasting wood on exterior walls is not enough. One has to first create an ambiguous state where internal and external spaces are integrated that is so peculiar to wooden architecture. In this project, the rooftop chapel was designed as a glass box in a garden, and by setting up a number of semi-outdoor spaces there, integration of internal and external spaces came to be realized.

Another unique approach was breaking down the wood-sided exterior walls into square units whose sides are 2 to 3 meters long. When a mid-rise architecture of such volume is covered with wood panels in a regular detail, it tends to look flat and bland like painted concrete even if real wood were being used, and any texture or lightness of wood as a material are ruined. By making use of wide grids and segmentalizing exterior walls into granular units, we have challenged the possibilities of exterior wall design that is equipped with a touch of wooden texture in an architecture of enoumous volume. In addition, subtle irregularities and misalignments were introduced to the positioning and sizing of apertures in the exterior walls in an attempt to create fluctuation and looseness on the wall surfaces.

133

West elevation of main building　本館西面

East elevation of main building　本館東面

ガーデンテラス長崎

長崎の港を見下ろす丘の上に, 木でできたホテルをつくろうと考えた。あるヴォリュームを持つ建築を「木の建築」と感じさせるためには, 外壁に木を貼り付けるだけでは不充分である。まず,「木の建築」に固有の内外空間が融合した, 曖昧な状態をつくり出さなければならない。本プロジェクトでは, 屋上部分のチャペルを庭園の中のガラスボックスとしてデザインし, そこにたくさんの半屋外空間を用意することで内外空間の融合を実現した

もうひとつの工夫は, 木の羽目板貼りの外壁を1辺2～3mのユニットへと分解することであった。このヴォリュームを持つ中層建築に, 普通のディテールで木の羽目板を貼り付けると, 本物の木の板を用いているにもかかわらず, コンクリートの上に塗装を施したようにのっぺりとしてしまって, 木という素材の持つ質感も軽さもすべて吹き飛んでしまう。われわれは, 幅の大きな目地によって, 外壁を粒子状のユニットへと分節することで, 巨大なヴォリュームを持つ建築においても, 木の質感が感じられる外壁デザインの可能性に挑戦した。さらに, 外壁にあけられた開口部の位置や大きさにも, 微妙な不規則性, ズレを導入することで, 大きな壁面の中にゆらぎとゆるさを生み出そうとした。

Entrance lobby of main building　本館エントランス・ロビー

Roof terrace and chapel (right)　ルーフ・テラスとチャペル (右)

Restaurant on left, cottage B on right　左がレストラン棟，右がコテージB

1　BAR AND LOUNGE
2　BEAUTY SALON
3　POOL
4　JAPANESE RESTAURANT
5　GUEST ROOM

Japanese restaurant　和食レストラン

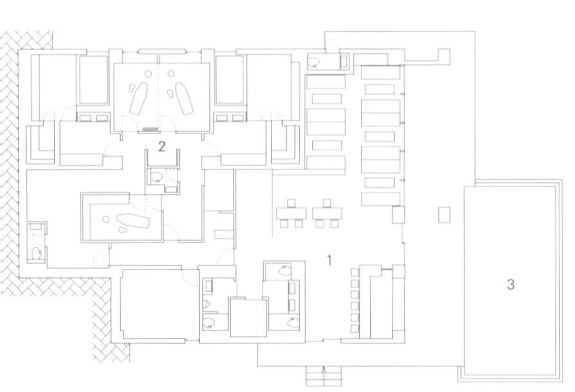

First floor S=1:400

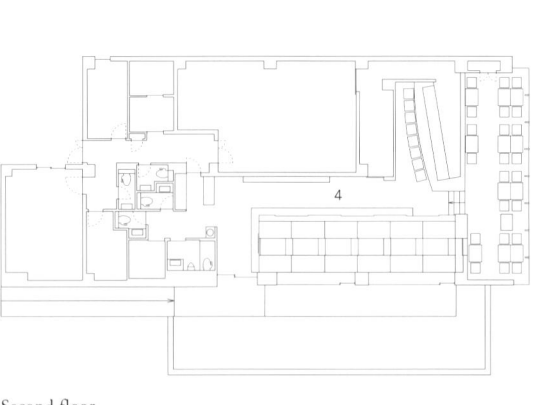

Second floor

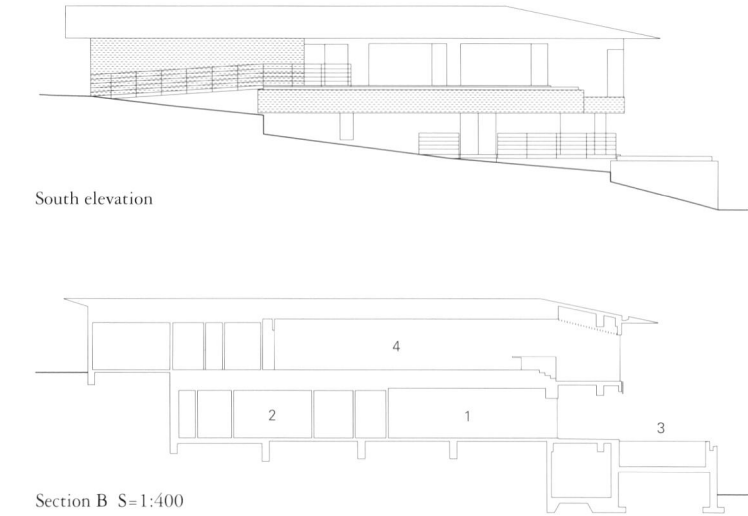

RESTAURANT

East elevation

Section A

South elevation

Section B S=1:400

COTTAGE A

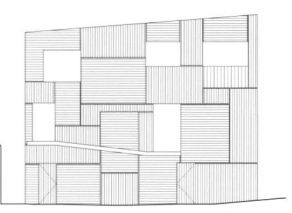

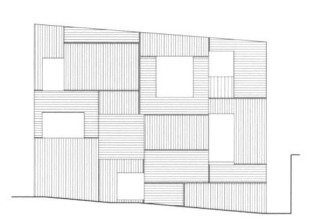

Cottage A コテージA

Guest room of cottage A コテージAの客室

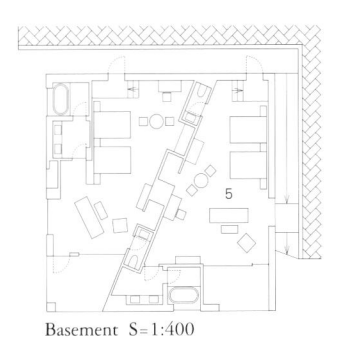

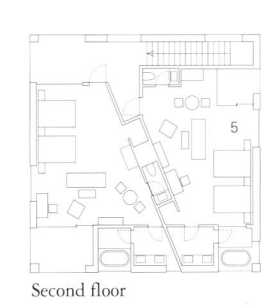

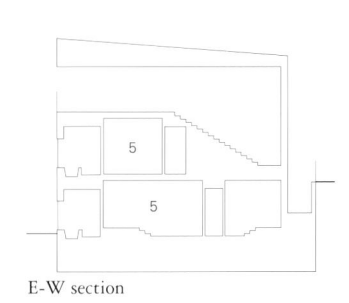

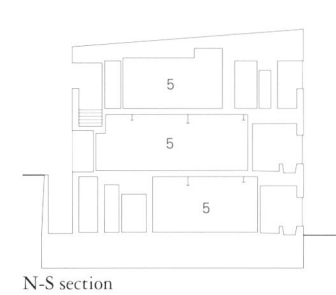

West elevation

North elevation

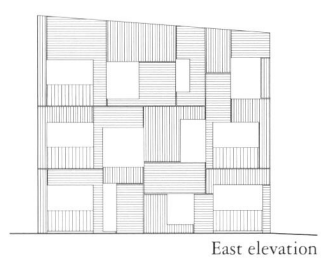

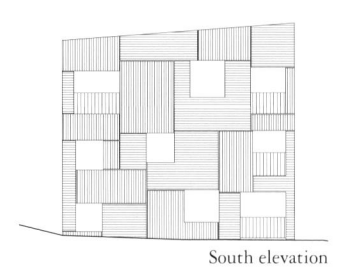

East elevation

South elevation

Basement S=1:400

First floor

Second floor

E-W section

N-S section

COTTAGE B

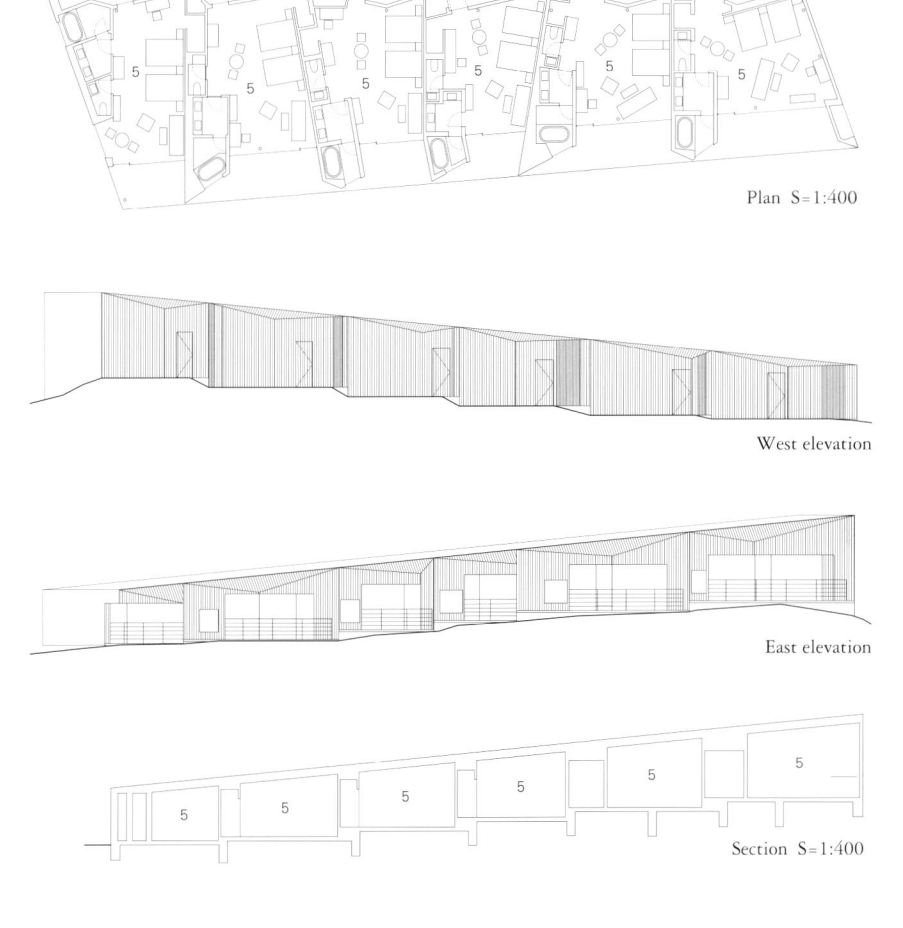

Cottage B コテージB

Plan S=1:400

West elevation

East elevation

Section S=1:400

2007-10 Akagi Jinja & Park Court Kagurazaka
Shinjuku, Tokyo, Japan

Overall view from stair on artificial terrain　人工地盤上の参道階段より見る全景

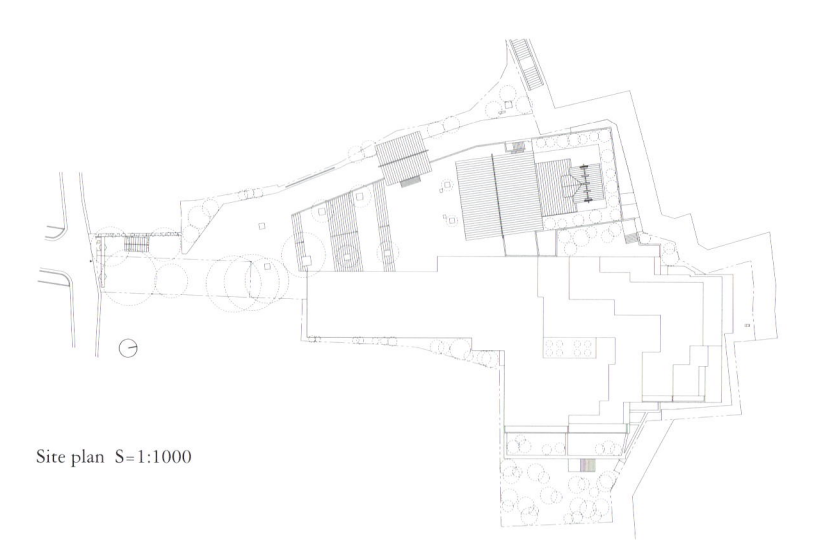

Site plan　S=1:1000

The project is a revitalization plan of Akagi Shrine, built in the midst of Kagura-zaka. A middle-rise condominium was additionally built so as to optimize the use of the site. We revitalized the space from the approach to the shirine building as much attractive community space without loosing the original quality. A multi-functional hall open to community was constructed beneath the shrine. The upper part was defined as an artificial terrain and a shrine was built above it.

The approach to the shrine is a big staircase giving relaxed sense of ascending. A transparent glass shrine was placed at the end. Ancient Izumo Taisha inspired the arrangement of the shrine at the end of the big staircase.

We adopted a detail called renjikoushi, a 45 degrees slanted lattice, for the lattice of the shrine. The roof was covered with Yamato-buki, which alternately covers metal plates with small gaps. Both are Japanese traditional details that avoid heavy impression of surfaces.

The details were used for the adjacent condominium's balcony balustrades and screens hiding machine and afforded lightness to the condominium. Furthermore, the tiled wall was designed in mosaic of different colors and evaded the weightiness as a surface.

View under eave of front shrine from east　拝殿の軒下を東より見る

赤城神社・パークコート神楽坂

神楽坂の中腹に建つ，赤城神社の再生計画。中層の集合住宅を併設することで，敷地の高度利用を図りながら，しかも参道から社殿へと至る空間の特質を損なうことなく，より魅力的な地域のための空間として再生させた。社殿の下に地域に開放された多目的ホールを設け，上部を人工的な大地と設定して，その人工地盤の上に社殿をたてた。

社殿へ至るアプローチは，ゆったりとした上昇感をもたらす大階段となり，その終点に透明なガラス張りの社殿が配置された。大階段の突き当たりに社殿を配する計画は，古代の出雲大社からインスピレーションを得た。

社殿の格子に，通常の格子を45度に傾けた連子格子と呼ばれるディテールを採用し，屋根は小さな段差をつけた金属板を互い違いに葺いていく大和葺きというディテールとした。ともに，面がべたっとして重い印象を与えることを避ける，日本の伝統的ディテールである。

このディテールは隣接する集合住宅棟のバルコニーの手摺，屋外機隠しのスクリーンにも応用されて，集合住宅に軽さを与えた。さらに壁面のタイルも，色違いのタイルをモザイク貼りとすることで，面としての重さを回避した。

Evening view of front shrine　透明度の高い拝殿の夕景

Interior of front shrine　拝殿内部

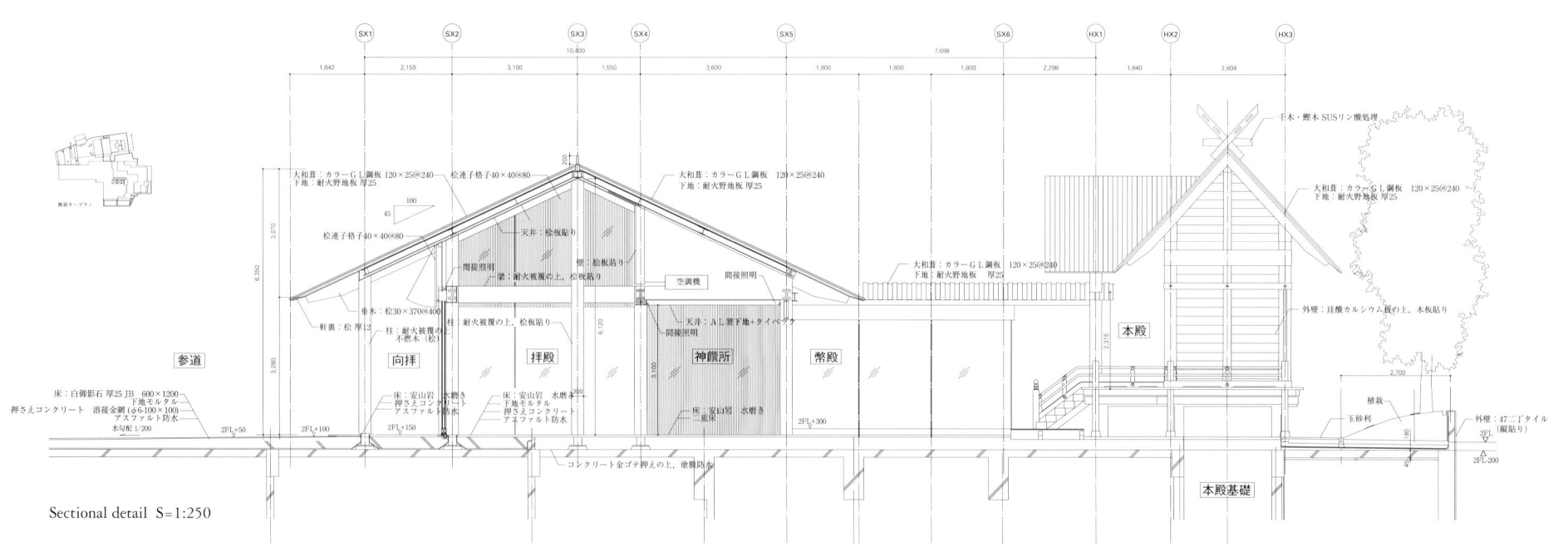

Sectional detail S=1:250

Facade of condominium　住宅棟ファサード

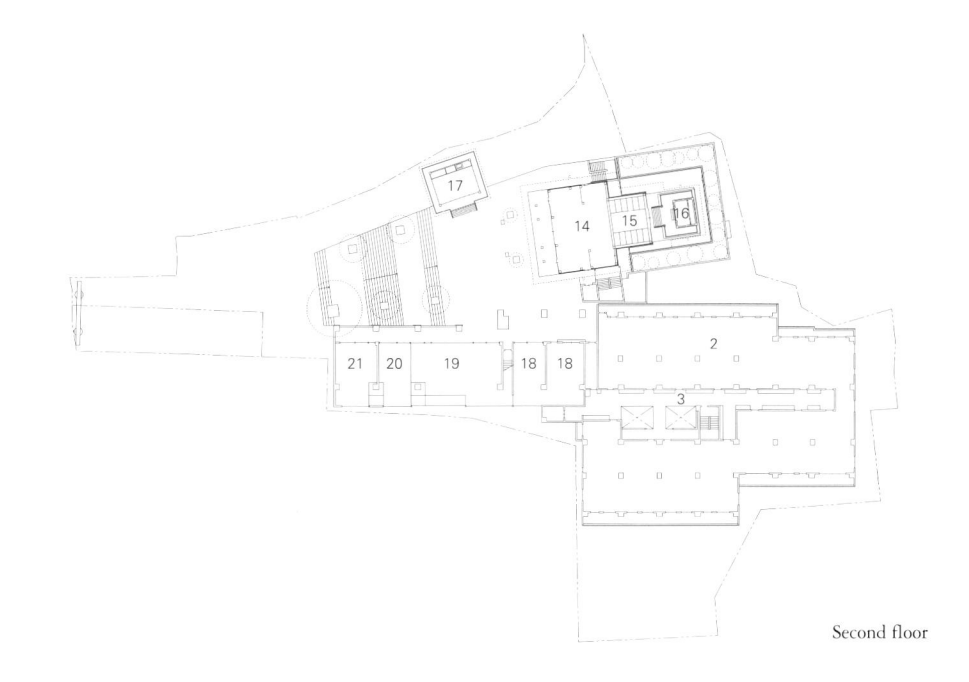

Second floor

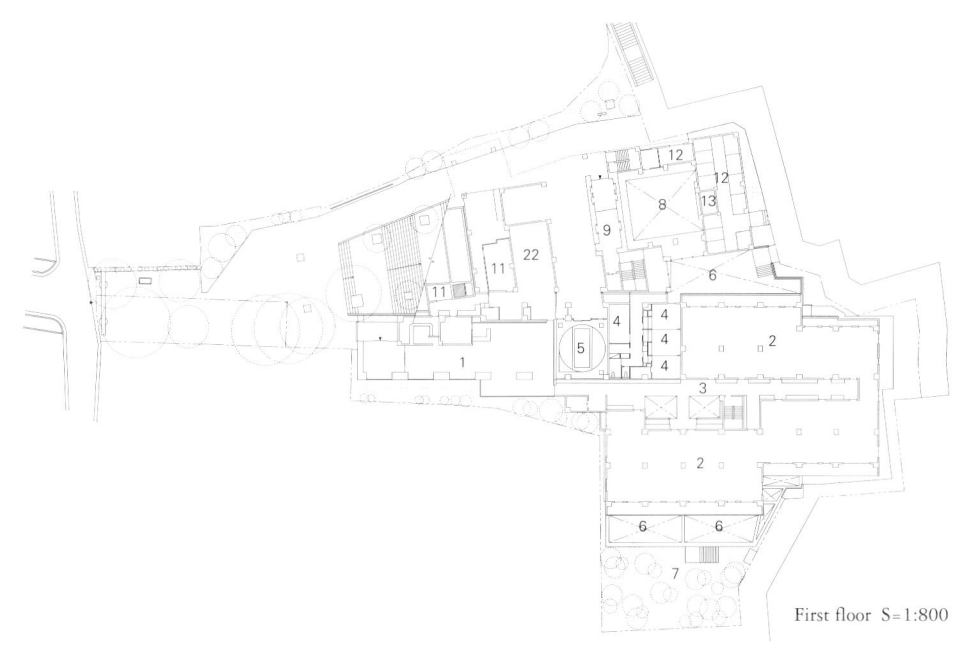

First floor　S=1:800

1	ENTRANCE HALL OF CONDOMINIUM	12	STORAGE OF PORTABLE SHRINE
2	DWELLING UNIT	13	BASE OF MAIN SHRINE
3	CORRIDOR	14	FRONT SHRINE
4	ANTEROOM	15	HALL OF OFFERINGS
5	PARKING	16	MAIN SHRINE
6	DRY AREA	17	KAGURA HALL
7	GARDEN	18	OFFICE
8	HALL	19	CAFE
9	ENTRANCE OF HALL	20	STORAGE
10	FOYER OF HALL	21	COMMUNITY FACILITY
11	GARBAGE DUMP	22	PARKING FOR BICYCLES

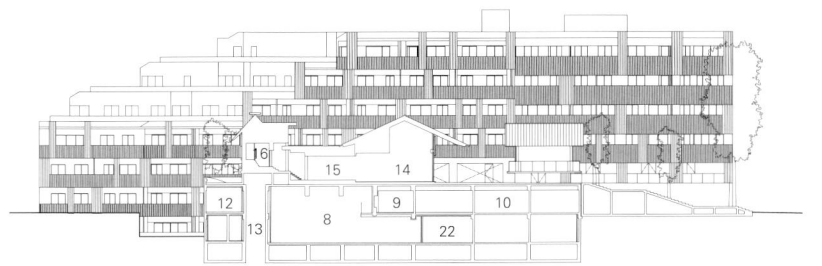

Entrance of condominium　住宅棟エントランス

Section　S=1:800

141

2007-10 Sanlitun SOHO
Beijing, China

Overall view from east 東より見る全景

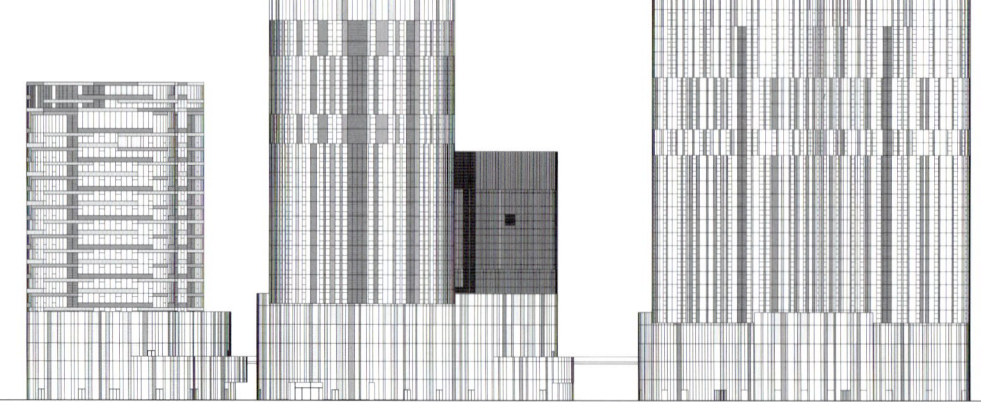

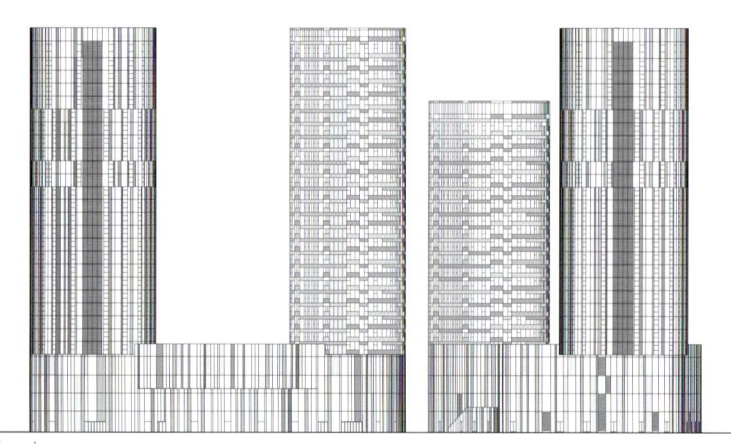

West elevation S=1:1500

South elevation

View of towers from southwest　南西よりタワー群を見る

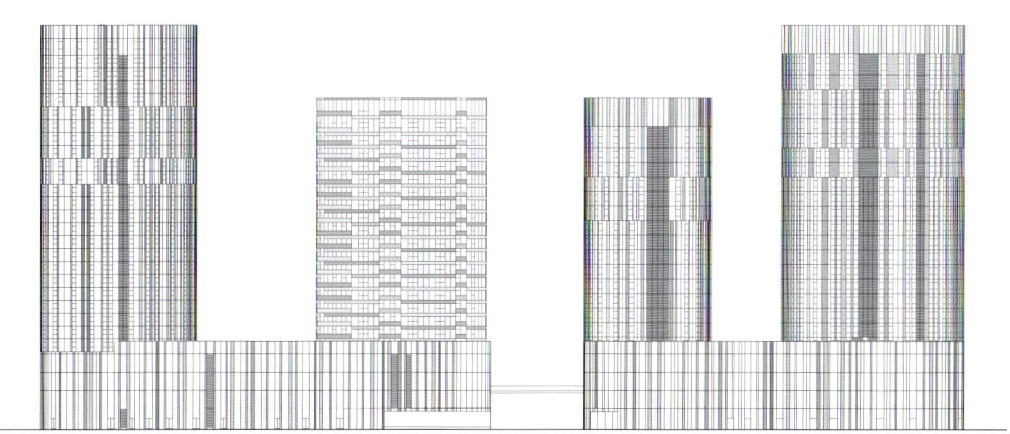

East elevation

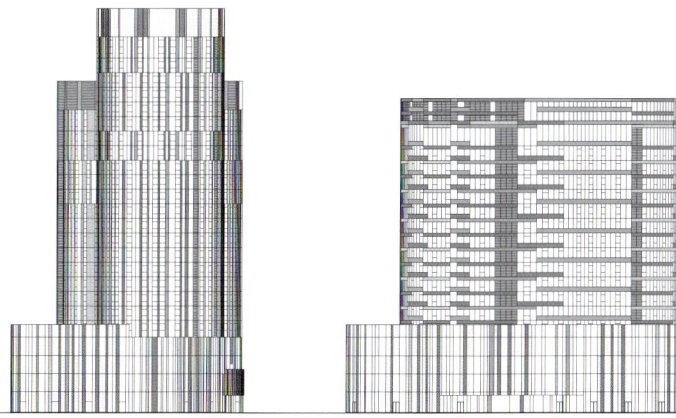

North elevation

143

Valley between towers　タワー群の谷間

Third floor

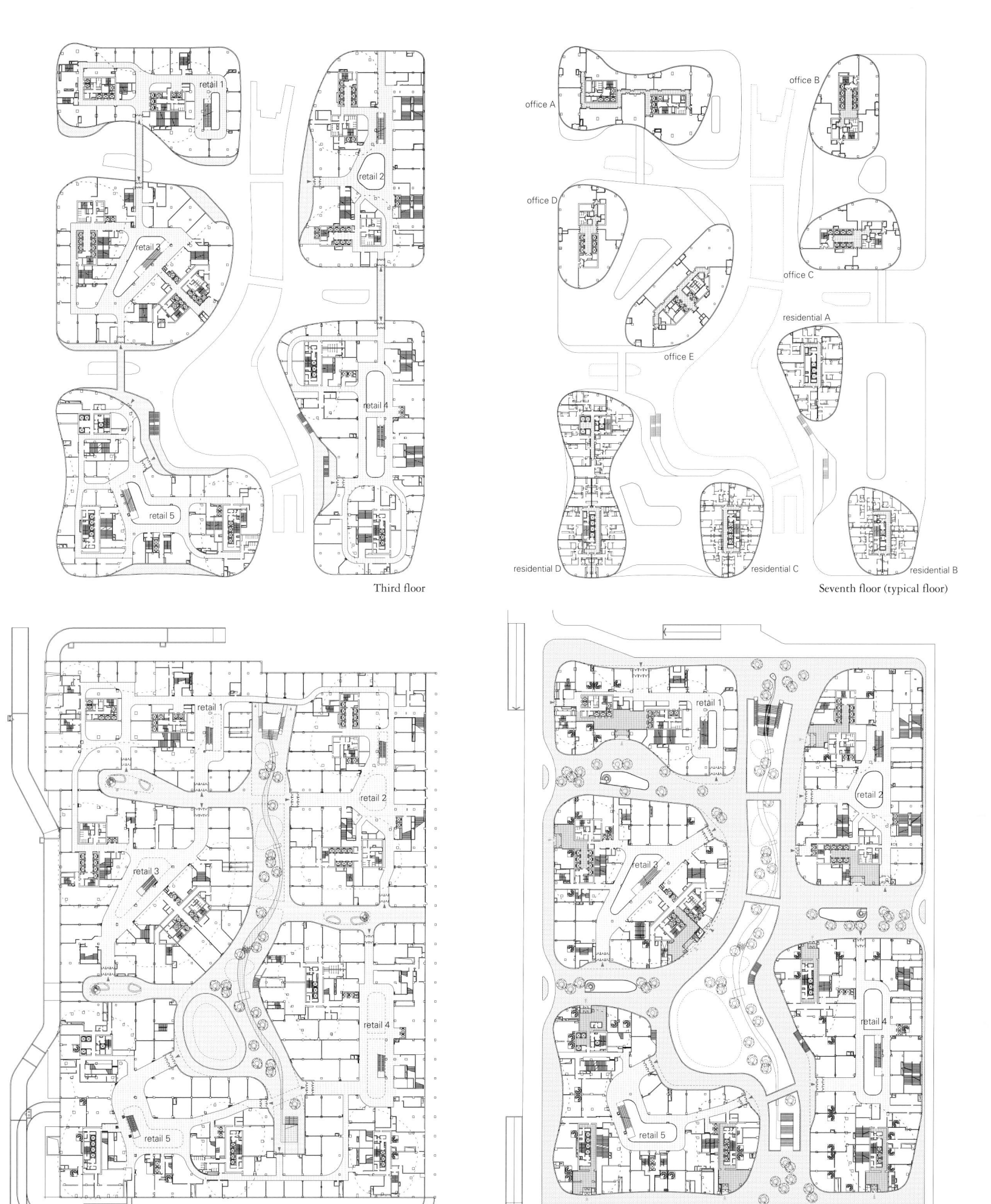

Seventh floor (typical floor)

Basement S=1:2000

First floor

I contemplated here to deny an ordinal high-rise buildings' image that one tall tower dominates a landscape, by a scheme of creating a scenery alike San Gimignano in Italy where multiple towers were erected in a crowd. Specifically, we created a panorama of a high-rise 'village' with nine 100 m-high towers in similar design standing in a row.

Conventional high-risen buildings are aimed at standing out a single being's character by unusual heights and forms. However, the 'village of towers' does not race conspicuous characters but shares loose rules by a multiple whole and create a harmonious condition of peace.

In order to manage the tactic, each tower needs to slightly differ in variation, though some parts should share a same look. In order to create the condition, we attempted a mosaic facade design that panels and glasses alternately align. By the similarity of the pattern and pixel size, we achieved a old village-like gentle and permissive harmony. Each tower's facade is divided vertically by a manipulation of shifting patterns. It is composed that several middle-high-rise architecture is piled up and therefore one flexible tower is erected. The method of dividing a tower resembles Asakusa Cultural Tourism Center. In between the towers valley-like space continues and water flow in the valley. An informal and wet public space like a village in a valley was created, contrary to a western type of formal open space.

Retail 4　リテール 4

Void of retail 4　リテール4の吹抜け

Retail 5　リテール5

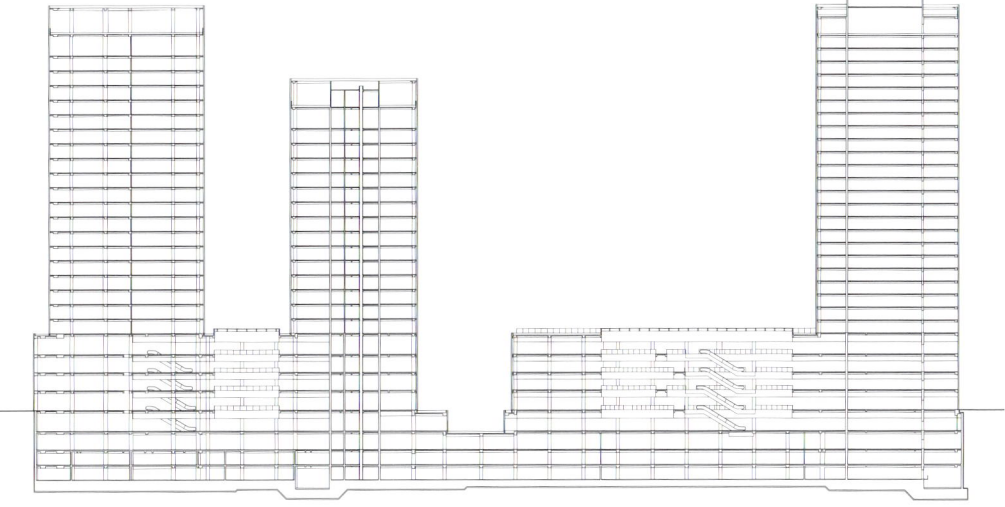

Section　S=1:1500

三里屯SOHO

複数の塔が群れて立ち並ぶ，イタリアのサンジミニァーノのような風景をつくり出すことによって，「1本の高い塔が風景を支配する」という従来の超高層ビルのイメージを否定したいと考えた。具体的には，相似したデザインを持つ高さ100mの塔が9本並んで立つことによって，超高層の「村」のような風景をつくった。

　従来の超高層は，ひとつの個（個人か企業）がその異常な高さと形態を用いて，その個性を突出させることが目的であった。しかし，この「塔の村」では，個性の突出ではなく，複数の全体がゆるやかなルールを共有することで，調和した平和な状態をつくり出そうとした。

　そのためには，それぞれの塔は，似ていながらも微妙に違わなければならない。その状態をつくるために，パネルとガラスを交互に並べるモザイク状のファサードデザインを試み，そのパターンとピクセルサイズの相似性によって，「村的」なやわらかく寛容なハーモニーを実現した。それぞれの塔のファサードは，パターンをずらすという操作によって垂直にも分割されて，中層の建築が幾つか積み重ねられてひとつのやわらかな塔をつくる構成となっている。「浅草文化観光センター」(2012年)と同じ様な，塔を分割する方法である。塔の隙間には谷状のスペースが連続し，その谷には水が流れ，西洋的なフォーマルな広場とは異なるインフォーマルでウェットな，谷間の集落のようなパブリックスペースが生まれた。

Retail 3　リテール 3

Void of retail 3　リテール3の吹抜け

Retail 3: upper view of void　リテール3：吹抜けの見上げ

2007-12 Water/Cherry
Japan

Approach from parking　駐車場からのアプローチ

Downward view from terrace on second floor of living room/dining wing toward bedroom wing　居間／食堂棟２階のぬれ縁より、主寝室棟を見下ろす

Night view from east. living room/dining wing on left, bedroom wing on right　東より見る夕景。右に主寝室棟、左に居間／食堂棟

1 GUEST ROOM
2 LAVATORY
3 SPA
4 KITCHEN
5 STUDY
6 BEDROOM
7 BATHROOM
8 CLOSET
9 ENTRANCE
10 LIVING ROOM/
   DINING
11 PANTRY

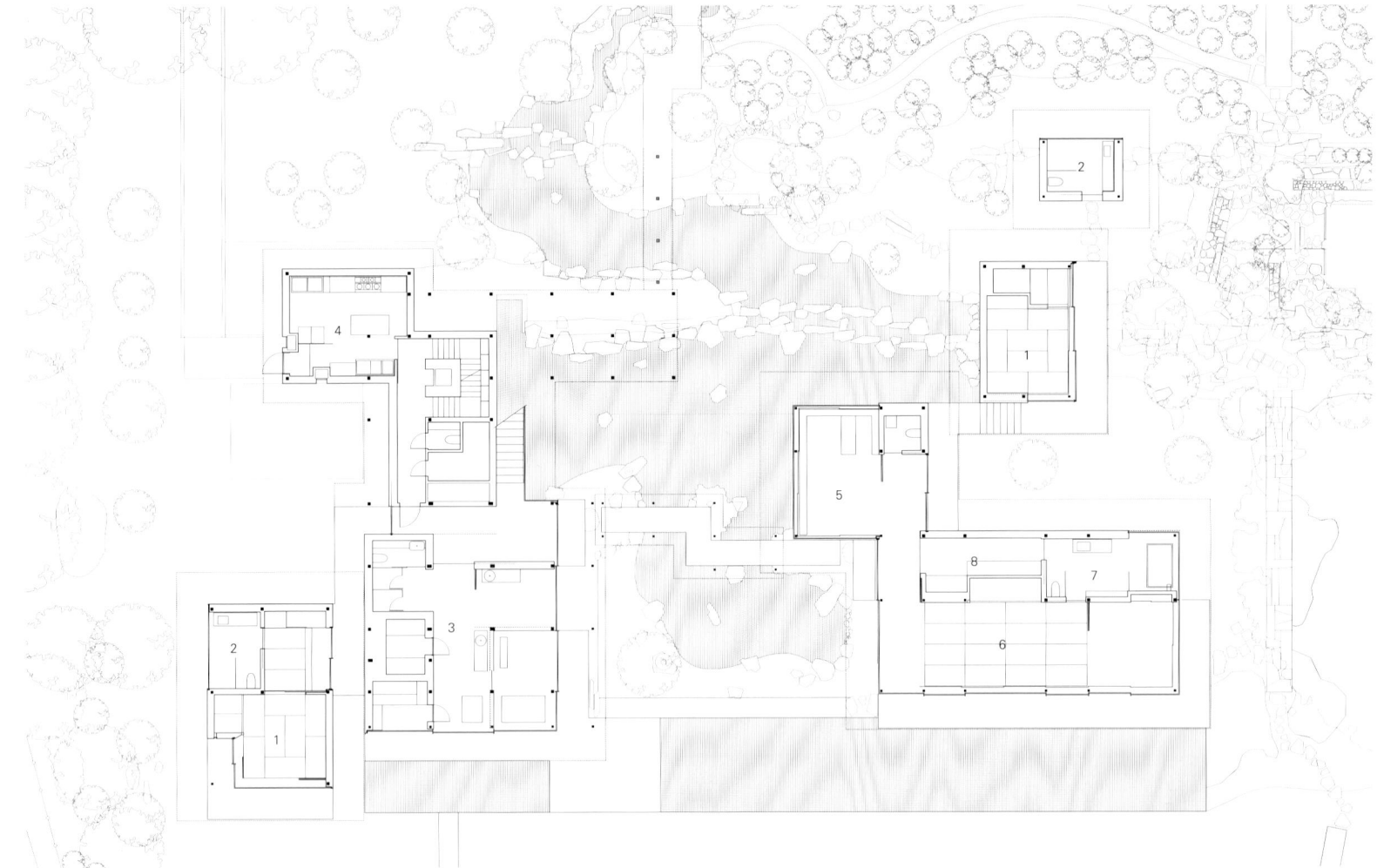

First floor S=1:300

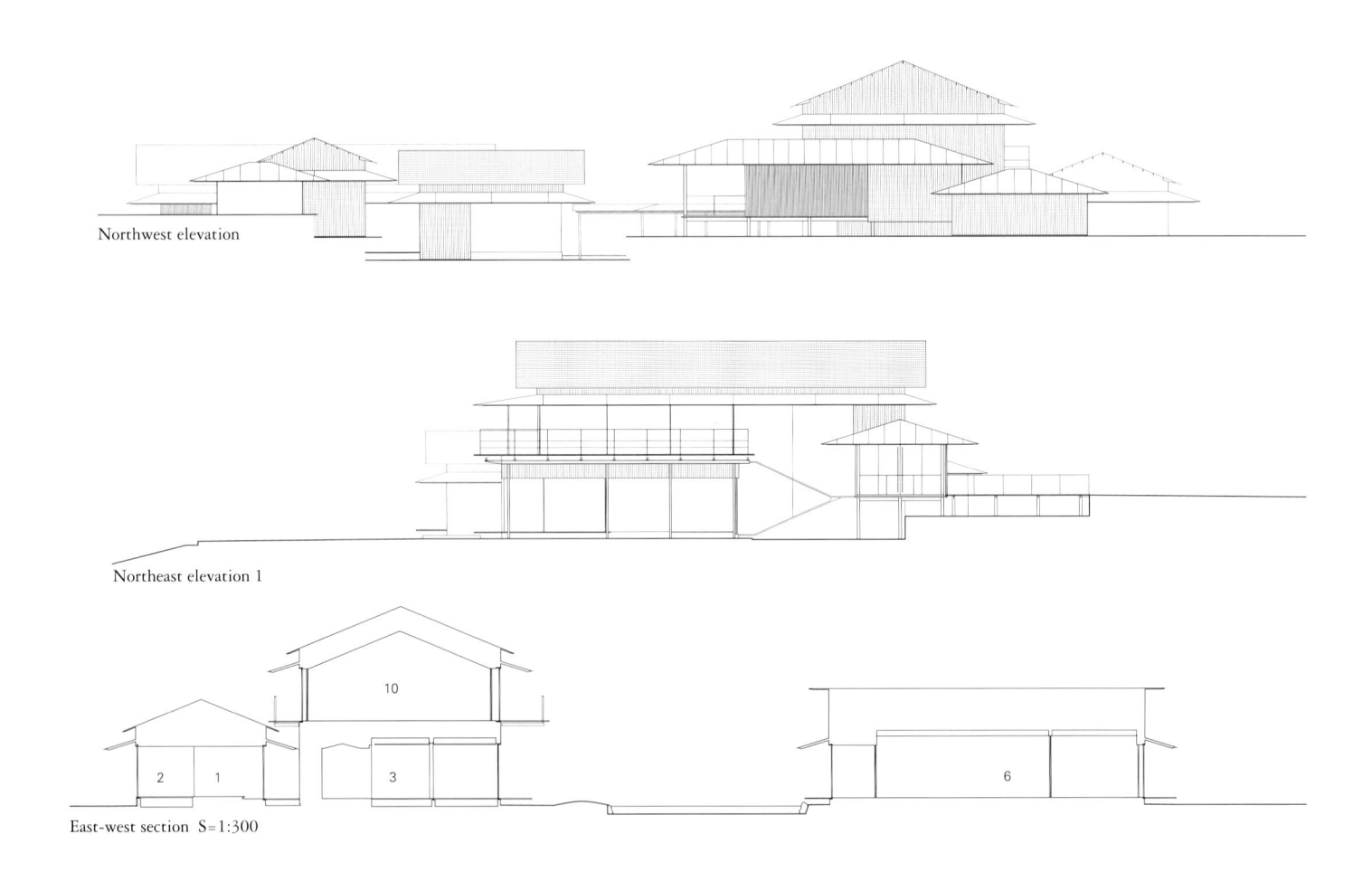

Northwest elevation

Northeast elevation 1

East-west section S=1:300

Second floor

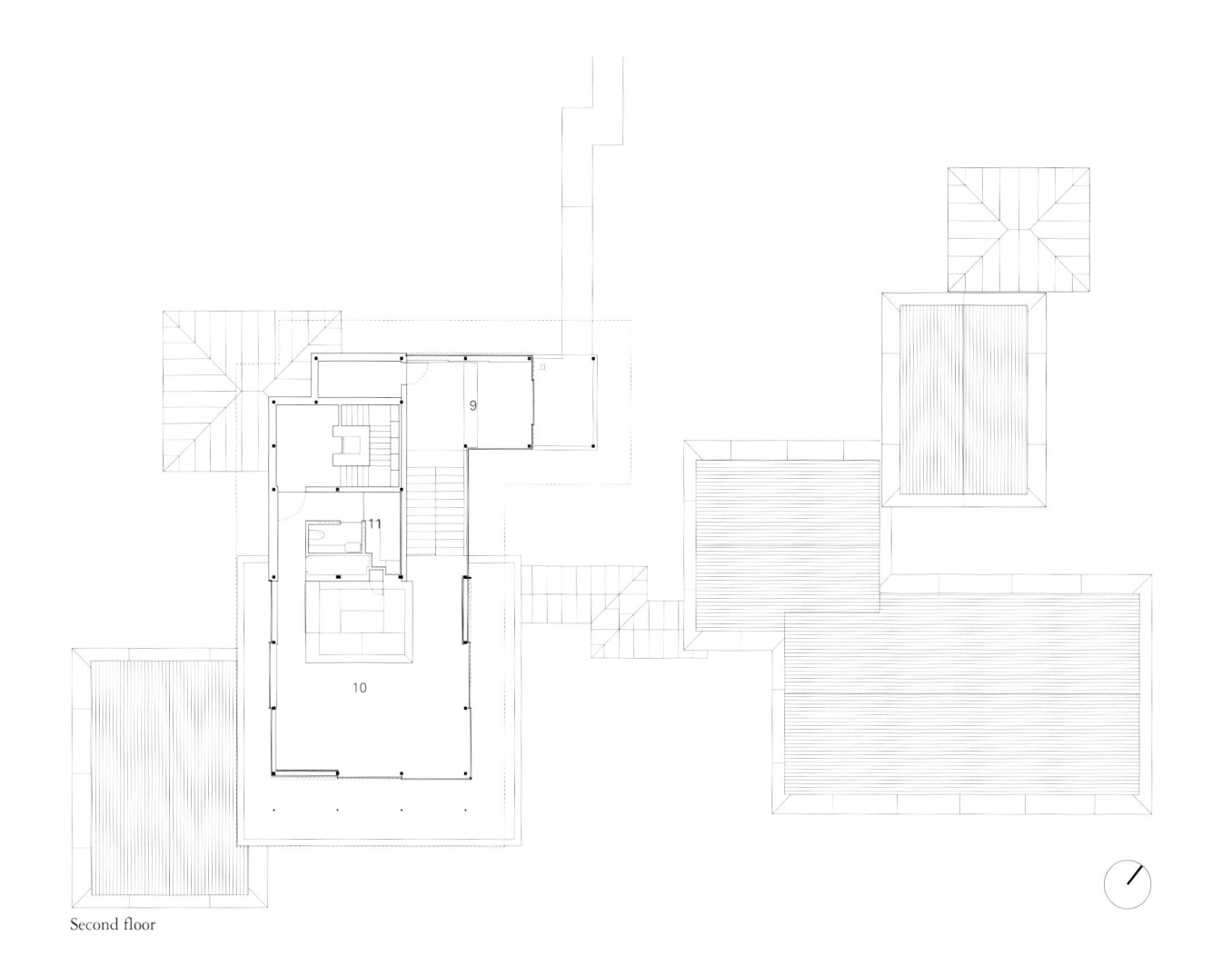

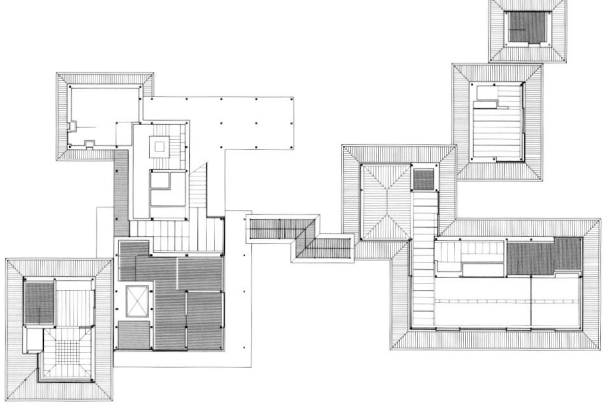

Reflected ceiling of first floor

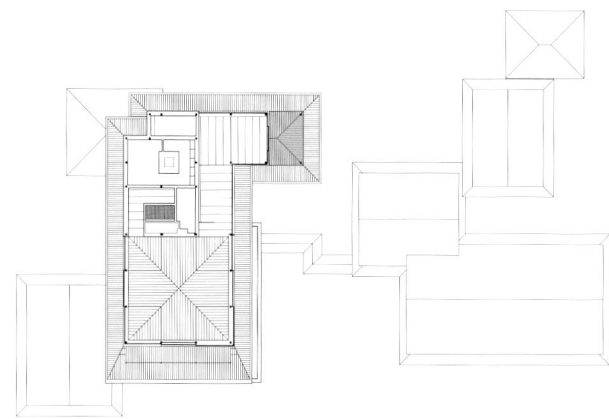

Reflected ceiling of second floor S=1:600

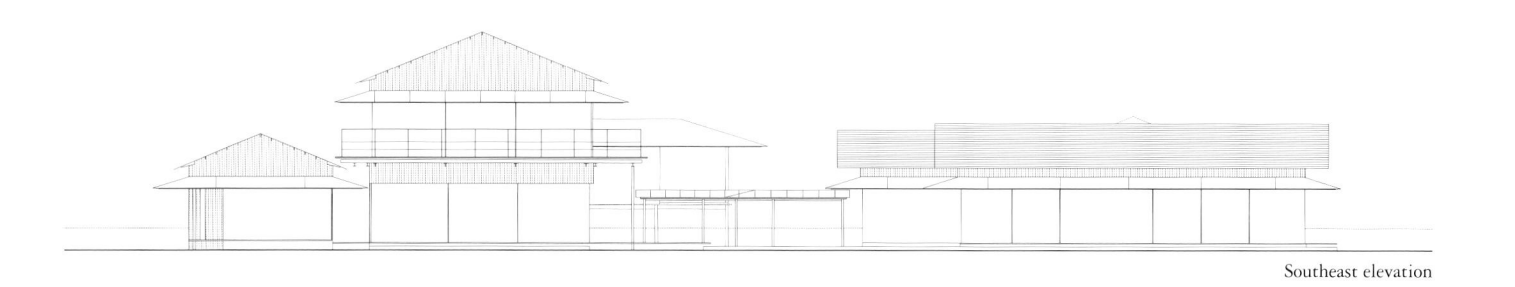

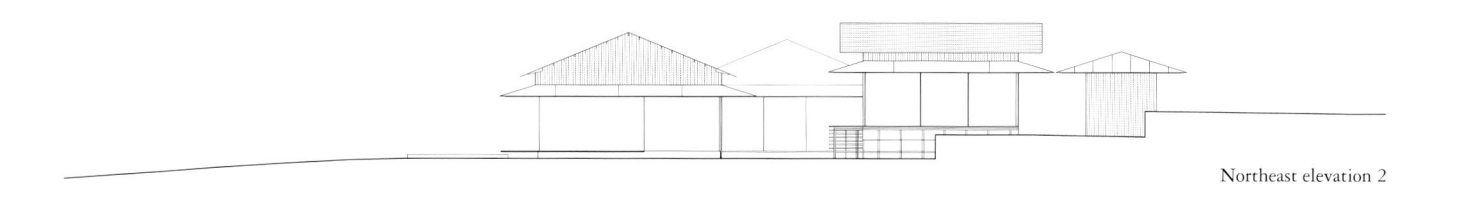

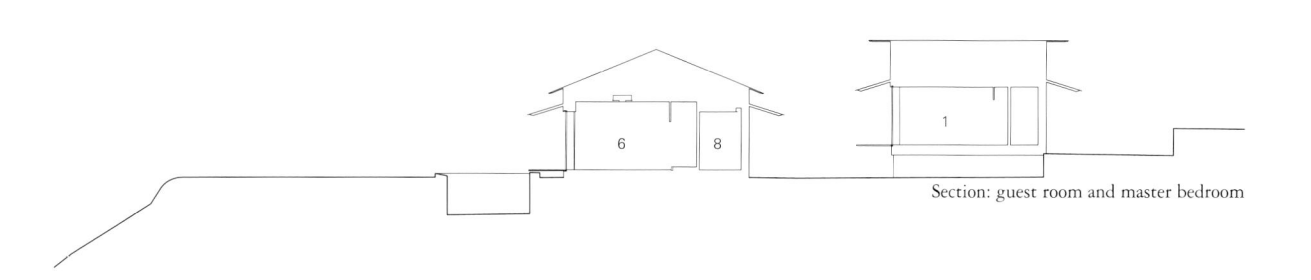

Southeast elevation

Northeast elevation 2

Section: guest room and master bedroom

153

View toward entrance of living/dining wing　居間／食堂棟2階、エントランス周り

View toward ocean through outdoor corridor　渡廊越しに海を望む

Southeast corner of master bedroom wing　主寝室棟の南東隅部

We thought to create a state where thin and light particles are scattered on a cliff facing the Pacific Ocean. A cherry blossom's petal was one of the inspirations. The ideal was thin and light components like cherry blossom's petal dance in the air above white sand.

Firstly, we separated the buildings. The residences which is not small at all are divided into small blocks and a light passage connected them to each other. We made a condition that enables people to look at the sea between the blocks. Roofs and exterior walls were split into small and light elements as much as possible. The walls were composed of an aggregate of thin 40 mm wide cedar. The interior was also designed as a collective of small and light parts. As for the ceiling, hinted by a Japanese traditional detail called Yamato-bari, 220 mm wide boards were aligned continuously in different levels. We gained an effect of particles, similar to fish scale, standing out. We tried to compose every part of the house as a loose collection of small features.

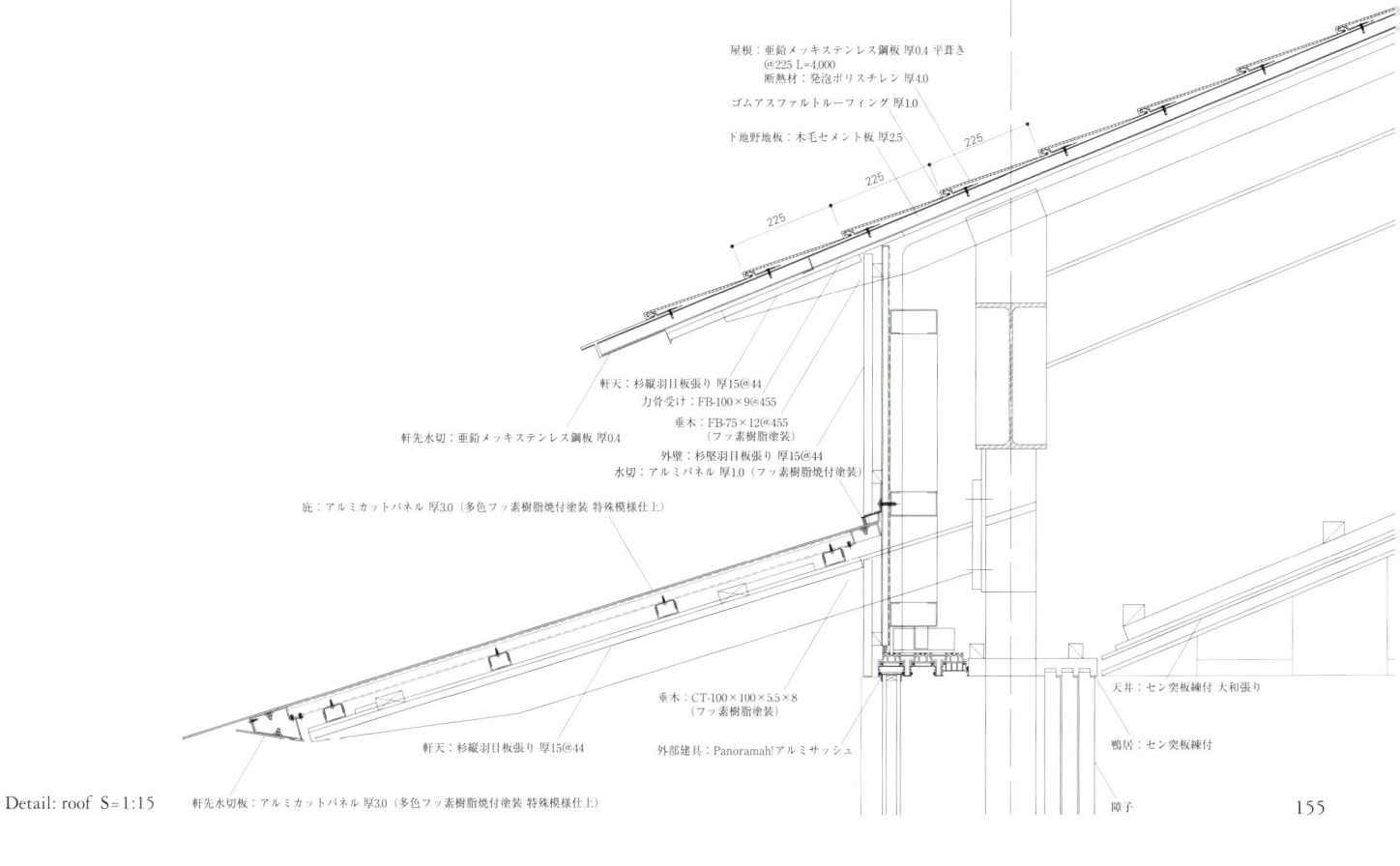

Eave on southwest of master bedroom wing. View toward ocean over pool　主寝室棟南西面の軒先。プール越しに海を望む

Detail: roof　S=1:15

Northeast corner of master bedroom wing　主寝室棟。北東側の軒先とぬれ縁

Annex wing of guest room. View toward garden on northeast　客室別棟。北東の庭園を見る

Water/Cherry

太平洋に面した崖の上に、薄く、軽やかな粒子がばらまかれたような状態をつくろうと考えた。桜の花ビラが、ひとつのヒントとなった。桜の花ビラのような薄く軽いエレメントが、白い砂の上に舞うような状態が理想だった。

　まず、分棟とした。決して小さくはない住宅を小さな棟にわけ、それを軽やかな渡り廊下でつないだ。棟と棟の隙間から、海が見える状態をつくった。屋根も外壁も、可能な限り小さくて軽いエレメントへ分解した。壁は、40mm幅の細い杉材の集合体とした。内装もまた、小さく軽いエレメントの集合体とした。天井は、大和張りと呼ばれる日本の伝統的なディテールにヒントを得て、220mm幅の板が段違いに連続していく収まりで、魚のウロコのような粒子性が際立つ効果を得た。小さなエレメントのゆるい集合体として、家のすべての部分を構成しようとした。

Living/dining room on second floor　2階居間／食堂

Entrance of living/dining wing. Northwest view　居間／食堂棟のエントランス。堅格子越しに北西を見る

Spa on first floor of living/dining wing　居間／食堂棟の1階スパ

2007-09 Cavamarket Headquarters
Salerno, Campania, Italy

This is the headquarters for the CAVA Market at Cava dei Tirreni in the Campania region of Italy. By placing retail outlets on the ground floor open to the courtyard we strove to create a courtyard office building that the public can enjoy.

The soft volcanic stone called Tufo is mined locally and used for the exterior walls and roofs. Tufo is compressed volcanic ash from nearby Mt. Vesuvio, and almost all the architecture in Cava was once built with this stone. But concrete became prevalent during the 20th century and the character of the town is being eroded. This architecture we designed will have all the roofs and walls covered by Tufo, and also there will be many slender slits cut into the Tufo.

Once seeds settle in these slits, we anticipate that plants will grow. This material has an intermediate quality between stone and soil and we expect the building will gradually turn into a green volume.

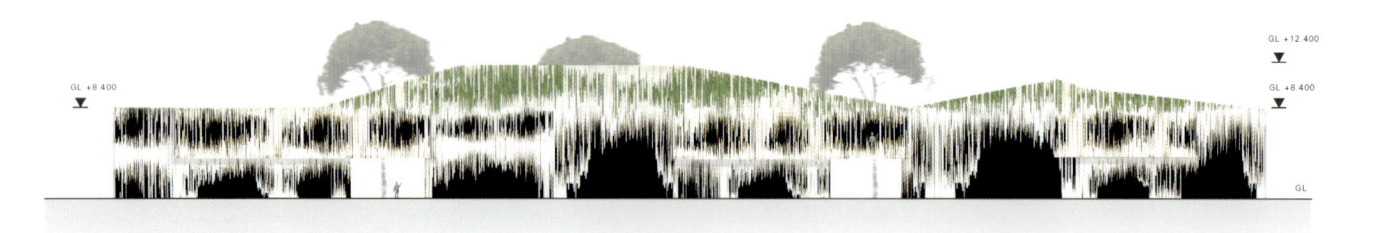

West elevation S=1:700

Restaurant レストラン

Patio パティオ

カヴァマーケット・ヘッドクォータース

イタリア,カンパーニャ地方,カヴァ・デイ・ティレーニの中心地区に計画されているCAVA Market社のヘッドクォーター。閉じたオフィスビルをつくるのではなく,中庭型のオフィスとして1階に店舗をいれ,中庭を市民に開放することで,市民に開かれた市民に親しまれるオフィスをつくろうと考えた。

外壁,屋根には,地元で採掘されているトゥーホという名のやわらかい火山岩を用いている。近くのベスビオ火山の火山灰が固まってできたこの石で,かつてのカヴァの町の建築はほとんどつくられていたが,20世紀にはコンクリートの建築群で町の質感が失われつつある。われわれが計画中の建築は,屋根も壁もすべてトゥーホで覆われ,さらにトゥーホには細かいスリットが無数に掘り込まれる。

このスリットに植物の種が落ちると,そこから根がのびて植物が育つことが知られている。この石と土との中間的性質をもつ素材で覆われた建築は,時と共に緑のヴォリュームへと近づいていくだろう。

Ground floor S=1:2000

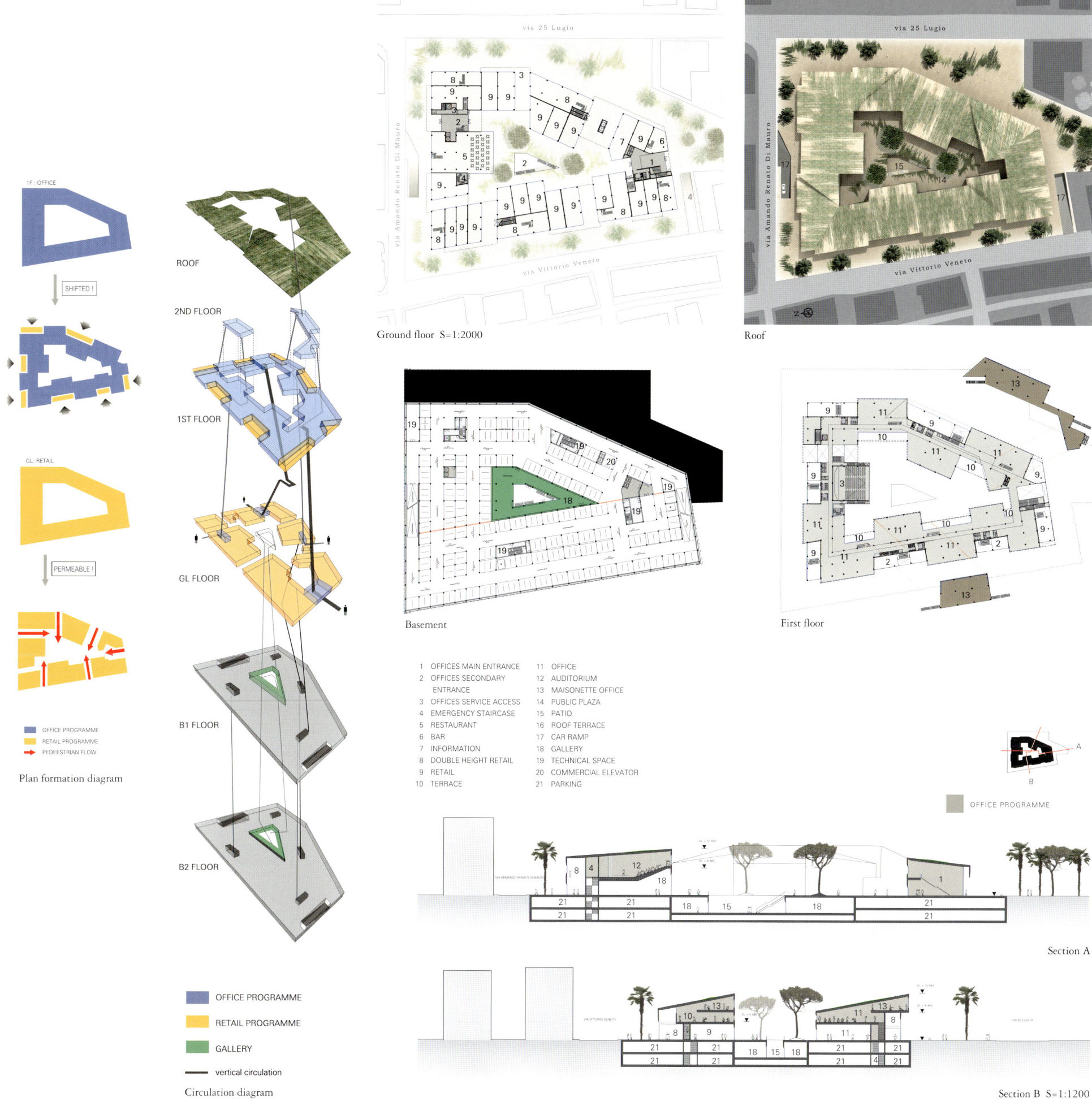

Roof

Basement

First floor

1	OFFICES MAIN ENTRANCE	11	OFFICE
2	OFFICES SECONDARY ENTRANCE	12	AUDITORIUM
3	OFFICES SERVICE ACCESS	13	MAISONETTE OFFICE
4	EMERGENCY STAIRCASE	14	PUBLIC PLAZA
5	RESTAURANT	15	PATIO
6	BAR	16	ROOF TERRACE
7	INFORMATION	17	CAR RAMP
8	DOUBLE HEIGHT RETAIL	18	GALLERY
9	RETAIL	19	TECHNICAL SPACE
10	TERRACE	20	COMMERCIAL ELEVATOR
		21	PARKING

OFFICE PROGRAMME

Section A

Section B S=1:1200

OFFICE PROGRAMME
RETAIL PROGRAMME
PEDEESTRIAN FLOW

Plan formation diagram

ROOF
2ND FLOOR
1ST FLOOR
GL FLOOR
B1 FLOOR
B2 FLOOR

OFFICE PROGRAMME
RETAIL PROGRAMME
GALLERY
vertical circulation

Circulation diagram

159

2007-08 Casa Umbrella
Milan, Italy

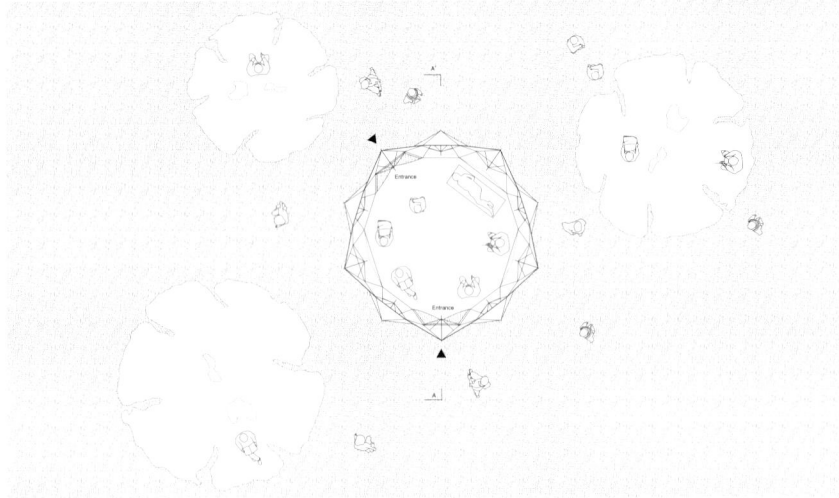

Consept

Plan S=1:200

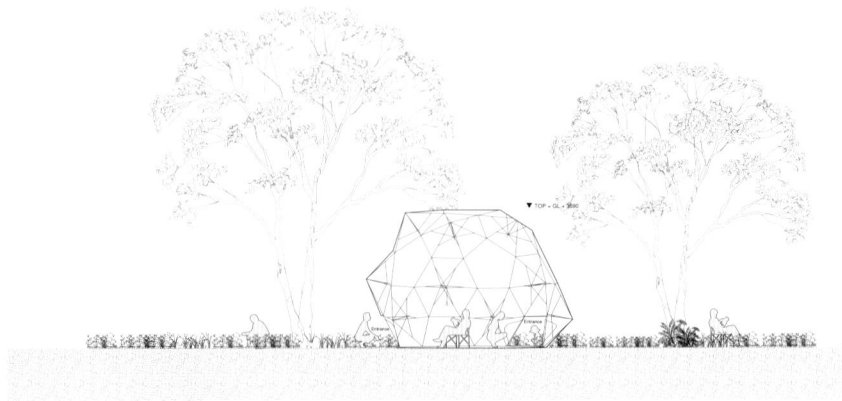

Section S=1:200

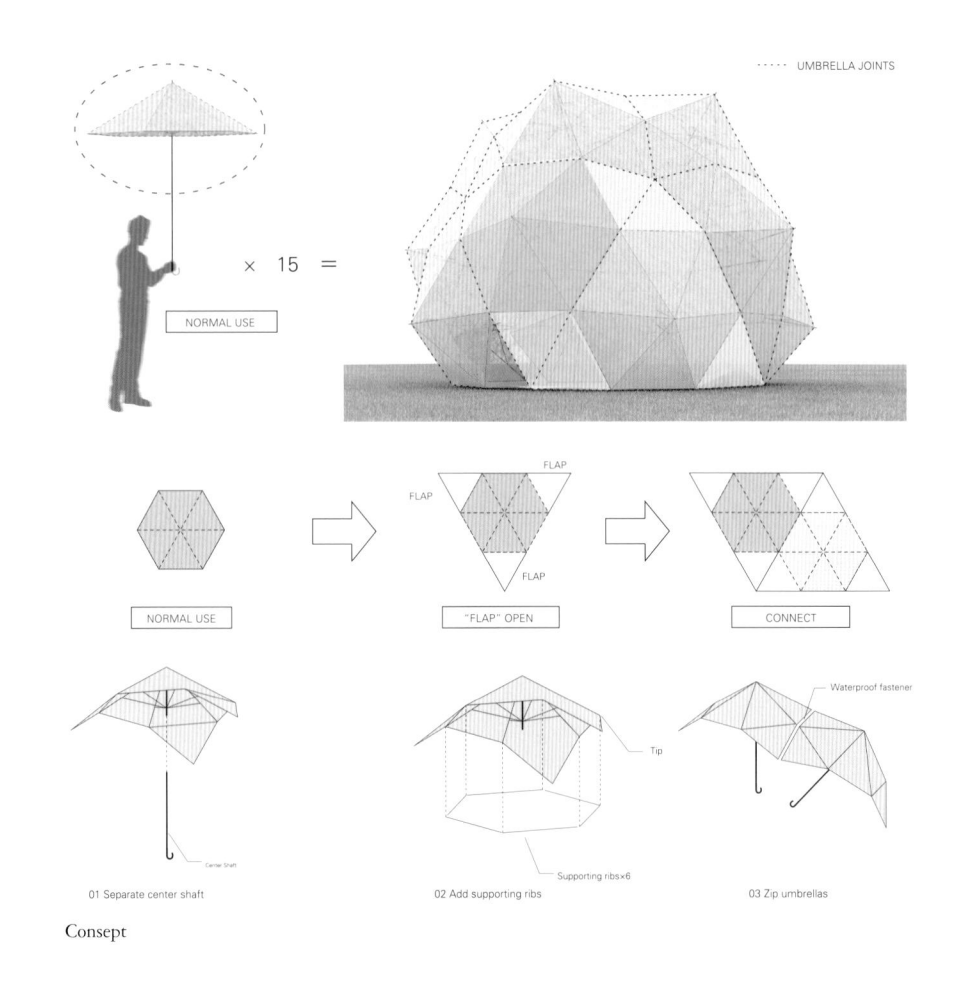

The project is a temporal pavilion for an exhibition titled "Casa de Toute", held in Milano Triennale in 2008. I considered making a temporal residence by a gathering of umbrellas that everyone brings from his or her home. I am interested in a challenge to reach to a large construction in a disaster situation, assembling small daily objects (umbrellas) by amateurs. We call the method of making architecture by not relying on 'large power' such as government and construction companies 'democratization of architecture'. Polythene Water Bricks and aluminum Polygonium also belong to the system.

The fundamental unit of the umbrella is made of Tyvek sheet. Each umbrella is connected with watertight zipper used for diving suits. The idea of creating an icosahedral by collecting 15 umbrellas is based on a similar geometry to Buckminster Fuller's Fuller Dome. However, what is unique about Casa Umbrella is the structural use of membrane's tension and frame's compression at the same time. The structural solution enables to support a pavilion with as thin frame as ordinal umbrellas and completed a far much delicate dome than Fuller Dome.

Casa Umbrella

2008年のミラノトリエンナーレで開催された"Casa de toute（みんなの家）"展のための仮設パビリオン。皆が玄関に置いているカサを持ち寄ることで、ひとつの仮設住宅をつくろうと考えた。小さな日用品（＝カサ）を素人が自分たちの力だけで組み立てて、災害時のための大きな構築物に到達する試みに興味がある。政府や建設会社などの「大きな力」に依存せず、このような方法で建築をつくることを、われわれは「建築の民主化」と呼んでおり、ポリエチレン製のウォーター・ブロックやアルミ製のポリゴニウムもこの系統に属する。

基本ユニットとなるカサは、タイベックシート製で、カサとカサとはダイバースーツ用の止水ジッパーで緊結される。15個のカサを集めて正20面体を構成する考え方は、バックミンスター・フラーのフラードームと同様の幾何学に基づいているが、「Casa Umbrella」のユニークな点は、膜材の張力とフレームのコンプレッションを、共に構造的に用いることである。その構造的解決によって、通常のカサと同じ細いフレームでパビリオンを支えることが可能となり、この解決によってフラードームよりはるかに繊細なドームが完成した。

2008-
Water Branch House
New York, U.S.A.

We began a research of constructing a temporal and transportable architecture by piling up polyethylene tanks from 2004. We started with an idea of making a unit of masonry architecture by first designing a tank that can tune its weight by adjusting the amount of water in the tank. We named the unit 'Water Block'.

Then in 2008, we were invited to House Delivery exhibition from MoMA in New York. As a unit to create a temporal house, we designed a new plastic tank named 'Water Branch'. The Water Branch was formed by shifting and linearly connecting 100 mm long cubes. There are two caps attached at the both ends of the unit. Because of the two caps, it became possible to pour hot and cold water from unit to unit when units are connected with a thin tube. Various liquid flow in the architecture just like blood run in a human body. So to speak, architecture became closer to organism. Furthermore, as Water Branch is long and thin in its shape, it is possible to corbel. Therefore, we were able to gain a free structural shape that surpasses masonry structure. In 2009 we constructed in reality a completely self-supporting experimental residence that does not rely on infrastructure using Water Branch in Nogizaka, Tokyo.

Water Branch House

ポリエチレン製のタンクを積み重ねて, 仮設, 移動型建築をつくる研究を2004年から始めた。まずは水を出し入れして重さを調整できるタンクをデザインし, それをユニットとして組積造の建築をつくるアイディアからスタートし, そのユニットを「ウォーター・ブロック」と名づけた。

続いて2008年, NYのMoMAからハウスデリバリー展に招待され, 仮設住宅をつくるためのユニットとして, 「ウォーター・ブランチ」という新しいポリタンクをデザインした。「ウォーター・ブランチ」は, 100mm角のキューブをずらしながらリニアに連結した形状で, キャップがユニットの両端に二つ付いている。キャップが二つなので, ユニット同士を細いチューブで連結すると, ユニットからユニットへと温水, 冷水を流すことが可能となる。建築体の中を, 体の中を血が流れるように様々な液体が流れるのである。いわば建築の生物化が起きる。さらに, 「ウォーター・ブランチ」は形状が細長いので, 持ち送り構造が可能となり, 組積造を超えた自由な構造形態を獲得することができた。「ウォーター・ブランチ」を使って, 2009年には完全自律型のインフラに依存しない実験住宅を, 東京の乃木坂に実際に建設した。

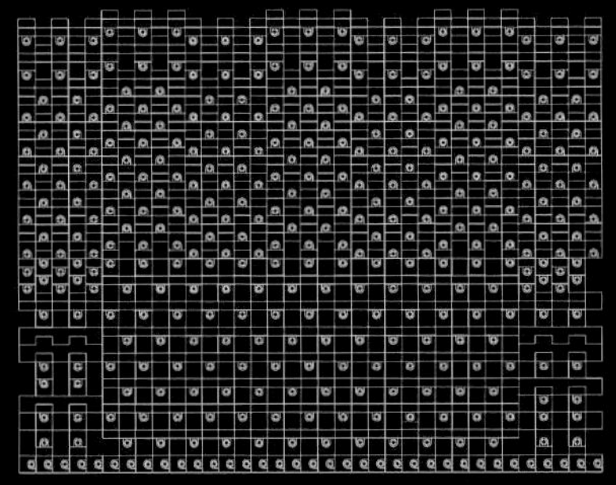

East elevation S=1:70 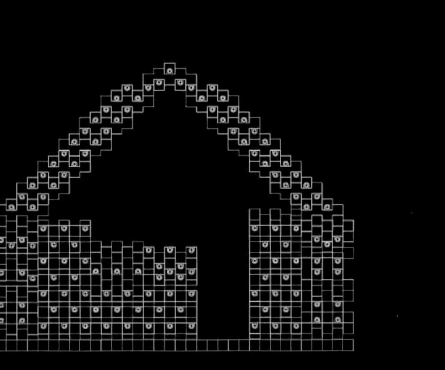　　South elevation 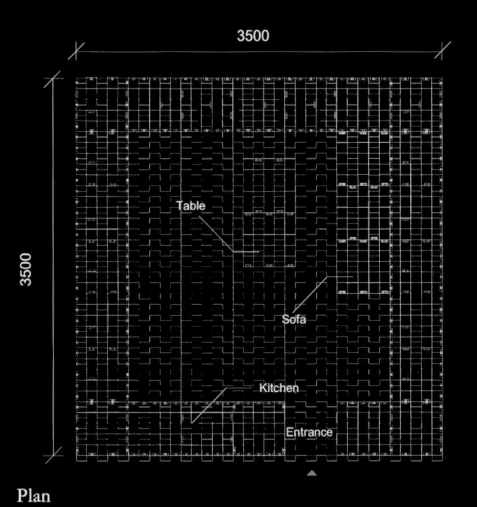　　Plan 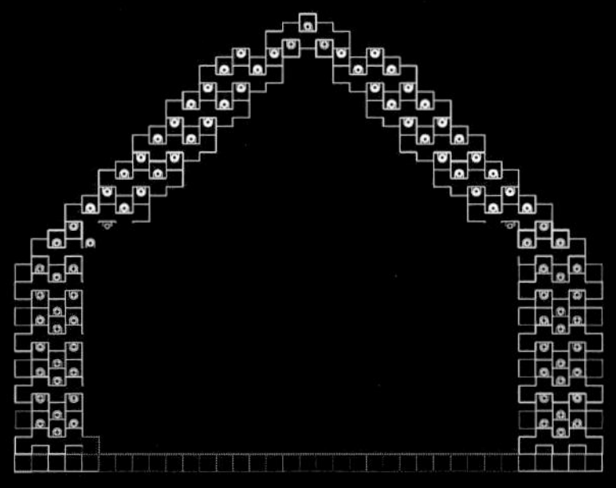　　Section

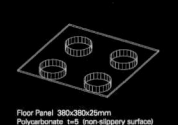

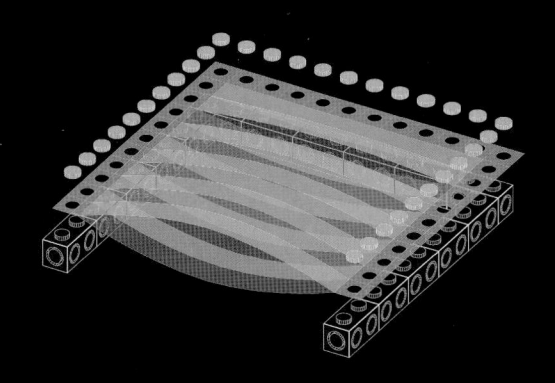

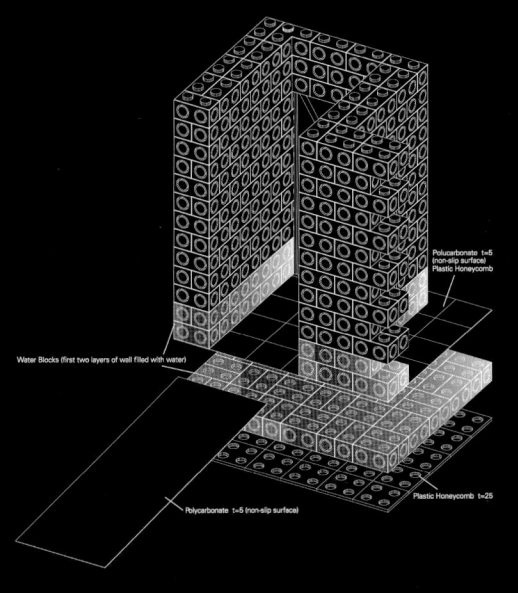

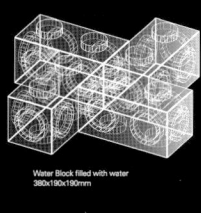

2008-10 Bamboo/Fiber
Japan

Evening view from south　南より見る夕景

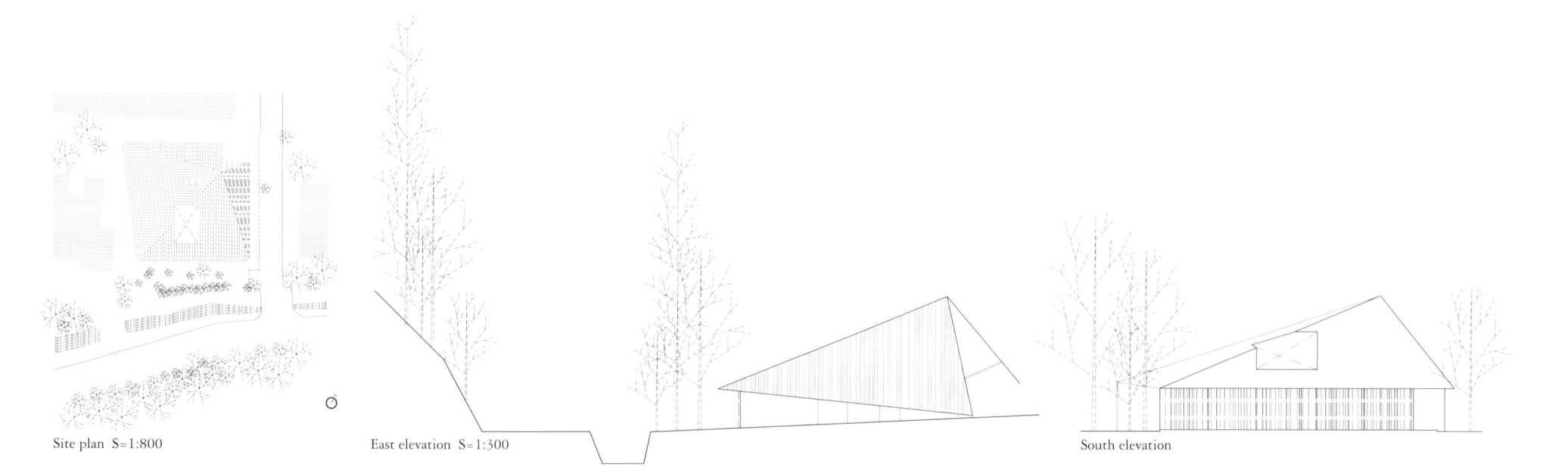

Site plan S=1:800

East elevation S=1:300

South elevation

Eaves of fiber reinforced plastic　FRP製の軒下

Courtyard　中庭

163

Hall　ホール

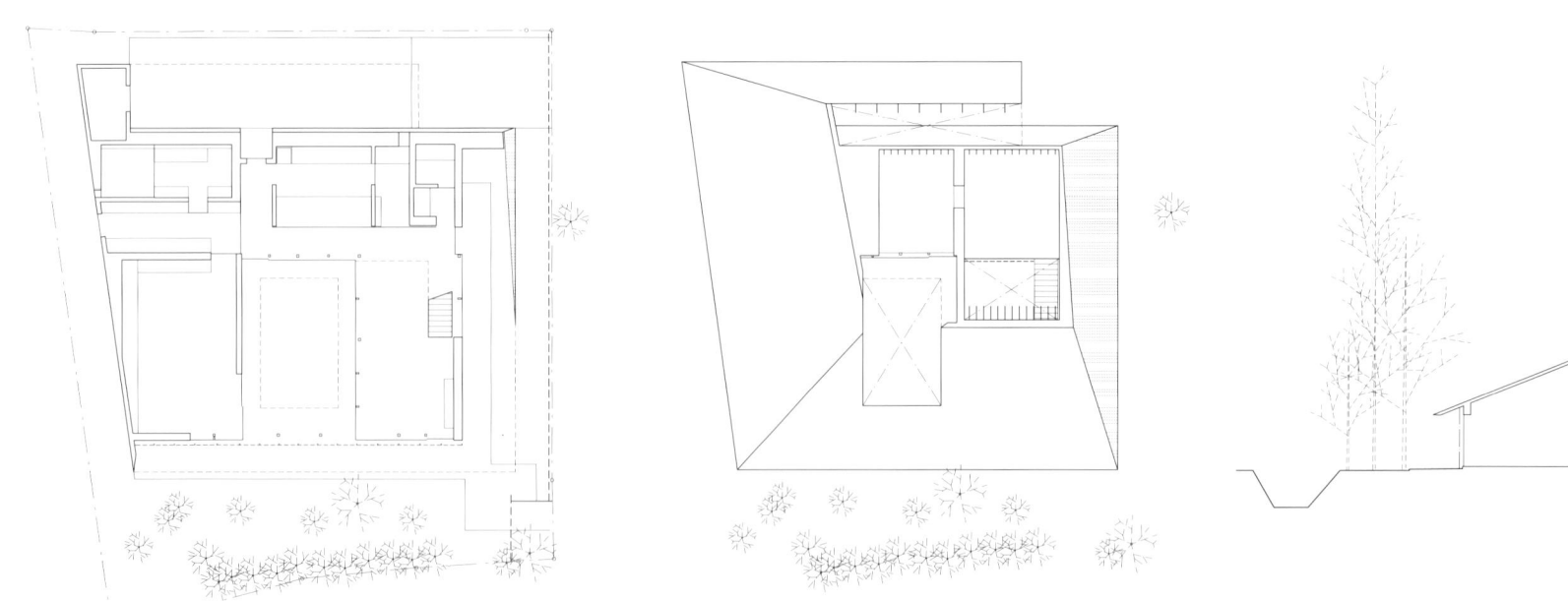

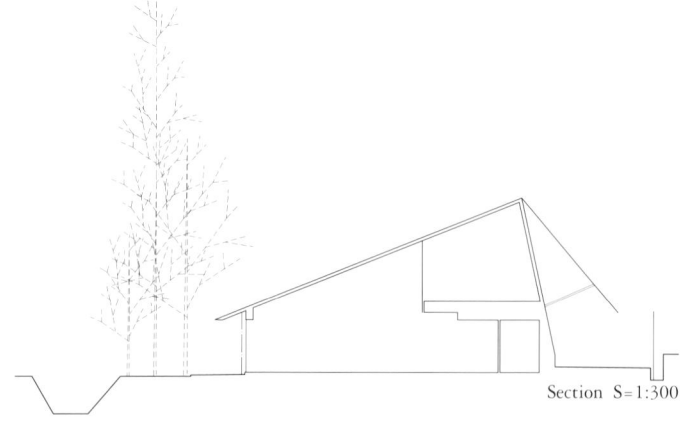

First floor S=1:300

Second floor

Section S=1:300

Hall: kitchen is behind partition of bamboo-fiber　ホール：竹繊維を含むパーティション後方は台所

Inspired by the bamboo grove adjacent to this site, this house is an attempt to explore bamboo's many potentials.

To start with, we found a structural material consisting of decomposed bamboo fiber solidified through 3,000-ton compression. Taking advantage of its high strength/low elasticity, it was adopted for the rafter of the large cantilever structure. Next, FRP made of bamboo fiber was used for the roof and the interior. FRP is usually made by mixing glass fiber into polyethylene resin. Here, bamboo fiber was mixed instead of glass, accounting for its soft, warm texture of amber. By using this bamboo FRP on the roof over the approach, a new type of space filled with magical light came to be created under the eaves.

Facing the front road is a screen inspired by 'takekomai' (bamboo lath), serving as a filter between the road and the house. Originally a type of groundwork for earthen walls, takekomai with its aesthetic beauty and lightness has been a source of inspiration for the teamaster Rikyu who invented an outrageous detail called 'shitajimado' (groundwork window) where instead of covering it with earth, the groundwork is left bare. This project features takekomai screens that make up the entire wall surfaces in order to expand and develop the idea of shitajimado. Moreover, use of bamboo parts of different sizes (20 mm, 30 mm, 40 mm) arranged at random pitch, and wire rather than normal rope cords to tie them together, have contributed in creating a bamboo screen with a cool, dry feeling that better suits the modern times. This bamboo screen became a medium that integrates the architecture with the bamboo grove across the pathway.

Bedroom　寝室

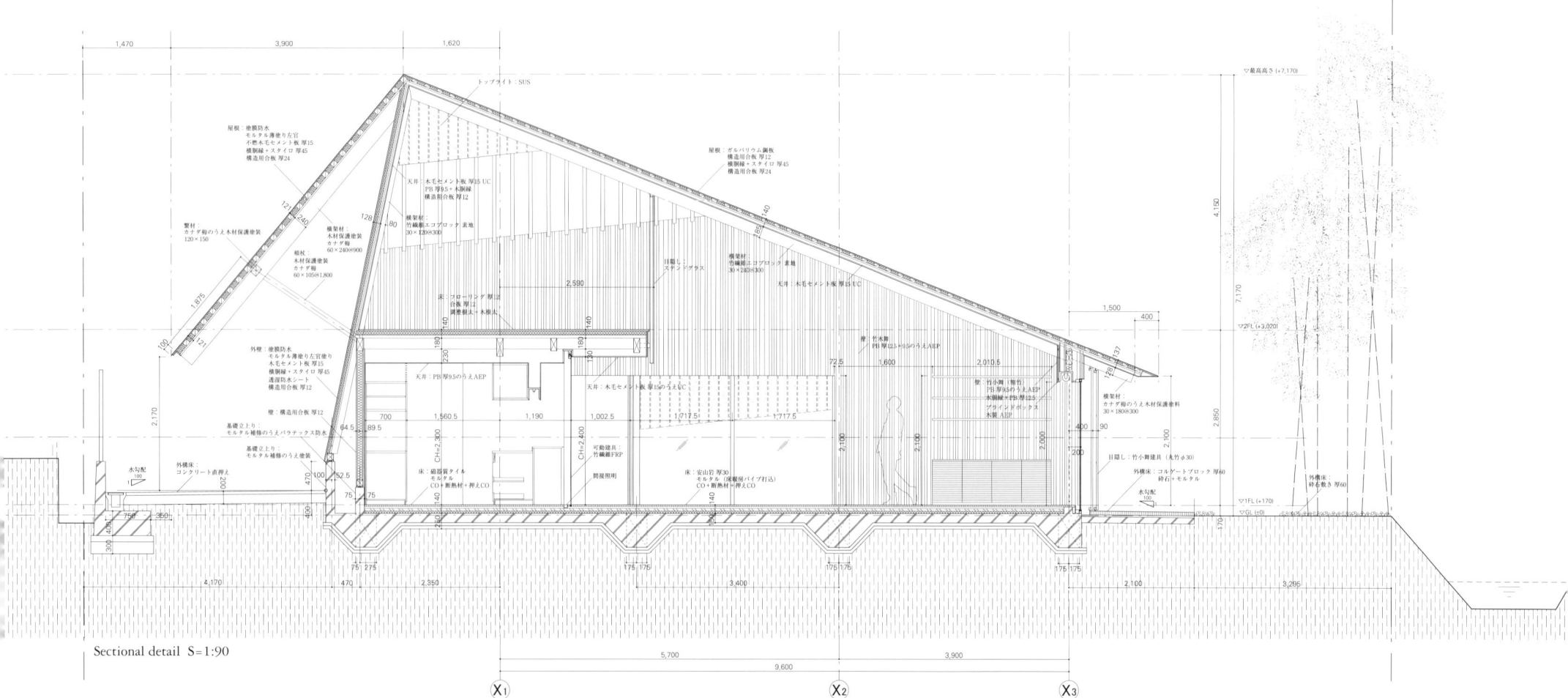

Sectional detail　S=1:90

Tatami room on second floor　2階和室△▽

Skylight on second floor　2階スカイライト

Bamboo/Fiber

竹林に隣接する敷地にインスピレーションを受けて,竹の様々な可能性に挑戦する家をつくった。

　まず,繊維に分解した竹を3,000 t のプレスで固形化した構造材料をみつけ,高強度,低伸縮である性質を利用し,大きなキャンティレバー構造の垂木として用いた。次に,竹の繊維を用いたFRPを,屋根材,内装材に用いた。通常,FRPはポリエチレン樹脂にガラス繊維を混入してつくられるが,ここはガラスのかわりに竹の繊維を混入するため,やわらかく暖かい琥珀の質感が生まれた。この竹FRPをアプローチ部分の屋根材に用いることで,不思議な光で満たされた,新しい軒下空間をつくることができた。

　前面道路との間には,竹小舞にヒントを得たスクリーンを配し,道路との間のフィルターとした。竹小舞はそもそも土壁の下地であったが,千利休はその美しさ,軽やかさに刺激され,土を塗らずに下地を露出する下地窓と呼ばれる奇抜なディテールを創案した。本プロジェクトでは,壁面全体をこの竹小舞のスクリーンで構成することで,下地窓の概念を拡張,発展させた。さらに竹にバラツキを与え(直径＝20mm, 30mm, 40mm),竹のピッチもランダムとし,竹を結ぶのにも通常の縄ヒモのかわりにワイヤーを用い,現代にふさわしいドライな竹のスクリーンを創造した。この竹スクリーンを媒介にして,路地の向こうの竹林と建築とがひとつにつながった。

2008-10 The Momofuku Ando Center of Outdoor Training
Komoro, Nagano, Japan

Overall view from northeast　北東より見る全景

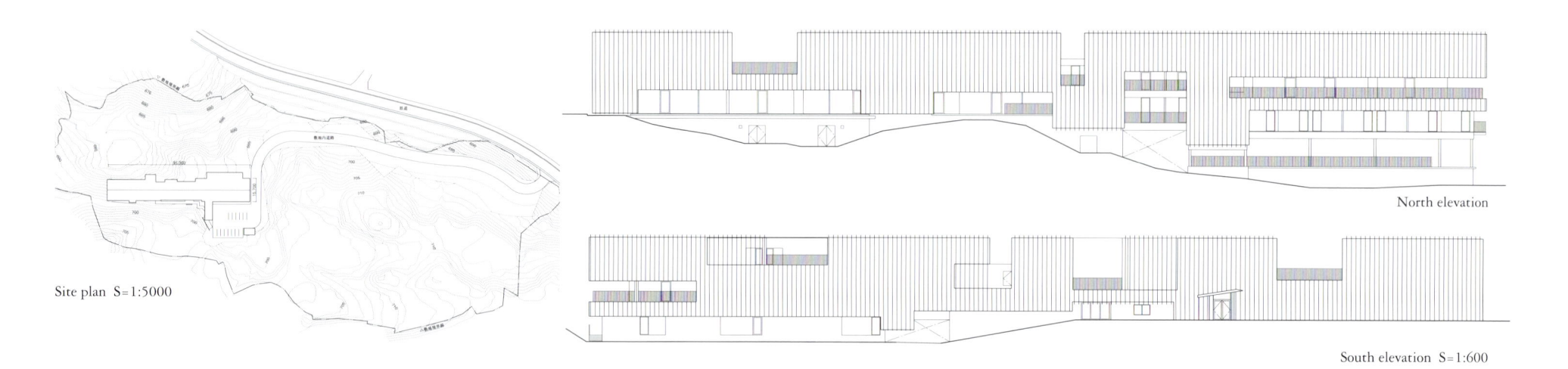

Site plan S=1:5000

North elevation

South elevation S=1:600

Basin on first floor　1階水盤テラス

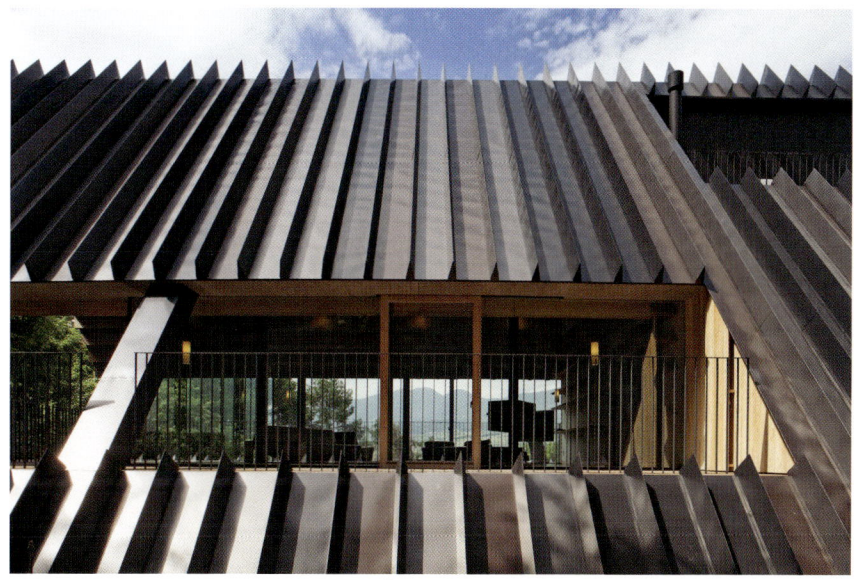

Terrace of communicatin room on second floor　2階談話室脇のテラス

North side terrace on first floor　1階北側テラス

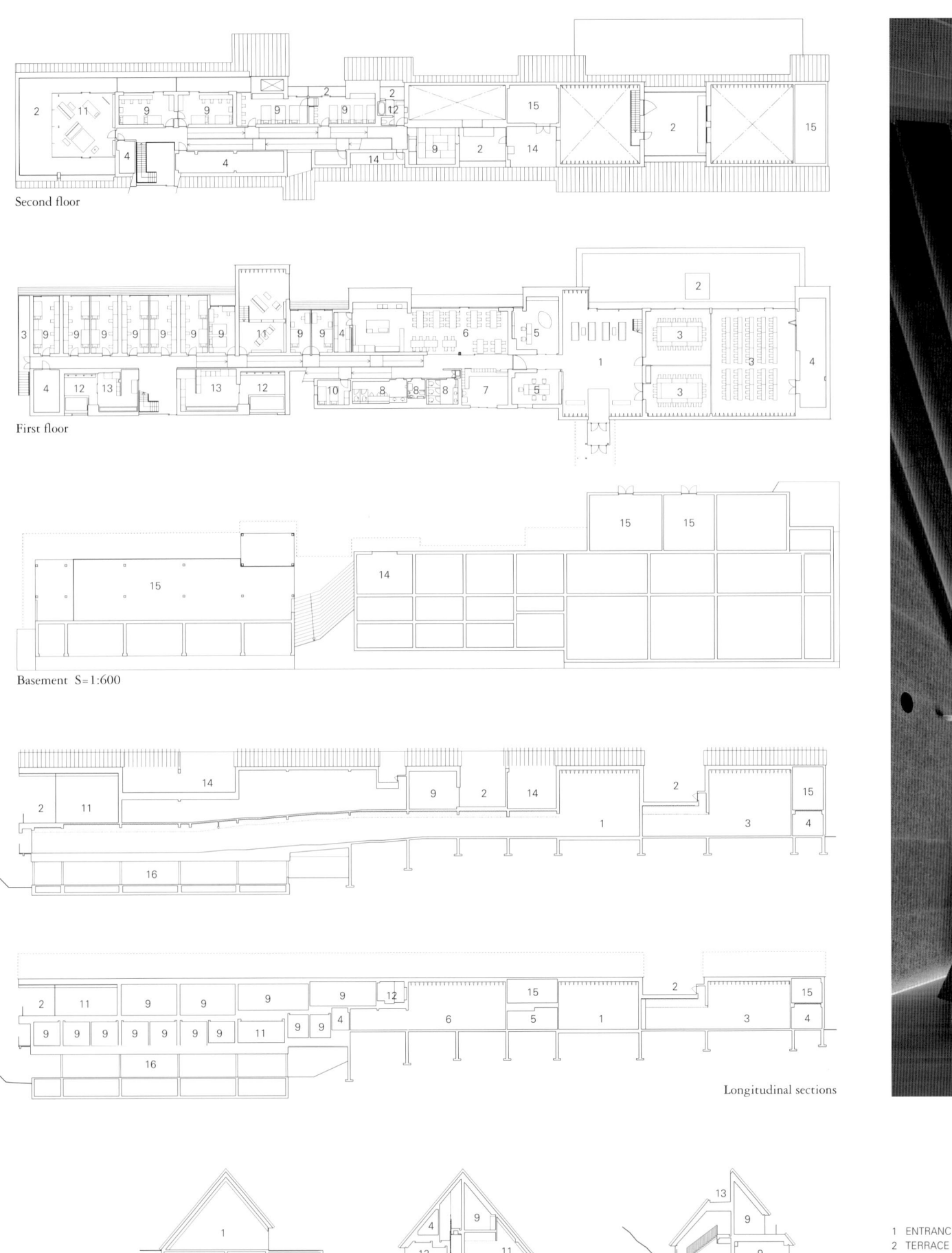

Second floor

First floor

Basement S=1:600

Longitudinal sections

Cross sections

1	ENTRANCE HALL	9	BEDROOM
2	TERRACE	10	NIGHT DUTY
3	MEETING ROOM	11	COMMUNICATION ROOM
4	STORAGE	12	BATHROOM
5	OFFICE	13	DRESSING ROOM
6	DINING ROOM / KITCHEN	14	OUTDOOR UNIT
7	EARTH FLOOR	15	MECHANICAL
8	WC	16	WORKSHOP

◁ △ Entrance hall on first floor　1階エントランスホール

This is an architecture to cultivate leaders for youth outdoor activities. We placed one long linear roof in the forest. We imagined a free and generous roof, underneath of which various activities to connect people to nature—such as exercise, learning, eating and sleeping—are conducted randomly. A box constrains people but a roof has more freedom because as a canopy it is like the crown of a tree which protects itself below from the harsh environment, a canopy protects people.

We had two devices to bring the architecture of a box closer to a roof. One was to create a metal roof that approximates a crown. The idea of 150 mm vertical fins used on the Baiso-in Temple (2003) was further developed here with 300 mm fins—hoping to approximate as much as possible the deep and subtle shading that leaves and branches create—in the architecture. In addition, using three different colors on the metal roof to tessellate, we tried to approximate the variety of colors of the forest.

The other device was uniting the interior space by one slope to provide the gentle continuity and variance similar to the ground in the forest. This slope is determined by the natural contour. We hoped to regenerate the sense of walking under the trees in this manmade environment called architecture.

Sectional detail S=1:150

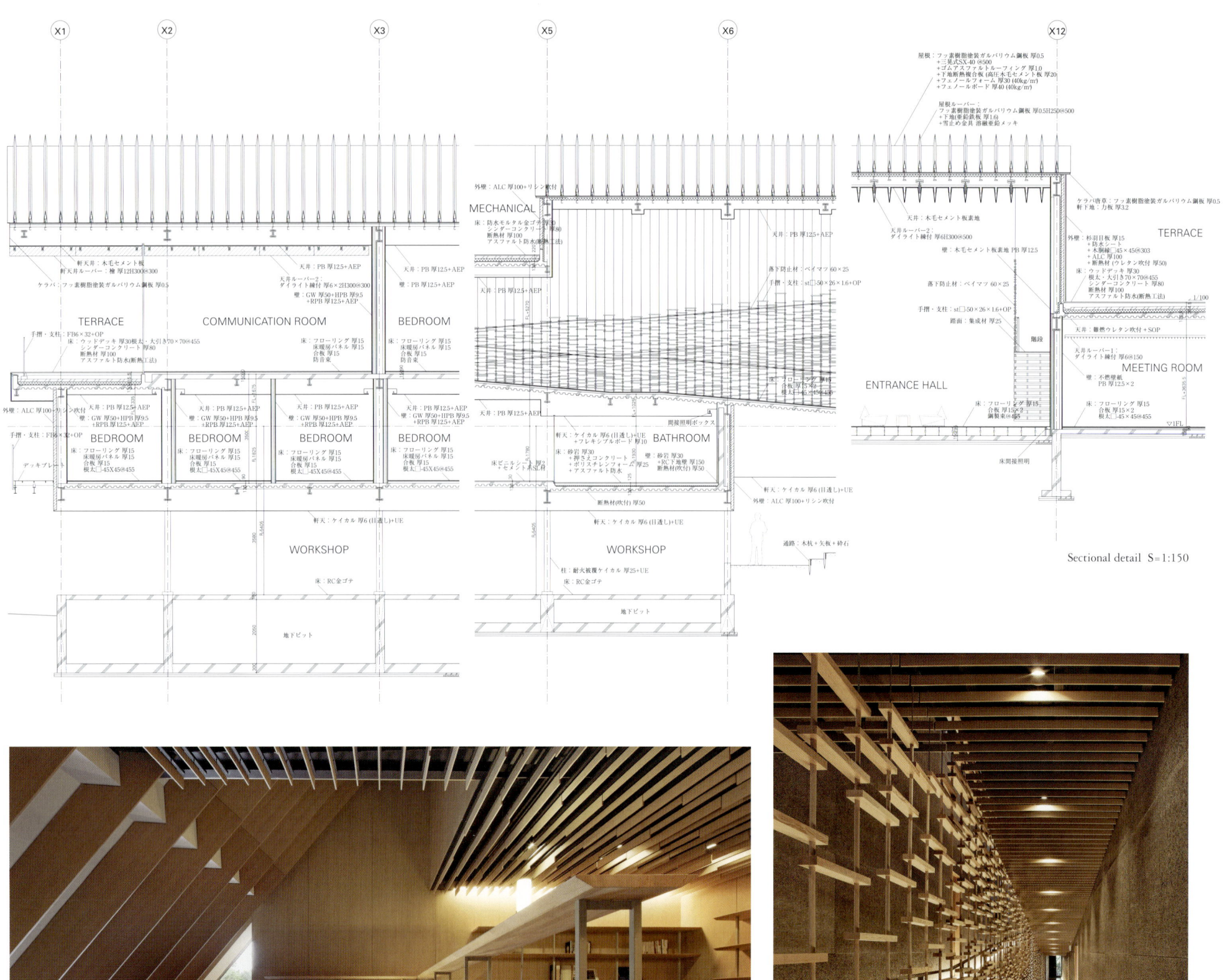

Communication room on first floor　1階談話室

Slope along bedroom　宿泊室に沿ったスロープ

Dining room on first floor　1階食堂

安藤百福記念 自然体験活動指導者養成センター

青少年の野外活動の指導者を,育成するための建築である。森の中に,ひとつの長い屋根を置いた。その長いリニアな屋根の下で,自然と人間とをつなぐ様々な活動が──運動,学習,食事,睡眠──ランダムに繰り広げられるような,自由で寛容な屋根をイメージした。箱は人を拘束するが,屋根は箱よりも自由であり,それは,樹冠(キャノピー)が過酷な環境から身体を守るようにして,人々を保護するからである。

建築を箱から屋根へと近づけるために,二つの工夫をした。ひとつは,金属板で葺かれた屋根を樹冠へと近づけるための工夫である。かつて,「梅窓院」(2003年)で試みた150mmの立ち上がりのハゼのアイディアをさらに発展させ,300mmのデプスをもつ彫りの深いハゼをつくることで,葉と枝とがつくる樹木の深く細かい陰に,建築を少しでも近づけたいと考えた。さらに,金属板に三つの異なる色を与えて,屋根をモザイク状に塗り分けることで,森の樹木のもつ多様な色彩に近づけたいと考えた。

もうひとつの工夫は,室内をひとつのスロープで統合し,そこに森の地面と同様のゆるやかな連続性と変化を与えようとした。このスロープは現地の地形の傾斜に従って決定され,屋根=樹冠の下の大地を歩くという感覚を,建築という人工環境の中でもう一度再生させたいと考えた。

Communication room at west end on second floor　2階東端の談話室

Tatami room on second floor　2階和室

2008-10　Prostho Museum Research Center
Kasugai, Aichi, Japan

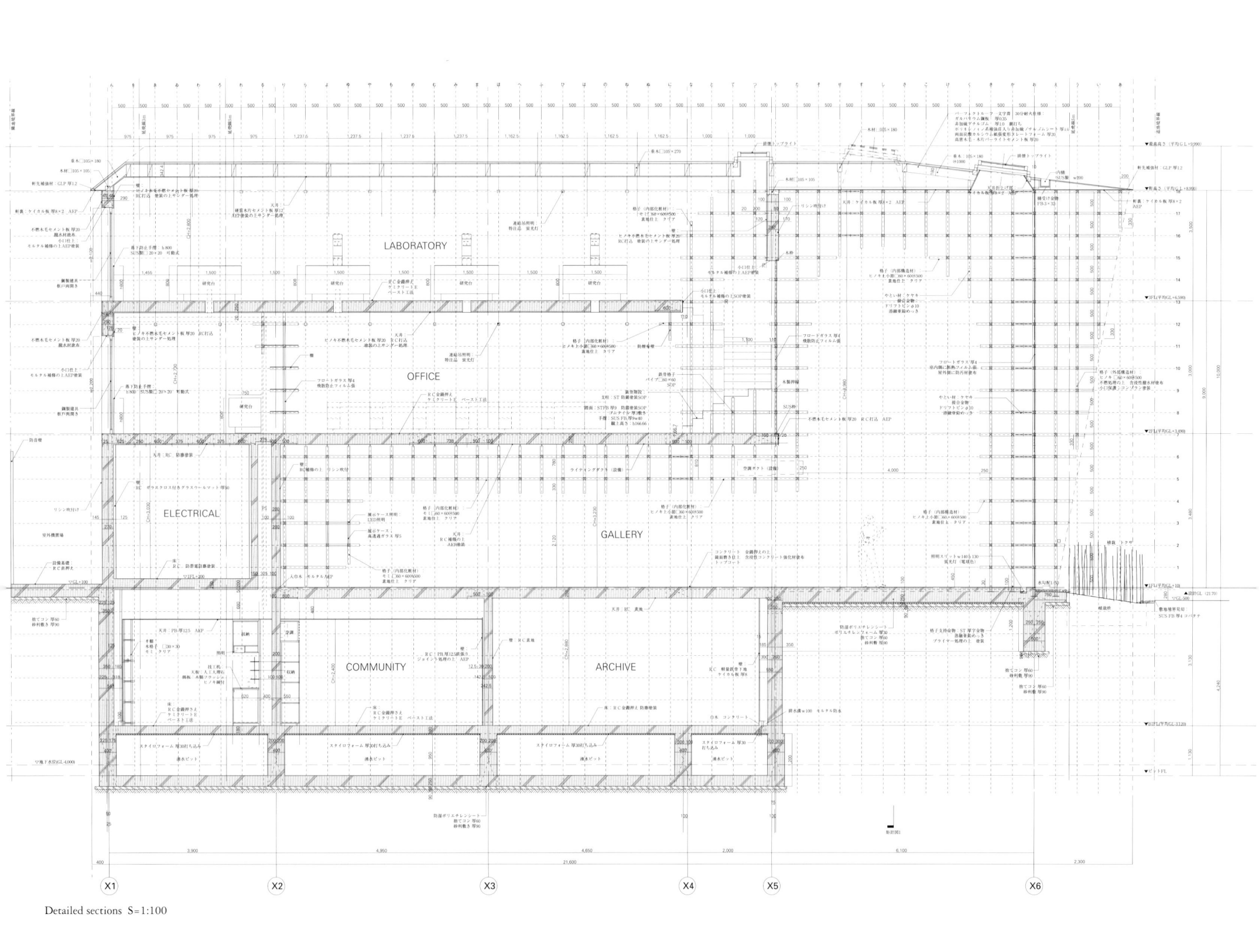

Detailed sections S=1:100

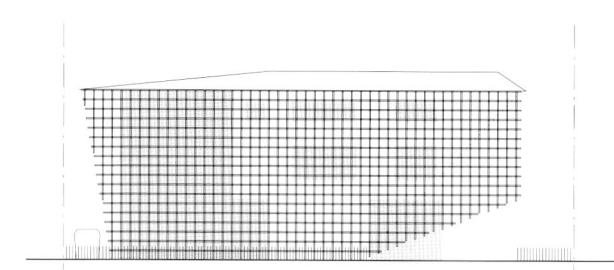

North elevation S=1:400

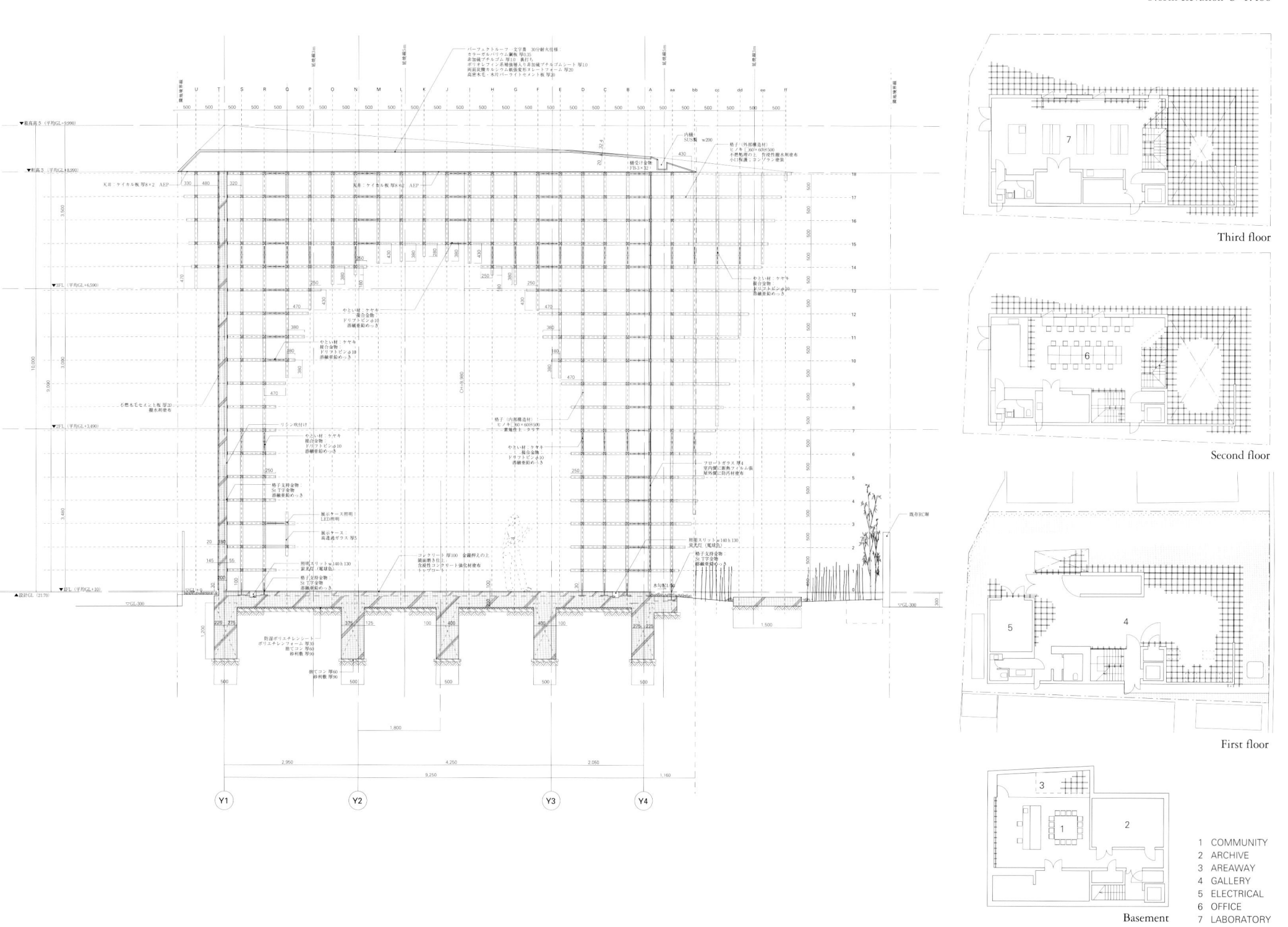

Third floor

Second floor

First floor

Basement

1 COMMUNITY
2 ARCHIVE
3 AREAWAY
4 GALLERY
5 ELECTRICAL
6 OFFICE
7 LABORATORY

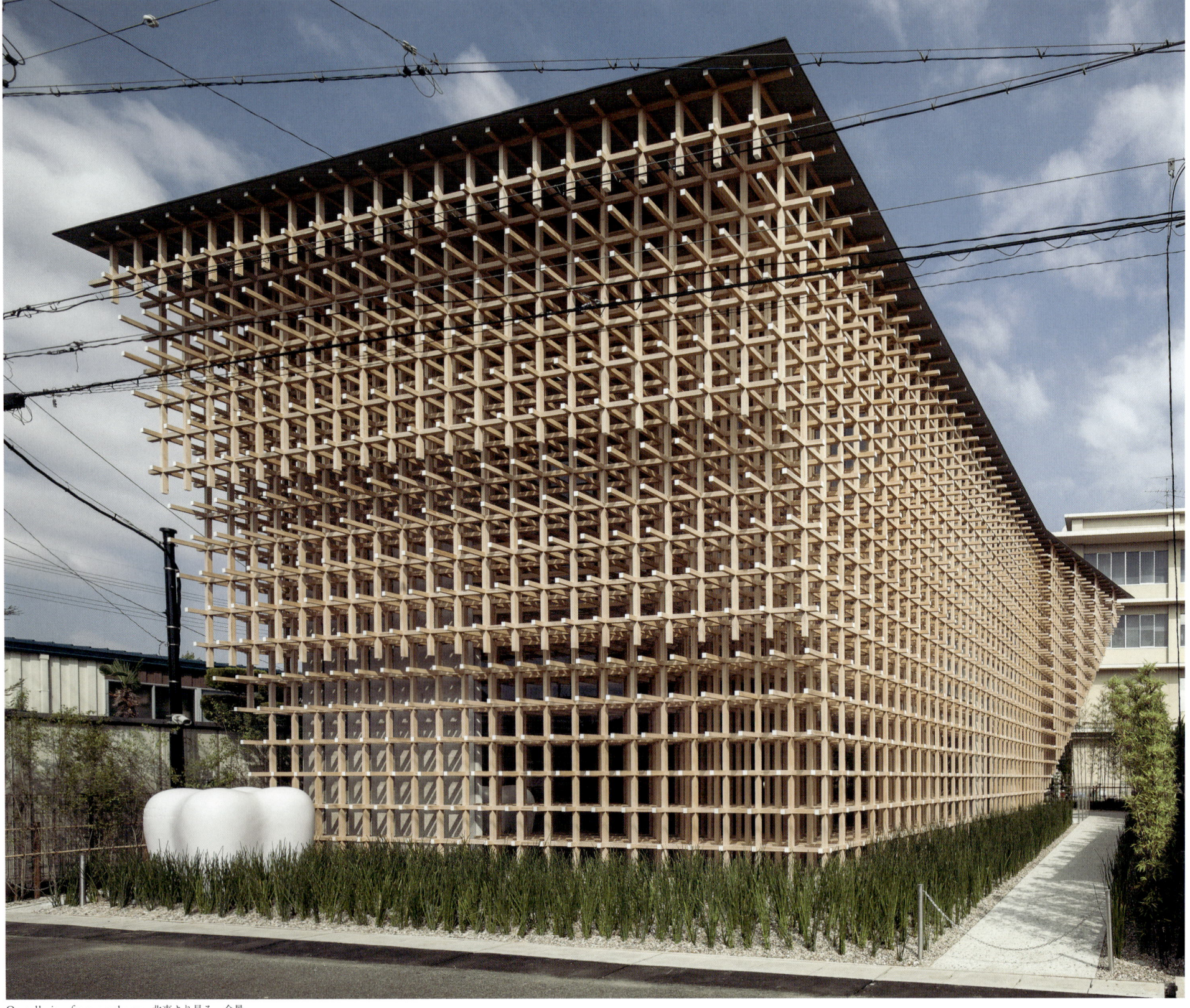

Overall view from northeast　北東より見る。全景

The architecture was built by expanding houndstooth system that adopts thin sticks to be three-dimensionally assembled with a simple action of twisting and fixing wooden rods and does not use any kind of nail or metal fittings. The hound's-tooth is one of the space frames called 'three-sides-hardening' or 'three-sides-tightening', fostered by Japanese carpenters who disliked metal fittings joints. Transmitted as children's toy, 'chidori', in Hidatakayama, we expanded the use of the 'chidori' system as a structure that supports architecture by basing a three-dimensional 50 cm cube grid consisted of thin 60 mm x 60 mm x 200 cm wooden sticks.

The three-dimensional 50 cm cube grid will be directly used as a showcase in the museum. The space, surrounded by six 50 cm cube grid, about 3 meters thick wall, produces tender and warm feeling like in a wooden cave. Because the grid protrudes out as it gets higher, the facade is protected from damages caused by rain.

Exhibition space　展示空間

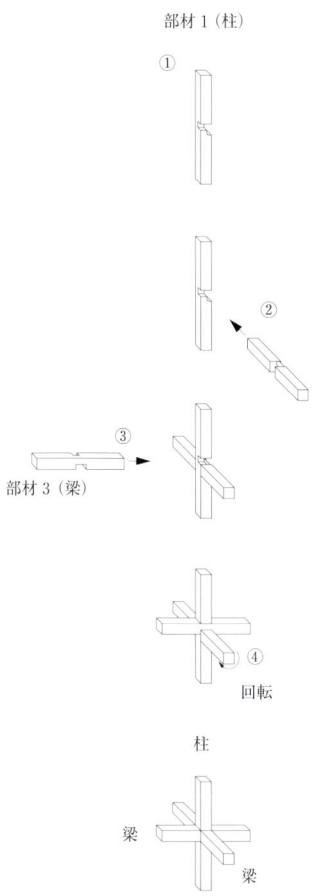

Diagram: 'chidori' structure

Detail: 'chidori'

プロソミュージアム・リサーチセンター

木の棒をひねって固定するという単純な動作だけで、いかなる釘も金物も用いずに木の細い棒を立体的に組み立てていく千鳥格子のシステムを拡大して、実際の建築をたてた。この千鳥格子は、金物によるジョイントを嫌う日本の大工によって育てられた、三方固め、三方締めなどと呼ばれるスペースフレームのひとつであり、飛騨高山では子供の玩具「千鳥」として伝えられてきた。われわれは、この「千鳥」のシステムを拡張し、60mm×60mm×200cmの細い木の棒を基本として、50cm角の立体グリッドを組み上げ、建築を支える構造体とした。

この50cm角の立体グリッドは、そのままこのミュージアムの展示ケースとしても用いられる。50cm角のグリッド6個分、約3mの壁厚で囲まれた空間は、木の洞窟のような、やわらかく暖かい雰囲気となった。ファサードにおいては、グリッドを上にいくに従ってせり出し、雨による劣化から守った。

2008-11 Lake House
Japan

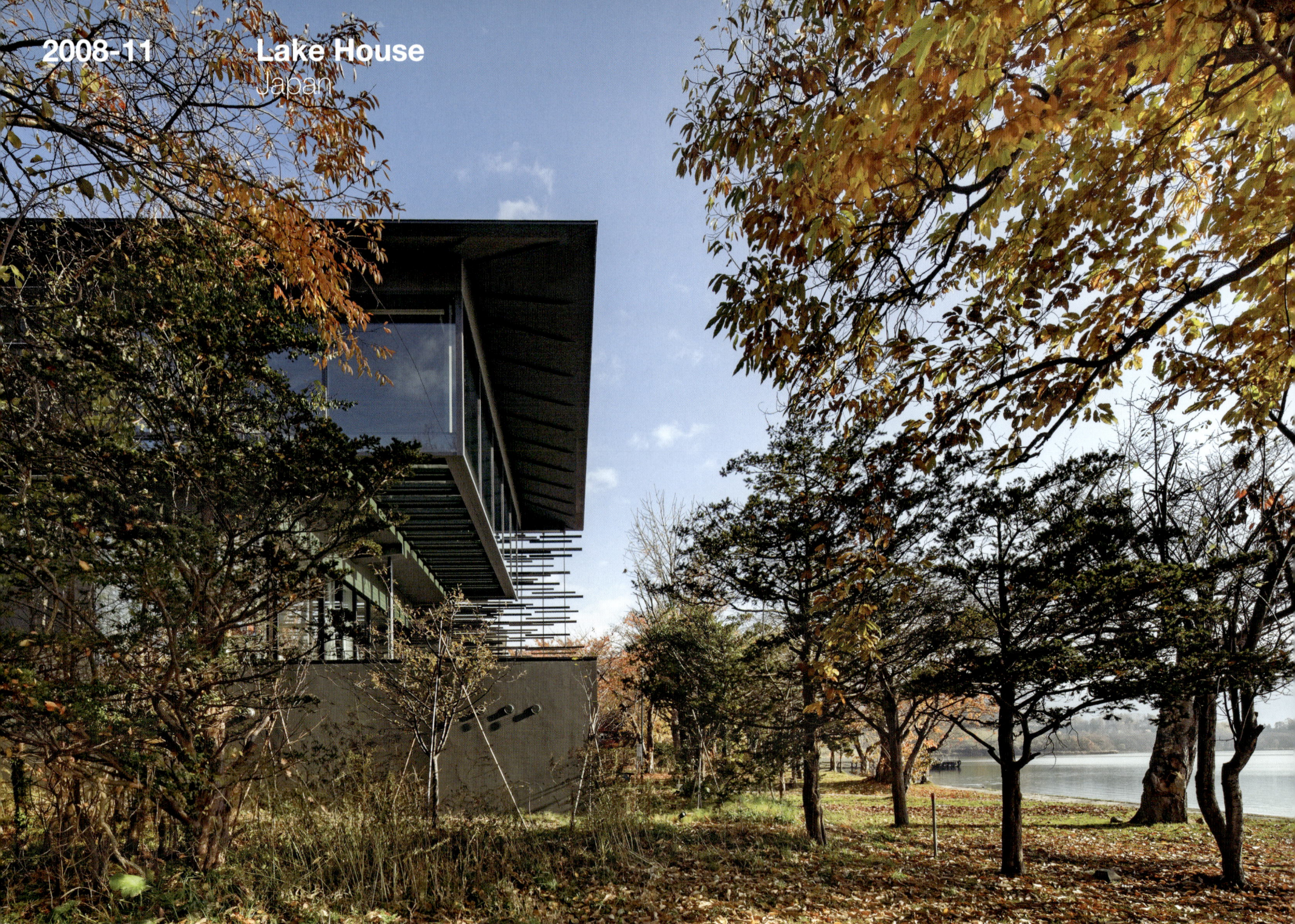

View from southwest　南西より見る

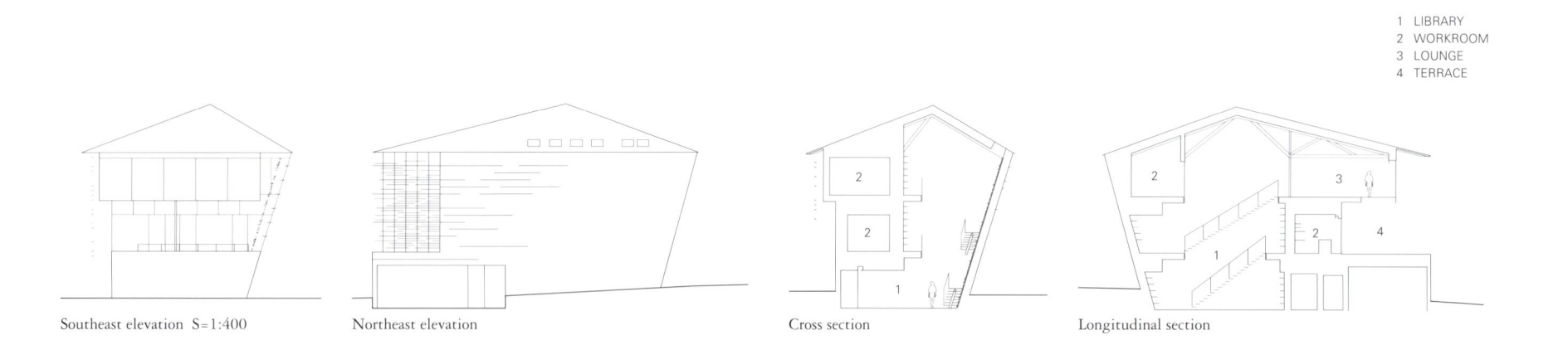

1　LIBRARY
2　WORKROOM
3　LOUNGE
4　TERRACE

Southeast elevation　S=1:400

Northeast elevation

Cross section

Longitudinal section

Terrace テラス

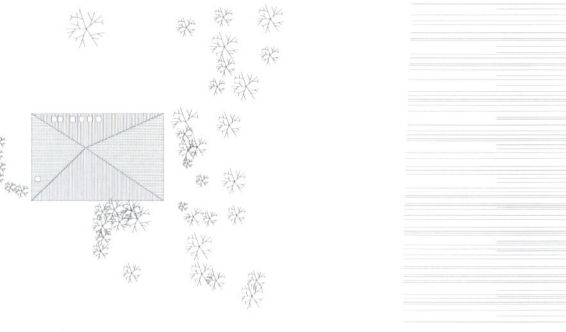

Site plan S=1:1200

1 LIBRARY
2 WORKROOM
3 LOUNGE
4 TERRACE
5 EV

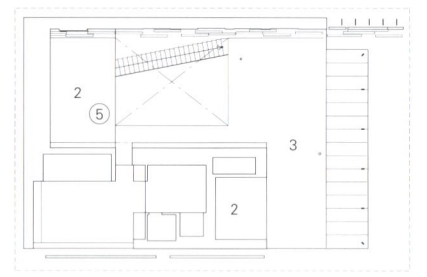

Level 3

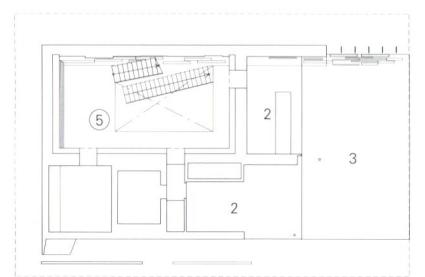

Level 2

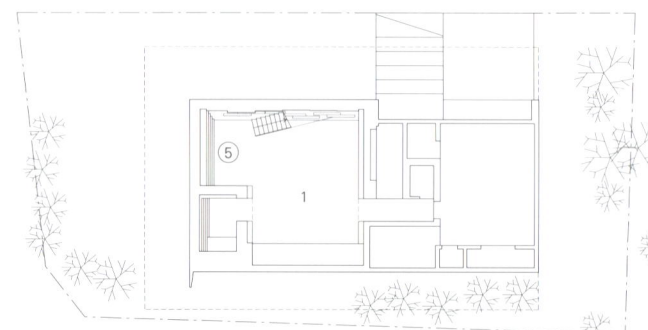

Level 1 S=1:400

Library: view toward workroom 3 on level 3　ライブラリー：3階，作業室3を見る

Sectional details: stacked stone pieces S=1:6

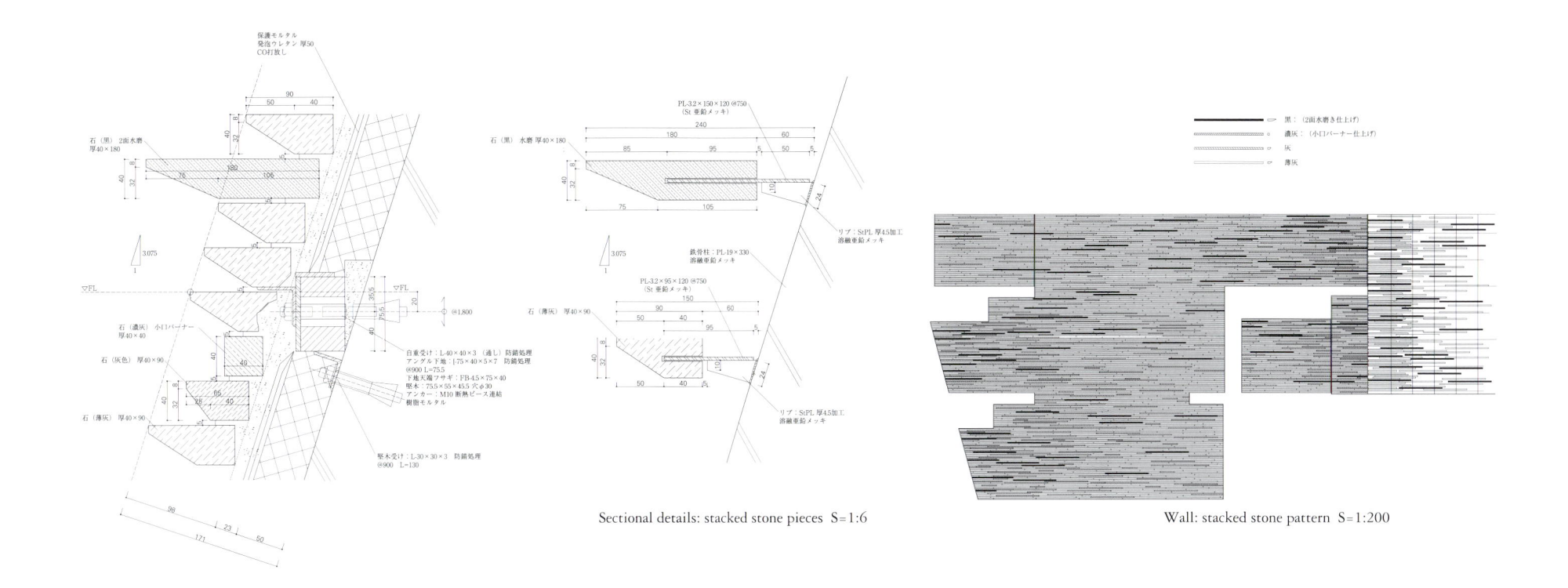

Wall: stacked stone pattern S=1:200

Library at level 1: void with staircase　1階ライブラリー：吹抜けを巡る階段

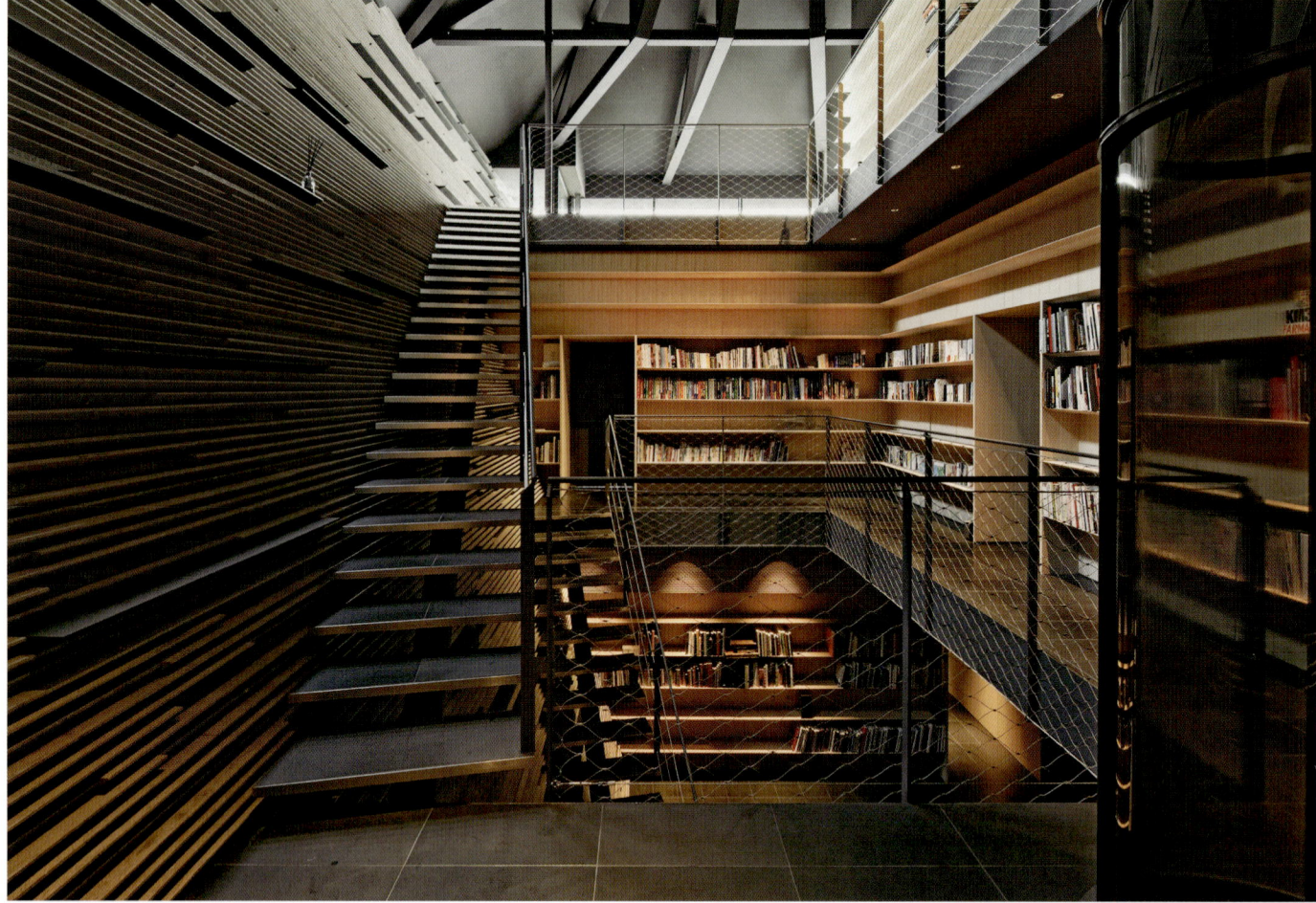

A resort villa, surrounded by a forest beside a lake.

As if leaves expand as trees grow higher, the form of the section was designed to look like a wedge. We often design architecture that has a bottom large section form like a mountain. However, this time, because the space above ground had a character as a lakeside park and it was difficult to eliminate public accesses, the upper floors were designed to be private spaces that is as if floating on the lake and made its mass small. As a result tree-like section emerged.

The tree-like architecture's center is a large three-storey cave-like library. The composition that living spaces surround the cave implies inheritance of the flux of time through books, which is the main theme of the house. It also suggests what would happen in the focus of lives in the house.

The exterior and the interior walls are made of a pile of sheet andesite that is found plenty around the site. The boards that are 40 mm thick and 1,500 mm long were sliced off in oblique up to 8 mm at the edge. Furthermore, using four slightly different colored stone helped to create the impression of thin leaves. The stone that floats like leaves is a sensor that transcends variations of light in a day beside the lake and changes of four seasons.

Library at level 2: view toward southeast　2階ライブラリー：南東を見る

Lake House

湖のほとりに樹木に囲まれて建つ別荘である。

　樹木が枝葉を広げるように，上層にいくほど大きいくさび形の断面形状とした。われわれは山のような底部の大きい断面形状をもつ建築を設計することが多いが，今回は地上部分が湖畔の公園的な性格を持ち，パブリックアクセスを排除することが難しかったため，上層階に湖上に浮遊するようなプライベート空間を確保して，地上部を小さくし，結果として樹木状の断面形状が出現した。

　この1本の樹木状建築の中心部は，3層吹抜けの大きな洞（ホラ）状の書庫となっている。その洞の周囲を生活空間が取り囲む構成は，書庫──本──時間の継承──こそがこの家の中心的テーマであり，この家でとり行われる生活の中心でもあることを暗示している。

　外壁，内壁には，敷地周辺に豊富な安山岩を板状にして積み上げている。厚さ40mm，長さ1,500mmの板を先端8mmにまで斜めに削ぎ落とし，さらに4種類の微妙に色の異なった石を使うことで，薄い木の葉のような印象をつくり出すことができた。木の葉のように漂う石は，湖畔の1日の光の変化，四季の移ろいを伝えてくれるセンサーである。

Lounge　ラウンジ

View toward southeast from workroom 4 on level 3　3階，作業室4より南東を見る

Lounge: looking east　ラウンジ：東を見る

Lounge: view toward southeast　ラウンジ：南東を見る

2008-11 Xinjin Zhi Museum
Chengdu, Sichuan, China

Overall view from northwest　北西より見る全景

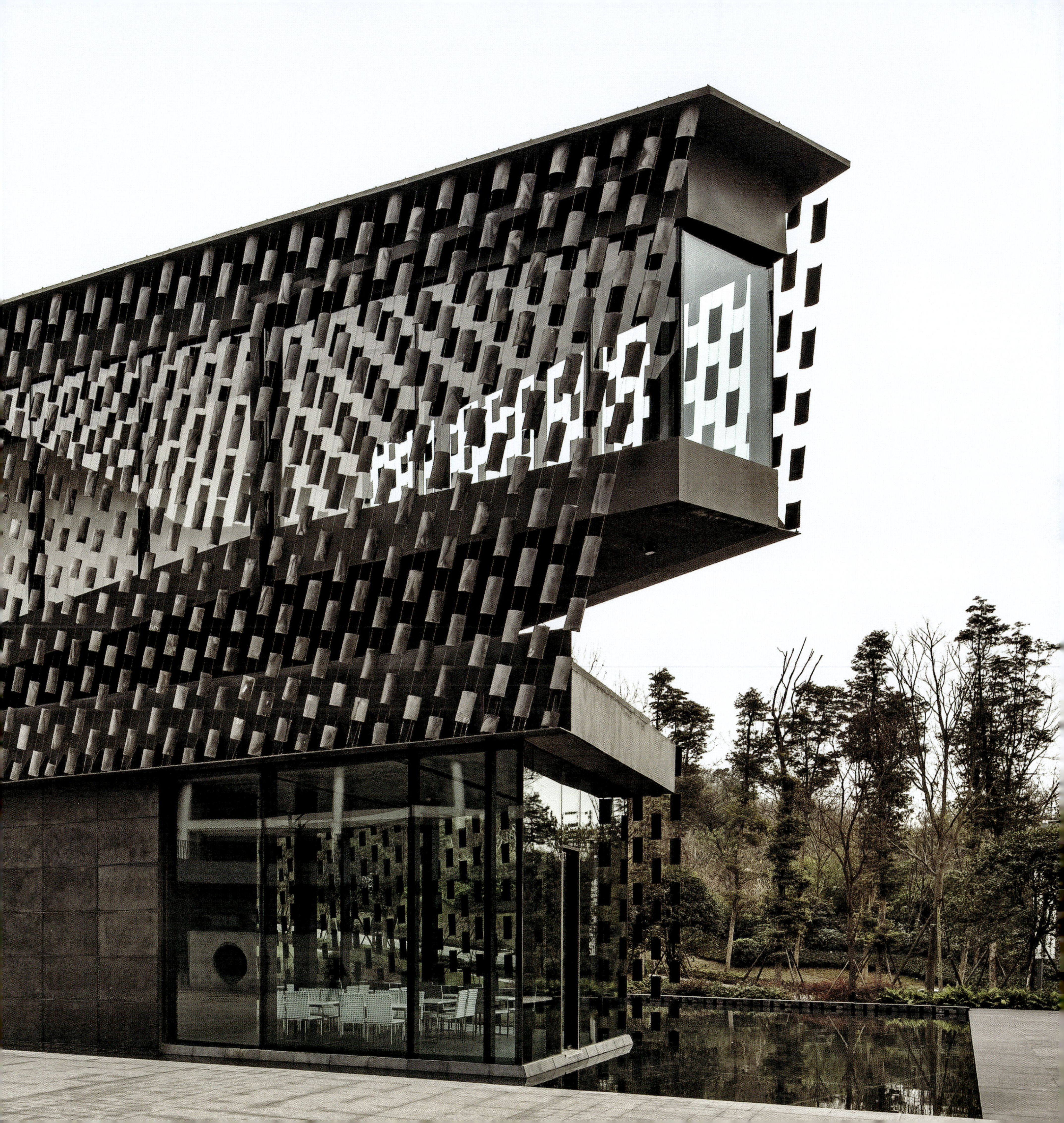

Evening view from southwest　南西側夕景

Corner of southeast　南東隅部

Curved wall with tile-screen on east　東面，カーブする瓦スクリーンのディテール

Exhibition room on basement　地下1階展示室

Entrance from parking on basement to exhibition room　地下1階駐車場から展示室へ至るエントランス

Exhibition room on basement　地下1階展示室

Site plan S=1:10000

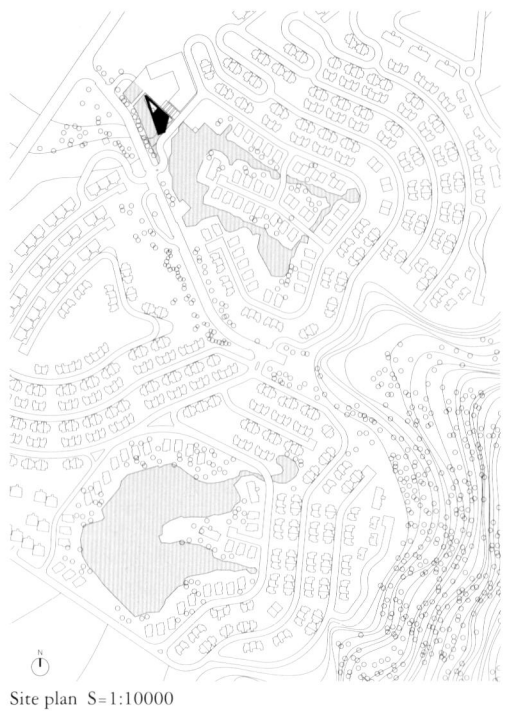

The museum was built at the foot of Mt. Laojunshan, Taoism's sacred place, located in the suburb of Xinjin County in Sichuan, China. The building was designed not as a box, but as a spiral route that reaches to Mt. Laojunshan. In order the spiral museum to harmonize with the surrounding environment, two devices such as water surfaces and a tile screen were utilized. The method of using a water surface for a purpose to connect architecture and a setting has been developed since Water/Glass (1995). This time, however, I considered to link the building and the milieu three dimensionally by employing two water surfaces, each in a different level.

The local tiles fabricated by burning them off on a field were used as a screen that covers the building. Chinese tiles are much thinner than Japanese ones and I was always fascinated by the lightness and the thinness. The unevenness of colors and shapes of the tiles produced with a primitive method of field burning was utilized as much as possible. By showing the tiles' unevenness that is not seen in Japanese manufactured tiles, we expected an organic architecture that is only possible to be built in China.

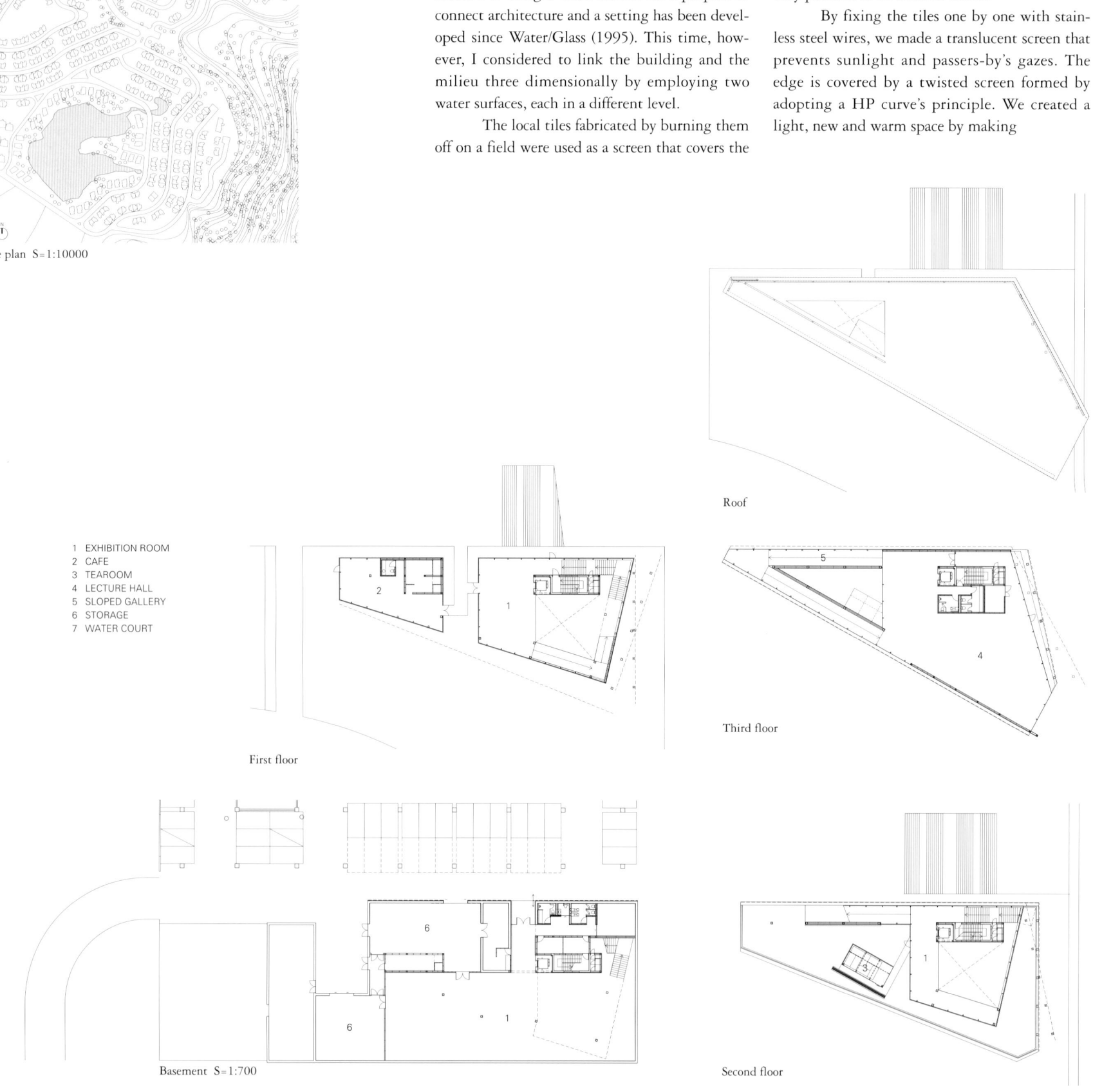

By fixing the tiles one by one with stainless steel wires, we made a translucent screen that prevents sunlight and passers-by's gazes. The edge is covered by a twisted screen formed by adopting a HP curve's principle. We created a light, new and warm space by making

1 EXHIBITION ROOM
2 CAFE
3 TEAROOM
4 LECTURE HALL
5 SLOPED GALLERY
6 STORAGE
7 WATER COURT

First floor

Basement S=1:700

Roof

Third floor

Second floor

新津 知・芸術館

中国四川省新津郊外,道教の聖地老君山のふもとに立つ美術館。箱としての美術館ではなく,老君山へと到るスパイラル状の経路としての美術館を創造した。その経路状の美術館を,周囲の環境と融合させるために,水面と瓦のスクリーンという二つの装置を用いた。水面によって建築と環境を接続する手法は「水／ガラス」(1995年)以来展開してきた方法だが,今回はレベルの違う二つの水面を用いて建築と環境とを立体的につなごうと考えた。

建物を覆うスクリーンには,野焼きの工法で製造された地元の瓦を用いた。中国の瓦は日本の瓦よりもはるかに薄く,その軽さ,薄さに魅力を感じていた。野焼きという原始的工法で製造された瓦の,色のムラ,形のバラツキも可能な限り活かした。日本の工業化された瓦にはないバラツキを使って,中国でしかつくれない有機的建築を目指した。

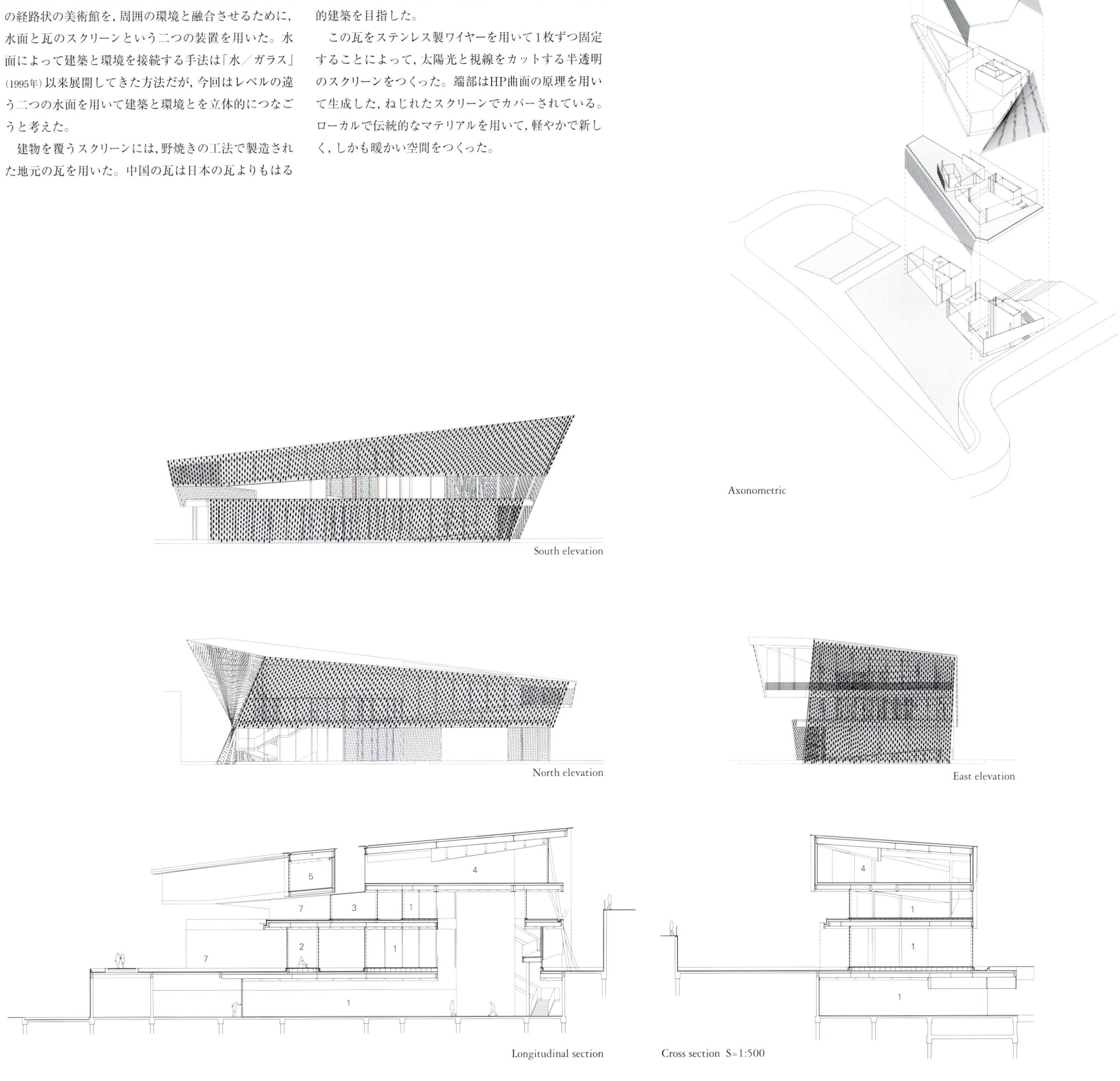

この瓦をステンレス製ワイヤーを用いて1枚ずつ固定することによって,太陽光と視線をカットする半透明のスクリーンをつくった。端部はHP曲面の原理を用いて生成した,ねじれたスクリーンでカバーされている。ローカルで伝統的なマテリアルを用いて,軽やかで新しく,しかも暖かい空間をつくった。

Axonometric

South elevation

North elevation

East elevation

Longitudinal section

Cross section S=1:500

Exhibition room on first floor　1階展示室

Exhibition room on second floor: view toward tearoom　2階展示室：茶室を見る

Sectional detail S=1:100

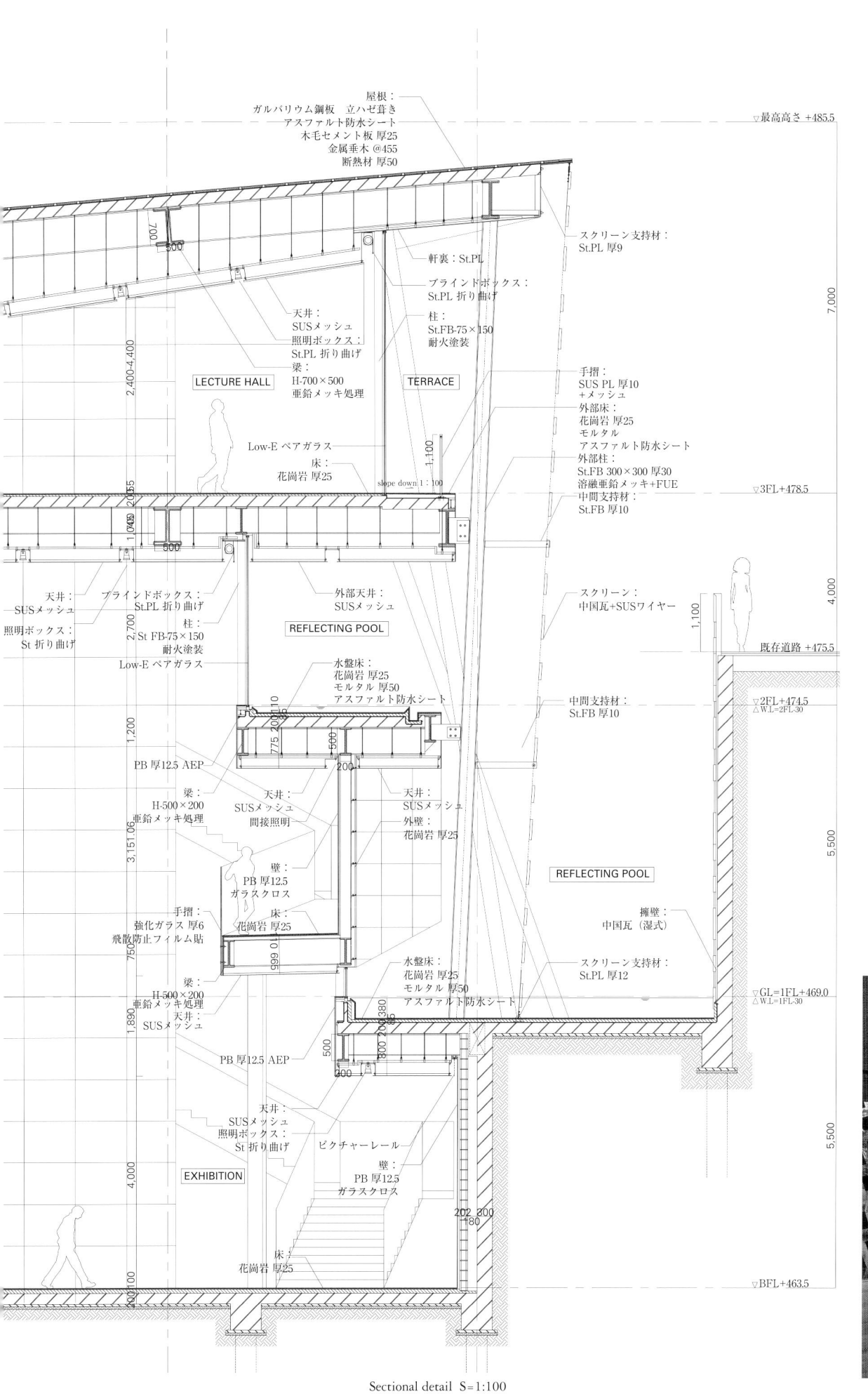

Tile-screen 瓦スクリーン

View toward cafe from exhibition room on first floor　1階展示室よりカフェを見る

2008-12 **Aore Nagaoka**
Nagaoka, Niigata, Japan

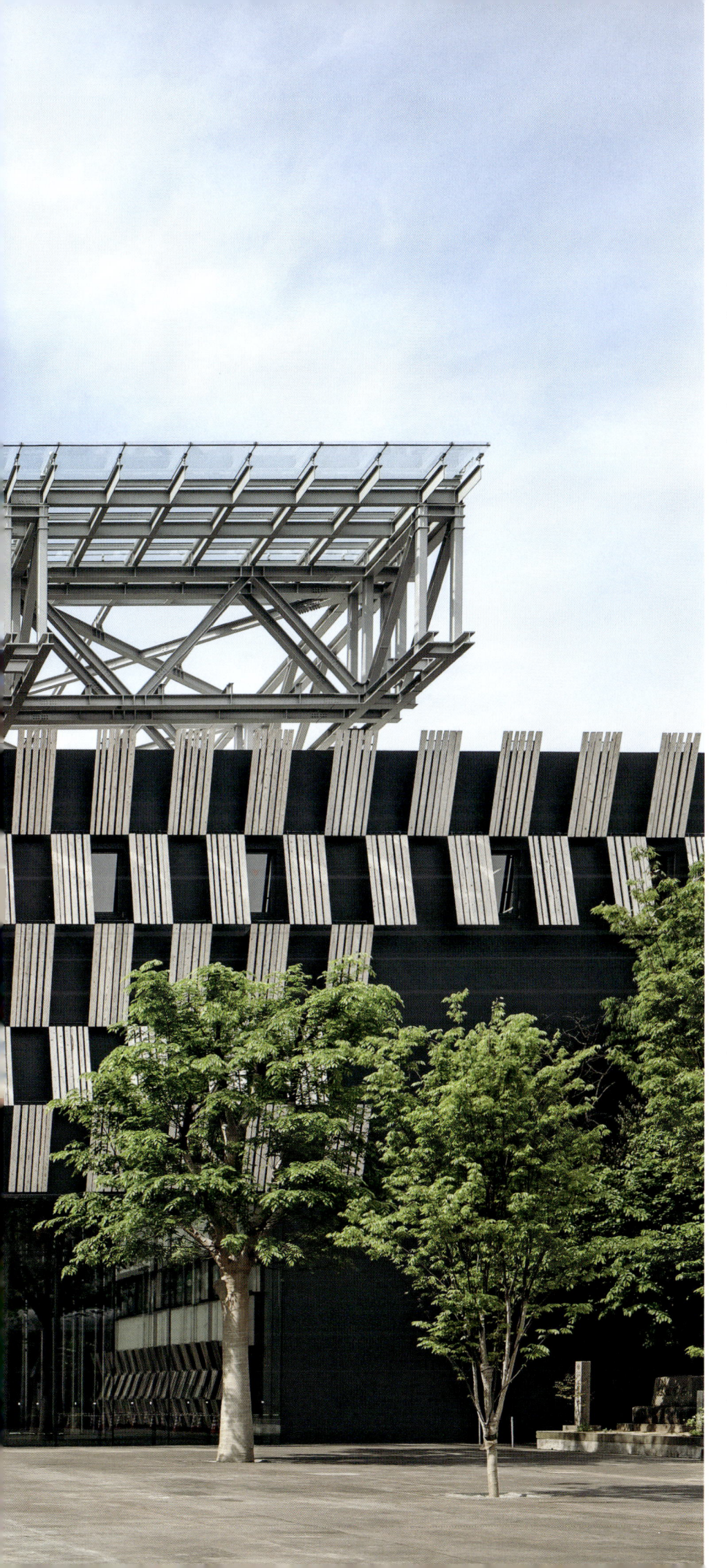

The public buildings in the 20th century were driven away from the centers of the city seeking larger sites and it was a kind of destiny to be a concrete container isolated in the middle of an asphalt car park at the outskirts of town. We reversed that flow and tried to create a timber public building in the middle of the city with a courtyard that opens to the city.

The courtyard we aimed for was a soft and warm intermediate space like the Doma of traditional Japanese houses, 'Naka-Doma' rather than a western style 'hard square'. To invite people in, even in a heavy snow area, this Doma has a glass roof and the dappled sunlight comes in from between the gaps in the solar panels and timber panels. The ground of the Doma is made based on the traditional method called 'Tataki' (firm the ground) and we improved the durability to resist the hard use. This 'Naka-Doma' is in the center of the complex and unites with the low-rise city hall, local council assembly and arena annexes. The local assembly room at the corner on the ground floor covered by glass is not just a symbol of an open venue to the citizen assembly but we also assume it could be used as an event hall for the citizens, for weddings etc.

Local cedar from within a 15 km radius is used extensively for both the exterior and interior. Applying it randomly with bark, we pursued a softness and warmth that industrial products cannot achieve. We aimed to overcome the hard and cold box container of 20th century public buildings.

アオーレ長岡

20世紀の公共建築は, 広い敷地を求めて街の中心から離れ, 町外れのアスファルトの駐車場の中に孤立する, コンクリートのハコモノとなる宿命をたどった。その流れを反転し, 街の中心に, 街に開かれた中庭型の「木の公共建築」をつくろうと考えた。

中庭は西洋型の「固い広場」を目指さずに, かつての日本の民家の土間のようなやわらかく温もりのある中間領域「ナカドマ」を目標としてデザインされた。雪国の冬でも人々が集まる屋根付きの土間となるよう, 屋根はガラス張りとし, 太陽光パネル, 木製パネルの隙間から木漏れ日状のやさしい光が中庭にふりそそぐ。床は, 昔ながらの土を固めたタタキを基本とし, 耐久性を改良して苛酷な使用にも耐える仕様とした。この市民が集い語り合う「ナカドマ」を中心として, 低層の市役所棟, 議会棟, アリーナ棟がひとつに統合される。議場はガラス張りとして1階のコーナー部に置かれ, 開かれた議会のシンボルとなるだけではなく, 結婚式などの様々な市民イベントの会場としての利用も想定した。

外装, 内装には地元産(15km以内)の杉材を多用し, しかも皮つきでランダムな貼り方をすることで, 工業製品にはない, やわらかさ, 暖かさを徹底して追求した。20世紀型のかたく冷たいハコモノからの脱却を目指した。

View of northern entrance of 'Naka-Doma' from plaza　マエニワよりナカドマの北側入口を見る

View of 'Naka-Doma' from main arena　メインアリーナよりナカドマを見る

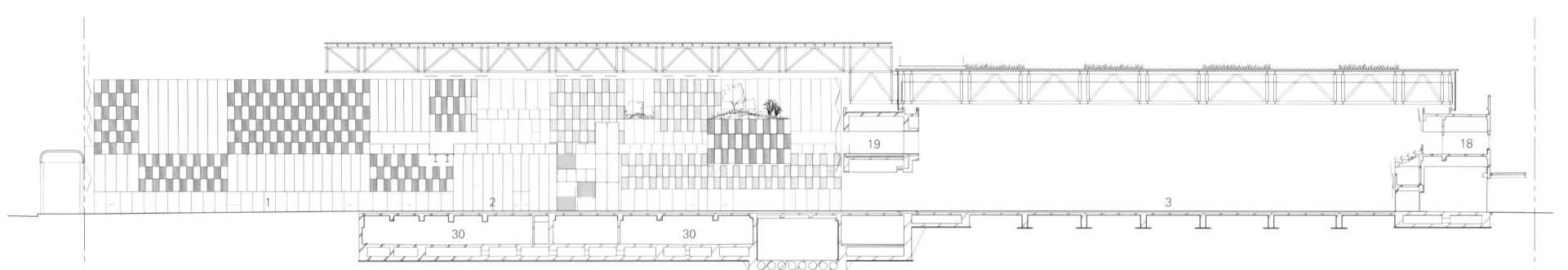

'Naka-Doma': east elevation and section S=1:750

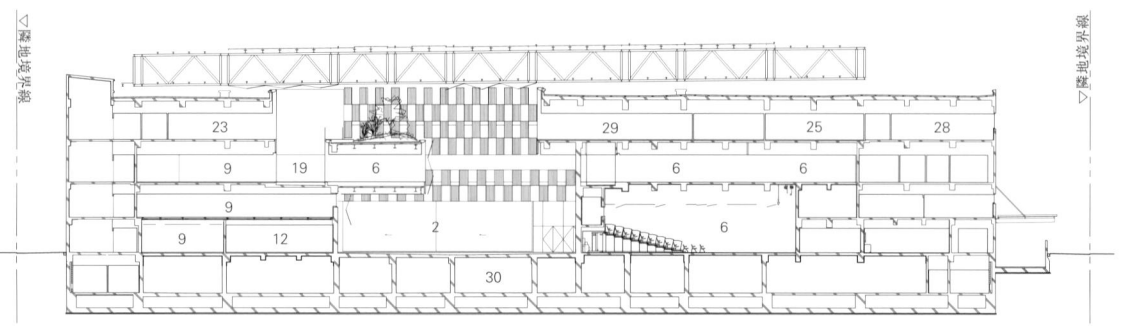

'Naka-Doma': south elevation and section

View toward east wing from terrace on third floor of west wing　西棟３階テラスよりブリッジ越しに東棟の連なりを見る

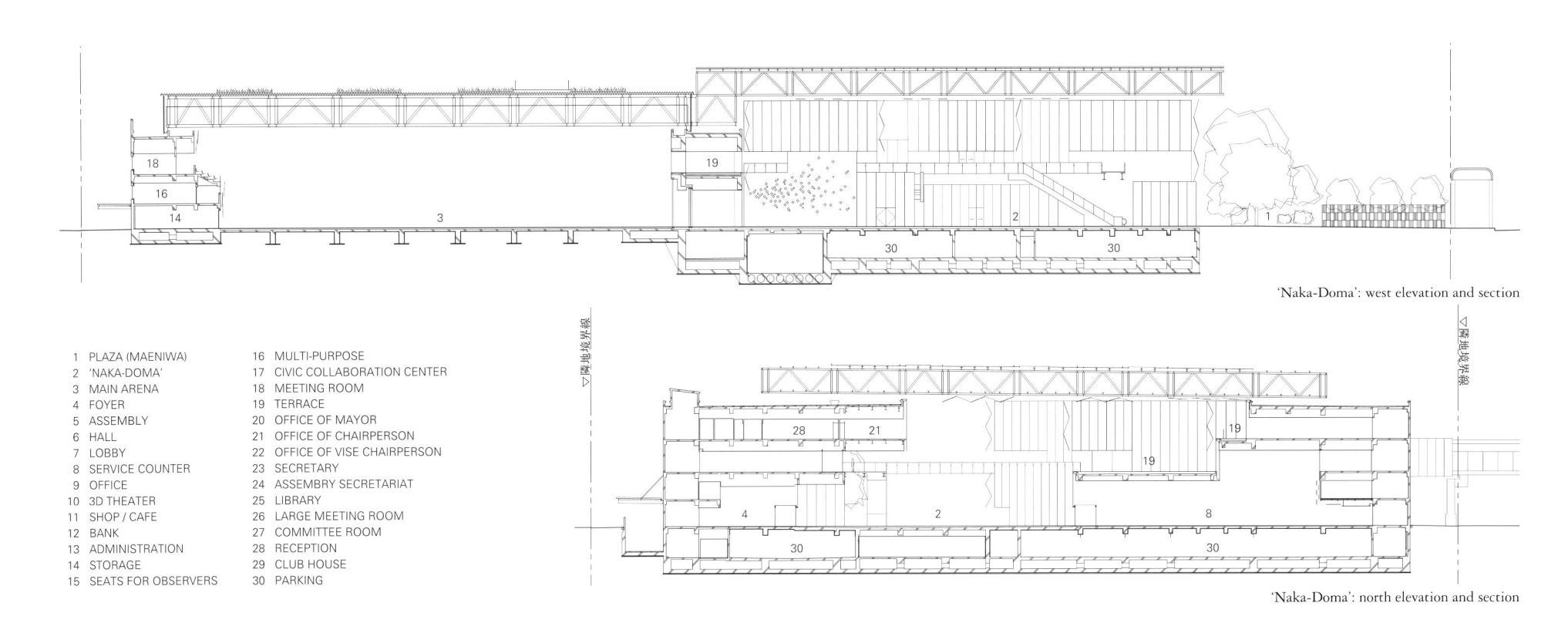

'Naka-Doma': west elevation and section

1	PLAZA (MAENIWA)	16	MULTI-PURPOSE
2	'NAKA-DOMA'	17	CIVIC COLLABORATION CENTER
3	MAIN ARENA	18	MEETING ROOM
4	FOYER	19	TERRACE
5	ASSEMBLY	20	OFFICE OF MAYOR
6	HALL	21	OFFICE OF CHAIRPERSON
7	LOBBY	22	OFFICE OF VISE CHAIRPERSON
8	SERVICE COUNTER	23	SECRETARY
9	OFFICE	24	ASSEMBRY SECRETARIAT
10	3D THEATER	25	LIBRARY
11	SHOP / CAFE	26	LARGE MEETING ROOM
12	BANK	27	COMMITTEE ROOM
13	ADMINISTRATION	28	RECEPTION
14	STORAGE	29	CLUB HOUSE
15	SEATS FOR OBSERVERS	30	PARKING

'Naka-Doma': north elevation and section

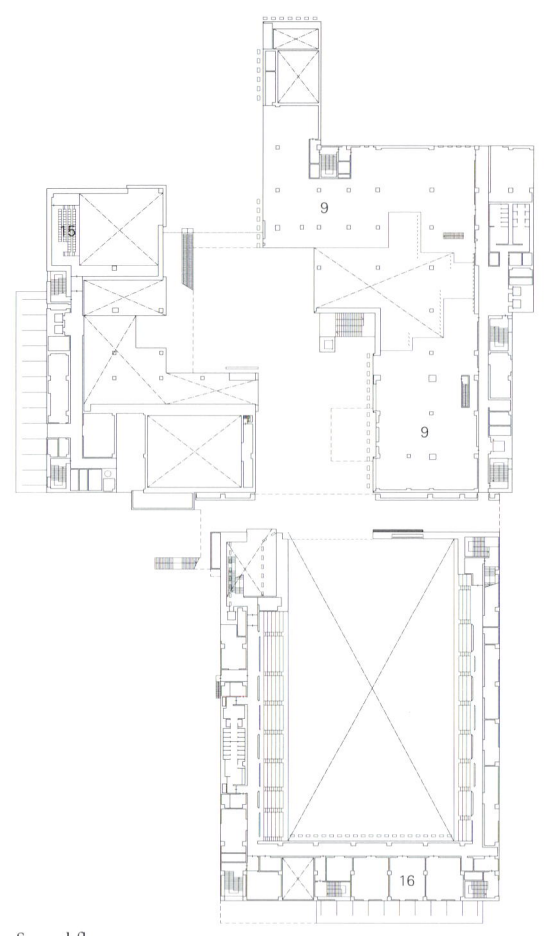

Second floor

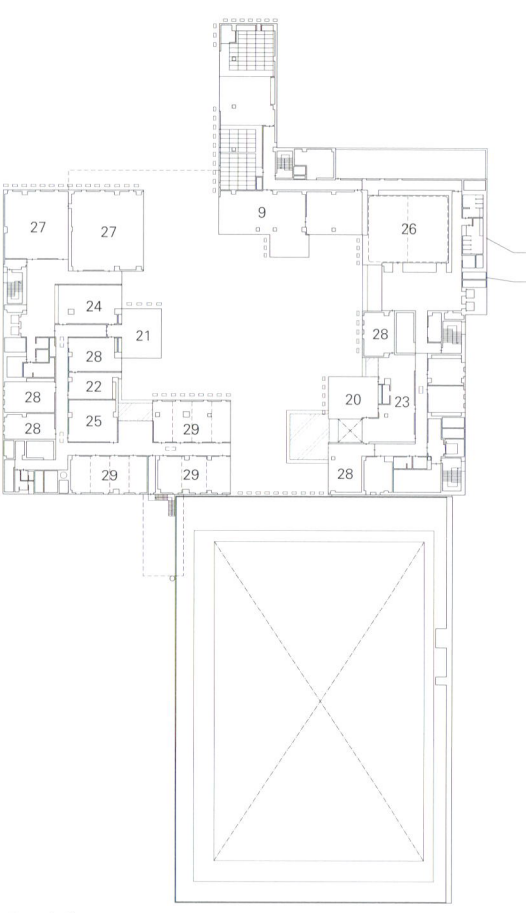

Fourth floor

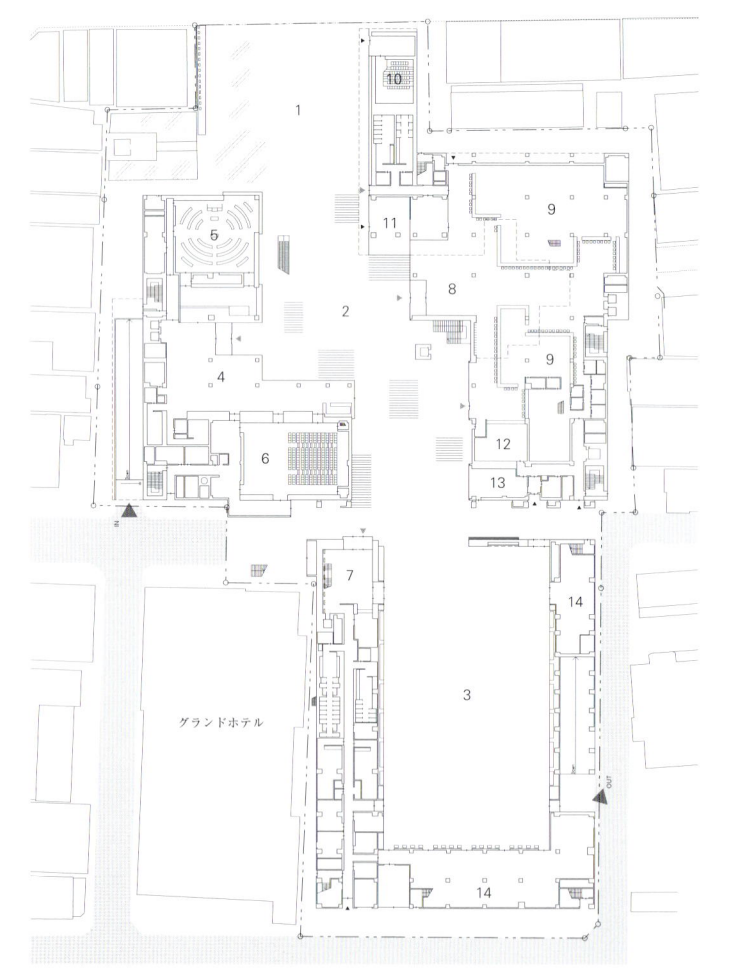

Ground floor S=1:1500

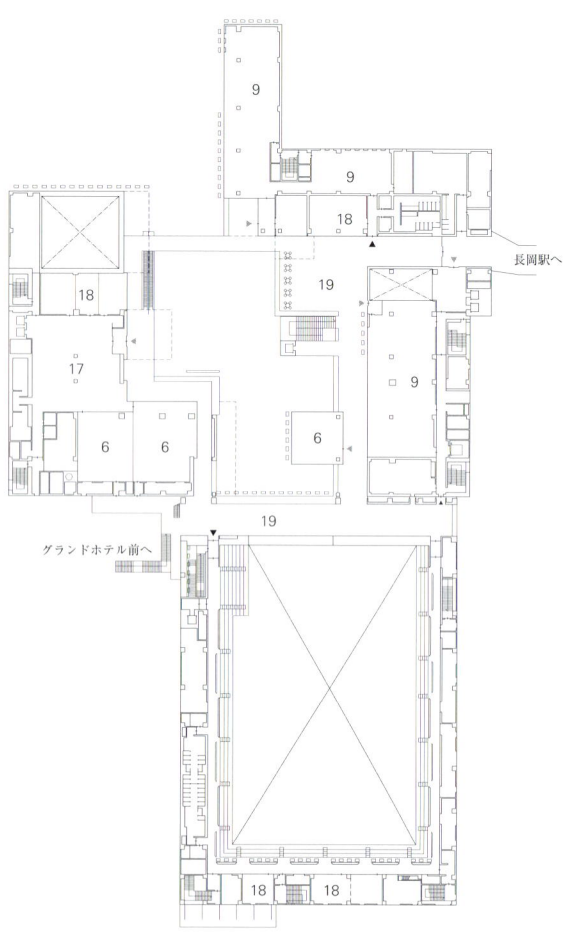

Third floor

198

'Naka-Doma': view from northern bridge on third floor　ナカドマ。3階北側ブリッジより見る

Downward view of service counter from office on third floor of east wing　東棟3階，市役所執務室より総合窓口を見下ろす

Service counter on first floor of east wing　東棟1階，市役所総合窓口

Civic hall 市民交流ホール

Assembly 市議会議場

2006-13 Kabuki-za Building
Chuo, Tokyo, Japan

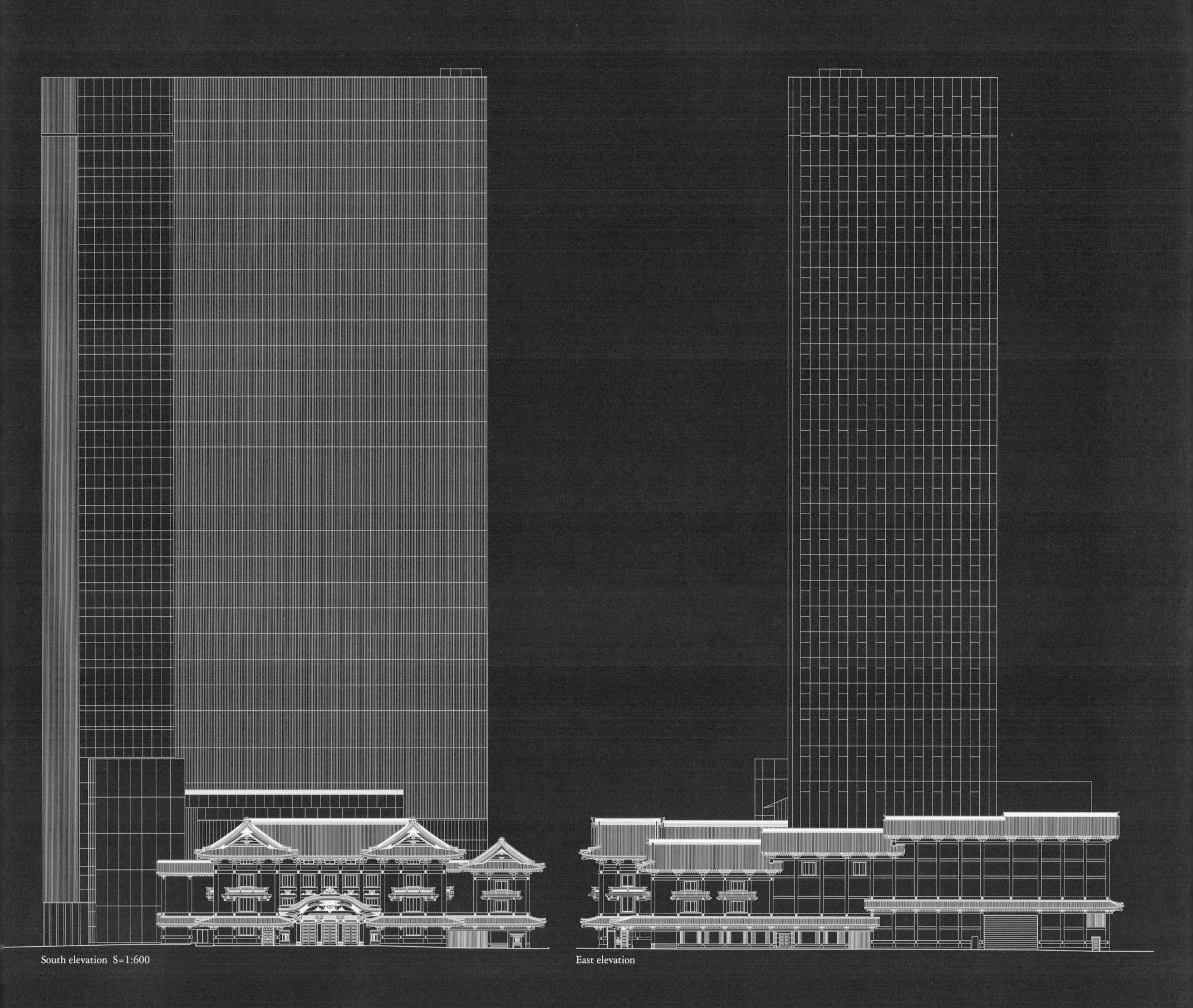

South elevation S=1:600

East elevation

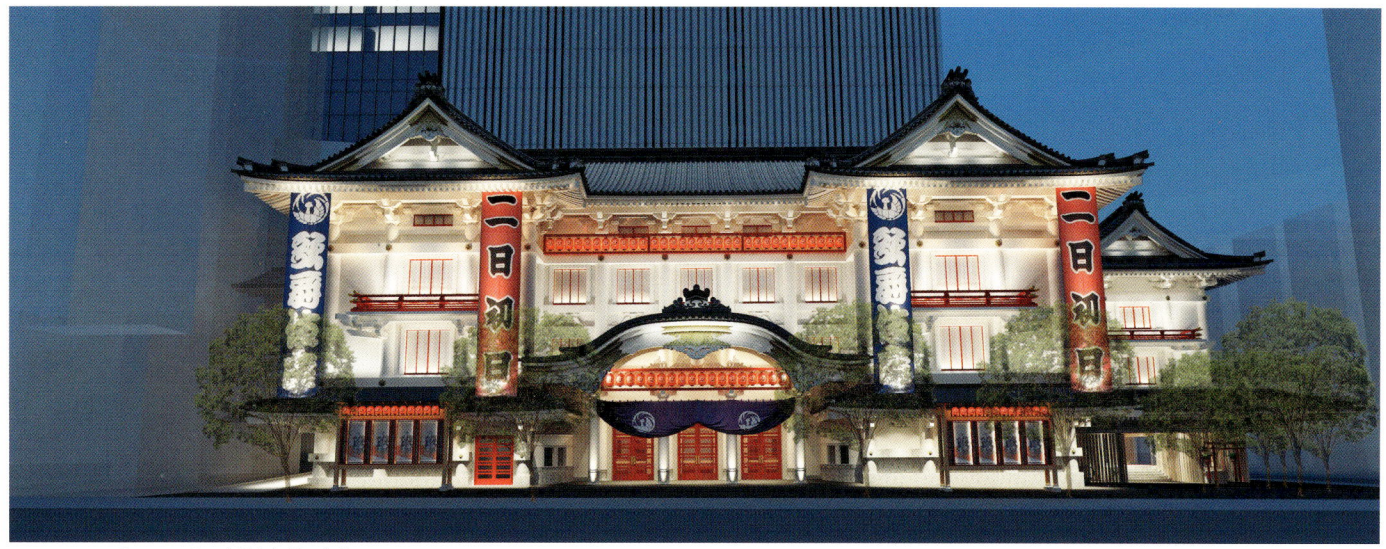

Evening view from south　南側より見る夕景

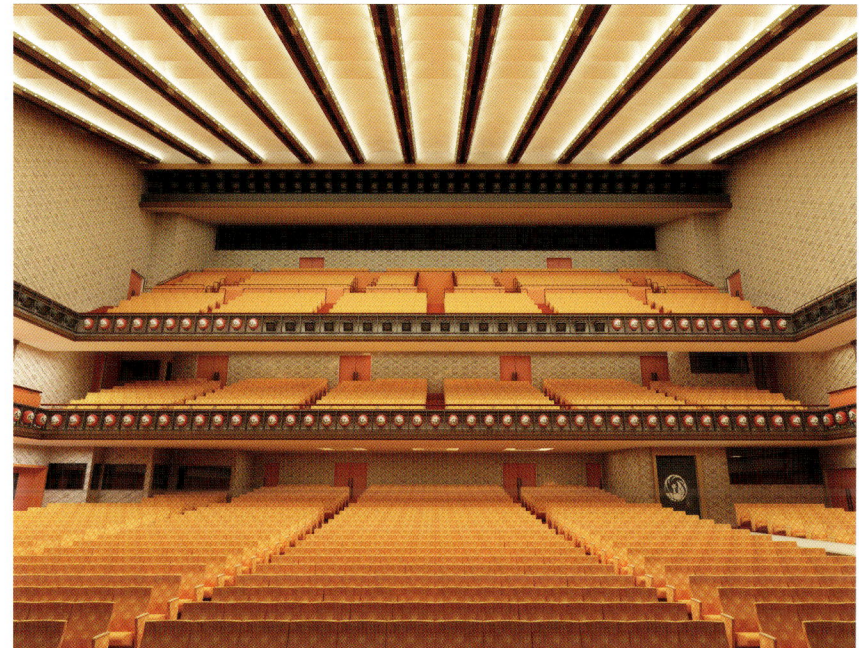

Theater　劇場

Rooftop garden　屋上庭園

Theater lobby　劇場のロビー

Theater foyer　劇場のホワイエ

The first Kabuki-za was constructed in Ginza, expected to serve as Japanese l'Opéra, exporting Japanese culture towards the world, after Edo Shiza (four za) were combined in Meiji 22 (1889). In later days, it was rebuilt every time disaster such as fire, earthquake and war struck the building and what we now design is the fifth Kabuki-za.

　　We targeted at a design that reconstructs baroque architectural space in the city. On top of the large Japanese-style baroque roof called Azuchi-Momoyama style that Shinichiro Okada (the third designer) and Isoya Yoshida (the fourth designer) established, a 145.5 m high-rise building was built, attempting to regain the power of new shape of the roof in the city. The design of the high-rise's facade at the back of the roof referred to neriko-renji-koushi detail (one kind of lattice made with finely aligned thin wooden bars), which has 45 degrees tilt. The columns that vertical lines were emphasized continue and a harmony of the tiled roof and the facade was created.

　　Facing the adjacent alley (Kobikicho-dori), semi-exposed openings attached with eaves and lattice align. We tried to reconstruct a 'playhouse' -type theatrical space that is open and integrated with the city, rather than creating a 20th century closed-type theatrical space.

(仮称) 歌舞伎座ビル

明治22年(1889年)江戸四座を統合し、世界に向けて日本文化を発信する拠点を目指し、日本のオペラ座となるべく第一期の歌舞伎座が銀座に建設された。その後、火災、震災、戦災のたびに再建され、われわれの設計するものは第5期の歌舞伎座となる。

　都市の中にバロック的な建築空間を再構築することを、デザインの目標に掲げた。岡田信一郎(第3期設計者)、吉田五十八(第4期設計者)によって確立された安土桃山風と呼ばれるバロック的和風の大屋根の上に、高さ145.5mの超高層を載せることで、都市の中に新しい形の屋根を復権させようとした。屋根の背後の超高層のファサードは、45度に角度を振った捻子連子格子と呼ばれるディテールを参考にして、垂直線を強調した柱が連続するディテールとし、瓦の屋根とファサードのハーモニーをつくり出した。

　脇の路地(木挽町通り)に面しても、庇と格子のついたセミオープンな開口部を連続することで、都市に閉じた20世紀型劇場空間ではなく、都市に開き都市と一体化した「芝居小屋型」の劇場空間を再構築しようと考えた。

2009　Lucien Pellat-Finet Shinsaibashi
Chuo, Osaka, Japan

Main facade facing Mido-suji street　御堂筋に面するメインファサード

Sections S=1:140

We tried to create a warm and affable cave by using low-cost plywood in a concrete box. Humans divide the gentle spatial associations of the world tastelessly with names like 'floor', 'wall', 'ceiling' or 'furniture'. However the cave denies such abstract divisions and wraps the body with a subtle gathering that forms an inner skin. In order to make the gentle and continuous gathering, we prepared three kinds of aluminum joints and two kinds of plywood with different widths. In terms of geometry, the combination of pentagon and parallelogram shelves are installed three dimensionally, and so it gains a cave-like complex and integrity. In this space, not only the division of the walls and ceilings but also the shop fittings and furniture are eliminated, and all becomes part of the architecture. The adorable items designed by Lucien Pellat-Finet are scattered within the soft gatherings of this cave.

Shop on first floor: cave-like space with complex and integrity　1階売り場。空間全体をペジブル・パターンが覆う

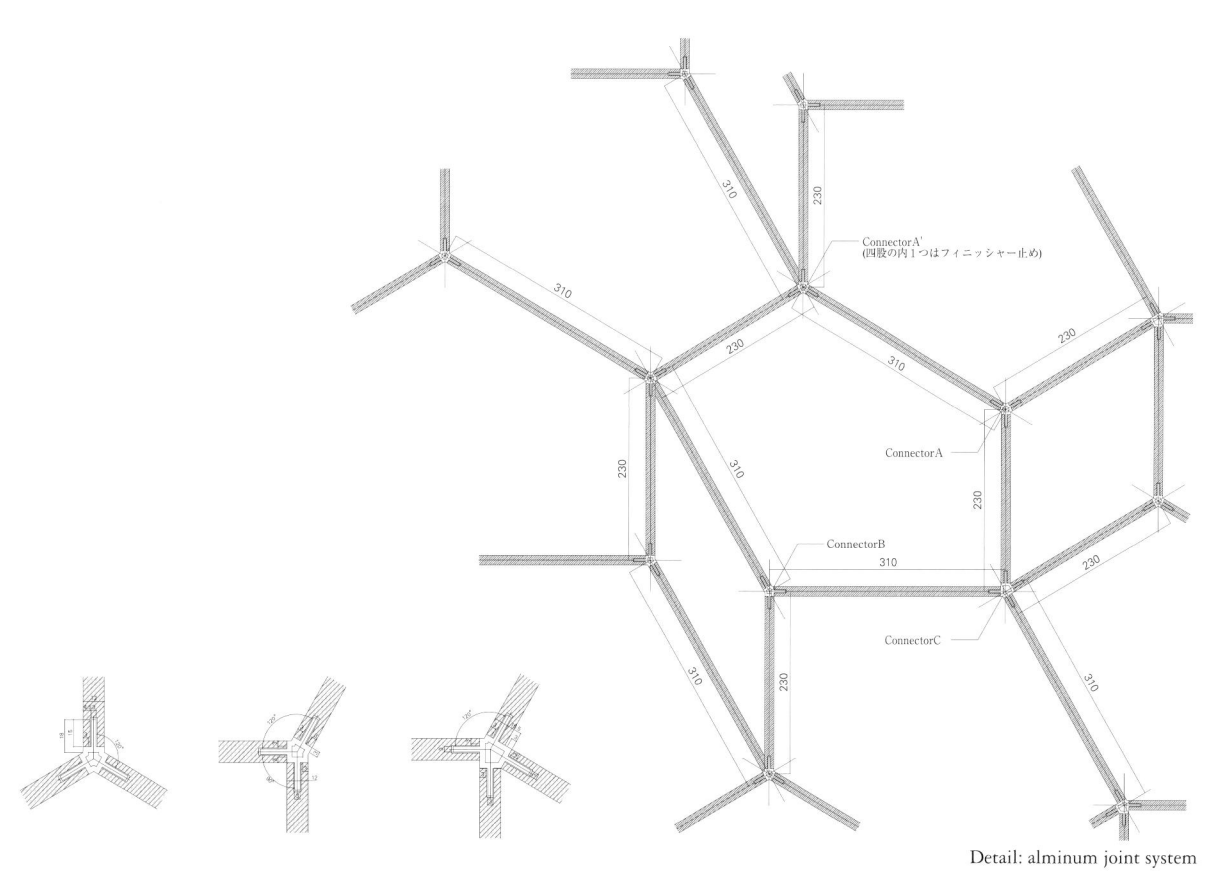

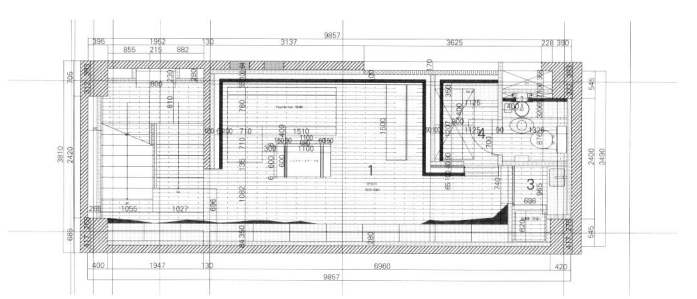

Third floor

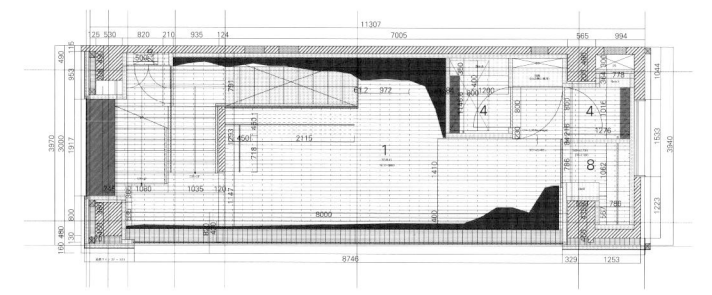

Second floor

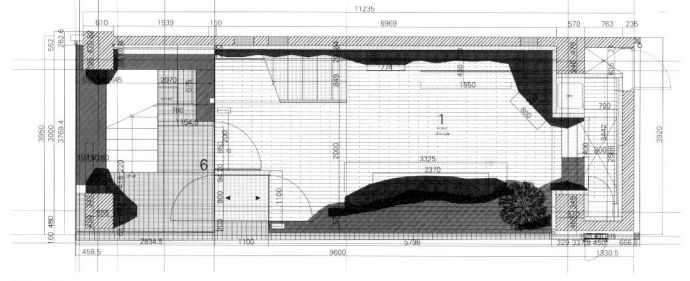

First floor

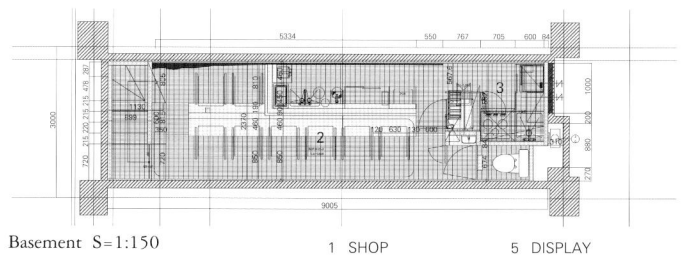

Basement S=1:150

1　SHOP
2　CAFE
3　KITCHEN
4　FITTING ROOM
5　DISPLAY
6　ENTRANCE OF CAFE
7　LIBRARY
8　STORAGE

Detail: alminum joint system

ルシアン・ペラフィネ心斎橋

コンクリートの箱の中に, 安価な構造用合板を用いて暖かくやさしい洞窟をつくろうと試みた。人間は床, 壁, 天井, 家具などの名前をつけて, 世界というゆるやかなつながりを無粋に分節する。しかし, 洞窟は分節を拒否し, その襞のようなゆるい内皮をもって, ゆるやかに身体を包み込む。そのゆるやかで連続的な襞をつくるために, 3種類のアルミ製のジョイントと, 2種類の幅を持つ構造用合板を用意した。幾何学的には五角形と平行四辺形の単純な組み合わせでできた棚が3次元化されることにより, 洞窟のような複雑な全体性を獲得した。ここでは, 壁, 天井の分節が排除されただけでなく, 建築, 什器, 家具という分節も排除され, 洞窟のやわらかい襞の中に, ルシアン・ペラフィネのデザインしたかわいらしいアイテムが散りばめられている。

2009-10 Community Market Yusuhara
Takaoka, Kochi, Japan

Overall view from south　南より見る全景

Wall with thatch　茅葺きの壁

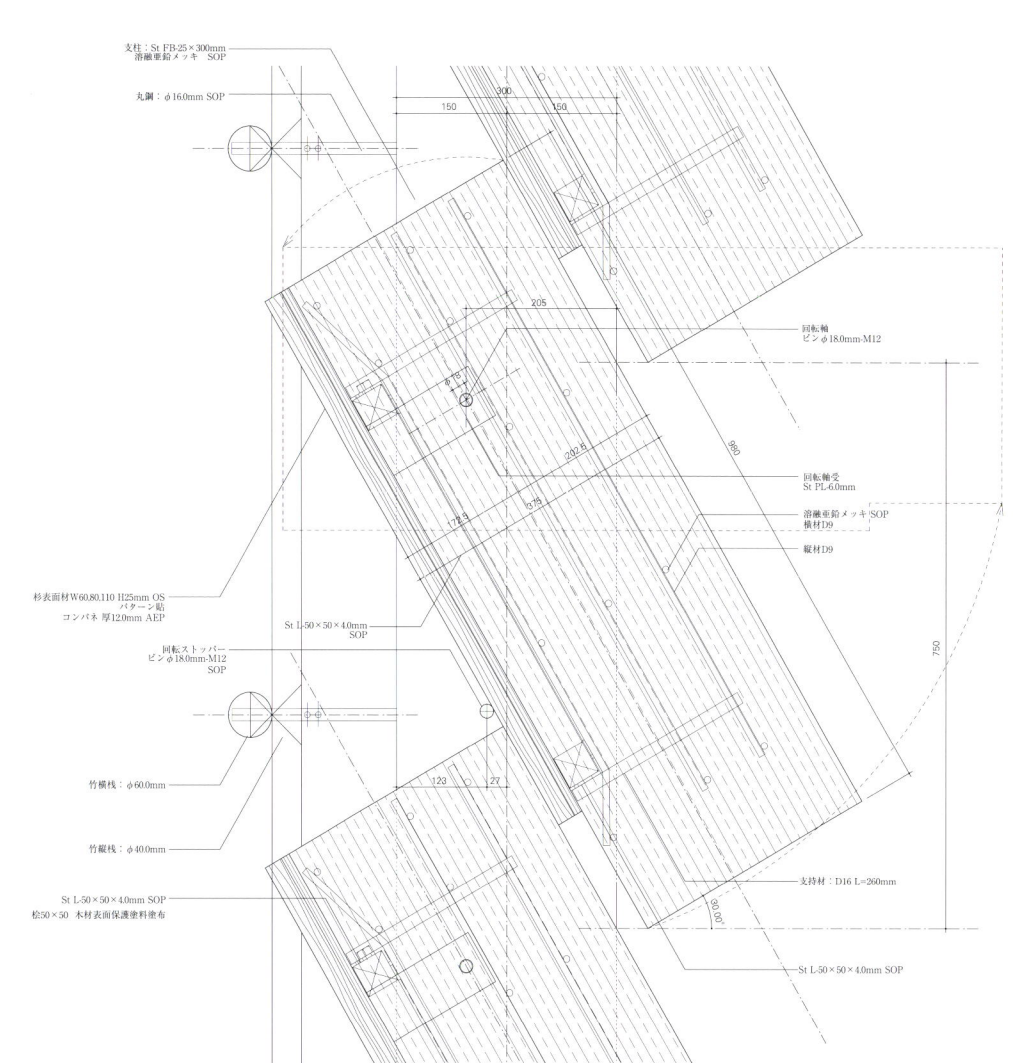

Detail: wall with thatch unit　S=1:10　茅葺き壁ユニット詳細

Yusuhara town in Kochi prefecture is known as a town besides Main Street where Ryoma Sakamoto left his domain. A group of arbors roofed with thatch along the main road is called 'Sadou' and the culture of providing tea to unknown travellers is a symbol of hospitality of Yusuhara town and is proud of the town's people.

It was pursued for the accommodation facility run by the town to sustain the tradition of 'Sadou' with thatch roof. However, as the site is located at the center of the town and three-layered volume was sought, thatch was not used for the roof but was used as wall material, and responded to the required volume. The thatch was made in 2 m by 1 m by 40 cm unit. The steel frame in each unit rotates centering the horizontal axis and it was detailed to take in fresh air. The detail enables the thatch to be treated as fittings and not as an exterior wall material and made it possible to create the exterior wall of the three-layered special architecture with thatch.

15 guest rooms were built to face a triple-height hall. Morning market selling local vegetable is held at the hall every morning. Eating breakfast beside the market, guests can experience something specific to a town between mountains.

まちの駅「ゆすはら」

高知県梼原町は，龍馬脱藩の街道の町として知られる。街道沿いの茅葺きの東屋群は茶堂とも呼ばれ，見ず知らずの旅人に茶を供する文化は，梼原町のホスピタリティ精神の象徴として，いまだに町民の誇りである。

町営の新たな宿泊施設も，この茅葺きの茶堂の伝統を継承しようと考えた。しかし，敷地は町の中心部で3層のヴォリュームが求められたため，茅を屋根材としてではなく外壁材として用いることで，要求のヴォリュームに対応した。茅は2m×1m×40cmのユニットとされ，ユニットそれぞれのスティール・フレームが軸を中心として横軸回転し，外気の取り入れが可能になるディテールとした。このディテールによって，茅は外壁材としてではなく，建具という扱いを受けて，3層の特殊建築物の外壁を茅でつくることが可能となった。

客室は吹き抜けに面して15室設けられ，吹き抜け部分は毎朝地産の野菜が並ぶ朝市が開かれ，その脇で朝食を食べるという，山間の町ならではの体験を味わうことができる。

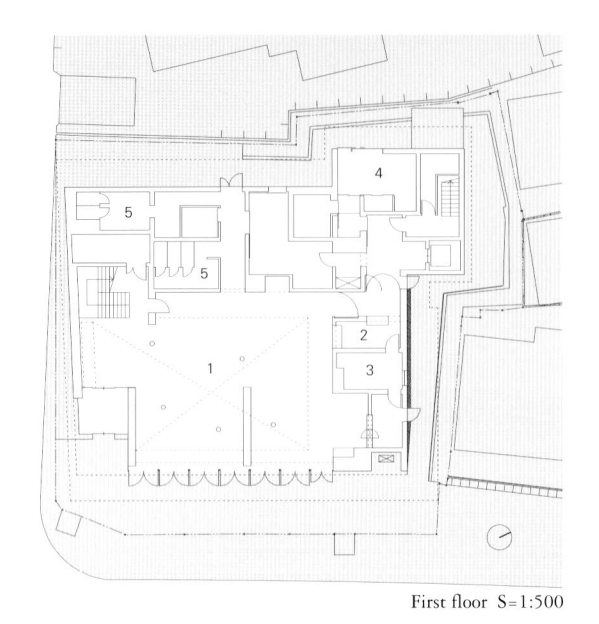

First floor S=1:500

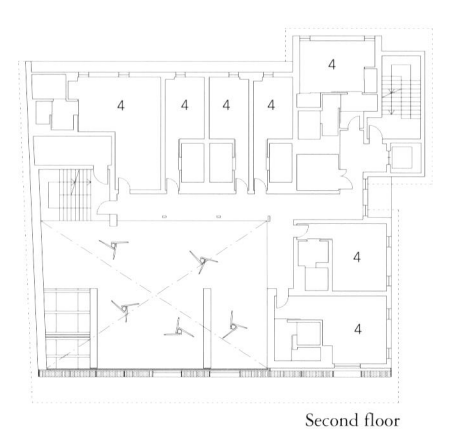

Second floor

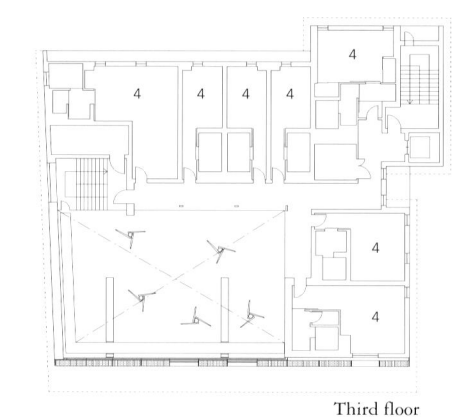

Third floor

1 SHOP / EXHIBITION
2 RECEPTION
3 OFFICE
4 GUEST ROOM
5 WC
6 PANTRY

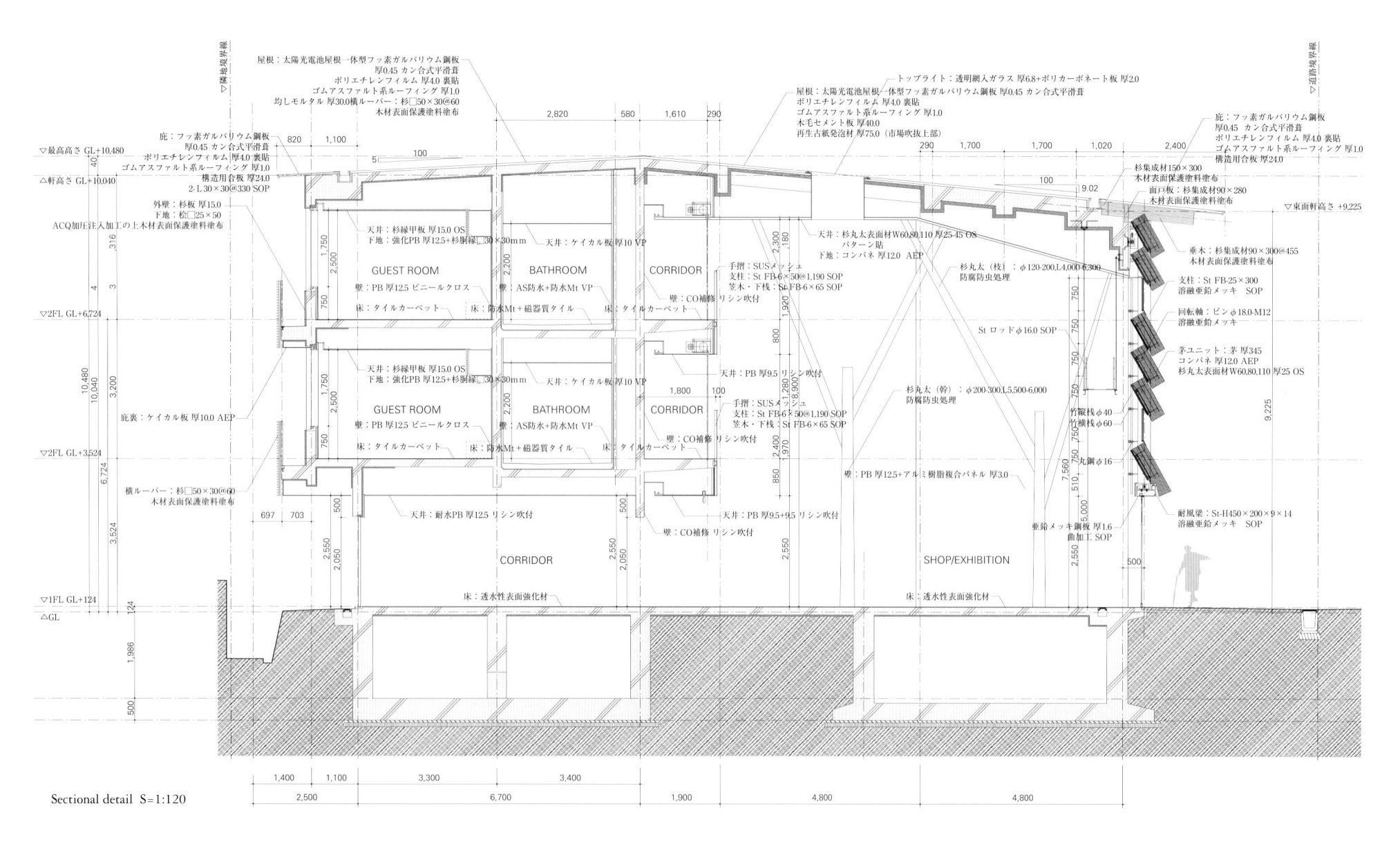

Sectional detail S=1:120

Shop/exhibition 市場／展示

2009-10 Yusuhara Wooden Bridge Museum
Takaoka, Kochi, Japan

Evening view 夕景

Distant view from north　北より見る遠景

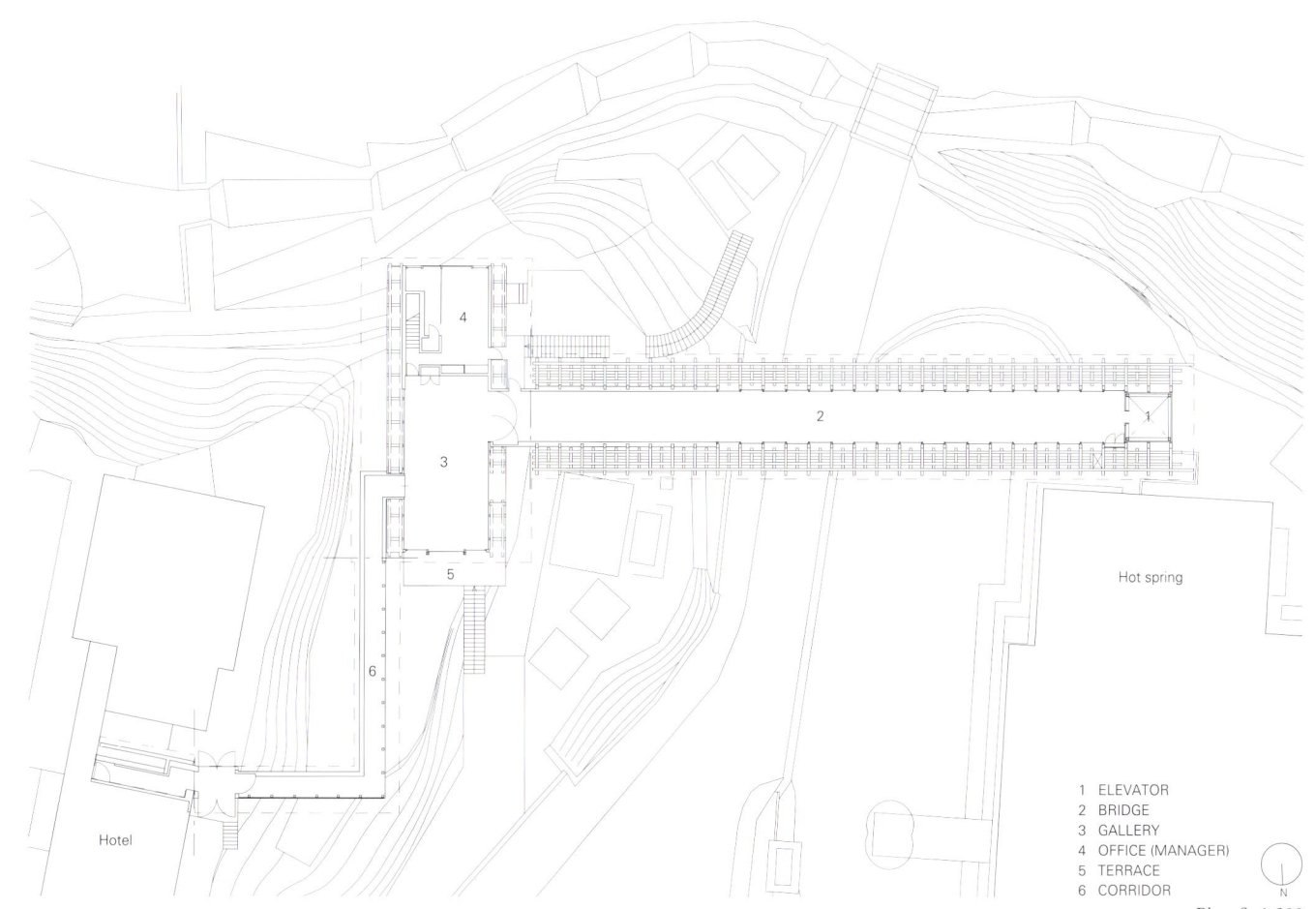

1　ELEVATOR
2　BRIDGE
3　GALLERY
4　OFFICE (MANAGER)
5　TERRACE
6　CORRIDOR

Plan　S=1:500

We challenged to create a large span wooden bridge by only using laminated local cedar in a small section available for production in local wooden shops. I am interested in a method of gathering small elements and create a large loose whole. The merit was an important point that laminated materials in a small section are possible to be created in a small local shop. I think a grass root method of making architecture by consuming material that can be obtained by us and using our power will change architecture.

We adopted a structural method of creating a large span bridge by pushing out laminated materials in 18 cm by 30 cm section little by little and piling them up. The format was inspired by a structural style of Saru-hashi in Yamanashi prefecture, which is assumed to be one of the three prominent bridges in Japan. Unlike Saru-hashi, a column was erected at the center and it was not designed as an arch type with supports at edges. Members were gradually taken out from the center and reversed the style, so that lightness that cannot be found in Saru-hashi was able to acquire. Because Saru-hashi was remodeled with steel structure, the Yusuhara Bridge remains the only wooden bridge that is made with a structural style called Saru-hashi.

It is often the case with wooden bridges to build a roof so as to avoid rain. Likewise, a roof covers the bridge and creates an indoor passage. The interior space will also be used for art and handicrafts' exhibition space. A studio for artist-in-residence were built at a part of the pier.

Wooden frame 'Kigumi' and pillar　木組と柱

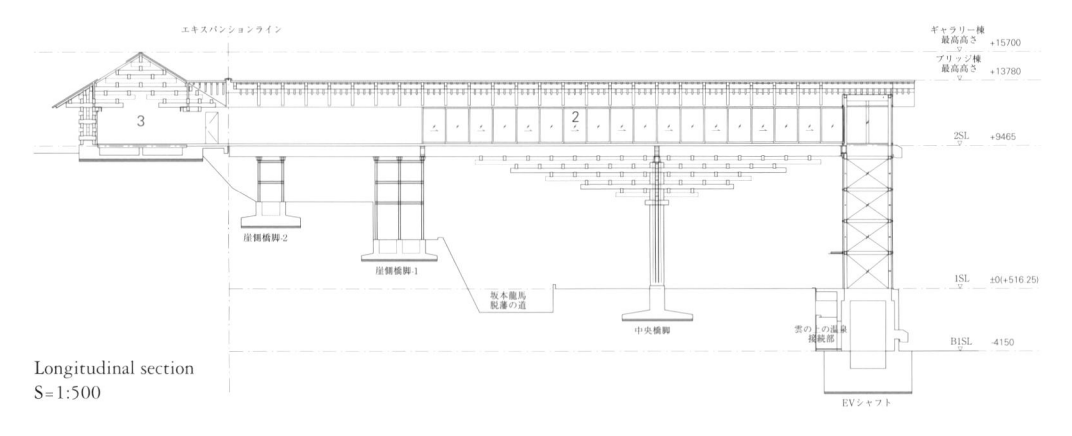

Longitudinal section
S=1:500

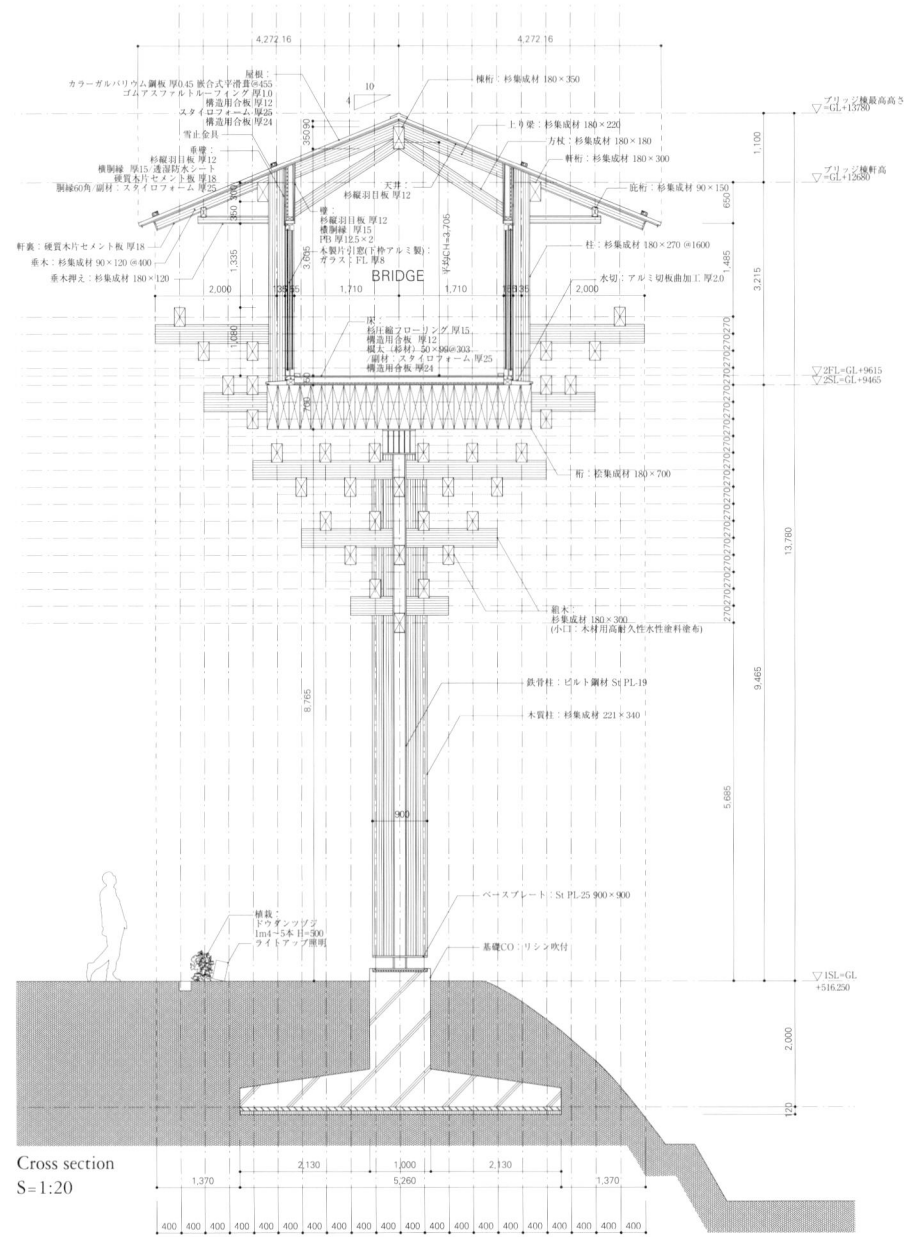

Cross section
S=1:20

Bridge ブリッジ

Gallery ギャラリー

梼原・木橋ミュージアム

地元の杉材を用い，地元の木材工場で加工可能な小断面の集成材だけを使って，大スパンの木橋をつくることに挑戦した。小さなエレメントを集合させて，大きくてゆるやかな全体を生成する方法に関心がある。小断面集成材ならば地元の小さな工場でもつくれるという利点も，われわれにとっては重要なポイントだった。大都市の大工場に依存せずに，自分たちの力で，自分たちで手に入る材料を使って建築をつくる，草の根的方法が建築を変えていくと考えている。

18cm×30cmの断面寸法の集成材を少しずつ持ち出して積み上げていくことによって，大スパンを架橋する構造方式を採用した。この形式は，日本三大橋のひとつと言われる山梨県の「猿橋」の構造様式にヒントを得たものであるが，両端に支点のあるアーチ状の形式ではなく，中心に支柱をたてて，中心から少しずつ持ち出す形式へと反転させることで，「猿橋」にはない軽やかさを獲得することができた。「猿橋」は現在，鉄骨造でつくり変えられてしまったため，この「猿橋」と呼ばれる構造形式でつくられている木橋は，この梼原の橋のみとなる。

木橋は木材を雨がかりにしないために，屋根を架けることが多く，今回も屋根を用いて通路空間を室内化した。さらに，この室内空間は，アート，工芸の展示空間としても用いられ，付随してアーティスト・イン・レジデンスのためのスタジオも，橋脚の一部に設けられている。

2009-10 Stone Roof
Nagano, Japan

Overall view from north　北より見る全景

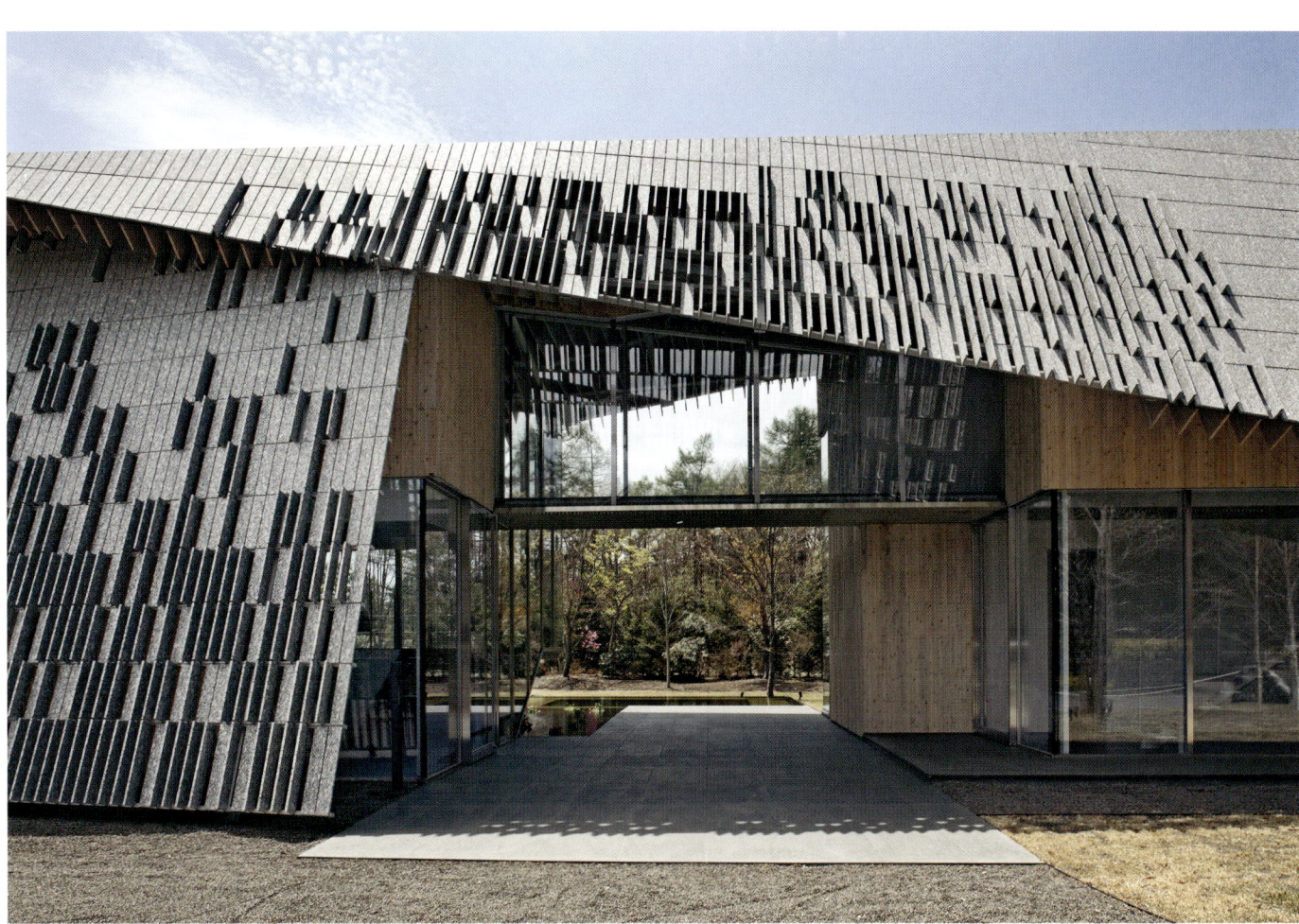

Court: view toward basin　中庭：水盤方向を見る

Stone roof: wooden joist and oyster stone strips
ストーン・ルーフ：木製ジョイストと石ルーバー（オイスター・ストーン）

Under eaves of stone roof　ストーン・ルーフの軒裏

Living room　居間

This is a second house located in Karuizawa. However since the site had already been leveled, it is far from the typical image of Karuizawa where there is a resort area deep in the forest, but it is a strangely bright place. Here we searched for an equivalent style which can maintain privacy but at the same time, openness in this peculiar environment that is somewhere between resort and urban.

As a result, we chose to challenge this by using three different characteristic elements to constitute this architecture.

The first is a stone roof which is folded into six planes. This roof consists of stone tiles 125 mm x 500 mm, and 20 mm thick. A part of the roof is louver and natural sunlight drops through small openings between the stones. The second is a functional skip floor, and the last is an undulating green garden which has a wild texture created by nature.

Some parts of the stone roof are close to the green garden and operate to protect daily life like a kind of armor and some parts are close to the sky and connect daily life and nature. A part of the green garden is sloped and continues to the floor and other parts continue out to the surrounding nature.

Relating these three different elements creates various different spaces with different characters.

Designing this house was just like folding three different kinds of fabrics and piling them neatly. We hope that a happy life connected to the environment will be generated in the spaces within the creases of the three fabrics.

View toward terrace from bathroom on second floor
2階浴室よりテラスを見る

View toward living room wing through glazed wall　ガラス越しに居間棟を見る

Living room on second floor: view from dining room　2階居間：食堂より見る

Master bedroom on second floor　2階主寝室

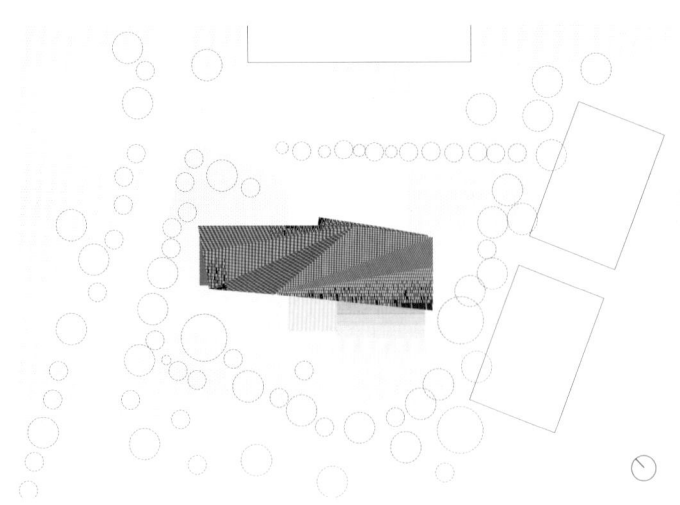

Site plan S=1:1200

1 HALL
2 COURT
3 LIVING / DINING ROOM
4 TERRACE
5 KITCHEN
6 BEDROOM
7 STORAGE
8 GYM
9 POOL
10 COLD BATH
11 BATHROOM
12 SAUNA
13 BASIN
14 AREAWAY

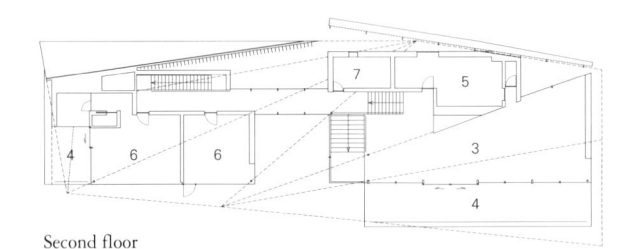

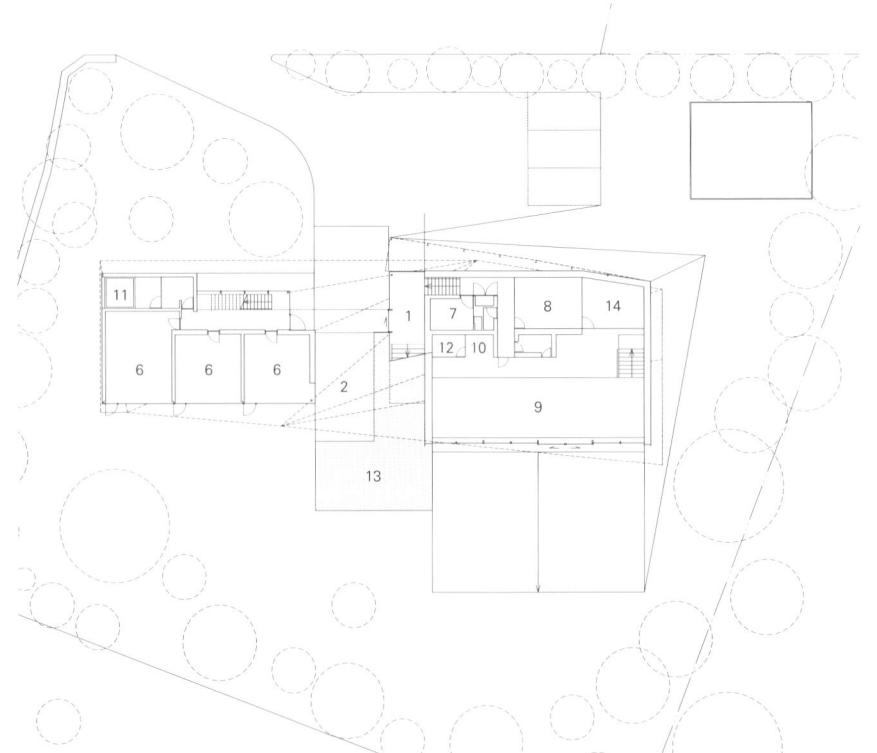

Second floor

First floor S=1:500

Stone Roof

軽井沢に建つ別荘である。しかしながら,敷地は別荘地として整えられていて,軽井沢と言えば思い出される「深い森の中のリゾート」というイメージを離れた奇妙に明るい場所である。リゾートとアーバンの狭間に位置するような特異な環境の中で,プライバシーを確保しながら同時に開放的であるような両義的な形式を探った。

結果として,建築を性格の異なる三つの要素で構成することでこれに挑戦した。

ひとつめは,六つの面に折り畳まれた石葺きの屋根である。125mm×500mm,厚み20mmの小さな石を単位として構成される屋根をつくった。石屋根の一部はルーバーになっていて,石の隙間の小さな開口から光が落ちる。二つめは,機能的なスキップフロアの床。三つめは,幾つかの勾配がつけられた緑の庭で,自然がつくり出す野生のテクスチャーを持っている。

石屋根は,ある所では緑の庭に近づき鎧のように生活を守り,またある所では空に近づき自然と生活を繋ぐ。緑の庭は,ある所ではスロープになって床に接続し,別の所では周りの自然に連続していく。

三つの異なる要素が互いに多様な関係を結ぶことで,多様な性格の空間が生まれる。

設計は,あたかも異なる種類の3枚のファブリックを丁寧に折りたたみ,順々と重ねていく作業のようであった。3枚のファブリックがつくり出すシワとシワの間に,環境と結ばれた幸福な生活が生まれることを期待した。

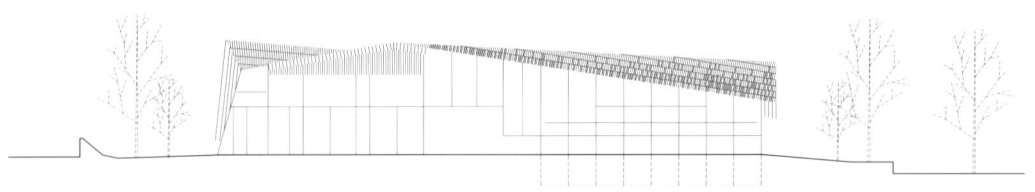

Southwest elevation

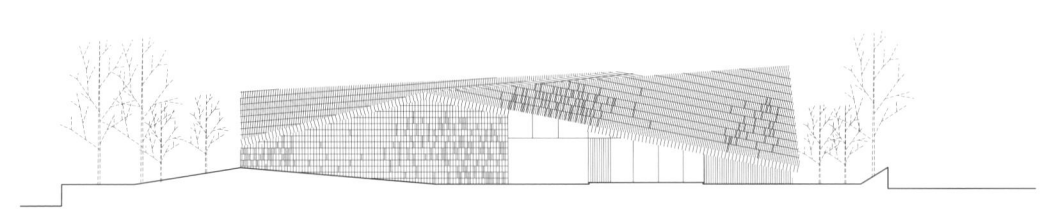

Northeast elevation S=1:500

Evening view from southwest　南西より見る夕景

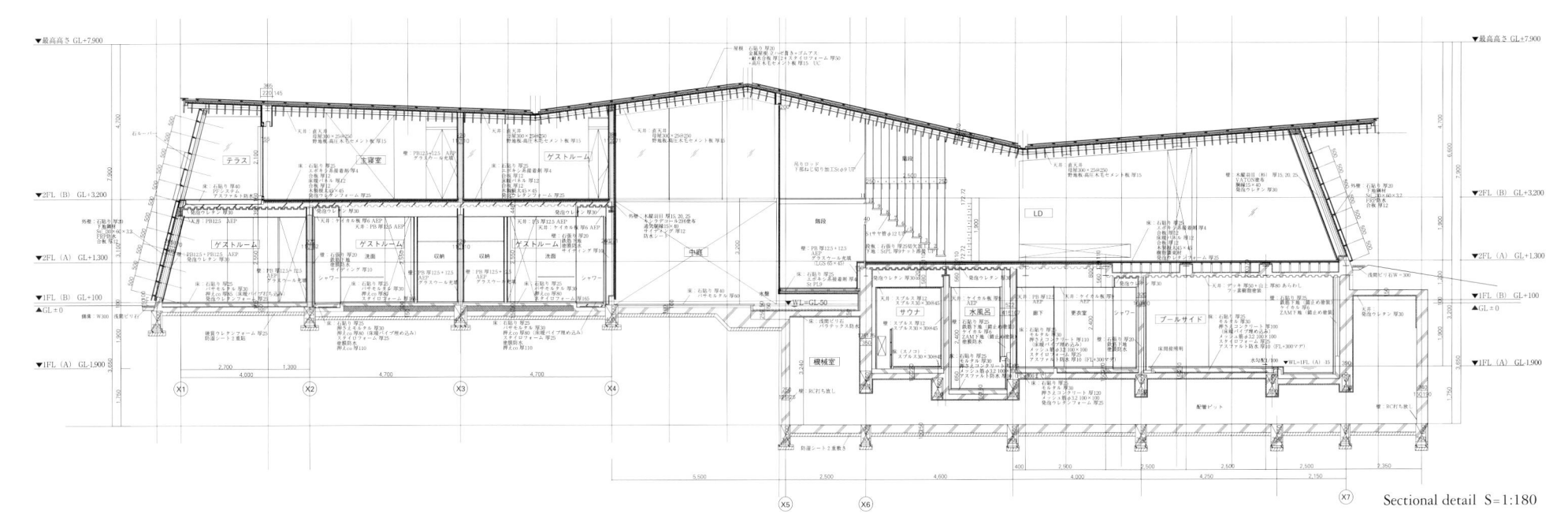

Sectional detail　S=1:180

2009-   Museum at The China Academy of Art
Xiangshan, China

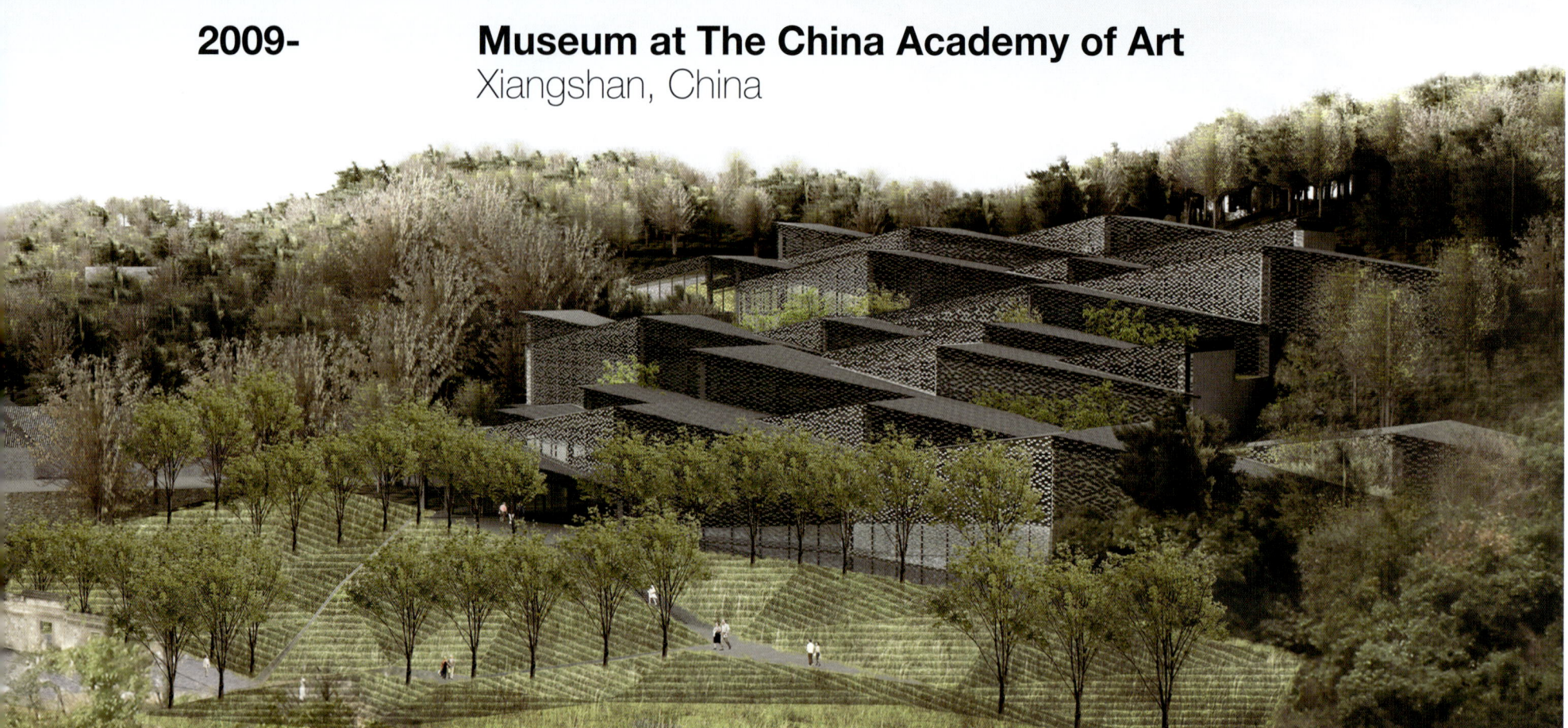

Overall view 全景

1 ENTRANCE LOBBY
2 LOBBY
3 FOYER
4 EXHIBITION
5 CORRIDOR
6 CONFERENCE
7 MEETING ROOM
8 CAFE

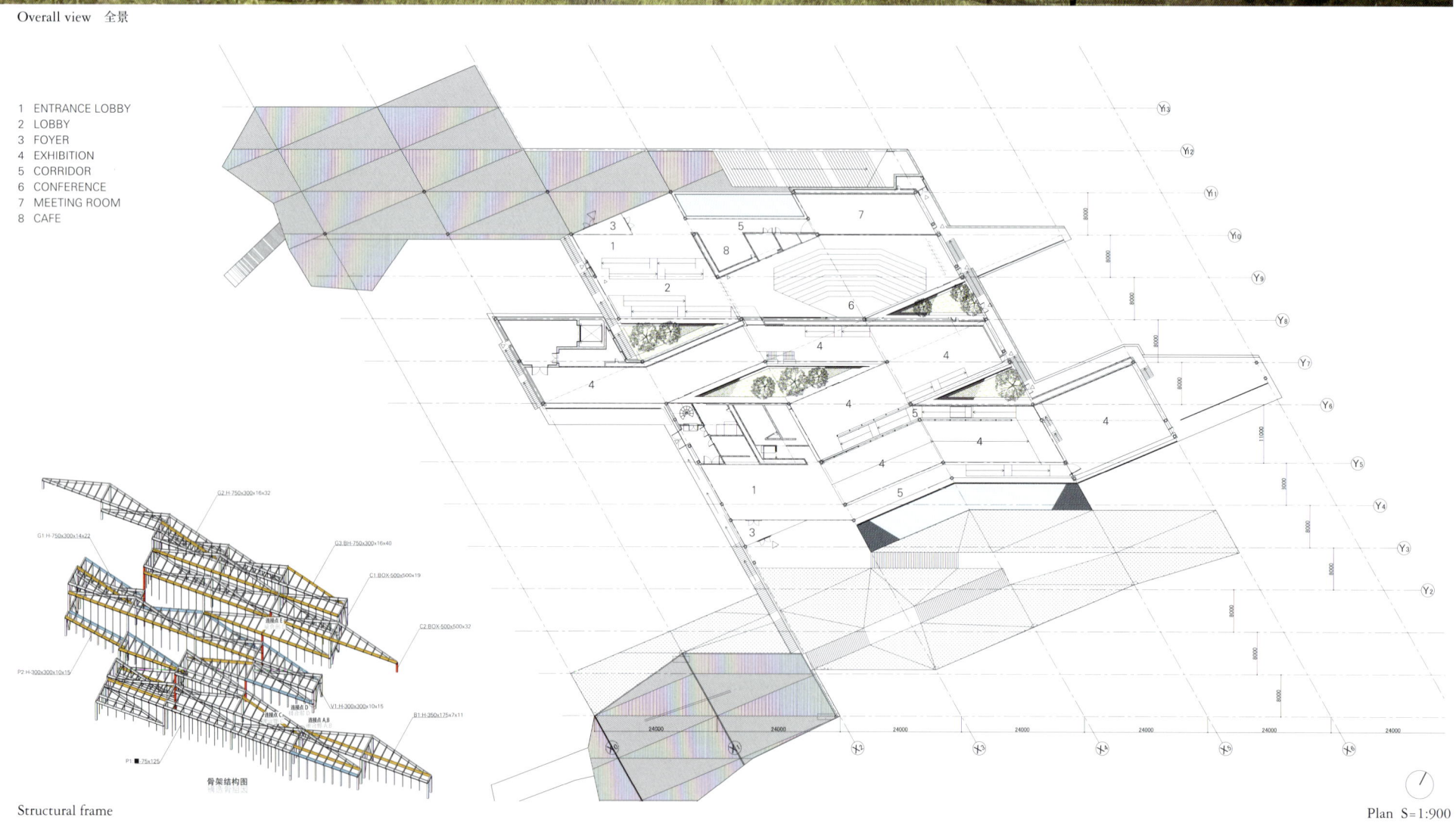

Structural frame

Plan S=1:900

220

Conference 会議室

Lobby ロビー

Exhibition area 展示エリア

China Academy of Art is a national art College and one of the centers of art education in China. The campus is in a beautiful natural setting in a suburb of Hangzhou.

Located along a hill side, we proposed an architecture that would unite with the hill. To achieve this, we divide the large volume of the museum into small diamond shaped cells and lay these along the slope of the hill. On the roof of each cell, the same roof tile as on the local houses is used. This makes the whole building look like one village from a distance. We believed that the most important factor in creating the scenery of this area is the roof tiles. The local roof tiles we used were burnt on the ground and varied in color and size. We also hung the roof tiles with wires on the wall to control the sunlight.

The continuous diamond shaped spaces with gentle changes in floor level that run along the slope gives a fluent spatial experience and differs from the ordinary box museum found in the city.

中国美術学院博物館

中国美術学院は国立の美術大学で，中国の美術教育の中心のひとつであり，そのキャンパスは杭州郊外の美しい自然の中にある。

われわれは，丘の傾斜面に沿ってたつ，丘と一体化した建築を計画した。そのために，美術館の大きなヴォリュームを，小さな菱型のセルに分割し，その菱型のセルを斜面に沿うように配置した。それぞれのセルは地元の民家と同様の瓦の屋根がのり，遠方からみると，ひとつの村のようでもある。瓦こそがこの地域の景観を構成する最も重要な要素であると考えて，野焼きの方法でつくられた色，サイズともにばらつきのある地元の瓦を全面的に用いた。壁にも瓦をワイヤーで吊り下げたスクリーンを用い，外からの光をコントロールしている。

斜面に沿って床レベルが変化する菱型の空間のゆるやかな連続体は，従来の都会的な箱型の美術館とは異なる，流動的な空間体験を与えてくれる。

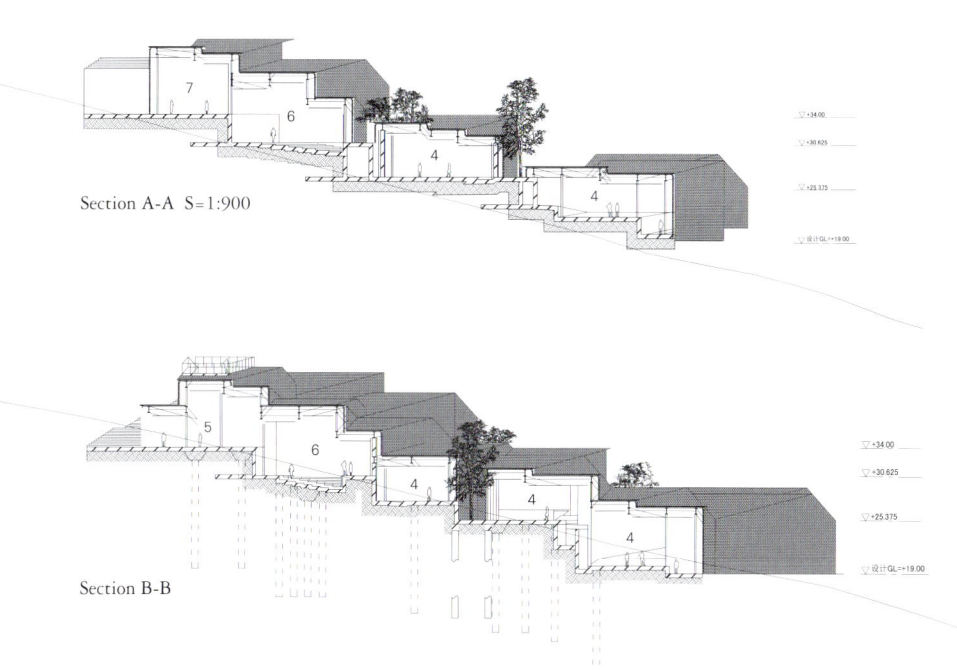

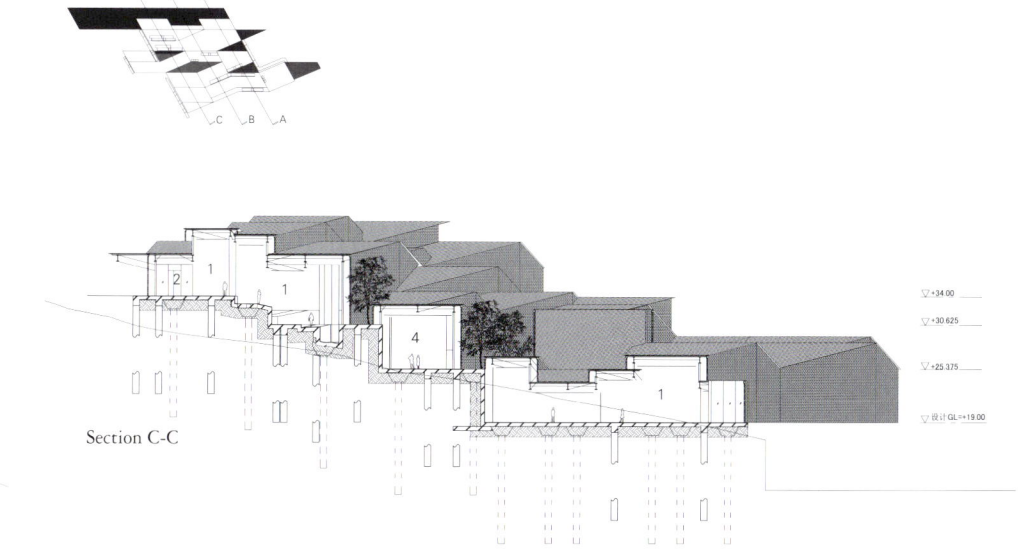

Section A-A S=1:900

Section B-B

Section C-C

2009- Granatum-Granada Performing Arts Centre
Granada, Spain

Wooden model 木製の模型

This is an Opera theater located at the perimeter of Granada city, famous for the Alhambra, in Spain. Our organic design proposal supported by a honeycomb structure was selected by competition.

We had been researching the method to divide a big volume into small cells, and so we took up the challenge to create an ensemble of hexagonal cells. This method results in a honeycomb structure, and these hexagonal cells divide the auditorium seating, providing a comfortable human scale for the 1,500-seat opera theater. Toward the outside, intermediate hexagonal spaces were created. These spaces are facing the city and are open, providing a comfortable foyer space where is protected from the strong sunlight. In terms of structure, it enables a huge space with no columns without relying on a truss, or a space frame.

It was indicated to us that this honeycomb structure is similar to the Islamic geometry of the ceiling in the Alhambra and also the granular composition of a pomegranate which the name of the city, Granada (Granatum), comes from.

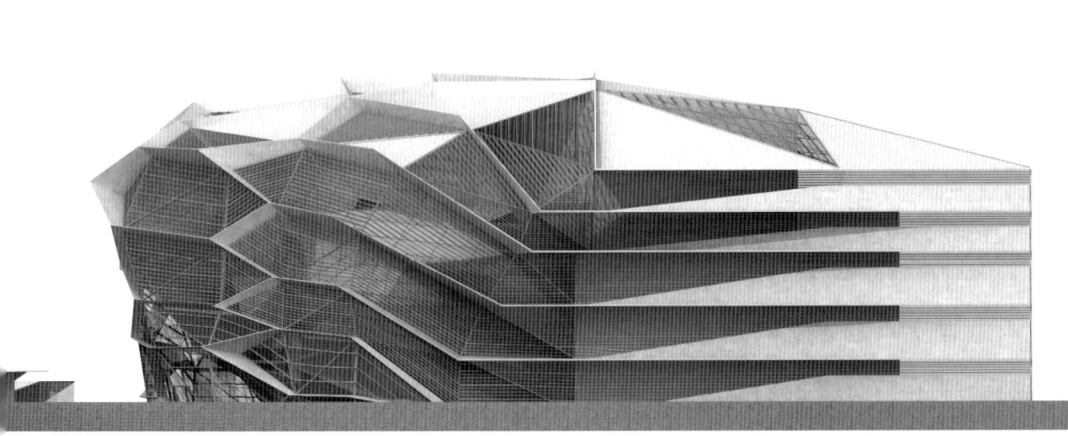

South elevation S=1:800

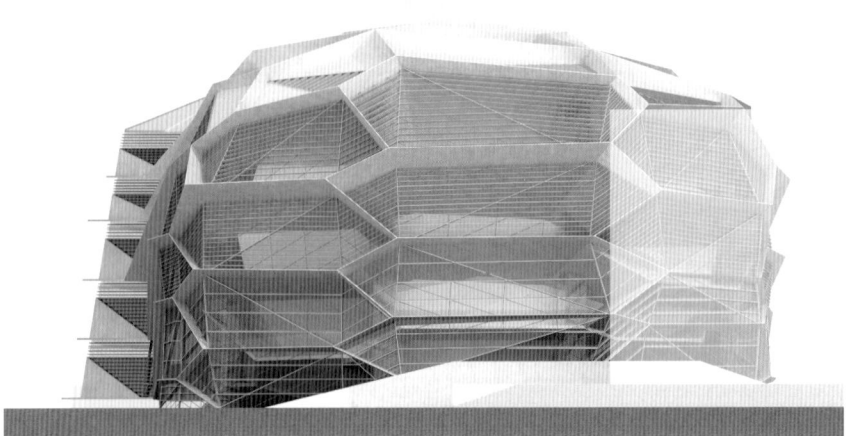

West elevation

Second floor

Fourth floor

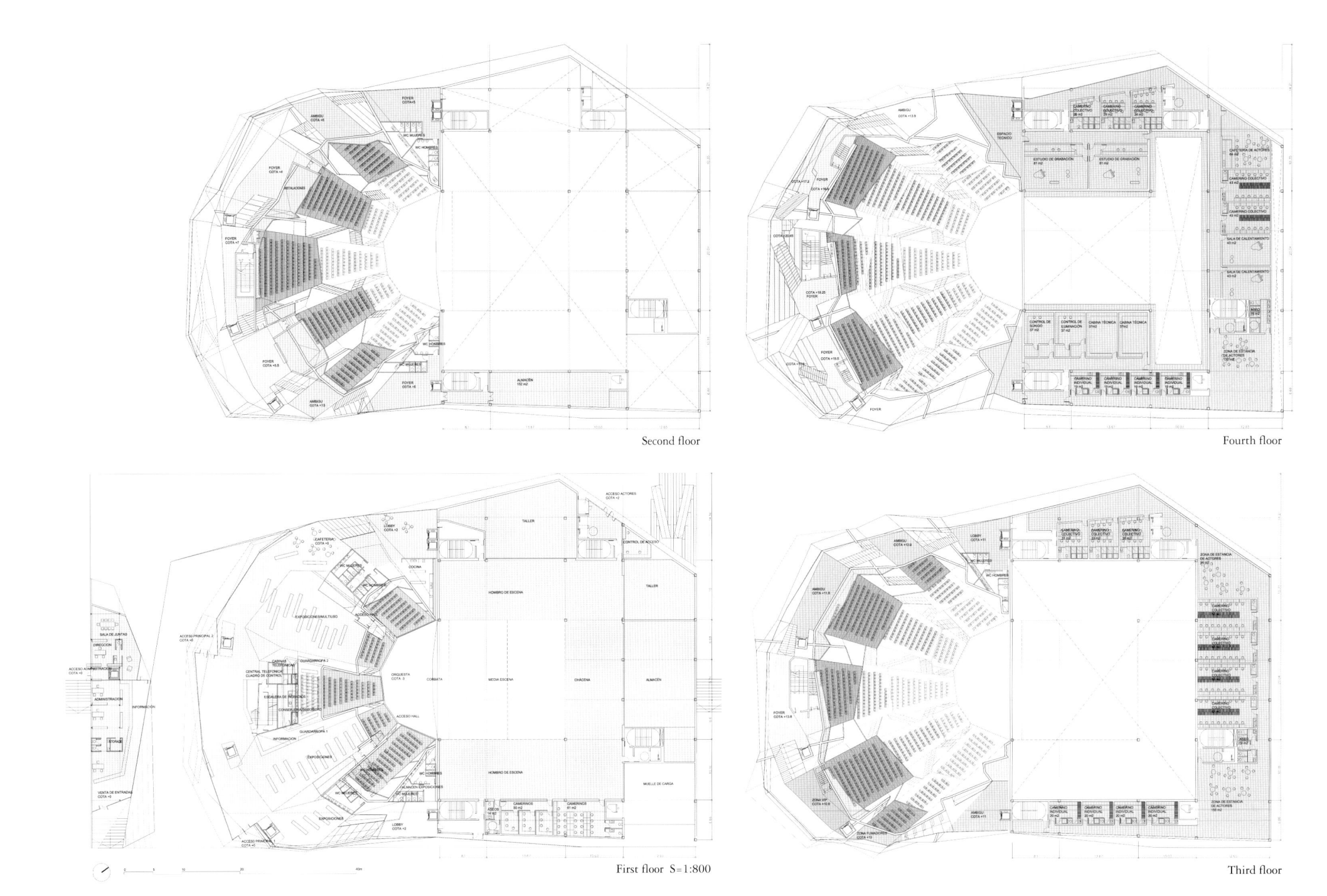

First floor S=1:800

Third floor

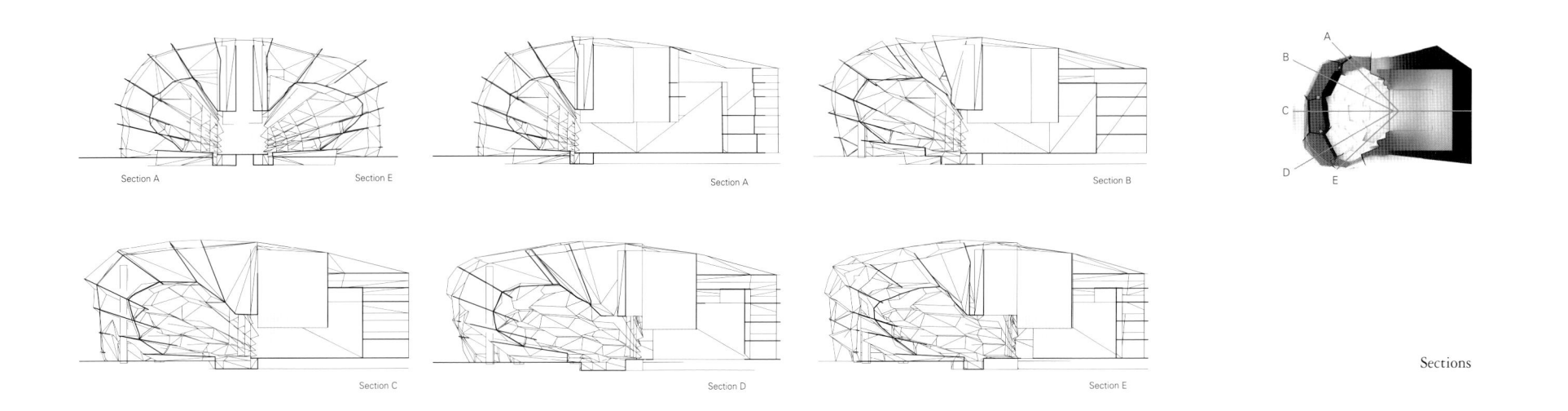

Section A Section E

Section A

Section B

Section C

Section D

Section E

Sections

223

View toward south elevation from approach　アプローチより南立面を見る

Access lobby　ロビー

LOS ASCENSORES PUBLICOS

ESCALERAS DE EMERGENCIA

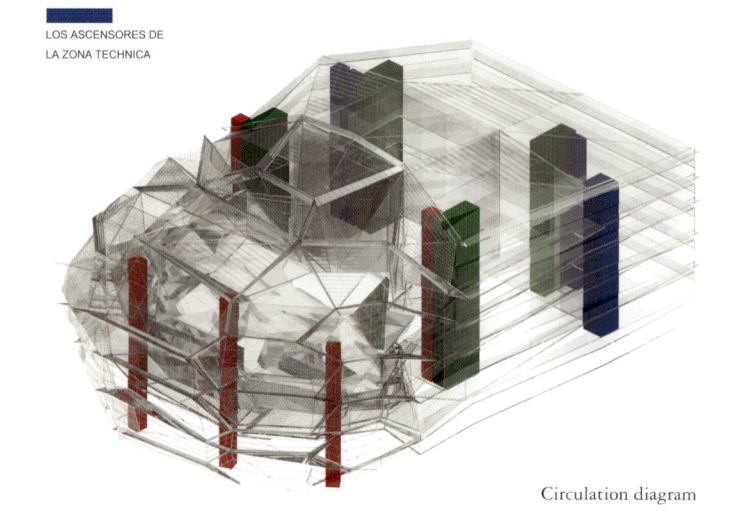

LOS ASCENSORES DE LA ZONA TECHNICA

Circulation diagram

Night view 夜景

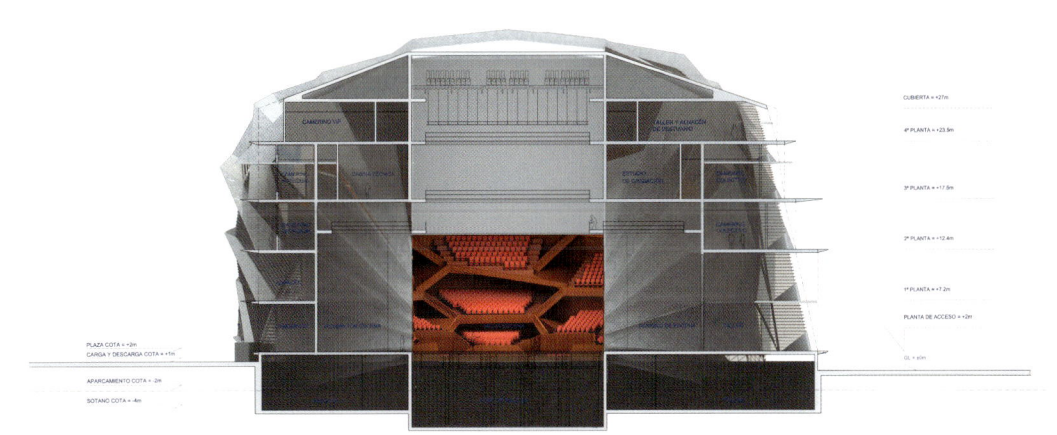

Cross section

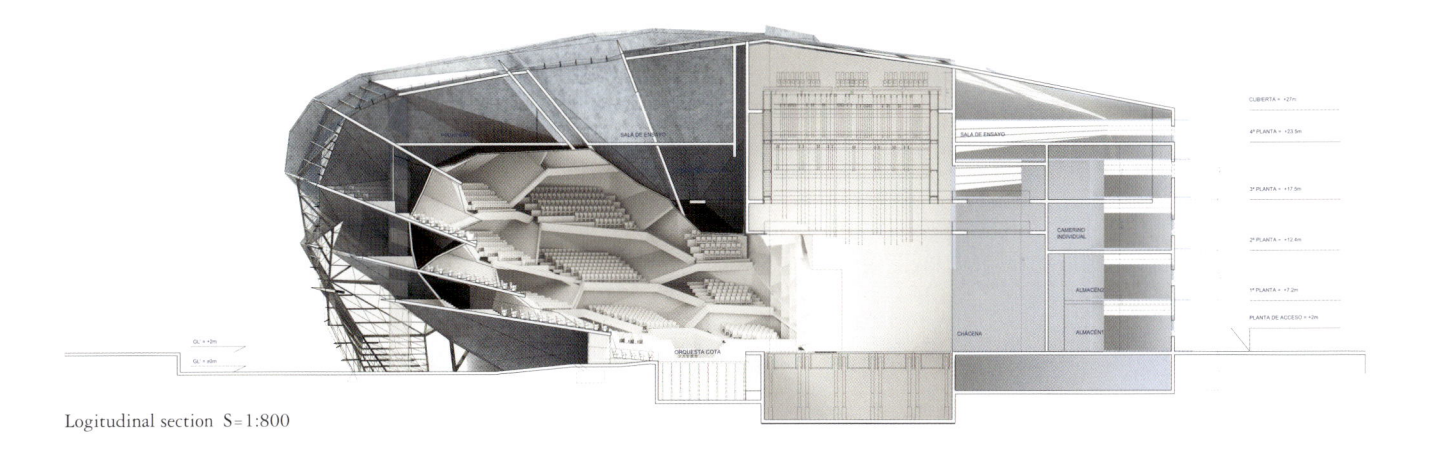

Logitudinal section S=1:800

グラナトゥン（グラナダ・パフォーミング・アーツセンター）

アルハンブラ宮殿で知られる、スペイン・グラナダ市の外周部に計画されたオペラ劇場。ハニカム状の構造システムで支えられた、有機的形態を提案したわれわれが、コンペティションで選ばれた。

大きなヴォリュームを小さなセルへと分割する方法をわれわれは探究してきたが、ここでは、六角形のセルの集合体という方法にチャレンジした。小さな六角形で球状の立体を構成していく方法は、まさに蜂の巣の構造システムである。ここでは、その六角形が室内側で劇場の客席を分割し、オペラのための1,500人収容の劇場に心地よいヒューマンスケールを与えている。また、外部に面しても、六角形の形をした中間領域が創造され、都市に面した開放的で、しかも強い直射日光から守られた快適なホワイエ空間をつくり出している。また構造的には、このシステムによって、トラスやスペースフレームに頼ることなく、巨大な無柱空間が実現した。

この蜂の巣状の構造は、アルハンブラ宮殿のイスラム的幾何学による天井と似ているとも、グラナダの名前の由来であるザクロ（グラナトゥン）の粒子状構成と似ているとも、指摘された。

225

2009-11 Mesh/Earth
Japan

It came into an idea to cover a residence in a park with something 'transparent, but also dirt-sensing and warm'.

Collaborating with a plasterer, Syuhei Hasado, we invented a new construction method of double and triple overlaying welding wire netting in different dense and spray dirt onto them. Mix-using 3.2 mm and 4 mm diameter wire netting and mixing carbon fiber instead of susa (natural fibers) that are often used in ordinal dirt wall, an adhesive property between the wire netting and soil enhanced and, thus, the 'transparent soil wall' was completed. 60 cm by 30 cm wire netting was chosen for the basic unit (pixel size). As each unit differs in directionality, density and the overlapping method, it was made possible to acquire various looks that are not found in industrial goods.

For the ceiling of the second and the third floor, rough plaster kneaded with unprocessed bamboo and bamboo grass was applied. For the first floor's tearoom wall, ash made out of Oak was kneaded so as to make black dirt wall that is smooth like human skin. There is a fireplace at the center of the tearoom and burning charcoal makes ash. The idea was to use the ash directly to the wall's material. It is an experiment to connect the software of what will be done in the room and the hardware of the composing space.

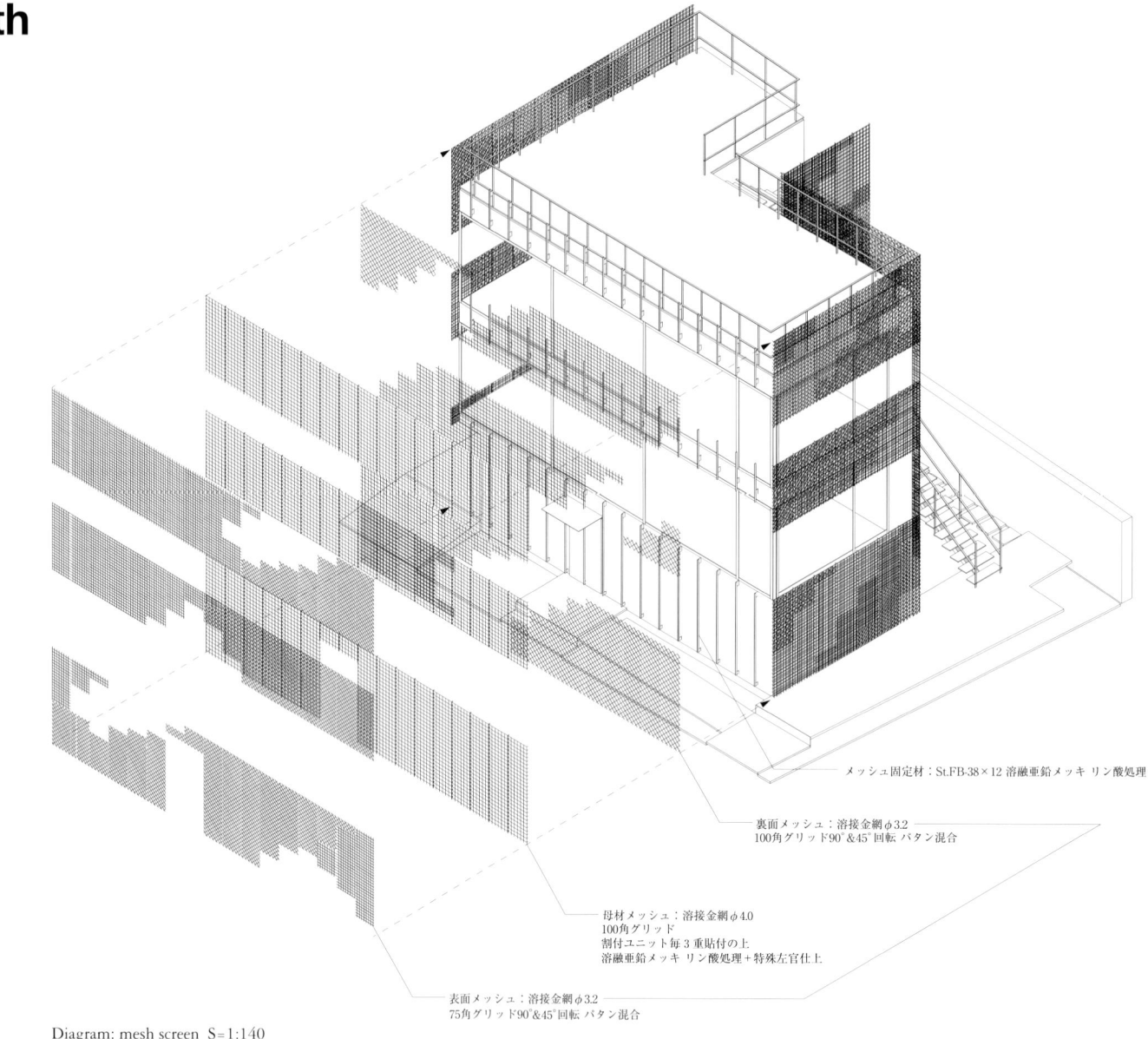

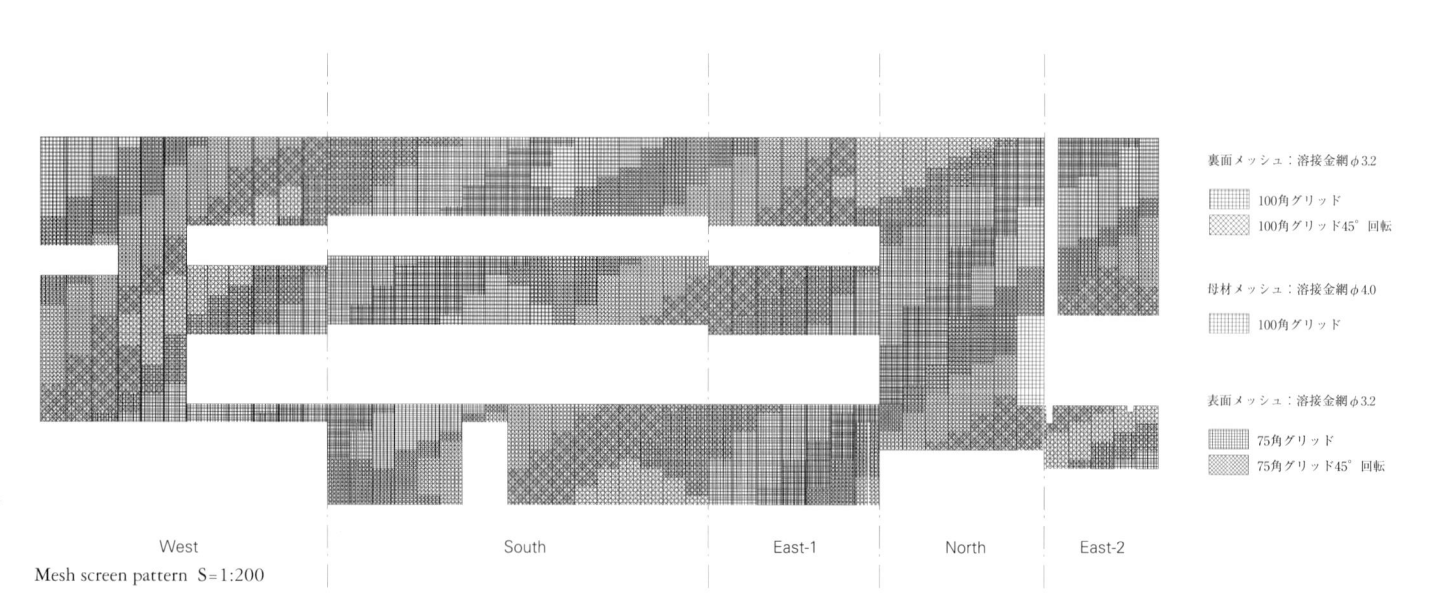

Diagram: mesh screen S=1:140

Mesh screen pattern S=1:200

West   South   East-1   North   East-2

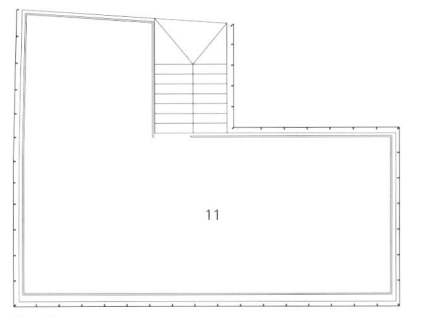

Roof

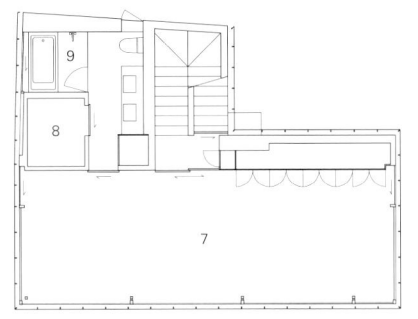

Third floor

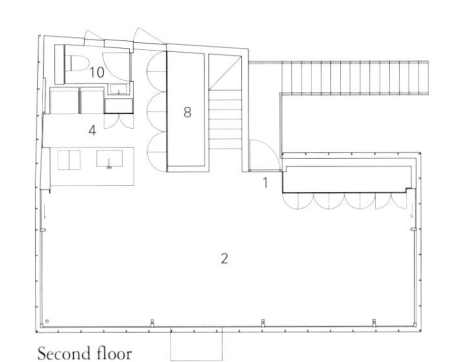

Second floor

First floor S=1:200

1 ENTRANCE
2 LIVING/DINING ROOM
3 LIVING ROOM/BEDROOM
4 KITCHEN
5 TATAMI ROOM
6 MIZUYA
   (PREPARATION ROOM FOR TEA CEREMONY)
7 BEDROOM
8 CLOSET
9 BATHROOM
10 WC
11 ROOF TERRACE
12 BASIN

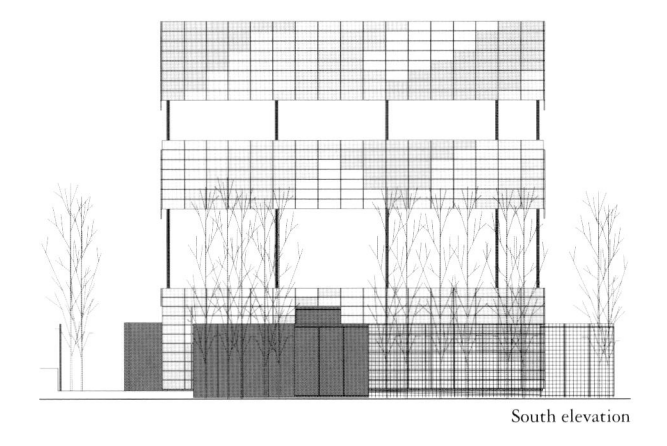

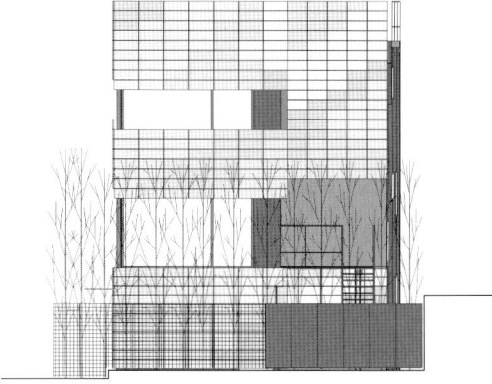

South elevation

East elevation

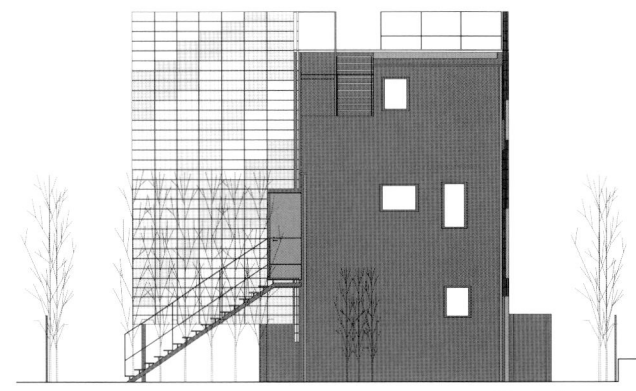

North elevation

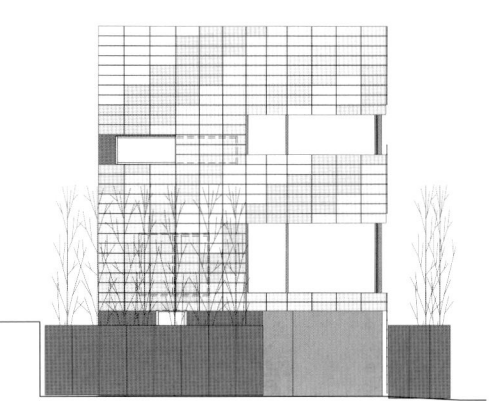

West elevation

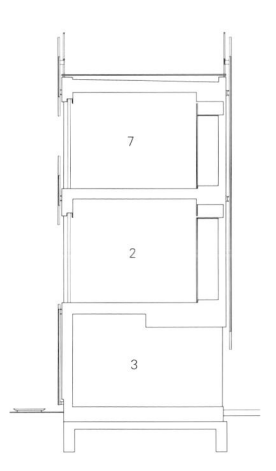

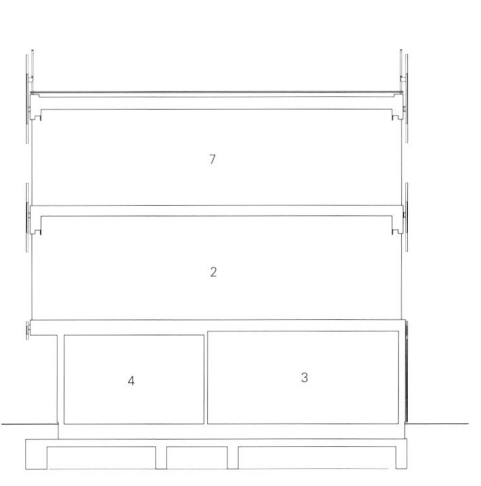

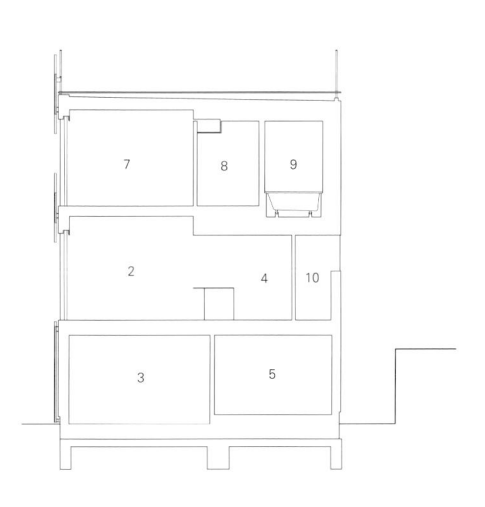

Sections

House facing Ume, Cherry and Peach trees on south　梅や桜，桃の木越しに見る南面

Overall view from southeast　南西より見る全景

Approach　露地

229

Approach and basin facing tearoom　茶室前の露地と水盤

Upward view of corner　角部の見上げ

Basin: tearoom on left　水盤：左が茶室

Living/dining room on second floor　2階居間／食堂

Bedroom on third floor　3階寝室

Tearoom "Hai-an"　茶室「灰庵」

Mesh/Earth

「透明でありながら, しかも土臭く暖かいもの」で公園の中の住宅を覆おうと考えた。

　密度の異なる溶接金網を二重, 三重に重ね, そこに土を吹き付けるという新しい工法を, 左官職人・挾土秀平とともに編み出した。金網の径は3.2mmと4mmを混用し, 通常の土壁に用いるスサの代わりに炭素繊維を混入することで金網と土との接着性を高め, この「透明な土壁」が実現した。金網は基準となる単位寸法(ピクセル寸法)を60cm×30cmとし, 単位毎に方向, 密度, 重ね方に差をつけることで, 工業製品にはない多様な表情を獲得することが可能となった。

　2, 3階の天井には竹, 笹の葉をそのまま練り込んだ粗々しい左官を施した。1階茶室の壁はナラを焼いてできる灰を練り込むことで, 人の肌のようにスムーズな黒い土壁とした。茶室の中心には炉があり, 炭を焼いて灰がつくられる。その灰を, そのまま壁の材料にするというアイディアである。空間の中で行われるソフトと, 空間を構成するハードとを連続させる試みである。

2009-12

Asakusa Culture Tourist Information Center
Taito, Tokyo, Japan

Crossing in front of Kaminari-mon.
West view
雷門前の交差点。西より見る

First floor
Fourth floor
Seventh floor
Roof

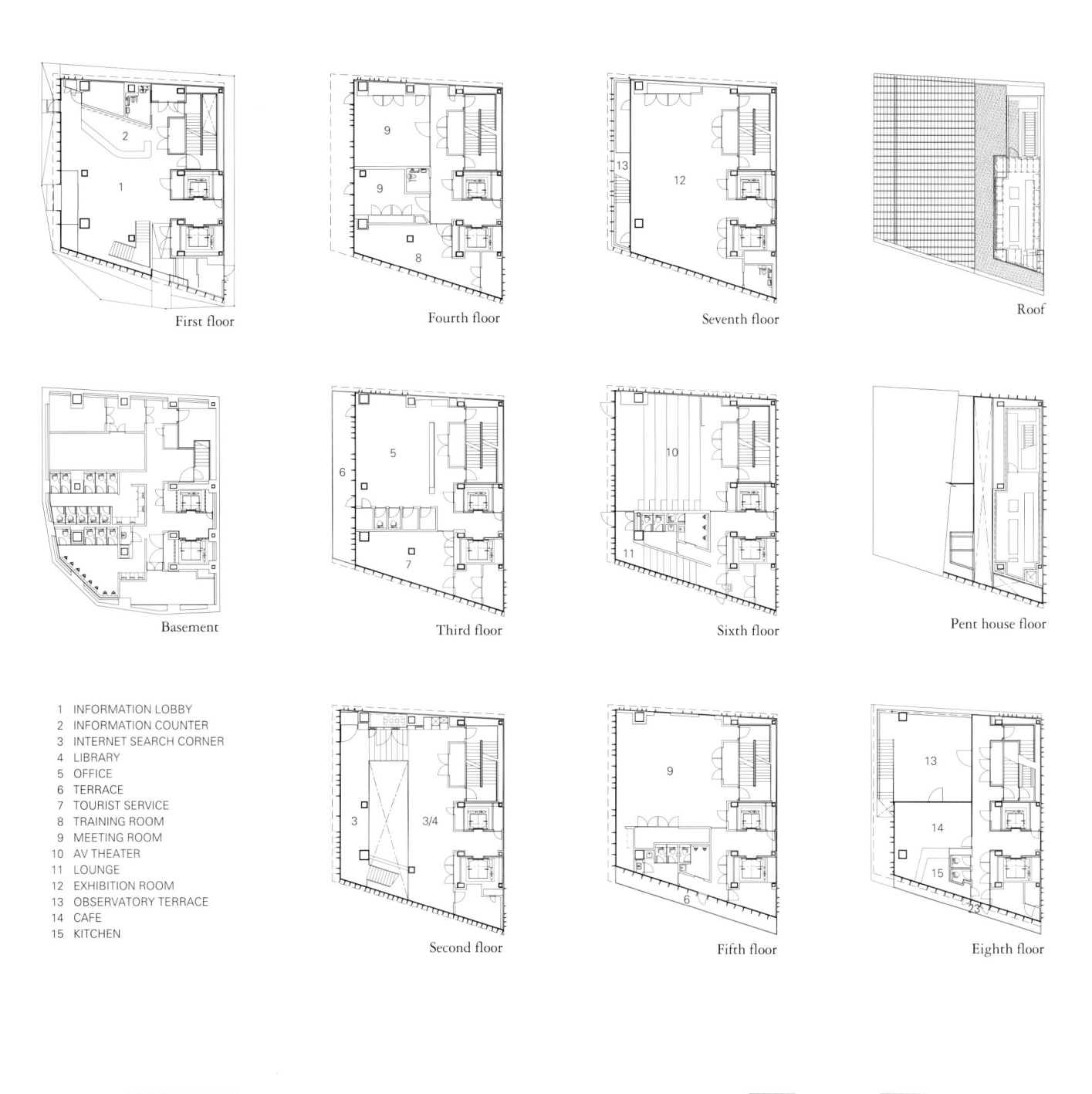

Basement
Third floor
Sixth floor
Pent house floor

1 INFORMATION LOBBY
2 INFORMATION COUNTER
3 INTERNET SEARCH CORNER
4 LIBRARY
5 OFFICE
6 TERRACE
7 TOURIST SERVICE
8 TRAINING ROOM
9 MEETING ROOM
10 AV THEATER
11 LOUNGE
12 EXHIBITION ROOM
13 OBSERVATORY TERRACE
14 CAFE
15 KITCHEN

Second floor
Fifth floor
Eighth floor

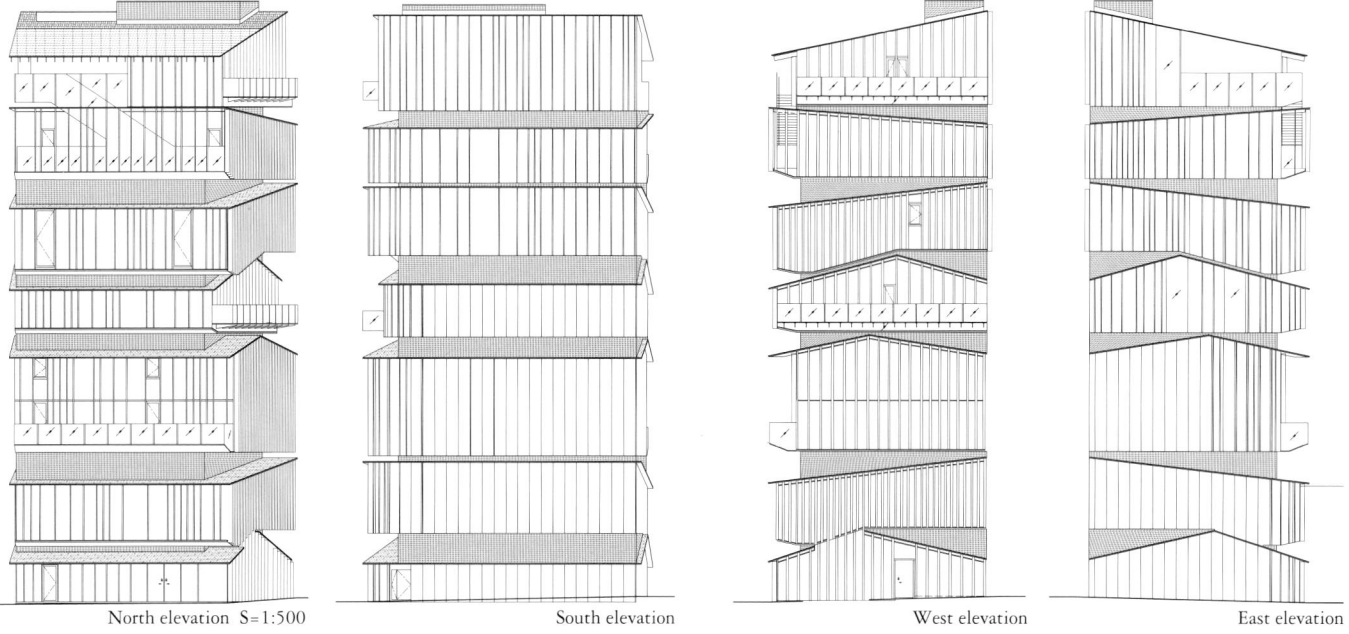

North elevation S=1:500
South elevation
West elevation
East elevation

On a corner plot of the other side of Tokyo representative Senso-ji Temple's Kaminari-mon, a three-dimensional tourism and cultural center compounded with a tourist center, conference rooms and a multi-purpose hall were requested. We endeavored to vertically laminate eight flat wooden buildings and to retrieve ground and roof to every floor. Between each 'flat building = house' a diagonally cut gap was created and the gap is used as minimized mechanical space. Hence, it was made possible to acquire large air volume space that has varying sectional shape, although the floor height is comparable to ordinal middle-rise architecture.

Continuous sequence that can feel the two different roof pitches at the same time was created on the first and the second floor. Though it is a middle floor, the fifth floor's roof inclination provided a stepped floor hall on the sixth floor. We confirmed it is possible to reconnect the space in the air to the ground by inclinations of the roof and the floor even on upper floors. The Senso-ji Temple's shopping street conveys fascination of humane streetscape composed of a row of wooden low-rise architecture in Edo era's Tokyo to the modern. We thought to regain the attraction of low-rise wooden architecture represented in the shopping street in the 38 m-high middle-rise architecture.

浅草文化観光センター

東京を代表する寺院，浅草寺の雷門の向い側の角地に，観光案内所，会議室，多目的ホールが複合した，立体的な観光・文化センターが求められた。八つの木造平屋建築を垂直に積層させ，それぞれのフロアに，大地と屋根を取り戻すことを試みた。それぞれの「平屋建築＝家」の間に，斜めに切り込まれた隙間が生まれ，その隙間をミニマムな設備スペースとすることで，通常の中高層建築と同等の階高でありながら，変化のある断面形状をもつ，大きな気積の空間を獲得することができた。

1,2階では，同時に二つの屋根の勾配を感じられる連続的なシークエンスをつくり出し，6階には，直下の5階の屋根の傾斜を利用することで，中間階でありながら階段状の床を持つホールを設けた。上層階であっても，屋根の角度，床の角度によって，空中の空間を大地に再接続することが可能であることを確認した。向かい側の浅草寺の仲見世は，江戸時代の東京の木造平屋建築が連なるヒューマンな街並みを現代に伝えている。この仲見世に代表される木造平屋建築の魅力を，高さ38mの中層建築の中で再生しようと考えた。

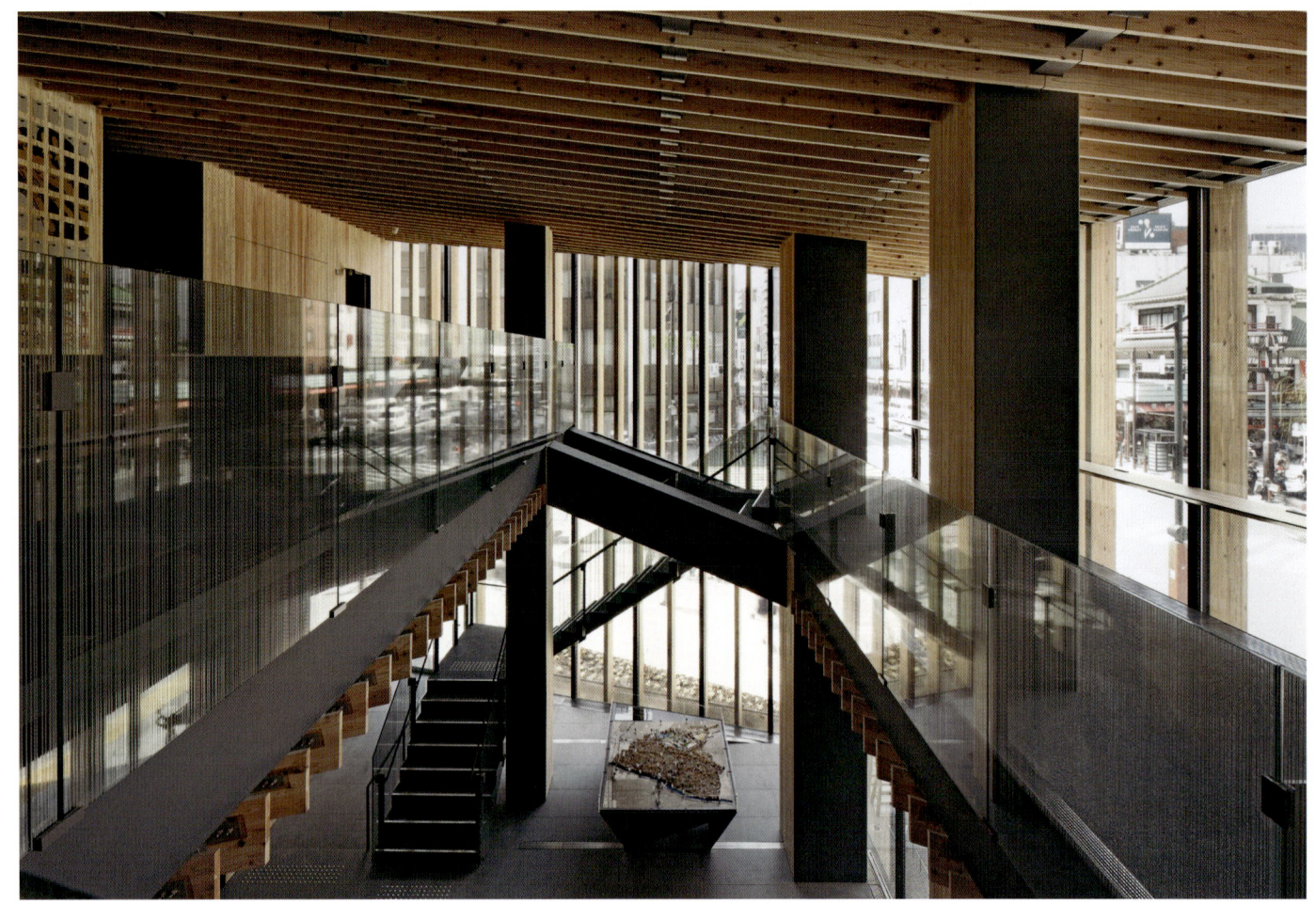

△▽Information lobby on first floor. Internet search corner above.　1階案内ロビー。2階はインターネット検索コーナー

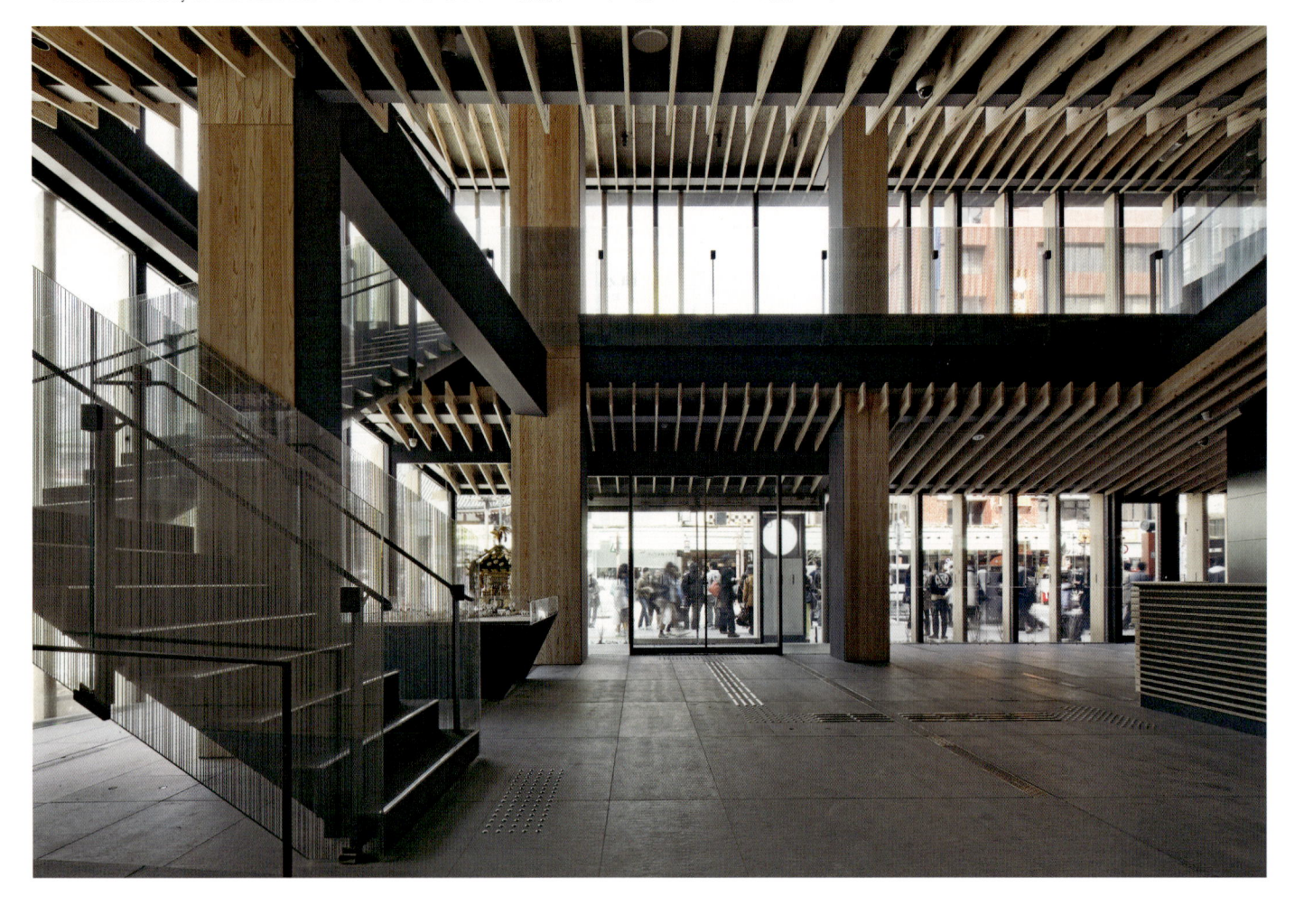

Sectional detail S=1:180

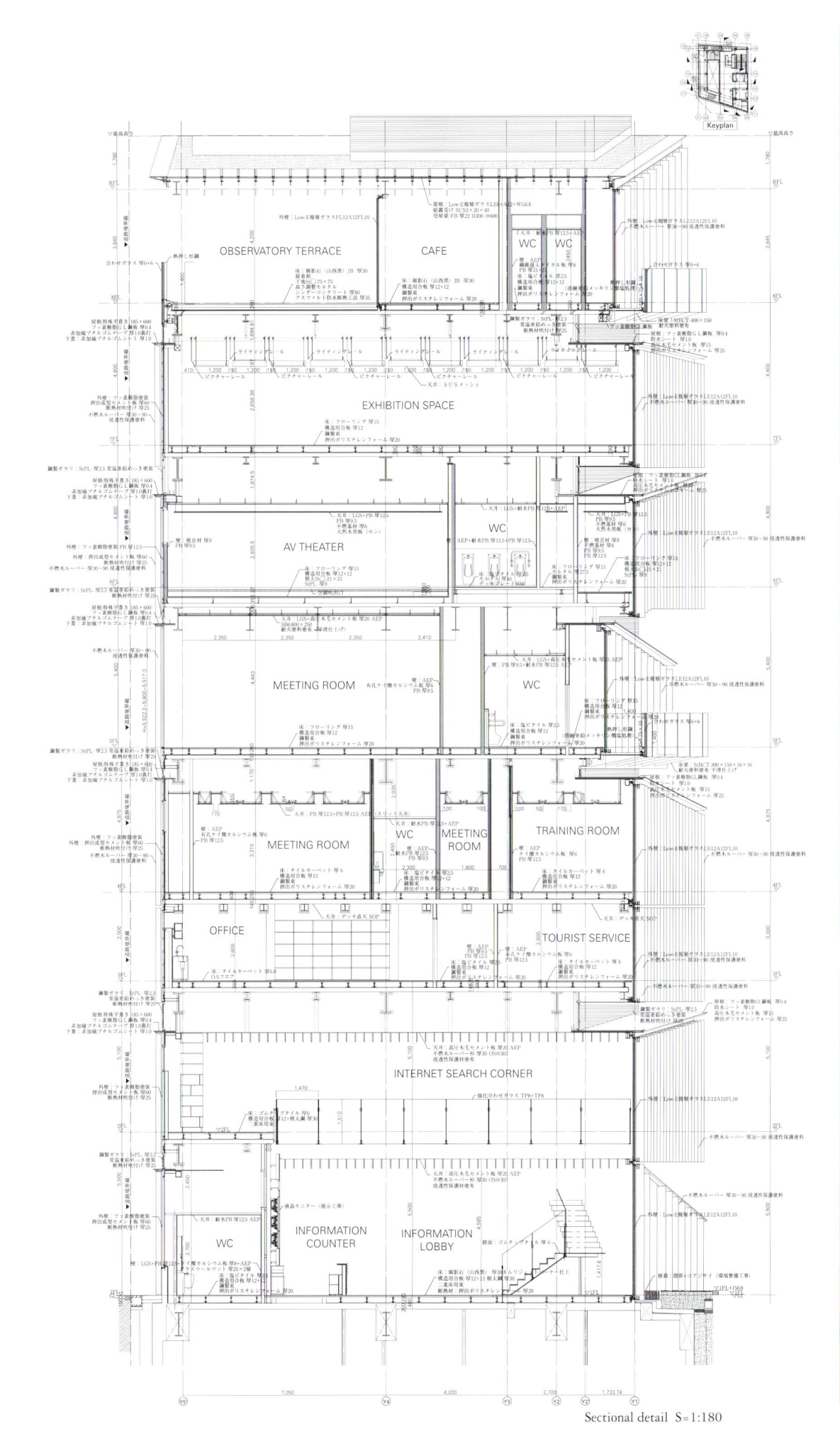

Observatory terrace on eighth floor　8階展望テラス

Exhibition space on seventh floor　7階展示スペース

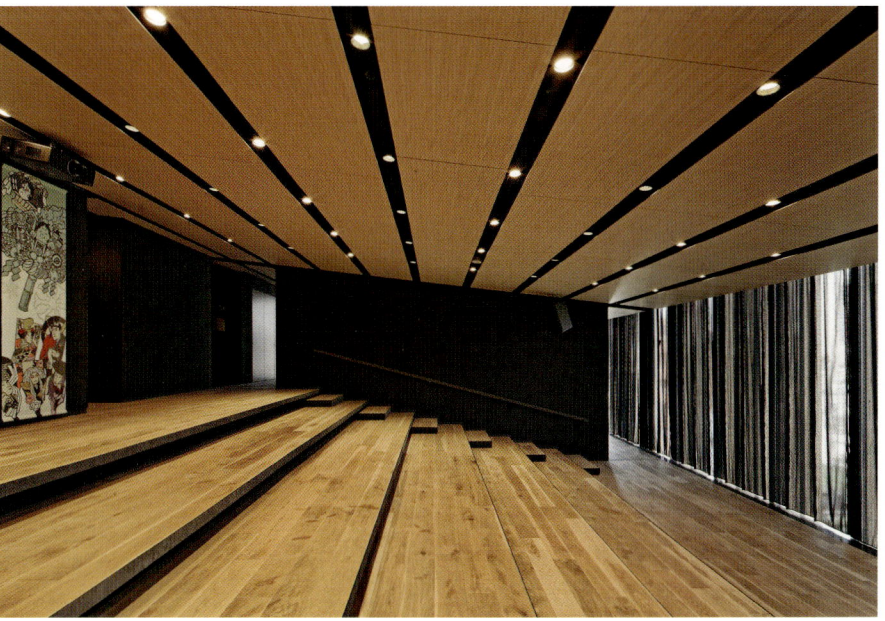

AV theater on sixth floor　6階映像展示室

Jeju Ball
Jeju, South Korea

Master plan S=1:3000

Jeju Ball

済州島を訪れた時，黒いポーラスな火山岩に出会い，このまるくやわらかな感じ，ポーラスな感じを建築化したいと考えた。ここでは，ひとつの家自体が，黒くまるい石として出現した。遠くから見れば，家がひとつの石ころであり，近寄ってみれば，家の様々な部分が黒い石でつくられている。

　なかでも石でできた石庇が，この家では最も重要なディテールである。黒い石ころの隙間から光がもれてくるようなディテールをつくりたいと思った。光がもれてくるディテールによって，黒いポーラスな石の質感を強調することができ，曖昧な屋根のエッジで，地面と屋根が接続されるからである。スティールメッシュの上に，黒い石をのせて庇をつくるというディテールが，その曖昧なエッジを実現した。黒いポーラスの質感が，済州島の景観を決定している。その質感を家のスケールに昇華させた。

DB type (two stories)

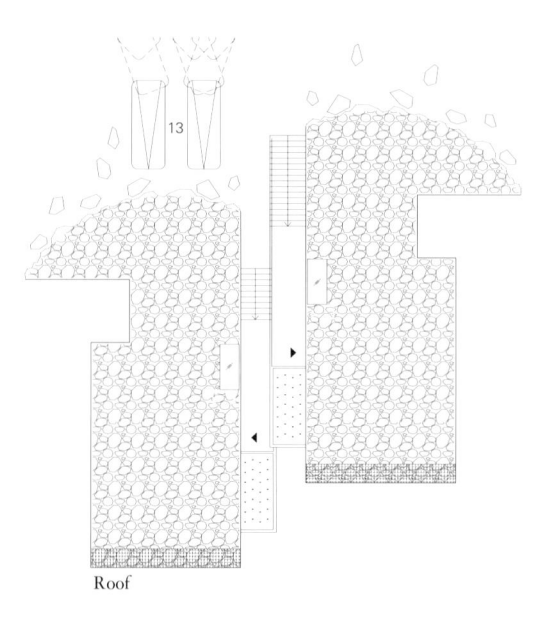

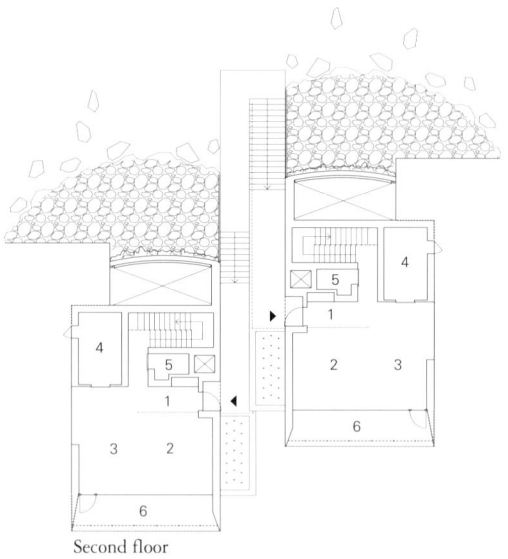

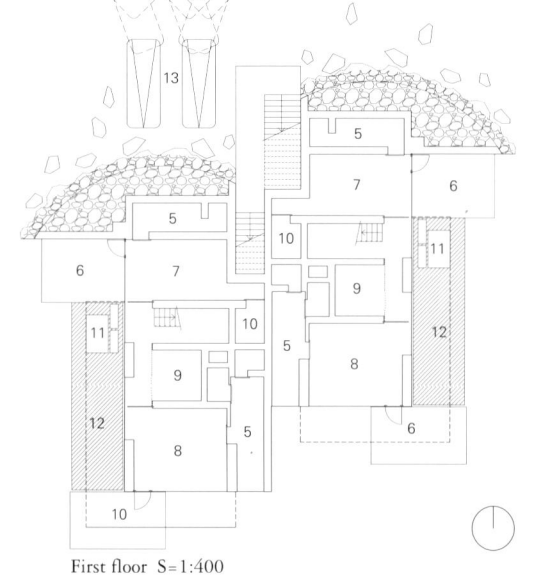

Roof

Second floor

1 ENTRY
2 LIVING ROOM
3 DINING ROOM
4 KITCHEN
5 BATHROOM
6 TERRACE/POACH
7 GUEST ROOM
8 BEDROOM
9 TEA ROOM
10 CLOSET
11 JACUZZI
12 POOL
13 CARPORT

First floor S=1:400

South elevation 南面

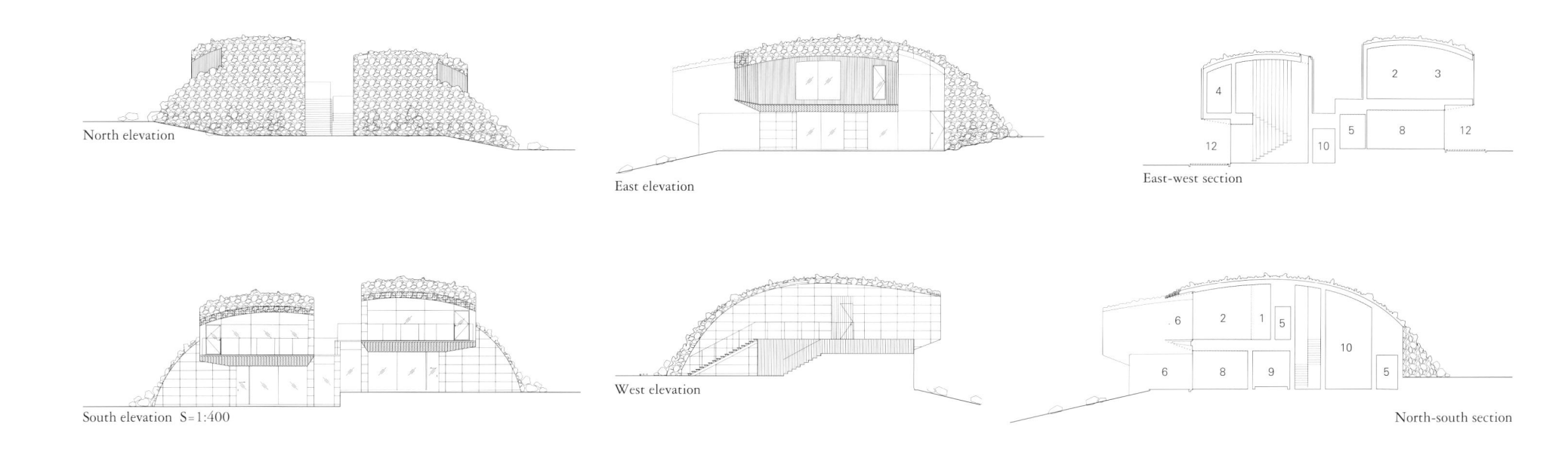

North elevation

East elevation

East-west section

South elevation S=1:400

West elevation

North-south section

Second floor: view toward living room from dining room. Entrance on right　2階：食堂より居間を見る。右は玄関

Guest room on first floor　1階，客室

West elevation　西面

Second floor: living/dining room facing terrace on south　2階：南側テラスに面する居間・食堂

Terrace on second floor: living/dining room on left
2階テラス：左は居間・食堂

DA type (one story)

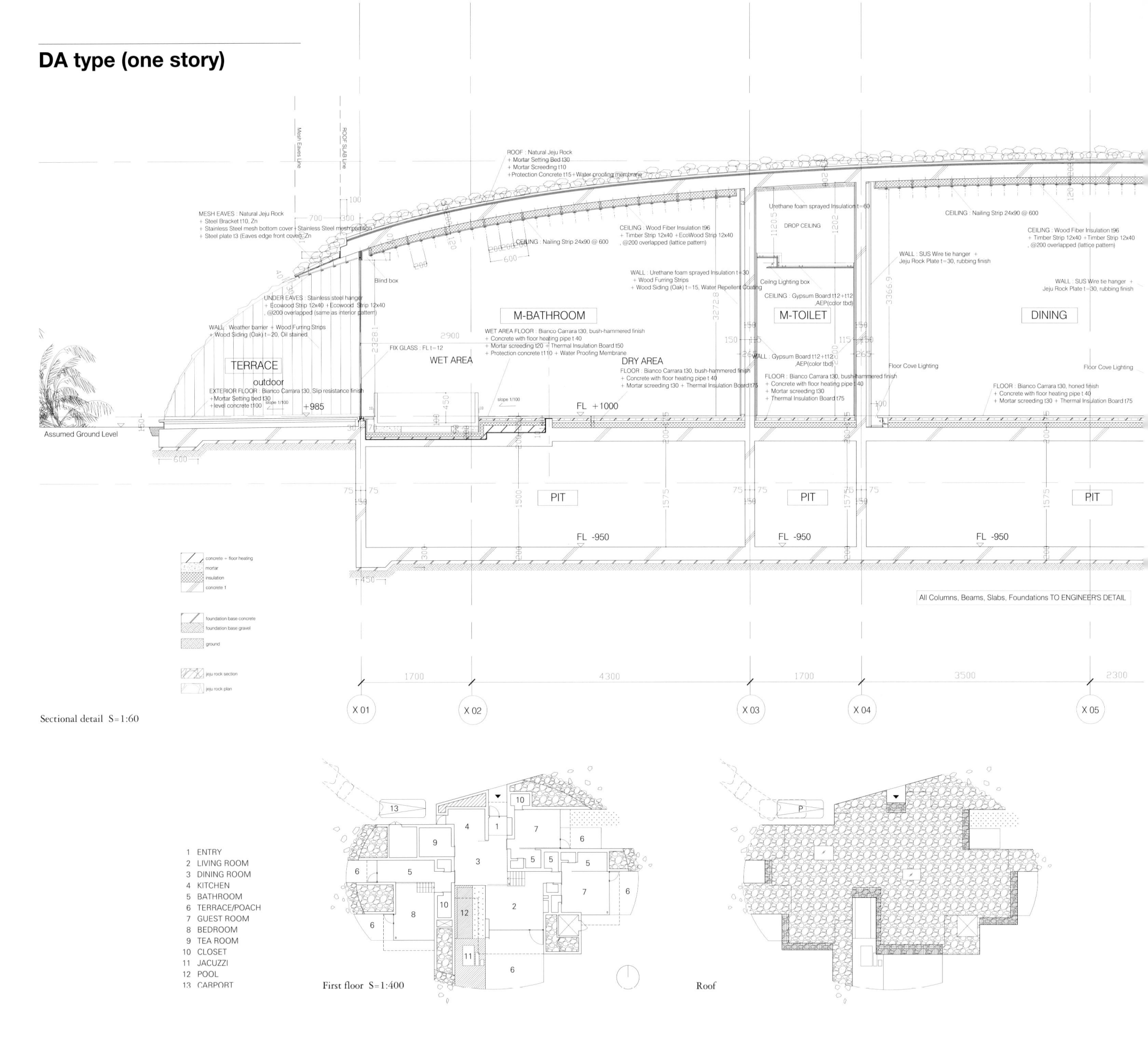

Sectional detail S=1:60

1 ENTRY
2 LIVING ROOM
3 DINING ROOM
4 KITCHEN
5 BATHROOM
6 TERRACE/POACH
7 GUEST ROOM
8 BEDROOM
9 TEA ROOM
10 CLOSET
11 JACUZZI
12 POOL
13 CARPORT

First floor S=1:400

Roof

East elevation

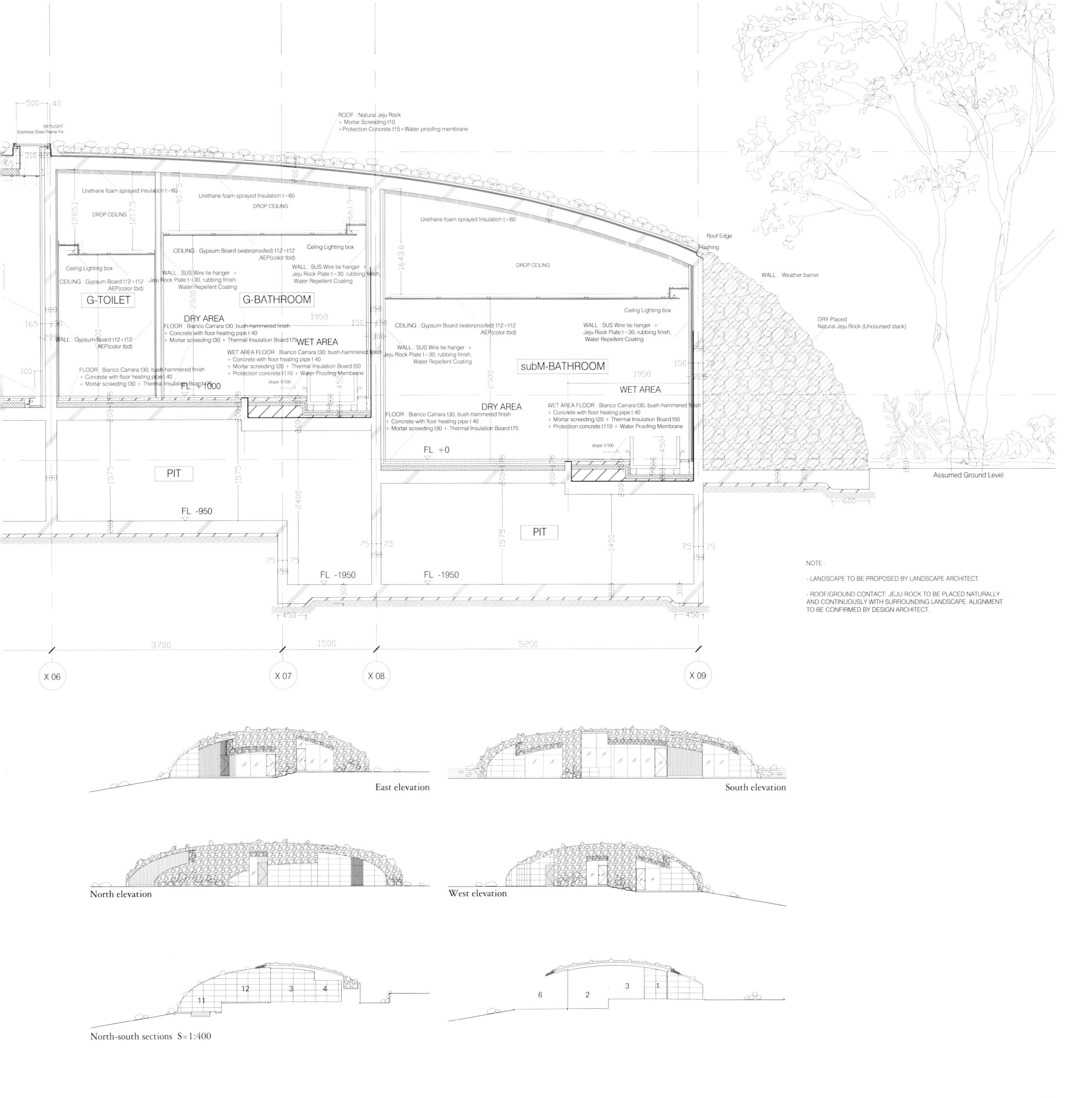

South elevation

North elevation

West elevation

North-south sections S=1:400

Evening view from south toward living room over terrace　夕景。南よりテラス越しに居間を見る

View from entrance toward living room. Dining room on right
玄関より居間を見る。右は食堂

Living room. View toward dining room　居間。食堂を見る

Bedroom: looking south　寝室：南を見る

243

2010 Shang Xia
Shanghai, China

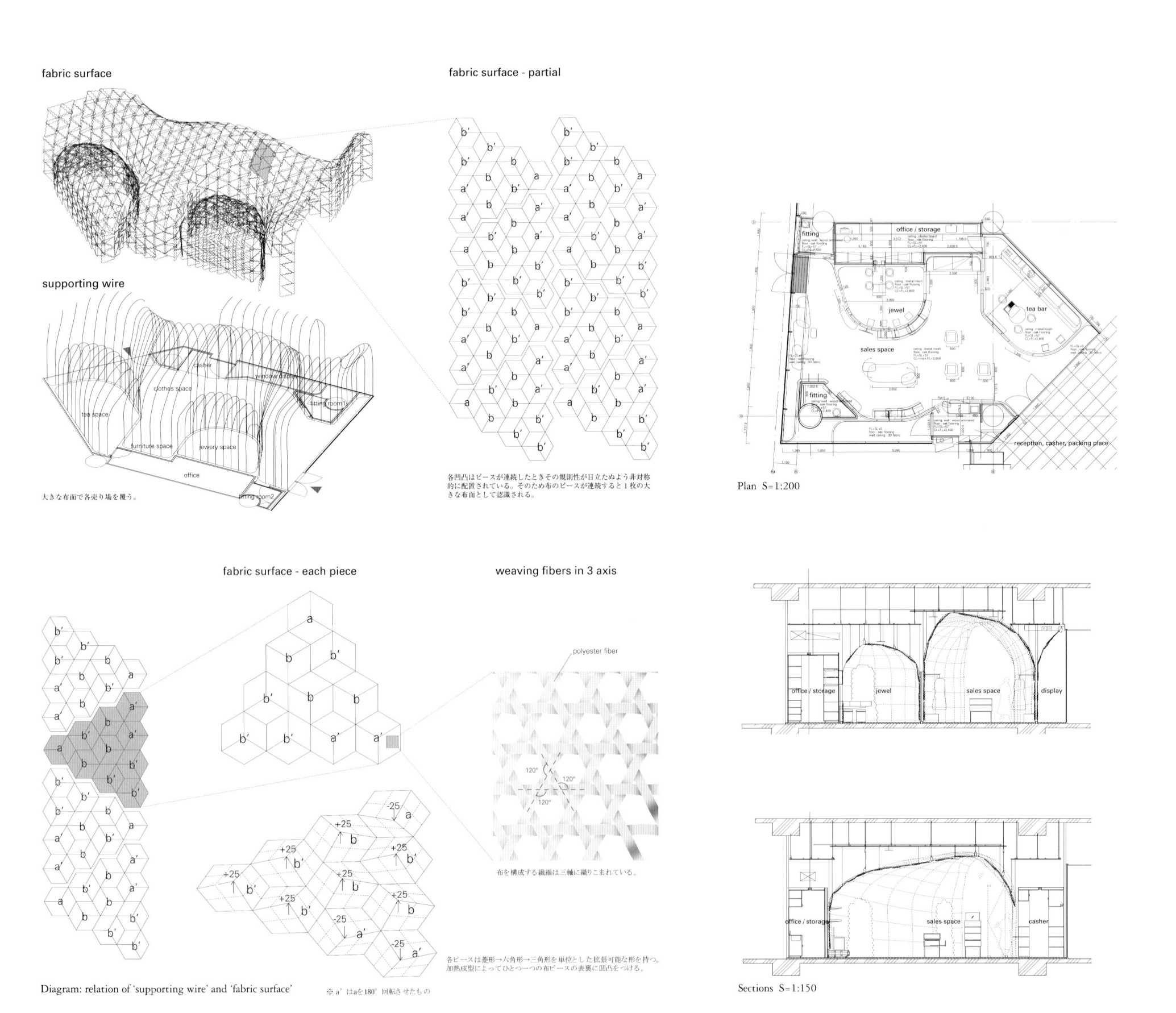

fabric surface

supporting wire

fabric surface - partial

各凹凸はピースが連続したときその規則性が目立たぬよう非対称的に配置されている。そのため布のピースが連続すると1枚の大きな布面として認識される。

大きな布で各売り場を覆う。

Plan S=1:200

fabric surface - each piece

weaving fibers in 3 axis

布を構成する繊維は三軸に織りこまれている。

各ピースは菱形→六角形→三角形を単位とした拡張可能な形を持つ。加熱成型によってひとつ一つの布ピースの表裏に凹凸をつける。

Diagram: relation of 'supporting wire' and 'fabric surface'   ※ a' はaを180°回転させたもの

Sections S=1:150

Shang Xia is a new brand affiliated to Hermes and it schemes to fuse Chinese craftsmanship and modern design. The project is their first store. We made three-dimensional fabric that uses polyester fiber interlaced by so-called three-axes-weave method. By hanging the fabric, we created flexible and amorphous space that can be called a fabric cave. Although the cloth maintains transparency, it gains geometrical concave and convex shape by the three-dimensional process and accordingly creates shades. Therefore, it was possible to make intermediate and vague space that jumps various dichotomies that we used to express space until then, such as light and shade, trueness and falseness and opaqueness and transparency.

「上下」上海店

「上下」は，中国のクラフトマンシップと現代デザインの融合をコンセプトとするHermes傘下の新ブランドで，これはその第1号店。ポリエステル繊維を用いる三軸織りと呼ばれる立体的な布をつくり，その布を吊り下げて布の洞窟ともいうべき，やわらかで不定形な空間をつくりあげた。布は透明性を持ちながらも，立体加工によって幾何学的な凹凸を獲得し，陰影を生じるため，光と影，実と虚，不透明性と透明性等々，今までわれわれが空間を形容する時に用いてきた様々な二項対立を飛び越えた，中間的で曖昧な空間をつくり上げることができた。

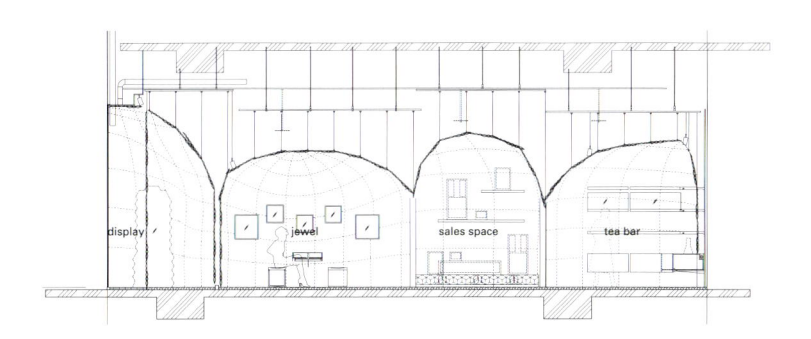

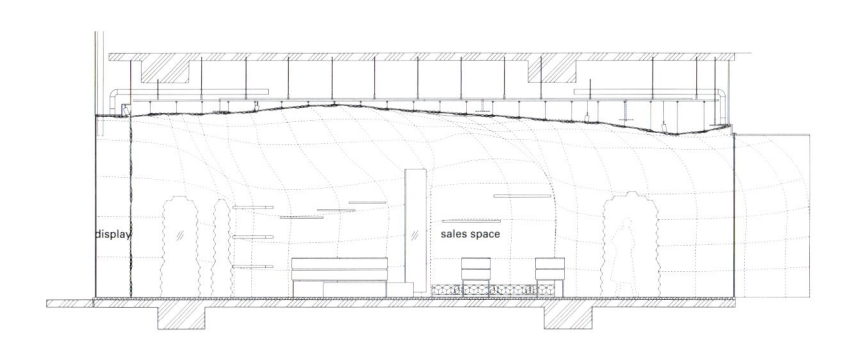

Cave-like interior of store 'clothes space'　ブティックのインテリア「clothes space」

View from entrance toward fitting room', 'jewely space' on right　エントランス周り。奥は「fitting room」，右の開口を潜ると「jewely space」

View toward shoes display through 'furniture space'　「tea space」より「furniture space」越しにshoes displayなどを見る

2009-10 Ceramic Cloud
Casalgrande, Bologna, Italy

This is a monument located in the middle of a traffic roundabout on the road at Reggio Emilia, Italy. The sponsor is a leading Italian ceramic tile manufacturer, Casalgrande Padana. To avoid producing another traditional tile monument that uses tiles as a cladding on a shaped concrete base which could be described as a 'Gaudi type', we used tiles as a structural component by taking advantage of its planar rigidity.

We wove together 20 mm diameter stainless rods as a vertical thread, and 600 mm x 1200mm x 14mm ceramic tiles as a horizontal thread to create a 5.4 m high wall-like monument.

Its plan is a 45 m long spindle shape with each end finished sharply to realize a strongly contrasting effect. As drivers approach from the distance it appears as a thin vertical element but as they negotiate the roundabout a 45m wall suddenly appears. We pursued the possibility of a phenomenological entity whose form can vary tremendously depending on the (moving) position of the viewer.

This porous monument made of white ceramic tiles set at a variety of angles also varies its appearance depending on the direction and strength of the natural daylight. In much the same way mist and clouds are remarkable for the way their water vapor molecules appear in various forms depending on the condition of the light or the relationship with the observer. We named this monument ' Cloud ' aspiring to the idea that this new but subtle work can evoke such an ephemeral phenomenon.

Ceramic Cloud

イタリア、レッジオ・エミリアの幹線道路のロータリーの中央に計画されたモニュメント。スポンサーは、イタリアを代表するタイルメーカーであるカザルグランデ・パダナ社である。通常、タイルのモニュメントというと、奇妙な形態のコンクリートの躯体の上にタイルを化粧材として貼り付ける、「ガウディ型」のものが多い。しかし、このプロジェクトではタイルの面的剛性を利用し、タイルそのものを構造材として用いた。

直径20mmのステンレス・パイプを縦糸に、600mm×1,200mm、厚さ14mmのタイルそのものを横糸として、それを織り上げるように高さ5.4mの壁状のモニュメントを組み上げていった。

平面形状は長さ45mの細長い紡錘形であり、両端は鋭角的に尖らせてある。遠方よりこのロータリーに近づく車に対して、このモニュメントはまず細い線として出現し、ロータリーを廻る時には突如として45mの長さの大壁面として出現するという対比的な効果を狙って、この形状が決定された。移動に応じて極端に形態が異なって認識される、現象学的な物質のあり方を追求した。

様々な角度をもつ白いタイルでできたポーラスなモニュメントは、光の向き、強さによっても多様な姿、形態をもって出現する。霧や雲とは、水蒸気の粒子が、光の状態、観察者との関係に応じて、多様な形で出現するところが興味深い。そのような現象学的とも呼べる新しい曖昧なモニュメントを目指して、名前をクラウド(=雲)とした。

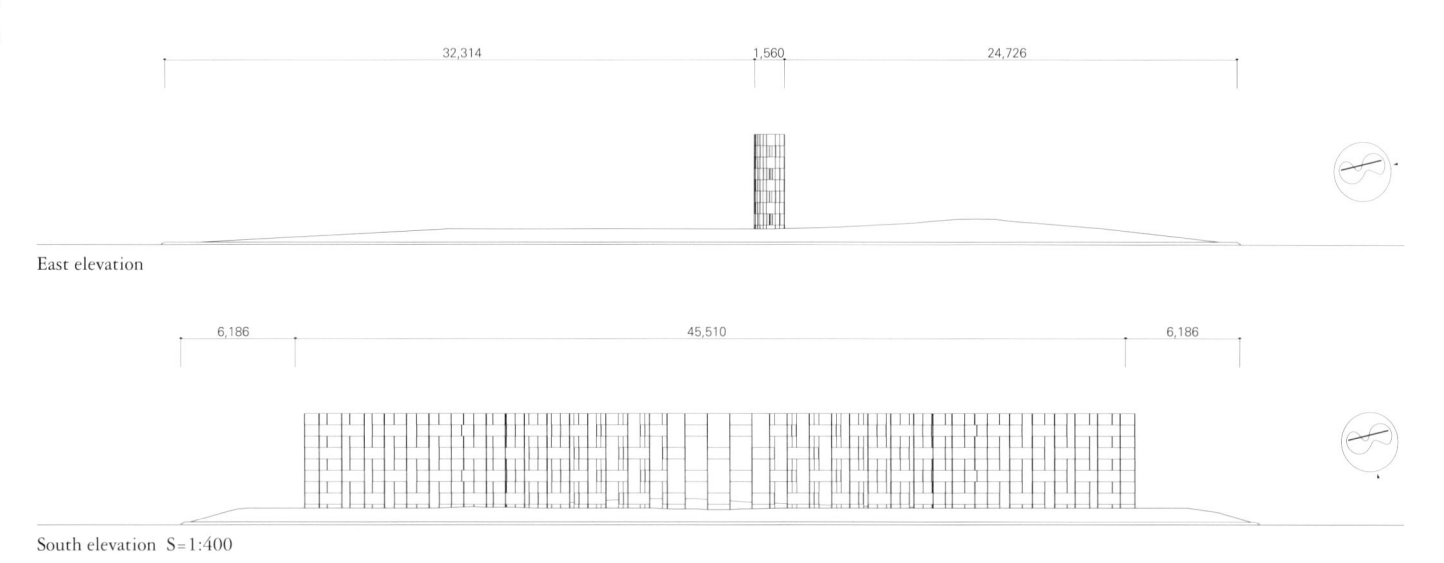

East elevation

South elevation S=1:400

Overall view from south　南より見る。全景

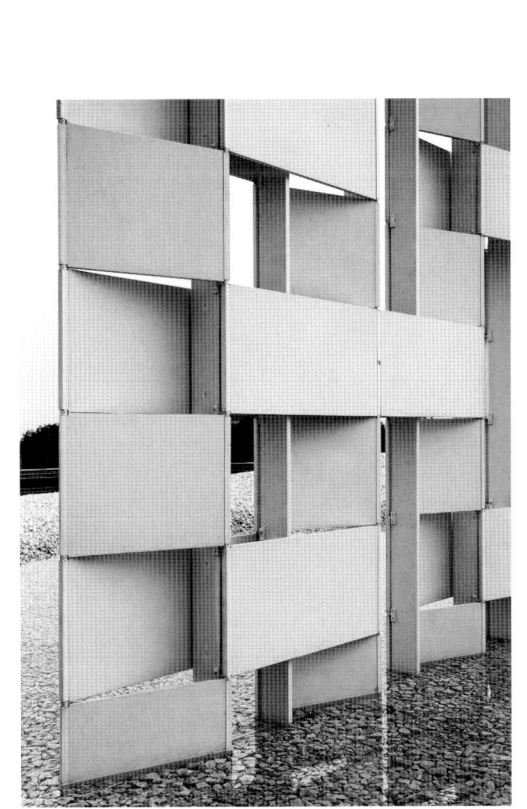

Eastern end　東側端部を見る

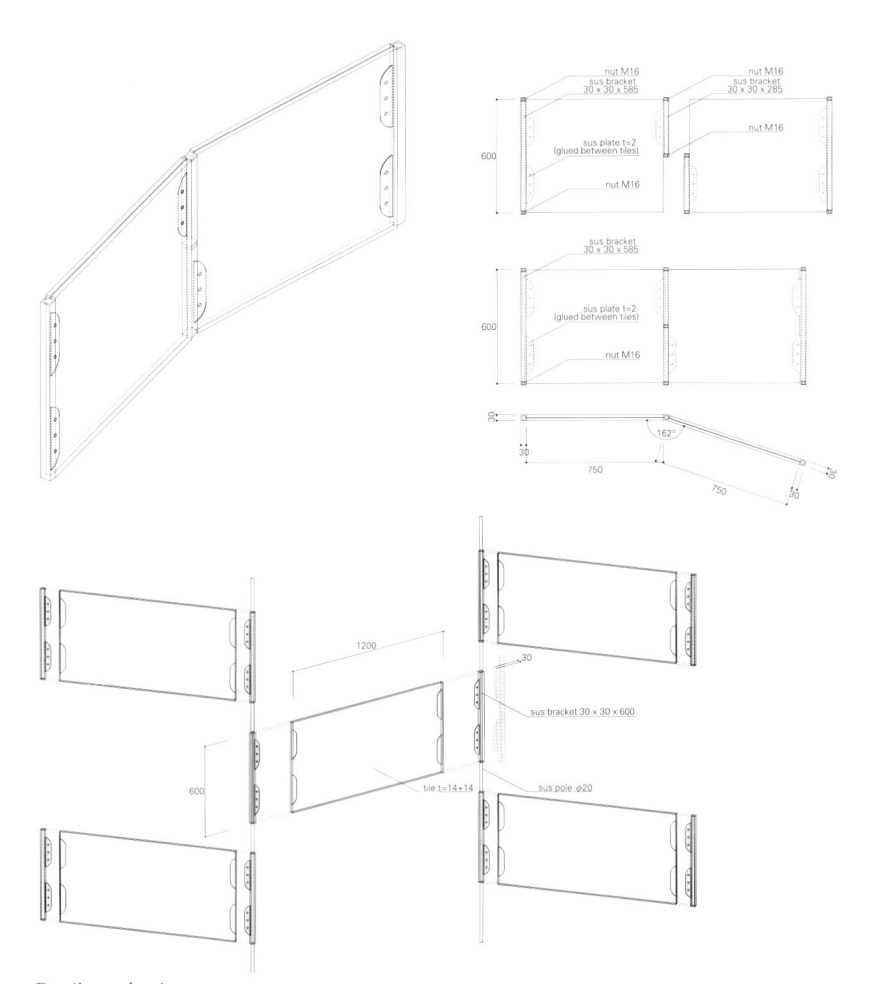

Detail: panel unit

247

2010- Chikugo Art and Culture Center
Chikugo, Fukuoka, Japan

Overall view from Chikugo-funagoya station / Left: Annex 1 (designed by SUEP), center: main building, right: Annex 2 (designed by Kengo Kuma and Associates)
筑後船小屋駅より見る全景／左：Annex 1（設計：SUEP），中央：本館，右：Annex 2（共に，設計：隈研吾建築都市設計事務所）

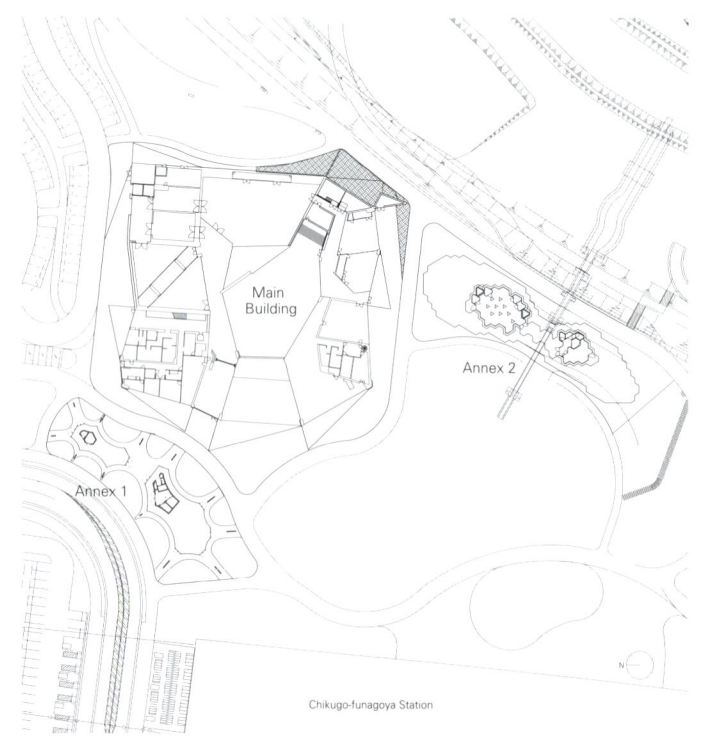

Site plan S=1:1500

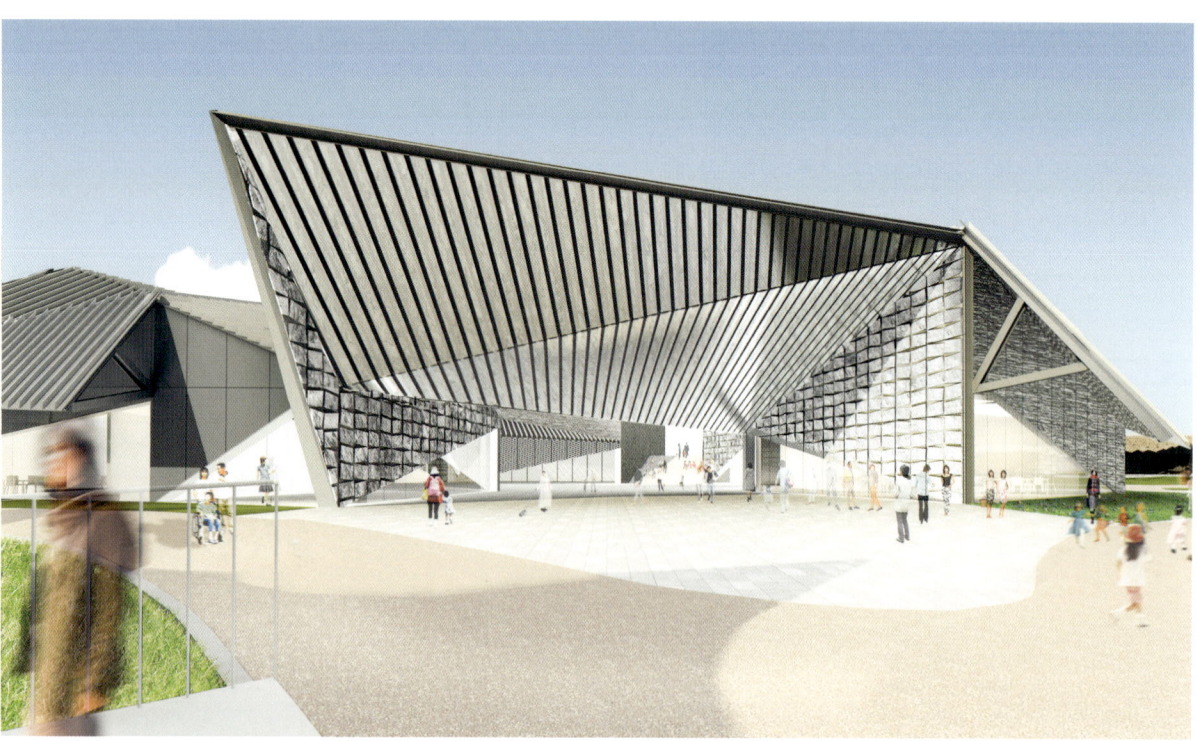

Entrance of main building 本館エントランス

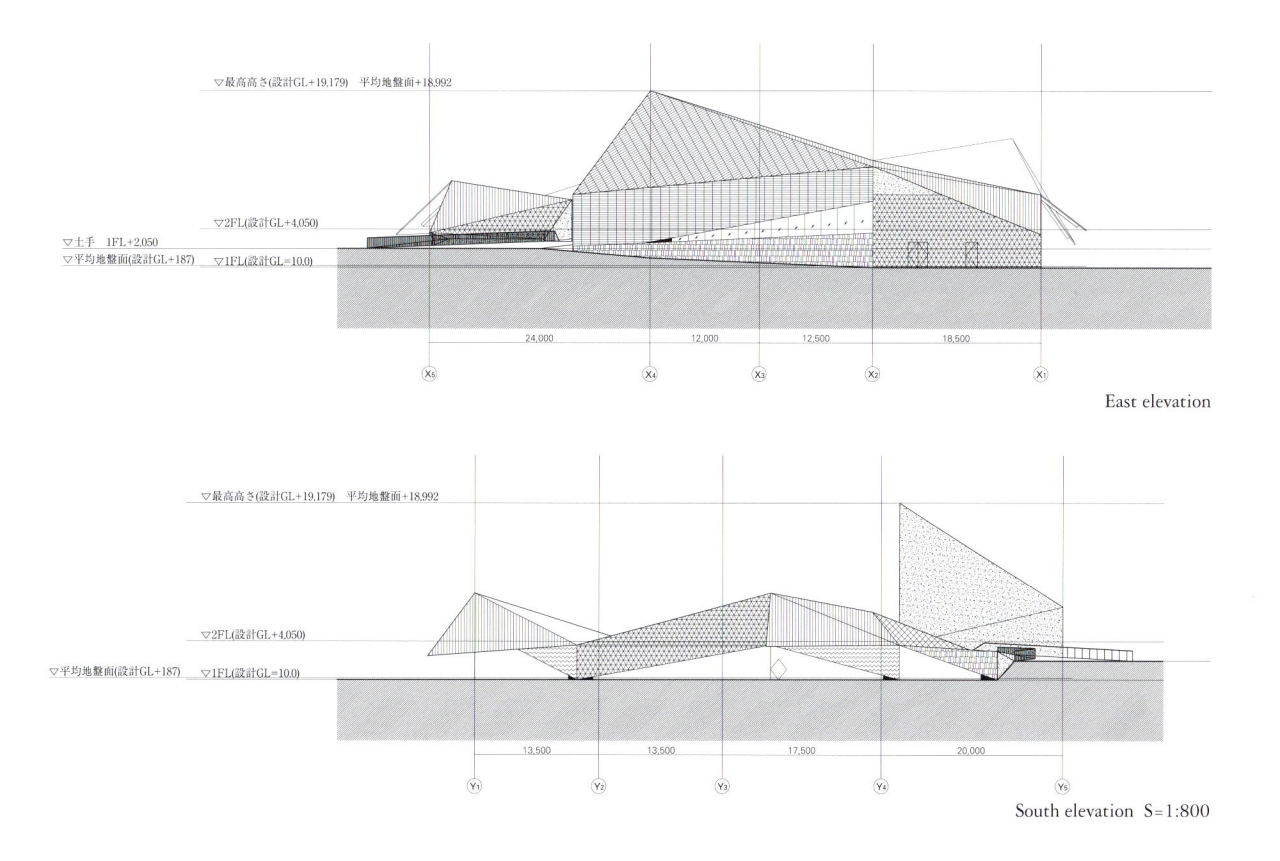

We searched for a possibility of a gate-type and a roofed-type cultural facility that replaces box-type one. The site was on an exceptional location in front of Kyushu Shinkansen's Chikugo-funagoya station and besides the Yabe River on east side. By designing the architecture as a kind of gate, we thought artificial objects and nature such as the station, river and railway are connected as one and the distance between the nature and human become closer.

In order the gate-type architecture to get familiar with the surrounding park and river, it was decomposed into an assembly of small roofs. A diverse texture was afforded to the created small roofs and walls. A way to decompose a large rectangle box into various triangles was a theme. Further, the decomposed elements were not just thrown on the ground, but were loosely united, a large gate was made and then they re-connected human and the nature.

For the each small triangle, texture of galvanized steel plate, stainless steel mesh and granite stone were given, but it was detailed that each triangle further decomposes into particles. In detail, the roof's galvanized steel plate was roofed by shingle with a large riser (200 mm), and stone was accentuated the each unit by changing the length of the stainless steel 'leg'. Owing to these details, large entity was converted into a collection of small things. Small things variously transform the shade and materiality responding to the alteration of seasons, and the architecture keeps on changing its state like rich nature.

On the adjacent site along the river we designed a pavilion for pottery making using local cedar. Cedar was made into laminated material and created into 2.4-meter–long home base type beams. The unit beam was assembled with a joint system using bolts based on a geometry that sources triangle like the main building. It is an experiment to create an expandable loose whole using small units.

East elevation

South elevation S=1:800

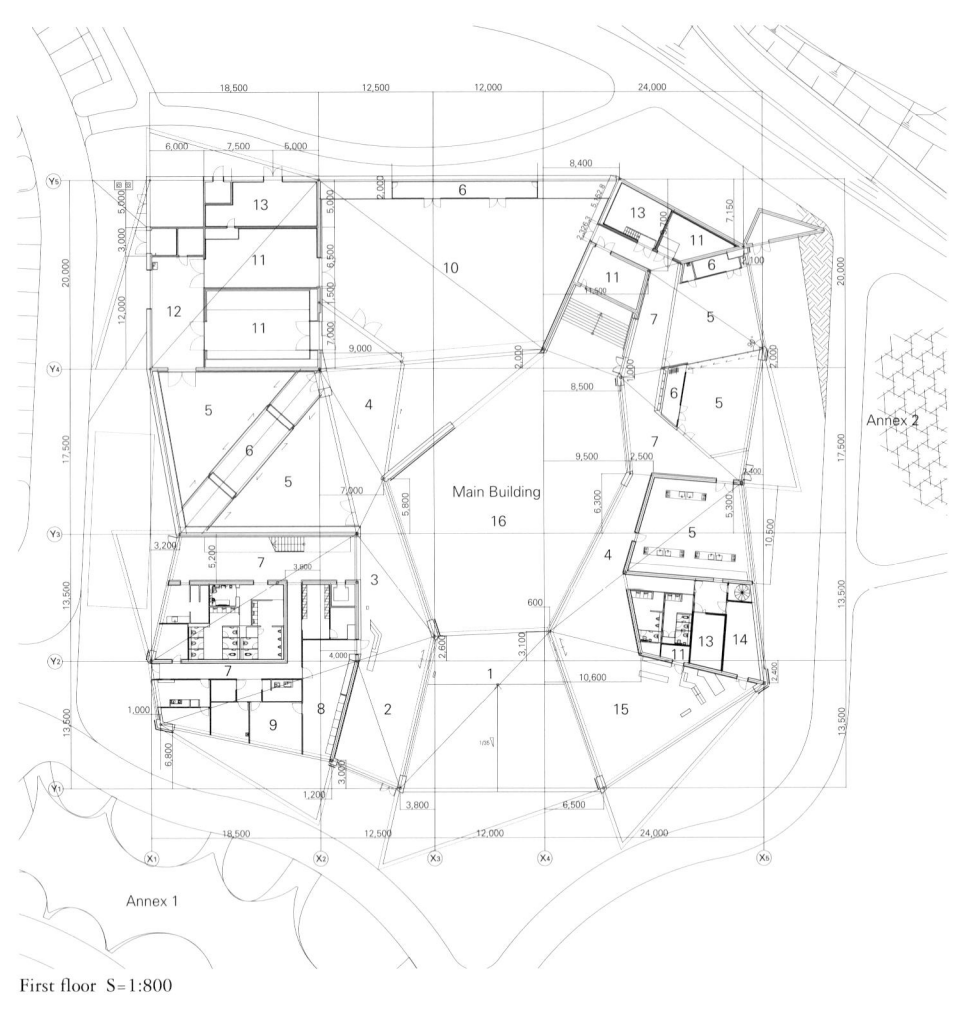

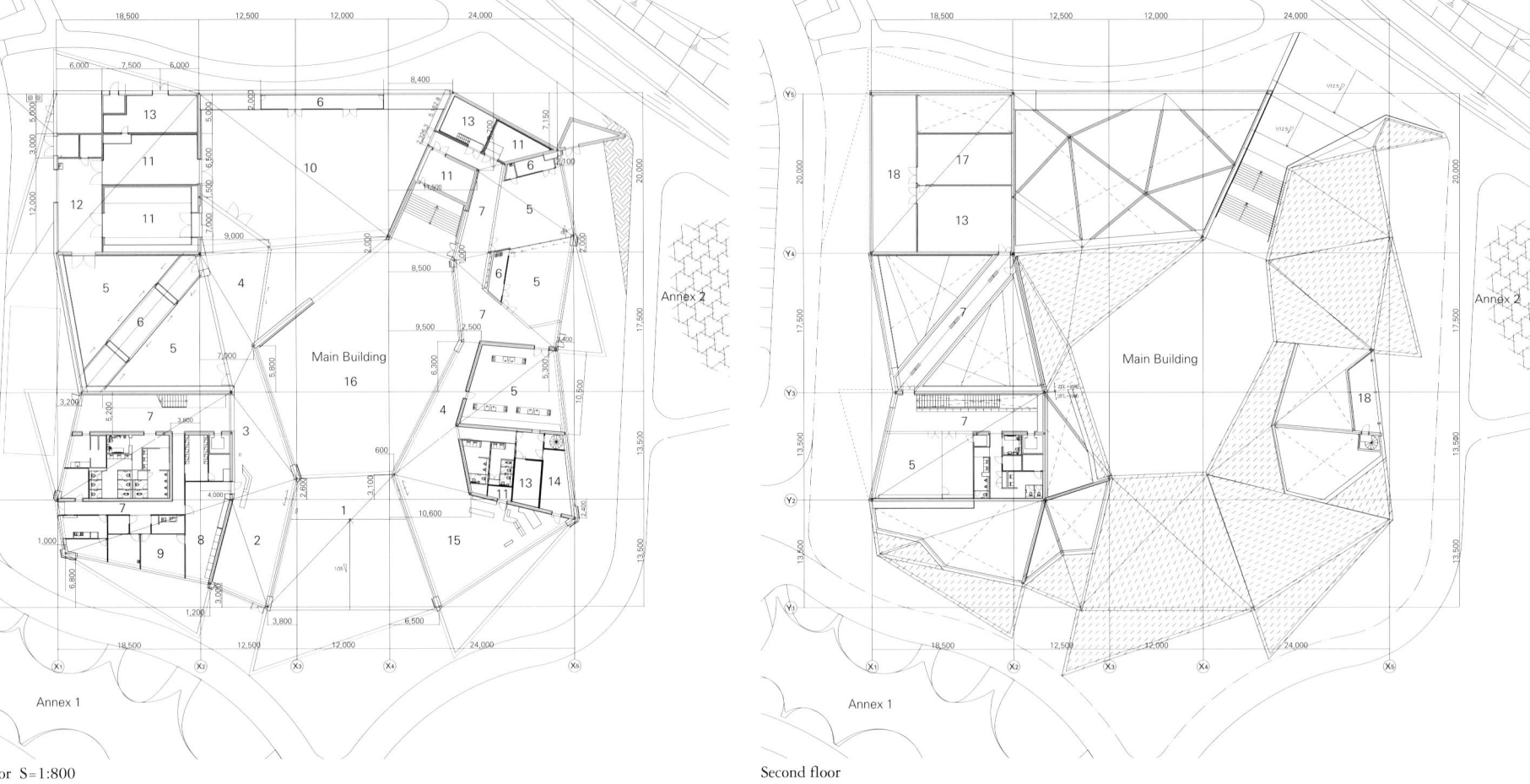

First floor S=1:800

Second floor

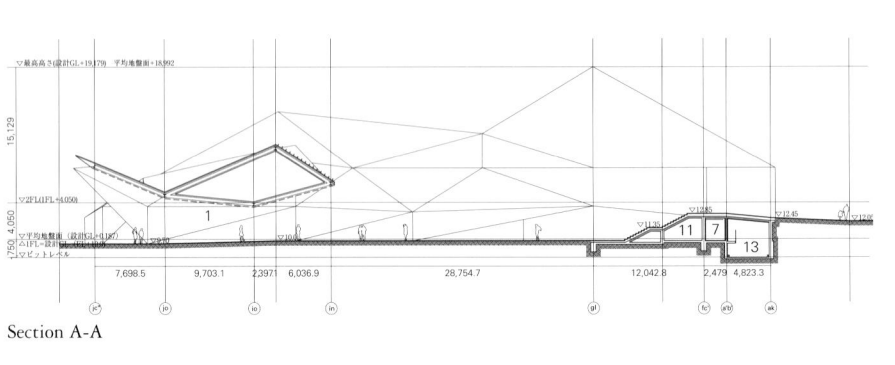

Section A-A

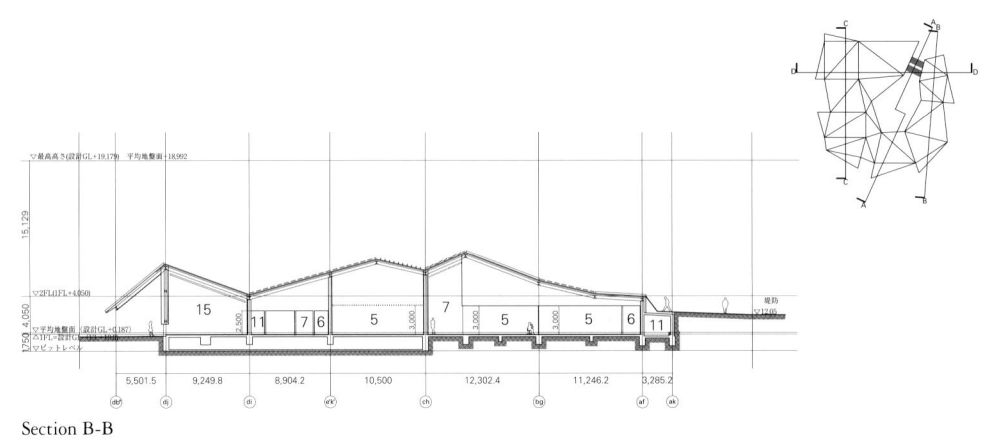

Section B-B

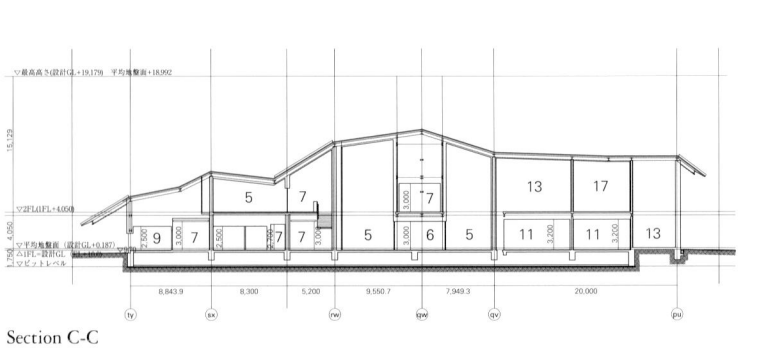

Section C-C

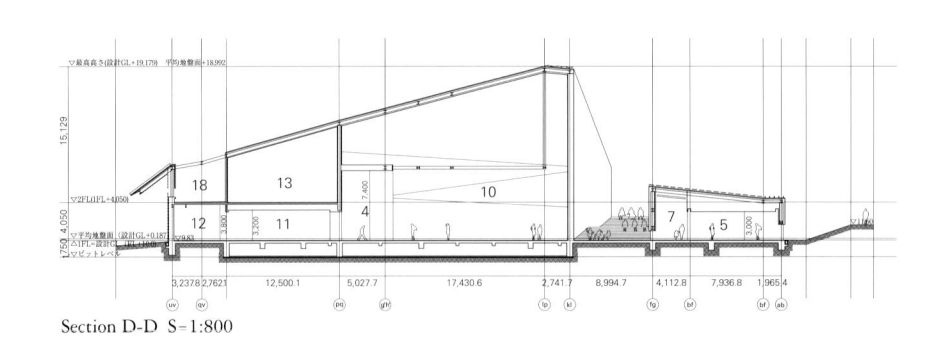

Section D-D S=1:800

1 ENTRANCE	6 SHELF	11 STORAGE	16 PLAZA
2 GALLERY	7 CORRIDOR	12 UNLOADING	17 ELECTORICAL
3 INFORMATION	8 OFFICE	13 MECHANICAL	18 OUTDOOR MECHANICAL UNIT
4 FOYER	9 MEETING ROOM	14 KITCHEN	
5 WORKSHOP	10 COMUNICATION ROOM	15 CAFETERIA	

PAVILION (Annex 2)

Exterior of Annex 2　アネックス2の外観

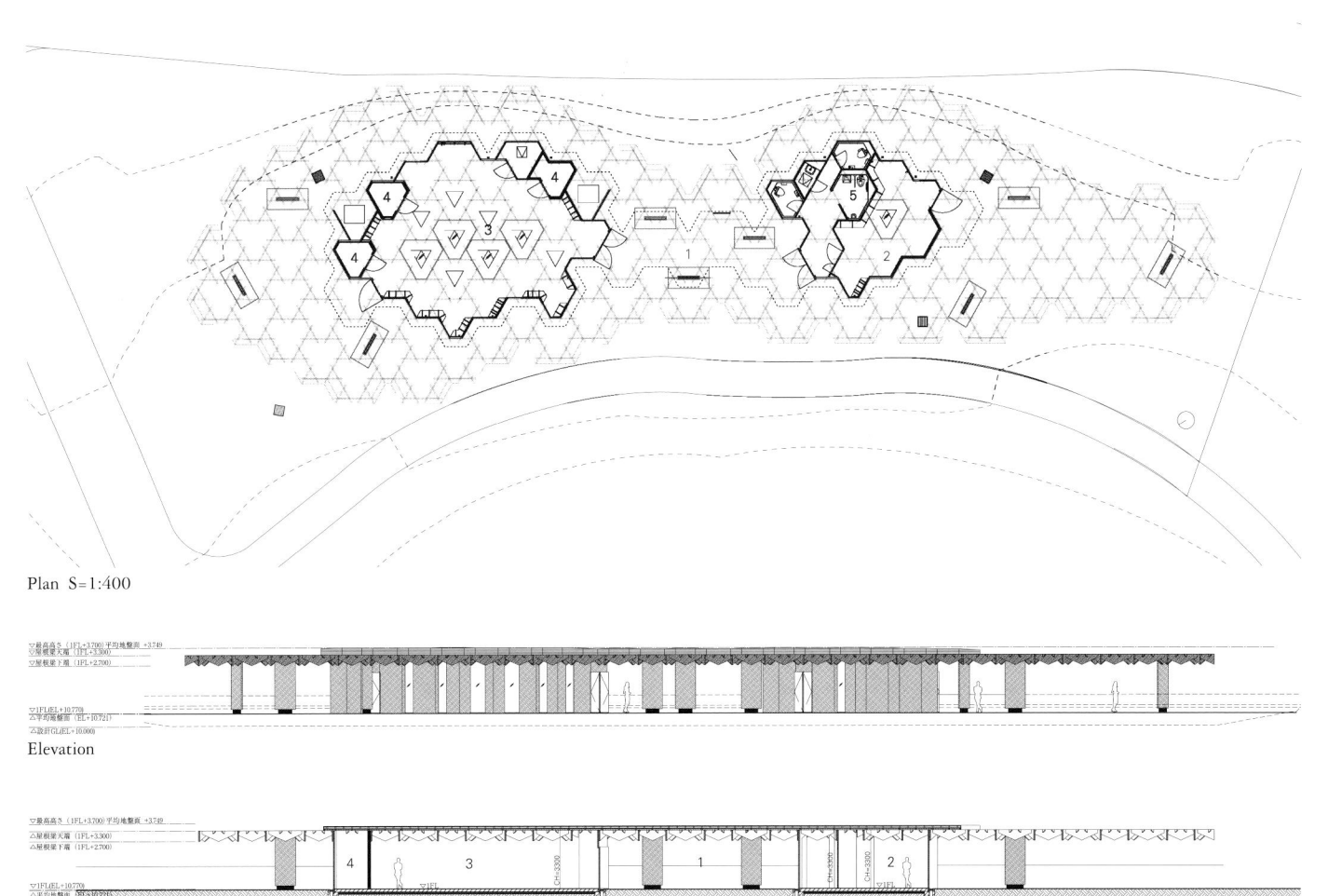

Studio　教室工房

Plan S=1:400

Elevation

Longitudinal section S=1:400

1　ENTRANCE PORCH
2　WORKSHOP
3　STUDIO
4　MECHANICAL
5　WC

筑後広域公園芸術文化交流施設(仮称)

ハコ型の文化施設にかわる，ゲート型，屋根型の文化施設の可能性を探った。九州新幹線筑後船小屋駅の駅前，東側は矢部川という類い希な敷地が与えられた。この建築を一種のゲートとしてデザインすることで，駅と川，鉄道という「人工物と自然」をひとつにつなぎ，自然と人間との距離を近づけようと考えた。

周囲の公園，川と建築とを馴染ませるために，このゲート型建築は小さな屋根の集合体へと分解され，その結果生まれた小さな屋根，小さな壁に対しては多種多様なテクスチャーが与えられる。大きな四角いハコを，如何に小さくて多様な三角形に分解するかがひとつのテーマである。そして分解されたものが，ただ地上に投げ出されるのではなく，分解されながらゆるく結合して大きなゲートが構成され，それによって人と自然とが再接続される。

小さな三角形それぞれには，ガルバリウム鋼板，ステンレス・メッシュ，御影石などのテクスチャーが与えられるが，それぞれの三角形がさらに粒子へと分解されるディテールとした。具体的には，屋根のガルバリウム鋼板は，立ち上がりの大きな200mmの竪ハゼ葺き，石はステンレス製の「脚」の長さを変えることで段差をつけ，1枚1枚の単位の存在を際立たせた。これらのディテールによって，大きなものが小さなものの集合体へと変換され，小さなものは光の変化，季節の変化によっても様々に影が変化し，質感を変えて，豊かな自然の変化の中で自然と同じように建築もまたその様相を変化させ続ける。

川沿いの隣地には，地元産の杉材を用いてつくった陶芸のためのパビリオンをデザインした。杉を集成材として，長さ2.4mのホームベース型の梁をつくり，その単位となる梁を本館と同じく三角形を基本とする幾何学に基づいて，ボルトを用いたジョイントシステムで組み上げた。小さな単位を用いて，拡張可能なゆるい全体をつくる試みである。

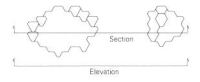

2010-12　**Teikyo University Elementary School**
Tama, Tokyo, Japan

Distant view from south　南より見る遠景

North elevation

South elevation　S=1:600

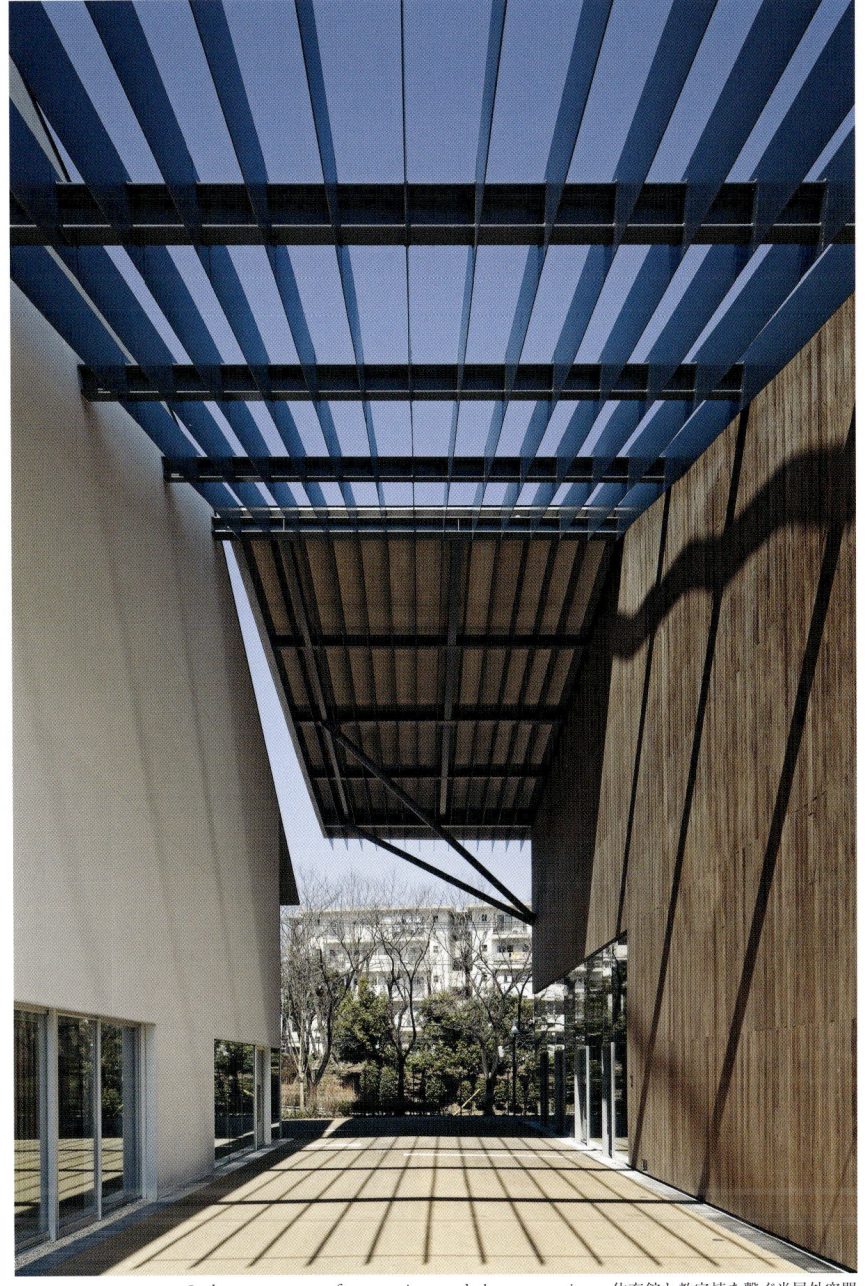

In-between space of gymnasium and classroom wing　体育館と教室棟を繋ぐ半屋外空間

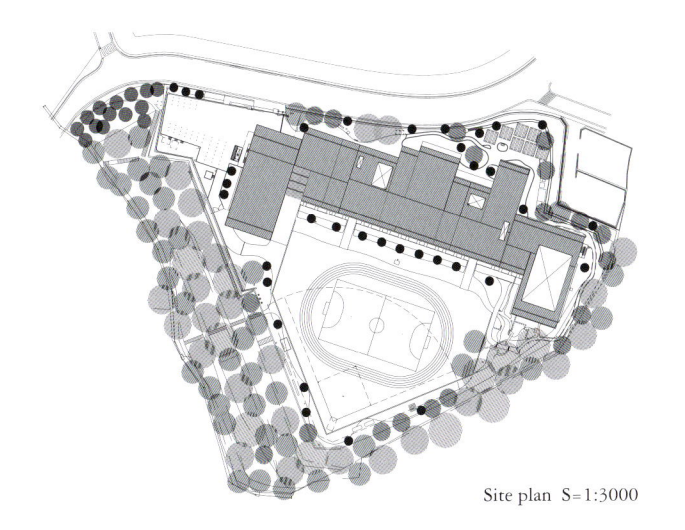

Site plan S=1:3000

View toward entrance from school gate　校門より昇降口を見る

Sectional detail S=1:125

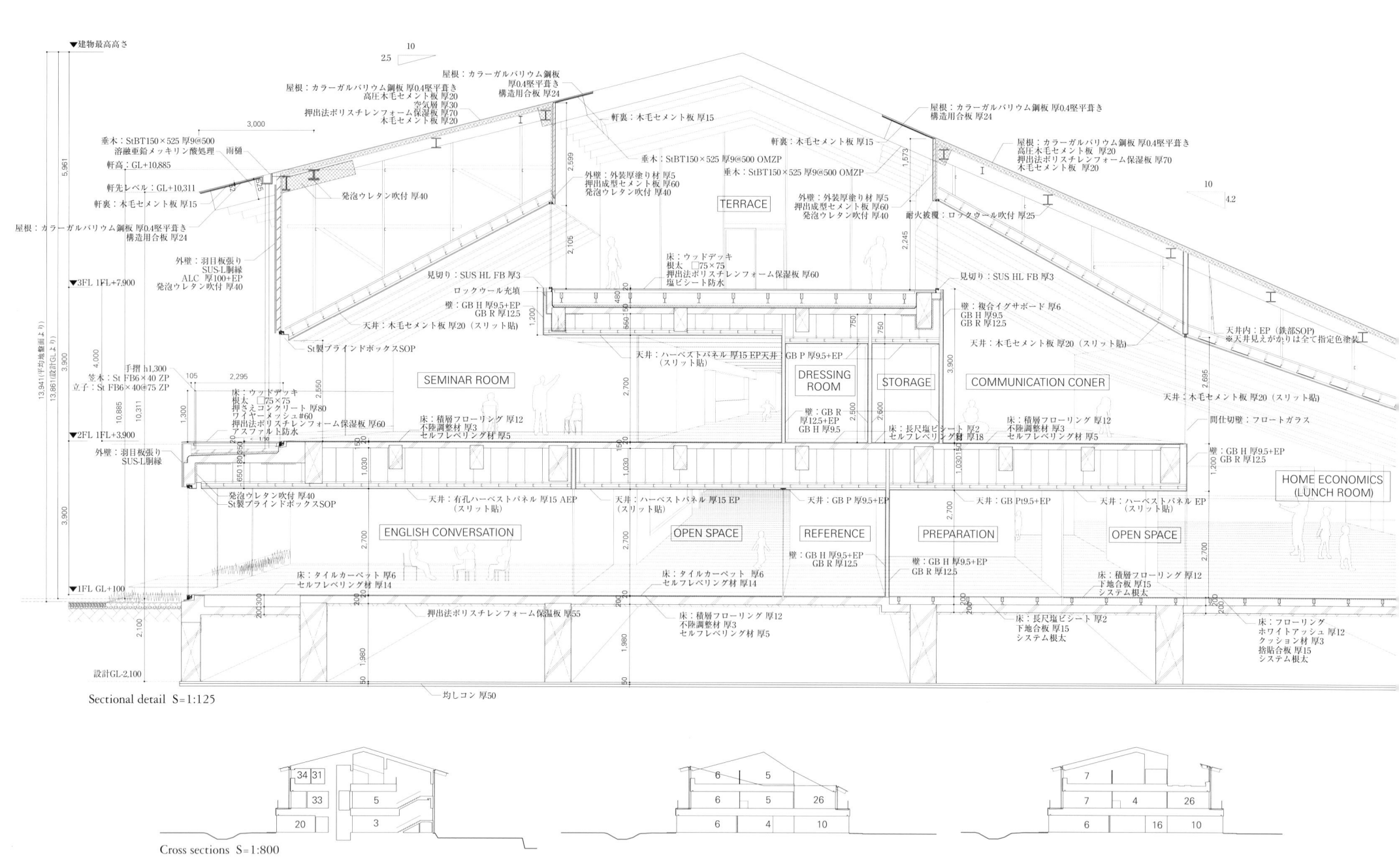

Cross sections S=1:800

We aimed to design a contemporary timber school building. Here a timber building means a big 'Timber house' for the students. This timber house consists of a sloping roof and the materiality of timber on the interior and the exterior.

We created various flexible spaces which can respond to the surrounding environment and inner programs by changing the pitch of the roof and the height of the eaves. A timber house with a collection of 12 roofs provides a harmony with the surroundings and gains a variety of sections that a flat roof cannot achieve.

We tried to bring the warm quality of a timber school back into the city by using cedar on the exterior. A layered detail called 'Yamato-Bari' (vertical cedar boards are off-set and overlapped to form a kind of layered timber wall) and timber louvers are applied on the facade in accordance with interior spaces and functions to provide a variety of expressions on the building.

We did not use timber just as a material for the interior but we tried to make use of the pliability and softness of timber. A recycled material made of compressed chips of straw, rushes (Igusa) and Poplar, which can also be a soft message board where pins can be used directly is used for the interior walls. The roof cuts the sunlight on the south side and we installed a heat collector device on the southern facing roof. This system works to blow warm air, which is warmed in the air gap between the roof and ceiling during the winter, from under the floor. The rain water collected from the roof flows into the water conduit at the south and it nurtures a biotope in front of the science room. In these ways, we tried to reintroduce a timber school building which connects with the greater natural environment.

帝京大学小学校

現代の木造校舎をめざした。木造校舎とは大きな「木の家」である。「木の家」は，勾配屋根と内外装におけるマテリアリティで構成される。

屋根勾配と軒の高さを場所場所で変えることで，周辺環境と内部プログラムに柔軟に対応した空間，多様性をつくり出した。本プロジェクトでは，12個の屋根の集合体としての「木の家」をつくることで，周辺環境との調和を図り，フラットルーフでは得ることのできない多様な断面形状を獲得した。

外壁には杉材を使用し，木の小学校の暖かい質感を都市に取り戻そうと試みた。ファサードでは，大和張りと呼ばれる彫りの深いディテールと透明な木製ルーバーを場所と機能に応じて使いわけ，建物の表情に多様性を与えた。

内装では単に素材として木を使うのではなく，木の可塑性とやわらかさを生かす計画とした。藁やイグサ，

1	ENTRY (GENERAL)	10	WORKSHOP	19	STORAGE	27	HALL	34	CAREER COUNSELING	43	STAGE
2	ENTRY (CHILDREN)	11	HOME ECONOMICS	20	INFIRMARY	28	ROOF PLAZA	35	CUSTOMER'S ROOM	44	GUARD PERSON'S ROOM
3	ENTRANCE HALL	12	ENGLISH	21	TEACHER'S ROOM	29	SEMINAR ROOM	36	PRINCIPAL'S OFFICE	45	TEACHER'S ROOM (GYMNASIUM)
4	OPEN SPACE	13	MUSIC	22	SERVICE ENTRY (SCHOOL MEALS)	30	COMMUNICATION CORNER	37	ANTEROOM	46	PUMP
5	LOUNGE	14	LIFE ENVIRONMENTAL	23	HOT WATER SUPPLY	31	DRESSING ROOM (CHILDREN)	38	SUPPORTER'S OFFICE	47	CONTROL ROOM
6	CLASSROOM	15	LABORATORY	24	PRINTING	32	BALCONY	39	MECHANICAL	48	AIR CONDITIONER UNIT
7	MULTIPURPOSE ROOM	16	PREPARATION	25	SUB ENTRY	33	BROADCASTING	40	ENTRY (GYMNASIUM)	49	OUTSIDE CORRIDOR
8	MUSIC HALL	17	REFERENCE	26	MEETING ROOM			41	HALL (GYMNASIUM)		
9	MEDIA CENTER	18	TERRACE					42	GYMNASIUM		

Third floor

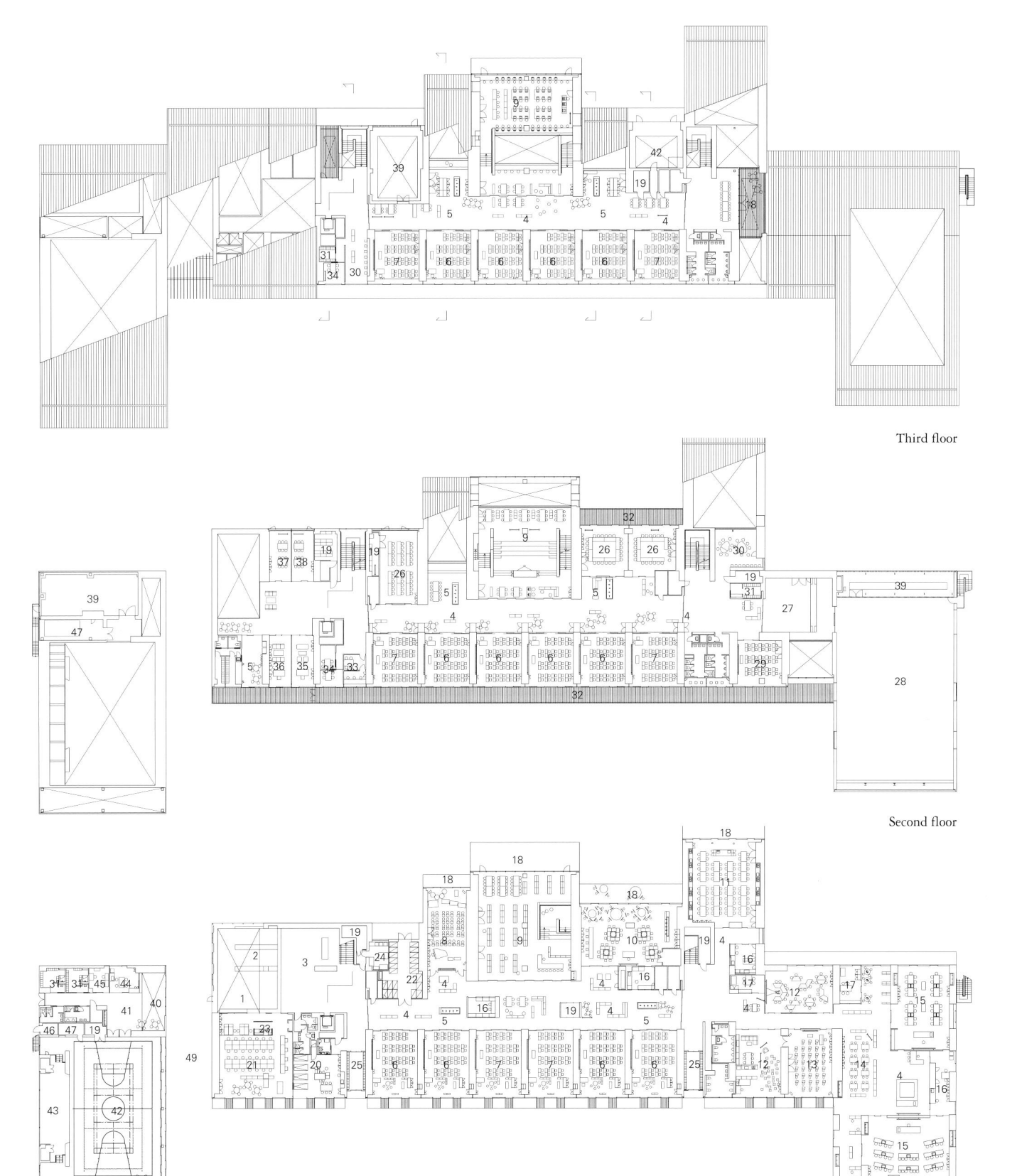

Second floor

First floor S=1:800

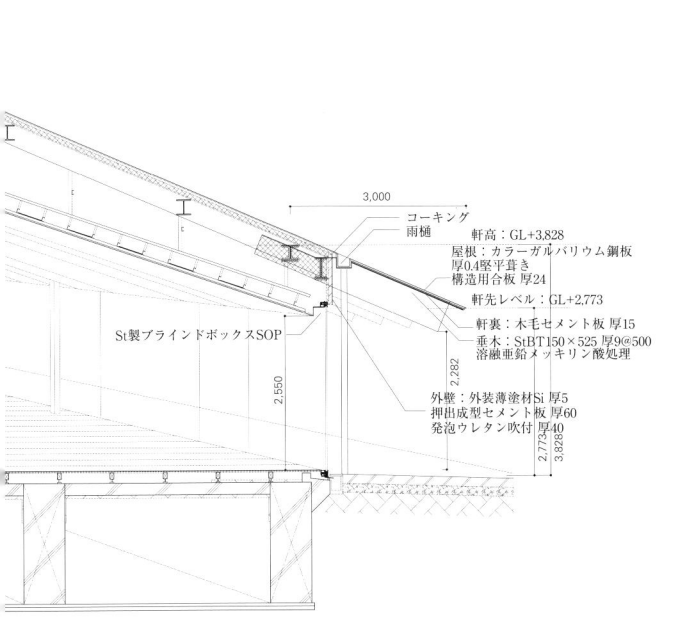

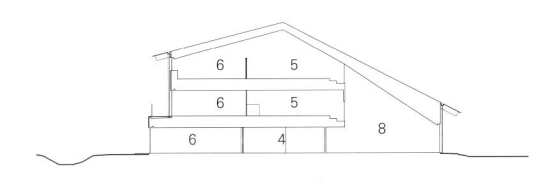

ポプラの端材を押し固めた再生建材を利用し、そのまま画鋲をさすことのできる、やわらかい掲示板として壁面を構成した。屋根は南側の日射をカットし、さらに南面の屋根を利用して、集熱装置を組み込んだ。冬場は、屋根と天井との間の空気層で暖められた空気を床下から吹き出す暖房システムを採用した。屋根で集めた水は、南側の水路に流し、理科室前でビオトープをつくった。大きな自然環境とひとつに融合した、木の校舎を取り戻そうと試みた。

Lounge on third floor. Classroom on right, media center and meeting room on left　3階ラウンジ。右に普通教室，左にメディアセンターや会議室

Entrance　一般玄関及び児童昇降口

Terrace of eastern end on third floor　3階東端のテラス

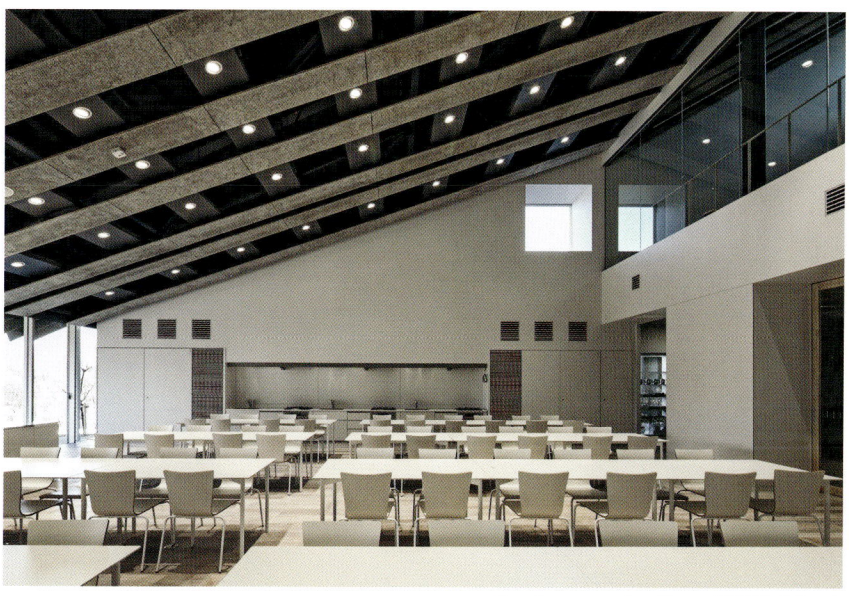

Lunch room on first floor　1階ランチルーム

2010- Victoria and Albert Museum at Dundee
Dundee, Scotland, U.K.

Site plan

Level 2

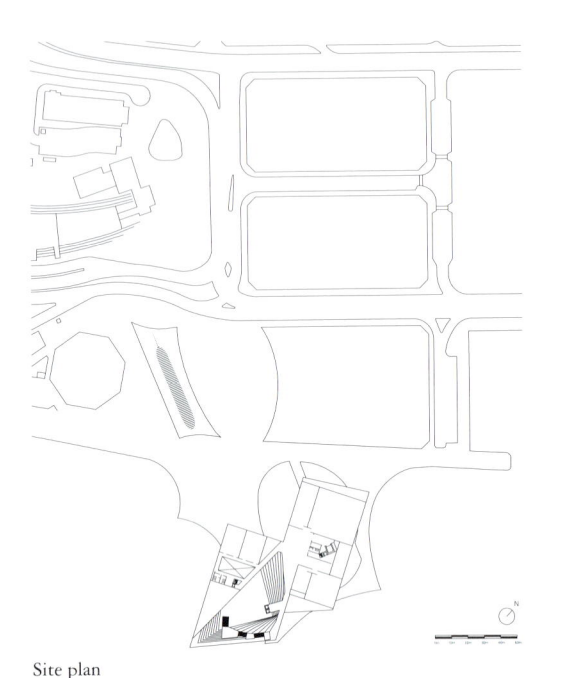

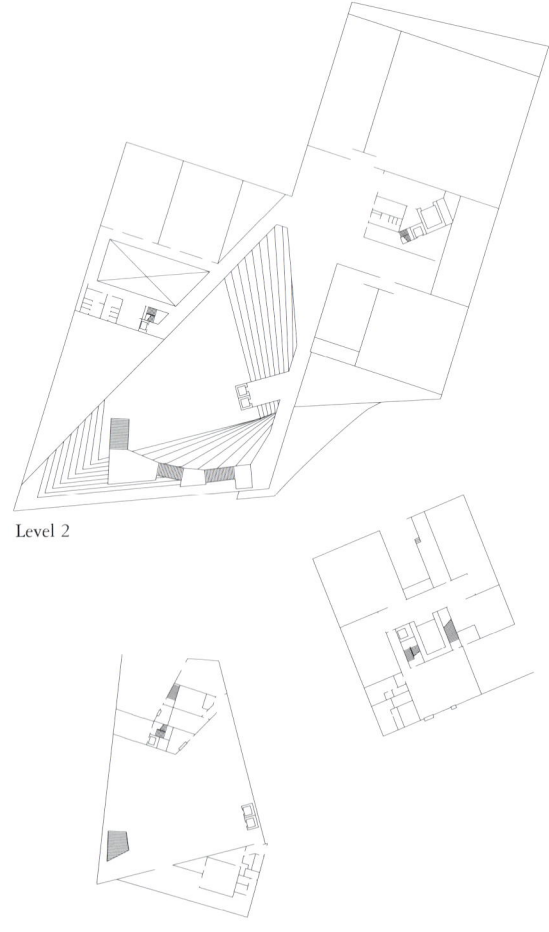

Level 0 S=1: 1500

The project is an annex of Victoria and Albert Museum planned in River Tay in Dundee City located at the southern shore of Scotland. Our plan that proposed shifting and laminating precast concrete panels to create a gate-shaped architecture was selected in the competition.

The idea of reconnecting existing urban network and nature with gate-form architecture is our trial since Hiroshige Museum (2000) and Besançon City Arts and Culture Center (2007-). We expected a new relationship is born between nature and architecture by letting people walk around on a floating pedestrian road made on the periphery of the architecture, after erecting piles on the river bottom to build architecture from the water.

The cone-shaped foyer that is made by a method of shifting and piling up precast concrete panels is an indoor open space that allows multi-purpose events such as concerts and plays to take place. We hope it will serve as a new communication space for the citizens, who endure Scotland's harsh winter.

ヴィクトリア&アルバート・ミュージアム・ダンディ

スコットランド南岸ダンディ市のテイ川の中に計画された、ヴィクトリア&アルバート・ミュージアムの分館。プレキャスト・コンクリートをずらしながら積層して、ゲート状の建築をつくるわれわれの提案がコンペティションで選定された。

ゲート状建築で、既存の都市ネットワークと自然とを再接続するというアイディアは「那珂川町 馬頭広重美術館」(2000年)や「ブザンソン芸術文化センター」(2007年〜)以来、われわれが試行を重ねてきたものである。川底にパイルを打ち込み水中から建築をたて、建築の周囲に水に浮いた遊歩道を設けて人々を回遊させることで、自然と建築との間に、新しい関係性が生まれることを期待した。

プレキャスト・コンクリートをずらしながら積み上げる工法によって生まれるすり鉢状のホワイエ空間は、コンサートや演劇などの多目的なイベントを許容する室内型の広場であり、スコットランドの冬の厳しさに耐える、新しい市民のコミュニケーションスペースとなることを期待している。

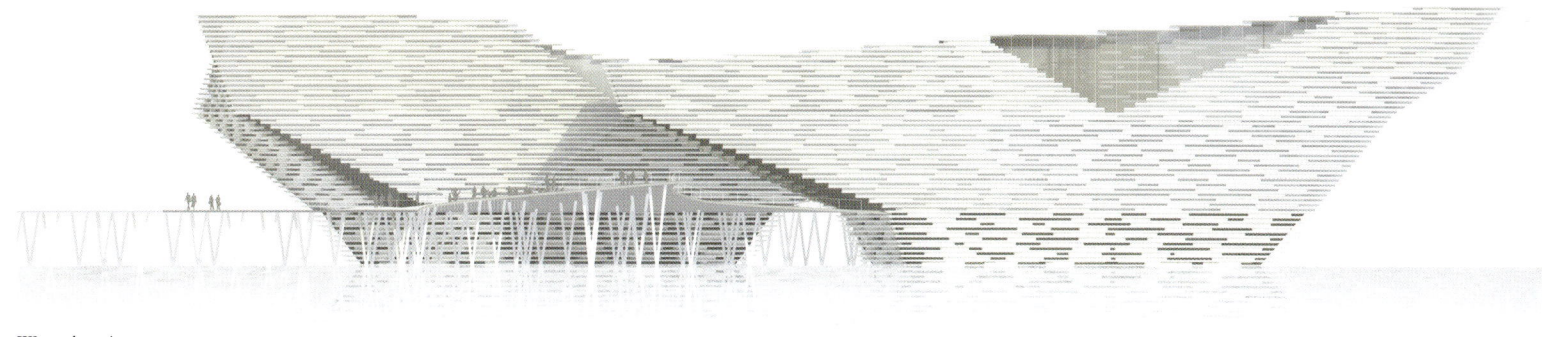

West elevation

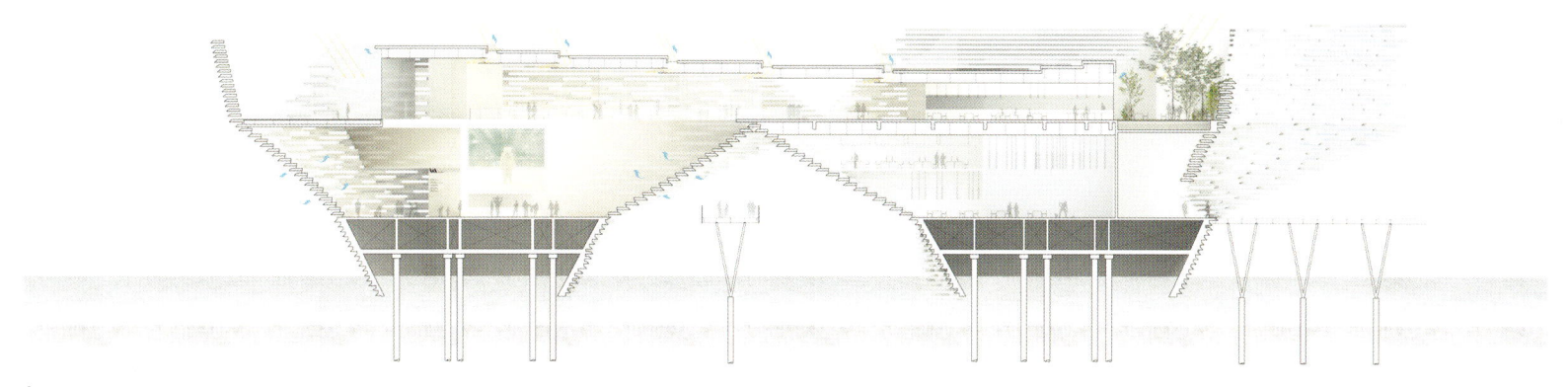

Section

View from riverside　川岸より見る

Approach　アプローチ

Main hall. Downward view from mezzanine　メインホール。メザニンより見下ろす

Main hall. View from entrance　メインホール。エントランスより見る

2010-12 Garden Terrace Miyazaki
Miyazaki, Japan

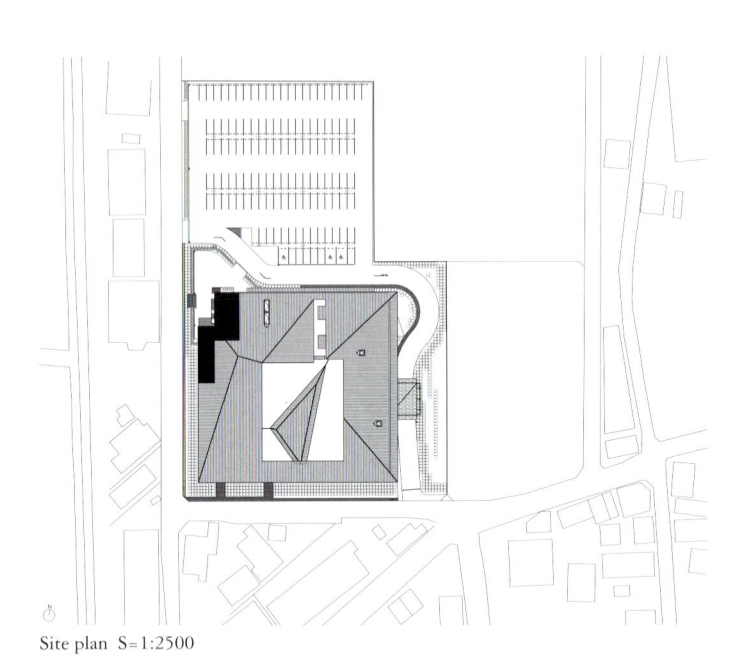

Site plan S=1:2500

East elevation 東立面

260

Overall view from south　南より見る全景

Large eaves. Entrance on left　大庇。左はエントランス

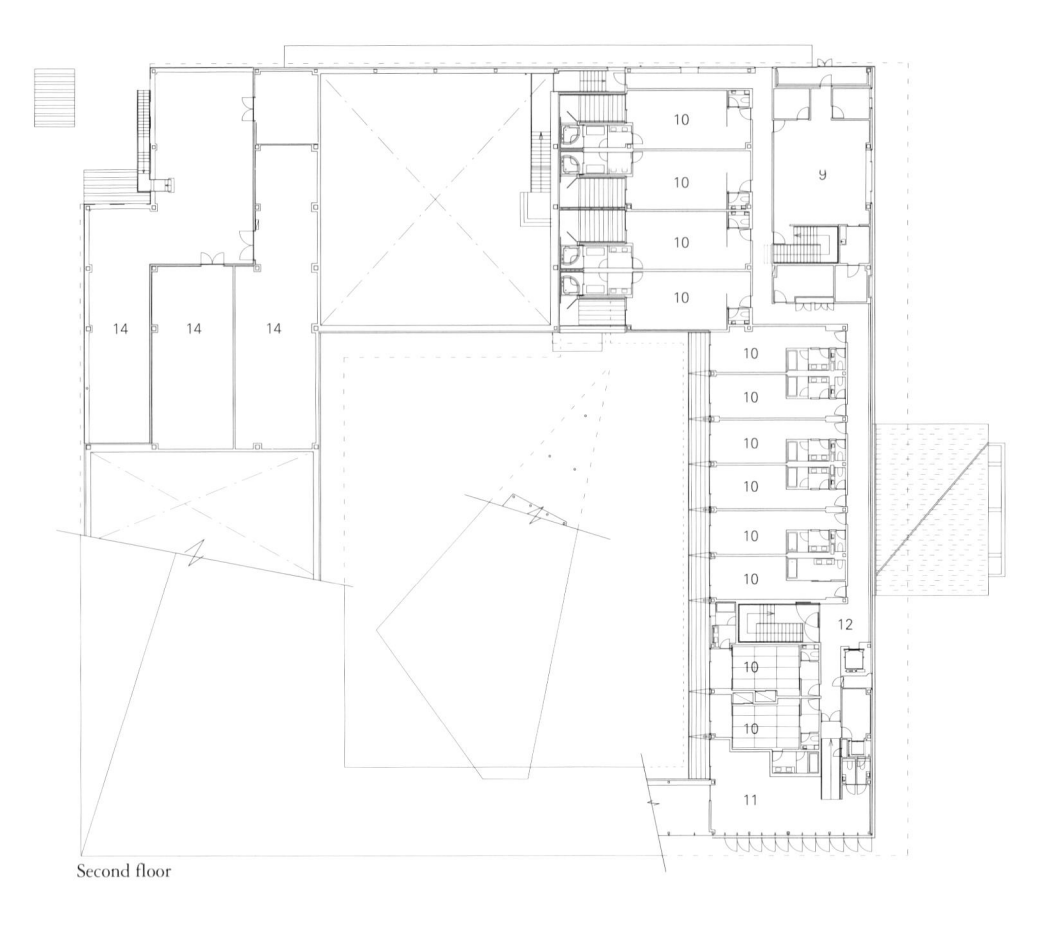

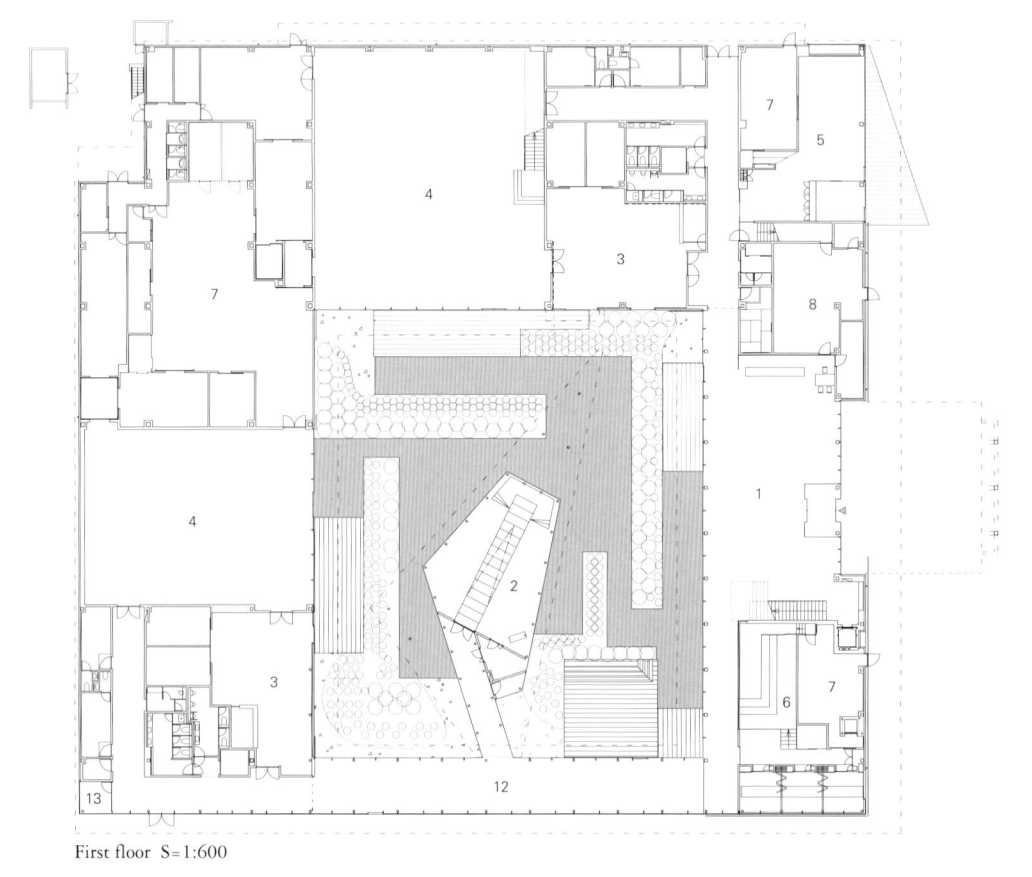

1	LOBBY
2	CHAPEL
3	FOYER
4	BANQUET ROOM
5	RESTAURANT
6	RESTAURANT (JAPANESE)
7	KITCHEN
8	OFFICE
9	BRIDAL SALON
10	GUEST ROOM
11	LOUNGE
12	CORRIDOR
13	SMOKING ROOM
14	MECHANICAL

Second floor

First floor S=1:600

Miyazaki is renowned for a production hub of bamboo and is also branded for beautiful bamboo handiworks. Dealing bamboo as a theme, we planned a low-rise hotel that is integrated with a bamboo forest. Guest rooms, banquet rooms and restaurants were arranged around the courtyard. In the middle of the courtyard of the forest and a water basin, a pentagon-shaped glass box was placed that will be operated as a chapel.

Targeting at creating a dissimilar world from the nearby urban settings, it was designed as a courtyard-type, composed of bamboo and the water basin. Bamboo is repeatedly used for the building's exterior and the interior. In Japan, there is folklore of Princess Kaguya and there is a historical story of the "seven wise men in a bamboo grove" in a Chinese classic. In both cases bamboo is depicted as a mysteriously powered plant that creates unrealistic world. Frequently, courtyard falls into a static space. However, in the project, the insertion of a glass box in the shape of unequal sided pentagon produced a flux similar to a whirl. Thus, the courtyard was united to the universe.

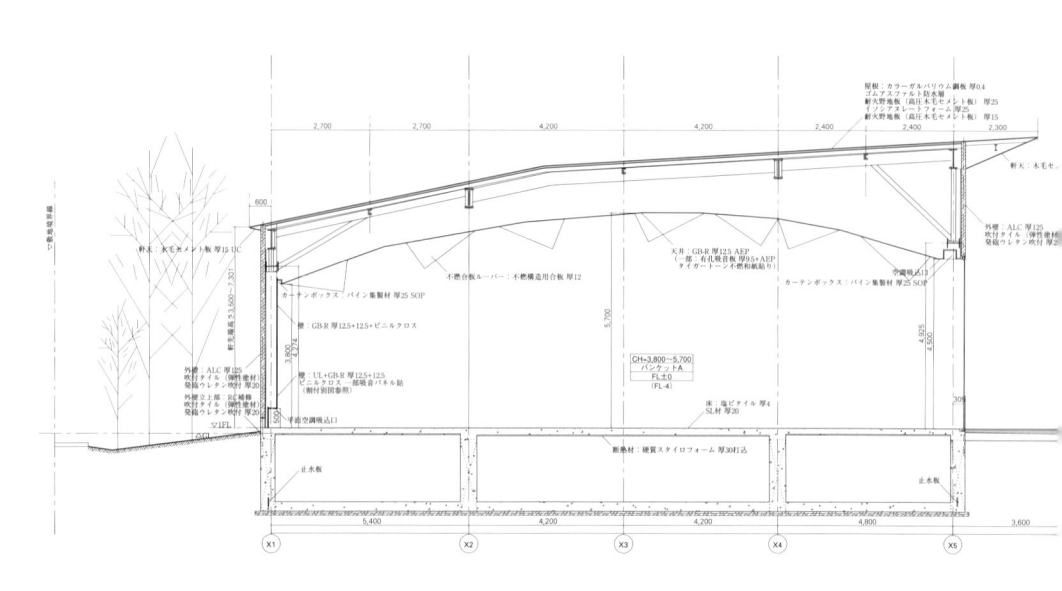

ガーデンテラス宮崎

宮崎は竹の産地として有名で,美しい竹細工でも知られる。竹をテーマにした,竹林と一体となった低層のホテルを計画した。中庭のまわりに客室,宴会場,レストランを配置し,竹林と水盤の中庭の真ん中には,五角形のガラスボックスが置かれ,チャペルとして用いられる。

周辺の都市的環境の中に,いかに別世界を創出するかをめざして,竹と水盤を用いて構成された中庭型とした。竹は建築の外装,内装にも繰り返して用いられている。日本にはかぐや姫の民話があり,中国には「竹林の七賢」の故事があり,どちらの場合も,竹は非現実的世界を創出する不思議な力を持った植物として取り扱われている。中庭型は得てしてスタティックな空間となりがちだが,このプロジェクトは不等辺五角形のガラスのボックスを挿入することで,空間に渦のような流れが生まれて,中庭と宇宙とがつながった。

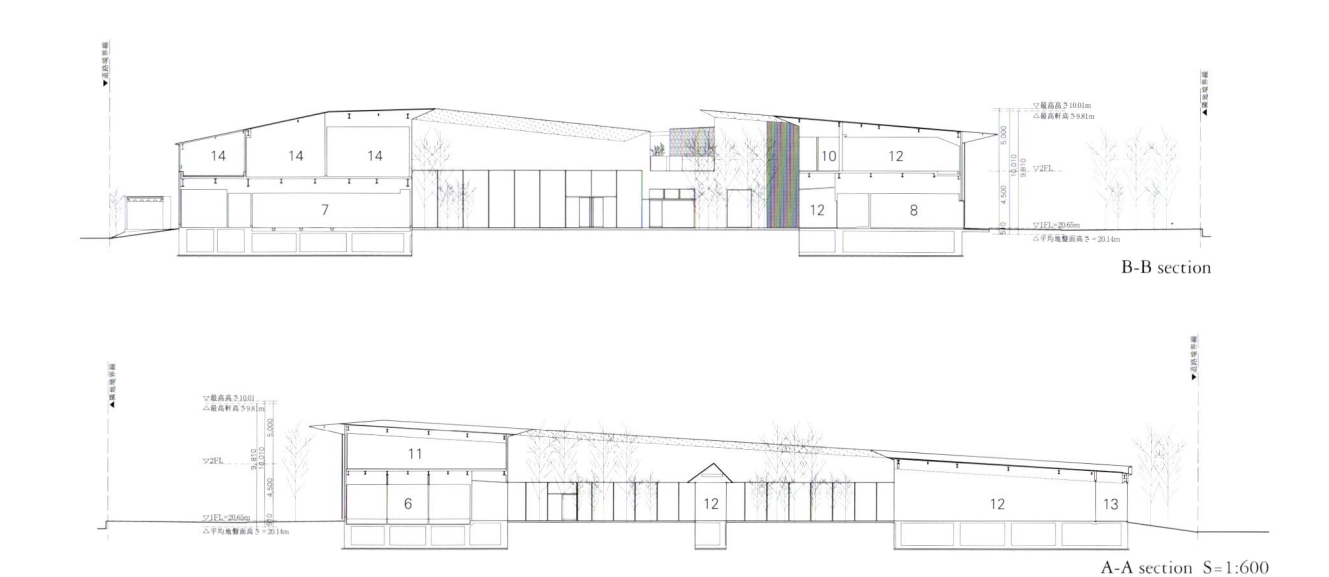

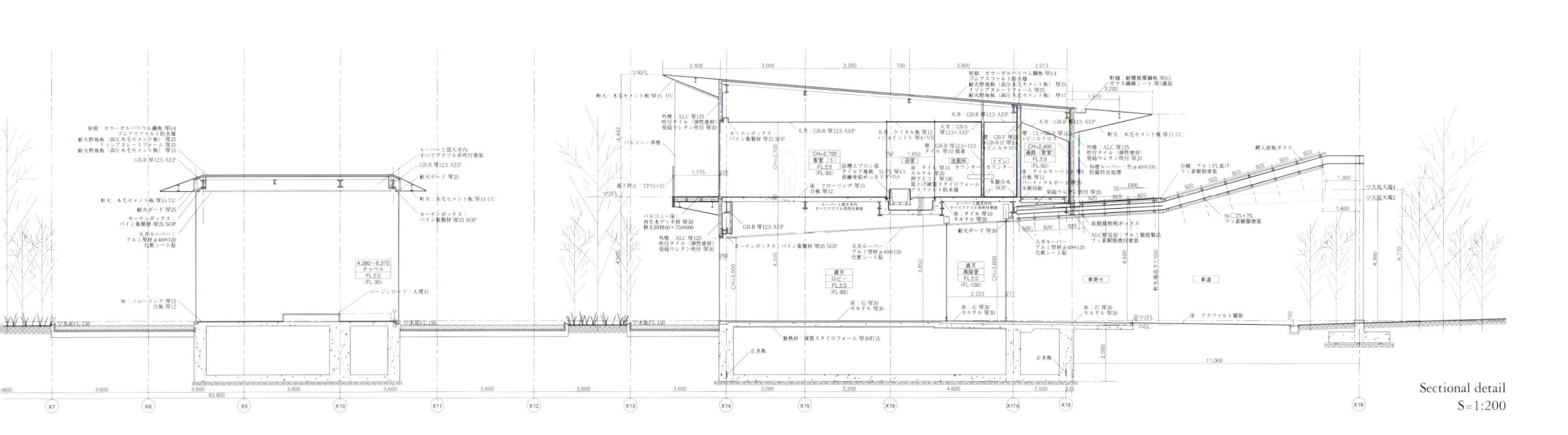

East elevation

South elevation

B-B section

A-A section　S=1:600

Sectional detail　S=1:200

Evening view of court　中庭の夕景

View toward court from lobby　ロビーより中庭を見る

Banquet room at west area　西側のバンケット

Corridor: view toward banquet room　回廊：バンケット方向を見る

Banquet room at north area　北側のバンケット

2011

Starbucks Coffee
Dazaifu-Tenmangu Omotesando
Dazaifu, Fukuoka, Japan

The coffee shop is located at a unique location facing an approach to Dazaifu Tenman-gu. Daizaifu Tenman-gu is one of the representing shrines of Japan. It was built in 919 and is known as 'the god of examinations'. Two million people visit here annually. Traditional one-storey and two-storey Japanese-style buildings align in a row and create original townscape on the approach to the shrine. The project's goal was to create a modern wooden architecture that harmonizes with the look of the town by employing a special wooden structural system that is created by diagonally weaved thin wooden sticks. Suiting the short width and long depth site shape besides the approach, a fluid space that invites people deep inside was accomplished by a crosswise wooden space frame.

The structure was built by interweaving two thousand stick-shaped members in 1.3m to 1.4 m-long in 6 cm square sectional dimension. The total length of the stick reached up to 4.4 km. The method of lacing thin and long members was attempted in projects such as CIDORI and Prostho Museum Reserch Center. In this project, we tried a method of intertwining sticks obliquely and introduced directionality and a flux in the space.

In CIDORI and Prostho Museum three sticks intersect at one point. However, in this project more challenging joints that four sticks intersect at one point was needed, because sticks were assembled diagonally. A manipulation to slightly shifted intersections of the members avoided four members to intersect at one point and connected a set of two members. Hence, the difficult problem was solved.

The technique of supporting roofs by assembling small structural members that were easy to obtain and not using thick wooden members was developed to a high degree in old Chinese and Japanese architecture and became one of the utmost attractions of Asian wooden architecture. Here in the project, we combined the method and a cutting-edge modern structural technique and formed a fluid and cave-like space.

View from approach to Dazaifu Tenman-gu　太宰府天満宮への参道より見る

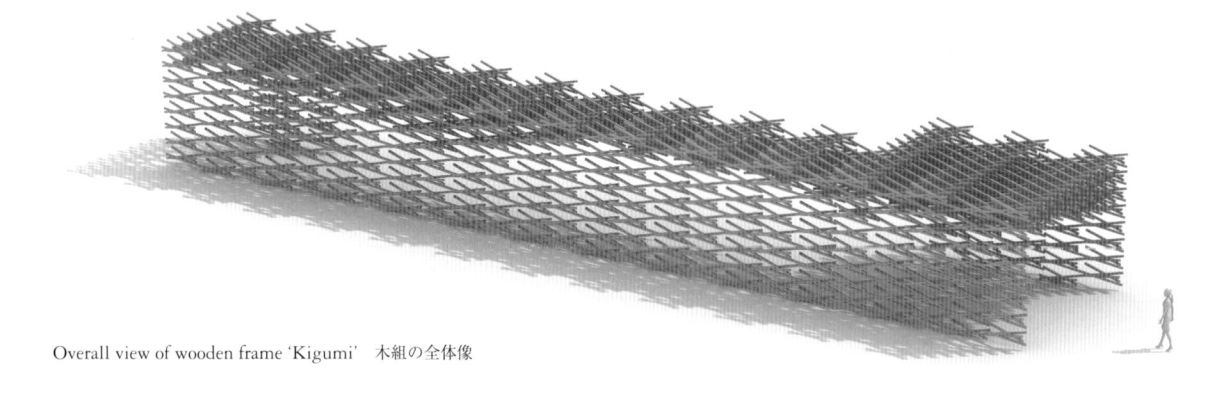

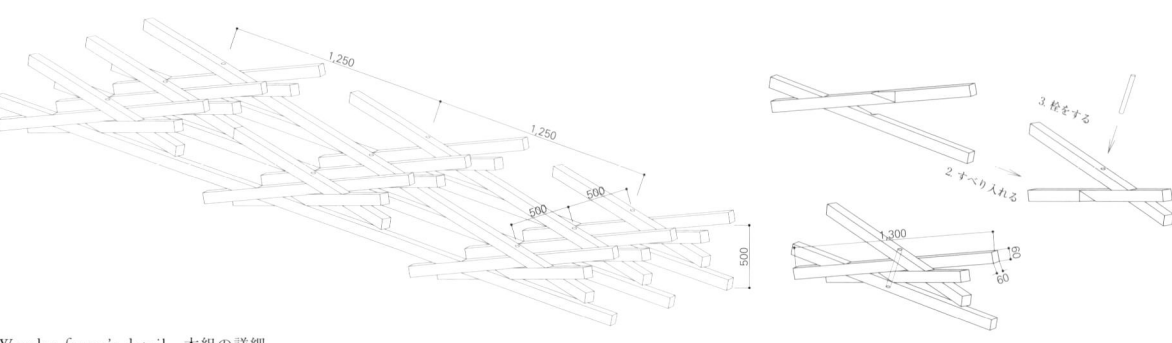

Overall view of wooden frame 'Kigumi'　木組の全体像

Wooden frame's detail　木組の詳細

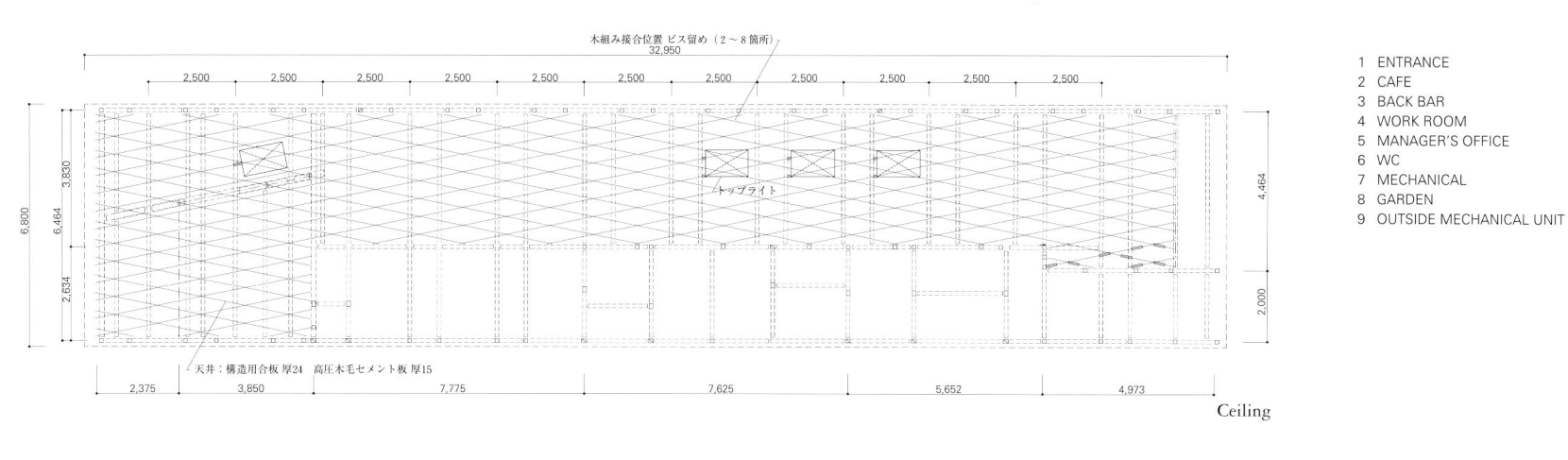

1 ENTRANCE
2 CAFE
3 BACK BAR
4 WORK ROOM
5 MANAGER'S OFFICE
6 WC
7 MECHANICAL
8 GARDEN
9 OUTSIDE MECHANICAL UNIT

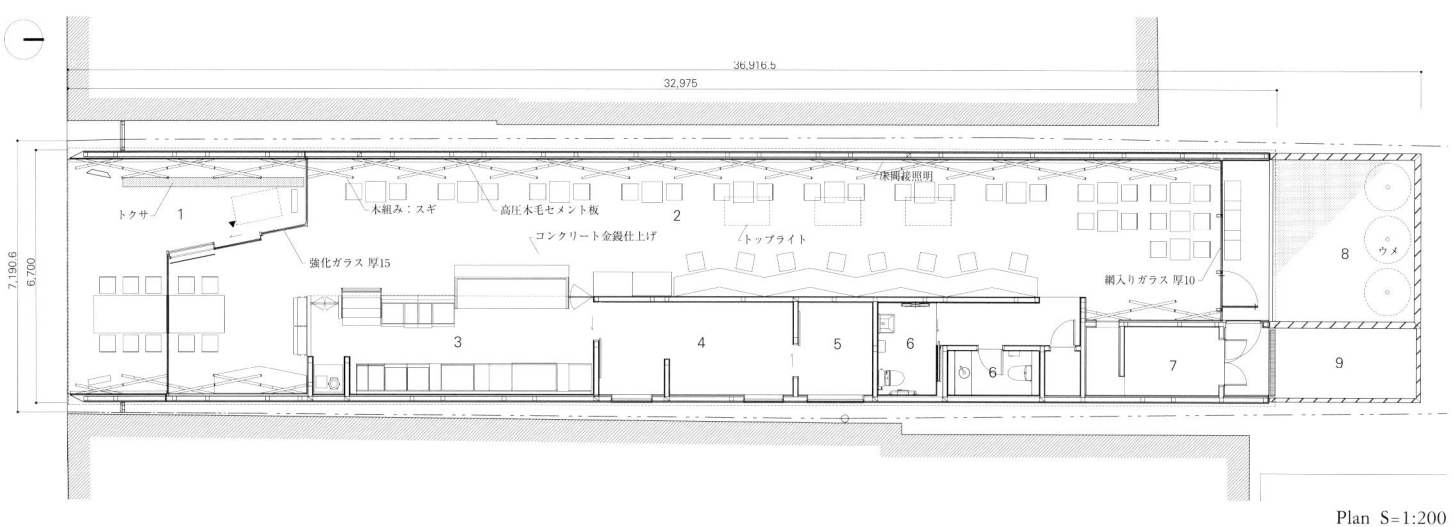

Ceiling

Plan S=1:200

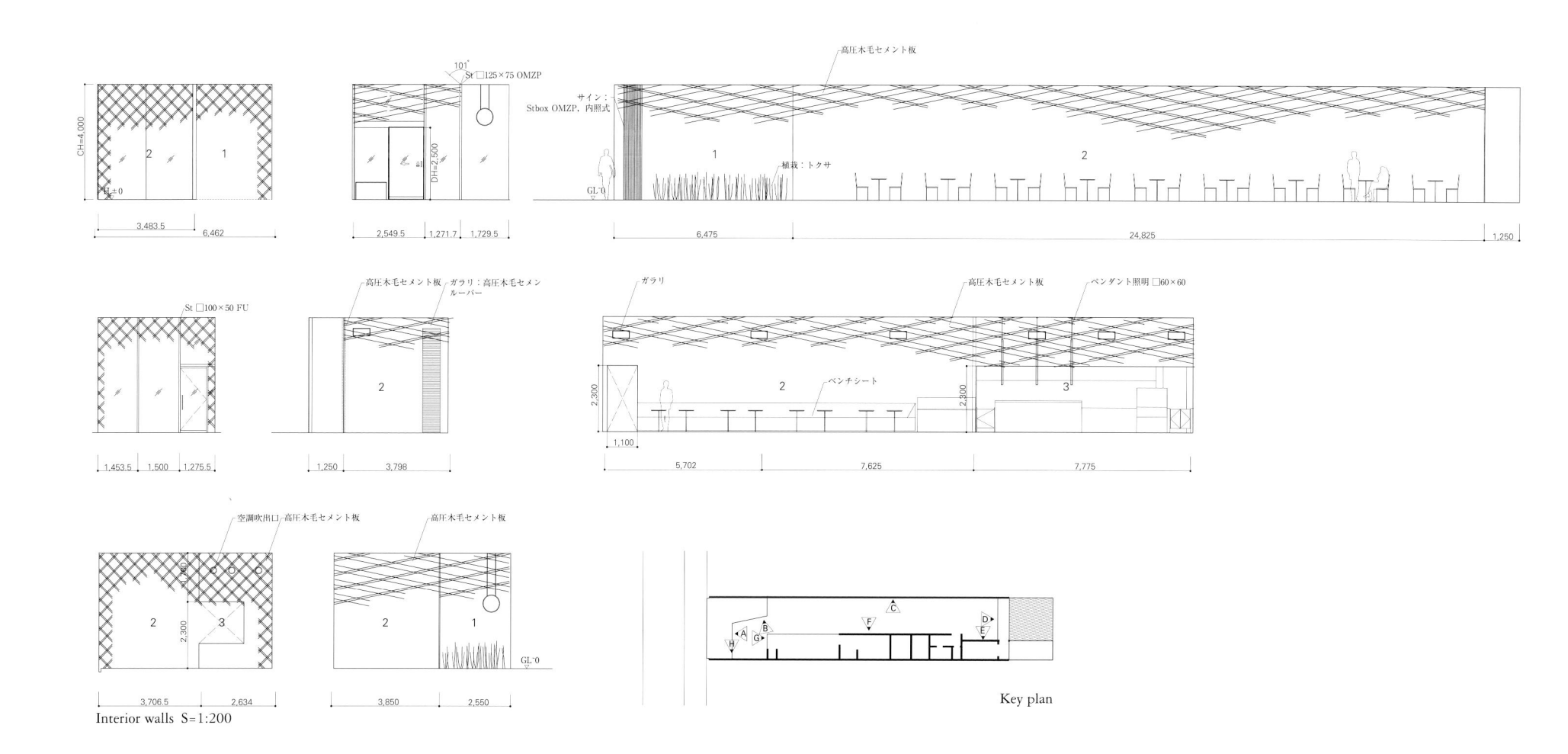

Interior walls S=1:200

Key plan

Interior of cafe　カフェのインテリア

Wooden frame 'Kigumi'　木組

スターバックスコーヒー太宰府天満宮表参道店

太宰府天満宮参道という,特殊なロケーションに立つコーヒーショップ。太宰府天満宮は,日本を代表する神社のひとつで,建立は919年。「試験の神様」として知られ,年間200万人が参拝に訪れる。その神社の前の参道には,平屋か2階建ての伝統的日本建築が立ち並び,独特の街並みを形成している。細い棒状の木をダイアゴナルに織りあげる特殊な木構造システムによって,その街並みと調和する現代的な木造建築をつくることが,プロジェクトの目標であった。参道沿いの,間口が狭く,奥行きの深い敷地形状にふさわしい,奥へ奥へと人を引き込むような流動的空間を,ダイアゴナルな木のスペースフレームで実現することができた。

6cm角の断面寸法を持つ,長さ1.3～4.0mの棒状の部材約2,000本を織りあげることで,この構築物ができ上がった。棒の総長は4.4kmに及んだ。細長い部材を織りあげる手法は,「CIDORI」(2007年),「プロソミュージアム・リサーチセンター」(2010年)等のプロジェクトで試みたが,今回はダイアゴナルに織りあげていく方法を試み,空間に方向性,流動性を導入した。

「CIDORI」や「プロソ」では三つの棒が1点で交わるが,このプロジェクトでは棒をダイアゴナルに組むために,4本が1点で交わるという難易度の高いジョイントが必要になった。部材の交点をわずかにずらすことで,4部材が1点でまじわることを避け,2部材ずつを接合することで,この難問を解決した。

太い木材を使わずに,手に入り易い細かい構造部材を組み上げて屋根を支える方法は,かつての中国建築,日本建築で高度な発展をとげ,アジアの木造建築の最大の魅力のひとつとなっていた。今回はこの方法と,現代の最先端の構造技術を組み合わせ,流動性の高い,洞窟状の空間をつくることができた。

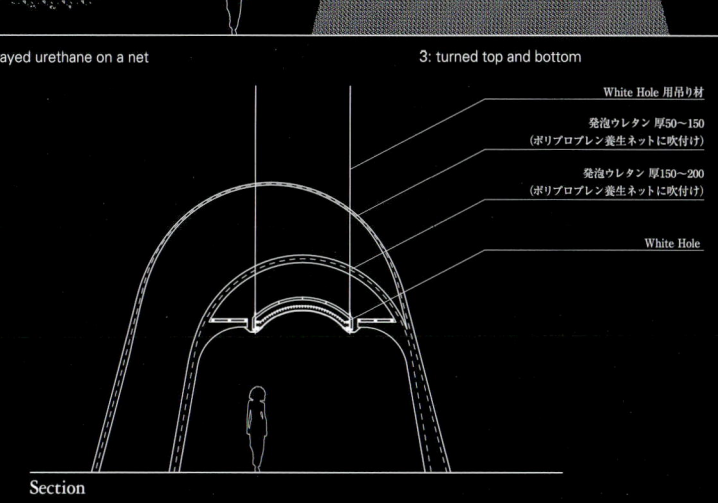

2011

Bubble Wrap
Fukushima, Osaka, Japan

By using urethane foam which is usually sprayed on walls as insulation, we created a dome space to wrap the artwork 'White Hole' by the artist, Mariko Mori. We thought that the extraordinary lightness of urethane foam would suit her artworks which are inspired by cosmic phenomenon.

We hung a double layer of polypropylene mats, typically used on construction sites, from the ceiling and this naturally formed a catenary which we sprayed with urethane. We flipped over the dome after it hardened and thus created a double-layered structural dome. Even though urethane is a soft material, since the outer and the inner domes support each other, the five meter height of the structure became possible. The catenary is a highly rational curved surface shape that Gaudi used for the Sagrada Familia. The thickness of the urethane foam is 60 cm at the lower part and 10 cm at the upper part. From the thin walls of the upper parts of the dome, soft cosmic light appears.

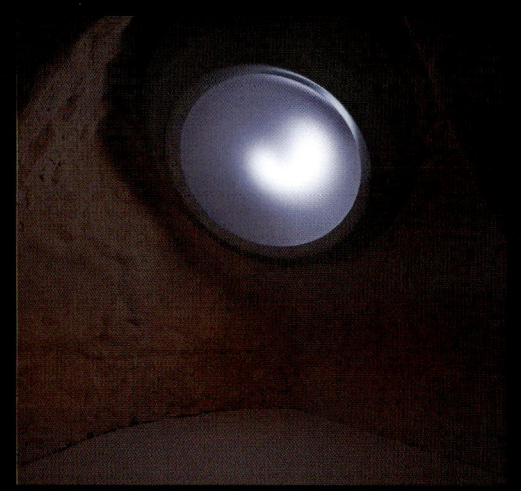

Exhibition space. 'White Hole' by Mariko Mori
展示スペース。森万里子氏による「White Hole」

Overall view　全景

Bubble Wrap
断熱素材として壁に吹き付けて用いられる発泡ウレタンを構造材として用い、アーティスト森万里子の作品「White Hole」を包み込むドーム状の空間をつくった。森万里子の作品は、宇宙現象にヒントを得たもので、発泡ウレタンのもつ非日常的な軽さがその作品にフィットすると考えた。

ポリプロピレン製の工事用養生マットを天井から二重に吊るして、まず基準となるカテナリー曲面をつくり、そこにウレタンを吹き付けて二重の構造のドームとした。吹いたウレタンが固まった後、天地を反転させるとドームが完成する。外のドーム、内のドームがそれぞれに支え合うことで、ウレタンというやわらかな素材を構造材に用いて、高さ5mという構造体が可能になった。カテナリー曲面は、ガウディがサグラダファミリアで用いた合理性の高い曲面形状である。吹き厚は下部で60cm、上部で10cm程度とし、上部の薄い壁からはやわらかに光が透過する効果があって、宇宙的な光の状態が出現した。

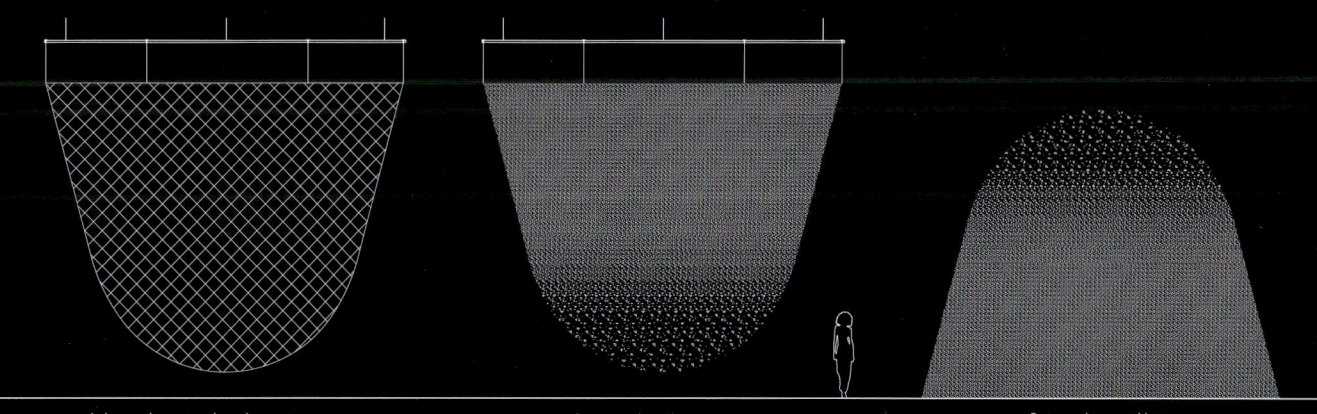

1: hanged a net and made a catenary curve
2: sprayed urethane on a net
3: turned top and bottom

Construction diagram

1　EXHIBITION SPACE
2　MECHANICAL FOR 'White Hole'

Plan　S=1:150

White Hole 用吊り材
発泡ウレタン 厚50～150
（ポリプロピレン養生ネットに吹付け）
発泡ウレタン 厚150～200
（ポリプロピレン養生ネットに吹付け）
White Hole

Section

2011

Polygonium House
Minato, Tokyo, Japan, and others

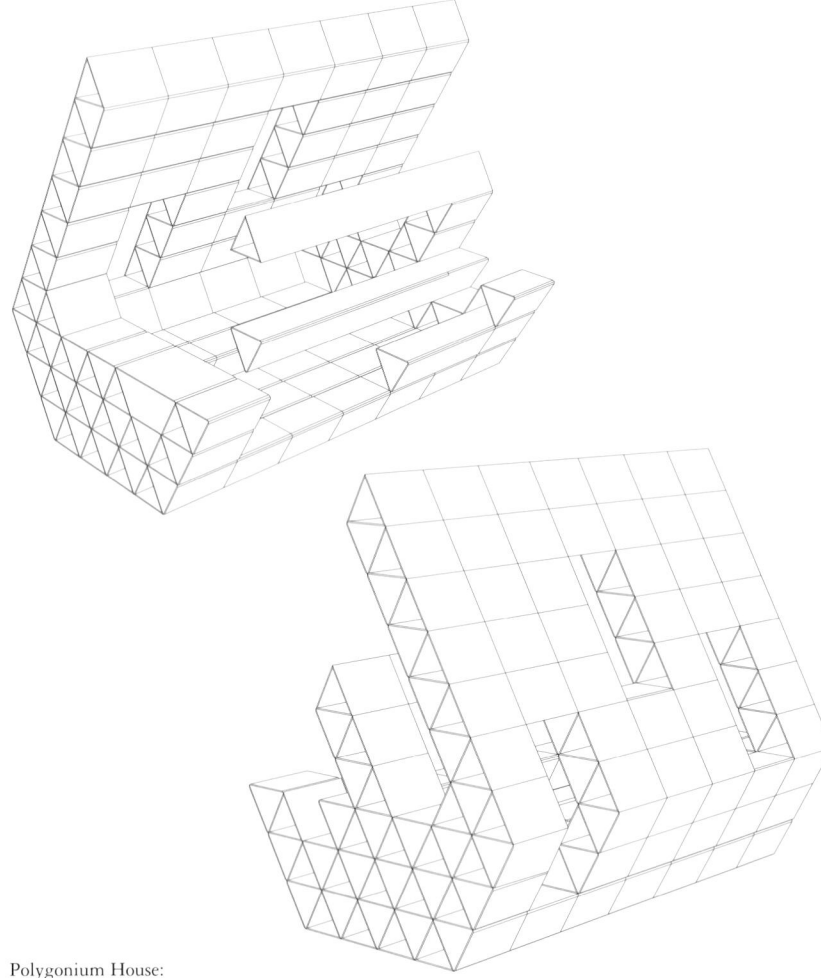

Polygonium House ポリゴニウム・ハウス

Polygonium House:
'Kanaya-machi RAKUICHI and Kengo Kuma' in Tokyo, 2011

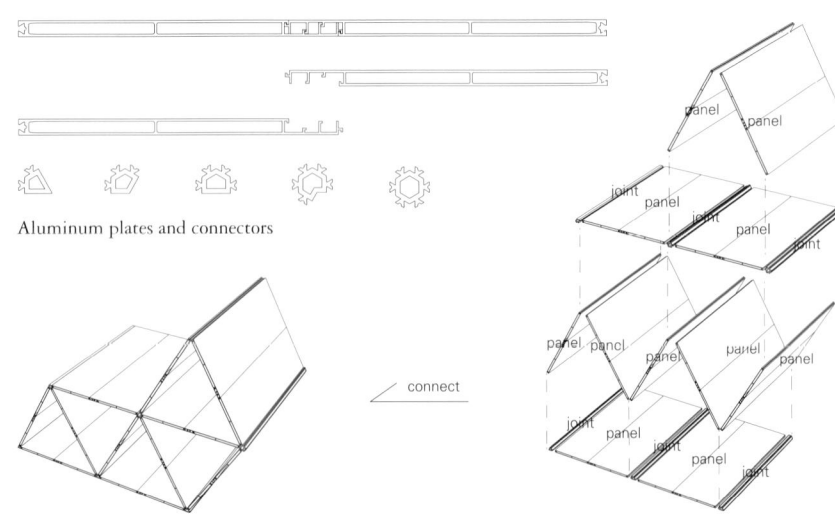

Aluminum plates and connectors

Basic unit of polygonium:
Basic dimensions of aluminum panels are 400mm x 600mm.
Various displays can be made up by five connectors.

We collaborated with Sankyo Tateyama Aluminum to develop a reversible joint system using aluminum boards, inspired by a play called 'card castle' that makes a castle-like structure by assembling thin trump cards in trusses.

10 mm-thick extruded hollow-core aluminum material was chosen for the board. Two 20 cm-thick boards are connected and compose a triangle made of 40 cm-long sides. Five types of joints made of extruded aluminum connect each board. By the use of five different types, it was possible to freely extend the system into any direction and we challenged to create a building that is like a real house with students of Toyama University.

The joints' tightening was done with one action, using bent steel pins. Thus, the system became extremely easy to fix and deconstruct panels. The ordinal system of this kind uses bolts for tightening, so it took time to assemble and dismantle panels. Also it often happened that a screw wrecks and disabled to disassemble panels and consequently reversibility is lost.

The system that was devised for an event that took place in an old townscape of Takaoka Kanayamachi in Toyama prefecture renowned for metal work craftsmanship balanced well a sensitive dimension of traditional architecture's wooden lattice and aluminum's sharpness.

ポリゴニウム・ハウス

薄いトランプカードをトラス状に組み上げて城のような構造体をつくる「カード・キャッスル」という遊びからインスピレーションを得て、アルミの板を使った可逆的ジョイントシステムを、三協立山アルミと共同で開発した。

板材として用いたのは10mm厚のアルミ中空押出材で、幅20cmのものを2連結して1辺40cmの三角形を構成する。その板材同士は、アルミ押出し材を用いてつくった5タイプのジョイントで連結される。5タイプを組み合わせることで、どの方向にも自由に拡張していくことが可能となり、富山大学の学生たちとともに、実際の家のような建築をつくることにも挑戦した。

ジョイントの締め付けは、曲げ加工を施したスティールピンを用いたワンアクションとし、留め付け、解体がきわめて容易なシステムとなった。従来のこの手のシステムはボルトを用いて締め付けるため、組み立て、解体に時間が掛かり、ねじが切れて分解不能となって可逆性が失われることも多かった。

金物細工の職人の町として知られる富山県高岡市金屋町の古い街並みで行われるイベントのために考案されたシステムによって、伝統建築の木格子の繊細な寸法と、アルミのシャープさとがうまくバランスをとった。

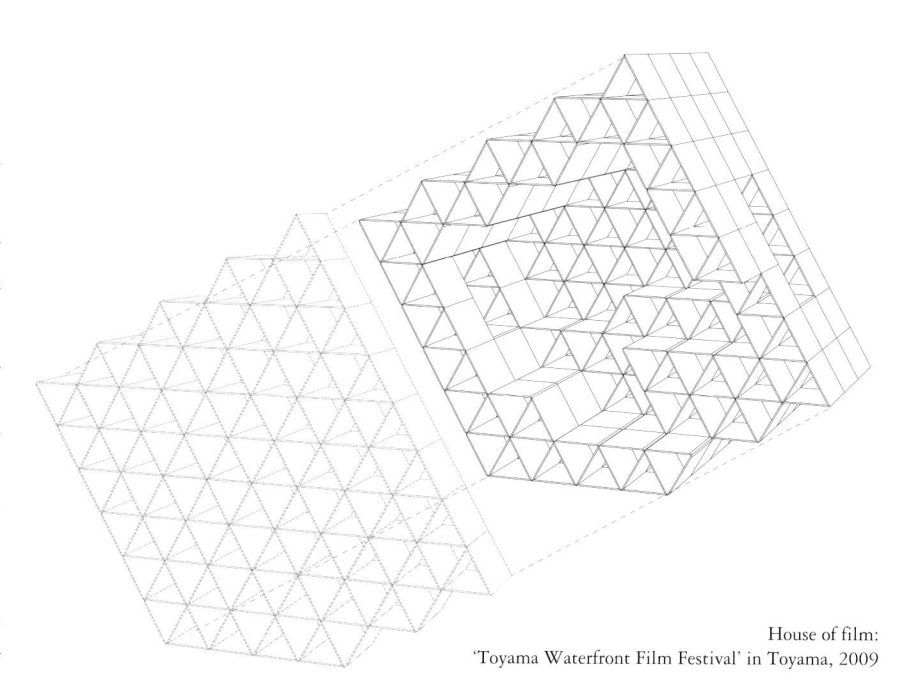

Display　展示什器

House of film: 'Toyama Waterfront Film Festival' in Toyama, 2009

Display: 'International Triennale of Kogei in Kanazawa' in Ishikawa, 2011

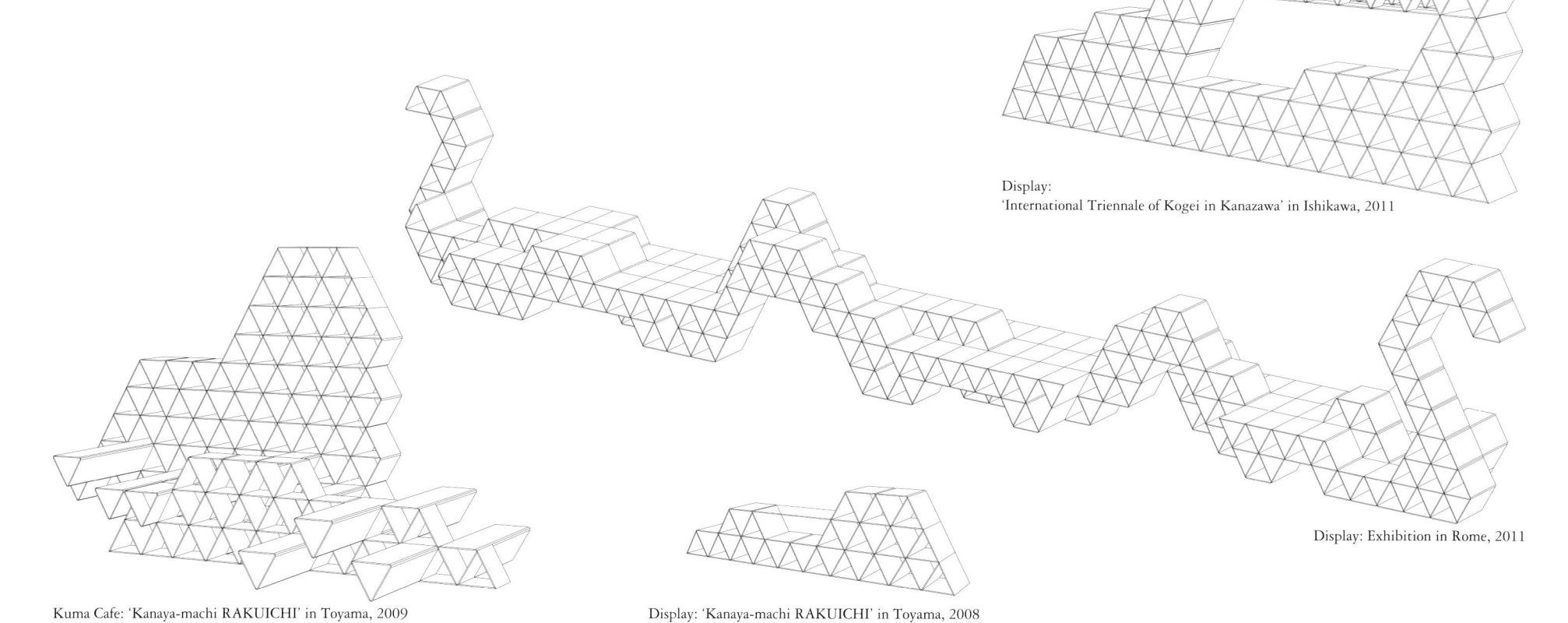

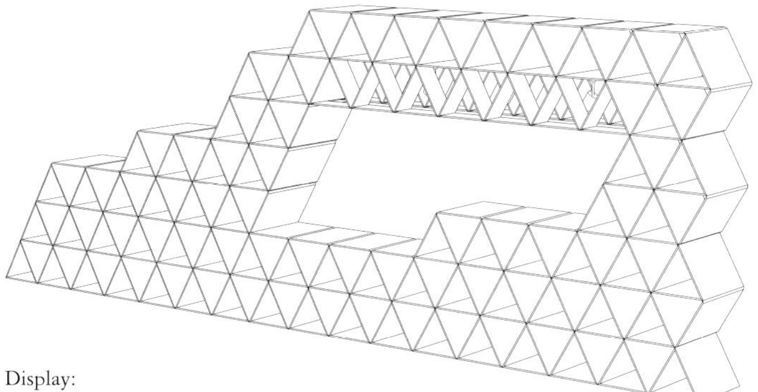

Display: Exhibition in Rome, 2011

Kuma Cafe: 'Kanaya-machi RAKUICHI' in Toyama, 2009

Display: 'Kanaya-machi RAKUICHI' in Toyama, 2008

2009-11 Green Cast
Odawara, Kanagawa, Japan

It is a multi-functional building located on a hillock near Odawara station.

The facade is covered by planters made of aluminum cast panels that also function as equipment space. We designed the integral exterior wall system that unifies a ventilation opening, a storm water drain spout, a planter box, a vegetation base and irrigation equipment.

A diverse facade that does not look industrially manufactured was realized by a combined unit of 12 mm thick aluminum panels and a vegetation base (300 mm x 300 mm) that is fixed slightly rotated and slanted. By giving porous texture like a rock surface to the aluminum surfaces, we wanted to create a condition that various plants grow thickly on an aluminum cliff in the city.

As for the vegetation, five different kinds of plants tolerant of severe condition grow mingled together. Especially the plants that blossom flowers were frequently chosen so as the exterior wall to bloom flowers in each season. In order to gain rocky texture on the aluminum, a mold was made by sprinkling solution over styrene foam and randomly corroding it. Aluminum was then poured into the mold to make a product. We tried to reappear the process of a rocky surface eroded by rain and become porous on an industrial manufacture of aluminum.

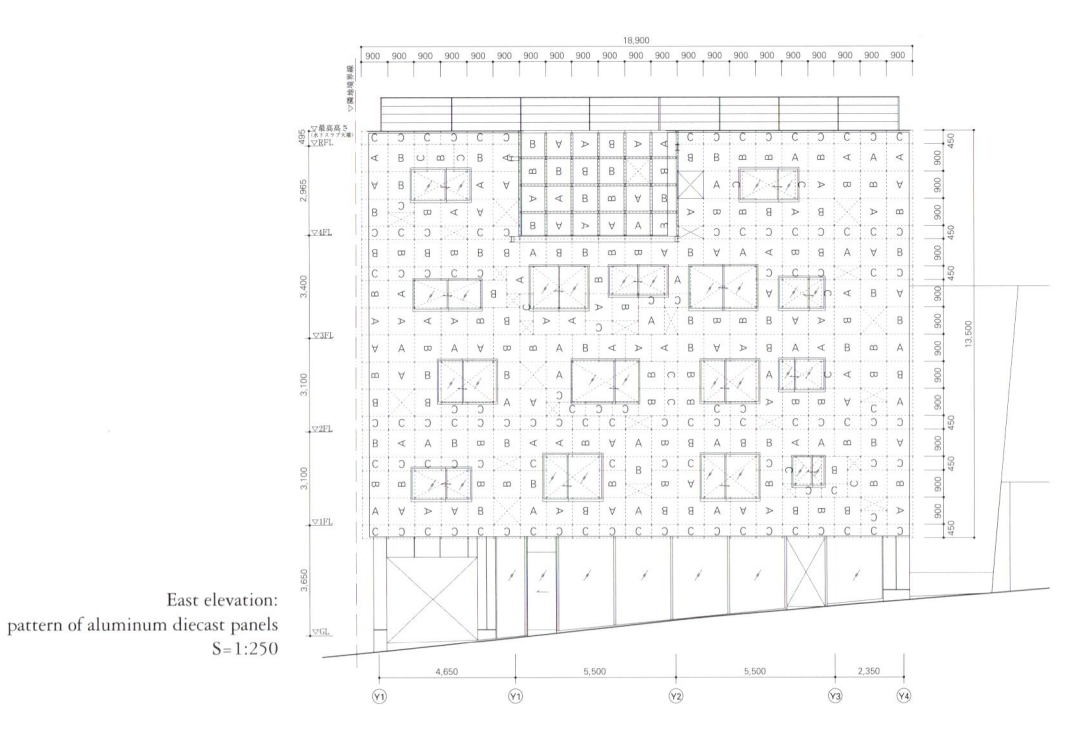

Overall view from east　東より見る全景

East elevation: pattern of aluminum diecast panels
S=1:250

グリーン・キャスト

小田原駅近くの丘陵地に建つ複合ビル。

　ファサードは，設備スペースを兼ねたアルミキャストパネルでつくったプランターに覆われている。換気口，雨水立樋，プランターボックス，緑化基盤，灌水設備が一体化された，複合的な外壁システムをデザインした。

　12mm厚のアルミキャストパネルを用いて緑化基盤（300mm×300mm）と一体化したユニットをつくり，ユニットを少しずつ回転，傾斜させることで，工業製品とは思えないような多様性のある変化に富んだファサードを実現した。アルミの表面に岩肌の様な多孔質のテクスチャーを与えることで，アルミの崖に多様な植物が繁茂するような状態を，都市の中につくり出そうと考えた。

　植物は耐候性の高い5種類を混生させ，特に花が咲くものを多く用いて，季節ごとに花が咲く外壁とした。アルミに岩肌のテクスチャーを獲得するため，発泡スチロールのボードに溶液をふりかけて，スチロールをランダムに腐食させるという方法で型をつくり，そこにアルミを流し込んで鋳造した。岩肌が雨水に腐食されて多孔質となるプロセスを，アルミという工業製品において再現しようと試みた。

Vegetation panels. Rear side　緑化パネル。裏側

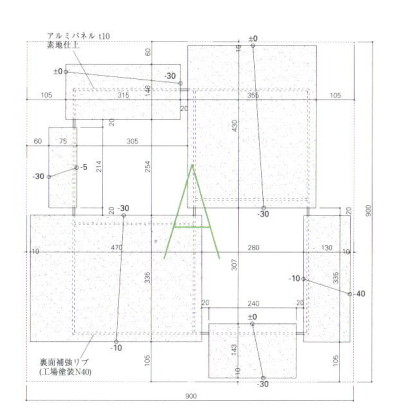

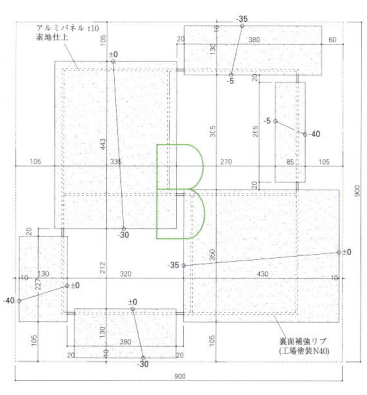

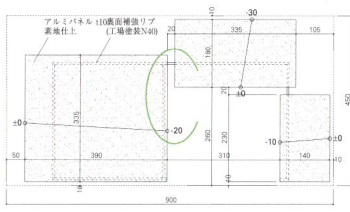

Vegetation panel: partial detail　S=1:15

Upward view of vegetation panel　緑化パネルの見上げ

Aluminum diecast panels　S=1:15

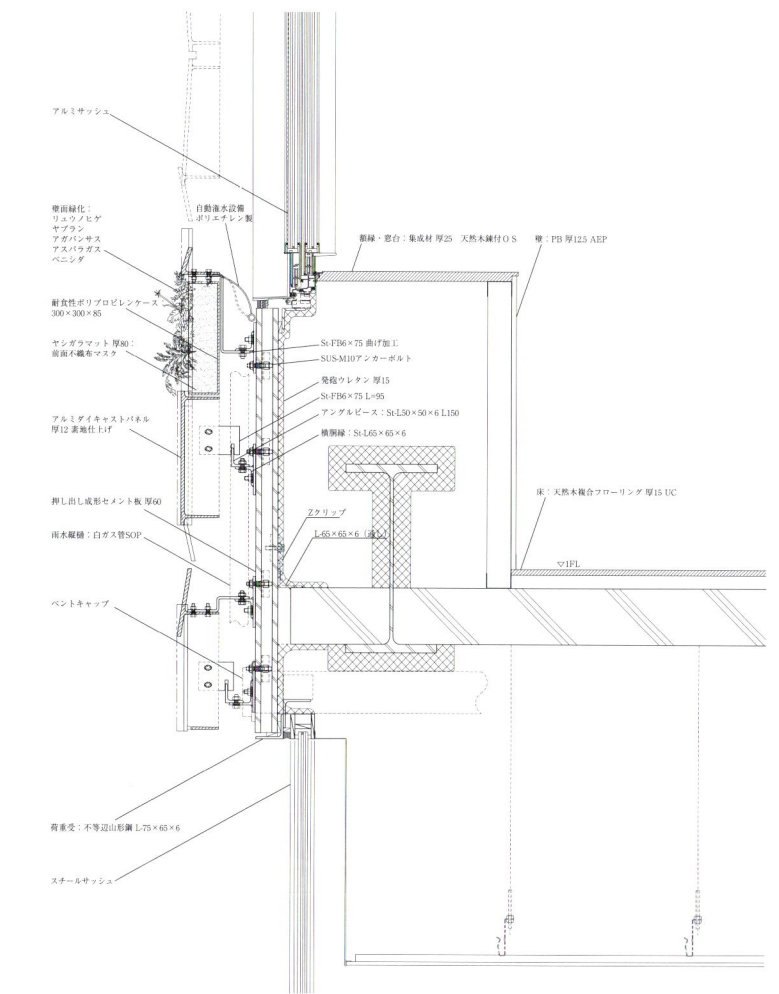

View of vegetation panels from terrace　テラスより緑化パネルを見る

273

2012–   Iiyama Plaza
Iiyama, Nagano, Japan

Overall view 全景

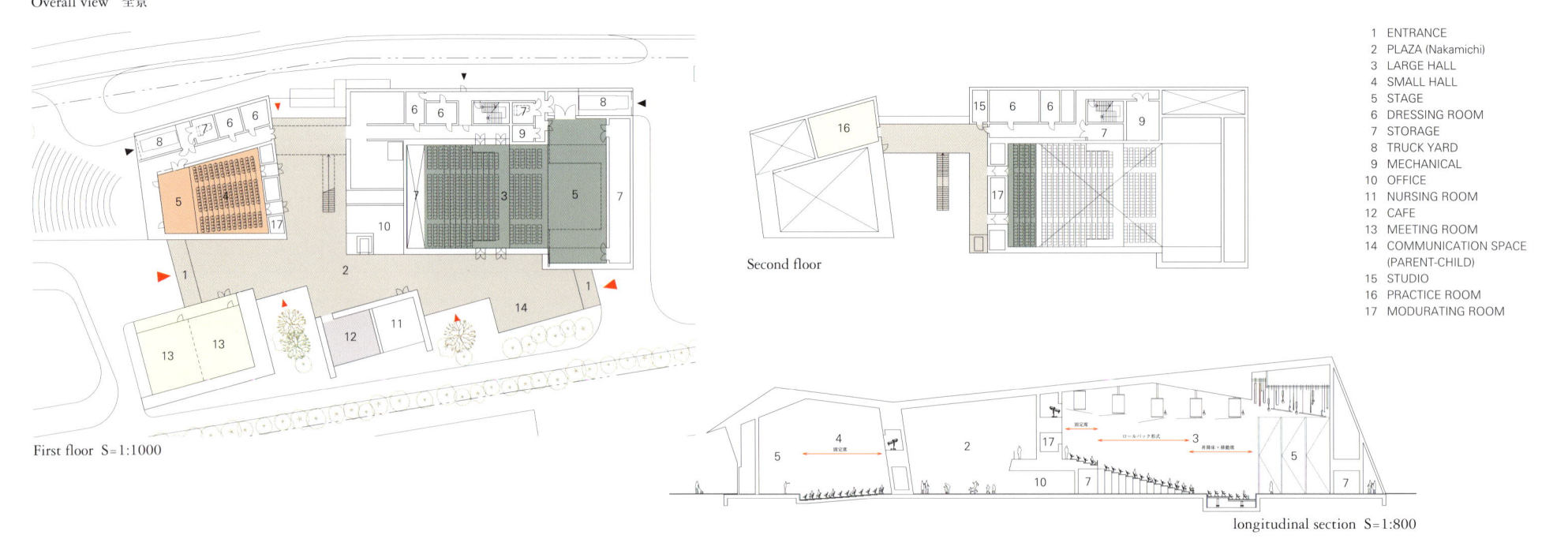

First floor S=1:1000

Second floor

longitudinal section S=1:800

1 ENTRANCE
2 PLAZA (Nakamichi)
3 LARGE HALL
4 SMALL HALL
5 STAGE
6 DRESSING ROOM
7 STORAGE
8 TRUCK YARD
9 MECHANICAL
10 OFFICE
11 NURSING ROOM
12 CAFE
13 MEETING ROOM
14 COMMUNICATION SPACE (PARENT-CHILD)
15 STUDIO
16 PRACTICE ROOM
17 MODURATING ROOM

Small hall　小ホール

Plaza (Nakamichi)　ナカミチ

View from southeast　南東より見る

This is a complex facility for a cultural and community hall to be located in front of the Iiyama Station for the newly developed Hokuriku Shinkansen in 2014.

Community halls tend to be huge and something foreign so we tried to open the hall to the city allowing it to merge into the nature of Iiyama City. We placed two halls, one large one small, independently, and connected them to the street with a roof—thus forming a 'Naka-Michi'. By opening Naka-Michi to the city in many directions, we aimed to give a new festivity to the city and to seamlessly connect this facility and the city. The space of the big hall with 600-seat can vary from a sloping theater style to a flat seated on-the-ground style. Realizing a big opening facing the Naka-Michi makes the big hall a part of the Naka-Michi.

Fast mass-transportation by Shinkansen will make a big impact on the local society and the economy. We believe that at this moment the paths local people walk and the places where people get together have to be revived and the connection between the earth and the people has to be maintained.

(仮称) 飯山ぷらざ

2014年度末に開業予定の北陸新幹線飯山駅の駅前に計画された，文化ホールと交流施設の複合体。

大きなヴォリューム，大きな「異物」となりがちなホールを町に対して開き，飯山の自然環境に融合させようと試みた．大小二つのホールと交流機能をつなげずに，独立した建築として敷地にばらまき，その隙間に「ナカミチ」と名づけた屋根つきのストリート空間を通した．「ナカミチ」は，多方向に開くことで新しい賑わいを町に与え，町と公共建築がシームレスにつながる状態をめざした．600席の大ホールは，劇場形式から平土間形式まで，様々な空間形式をとることが可能である．「ナカミチ」に面する大きな開口を開けば，大ホールも「ナカミチ」の一部となる．

新幹線による高速大量輸送は，地域社会や経済に大きなインパクトを与える．その時にこそ，町に人間の歩く道，人間の集まる場所を復活させて，大地と人間とをつなぎとめなくてはいけない．

2012- Towada City Plaza for Social Communication
Towada, Aomori, Japan

Overall view from southwest　南西より見る全景

The project is a compound facility of welfare and lifetime-education, intending at citizens' interactions. It was planned along a central shopping street in Towada city. Our proposal of the passage type linear space under an natural mountain-shaped roof was selected in the competition.

Firstly, we walked around the existing shopping street in Towada city and found fascination and potential in the spaces under a covered passage that intersects a large road. Utilizing the passage space, rooms for welfare education were connected. Further, the passage space was folded and foyer and shades were given in the linear space. In this way, we tried to induce various citizens' activities, which will not fit in rooms, and their communications. The roof is folded based on logic of 'city' and 'snow', unrelated to the division of the rooms below. The encounter of the Origami shaped organic form and the planning of the below space creates spatial diversity.

△▷ Plaza (Michi-no-Hiroba)　みちの広場

Tatami room　和室

Play room　プレイルーム

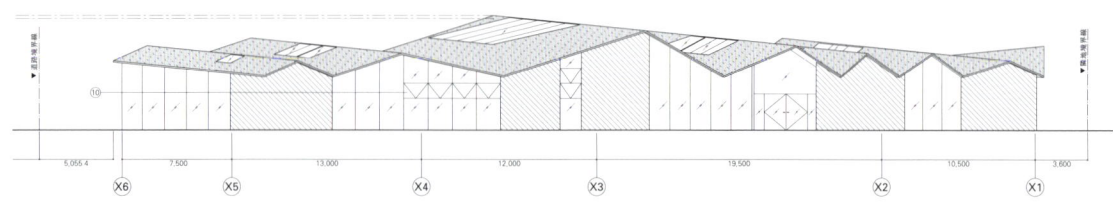

West elevation S=1:500

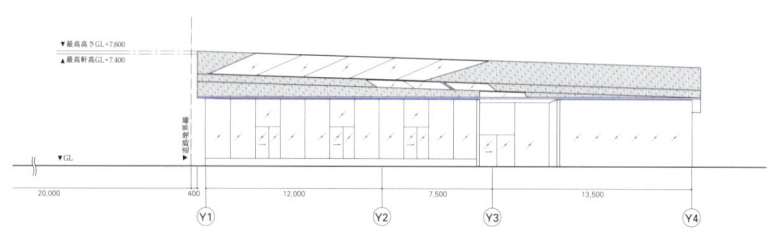

South elevation

1 ENTRY
2 PLAZA (Michi-no-Hiroba)
3 MULTIPURPOSE SEMINAR ROOM
4 SMALL OFFICE
5 WORK STATION
6 STORAGE
7 HOT WATER SUPPLY
8 ANTEROOM
9 OFFICE
10 MEETING ROOM
11 WC
12 EXHIBITION ROOM
13 PLAY ROOM
14 COMMUNICATION ROOM (PARENT-CHILD)
15 NURSING ROOM
16 TATAMI ROOM
17 KITCHEN STUDIO
18 KILN
19 MECHANICAL
20 PUMP
21 ELECTRICAL
22 BOILER
23 SILO

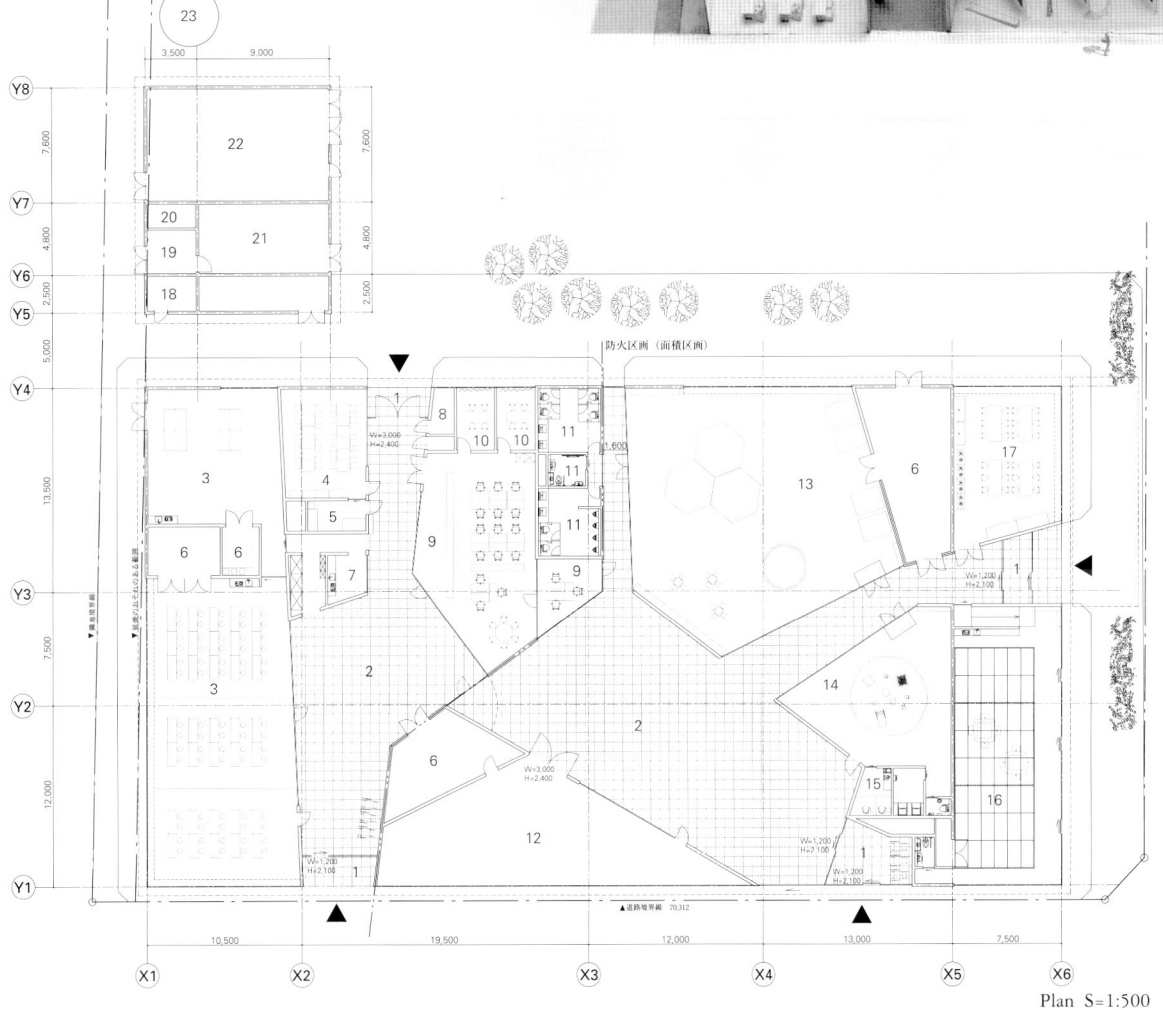

Model: looking interior through roof
模型：屋根を透かしてインテリアを見る

Plan S=1:500

Cross section

Longitudinal section

(仮称) 十和田市市民交流プラザ

十和田市の中心商店街に沿って計画された, 福祉と生涯教育施設が複合した市民交流施設。山のような有機的形態を持つ屋根の下に, パッサージュ型のリニアな空間を提案したわれわれが, コンペティションで選出された。

まず, 十和田市の既存商店街を歩きまわり, 大通りと直交する屋根付きのパッサージュ空間に, 魅力と可能性を感じた。そのパッサージュ空間によって福祉教育機能をもつ諸室をつなぎ, さらにこのパッサージュ空間を折り曲げてリニアな空間にタマリと陰影を与えることで, 諸室の中には収まりきらない多様な市民活動やコミュニケーションを誘発しようと考えた。屋根は, 下部の室内の分割とは無関係に, 「街」と「雪」のロジックに基づいて折りたたまれる。その折り紙状の有機的形状と下部のプランニングとの出会いによって, 空間の多様性が創造される。

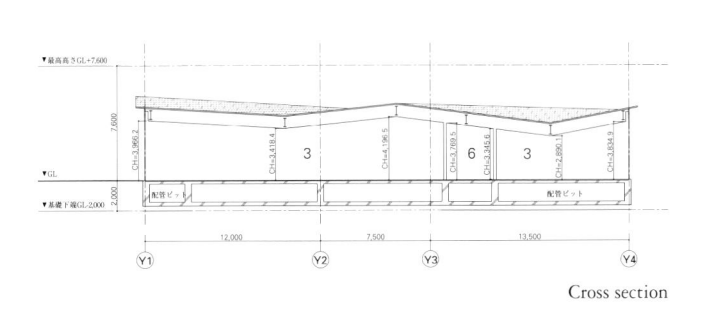

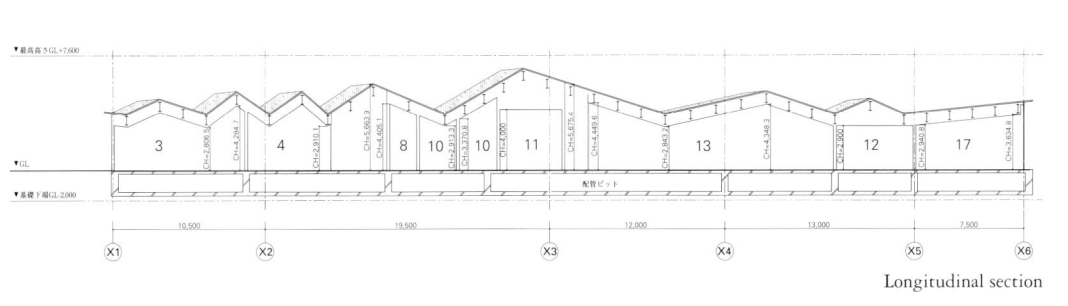

2012-
Under One Roof
Lausanne, Switzerland

Overall view from southeast　南東より見る全景

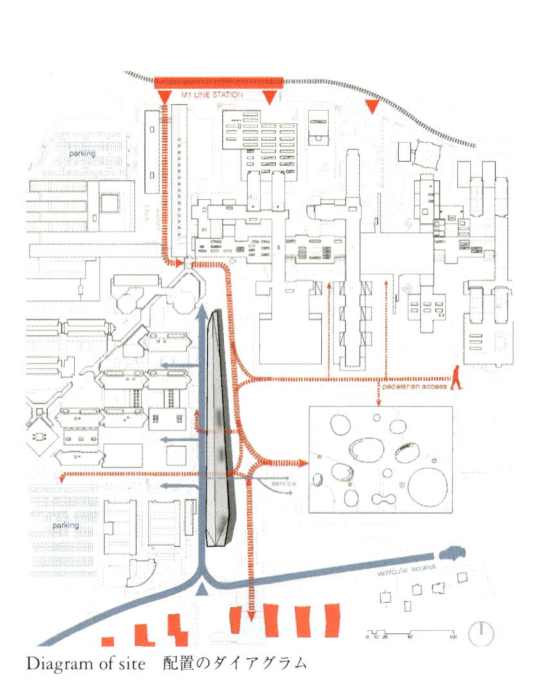

Diagram of site　配置のダイアグラム

Diagram of structure　構成のダイアグラム

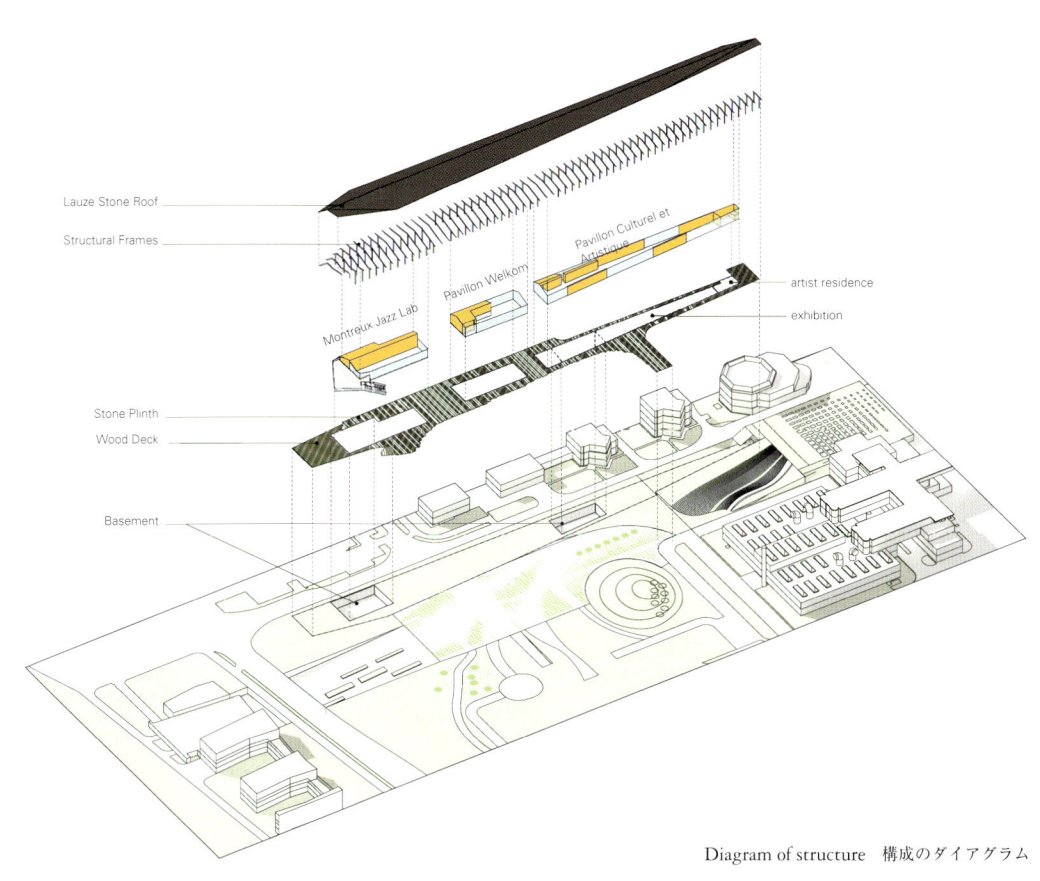

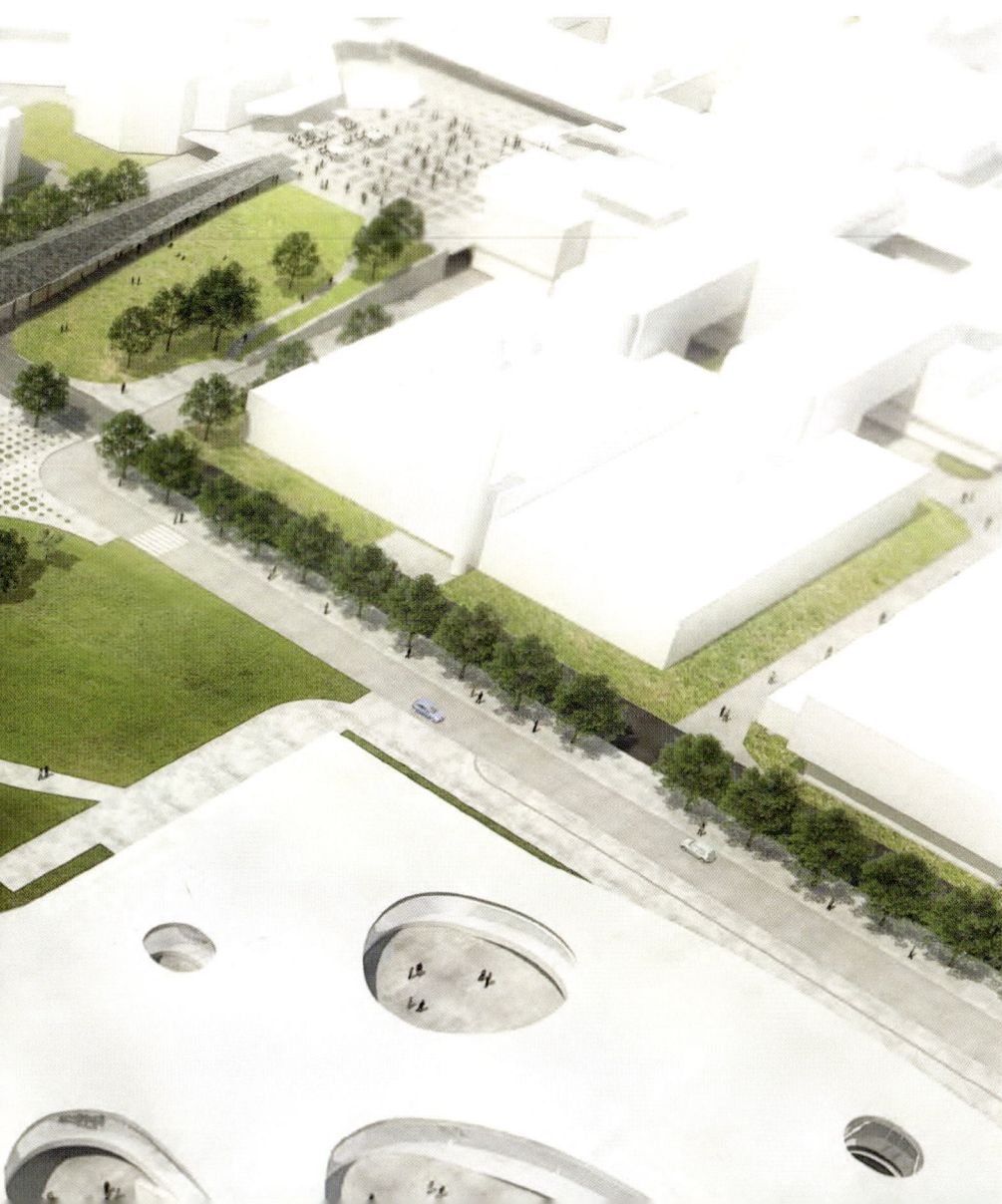

This is an attempt to insert a new infrastructure, rather than an architecture, to a university campus. Inside the 260 m-long infrastructure are a number of activities that are rarely found on a conventional university campus ground, such as an archive of Montreux Jazz Festival. A 'gap' is prepared between each activity—an ambiguous space that is neither a box nor a plaza.

While the adjacent 'ROLEX Learning Center' (2009) designed by SANAA creates a sense of ambiguous domains through its undulating floors, we tried to create a sense of ambiguous domains through the use of semi-outdoor space under the roof.

For its roof, we took our hint from the stone roof of local private houses. By using granular metal plates, natural light is introduced through the 'gaps' between granules in a controlled manner.

Similarly, we took our hint from the local private houses for its wooden structure, but made it a composite structure of wood and aluminum in our challenge to explore new possibilities of traditional materials.

Under One Roof

大学キャンパスの中に，建築ではなく，新しいインフラストラクチャーを挿入しようと考えた。260mの長さを持つインフラストラクチャーの中には，従来の大学キャンパスには存在しなかった複数のアクティビティ——例えば，モントルー・ジャズ・フェスティバルのアーカイブ——が配置されている。それぞれのアクティビティの間には「隙間」が用意される。その「隙間」空間はボックスでもないし，広場でもない曖昧な場所である。

隣接するSANAA設計の「ROLEXラーニングセンター」(2009年)が隆起する床によって曖昧な領域性を創造したのに対し，われわれはルーフの下の半屋外空間を用いて曖昧な領域性を生み出そうと試みた。

屋根には，この地域の民家の石屋根にヒントを得た。粒子状の金属板が用いられ，粒子と粒子の「隙間」から，自然光がコントロールされた形で導入される。

構造もまた，この地域の民家からヒントを得た木構造だが，木とアルミの板との複合構造とすることで，伝統的素材の新しい可能性に挑戦した。

Aerial view　鳥瞰全景

First floor S=1:600

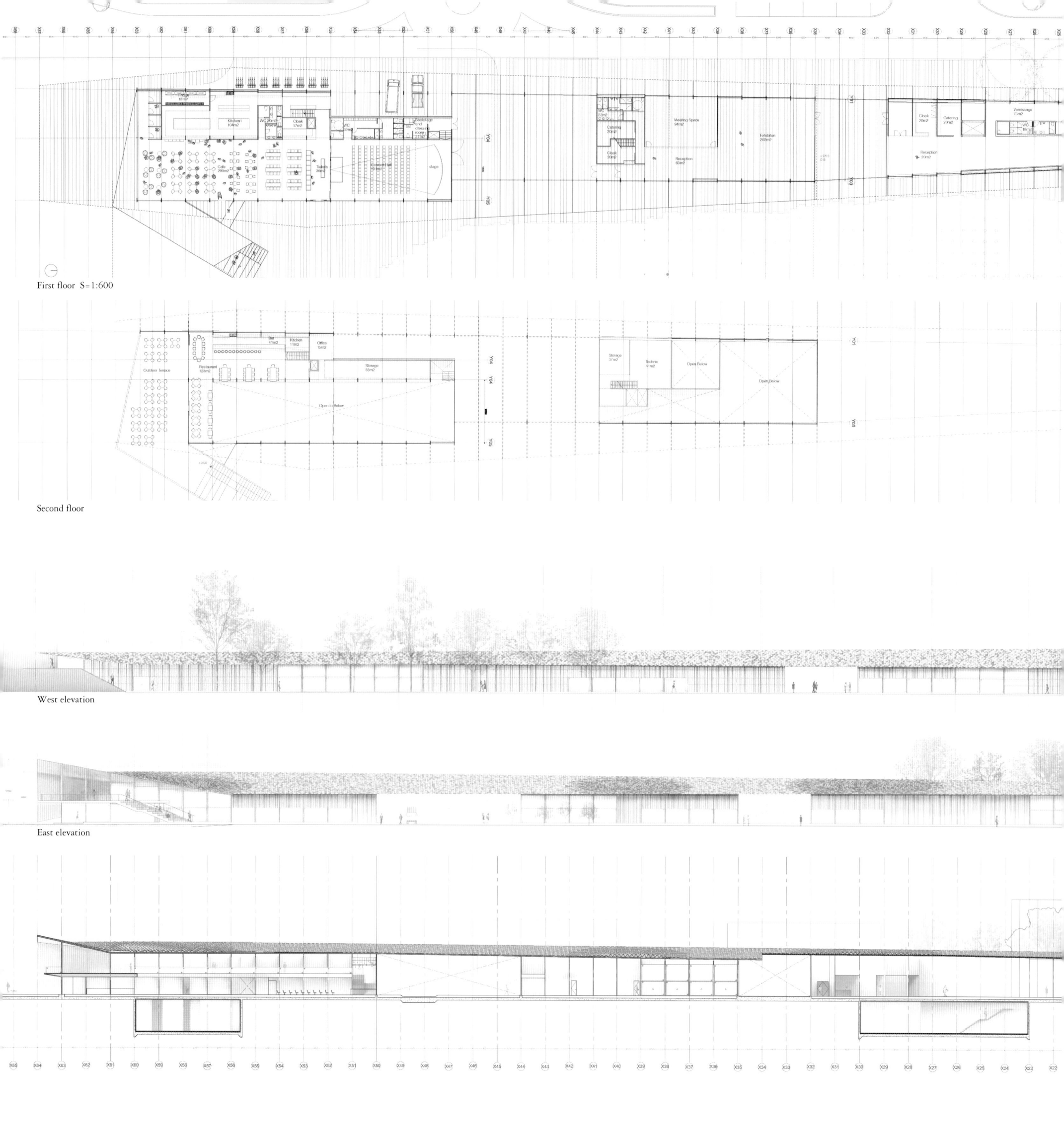

Second floor

West elevation

East elevation

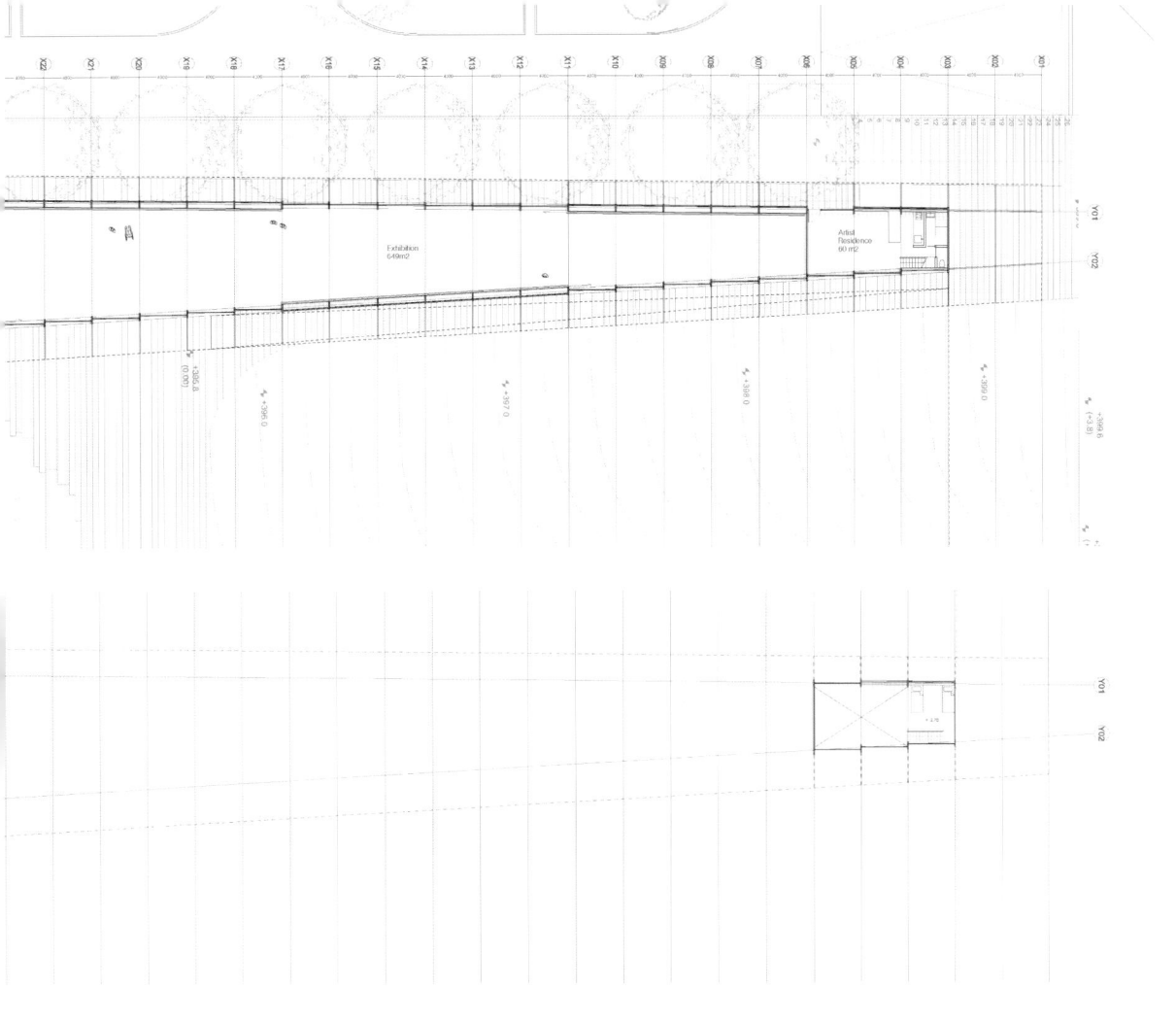

Art and culture pavilion　芸術文化パヴィリオン

Welcome pavilion　ウェルカム・パヴィリオン

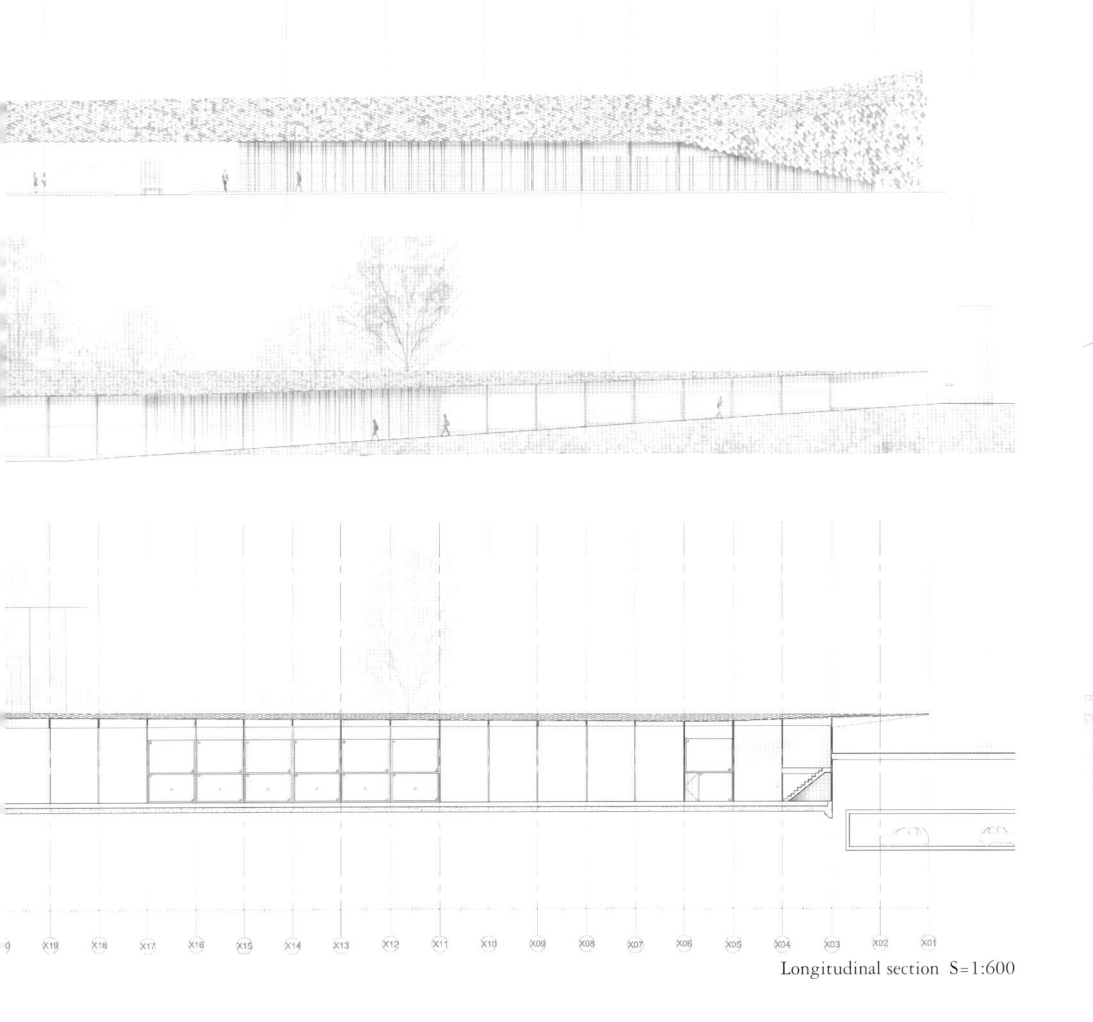

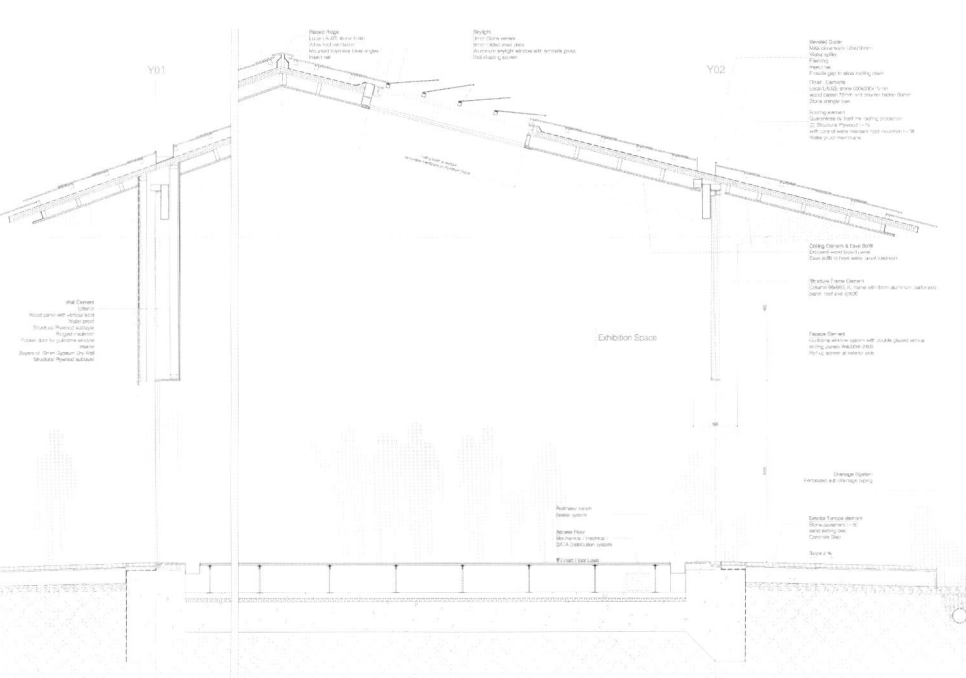

Longitudinal section　S=1:600

Cross section　S=1:100

2012- Susa International Train Station
Susa valley, Turin, Italy

Overall view from southwest　南西より見る全景

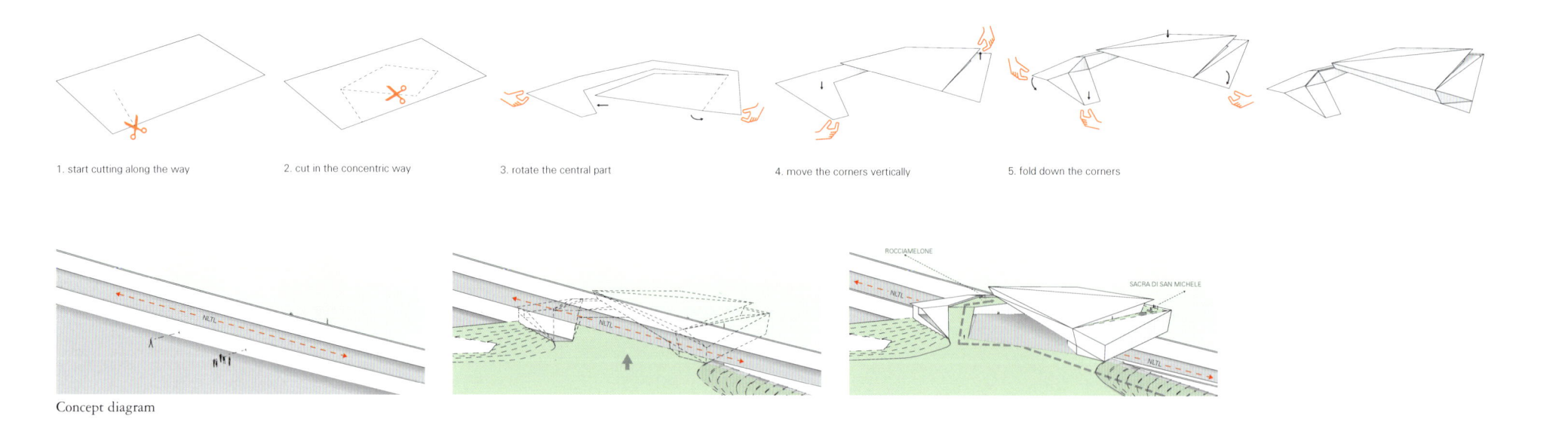

1. start cutting along the way
2. cut in the concentric way
3. rotate the central part
4. move the corners vertically
5. fold down the corners

Concept diagram

The station will serve as a gate of the Italian side new express railway that connects France and Italy. Our proposal was selected in an international competition.

We considered that a station is not only a node of a railway and neighborhood, but also a connection of the ground and the sky and a link of human and constructed objects. There, as a composition that the ground rise up in a spiral and becomes a roof terrace and, further, gradually connects to a sloped roof, we blended the architecture and the earth. Covering the architecture with a roof inspired by 'tetto della rosa' (stone plate roof), which is used in the district's traditional houses, and controlling light and ventilation through the stone boards, sustainability was achieved.

It was suggested by jurors that the roof shape reminded them of Carlo Mollino 'Chalet Lago Negro' (1947), which is placed close to the site.

As for program, we proposed a compound of station and the district's community facility. Expecting the express railway's station to act as a generous saucer that catches the areas' various activities, it was designed open so as to contribute to the region with half outdoor space unified with architecture and half outdoor space.

Aerial view　鳥瞰

Cafe on third floor　3階カフェ

Foyer on second floor　2階ホワイエ

スーザ国際駅

フランスとイタリアを結ぶ新しい高速鉄道のイタリア側のゲートとなる駅で, 国際コンペティションでわれわれの案が選ばれた。

駅は, 鉄道と地域の結節点であるだけでなく, 地面と空とをつなぐ結節点であり, また, 人間と構築物とをつなぐ結節点であると考えた。そのために, 大地がスパイラル状に隆起してルーフテラスとなり, さらに勾配屋根へとゆるやかに連続する構成として, 建築と大地とを融合した。地域の伝統的民家で用いられてきた,「テット・デッラ・ローザ(＝石板の屋根)」にヒントを得た屋根で建築を覆い, 石板の隙間からの光や通風をコントロールすることで, サステイナビリティを達成した。

屋根の形態は, 近くに建つカルロ・モリーノの「ラゴネグロのシャレー」(1947年)という作品を想起させると審査員から指摘された。

プログラムにおいては, 駅と地域のコミュニティ施設との複合を提案した。高速鉄道の駅が, 地域の様々な活動を受け入れる寛容な受け皿となることを期待し, 建築と一体化した屋外空間, 半屋外空間, 地域に貢献するような開放的デザインとした。

2012-   Tomioka City Hall
Tomioka, Gunma, Japan

Site plan

Tomioka city, which is renowned for a silk mill, is not an exception to many other Japanese countryside cities in problems such as hollow center due to automobile transportation and a managerial crisis of railways.

Centering a courtyard, we proposed separate blocks of city hall by utilizing the vicinity to the railway station and redefined the city hall as a comprehensive base for citizens' interactions revitalizing the central city.

Respecting the tiled roofs of the existing city's local houses and the silk mill, which is the symbol of the city, roof was designed with tiles and we endeavored to blend public architecture into the city fabric.

Each building has a roof following 'monitor roof', which has a unique sectional shape for ventilation of a sericulture farmhouse. The lower part is defined as a half-outdoor open communication space by tile louver's detail. The shape of the open space also followed Tomioka's traditional street pattern, 'kaimagari' (a cranked passage), and made an outdoor space full of variations coexisting with halt and flow, which cannot be found in square type open spaces.

Bird's eye view from northeast　北東より見る鳥瞰

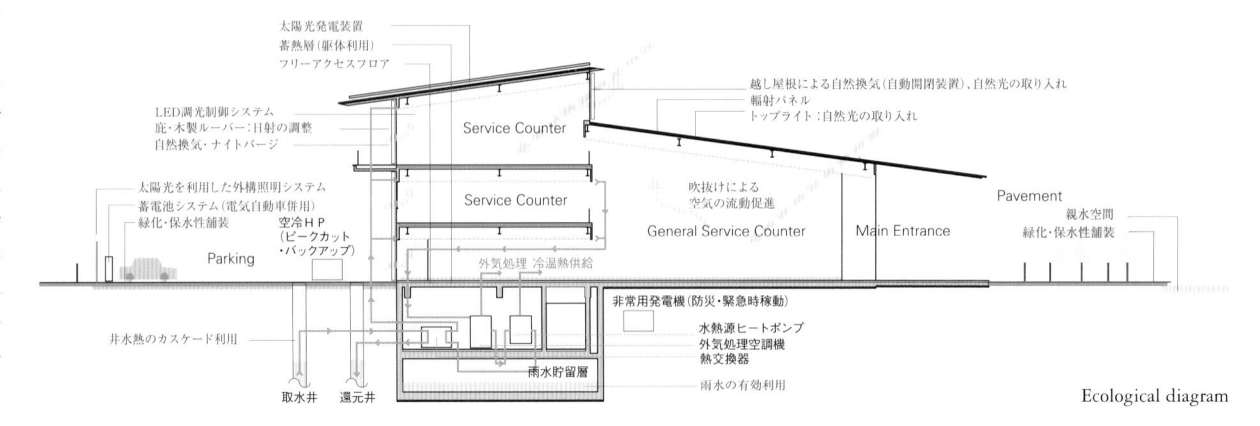

Ecological diagram

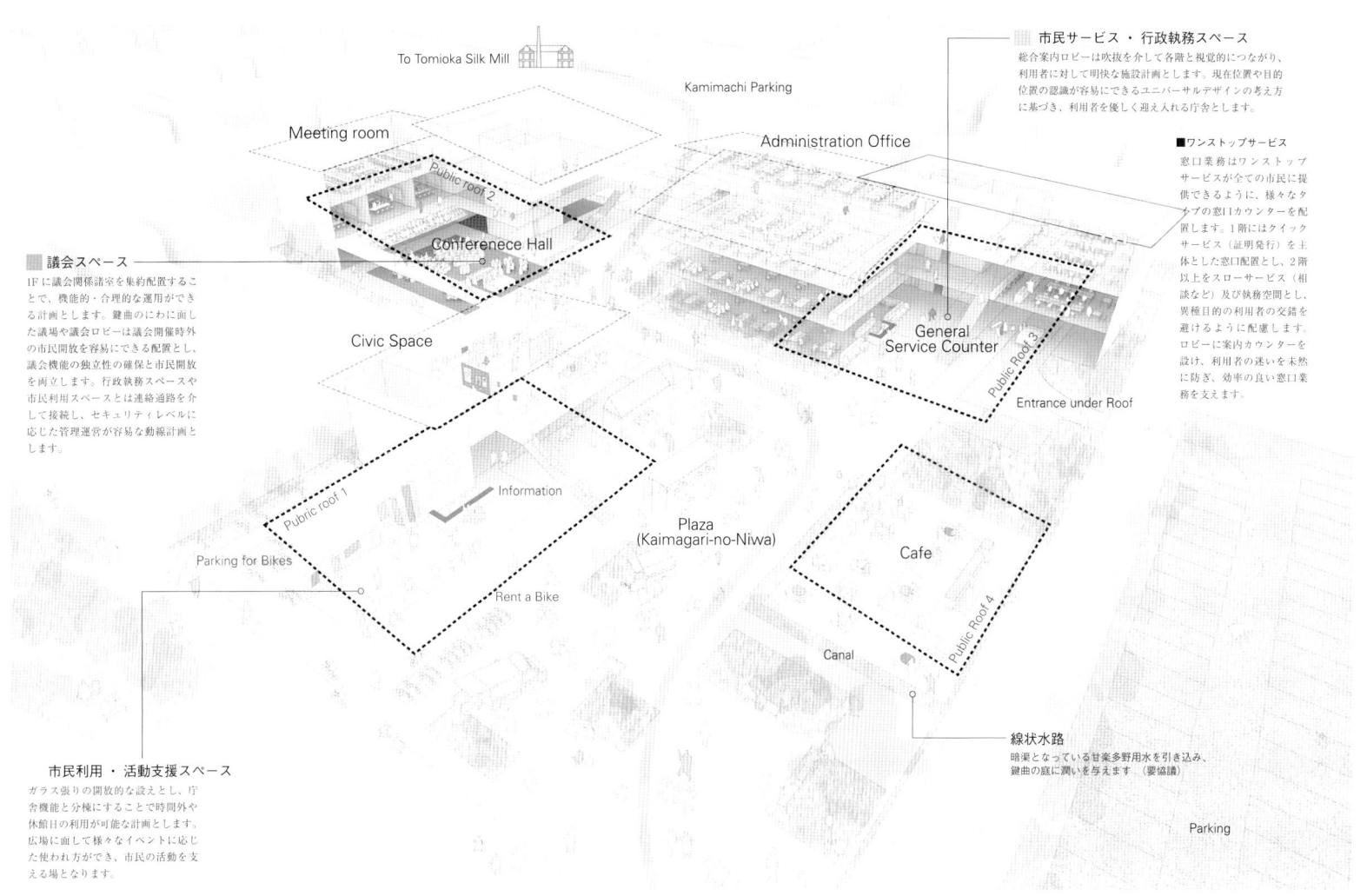

市民サービス・行政執務スペース
総合案内ロビーは吹抜を介して各階と視覚的につながり、利用者に対して明快な施設計画とします。現在位置や目的位置の認識が容易にできるユニバーサルデザインの考え方に基づき、利用者を優しく迎え入れる庁舎とします。

■ワンストップサービス
窓口業務はワンストップサービスが全ての市民に提供できるように、様々なタイプの窓口カウンターを配置します。1階にはクイックサービス（証明発行）を主体とした窓口配置とし、2階以上をスローサービス（相談など）及び執務空間とし、異種目的の利用者の交錯を避けるように配慮します。ロビーに案内カウンターを設け、利用者の迷いを未然に防ぎ、効率の良い窓口業務を支えます。

■議会スペース
1Fに議会関係諸室を集約配置することで、機能的・合理的な運用ができる計画とします。鍵曲のにわに面した議場や議会ロビーは議会開催時外の市民開放を容易にできる配置とし、議会機能の独立性の確保と市民開放を両立します。行政執務スペースや市民利用スペースとは連絡通路を介して接続し、セキュリティレベルに応じた管理運営が容易な動線計画とします。

■市民利用・活動支援スペース
ガラス張りの開放的な設えとし、庁舎機能と分棟にすることで時間外や休館日の利用が可能な計画とします。広場に面して様々なイベントに応じた使われ方ができ、市民の活動を支える場となります。

線状水路
暗渠となっている甘楽多野用水を引き込み、鍵曲の庭に潤いを与えます。（要協議）

Concept diagram

General service lobby　総合窓口ロビー

Cafe　カフェ

Conference hall　議場

Information counter of civic space
市民利用スペースの情報カウンター

富岡市新庁舎

富岡製糸場で知られる富岡市は，日本の多くの地方都市の例にもれず，自動車交通によって中心市街地の空洞化や鉄道の経営危機から脱出できずにいる。

われわれは，鉄道駅の近くという立地を生かして，市役所を中心市街地を活性化する包括的市民交流の拠点として再定義し，広場を中心とする分棟型の市役所を提案した。

既存市街地の瓦屋根の民家，そして市のシンボルである富岡製糸場に敬意を払い，屋根には瓦をのせて，都市のファブリックに公共建築も溶け込ませようとした。

それぞれの棟は，養蚕農家の換気のための特徴的断面形状「越屋根」を踏襲する屋根とし，低い部分は瓦ルーバーのディテールによって，半屋外的雰囲気を持つ開放的なコミュニケーション空間と定義した。広場の形状は，同じく富岡の伝統的街路パターンである「鍵曲」を踏襲し，スクエアの広場にはない，溜まりと流れの共存する変化に富んだ外部空間とした。

2007-13 Besançon City Arts and Culture Center
Besançon, Doubs, France

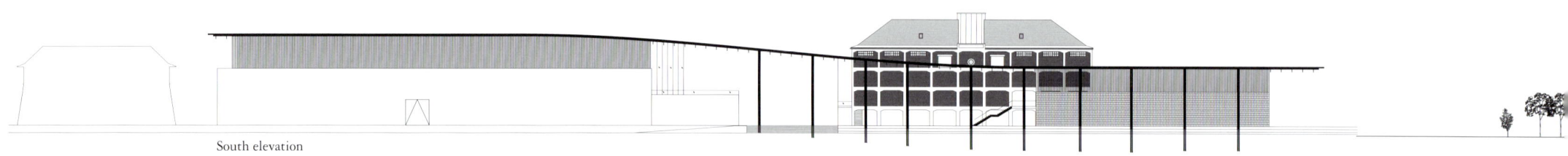

Aerial view　上空より見る

South elevation

Site plan

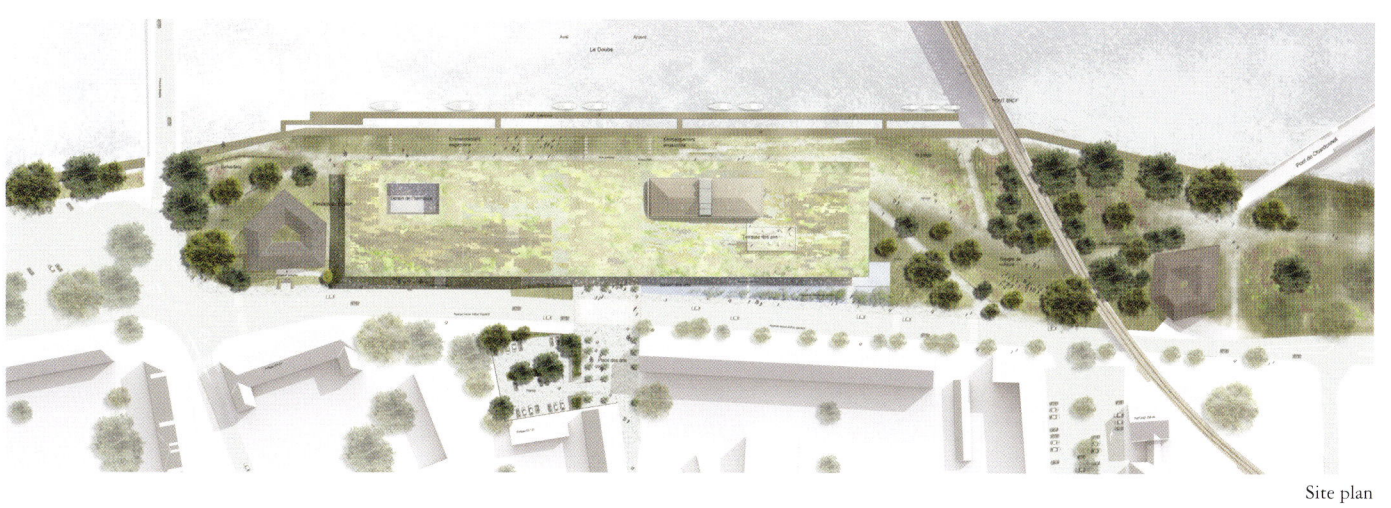

View from southeast: front volume is museum of contemporary art
南東より見る：美術館棟

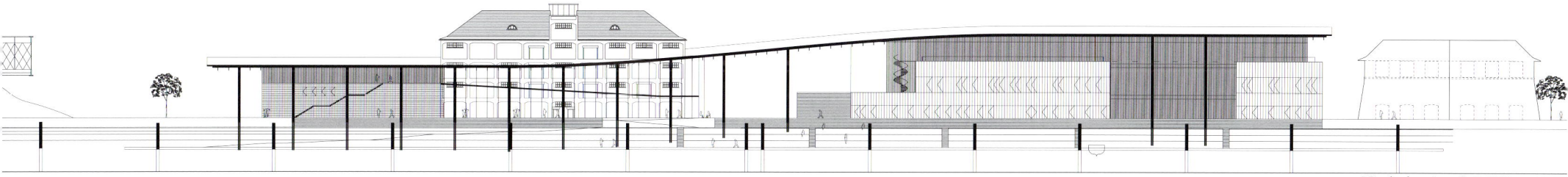

North elevation S=1:1000

287

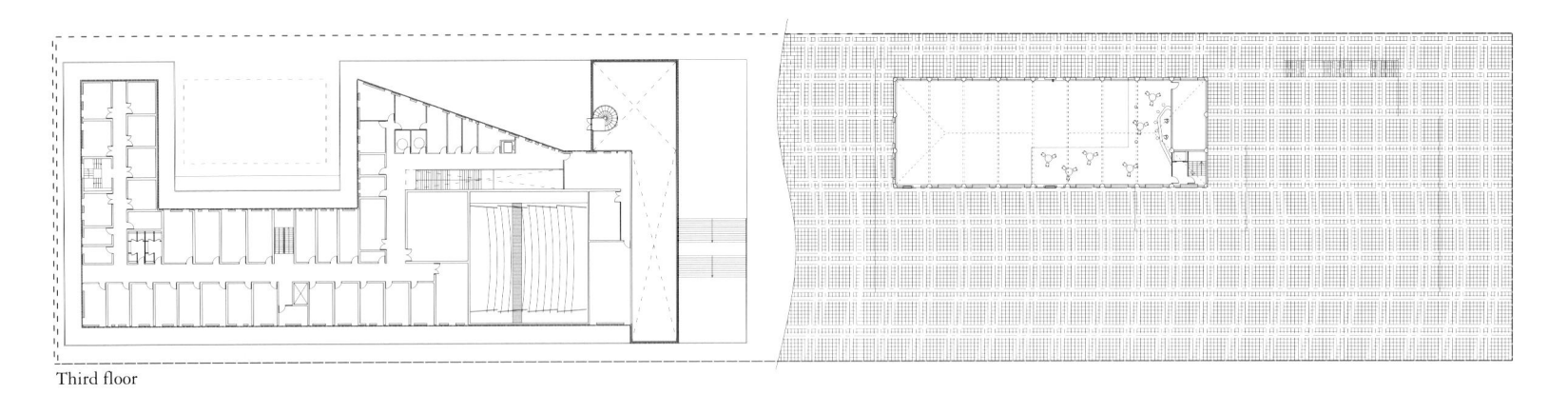

Third floor

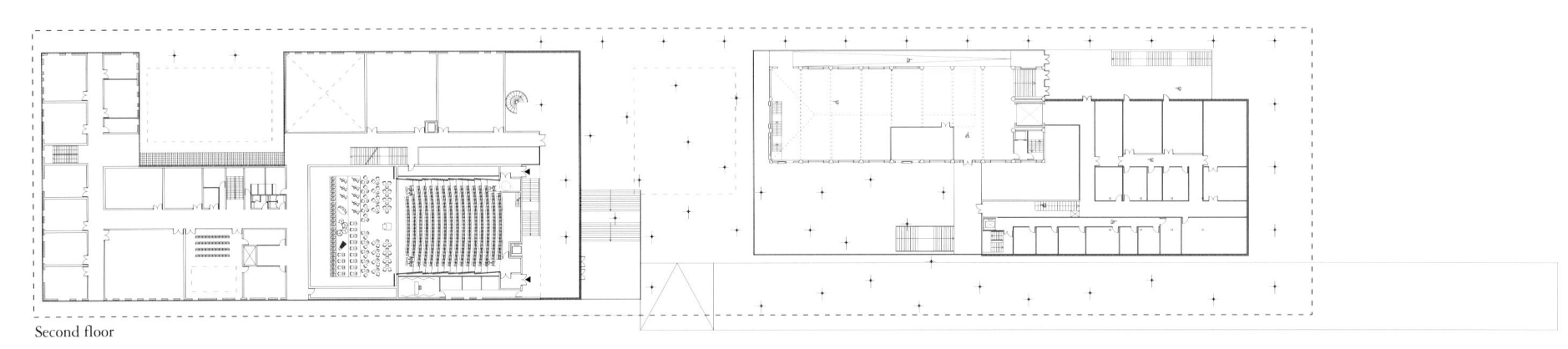

Second floor

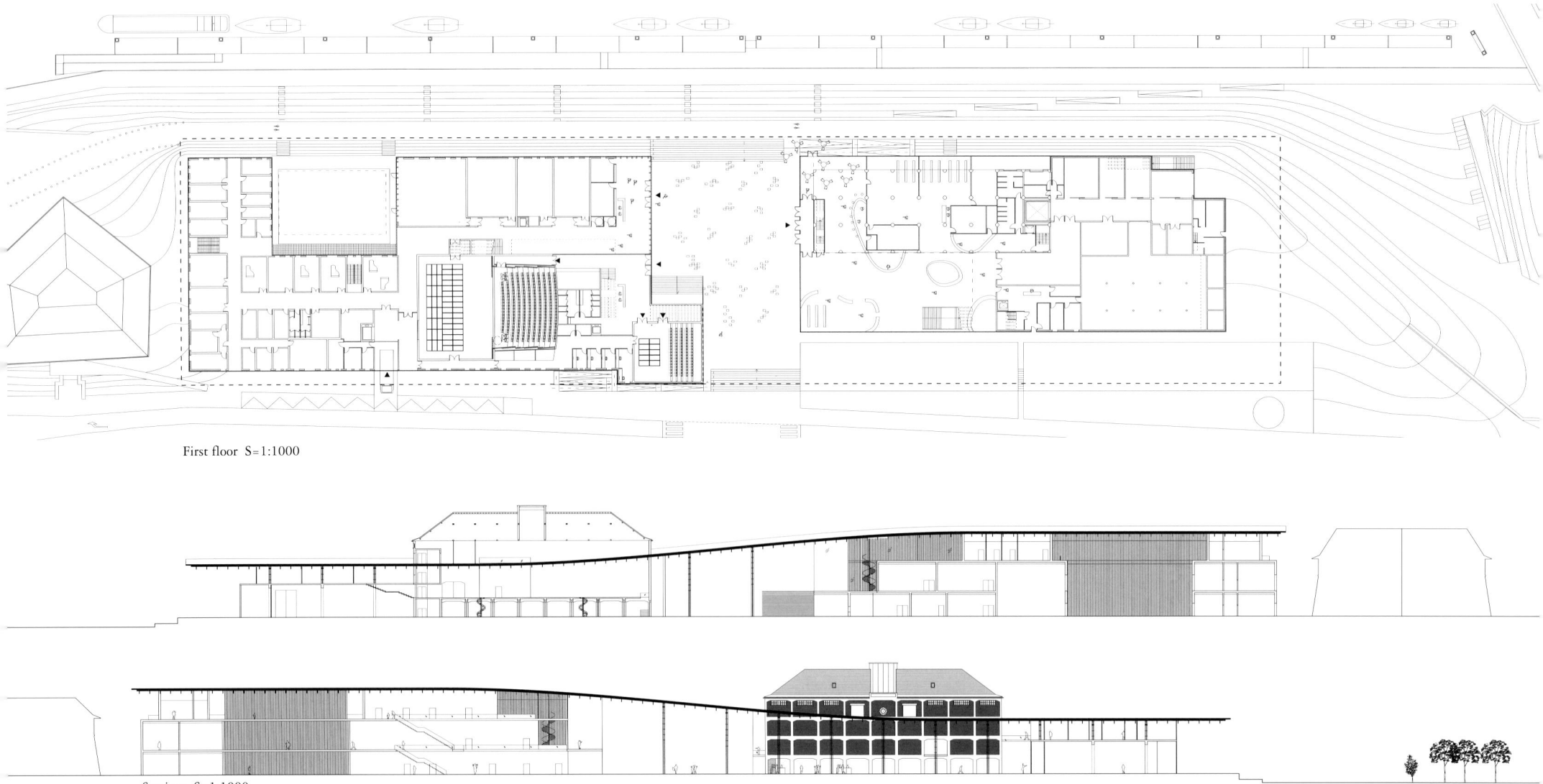

First floor S=1:1000

Sections S=1:1000

288

Our proposal which aimed for a 'soft' cultural facility using local timber was chosen by competition in 2007.

The site is facing the Doubs River, which originates in Switzerland, and an old city to the north while to the south on the top of the hill, there is a citadel famed as the place Caesar stayed at to write 'Gallic War'.

We proposed a gate-style cultural facility which connects the city and nature. By adding a timber roof around the existing brick warehouse, the 'semi-open' space underneath acts as a vehicle to connect the city and nature. The space under the roof will provide a place to communicate for citizens, or for students studying at the conservatoire, or perhaps an outside concert.

Considering the view from the citadel on the hill, planted panels and solar panels are laid in a mosaic pattern on the roof which is considered the fifth facade. The locally grown cedar has been laid in a mosaic pattern on the exterior wall. The sunlight and the wind flow through the spaces in between the buildings and from the gaps between the timber panels, thus uniting architecture and nature.

Semi-open space under timber roof (under construction)　木造屋根の下にできる半屋外空間（工事中）

Museum of contemporary art　美術館棟

View from riverside　河岸より見る

ブザンソン芸術文化センター

地元の木を用いて「やわらかな」文化施設をめざしたわれわれの提案が、2007年のコンペティションで選出された。

スイスから流れるドゥー川に面し、北側に旧市街、南側の丘の上にはカエサルが逗留し「ガリア戦記」を執筆したことでも知られる要塞が残っている。

都市と自然（川）とをつなぐ、ゲート型の文化施設を提案した。既存のレンガ倉庫の上に、木造の屋根をのせ、その下にできる「半屋外空間」を媒介として、都市と自然をつなぐのである。屋根の下の空間は、市民やコンセルバトワールの学生たちのためのコミュニケーション、屋外コンサートの場所となるだろう。

要塞からの建物を見下ろす視点を考慮して「5番目のファサード」である屋上には緑化パネルと太陽光パネルとがモザイク状に配置され、外壁は地元のカラマツ材を用いたパネルがモザイク状に配置される。棟と棟との隙間、粒子状の木製パネルの隙間から光や風が室内に導かれ、川の自然と建築とが一体化される。

2006-12   List of Works

2002–06
Ginzan-Onsen Fujiya
Yamagata, Japan
—
Program: Japanese style hotel
Total floor area: 927.99m²
Site area: 558.13m²
Structure: timber frame
3 stories, 1 basement

銀山温泉 藤屋
所在地：山形県尾花沢市大字銀山新畑443
設計：200204-0503
工事：200504-0607
建築主：藤敦
主要用途：旅館
構造：中田捷夫研究室
設備：森村設計
照明：小西武志＋建築照明計画
ステンドグラス：アトリエ・ルブランス
施工：愛知建設
主体構造・規模：木造／地下1階，地上3階
敷地面積：558.13m²
建築面積：366.09m²
延床面積：927.99m²

2003–06
Z58
Shanghai, China
—
Program: office, showroom
Total floor area: 3,159.34m²
Site area: 961.91m²
Structure: reinforced concrete
4 stories, 1 basement

Z58
所在地：中国上海市番禺路58
設計：200310-0405
工事：200405-0607
建築主：Zhongtai Lighting Group
主要用途：事務所，ショールーム
構造：Chen Ke
設備：Zhongtai Qingyu
事務所内装：ZLG Architects
施工：Zhongtai Decoration Engineering Co., Ltd.
主体構造・規模：鉄筋コンクリート造，一部鉄骨造
地下1階，地上4階
敷地面積：961.91m²
建築面積：860.80m²＋90.48m²
延床面積：3,159.34m²

2003–08
Asahi Broadcasting Corporation
Osaka, Japan
—
Program: broadcasting station, parking, shop
Total floor area: 43,401.27m²
Site area: 8,500.04m²
Structure: steel frame
16 stories, 1 basement, 2 rooftops

朝日放送
所在地：大阪府大阪市福島区福島1-1-30
設計：200309-0509
工事：200510-0801
建築主：朝日放送
主要用途：放送局，駐車場，店舗
共同設計・構造・設備：NTTファシリティーズ
ランドスケープ：PLACEMEDIA
照明：松下電工
施工：竹中工務店
主体構造・規模：鉄筋コンクリート造，
鉄骨鉄筋コンクリート造／地下1階，地上16階，塔屋2階
敷地面積：8,500.04m²
建築面積：6,959.85m²
延床面積：43,401.27m²

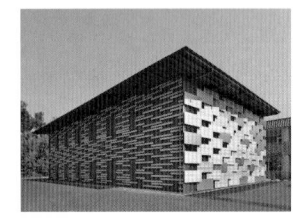

2004–06
Hoshinosato Annex
Kudamatsu, Yamaguchi, Japan
—
Program: special nursing home for the aged
Total floor area: 852.35m²
Site area: 11,233.1m²
Structure: steel frame
2 stories

ほしのさとアネックス
所在地：山口県下松市生野屋南1-13-1
設計：200411-0508
工事：200510-0603
建築主：社会福祉法人くだまつ平成会
主要用途：特別養護老人ホーム
構造：牧野構造計画
設備：森村設計
照明：松下電工
施工：鏡高組
主体構造・規模：鉄骨造／地上2階
敷地面積：11,233.1m²
建築面積：512.3m²
延床面積：852.35m²

2004–06
Y Hütte
Japan
—
Program: villa
Total floor area: 90.51m²
Site area: 1,127.8m²
Structure: timber frame
2 stories

Y Hütte
所在地：東日本
設計：200412-0507
工事：200510-0603
主要用途：別荘
構造：江尻建築構造設計事務所
設備：森村設計
施工：第一建設
主体構造・規模：木造／地上2階
敷地面積：1,127.8m²
建築面積：73.37m²
延床面積：90.51m²

2004–06
Yusuhara Town Hall
Kochi, Japan
—
Program: city hall
Total floor area: 2,970.79m²
Site area: 6,020.94m²
Structure: timber frame
2 stories, 1 basement

梼原町総合庁舎
所在地：高知県高岡郡梼原町梼原1444-1
設計：200404-0502｜工事：200505-0610
建築主：梼原町
主要用途：総合庁舎
共同設計：慶應義塾大学理工学部システムデザイン工学科
構造：中田捷夫研究室
監理協力：ケイズ設計
施工：飛鳥・ミタニ建設工事共同企業体
主体構造・規模：木造，一部鉄筋コンクリート造（地下，外周部）
地下1階，地上2階
敷地面積：6,020.94m²
建築面積：1,628.25m²
延床面積：2,970.79m²

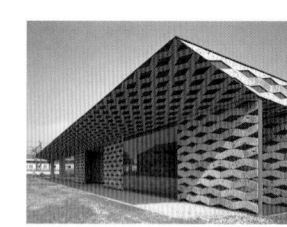

2004–06
Chokkura Plaza
Takanezawa, Tochigi, Japan
—
Program: assembly hall, exhibition hall
Total floor area: 607.66m²
Site area: 2,668.52m²
Structure: masonry, steel plate
1 story

ちょっ蔵広場
所在地：栃木県塩谷郡高根沢町
設計：200403-0503
工事：200507-0603
建築主：高根沢町長 高橋克法
主要用途：集会場，展示場
構造：オーク構造設計
設備：森村設計
照明：松下電工
施工：渡辺建設
主体構造・規模：組積造，鉄板造／地上1階
敷地面積：2,668.52m²
建築面積：728.18m²
延床面積：607.66m²

2004–07
Suntory Museum of Art
Tokyo, Japan
—
Program: museum
Total floor area: 4,700.00m²
Site area: 68,891.63m²
Structure: steel reinforced concrete
3 stories, 6 basements

サントリー美術館
所在地：東京都港区赤坂9-7-4 東京ミッドタウンガーデンサイド
設計：200404-0702｜工事：200405-0703
建築主：サントリー・ホールディングス他6社
主要用途：美術館
共同設計：日建設計（外装・躯体），次交社（茶室），
ミュージアムプランニング & オペレーターズ（ショップ・カフェ）
構造・設備：日建設計
展示室階段構造：オーク構造設計，竹中技術研究所
展示室内装：キルトプランニングオフィス
和紙：門出和紙，アサノ不燃木材
施工：竹中工務店
主体構造・規模：鉄骨鉄筋コンクリート造，一部鉄筋コンクリート造，鉄骨造，木造／地下3階，地上6階
敷地面積：68,891.63m²／延床面積：4,700.00m²

2004–07
Kure City Ondo Civic Center
Hiroshima, Japan
—
Program: city hall, public hall, library, multipurpose room
Total floor area: 4,642.91m²
Site area: 4,424.39m²
Structure: steel frame
3 stories

呉市音戸市民センター
所在地：広島県呉市音戸町南隠渡1丁目7番
設計：200407-0602
工事：200606-0712
建築主：呉市
主要用途：市役所支所，公民館，図書館，多目的ホール
構造：オーク構造設計
設備：森村設計 担当／鈴木幸正，袖川政憲
施工：鴻池・日興特定建設工事共同企業体
主体構造・規模：鉄骨造／地上3階
敷地面積：4,424.39m²
建築面積：2,581.08m²
延床面積：4,642.91m²

2004–07
Steel House
Bunkyo, Tokyo, Japan
—
Program: house
Total floor area: 265.12m²
Site area: 202.71m²
Structure: reinforced concrete, folded steel plate
3 stories, 1 basement

「鉄」の家
所在地：東京都文京区
設計：200409-0604
工事：200605-0703
建築主：廣瀬 通孝
主要用途：住宅
構造：江尻建築構造設計事務所
設備：森村設計
カーテン：NUNO
施工：アイガー産業
主体構造・規模：鉄筋コンクリート造，鉄骨造
地上3階，地下1階
敷地面積：202.71m²
建築面積：113.13m²
延床面積：265.12m²

2004–09
Nezu Museum
Tokyo, Japan
—
Program: museum
Total floor area: 4,014.08m²
Site area: 15,372.33m²
Structure: steel frame, steel reinforced concrete
2 stories, 1 basement

根津美術館
所在地：東京都港区南青山6-5-1
設計：200411-0708｜工事：200708-0902
展示ケース工事／200902-0906
造園工事／200902-0909
建築主：根津美術館
主要用途：美術館
構造・設備：清水建設
照明：パナソニック電工　造園：晴風苑
ケース：コクヨファニチャー（展示）、東急心傳庵（茶室）
展示照明：キルトプランニング｜施工：清水建設
主体構造・規模：鉄骨造、鉄骨鉄筋コンクリート造
地下1階、地上2階
敷地面積：15,372.33m²｜建築面積：1,947.49m²
延床面積：4,014.08m²

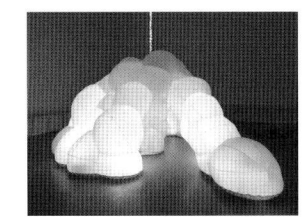

2005
T-Room
Ishikawa, Japan
—
Program: tee room
Total floor area: 8m²
Structure: air film
1 story

t-room
所在地：石川県金沢市広坂1-2-1
展示：200511-0603
建築主：金沢21世紀美術館
主要用途：茶室
コラボレーションデザイナー＆アーティスト：
岩井俊雄（LED light/sound）、
原研哉（TSUKUBAI、展示グラフィックデザイン）、
深澤直人（IISHI、T-server）
照明：カラーキネティクス・ジャパン
展示付属製作：ナカダ
施工：乃村工藝社
主体構造：空気膜構造
延床面積：8m²

2004–10
Tokyu Capitol Tower
Tokyo, Japan
—
Program: hotel, office, housing, shop
Total floor area: 87,428.28m²
Site area: 7,938.25m²
Structure: steel frame, steel reinforced concrete, reinforced concrete
29 stories, 4 basement

東急キャピトルタワー
所在地：東京都千代田区永田町2-10-3
設計：200407-0801｜工事：200803-1007
建築主：東京急行電鉄
主要用途：ホテル、事務所、共同住宅、店舗
建築：東急設計コンサルタント・観光企画設計社設計共同企業体
デザイン監修：隈研吾建築都市設計事務所
構造：構造計画研究所
設備：東急設計コンサルタント、建築設備設計研究所
外構：プレイスメディア｜照明：パナソニック電工
施工：清水建設｜企画・総合プロデュース：東京急行電鉄
主体構造・規模：鉄骨造（地上部）、鉄骨鉄筋コンクリート造（地下部）、
鉄筋コンクリート造、一部CFT造（高層直下柱）｜地下4階、地上29階
敷地面積：7,938.25m²｜建築面積：5,425.92m²
延床面積：87,428.28m²

2005–07
Tee Haus
Frankfurt, Germany
—
Program: tee room
Total floor area: 31.3m²
Site area: 31.3m²
Structure: double air film
1 story

Tee Haus
所在地：Schaumainkai 17, Frankfurt an Main, Germany
設計：200505-0704
工事：200705-0707
建築主：フランクフルト市
主要用途：茶室
構造：Form TL GmbH, Taiyo Europe GmbH
茶室しつらい・監修：木村宗愼（裏遠家）
主体構造・規模：二重空気膜構造／地上1階
敷地面積：31.3m²
建築面積：31.3m²
延床面積：31.3m²

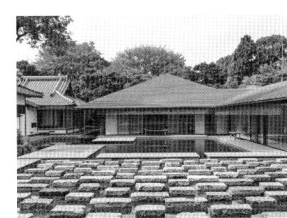

2005–07
Yien East
Japan
—
Program: villa
Total floor area: 394.15m²
Site area: 1,609.97m²
Structure: steel frame, timber frame
1 story

Yien East
所在地：日本
設計：200509-0607
工事：200608-0710
主要用途：別荘
構造：オーク構造設計
設備：森村設計
照明：小西武志＋建築照明計画
キッチン：ポンテピッコロ
施工：大成建設
主体構造・規模：鉄構造（母屋）、木造（離れ）／地上1階
敷地面積：1,609.97m²
建築面積：490.89m²
延床面積：394.15m²

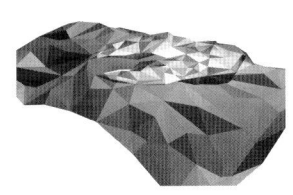

2006–
Kenny Heights Museum
Kuala Lumpur, Malaysia
—
Program: museum
Total floor area: 3,914.9m²
Site area: 67,865.7m²
Structure: steel frame
2 stories

ケニー ハイツ ミュージアム
所在地：クアラルンプール、マレーシア
設計：200606-0703
建築主：Olympia Land Berhad
主要用途：美術館＋多目的
構造：江尻建築構造設計事務所
設備：Jurutera Perundig Urus Jaya Sdn. Bhd.
主体構造・規模：鉄骨／地上2階
敷地面積：67,865.7m²
建築面積：7,178.1m²
延床面積：3,914.9m²

2005–08
Hoshakuji Station
Tochigi, Japan
—
Program: free passage, station
Total floor area: 862.06m²
Site area: 5,528.61m²
Structure: steel frame
2 stories

宝積寺駅
所在地：栃木県塩屋郡高根沢町大字宝積寺2374-1
設計：200508-0603｜工事：200609-0803
建築主：高橋克法（高根沢町長）、東日本旅客鉄道大宮支社
主要用途：自由通路、駅舎
監修：隈研吾建築都市設計事務所
構造監修：オーク構造設計
設計・構造・設備・サイン：東日本旅客鉄道大宮支社 JR東日本建築設計事務所
照明：松下電工
施工：東鉄工業
主体構造・規模：鉄骨造／地上2階
敷地面積：5,528.61m²
建築面積：802.89m²
延床面積：862.06m²

2006–07
Sake no Hana
London, U.K.
—
Program: restaurant
Total floor area: 436.3m²
2 stories, 1 basement

Sake no Hana
所在地：23 St. James's street, London, U.K.
設計：200603-0612
工事：200701-0710
建築主：Hakkasan ltd.
主要用途：レストラン
共同設計：Denton Corker Marshall
構造：Michael Hadi Associates
設備：E+M Technica
照明：Isometrix Lighting+Design
施工：Goodman hichens PLC
規模：地下1階、地上2階
延床面積：436.3m²（厨房除く）

2005–08
The Opposite House
Beijing, China
—
Program: hotel
Total floor area: 14,327m²
Site area: 4,584m²
Structure: reinforced concrete
6 stories, 2 basements

The Opposite House
所在地：中国北京市朝陽区三里屯
設計：200508-0706｜工事：200710-0807
建築主：Swire Hotels
主要用途：ホテル
客室内装設計協力：nSTUDIO
構造：Arup, Beijing Architectural & Engineering Design
設備：China/Team
照明：Isometrix
施工：Yearfull Contracting Limited（共用部内装）、
Beijing Yan Jia Construction Engineering Co. Ltd.（客室内装）
主体構造・規模：鉄筋コンクリート造／地下2階・地上6階
敷地面積：4,584m²
建築面積：2,454m²
延床面積：14,327m²

2006–08
Ryotei Kaikatei Annex "sou-an"
Fukui, Japan
—
Program: restaurant
Total floor area: 378.4m²
Site area: 310.74m²
Structure: reinforced concrete
2 stories

料亭開花亭別館「sou-an」
所在地：福井県福井市中央3-9-21
設計：200606-0706
工事：200706-0801
建築主：開発毅
主要用途：飲食店
構造：中田捷夫研究室
設備：森村設計
施工：村中建設
主体構造・規模：鉄筋コンクリート造、一部鉄骨造
地上2階
敷地面積：310.74m²
建築面積：202.55m²
延床面積：378.4m²

2006–08
Wood/Berg
Japan
—
Program: house
Total floor area: 1,422.31m²
Site area: 452.65m²
Structure: steel frame
5 stories, 2 basements

Wood/Berg
所在地：東日本
設計：200601-0705
工事：200706-0810
主要用途：住宅
構造：オーク構造設計
設備：電気／森村設計
インテリア（一部）：MLINARIC HENRY & ZERVUDACHI. LTD, TCKW
施工：大成建設
主体構造・規模：鉄骨造，一部鉄筋コンクリート造
地上5階，地下2階
敷地面積：452.65m²
建築面積：266.98m²
延床面積：1,422.31m²

2006–
Hamada Soy Sauce Cellar Renovation
Kumamoto, Japan
—
Program: manufacturing, shop, house
Total floor area: 1,422.2m²
Site area: 20,92.4m²
Structure: timber and bamboo frame
2 stories

濱田醤油蔵改修計画
所在地：熊本県熊本市小島中町
設計：200607-0803
工事：200708-
建築主：酒田　油
主要用途：工場，店舗，住居
構造：江尻建築構造設計事務所
照明：Panasonic電工
設備・施工：クリーン・スペース
主体構造・規模：木造／地上2階
敷地面積：20,962.4m²
建築面積：1,104.4m²
延床面積：1,422.2m²

2006–09
Museum of Kanayama Castle Ruin, Kanayama Community Center
Gunma, Japan
—
Program: museum office
Total floor area: 1,676.89m²
Site area: 3,318.69m²
Structure: steel reinforced concrete
2 stories (3 layers)

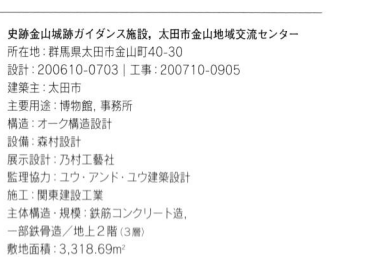

史跡金山城跡ガイダンス施設，太田市金山地域交流センター
所在地：群馬県太田市金山町40-30
設計：200610-0703 ｜ 工事：200710-0905
建築主：太田市
主要用途：博物館，事務所
構造：オーク構造設計
設備：森村設計
展示設計：乃村工藝社
監理協力：ユウ・アンド・ユウ建築設計
施工：関東建設工業
主体構造・規模：鉄筋コンクリート造，一部鉄骨造／地上2階（3層）
敷地面積：3,318.69m²
建築面積：1,319.45m²
延床面積：1,676.89m²

2007
Fu-an
Shizuoka, Japan
—
Program: tee room
Total floor area: 7.29m²
1 story

浮庵
会場：世界お茶まつり2007　新・緑茶空間
設計：200706-0710
工事：200710-0711
建築主：世界お茶まつり2007実行委員会
主要用途：茶室
バルーン・構造・製作：D.Pバルーン
布　　　：NUNO
床　　　：イノウエインダストリィズ
畳　　　：岡田畳本店
協創：生地／天池合繊　畳／岡田畳本店
施工：イノウエインダストリィズ
延床面積：7.29m²

2006–09
Shimonoseki City Kawatana-Onsen Visitor Center and Folk Museum
Yamaguchi, Japan
—
Program: museum
Total floor area: 1,242.85m²
Site area: 2,349.06m²
Structure: steel frame

下関市川棚温泉交流センター「川棚の杜」
所在地：山口県下関市豊浦町大字川棚字湯町5181他
設計：200612-0705
工事：200804-0911
建築主：下関市
主要用途：博物館
構造：佐藤淳構造設計事務所
設備：森村設計
外構共同設計：中央コンサルタンツ
施工：広成建設株式会社規模
主体構造：鉄骨造
敷地面積：2,349.06m²
建築面積：1,107.81m²
延床面積：1,242.85m²

2007–08
Tiffany Ginza
Tokyo, Japan
—
Program: shop, office
Total floor area: 5,870.35m²
Site area: 702.84m²
Structure: steel reinforced concrete (existing), steel frame (new)
9 stories, 1 basement

ティファニー銀座
所在地：東京都中央区銀座2-7-17
設計：200708-0803 ｜ 工事：200803-0810
建築主：TIFFANY&Co. JAPAN
主要用途：店舗，事務所
内装共同設計：ア・ファクトリー
構造：オーク構造設計
店内家具：Kevin Cherry
外装照明：内原智史デザイン事務所
カーテン：NUNO
施工：大成建設
主体構造・規模：鉄骨鉄筋コンクリート造（既存），鉄骨造（新設）
地上9階，地下1階
敷地面積：702.84m²
延床面積：5,870.35m²

2006–10
Glass/Wood
U.S.A.
—
Program: house
Total floor area: 830m²
Site area: 10,000m²
Structure: timber frame (existing), steel frame (annex)
1 story, 1 basement

Glass/Wood
所在地：ニューキャナン，コネチカット州，アメリカ
設計：200602-0805 ｜ 工事：200704-1006
建築主：Susan Leaming Pollish & Eric Pollish
主要用途：住宅
構造：牧野構造計画（基本設計），
The Di Salvo Ericson Groupe（実施設計）
設備：Kohler Ronan, LLC
ローカルアーキテクト：Gregory T. Waugh, 勝野一起
施工：Prutting & Company Custom Builders, LLC（既存），
The Deluca Construction Co.（アネックス）
主体構造・規模：木造（既存棟），鉄骨造（アネックス）
地下1階，地上1階
敷地面積：10,000m² ｜ 建築面積：600m²
延床面積：830m²

2007–08
Casa Umbrella
Milan, Italy
—
Program: shelter
Total floor area: 15m²
Built area: 15m²
Structure: steel rods, aluminium shafts
1 story

Casa Umbrella
所在地：イタリア，ミラノ市
設計：200711-0803
工事：200802-0805
建築主：La Triennale di Milano
主要用途：シェルター
構造：江尻建築構造設計事務所
傘：イイダ傘店
生地：DuPont
照明：ismi design office
接合：super-robot
技術協力：日吉屋，ムーンバット
主体構造・規模：鋼棒，アルミ棒／地上1階
建築面積：15m²
延床面積：15m²

2006–13
Kabuki–za Building
Chuo, Tokyo, Japan
—
Program: theater and office
Total floor area: 94,097m²
Site area: 6,996m²
Structure: steel frame, steel reinforced concrete
29 stories, 4 basement

(仮称) 歌舞伎座ビル
所在地：東京都中央区
設計：200606-1010 ｜ 工事：201010-1302
建築主：オフィス／KSビルキャピタル特定目的会社，
劇場／歌舞伎座
主要用途：劇場，オフィス
共同設計：三菱地所設計
構造・設備：三菱地所設計
外装照明：石井幹子デザイン事務所
施工：清水建設
主体構造・規模：鉄骨造（地上部），鉄骨鉄筋コンクリート（地下部）
地上29階，地下4階，塔屋2階
敷地面積：6,996m²
建築面積：5,985m²
延床面積：94,097m²

2007–09
Garden Terrace Nagasaki
Nagasaki, Japan
—
Program: hotel, ceremony hall
Total floor area: 7,104.18m²
Site area: 10,034.47m²
Structure: reinforced concrete, steel frame
3 stories, 1 basement

ガーデンテラス長崎
所在地：長崎県長崎市秋月町2-3
設計：2007-08
工事：2008-09
建築主：メモリード
主要用途：ホテル，セレモニーホール
構造：牧野構造計画
設備：森村設計
施工：清水建設
主体構造・規模：鉄骨造，鉄筋コンクリート造
地下1階，地上2階
敷地面積：10,034.47m²
建築面積：3,191.85m²
延床面積：7,104.18m²

2007–09
Cavamarket Headquarters Project
Salerno, Campania, Italy
—
Program: office, shop, parking
Total floor area: 11,850m²
Site area: 14,000m²
Structure: reinforced concrete

カヴァマーケット・ヘッドクォーターズ
所在地：カンパニア、イタリア
設計：200711-0811
工事：200811-0911
建築主：Cavamarket
主要用途：オフィス、商業施設、駐車場
Local architects : Studio Apicella Pagano
構造：Arup Italia
設備：Hilson & Moran Italia
Local coordination : Giovanni Pagano, Luigi Alini
主体構造：鉄筋コンクリート造
敷地面積：14,000m²
建築面積：6,535m²
延床面積：11,850m²

2007–13
Besançon City Arts and Culture Center
Besancon, Doubs, France
—
Program: music school, FRAC (regional art contemporary foundation)
Total floor area: 11,925m²
Site area: 23,000m²
Structure: reinforced concrete, timber frame
3 stories

ブザンソン芸術文化センター
所在地：ブザンソン、フランス
設計：200711-0912｜工事：201002-1301
建築主：ブザンソン市、グランブザンソン広域公共団体、フランシュ・コンテ州
主要用途：音楽学校、音楽ホール、アートセンター、展示室、オフィス、カフェ、図書室
共同設計：Archidev｜構造・設備：EGIS GRAND EST
音響：J.P LAMOUREUX　舞台効果：Changement à Vue
ランドスケープ：Agence L'ANTON｜施工：CAMPENON BERNARD Franche- Comté、AVENIR BOIS STRUCTURES
主体構造・規模：鉄筋コンクリート造、一部木造／地上3階
敷地面積：23,000m²
建築面積：2,785m²（音楽学校）＋2,210m²（現代美術館FRAC）
延床面積：11,952 m²

2007–10
Akagi Jinja & Park Court Kagurazaka
Tokyo, Japan
—
Program: shrine, apartment
Total floor area: 9,975.76m²
Site area: 4,069.23m²
Structure: reinforced concrete (apartment), steel frame+reinforced concrete (shrine)
6 stories, 1 basement

赤城神社・パークコート神楽坂
所在地：東京都新宿区赤城元町1-10
設計：200711-0903
工事：200902-1008
建築主：宗教法人 赤城神社、三井不動産レジデンシャル
主要用途：神社、集合住宅
デザイン監修：隈研吾建築都市設計事務所
設計・施工：熊谷組
主体構造・規模：鉄筋コンクリート造（住宅棟）、鉄骨造＋鉄筋コンクリート造（神社棟）／地下1階、地上6階
敷地面積：4,069.23m²
建築面積：2,425.09m²
延床面積：9,975.76m²

2007–
Complex of Government Buildings related to Area of "Eiffel Hall"- Western Railway Station of Budapest
Budapest, Hungary
—
Program: government office
Total floor area: 8,870m² / Site area: 33,000m²
Structure: reinforced concrete
8 stories, 1 basement

ハンガリー中央官庁舎及びブダペスト西駅地区都市計画
所在地：ハンガリー、ブダペスト
設計：200706-0806
建築主：ハンガリー政府
主要用途：各省庁
Local architects : Janesch Peter and Teams
構造：Molnar Gyorgy and teams
主体構造・規模：鉄筋コンクリート造／地下1階、地上8階
敷地面積：33,000m²
建築面積：11,500m²
延床面積：88,770m²

2007–10
Sanlitun SOHO
Beijing, China
—
Program: retail, office, residence
Total floor area: 465,680m²
Site area: 51,245m²
Structure: reinforced concrete
24 stories(office), 24 stories (residence), 4 basements, 2 rooftops

三里屯SOHO
所在地：中国北京市朝陽区工体北路
設計：200701-0905｜工事：200712-1010
建築主：SOHO CHINA
用途：商業施設、オフィス、住宅
設計補助：日本設計、日本設計インターナショナル、日本設計システム｜構造・設備：中国電子工程設計院 北京中聯環建文建築設計有限公司
ランドスケープ：設計組織PLACEMEDIA
照明：ぼんぼり光環境計画｜サイン：日本デザインセンター
施工：中建一局發展、中建一局五公司
主体構造・規模：鉄筋コンクリート造、一部S鉄筋コンクリート造
地下4階、地上オフィス24階、地上住宅28階、塔屋2階
敷地面積：51,245m²｜建築面積：23,500m²
延床面積：465,680m²

2008–10
Bamboo/Fiber
Japan
—
Program: house
Total floor area: 224.08m²
Site area: 459.15m²
Structure: timber frame
2 stories

Bamboo/Fiber
所在地：東日本
設計：200808-0904
工事：200905-1005
主要用途：住宅
構造：江尻建築構造設計事務所
設備：電気、森村設計
ブラインド：NUNO
施工：まつきとコーポレーション
主体構造・規模：木造／地上2階
敷地面積：459.15m²
建築面積：182.15m²
延床面積：224.08m²

2007–12
Water/Cherry
Japan
—
Program: villa
Total floor area: 755.12m²
Site area: 5,372.55m²
Structure: steel frame
2 stories, 1 basement

Water/Cherry
所在地：東日本
設計：200704-0808｜工事：200809-1202
主要用途：別荘
構造：牧野構造計画
設備：環境エンジニアリング
庭園：プレイスメディア
照明：岡安泉照明設計事務所
和室内装工事：中村外二工務店
造園：岩城
施工：大成建設
主体構造・規模：鉄骨造、一部鉄筋コンクリート造
地下1階、地上2階
敷地面積：5,372.55m²｜建築面積：595.47m²
延床面積：755.12m²

2008–10
The Momofuku Ando Center of Outdoor Training
Nagano, Japan
—
Program: training institute
Total floor area: 1,999m²
Site area: 37,282m²
Structure: steel frame, reinforced concrete
2 stories, 1 basement

安藤百福記念自然体験活動指導者養成センター
所在地：長野県小諸市大久保1100
設計：200803-0904
工事：200908-1005
建築主：財団法人安藤スポーツ・食文化振興財団
主要用途：研修施設
構造：金箱構造設計事務所
設備：森村設計
照明：パナソニック電工
施工：大成建設
主体構造・規模：鉄骨造、鉄筋コンクリート造
地下1階、地上2階
敷地面積：37,282m²
建築面積：1,421.32m²
延床面積：1,999m²

2007–13
Marseille Regional Foundation of Contemporary Art
Marseille, France
—
Program: Regional art contemporary foundation
Total floor area: 3,895m²
Site area: 1,580m²
Structure: steel frame, reinforced concrete
5 stories, 1 basement

マルセイユ・アートセンター
所在地：マルセイユ、フランス
設計：200706-1003｜工事：201012-1301
建築主：プロバンス・アルプ・コートダジュール州
主要用途：アートセンター、展示場、アーティストレジデンス、図書室、カフェ、オフィス、作品収蔵庫
共同設計：Agence Toury Valley
構造：CEBAT
設備：ETB Antonelli
音響：ACCORD ACOUSTIQUE
舞台効果：Changement à Vue
施工：LEON GROSSE
構造・規模：鉄筋コンクリート造、鉄骨造／地下1階、地上5階
敷地面積：1,580m²｜建築面積：1,540m²
延床面積：3,895m²

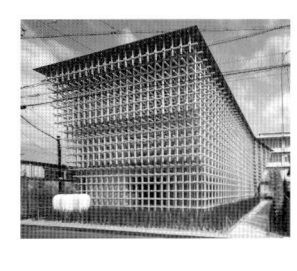

2008–10
Prostho Museum Research Center
Aichi, Japan
—
Program: museum, laboratory
Total floor area: 626.5m²
Site area: 421.55m²
Structure: reinforced concrete, timber frame
3 stories, 1 basement

プロソミュージアム・リサーチセンター
所在地：愛知県春日井市鳥居松町2-294
設計：200804-0905｜工事：200906-1005
建築主：ジーシー
主要用途：博物館、研究所
設計協力：松井建設寺建築部
木サッシュ設計協力：AGCガラス建材
構造：佐藤淳構造設計事務所
設備：森村設計｜照明：大光電気
サイン：日本デザインセンター・原デザイン研究室
施工：松井建設
主体構造・規模：鉄筋コンクリート造、木造
地下1階、地上3階
敷地面積：421.55m²｜建築面積：223.95m²
延床面積：626.5m²

2008–11
Lake House
Japan
—
Program: villa
Total floor area: 503.22m²
Site area: 533.69m²
Structure: reinforced concrete
2 stories, 1 basement

Lake House
所在地：日本
設計：200810-0910
工事：201003-1101
主要用途：別荘
構造：オーク構造設計
設備：森村設計
モザイクガラス：高臣大介、木下良輔
施工：大成建設
主体構造・規模：鉄筋コンクリート造／地下1階、地上2階
敷地面積：533.69m²
建築面積：262.71m²
延床面積：503.22m²

2008–11
Xinjin Zhi Museum
Chengdu, Sichuan, China
—
Program: museum
Total floor area: 2,353m²
Site area: 2,580m²
Structure: steel frame, reinforced concrete
3 stories, 1 basement

新津 知・芸術館
所在地：中国四川省成都市新津県
設計：200806-0909｜工事：201001-1112
建築主：花様年控股集団
主要用途：美術館
構造：オーク構造設計
設備：森村設計
サイン：日本デザインセンター
照明：岩井達弥光景デザイン
施工：中国二十冶金建築
主体構造・規模：鉄骨造、一部鉄筋コンクリート造（地上）、鉄筋コンクリート造（地下）／地下1階、地上3階
敷地面積：2,580m²
建築面積：787m²
延床面積：2,353m²

2008–12
Aore Nagaoka
Nagaoka, Niigata, Japan
—
Program: city hall, office, assembly hall, parking, shop, cafe, branch bank, open space with roof
Total floor area: 35,492.44m²
Site area: 14,938.8m²
Structure: prestressed concrete, steel frame
4 stories, 1 basement

アオーレ長岡
所在地：新潟県長岡市大手通1-4-10
設計：200802-0909｜工事：200911-1202
建築主：長岡市長 森民夫
主要用途：市役所本庁舎（事務所）、集会所、自動車車庫、店舗・飲食店、銀行支店、屋根付き広場
構造：江尻建築構造設計事務所　設備：森村設計
舞台装置・舞台照明：シアターワークショップ
舞台音響・建築音響：永田音響設計
ランドスケープコンサルティング：プレイスメディア
施工：大成・福田・中越・池田シティホール建築工事特定共同企業体
主体構造・規模：鉄筋コンクリート造、プレストレストコンクリート造（スパンの大きい部分）、鉄骨造（耐火抱化ヴォリューム、車棟2F床部）、屋根鉄骨／地下1階、地上4階｜敷地面積：14,938.81m²
建築面積：12,073.44m²｜延床面積：35,492.44m²

2008–
Water Branch House
New York, U.S.A.
—
Program: temporary house
Total floor area: 1.2m²
Site area: 1.2m²
Structure: plastic
1 story

Water Branch House
所在地：11 West 53 Street, between Fifth and Sixth avenues, NY, USA
設計：200801-0803
工事：200807
建築主：ニューヨーク近代美術館
主要用途：仮設住宅
施工：セルフビルド
主体構造・規模：プラスチック／地上1階
建築面積：1.2m²
延床面積：1.2m²

2008–
Yunnan Resort
Tengchong, Yunnan, China
—
Program: hotel, spa, commercial facilities
Total floor area: 82,500m²
Site area: 254,200m²
Structure: reinforced concrete (villa), steel frame (reception)
3 stories

雲南リゾート
所在地：中国雲南省騰冲雲峰山
設計：200808-1110
工事：201110-
建築主：雲南騰冲雲峰山風景区旅遊産業発展有限公司
主要用途：ホテル、スパ、商業施設
照明：岩井達弥光景デザイン
主体構造・規模：鉄筋コンクリート造（ヴィラ）、鉄骨造（レセプション）／地上3階
敷地面積：254,200m²
建築面積：81,900m²
延床面積：82,500m²

2009
Lucien Pellat-Finet Shinsaibashi
Osaka, Japan
—
Program: shop
Total floor area: 133m²
3 stories, 1 basement

ルシアン・ペラフィネ 心斎橋店
所在地：大阪府大阪市中央区西心斎橋1-1-1
設計：200904-0908
工事：200909-0911
建築主：コロネット
主要用途：店舗
構造アドバイス：江尻建築構造設計事務所
設備：森村設計
照明：パナソニック電工
キッチン：MANA
施工：スマイルデザイン
規模：地下1階、地上3階
延床面積：133m²

2009–10
Community Market Yusuhara
Kochi, Japan
—
Program: hotel, market
Total floor area: 1,132.00m²
Site area: 779.08m²
Structure: reinforced concrete
3 stories

まちの駅「ゆすはら」
所在地：高知県高岡郡梼原町梼原1196-1
設計：200908-0911
工事：200912-1007
建築主：梼原町長 矢野富夫
用途：ホテル、市場
構造：中田捷夫研究室
設備：シグマ設備設計室
監理協力：ケイズ設計
施工：大旺新洋
主体構造・規模：鉄筋コンクリート造／地上3階
敷地面積：779.08m²
建築面積：552.28m²
延床面積：1,132.00m²

2009–10
Yusuhara Wooden Bridge Museum
Kochi, Japan
—
Program: exhibition hall
Total floor area: 445.79m² (annex)
Site area: 1,4736.47m²
Structure: timber frame
2 stories, 1 basement

梼原・木橋ミュージアム
所在地：高知県高岡郡梼原町太郎川3799-3
設計：200908-0911
工事：201002-1009
建築主：梼原町長 矢野富夫
主要用途：展示場
構造：中田捷夫研究室
設備：シグマ設備設計室
監理協力：ケイズ設計
施工：四万十川総合建設
主体構造・規模：木造、一部鉄骨造、鉄筋コンクリート造／地下1階、地上2階
敷地面積：14,736.47m²
建築面積：574.15m²（今回増築部分）
延床面積：445.79m²（今回増築部分）

2009–10
Stone Roof
Nagano, Japan
—
Program: villa
Total floor area: 499.76m²
Site area: 2,565.71m²
Structure: steel frame
2 stories, 1 basement

Stone Roof
所在地：長野県
設計：200901-0911｜工事：200912-1011
主要用途：別荘
構造：森部康司研究室
設備：環境エンジニアリング
照明：ヤマギワ
ファブリック：マナトレーディング
ランドスケープ：グリーン・ワイズ
施工：北野建設
主体構造・規模：鉄骨造、一部鉄筋コンクリート造／地下1階、地上2階
敷地面積：2,565.71m²
建築面積：311.34m²
延床面積：499.76m²

2009–10
Shang Xia
Shanghai, China
—
Program: shop
Total floor area: 126m²
1 story

「上下」上海店
所在地：中国上海市盧湾区淮海路中路283号 香港プラザ内
設計：200908-0912
工事：201003-1006
建築主：Shang xia
主要用途：店舗
構造：江尻建築構造設計事務所
照明：コイズミ照明
施工：乃村工藝建築装飾（北京）
規模：地上1階
延床面積：126m²

2009-10
Ceramic Cloud
Casalgrande, Reggio Emilia, Italia
—
Program: monument
Site area: 2,967m²

Ceramic Cloud
所在地：イタリア、レッジオエミリア州、カザルグランデ
設計：200901-0911
工事：200910-1009
建築主：Casalgrande Padana S.p.a.
主要用途：モニュメント
構造：江尻建築構造設計事務所
照明：Progetto Luce Mario Nanni
敷地面積：2,967m²

2009-12
Jeju Ball
Jeju, South Korea
—
Program: villa, hotel
Total floor area: DA/245.0m², DB/210.0m²
Site area: 13181.9m²
Structure: reinforced concrete
2 stories

Jeju Ball
所在地：ジェジュ島、大韓民国
設計：200902-1005 ｜ 工事：201007-1203
建築主：LOTTE JEJU RESORT CO.LTD.
主要用途：ヴィラ、ホテル
Local architect：
DA GROUP Urban Design & Architecture Co., Ltd.
構造：MIRAE Structural Engineers Co., Ltd.
設備：YUNGDO Engineers, Ltd. ｜ 浴室：JAXSON CORP.
施工：LOTTE Engineering & Construction,
KINGSMEN Korea
主体構造・規模：鉄筋コンクリート造／地上2階
敷地面積：13181.9m2 (D地区)
建築面積：DA／313.2m², DB／166.4m²
延床面積：DA／245.0m², DB／210.0m²

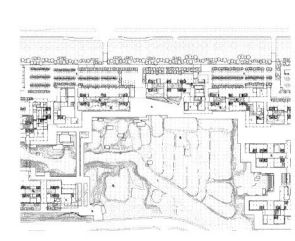

2009-11
Mesh/Earth
Japan
—
Program: row house
Total floor area: 182.82m²
Site area: 158.11m²
Structure: steel frame
3 stories

Mesh/Earth
所在地：東日本
設計：200911-1006
工事：201007-1102
主要用途：長屋
構造：オーノJAPAN
設備：環境エンジニアリング
照明デザイン：岡安泉照明設計事務所
施工：松井建設
主体構造・規模：鉄骨造／地上3階
敷地面積：158.11m²
建築面積：60.03m²
延床面積：182.82m²

2009-13
Alibaba Group "Taobao City"
Hangzhou, Zhejiang, China
—
Program: Office (canteen, gymnasium, auditorium, exhibition hall)
Total floor area: 260,000m²
Site area: 260,000m²
Structure: reinforced concrete, steel frame
7 stories, 1 basement

アリババグループ "タオバオシティ"
所在地：中国浙江省杭州市
設計：200901-1104
工事：201001-1304
建築主：Alibaba group
主要用途：オフィス（食堂、体育館、講堂、展示ホールを含む）
構造：Arup Japan
Local architect：中国联合工程公司
施工：躯体／中天集团、中冶成工、上海扬子江建设集团
主体構造・規模：鉄筋コンクリート造、鉄骨造
地上7階、地下1階
敷地面積：260,000m²
建築面積：60,000m²
延床面積：260,000m²

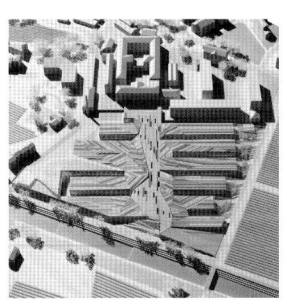

2009-11
Green Cast
Odawara, Kanagawa, Japan
—
Program: shop, clinic, office, private residence
Total floor area: 1,047.80m²
Site area: 424.50m²
Structure: steel frame, reinforced concrete
4 stories, 1 basement

グリーン・キャスト
所在地：神奈川県小田原市城山
設計：200902-0909
工事：201005-1106
主要用途：店舗、クリニック、事務所、住宅
構造：牧野構造設計
設備：森村設計
照明：パナソニック
施工：竹中工務店
主体構造・規模：鉄骨造、一部鉄筋コンクリート造
地上4階、地下1階
敷地面積：424.50m²
建築面積：207.64m²
延床面積：1047.80m²

2009-
Progetto Manifattura— Green Innovation Factory
Rovereto, Trento, Italy
—
Program: manufacturing, offices, research labs, auditorium, gym, learning center, cafe, greenhouse, publich roof garden (vegetation)
Total floor area: 32,000m²
Site area: 50,000m²
Structure: timber frame, concrete

ロヴェレート・マニファッチューラ
所在地：ロヴェレート、トレント、イタリア
設計：2009-
建築主：Manifattura Domani Srl
主要用途：工場、オフィス、研究室、オーディトリアム、ジム、学習センター、温室、屋上庭園、カフェ
共同設計：Carlo ratti associati, Arup (マスタープラン)
構造：AIA Engineering, Marco Zanuso
設備：PROGETTA di Broilo, Tamanini e Associati, Studio Ingegneria Luca Tomasi ｜ LEED and sustainability strategy：Arup Italia, Alejandro Gutierrez
Project Manager and Client Architect：Stefano Sani
主体構造：木造、コンクリート
敷地面積：50,000m² ｜ 建築面積：27,000m²
延床面積：32,000m²

2009-12
Même— Experimental House
Hokkaido, Japan
—
Program: house and other purposes
Total floor area: 79.50m²
Site area: 75.90m²
Structure: timber frame
1 story

実験住宅 Même
所在地：北海道広尾郡大樹町芽武158-1他
設計：200903-1010
工事：201011-1206
建築主：トステム建材産業振興財団
構造：森部康司（昭和女子大学）
設備：馬郡文平（東京大学生産技術研究所産学連携研究員、Factor M代表取締役）
施工：高橋工務店
主体構造・規模：木造／地上1階
建築面積：79.50m²
延床面積：79.50m²

2009-
Museum at The China Academy of Art
Hangzhou, Zhejiang, China
—
Program: museum
Total floor area: 4,556m²
Site area: 9,525m²
Structure: steel frame
1 Story (partially 2 Stories)

中国美術学院博物館
所在地：中国浙江省杭州市
設計：200904-1108
工事：2013-
建築主：中国美術学院
主要用途：博物館
構造：小西泰孝建築構造設計
設備：森村設計
主体構造・規模：鉄骨造／地上1階（一部2階）
敷地面積：9,525m²
建築面積：3,448m²
延床面積：4,556m²

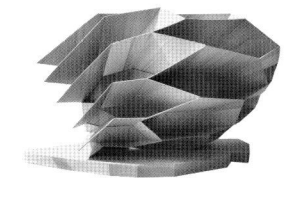

2009-12
Asakusa Culture Tourist Information Center
Taito, Tokyo, Japan
—
Program: tourist information center, office, exhibition hall, cafe
Total floor area: 2,159.52m²
Site area: 326.23m²
Structure: steel frame
8 stories, 1 basement

浅草文化観光センター
所在地：東京都台東区雷門2-18-9
設計：200901-1001 ｜ 工事：201008-1202
建築主：東京都台東区長 吉住弘
主要用途：観光案内所、事務所、展示場、飲食店
構造：牧野構造計画
設備：環境エンジニアリング
照明：岡安泉照明設計事務所
展示：SPフォーラム
カーテン：安東陽子デザイン　ロゴ・サイン：TOKYO PISTOL
施工：フジタ・大雄特定建設工事共同企業体
主体構造・規模：鉄骨造、一部鉄骨鉄筋コンクリート造（地階）
地下1階、地上8階
敷地面積：326.23m² ｜ 建築面積：234.13m²
延床面積：2,159.52m²

2009-
Granatum-Granada Performing Arts Centre
Granada, Spain
—
Program: multipurpose hall
Total floor area: 12,042m²
Site area: 6,553m²
Structure: reinforced concrete
5 stories, 1 basement

グラナトゥン
所在地：グラナダ、スペイン
設計：200905-
建築主：Junta de Andalucia (AndalousieRegional Government)
主要用途：多目的ホール
共同設計：Ana Julieta Peretz, David Navalon, Juan Hernandez, Francisco Quiles
Local architects：AH & asociados
構造：江尻建築構造設計事務所
ランドスケープ：Teresa Gali-Izard (Arquitectura Agronomia)
音響：永田音響設計
構造・規模：鉄筋コンクリート造／地下1階、地上5階
敷地面積：6,553m²
建築面積：4,780m²
延床面積：12,042m²

2010–11
Café Kureon
Toyama, Japan
—
Program: cafe
Total floor area: 197.73m²
Site area: 1484.02m²
1 story

カフェ・クレオン
所在地：富山県富山市呉羽町2247-3
設計：201003-1007
工事：201010-1103
主要用途：飲食店
構造：江尻建築構造設計事務所
設備・施工：正栄産業株式会社
規模：地上1階
敷地面積：1,484.02m²
建築面積：208.86m²
延床面積：197.73m²

2010–
Chikugo Art and Culture Center
Chikugo, Fukuoka, Japan
—
Program: arts and cultural facilities
Total floor area: 4157.32m²
Structure: reinforced concrete, timber frame
2 stories

筑後広域公園芸術文化交流施設（仮称）
所在地：福岡県筑後市
設計：2010-
主要用途：芸術文化交流施設
主体構造・規模：鉄筋コンクリート造、一部鉄骨造（本館）、木造（アネックス2）／地上2階
延床面積：4157.32m²
（本館／3,657m²、アネックス1／334.77m²、アネックス2／165.51m²）

2010–12
Teikyo University Elementary School
Tama, Tokyo, Japan
—
Program: elementary school
Total floor area: 7,781.52m²
Site area: 22,852.04m²
Structure: reinforced concrete
3 stories

帝京大学小学校
所在地：東京都多摩市和田1254-6
設計：201007-1102
工事：201102-1202
建築主：学校法人帝京大学
主要用途：小学校
共同設計・構造・設備・ランドスケープ：日本設計
施工：竹中工務店
主体構造・規模：鉄筋コンクリート造、一部鉄骨造、鉄骨鉄筋コンクリート造（3階、屋根）／地上3階
敷地面積：22,852.04m²
建築面積：4,405.11m²
延床面積：7,781.52m²

2010–
V&A at Dundee
Dundee, Scotland, U.K.
—
Program: museum
Total floor area: 6,200m²
Site area: 18,400m²

ヴィクトリア&アルバート・ミュージアム・ダンディ
所在地：イギリス、スコットランド、ダンディ
設計：2010-
建築主：Dundee Design Limited
主要用途：美術館
構造・設備：Arup
ランドスケープ：Optimised Environments
積material：CBA
Local architect：Cre 8 Architecture
敷地面積：18,400m²
建築面積：2,550m²
延床面積：6,200m²

2010–12
Garden Terrace Miyazaki
Miyazaki, Japan
—
Program: wedding ceremony hall, hotel
Total floor area: 4,562.04m²
Site area: 10,956.00m²
Structure: steel frame
2 stories

ガーデンテラス宮崎
所在地：宮崎県宮崎市下原町247-18
設計：201008-1110
工事：201111-1209
建築主：セレモニー宮崎
主要用途：結婚式場、ホテル
構造：福岡構造
設備：協同システム設計
家具：AURA CREATE
施工：大林組
主体構造・規模：鉄骨造／地上2階
敷地面積：10,956.00m²
建築面積：3,333.32m²
延床面積：4,562.04m²

2010–
Floating Cave
Seoul, South Korea
—
Program: memorial hall, house
Total floor area: 200m²
Site area: 330m²
Structure: reinforced concrete
2 stories, 1 basement

Floating Cave
所在地：ソウル市、大韓民国
設計：201008-1212
工事：2013
主要用途：過善館、住宅
構造：江尻建築構造設計事務所
照明：岡安泉照明設計事務所
主体構造・規模：鉄筋コンクリート造／地上2階、地下1階
敷地面積：330m²
建築面積：100m²
延床面積：200m²

2010–13
Aix en Provence Conservatory of Music
Aix en Provence, France
—
Program: music school
Total floor area: 7,430m²
Site area: 3,920m²
Structure: reinforced concrete
5 stories, 1 basement

エクサンプロヴァンス音楽院
所在地：エクサンプロヴァンス、フランス
設計：201003-1011
工事：201103-1306
建築主：エクサンプロヴァンス市
主要用途：音楽学校、音楽ホール
構造：AIA
設備：ETB Antonelli
音響：PEUTZ
施工：DUMEZ CAMPENON BERNARD AUER
主体構造・規模：鉄筋コンクリート造、一部鉄骨造
地上5階、地下1階
敷地面積：2,045m²
建築面積：1,984m²
延床面積：7,430m²

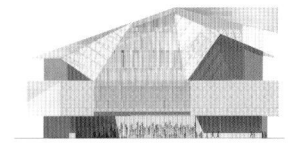

2011
Starbucks Coffee Dazaifu-Tenmangu Omotesando
Dazaifu, Fukuoka, Japan
—
Program: cafe
Total floor area: 210.03m²
Site area: 436.71m²
Structure: timber frame, steel frame
1 story

スターバックスコーヒー太宰府天満宮表参道店
所在地：福岡県福岡市太宰府市宰府3-2-43
設計：201101-1108
工事：201108-1111
建築主：満天
主要用途：飲食店
構造：佐藤淳構造設計事務所
照明：岡安泉照明設計事務所
施工：松本組
主体構造：木造
敷地面積：436.71m²
建築面積：212.98m²
延床面積：210.03m²

2010–14
Macdonald Public Facility Complex of General Education and Sports
Paris, France
—
Program: junior high school, elementary school, sport center, professors residence
Total floor area: 14,500m²
Site area: 7,600m²
Structure: Steel reinforced concrete
5 stories, 1 basement

マクドナルド公共複合施設
所在地：パリ、フランス
設計：201011-201111
工事：201205-201406
建築主：パリ市
主要用途：小学校・中学校、体育館、教員寮
構造・設備：AIA
音響：Peutz
施工：GCC (Ginie Civil et Construction)
主体構造・規模：鉄筋コンクリート 一部鉄骨造
地上5階、地下1階
敷地面積：7,600m²
建築面積：5,370m²
延床面積：14,500m²

2011
Bubble Wrap
Fukushima, Osaka, Japan
—
Program: installatioin
Total floor area: 34m²
Structure: catenary dome of polyurethane foam
1 story

Bubble Wrap
所在地：大阪府大阪市福島区福島1-1-17
設計：201105-1107
工事：201107
主要用途：インスタレーション
構造：江尻建築構造設計事務所
照明：森万里子
主体構造・規模：発泡ウレタン・カテナリードーム／地上1階
延床面積：34m²

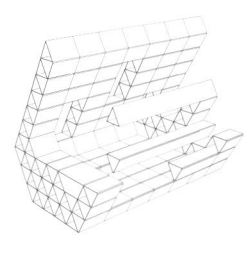

2011
Polygonium House
Tokyo, Japan
—
Program: house
Total floor area: 12m²
Site area: 130m²
Structure: aluminum panel
1 story

ポリゴニウム・ハウス
所在地：東京都千代田区丸の内2-4-1
丸の内ビルディング1F
設計：201104-1106
工事：201108
建築主：金屋町楽市実行委員会
主要用途：住宅
構造：三協立山アルミ、江尻建築構造設計事務所
施工：セルフビルド
主体構造・規模：アルミパネル／地上1階
敷地面積：130m²
建築面積：12m²
延床面積：12m²

2012
JP Tower Commercial Space
Tokyo, Japan
—
Program: commercial space
Total floor area: 212,043.05m²
Site area: 11,633.87m²
Structure: steel frame
38 stories, 4 basements, 3 rooftops

JPタワー 商業内装
所在地：東京都千代田区丸の内2-7-2
設計：200901-0910｜工事：200911-1205
建築主：郵便局株式会社、東日本旅客鉄道株式会社、三菱地所株式会社
主要用途：事務所、物販店舗、飲食店舗、郵便局、集会場、博物館、駐車場
共同設計：三菱地所設計
照明：内原智史デザイン事務所
構造・設備：三菱地所設計
施工：大成建設
主体構造・規模：鉄骨造、一部鉄骨鉄筋コンクリート造
地下4階、地上38階、塔屋3階
敷地面積：11,633.87m²
延床面積：212,043.05m²

2011–14
Lyon Confluence/HIKARI Project
Lyon, France
—
Program: office, residence, shop
Total floor area: 12,820m²
Site area: 3,370m²
Structure: reinforced concrete
office 7 stories, residence 8 stories, 1 basement

リヨン／HIKARIプロジェクト
所在地：リヨン、フランス
設計：201108-1301｜工事：201303-1412
建築主：BUYGUES IMMOBILIER
主要用途：オフィス、集合住宅、商業施設
共同設計：CRB
構造・設備：SETEC
音響：EAI
主体構造・規模：鉄筋コンクリート造
地上7階（オフィス棟）、地上8階（住宅棟）、地下1階
敷地面積：3,370m²
建築面積：469m²（NISHIオフィス＋住宅棟）＋506m²（MINAMI住宅棟）＋797m²（HIGASHIオフィス棟）
延床面積：12,820m²

2012–
Iiyama Plaza
Iiyama, Nagano, Japan
—
Program: multipurpose hall
Total floor area: 4,308m²
Site area: 9,926m²
Structure: reinforced concrete, steel frame
3 stories

（仮称）飯山ぷらざ
所在地：長野県飯山市
設計：201204-1308
工事：201310-
建築主：飯山市
主要用途：多機能的施設（芸術・文化機能／交流・賑わい機能）
構造：江尻建築構造設計事務所
設備：環境エンジニアリング
主体構造・規模：鉄筋コンクリート造、鉄骨造／地上3階
敷地面積：9,926m²
延床面積：4,308m²

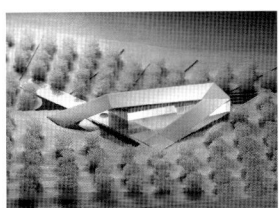

2011–
Chiva House
Chiva, Valencia, Spain
—
Program: house
Total floor area: 353m²
Site area: 9,157m²
Structure: steel frame, reinforced concrete retaining wall

Chiva House
所在地：チヴァ、ヴァレンシア、スペイン
設計：2011-
建築主：Martinez family
構造：オーノJAPAN
Local architect: Jose Luis Santolaria
主体構造・規模：鉄骨造、鉄筋コンクリート擁壁
敷地面積：9,157m²
建築面積：304m²
延床面積：353m²

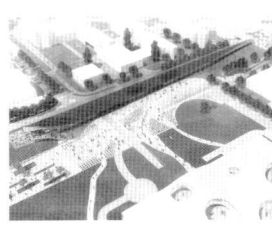

2012–
Under One Roof
Lausanne, Switzerland
—
Program: reception hall, exhibition hall, music hall, restaurant
Total floor area: about 3,500m²
Structure: timber frame, reinforced concrete
2 stories, 1 basement

Under One Roof
所在地：ローザンヌ、スイス連邦
設計：2013-
工事：2014-
建築主：スイス連邦工科大学ローザンヌ校（EPFL）
主要用途：レセプションホール、展示スペース、音楽ホール、レストラン
共同設計：Holzer Kobler Architekturen
構造：江尻建築構造設計事務所
施工：Buro Happold
施工：Marti SA
主体構造・規模：木造、一部鉄骨造（地上）、鉄筋コンクリート造（地下）／地上2階、地下1階
延床面積：約3,500m²（予定）

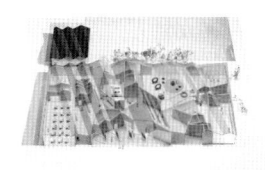

2011–
Towada City Plaza for Social Communication
Towada, Aomori, Japan
—
Program: community center
Total floor area: 1,826m²
Site area: 5,800m²
Structure: steel frame
1 story

（仮称）十和田市民交流プラザ
所在地：青森県十和田市
設計：201112-1212
工事：201304-
建築主：青森県十和田市
主要用途：コミュニティセンター
構造：佐藤淳構造設計事務所
設備：環境エンジニアリング
照明：岡安泉照明設計事務所
主体構造・規模：鉄骨造、一部鉄筋コンクリート造／地上1階
敷地面積：5,800m²
建築面積：1,894m²
延床面積：1,826m²

2012–
Susa International Train Station
Susa valley, Turin, Italy
—
Program: train station, cultural centre
Total floor area: 8,500m²
(+car parking 15,000m²) (as planed)

スーザ国際駅
所在地：スーザ、トリノ、イタリア
設計：2012-
建築主：Lyon Turin Ferroviaire SAS
主要用途：駅、文化センター
規模：地上3階、地下2階
延床面積：約8,500m²（+駐車場／15,000m²）（予定）

2012
Hojo-an
Kyoto, Japan
—
Program: installation
Total floor area: 9m²
Structure: semi tensegrity of magnet

方丈庵
所在地：京都市左京区下鴨泉川町59
設計：201207-1210
工事：201210
主要用途：インスタレーション
構造：江尻建築構造設計事務所
主体構造：磁石によるセミ・テンセグリティー
述床面積：9m²

2012–
Tomioka City Hall
Tomioka, Gunma, Japan
—
Program: City Hall
Total floor area: 9,000m²
Site area: 9,856m²
Structure: reinforced concrete, steel frame
3 stories, 1 basement

富岡市新庁舎
所在地：群馬県富岡市
設計：201211-1402
開庁予定：201604以降
建築主：富岡市
主要用途：庁舎
主体構造：鉄筋コンクリート造、鉄骨造
敷地面積：9,856m²
延床面積：9,000m²

2012

KENGO KUMA AND ASSOCIATES
Japan and Europe

KENGO KUMA ASSOCIATES

—

Kengo Kuma　隈研吾

—

Minoru Yokoo　横尾実
Akiko Shintsubo　新津保朗子
Kenji Miyahara　宮原賢次
Makoto Shirahama　白浜誠
Shuji Achiha　阿知波修二
Teppei Fujiwara　藤原徹平
Emiko Noguchi　野口恵美子
Kazuhiko Miyazawa　宮澤一彦
Yuki Ikeguchi　池口由紀
Eishi Sakamoto　坂本英史
Shin Ohba　大庭晋
Hiroaki Akiyama　秋山弘明
Tsuyoshi Kanda　神田剛
Takumi Saikawa　斎川拓未
Toshiki Meijo　名城俊樹
Yoshihiro Kurita　栗田祥弘
Javier Villar Ruiz
Satoshi Adachi　安達賢
Atsushi Kawanishi　川西敦史
Suguru Watanabe　渡辺傑
Takeyuki Saita　斎田武亨
Tomoyuki Hasegawa　長谷川倫之
Hirofumi Yamada　山田裕史
Jun Shibata　柴田淳
Hirokatsu Asano　浅野浩克
Ryohei Tanaka　田中亮平
Tessei Suma　須磨哲生
Ryota Torao　虎尾亮太
Nahoko Terakawa　寺川奈穂子

Masafumi Harigai　針谷將史
Shuhei Kamiya　神谷修平
Keiko Yoshida　吉田桂子
Hiroaki Saito　斉藤浩章
Ritsuko Ameno　飴野りつ子
Balazs Bognar
Tomoko Sasaki　佐々木倫子
Mariko Inaba　稲葉麻里子
Yoshihiko Seki　関佳彦
Shinya Kojima　小嶋伸也
Marcin Sapeta
Satoshi Onomichi　尾道理
Shi Hu (Minoru Ko)　胡実
Akio Saruta　猿田暁生
Xinxuan Jiang　江欣璇
Shuhei Yamane　山根脩平
Ryuya Umezawa　梅澤竜也
Naoki Okayama　岡山直樹
Kiyoaki Takeda　武田清明
Kazuyo Nishida　西田和代
Maurizio Mucciola
Maria-Chiara Piccinelli
Hajime Kita　喜多啓
Masaru Shuku　珠玖優
Kimio Suzuki　鈴木公雄
Taku Nishikawa　西川拓
Nahoko Yoshii　芳井菜穂子
Junki Wakuda　涌田純樹
Yuteki Dozono　堂園有的
Tetsuo Yamaji　山路哲生
Yu Momoeda　百枝優
Hiroyo Yamamoto　山本紘代
Kazuaki Hattori　服部一晃

Haiying Jin　金海英
Kazuya Katagiri　片桐和也
Kotaro Kitakami　北上紘太郎
Takashi Taguchi　田口誉
Rita Topa
Miguel Huelga De La Fuente
Ayako Takahashi　髙橋亜矢子
Huishan He　何慧珊
Yihang Zhang　張逸航
Yutaka Terasaki　寺崎豊
Tomonori Kusagaya　草ヶ谷友則
Akira Kindo　金道晃
Yoko Ushioda　潮田容子
Erina Kuryu　栗生えりな
Hironori Nagai　長井宏憲
Sungju Lee　李成柱
Mariko Abe　阿部真理子
Keita Watanabe　渡邉啓太
Masaki Kakizoe　垣副正樹
Fangfang Wei　魏芳芳
Ryukichi Tatsuki　田付龍吉
Nayoung Kim (Joenna Kim)　金奈映
Shengze Chen　陳勝澤
Jingwen Li　李静雯
Nicola Maniero
Masatoshi Tobe　戸部正俊
Jaime Fernandez Calvache
Miki Sato　佐藤未季
Masafumi Yukimoto　行本昌史
Noriko Ubukata　生方典子
Tian Qiu　秋天
Yuka Mukai　向井優佳
Chunsing Kwan (Magic Kwan)　關鎮陞

1986-2012   Published Writing
Japan

Taketo Ichise　一瀬健人

Kuniaki Tanaka　田中邦明

Masahiro Minami　南雅博

Yumi Ogawa　小川由美

Tanyaporn Anantrungroj

Ringo Tse　谢匡政

Seungjun Lee　李承俊

Chihiro Isono　磯野千紘

Tomohiro Matsunaga　松長知宏

Anteo Taro Sanada　眞田・アテオ・太郎

Kai Araki　荒木海威

Kengo Kuma Europe
—

Diego Lopez Arahuetes

Sarah Markert

Louise Lemoine

Matthieu Wotling

Miruna Constantinescu

Elise Fauquembergue

Chizuko Kawarada　河原田千鶴子

Charlotte Brussieux

Sebastien Yeou

Coralie Viguié

Aurelie Vernon

Silvia Fernandez

Jordi Vinals

François Arnwaout

Miguel Reyes

Baptiste Lobjoy

2012
つなぐ建築［岩波書店］
日本人はどう住まうべきか？［養老孟司との共著・日経BP社］
場所原論［市ヶ谷出版社］

2011
新・ムラ論TOKYO［清野由美との共著・集英社新書］

2010
境界［淡交社］
三低主義［三浦展との共著・NTT出版］

2008
素材の系譜［グラフィック社］
自然な建築［岩波新書］
新・都市論TOKYO［清野由美との共著・集英社新書］
Studies in Organic［TOTO出版］

2007
隈研吾：レクチャー／ダイアローグ［INAX出版］

2004
隈研吾読本 II —2004［A.D.A. EDITA Tokyo］
負ける建築［岩波書店］

2000
反オブジェクト［筑摩書房］

1999
隈研吾読本 —1999［A.D.A. EDITA Tokyo］

1995
建築の危機を超えて［TOTO出版］

1994
建築的欲望の終焉［新曜社］
新・建築入門―思想と歴史［ちくま新書］

1989
グッドバイ・ポストモダン―11人のアメリカ建築家［鹿島出版会］

1986
10宅論―10種類の日本人が住む10種類の住宅［ちくま文庫］

PHOTOGRAPHY CREDITS
GA photographers:
except as noted bellow
Kengo Kuma and Associates:
p.131, p.292 (Fu-an),
p.161, p.294 (Water Branch House),
p.222, p.295 (Granatum-Granada Performing Arts Centre),
p.296 (Café Kureon)
p.289 (except for above, Besancon City Arts and Culture Center)
Museum für angewandte Kunst Frankfurt:
p.127, p.291 (Tee Haus)
Yoshie Nishikawa:
p.160, p.292 (Casa Umbrella)
Nicolas Waltefaugle:
p.289 (above, Besancon City Arts and Culture Center)

COMPUTER GENERATED RENDERING CREDITS
Kengo Kuma and Associates:
except as noted bellow
Mir:
pp.282-283, p.283 (above),
p.297 (Susa International Train Station)

ENGLISH TRANSLATION
Lisa Tani:
pp.8-11, p.59, p.75, p.133, p.166, p.279
Satoko Hirata:
p.13, p.17, p.28, p.40, p.63, p.71, p.80, p.84, p.92, p.93,
p.96, p.103, p.117, p.123, p.127, p.128, p.131, p.138, p.146,
p.155, p.160, p.177, p.182, p.190, p.203, p.207, p.212,
p.226, p.233, p.236, p.245, p.249, p.262, p.266, p.270,
p.272, p.276, p.283, p.284
Peter Boronski
p.24, p.39, p.46, p.52, p.101, p.112, p.158, p.171, p.195,
p.204, p.216, p.221, p.222, p.246, p.254, p.258, p.275, p.289

隈研吾作品集 2006-2012
2012 年 11 月 22 日発行
2020 年 3 月 25 日 2 刷発行

企画・編集：二川由夫
撮影：GA photographers
序文・作品解説：隈研吾
ロゴ・デザイン：細谷巌
発行者：二川由夫
印刷・製本：大日本印刷株式会社
発行：エーディーエー・エディタ・トーキョー
東京都渋谷区千駄ヶ谷 3-12-14
TEL. (03) 3403-1581 (代)

禁無断転載

ISBN978-4-87140-433-4 C1352